THE SOCIAL TEACHING
OF VATICAN II

THE SOCIAL TEACHING OF VATICAN II

Its Origin and Development

Catholic Social Ethics: an
historical and comparative study

by

RODGER CHARLES, S.J.

with

DROSTAN MACLAREN, O.P.

OXFORD • PLATER PUBLICATIONS

SAN FRANCISCO • IGNATIUS PRESS

Cover design and calligraphy by Victoria Hoke

With ecclesiastical approval

Published simultaneously in Great Britain by Plater Publications
and in the United States by Ignatius Press

©Ignatius Press, San Francisco 1982
All rights reserved

ISBN 0-89870-013-2
Library of Congress Catalogue Number 81-83567

Printed in the United States of America

Dedication:

*To my mother
and to my sisters Margaret and Anne
for their faith and their love*

GENERAL CONTENTS

ANALYTIC CONTENTS   ix

ACKNOWLEDGEMENTS   xxv

INTRODUCTION   I

I   The Ultimate and Objective Ethical Norm: the Divine Law   9

     *The ultimate and objective ethical norm is the divine law—
     eternal, objective and universal, and man participates in this law
     through natural law* (Dignitatis Humanae *and* Gaudium et
     Spes).

2   The Proximate and Subjective Ethical Norm   73

     *The proximate and subjective ethical norm is man's conscience,
     guided by the sacred and certain teaching of the Church in-
     terpreting objective moral law* (Dignitatis Humanae *and*
     Gaudium et Spes).

3   The Ethics of Marriage and the Family   115

     *Marriage is divinely instituted as a loving, personal, monoga-
     mous and indissoluble relationship, by nature ordained to the
     procreation and education of children* (Gaudium et Spes).

4   The Ethics of Political Life   173

     *The political community and the authority of the state are based
     on human nature and so belong to God's design, though the
     method of government and the appointment of rulers is left to the
     citizens' free choice. The Church is not identified with any
     particular system but must be free to teach her whole doctrine
     (including her social doctrine) and pass moral judgement on
     political issues as required* (Gaudium et Spes).

5   The Ethics of Economic Life   261

*The purpose of economics is the service of men, their material
needs and those of their moral, spiritual and religious life.
Economic activity is to be carried out according to its own methods
and laws but within the limits of morality* (Gaudium et Spes).

6   Summary and Conclusions   359

APPENDIX: DOCUMENTATION   381

READING SUGGESTIONS   511

INDEX OF AUTHORS, NAMES AND TITLES   547

INDEX OF SUBJECTS   559

INDEX OF DOCUMENTATION   567

ANALYTIC CONTENTS

CHAPTER ONE

THE ULTIMATE AND OBJECTIVE ETHICAL NORM: THE DIVINE LAW

The ultimate and objective ethical norm is the divine law—eternal, objective and universal, and man participates in this law through the natural law (Dignitatis Humanae, *paragraphs 2 and 3 and* Gaudium et Spes, *paragraphs 63 and 79).*

I. THE TEACHING OF THE COUNCIL ON THE ULTIMATE NORM OF MORALITY AND THE CONTEXT IN WHICH THAT TEACHING IS GIVEN

A. THE CONTEXT OF THE COUNCIL'S STATEMENT: RELIGIOUS FREEDOM

The ethical assumptions of the Council (9); the context of its statement about the supremacy of divine law: *Dignitatis Humanae* (10); freedom to seek and live the truth (12); contrast with the liberal idea of freedom (13); restraints on freedom (14); the need for law to have a moral basis (15).

B. THE CHURCH AND FREEDOM: SOME HISTORICAL QUESTIONS

1. The Early Church and Roman Society
The freedom offered by the Church, one of its attractions to early converts (19); the reasons for the acceptance of the Church by the Roman Empire and the effects of that acceptance (20); Christ, the martyrs and the freedom of the Church (21); the Church/state conflict and European ideas of freedom: the two swords theory (22).

2. The Church and Medieval Society
Church and society: a general view: What we mean by "the Middle Ages" (23); medieval Europe, emergence, growth, decline (24); the role of the Church in this period (25); the papacy, the Franks and Christendom (26); the Church and the moral and intellectual life of the Middle Ages (27).

The decline of slavery: Undermining its intellectual foundations (28); the monasteries and the ideal of free labour: Christian ethics and the reduction in the supply of slaves (29); the development of a free peasantry: monastic influences and economic needs (30); summary: the medieval theologians, the Church and slavery (31).

Education: The Church as educator: the Irish monks and the Benedictines (34); the emergence of the universities (35); the intellectual synthesis of the thirteenth century: the role of the friars and the universities (36); intellectual enquiry and the sciences: Nicholas of Cusa, Copernicus and Galileo (37).

3. The Secular Power of the Church and Its Consequences
The Investiture Controversy: Origins of the Church's involvement with secular affairs: Leo the Great and Gregory the Great (38); the papacy and the Franks: the Papal States (39); the Church as landowner and the implications of this role in the feudal system (40); the growth of lay control in the Church in the ninth and tenth centuries: Gregory VII, the excommunication of Henry IV and its consequences (41).

The Crusades: The religious and political/military context (42); the Crusades, chivalry, the Church's efforts to reduce violence and the appeals for help from the East (43).

The Inquisition: Heresy in the Middle Ages and its social implications (44); reasons for violence in dealing with heresy: the heresy trials (45).

Conclusion: The lesson of the Church's over-involvement in secular affairs: her services to freedom summarised (46); the links between the medieval and the modern worlds: the universities and the development of the physical sciences: representative government: freedom under the law: trial by jury (47); the communes, the guilds, and the dignity of labour: education and social welfare: understanding the Middle Ages (48).

II. THE DIVINE ETERNAL LAW AS THE ULTIMATE MORAL NORM: THE
    TEACHING OF SCRIPTURE

A. THE OLD TESTAMENT

The continuity of the Old and New Testaments: the Old Testament and its role in the history of the Jews (49); the Covenant, the prophets and objective morality (50); the connection between belief in God and the moral life: the Jewish tradition and that of contemporary and classical cultures (51); the Commandments and their binding force (54); the moral, ceremonial and judicial precepts of the Old Testament (55).

B. THE NEW TESTAMENT

Moral teaching of the New Testament: the approach to the texts (56); Christ, ethics and religion: his teaching on the Commandments (58); ethics in the teaching of SS. Peter and Paul (59).

III. The Divine Eternal and the Natural Laws: The Council's Teaching and the Catholic Tradition

A. THE COUNCIL ON NATURAL LAW

The Council, and the Thomistic concept of natural law as a participation in divine law (60); St. Thomas and the natural law: the place of St. Thomas in Catholic theology (61).

B. THE ORIGIN OF NATURAL LAW THEORY AND ITS EMBODIMENT IN THE CATHOLIC TRADITION

The necessity for Catholic theology to come to grips with the concept of natural law: St. Paul's appeal to it (64); the Greeks: religion, drama, literature and morality (65); the development of scientific moral theory among the Greeks: *nomos* and *physis* (66); Socrates and the constant laws of human nature: Plato, the unchanging forms and the cardinal virtues: Aristotle: the Stoics and natural law (67); Roman jurisprudence and natural law (68); the Fathers of the Church and natural law (69); St. Thomas and natural law (70); Hume's attack on the concept: the Church as interpreter of natural law (71).

CHAPTER TWO

THE PROXIMATE AND SUBJECTIVE ETHICAL NORM

The proximate and subjective ethical norm is man's conscience (personal and social) guided by the sacred and certain teaching of the Church interpreting objective moral law (Dignitatis Humanae, paragraph 14 and Gaudium et Spes, paragraphs 16, 17, 26, 63).

I. The Objective Moral Law as the Norm of Personal Conscience: The Teaching of the Council and its Basis

A. THE COUNCIL, OBJECTIVE MORAL LAW AND CONSCIENCE

God's law the norm of human action: conscience and this norm: the teaching of the Council (73); objective criteria to be used: the Council's teaching (74); summary (75).

B. THE BIBLICAL TEACHING ON CONSCIENCE AND ITS DEVELOPMENT IN MORAL THEOLOGY

The scriptural idea of conscience: the influence of Greek philosophy in its clarification: St. Paul and St. Thomas Aquinas on conscience (76); the erroneous conscience and objective moral truth (77).

C. THE NATURE OF THE MORAL ACT ACCORDING TO THE NEW TESTAMENT, CLASSICAL
MORAL THEOLOGY AND THE COUNCIL

The New Testament and the duty of obeying God's will (78); the morality
of the human act: *finis operis* and *finis operantis*: human freedom and
imputability (79).

D. MODERN CATHOLIC OBJECTIONS TO THE CLASSICAL THEORY

Objective moral law and imputability of moral evil: the teaching of the
Council (80); circumstances and morality: the argument of Fuchs (81);
pre-moral, ontic and physical evil (82).

E. THE ROLE OF CASUISTRY IN MORAL THEOLOGY

The principle of totality (83); of the lesser of two evils (84); of double effect
(85).

II. THE OBJECTIVE MORAL LAW AS THE NORM OF SOCIAL CONSCIENCE:
THE TEACHING OF THE COUNCIL AND ITS BASIS

A. CHRISTIAN PERSONALISM

The foundations of personal and social morality (86); the Council and the
Church's social teaching: the truth of God as the foundation of the social
order: *Mater et Magistra* (87).

B. JUSTICE AND CHARITY

Complementarity of the two concepts (88); justice defined: divisions of
justice: legal, distributive and commutative (89); the concept of social
justice (90).

III. MODERN OBJECTIONS TO THE IDEA OF OBJECTIVE MORAL LAW AND THE
LIBERAL ROOTS OF THESE OBJECTIONS

A. THE LIBERAL PHILOSOPHY

Judaeo/Christian ethics rooted in God and unchanging in principle: the
modern rejection of this idea (91); liberalism and the absolute autonomy of
the individual: the classical and Christian ideas liberalism drew on (92);
liberalism and political and economic theory (93); liberalism as philosophy (94); its assumptions concerning objective and eternal truth: the
Christian and medieval origins of these assumptions (95); positivism, the
Church and liberalism (97).

B. SOME MODERN ETHICAL THEORIES

1. Moral Sense Theories: Kantianism and Positivism
Moral sense theories (97); Kant's moral theories and his Christian background (98); Comte and positivism (99).

2. Hegel, Marxism and Ethics
Hegel and nature as the objective expression of infinite spirit (99); Hegel's ideal and Marx's materialist dialectic (100); Marxist ethics: their ultimate and fundamental relativism (102).

3. Utilitarianism, Darwinism and Ethics
Utilitarianism and the pleasure principle (103); Darwin's scientific theories on the origin of animals and man (104); their potential implications for the Christian understanding of man: the theological content of Darwinism (105); Man's physical evolution and Christian belief (106).

4. Freud, Psychiatry and Ethics
The structure of the human psyche according to Freud: his treatment of the traditional categories of Judaeo/Christian belief and moral theory (108); the human psyche according to Freud and the liberal view of man (109); Freud, God and religion (110); Adler and Jung (111); psychiatry, religion and ethics (112).

5. Situation Ethics
Situationism as a reaction against narrow biblicism and unsound moral theology (112); the origins of situation ethics (113); the defects of the "love ethic" of situationism and the nature of its objective norms (114).

CHAPTER THREE

THE ETHICS OF MARRIAGE AND THE FAMILY

Marriage is divinely instituted as a loving, personal, monogamous and indissoluble relationship, by nature ordained to the procreation and education of children (Gaudium et Spes, paragraphs 48–50).

I. INTRODUCTION: MARRIAGE, ITS PERSONAL AND SOCIAL DIMENSION
Marriage as a loving union between equals in total community of life (115); the family as the basis of society: the unity of these two aspects of marriage (116).

II. THE CHRISTIAN UNDERSTANDING OF THE NATURE OF MARRIAGE AS A LOVING PERSONAL COMMITMENT AND THE IMPLICATIONS OF THIS COMMITMENT

A. THE BIBLICAL TEACHING ON MARRIAGE

Genesis: marriage as the union of equal partners (117); the importance of
the Genesis teaching concerning the proper understanding of sex (118);
the contrast with contemporary cultures (119); Christ's teaching on marriage (120); on divorce (121); St. Paul to the Ephesians on marriage: the
indissolubility of marriage: St. Augustine to Vatican II (122).

B. THE DEVELOPMENT OF CANON LAW AND THE THEOLOGY OF MARRIAGE

1. Canon Law and Annulment
The reasons for the development of canon law on marriage (123); the
Pauline and Petrine privileges (124); the traditional grounds for annulment: lack of free consent, moral or mental defect, marriage in defiance
of the Church's law, serious impediment: recent annulment decisions:
potentialities and problems (125).

2. The Development of the Church's Teaching
On the Ends of Marriage
Sexual pleasure, procreation and the weaknesses of human nature: the
awareness of the early Church that marriage did not do away with this
weakness; contraceptive practices in pre-Christian times (126); the Scriptures on the ends of marriage: the book of Tobit, the Song of Songs, St.
Paul to the Corinthians (127); the pessimism of the early Church regarding sexuality (129); the medieval penitentials and the continuance of this
pessimism (130); St. Augustine and the goods of marriage: *proles, fides* and
sacramentum: St. Thomas on the primary, secondary and tertiary ends of
marriage: St. Thomas' more positive approach to sexual love in marriage
(131); the importance of marital chastity: St. Thomas to Vatican II (132);
positive developments in the theology of marriage from the sixteenth
century: medical knowledge and further developments in that theology:
Pius XII and sexual love as the *finis operis* of marriage (133); the contraceptive mentality and permissiveness: dangers to health and happiness and
the stability of marriage (134); the naivety of the intellectual attacks upon
Christian teaching: the commercial pressures encouraging permissiveness
(137).

3. The Teaching of the Second Vatican Council and *Humanae Vitae* on the
Ends of Marriage
Marriage essentially ordered to the bringing to be of new life (138); true
marriage remains where children cannot be born of it: sincere intentions
and motives not enough in family planning (139); *Gaudium et Spes* and
Humanae Vitae (140); responsible parenthood means responsibility to

God, to the partner in the marriage, to the family and to society: neither the unitive nor the procreative aspects of the sex act may ever be deliberately denied (141); birth control for good reasons and by moral means is acceptable, contraception is not (142); the infertile period and natural family planning: the Billings and the symptothermal methods, the effectiveness and the value of N.F.P. (143); the summary of Catholic teaching on the proper use of sex in marriage, its rationality and its regard for psychological needs and the dignity of the human person (145); the teaching of *Humanae Vitae* is infallible from the ordinary magisterium (147); invalidity of arguments against *Humanae Vitae* from presumed previous errors of the magisterium regarding the Galileo case, the teaching on usury (148), slavery (149), and "no salvation outside the Church" (153); summary (154); contraception and population control (156).

III. Marriage as a Social Institution: The Family

A. THE COUNCIL ON THE FAMILY AND THE FAMILY AND SOCIETY TODAY

The high ideals of Christian marriage and family (156); the role of parents and children (157); the right of women to full personal development (158); the Church's historical role in safeguarding the dignity of women (159); woman's role in the family and her desire for personal fulfillment not opposed (161); the importance of the family to society and the need for society to protect it: society and divorce (162); the Christian teaching on the family does not assume any one particular sociological model of the family (163).

B. THE SCRIPTURES, THE PATRIARCHAL FAMILY AND MODERN NEEDS

The Scriptures and the patriarchal family (164); Christ's love of the family but his warning of the dangers that can come from family ties (165); the abuses of the patriarchal ideal: the Marxist critique of the patriarchal family and the weaknesses of that critique (167); the true patriarchal family and its advantages to human society (168).

C. EDUCATION: THE ROLE OF PARENTS, CHURCH AND STATE

The teaching of the Council (169); the primary educative role is that of the family: the importance of the school and the teaching profession (170); the rights of the state and parents in education (171); the need for the Catholic school (172).

CHAPTER FOUR

THE ETHICS OF POLITICAL LIFE

The political community and the authority of the state are based on human nature and so belong to God's design, though the method of government and the appointment of rulers is left to the citizens' free choice. The Church is not identified with any particular system but must be free to teach her whole doctrine (including her social doctrine) and pass moral judgement on political issues as required (Gaudium et Spes, paragraphs 74 and 76).

I. THE ORIGIN AND THE NATURE OF POLITICAL AUTHORITY

A. THE TEACHING OF THE COUNCIL

The state is based in the needs of human nature and is according to God's design; the method of government and the appointment of rulers is for the people to decide (173); the historical origin of the state (175).

B. THE HISTORICAL CONTEXT AND THE DEVELOPMENT OF CATHOLIC THOUGHT DOWN TO THE SIXTEENTH CENTURY

The Old Testament, politics and the state (175); Christ's teaching and that of the New Testament (176); the Fathers of the Church: St. Gregory and divine right (179); the influence of the Investiture controversy (180); Marsilio of Padua and William of Occam (183); the conciliar movement (184); the growth of representative government: the influence of city life (185); England, the development of common law and parliament (186); the Church and representative government (187); St. Thomas, the origin of the state and the nature of political authority (189); summary of the political ethics of the Middle Ages (190); the growth of absolute monarchy (192); sixteenth century scholasticism: the origin of the state: the limits of constitutionalism and of government by consent (193).

C. SOME NON-CATHOLIC AND SECULAR THINKERS SINCE THE RENAISSANCE

Machiavelli and political morality (195); Calvinism, Lutheranism and the right to revolt (196); absolutism: Protestant and Catholic states (197); Bodin, Hobbes and absolutism (198); Locke and liberalism (200); Montesquieu, Voltaire and liberalism (201); Rousseau and democracy (202); Hegel and the spirit of the nation: Marx, the state and revolution (203).

D. CONCLUSION

The traditional Catholic theory and democratic absolutism (204); Rousseau, Bellarmine, Leo XIII and the origin of political authority (205).

II. The Purpose, Attitude Towards and Proper Use of Political Authority

A.THE PURPOSE OF POLITICAL AUTHORITY: THE COMMON GOOD

The common good defined as the conditions in which individuals, families and organisations can fulfill themselves (207); socialisation and the welfare state (208); the principle of subsidiary function (209); political authority subject to the divine and natural laws (211).

B. THE ATTITUDE TOWARDS POLITICAL AUTHORITY AND THE RIGHT OF DISSENT

1. The Attitude Towards Political Authority
The need to respect political authority (213); the right of dissent: general: particular: party politics (215).

2. The Right of Dissent:
Conscientious Objection and the Just War Concept
The right of conscientious objection in a just war (215); the just war concept: the Council and the right to wage war (216); modern weapons and the morality of war (217); the need for public debate (218); the serviceman and conscientious objection to the use of modern weapons (219).

3. The Right and Forms of Dissent on Other Issues:
The Use of Non-Violent and Violent Means
The Council and the traditional teaching on resistance to legitimate authority (221); violent resistance: St. Thomas' teaching and *Populorum Progressio* (222); the difficulty of application of the traditional teaching (223).

III. The Christian, the Church and Politics

A. THE INDIVIDUAL CHRISTIAN AND POLITICS

Christians to respect their political opponents and work for the common good: the acceptability of party politics (223); the common good and the rights of man: the detailed teaching of *Pacem in Terris* (224); *Redemptor Hominis* and human rights (226).

B.THE CHURCH AND POLITICS: THE THEORY

Individuals to take their own options: the Church not identified with any political system (227); the independence and autonomy of Church and state (228); the historical experience, an introductory summary (229).

C. THE CHURCH AND POLITICS: THE EXPERIENCE IN THE MIDDLE AGES

The Church's refusal to oppose persecution by violence: the assumptions of the Gelasian theory of Church/state relationships under the Christian Roman Empire (230); the abuse by the secular authorities of the Investiture system (231); the conflict between empire and papacy, eleventh to fourteenth centuries (232); the motives for and effects of papal involvement in secular affairs (233).

D. THE CHURCH AND POLITICS: RENAISSANCE AND REFORMATION TO TODAY

The absolute monarchies in the Catholic states: Gallicanism, Febronianism and Josephism (234); the French Revolution and the civil constitution on the clergy: the suppression of the Society of Jesus (236); Ireland, Poland and the problem of the Papal States (237); Gregory XVI and liberalism: the condemnation of Lammenais (238); the papal dilemma illustrated by the experience of Pius IX (239); Pius IX and liberalism: the Syllabus of Errors (240); the papacy, Italian nationalism and liberalism (242).

E. THE CHURCH AND POLITICS TODAY

The implications of the Church's historical experience (243); the teaching of the Council on the relationship between Church and politics: the social teaching of the Church as a guide to Catholic thinking and action (244); liberation theology: its origins, growth and inspiration (245); violence: Marxism and social change (246); the Latin American experience and that of the European Church in the nineteenth century: the Catholic social movement (248); John Paul II at Puebla (252); his stress on the social teaching of the Church (253); the final document of the Puebla Conference (254); the Church and the Third World (255).

IV. INTERNATIONAL LAW AND INTERNATIONAL RELATIONS

The Council and the importance of a universally acknowledged international authority (256); the Church's historical experience and its reasons for interest in international relations: sixteenth century Thomists and international law (257); *Pacem in Terris, Gaudium et Spes*, and international relations (259); the United Nations Organization and the Church (260).

CHAPTER FIVE

THE ETHICS OF ECONOMIC LIFE

*The purpose of economics is the service of men, their material needs and those
of their moral, spiritual and religious life. Economic activity is to be carried
out according to its own methods and laws but within the limits of morality
(Gaudium et Spes, paragraph 64).*

I. INTRODUCTION: CHRISTIAN ECONOMIC ETHICS AND IDEALS

The dangers of wealth: the warnings of the New Testament and the
teaching of Vatican II (261); economic ethics, the Council and the social
encyclicals (262).

II. LIBERAL CAPITALISM AND MARXIST SOCIALISM: THEIR ETHICS AND
IDEALS IN THEORY AND IN PRACTICE

A. LIBERAL CAPITALISM

Economics and ethics: the implications of the development of the modern
science (263); mercantilism, Smith and the invisible hand (264); the
one-sided interpretation of Smith's theories by sectional interests (265);
Say, Malthus, Ricardo and J. S. Mill (266); the development of welfare
economics (267); Keynes (268); the use of classical economics against the
worker in Britain, on the Continent and in America (269); the standard of
life, the quality of life and the justice to the wage earner in the industrial
revolution (271); the defects of welfare capitalism: its materialism (272).

B. MARXIST SOCIALISM

Marx, the labour theory of value and the destruction of capitalism (273);
the failure of Marxist predictions (274); Marx's picture of the model
socialist society: the inevitability of Marxist tyranny (275); Leninism, war
communism and the N.E.P. in Soviet Russia (276); the collectivisation of
agriculture and its human cost (277); the industrial worker and freedom
(278).

III. ETHICS AND ECONOMIC SYSTEMS: THE MARKET ECONOMY, BASIC
LOGIC, CONCEPTS AND ETHICS

The market economy and welfare capitalism: the basic logic (278); key
concepts: production, demand and supply, money and banking, international trade, government policy (279); the ethics of competition: pro-

ducer ethics and consumer ethics (282); just price (283); taxation, and distribution of income and property (283); land speculation and rents (284); labour and the right to the whole product (285); capital, investment and interest (286); the historical problem of usury (287); profit (289).

IV. ETHICS AND ECONOMIC SYSTEMS: THE CENTRALLY PLANNED ECONOMY,
     BASIC LOGIC, CONCEPTS AND ETHICS

Central planning as the determinant of economic activity: the importance of the Soviet experience (290); Soviet planning: industry and agriculture (291); central planning: theory and practice (292); adjustments towards greater freedom in Russia and East European countries (293); free enterprise and communist systems: comparative performance (294); the exportability of the Soviet model to the Third World (295); the experience of Cambodia and its significance (296).

V. CONCLUSION: THE MARKET ECONOMY, SOVIET PLANNING AND CATHOLIC
    SOCIAL ETHICS

General theoretical preference for economic freedom (296); the readiness of the Church to live with the Soviet system: some advantages of that system (297); the option for freedom is not an option for the materialism of modern welfare capitalism: the significance of the experience of John Paul II (296).

VI. THE MORAL LAWS GOVERNING PRIVATE PROPERTY: ITS OWNERSHIP
     AND USE

The teaching of the Council on private property (299); its incompatibility with liberal capitalism: the reasonableness of the Church's teaching (300); private property: the scriptural teaching (302); the teaching of the Fathers of the Church (303); of St. Thomas (304); of *Rerum Novarum* and *Gaudium et Spes* (305); the problem raised by the division between ownership and control: *Quadragesimo Anno* (307); summary of Catholic teaching (308); private property, security and state welfare: *Mater et Magistra* and *Gaudium et Spes* (309); public ownership, confiscation and compensation: *Quadragesimo Anno*, *Gaudium et Spes* and *Populorum Progressio* (310).

VII. WORK, ITS SPIRITUAL AND MORAL SIGNIFICANCE, ITS RIGHTS AND
      ITS DUTIES

Christ, the New Testament and the dignity of work: the Jewish background (312); the medieval guild and Christian influences: the alienation of the modern worker (313); God the Creator, man as worker before the Fall and the results of the Fall (314); work as glorifying God: as personal and necessary (315); work and recreation (316); work as necessary: the right to work and a just wage: *Rerum Novarum* and *Quadragesimo Anno* (318); the state's duty in securing proper conditions of work (319).

VIII. The Enterprise and Industrial Organisation: The Rights and Duties of Capital and Labour

Gaudium et Spes, worker participation and strikes (319); the nature of the enterprise as it has developed from the nineteenth century (321); shareholders and social responsibility: *Quadragesimo Anno* (322); worker participation: *Quadragesimo Anno* and *Rerum Novarum* (323); rejection of Fascist corporativism by *Quadragesimo Anno* (324); strikes (325); difficulties of the just war theory applied to strikes (326); reducing strikes: the importance of sound industrial relations and collective bargaining (329); the norms governing a sound industrial relations and collective bargaining system (330).

IX. International Economics: The Developed and Underdeveloped Countries

A. DEVELOPMENT AND UNDERDEVELOPMENT: THE FACTS AND THE ETHICAL ISSUES

The context of the Council's teaching on economic development: international relations, justice and peace (333); *Populorum Progressio* and the concept of development (334); the indices of underdevelopment: the contrast between various areas in the underdeveloped world (336).

B. AID, TRADE AND DEVELOPMENT

Aid and trade (338); the World Bank and its origins; transfer of resources to the Third World (339); the distribution of aid and the overall performance of the developed countries regarding financial aid (340); technical aid (341); improving the trade position of the Third World: commodity prices and industrial development (342); the United Nations Commission on Trade, Aid and Development, 1964–1979 (343); population growth and the moral implications of population control (344); the concept of demographic transition (344); peasant societies and family planning (345); global population, global food resources and the problems of starvation and malnutrition in particular areas (346); the exploitation of resources and the protection of the environment (347); specific difficulties regarding resources (348); exploitation of resources and protection of the environment (349).

X. AGRICULTURAL ECONOMICS AND THE ETHICS OF AGRICULTURAL DEVELOPMENT

The importance of agriculture internationally (350); the Council's guidance regarding justice for the agricultural sector (351); urbanisation in the developed and underdeveloped worlds (352); land tenure and the problem of agricultural efficiency (353); land reform: the experience in Latin America and other areas (354); the importance to world food production of improving productivity on small farms; the significance of the success of Egypt, Taiwan, Japan and South Korea (356) the problems of African countries: the conditions for improving productivity on small farms in the underdeveloped world (357).

CHAPTER SIX

SUMMARY AND CONCLUSIONS

The Structure of the Study (359); Summaries: Chapter One (360); Chapter Two (363); Chapter Three (366); Chapter Four (370); Chapter Five (375); General Conclusions of the Whole Study (379).

APPENDIX:

DOCUMENTATION

I. Vatican II: *Declaration on Religious Freedom (Dignitatis Humanae)*, 1965 (381).

II. Vatican II: *Pastoral Constitution on the Church in the Modern World (Gaudium et Spes)*, 1965 (385).

III. Vatican II: *Declaration on Christian Education (Gravissimum Educationis)*, 1965 (423).

IV. Vatican II: *Decree on the Apostolate of Lay People (Apostolicam Actuositatem)*, 1965 (428).

V. Pope Paul VI: Encyclical Letter *On Fostering the Development of Peoples (Populorum Progressio)*, 1967 (436).

VI. Pope Paul VI: Encyclical Letter *On the Regulation of Birth (Humanae Vitae)*, 1968 (444).

VII. Pope Paul VI: Apostolic Letter *On the Eightieth Anniversary of Rerum Novarum* (*Octogesima Adveniens*), 1971 (453).

VIII. Sacred Congregation for the Doctrine of the Faith: *Declaration on Certain Questions Concerning Sexual Ethics*, 1975 (459).

IX. Pope John Paul II: *Address at the Opening of the Third General Conference of Latin American Bishops* (CELAM), Puebla, 1979 (463).

X. Third General Conference of Latin American Bishops (CELAM): *Conclusions* of the Conference, Puebla, 1979 (477).

XI. Pope John Paul II: *Address to the XXXIV General Assembly of the United Nations Organization*, 1979 (492).

XII. Pope John Paul II: *Concluding Address to the Synod of Bishops*, 1980 (498).

XIII. Pope John Paul II: Encyclical Letter *On Human Work* (*Laborem Exercens*), 1981 (500).

ACKNOWLEDGEMENTS

As I explain in a little more detail in the Introduction, this book is based on the research and the teaching that I did when I was running the Catholic Institute of Social Ethics from 114 Mount Street, London, in the years 1972 to 1979. Hence my thanks are first of all due to those who gave me permission to pursue the project and generously subsidised it—namely the two Provincial Superiors of the English Province of the Society of Jesus in that period, Frs. Bernard Hall and W. J. Maher, S.J. Secondly, they are due to the successive Superiors of the Farm Street Community, Frs. David Hoy, Richard Copeland and Peter Knott, S.J., who allowed me to use the facilities of the Jesuit house for the work, and above all to Brothers J. Harkess and M. Goodman, S.J.: being responsible for the administration of the house, it was they who bore the brunt of the practical arrangements for lectures and meetings over the years. Thirdly, I am indebted to those who helped me in the organisation of the C.I.S.E. or lent their names to the work: the Patrons, the original Advisory Committee, the Steering Committee which succeeded it, the Trustees of the C.I.S.E. and the long list of distinguished academics, an international group, who agreed to act as advisors. Since this group of friends and helpers numbers nearly one hundred in all, I hope they will forgive me if I do not mention each by name. I would just like each to know that I remember their support and encouragement with deep gratitude.

I owe much also to the two hundred or so who attended the lectures given at Farm Street in the years 1974/5 and 1975/6. The realisation of the depth of the problems that teaching social ethics presented was brought home to me in the questions and the discussions after these lectures; the realisation led to the decision to provide a one-year full-time course of study and, in time, to try to publish books such as this which we hope will help to deepen knowledge and understanding of the subject.

Because the work has grown out of teaching experience, a major debt is to Fr. Drostan MacLaren, O.P., whose name appears with mine on the title page. The work is in many ways a joint effort, though we are not indeed co-authors. The book was researched, planned and written by me, and I bear the ultimate responsibility for it and its contents. But I have consulted Fr. MacLaren throughout, and he has been watching over its development at every stage. As we have taught together, he has helped me to formulate my views on many matters, implicitly or explicitly, and he has also given me assurance on specific questions throughout. Above all, had he been less capable, less self-effacing and less wholeheartedly behind the project in the rather fluid situation that developed after he joined me in 1977 (and later when I took my sabbatical in late 1979), I would hardly have been able to put the book together. In the late stages I received great help also from the Principal of Plater College, Dennis Chiles, and from other members of the staff; Mike Blades, Harry Dodson, Fr. Nicholas Folan, O.P., Lionel St. Quintin and Ken Straw all read parts of the final draft most carefully, saved me from many errors and made many suggestions for its improvement in detail which I was glad to accept. Mr. K. Platt likewise gave valuable assistance with chapter 3. Responsibility for what finally appears is of course mine alone.

It is axiomatic that those who teach learn much from those they teach. Since the various drafts of the book have been used by one or both of us in seminars and classes at the Catholic Institute of Social Ethics, the Saint Ignatius Institute at the University of San Francisco, and now at Plater College, Oxford, Fr. MacLaren and I have had opportunities to benefit from the questionings of those who attended those seminars and classes. Time and again we had to rethink and research more deeply in consequence. The reader will be the judge of the value of our work. We can only say that the value it does possess owes much to them.

Extracts from the documents of the Second Vatican Council in both text and appendix are by permission of Fr. Austin Flannery, O.P., and those from the papal encyclicals and Vatican documents by that of the Incorporated Catholic Truth Society, 38–40 Eccleston Square, London, SW1V 1PD. The passages from the address of John Paul II to the 34th General Assembly of the United Nations are from *U.S.A.: Message of Justice, Love and Peace* published by St. Paul Editions, Boston, Mass. (1979), and the Pope's homily at Puebla and the final document of the bishops at Puebla from *Puebla: Evangelisation at Present and in the Future of Latin America*, St. Paul Publications, Slough, Buckinghamshire (1980). To these we would like to express our thanks.

The labour of getting a book to the press is lightened above all by patient and tireless secretarial assistance. Mrs. Pat Stevens was with me during the four years the book was in preparation and she well evidenced the possession of the virtues in question as successive drafts were typed and retyped. Miss Karen Varischetti, one of my students at the Saint Ignatius Institute, more briefly but with equal dedication organized and assisted in the preparation of a "final" version while I was in San Francisco. To Pat, Karen and her associates my grateful thanks also.

INTRODUCTION

As its title and subtitle indicate, this book considers the main principles of the social teaching or the social doctrine of the Church[1] (the principles of social, political and economic justice) as it is contained in the documents of the Second Vatican Council, examining the evolution of those principles from the Scriptures and through the Church's experience in history. It compares points of agreement and disagreement with other traditions and looks at developments since the Second Vatican Council, in both Catholic thinking and teaching, and considers the applicability of the social teaching of the Church to the changing situation in the world in general.

The relationship of the social teaching of the Church to Catholic social ethics[2] is that the latter is not only concerned with the theory of Catholic social teaching, its principles, but also with how it has evolved, what its relevance is today and how far it agrees with or differs from other theories about the nature of man's social, political and economic life and the moral values which should govern that life. The principles of this social teaching are binding on the Catholic conscience for reasons which are stated by the Council and are discussed below.[3] But that teaching cannot be properly applied unless it is understood in its context and in the light of its development. Social ethics, therefore, puts flesh on the bones of the

[1] This terminology, the "social teaching" or "social doctrine", was favoured by John XXIII in *Mater et Magistra* (London, C.T.S. edition, pars. 218–222), where he referred to the permanent validity of the "Church's social teaching" as admitting of no doubt, further stating that "this social doctrine is an integral part of the Christian conception of life." Paul VI also favoured this terminology, as we see in *Octogesima Adveniens* (London, C.T.S. edition, par. 42) and *Evangelii Nuntiandi* (London, C.T.S. edition, par. 38); John Paul II has recently referred to that "social doctrine" as a rich and complex heritage and called the bishops' special pastoral attention to "the urgent need to make your faithful people aware of this social doctrine of the Church." *Puebla: Evangelization at Present and in the Future of Latin America*. Third General Conference of Latin American Bishops (CELAM) (London, 1980), p. 13. (Address by Pope John Paul II, 28 January 1979.)

[2] The word *ethics* and the word *morals* both refer to the norms, the principles that govern human life and action in terms of "right" and "wrong", "good" or "bad". Ethics, strictly speaking, is concerned with the norms that are deducible by the aid of natural reason, human philosophy, only. Morals, strictly speaking, is concerned with the norms deducible from supernatural revelation, God's word in the Scriptures elucidated by the theologians and the Church's teaching. In practise the words are interchangeable—we speak of "theological ethics" and "moral philosophy" too.

[3] See below pp. 86 ff.

principles, facilitating the understanding of those principles by reference to their historical development and considering the findings of the
modern social sciences and the needs of modern society in order to judge
the soundness of the teaching and demonstrate its relevance.

The principles of Catholic social teaching accordingly are one element
in the presentation of its social ethic. They are concerned with the
conditions for a just social, political and economic order. As such, they
can be paralleled with the principles which should govern our personal
moral lives, but they are treated separately for obvious reasons. *Personal*
moral or ethical principles and *social* moral or ethical principles are both
equally binding on the Christian conscience. It is truncated Christianity
which is concerned with the proper ordering of personal moral life while
ignoring the moral governance of society in general and the need to work
for social justice. Yet it is much more difficult to apply the principles of
social justice with the same effectiveness, or to register their impact on the
conscience of the individual in such a way that they are seen to be of equal
importance to those which govern personal moral life.

Of its nature, the Christian ethic, the Christian moral code, is concerned
with my *personal* obligations to know, love and serve God above all things
and to love my neighbour as myself. This obligation grows out of
my status as a creature and my capacity and obligation to respond
to the love God has shown me. The norms laid down for us in the Ten
Commandments have formed, and still form, the basis of the Christian
obligation in this respect, the Christian *personal* ethic. Some of those
norms touch, indeed, upon what we can call the *social aspect of personal
ethics*—those which govern respect for property and for marriage, for
example. These are *personal* standards, *personal* norms, things we must, as
individuals, do or avoid doing. *But they impinge on society, they have a social
aspect*, a social implication, for all that they remain binding on us as
persons primarily. If I fulfill a personal obligation of righteousness in this
regard, then I serve society and my neighbour well too. But it is clear that
principles of this kind are of a different order from those principles which I
must try to put into practice in the social, political and economic order.

We can then usefully distinguish between *personal* ethics, the *social aspect
of personal ethics*, and *social ethics* proper. This distinction is seen most
readily if we imagine the case of a Swiss family Robinson, a family
marooned and isolated, and what would happen when they came back
into organised society. Living as a family alone, each member would
be bound by the moral law, by the needs of an ethically correct life
—truthfulness, respect for others, for property, honesty, and so on. These
are matters of personal morality or ethics which involve others on a
personal, man-to-man basis, although they also have a social aspect since

they affect others among whom we live. But the moment our Swiss family Robinson moved back into civil society, there would arise a whole new set of moral obligations, those which form the substance of social ethics: the moral obligation first of all to accept some responsibility for the affairs of the community—readiness to vote, to pay taxes and observe just laws. Work and its obligations would take on a new dimension; so would property ownership, education, social and cultural life generally.

The difficulty in meeting my obligation to have an effective attitude to social ethics is that that obligation involves me in collective decisions about matters of which I have either imperfect knowledge or limited control or both. For example, we all have the obligation to take an interest in the political life of the land, since those who wield political power have an important influence on our lives. Yet what that interest is depends on the abilities and opportunities of the individual, and once it is taken, I usually have to join with others in a collective decision, voting in a government for example, and have to judge extremely difficult alternatives at several removes. I vote for a party which forms a government— one vote among millions. If that party, when in power, does well by the common good, then I can take credit for that; if it does badly by the common good, I must take some of the blame. But in both cases credit and blame are less directly attributable to me than in the case, for example, of refusing to be dishonest in my personal life or, by contrast, choosing to be dishonest. There I freely choose to do an act, good or bad, of which I can foresee the consequences, and I must accept responsibility directly and fully for these consequences, good or bad. It is precisely because social decisions are collective decisions, because I am not able to affect things as directly as I can in a personal moral sphere, and because I have had to hand over my responsibility to a large extent to others, that it is harder for me to convince myself of the obligation to work for social justice through collective action. That obligation is there nonetheless and must be accepted—but that does not make it any easier for the moralist to give guidance or for the individual to feel the sense of personal responsibility as strongly as in personal matters.

This book on the social teaching of the Church, and the Catholic social ethic generally, is the result of the experience of some twenty years of teaching, writing and lecturing on the subject at various levels and in various contexts. My first book, *Man, Industry and Society* (1964), was an exploration of the ethics of industrial relations written during the 1950s and the early 1960s while I was studying for the priesthood. After ordination I continued these researches in industrial relations and sociology at Campion Hall, Oxford, while teaching social ethics as a general subject to the scholastics at Heythrop in the latter half of the 1960s. But it was while running the Catholic Institute of Social Ethics in the 1970s (the Institute is now merged with Plater College, Oxford) that the main structure of the book was formed. Father Maclaren joined me in 1977, and it was in the period when we taught our first two groups of students for the Institute's Diploma in Social Ethics, in 1977/78 and 1978/79, that the need for a comprehensive textbook of Catholic social ethics, related to the historical and "casework" approach we were taking in the Diploma course, became clear. There did not seem to be anything suitable available, and so, on the basis of the work we did in seminars in this period, the present volume took shape. The research that has gone into my previous publications in this area. *The Christian Social Conscience* (1970), *The Church and the World* (1973) and *Christian Ethics and the Problems of Society* (1975), provided me with an opportunity to clear the ground, but the present volume is very much a new departure in the light of the Second Vatican Council. Not until 1976 or so did I begin to see the importance of the new approach to Catholic social teaching made possible by the Council's insights.

The social teaching of the Church had suffered something of an eclipse in the 1970s,[4] partly, I think, because in the self-confident days before the Council, it was assumed that an acquaintance (however brief) with the social encyclicals was enough to enable one to "understand" the Church's social teaching. It was also assumed that the acceptance of the moral teaching of these and any other encyclicals could be taken for granted. Such assumptions, I suggest, account for the fact that much of the teaching and writing on the subject was perhaps a little too superficial and uncritical. The result was that those who had a basic confidence in the teaching were surprised by the sudden lack of interest in it and shocked by the open hostility that it was capable of receiving in Catholic circles. Certainly I shared these assumptions when I first started teaching the subject in the late 1960s to the Jesuits studying philosophy at Heythrop College in Oxfordshire. I thought I could begin a course on the social teaching of the Church with the background to *Rerum Novarum* and move from there on

[4] Indeed, on more than one occasion in the last ten years, it has been suggested that the teaching itself was no longer valid. For example, the Plater Memorial Lecturer in 1970 said that there was something "theologically bizarre about the attempt to formulate a systematic social doctrine" (*The Platernian*, vol. 1, no. 1, p. 10). Such a view was, of course, contrary to the understanding of the popes and the Church since Leo XIII. But, in the last ten years, many Catholics have lost confidence in the Church's tradition in these matters. At Puebla John Paul II had reason to remark that "placing responsible confidence in this doctrine—*even though some people seek to sow doubts and lack of confidence in it*—to give it serious study, to try to apply it, to teach it, to be faithful to it" is a guarantee, in a member of the Church, of a commitment to social justice. *Puebla: Evangelization at Present and in the Future of Latin America* (London 1980), p. 13.

ANALYTIC CONTENTS

CHAPTER ONE

THE ULTIMATE AND OBJECTIVE ETHICAL NORM: THE DIVINE LAW

The ultimate and objective ethical norm is the divine law—eternal, objective and universal, and man participates in this law through the natural law (Dignitatis Humanae, *paragraphs 2 and 3 and* Gaudium et Spes, *paragraphs 63 and 79).*

I. THE TEACHING OF THE COUNCIL ON THE ULTIMATE NORM OF MORALITY AND THE CONTEXT IN WHICH THAT TEACHING IS GIVEN

A. THE CONTEXT OF THE COUNCIL'S STATEMENT: RELIGIOUS FREEDOM

The ethical assumptions of the Council (9); the context of its statement about the supremacy of divine law: *Dignitatis Humanae* (10); freedom to seek and live the truth (12); contrast with the liberal idea of freedom (13); restraints on freedom (14); the need for law to have a moral basis (15).

B. THE CHURCH AND FREEDOM: SOME HISTORICAL QUESTIONS

1. The Early Church and Roman Society
The freedom offered by the Church, one of its attractions to early converts (19); the reasons for the acceptance of the Church by the Roman Empire and the effects of that acceptance (20); Christ, the martyrs and the freedom of the Church (21); the Church/state conflict and European ideas of freedom: the two swords theory (22).

2. The Church and Medieval Society
Church and society: a general view: What we mean by "the Middle Ages" (23); medieval Europe, emergence, growth, decline (24); the role of the Church in this period (25); the papacy, the Franks and Christendom (26); the Church and the moral and intellectual life of the Middle Ages (27).

The decline of slavery: Undermining its intellectual foundations (28); the monasteries and the ideal of free labour: Christian ethics and the reduction in the supply of slaves (29); the development of a free peasantry: monastic influences and economic needs (30); summary: the medieval theologians, the Church and slavery (31).

Education: The Church as educator: the Irish monks and the Benedictines (34); the emergence of the universities (35); the intellectual synthesis of the thirteenth century: the role of the friars and the universities (36); intellectual enquiry and the sciences: Nicholas of Cusa, Copernicus and Galileo (37).

3. The Secular Power of the Church and Its Consequences

The Investiture Controversy: Origins of the Church's involvement with secular affairs: Leo the Great and Gregory the Great (38); the papacy and the Franks: the Papal States (39); the Church as landowner and the implications of this role in the feudal system (40); the growth of lay control in the Church in the ninth and tenth centuries: Gregory VII, the excommunication of Henry IV and its consequences (41).

The Crusades: The religious and political/military context (42); the Crusades, chivalry, the Church's efforts to reduce violence and the appeals for help from the East (43).

The Inquisition: Heresy in the Middle Ages and its social implications (44); reasons for violence in dealing with heresy: the heresy trials (45).

Conclusion: The lesson of the Church's over-involvement in secular affairs: her services to freedom summarised (46); the links between the medieval and the modern worlds: the universities and the development of the physical sciences: representative government: freedom under the law: trial by jury (47); the communes, the guilds, and the dignity of labour: education and social welfare: understanding the Middle Ages (48).

II. The Divine Eternal Law As the Ultimate Moral Norm: The Teaching of Scripture

A. THE OLD TESTAMENT

The continuity of the Old and New Testaments: the Old Testament and its role in the history of the Jews (49); the Covenant, the prophets and objective morality (50); the connection between belief in God and the moral life: the Jewish tradition and that of contemporary and classical cultures (51); the Commandments and their binding force (54); the moral, ceremonial and judicial precepts of the Old Testament (55).

B. THE NEW TESTAMENT

Moral teaching of the New Testament: the approach to the texts (56); Christ, ethics and religion: his teaching on the Commandments (58); ethics in the teaching of SS. Peter and Paul (59).

into the twentieth century and its problems and the later documents of the social magisterium. Only in the teaching did it gradually occur to me that there was a need to consider the development of the ethical principles that were set forth in those documents, principles which had evolved from the Scriptures and through the dialogue of the Church with history. And it was not until I set up the C.I.S.E. in 1972 that I further realised it was essential also to establish the nature of Christian ethics or morality in order to show the validity of the social moral or the social teaching of the Church.

Through my work with the VIth Formers, first of all, then giving two series of popular evening lectures at Farm Street (1974–1976), and, finally, in the two years before the merger with Plater College in 1979—teaching a full-time one-year course mainly to graduates or people with professional qualifications—the problems clarified and the present volume evolved through seminars in the Institute. The use I have been able to make of my specialised studies in industrial sociology in the general teaching on social ethics, and in this book in particular, has been limited. But those studies have been of extreme importance to me in terms of deepening my conviction that the principles of the social teaching of the Church are valid in terms of social analysis. I know, in other words, from my use of them in research into industrial relations in the society I know best, that the prescriptions and the principles of the Church's social doctrine are an accurate and valid guide to understanding how to improve industrial relations in a free society. This knowledge gives me confidence in the social teaching in general—and the more I have to research into the historical and other situations to which the magisterium has responded in evolving its social teaching, the deeper has become my conviction of the value of that teaching.

The choice of the documents of the Second Vatican Council as the starting point of our seminar enquiry into the principles of Catholic social ethics was ultimately one that made itself. Initially we were at a loss where to start—so much was being questioned and none of the literature available seemed sufficiently relevant to developments since the Council or adequately rooted in the experience of the Church, or society, or helpful in understanding the relationship to present needs. It was when we came to realise the universal appeal that the "spirit of Vatican II" made as summing up the inspiration of the Holy Spirit and its guidance to the modern Church in the light of modern needs, that the document *Gaudium et Spes* stood out as the obvious place to start. There, surely, we thought, we could find the framework we needed, and I think we were not disappointed. The great advantage of *Gaudium et Spes* is that it sets out the main principles of the social teaching of the Church as it had been evolved in the social encyclicals until the time of the Council, and it does so very coherently, clearly and succinctly. Further, it brings in those questions of ethics of the family and of political ethics which are so much a part of the Church's social teaching, but which we were not used to seeing treated comprehensively in the social encyclicals.[5] The pre-Vatican II social encyclicals and *Gaudium et Spes* are, of course, not in any way in opposition. Indeed, it was the sophistication and the thoroughness with which those encyclicals had dealt with the political/economic issues in the years since 1891 which enabled the Council to bring together the elements of Catholic teaching on these matters with such effectiveness. But the earlier documents had been overwhelmingly concerned with questions of economic justice resulting from the impact of industrialisation. Apart from new issues in economic ethics which had arisen (some of which had already been dealt with in the social encyclicals of John XXIII which tended to be over-shadowed by the Council),[6] the centrality of the ethics of the family and of political ethics needed to be stressed. *Gaudium et Spes* provided this emphasis. Further, in *Dignitatis Humanae*, albeit in passing, the Council outlined the Catholic understanding of the nature of morality and also of the Catholic understanding of conscience, so reminding us of the essential guidelines of Catholic moral teaching. On such a firm and coherent framework we knew we would build. Again, we were not disappointed. Further statements of the magisterium since—for example, *Populorum Progressio* (1967) and *Octogesima Adveniens* (1971), above all the address of John Paul II to the Third General Conference of Latin American Bishops at Puebla on 28 January 1979, are all clearly elucidations or developments of the orthodox teaching summed up in Vatican II. Taking the statements of the Council on the foundations of Christian morality

[5] It has been the practice to refer to *Rerum Novarum* (1891) and *Quadragesimo Anno* (1931) as the social encyclicals, and these did mainly deal with the problems of industrialisation, liberal capitalism and Communism as an answer to the evils of that capitalism. But the full body of Catholic social teaching was much wider than this and contained much on the ethics of the family and political ethics, as we can see from such volumes as *The Pope and the People* (London: C.T.S., 1929), *The Church Speaks to the Modern World: The Social Teaching of Leo XIII* (Garden City, New York, 1954), and *The Church and the Reconstruction of the Modern World: The Social Encyclicals of Pius XI* (Garden City, New York, 1957). Yet that Catholic social ethics lacked this comprehensive approach can be seen from the fact that J. Y. Calvez and J. Perrin's *The Church and Social Justice* (London, 1961), originally published as *L'Église et la Société économique*, is entirely concerned with economic justice while E. Welty's *Handbook of Christian Social Ethics* (London, 1960) only deals very cursorily with economic justice, but is very full on political ethics and ethics of the family.

[6] In 1961 John XXIII issued the encyclical *Mater et Magistra* which was mainly concerned with problems of the Western world and, in 1963, *Pacem in Terris* which dealt with problems of international relations, peace and the underdeveloped countries.

and the nature of the Christian conscience as the basis of our enquiry into these matters, we were able to structure our discussion of the many problems in these areas on an agreed basis. So, too, in dealing with ethics of the family, political ethics and economic ethics, we found the way the Council dealt with these matters most enlightening and helpful. On the basis it provided, we could hope to structure a first-stage approach to the historical and contemporary issues.

We hope the book, therefore, will be useful to anyone who is seeking to study the social teaching of the Church as a serious academic subject. It is a textbook, therefore—but I hope it is more than that. I have tried to provide, in footnotes throughout the text, adequate references to reliable authorities who can enlighten the student further on the complicated and often controversial points an interdisciplinary survey of this kind can only touch on in passing. And in the bibliography I have tried to organise an annotated list of books for the same purpose. The book is intended to be one of a series that has grown out of our work with the Catholic Institute of Social Ethics over some nine years. Some will be original works we have planned ourselves, others will be reprints of standard works or collections of useful readings or texts, and we hope to commission other original work. In this way will be built up a useful literature on the Catholic tradition in social ethics so that there will be adequate material for other scholars, teachers and students.

R. Charles
Plater College
Oxford
6 April 1981

THE ULTIMATE AND OBJECTIVE ETHICAL NORM: THE DIVINE LAW

*The ultimate and objective ethical norm is the divine law–eternal, objective and universal, and man participates in this law through natural law (*Dignitatis Humanae, *paragraphs 2 and 3 and* Gaudium et Spes, *paragraphs 63 and 79).*

I. The Teaching of the Council On the Ultimate Norm of Morality And the Context in Which That Teaching Is Given

A. THE CONTEXT OF THE COUNCIL'S STATEMENT: RELIGIOUS FREEDOM

The idea that the standard for man in his moral life is God's eternal law, objective and universal, is central to the teaching of Vatican II.[1] By definition, such a law is absolute, allowing no higher authority that is, and it is unchanging and unchangeable. So basic is this assumption that it is taken for granted or mentioned in passing; it is not considered necessary to argue the case. The purpose of this chapter is to consider the clearest explicit statement made by the Council of this belief, and that is made in

---

[1] The word "objective" in ordinary language means that which is external to the mind, exists in reality independent of the mind of the thinker; "subjective" by contrast means that which is the result of my thinking it, which has existence only in my (the subject's) mind or consciousness. Though the *metaphysical* question (whether there can be a science beyond experience) and the *epistemological* question (whether we can indeed know anything apart from our ideas) are interrelated and as old as philosophy, the greatest philosophers of antiquity (for example, Socrates, Plato and Aristotle) were convinced that a metaphysical science was possible and necessary; they also argued to a knowledge which was objective, extramental, of "what is", not simply of "what I think to be". In this St. Augustine, St. Thomas and the scholastics were at one with them. They were similarly at one with them in their belief in an objective moral order, a "natural law"—an idea which had been more fully elaborated by the Stoics. Many modern philosophers, however, are less sure we can talk about metaphysics or objective reality, still less about objective morality. The Council's conviction about the knowability of objective truth and objective moral truth is based on the teaching of the Scriptures, of revelation. Yet that the same basic convictions can be arrived at on rational grounds is clear from classical Greek philosophy. Hence we may conclude that there is nothing in the nature of philosophy itself that suggests the Council's teaching is less than reasonable, however much out of sympathy with that teaching many modern thinkers are.

the document on religious freedom *Dignitatis Humanae*. We want to elaborate the statement and put it in its scriptural, historical and theological context and also to comment on another assumption made by the Council and growing out of that concerning divine law, namely that man participates in this law through natural law. The relevant passages of the Council's documents also introduce us to another fundamental assumption of Catholic moral thought which the Council shares, which is that the norm of conscience is the law of God authoritatively interpreted by the Church.

The context which the assertion about the supremacy of divine law is made is that of religious freedom. That it occurs in this context enables us to look also, in this chapter, at the question of the Church and freedom. This is convenient for several reasons.

Firstly, and most importantly, the question of religious and intellectual freedom, its necessity and its limitations, is a central one for social ethics. The obvious place to deal with it then is here where the Council's teaching on the matter provides the context in which the much more fundamental issue of the nature of Christian morality (which is our main concern) occurs. The second reason is that the argument from God's law is central to a proper understanding of man's right to spiritual and intellectual freedom and the other civil liberties which flow from that right. Thirdly and finally, it is a commonplace of objections to Catholicism that the Church has never been a friend of intellectual and spiritual freedom, yet here a claim is being made by the Council that the right to freedom flows directly from the law of God. Clearly, the whole credibility of the document is called into question, and with it the more central moral and theological propositions upon which it is based, if this objection is well-founded. To say something of the Church's role in the establishment of human freedom in the centuries when her influence was paramount is essential as an introduction to the whole subject.

The full context in which the relevant phrases about the divine, eternal, objective and universal law occur in *Dignitatis Humanae* is as follows:[2]

CHAPTER ONE

THE GENERAL PRINCIPLE OF RELIGIOUS FREEDOM

2. The Vatican Council declares that the human person has a right to religious freedom. Freedom of this kind means that all men should be immune from coercion on the part of individuals, social groups and every human power so that, within due limits, nobody is forced to act against his convictions in religious matters in private or in public, alone or in association with others. The Council further declares that the right to religious freedom is based on

---

[2] The italics in the text are the author's.

the very dignity of the human person as known through the revealed word of God and by reason itself.[2] This right of the human person to religious freedom must be given such recognition in the constitutional order of society as will make it a civil right.

It is in accordance with their dignity [a] that *all men, because they are persons, that is, being endowed with reason and free will and therefore bearing personal responsibility, are both impelled by their nature and bound by a moral obligation to seek the truth, especially religious truth.* They are also bound to adhere to the truth once they come to know it and direct their whole lives in accordance with the demands of truth. But men cannot satisfy this obligation in a way that is in keeping with their own nature unless they enjoy both psychological freedom and immunity from external coercion. Therefore the right to religious freedom has its foundation not in the subjective attitude of the individual but in his very nature. For this reason the right to this immunity continues to exist even in those who do not live up to their obligation of seeking the truth and adhering to it. *The exercise of this right cannot be interfered with as long as the just requirements of public order are observed.*

3. This becomes even clearer if one considers that *the highest norm of human life is the divine law itself—eternal, objective and universal, by which God orders, directs and governs the whole world and the ways of the human community according to a plan conceived in his wisdom and love. God has enabled man to participate in this law of his so that, under the gentle disposition of divine providence, many may be able to arrive at a deeper and deeper knowledge of unchangeable truth.* [b] For this reason everybody has the duty and consequently the right to seek the truth in religious matters so that, through the use of appropriate means, he may prudently form judgements of conscience which are sincere and true.

The search for truth, however, must be carried out in a manner that is appropriate to the dignity of the human person and his social nature, namely by free enquiry with the help of teaching or instruction, communication and dialogue. It is by these means that men share with each other the truth they have discovered, or think they have discovered, in such a way that they help one another in the search for truth. Moreover, it is by personal assent that men must adhere to the truth they have discovered.

It is through his conscience that man sees and recognizes the demands of the divine law. He is bound to follow this conscience faithfully in all his activity so that he may come to God, who is his last end. Therefore he must not be forced to act contrary to his conscience. Nor must he be prevented from acting according to his conscience, especially in religious matters. The reason is because the practice of religion of its very nature consists primarily of those voluntary and free internal acts, by which a man directs himself to God. Acts of this kind cannot be commanded or forbidden by any merely human authority.[3] But his own social nature requires that man give external expression to these internal acts of religion, that he communicate with others on religious matters, and profess his religion in community. Consequently to deny man the free exercise of religion in society, *when the just requirements of public order are observed*, is to do an injustice to the human person and to the very order established by God for men.

Furthermore, the private and public acts of religion by which men direct themselves to God according to their convictions transcend of their very nature the earthly and temporal order of things. Therefore the civil authority, the purpose of which is the care of the common good in the temporal order, must recognize and look with favour on the religious life of the citizens. But if it presumes to control or restrict religious activity, it must be said to have exceeded the limits of its power.

[2] Cf. John XXIII, Encycl. *Pacem in Terris*, 11 April 1963: AAS 55 (1963), pp. 260–61; Pius XII, Radio message, 24 Dec. 1942: AAS 35 (1943), p. 19; Pius XI, Encycl. *Mit brennender Sorge*, 14 March 1937: AAS 39 (1937), p. 160; Leo XIII, Encycl. *Libertas Praestantissimum*, 20 June 1888; Acta Leonis XIII, 8, 1888, pp. 237–38.

[a] *Author's Footnote.* A later paragraph (9) points to Christ's own example in patiently inviting and attracting disciples as evidence of the essential link between Christian belief and freedom.

[b] *Author's Footnote.* In the official Latin text a footnote referring to the *Summa Theologica* of St. Thomas I-II, q. 91 and q. 93 is given. It is omitted in the English translation. See below p. 61.

[3] Cf. John XXIII, Encycl. *Pacem in Terris*, 11 April 1963: AAS 55 (1963), p. 270; Paul VI, Radio message 22 Dec. 1964: AAS 57 (1965), pp. 181–82.

The general argument, therefore, is that man, because he is a person, possessing reason and free will, has an obligation to seek the truth, especially religious truth. The "especially" is important. It indicates that the right to seek the truth, though it is primarily one that pertains to religious matters, does not stop there. The whole burden of the document is the acceptance of the pattern of freedoms embodied in the modern constitutional state. Because that state is no longer marked by the aggressive agnosticism/atheism and rationalism that was typical of the nineteenth-century variety, the Church can recommend it and welcome it because in freedom men can seek the truth that she offers.[3]

The freedom to seek this truth and live it is founded in the nature of man and, subject to the needs of public order justly conceived, is not one that can be taken away from him. The inference is that *it is possible* to make the existence of this right an excuse for provoking public disorder. Clearly, the abuse of so important a right has to be condemned—as has the abuse of any other right. It is at this point that the argument about and from divine law in support of the right to seek the truth is introduced. It is pointed out that the highest norm of life is not *man's law*, but *God's law*, and this law is true and unchanging precisely because it is founded in the nature of God whose conception of things is eternal and unchanging. And since it is God who has given man the power to participate in his eternal and unchanging law so that he may know the truth more deeply, no human power can remove the duty to exercise that power from men. It is through its exercise that he forms true and sincere judgements of conscience.

[3] See H. Vorgrimler, ed., *Commentary on the Documents of Vatican II* (London, 1969), 4:83.

Is this, then, the Catholic Church embracing, late in the day and under pressure from the secular world, the ideals of liberalism, the Enlightenment and the Age of Reason? It is believed by many that the Church has encouraged repression rather than intellectual, spiritual and social freedom in times past. Surely if she now speaks out for freedom, it is because she has been shown the error of her ways. The argument and content of the document, let alone the historical facts, hardly justify such assumptions.

Liberal freedom was a claim, and is a claim, to absolute individual autonomy against the objective and universal law of God known to man through revelation and the teaching Church and the natural law in the context of that teaching Church.[4] Manifestly, the Council rejects such liberalism. The freedom it argues for is the freedom under the law of God. But since that embraces both the divine positive (the revealed) moral law and the natural law of right reason, through which man can attain to moral truth unaided,[5] there are inevitably sound elements in any claim to freedom which is based on right reason; not surprisingly, therefore, the liberal and Christian claims and rights overlap at many points.

In practice, the modern secular state accepts the need for some restraint on freedom. Public order is the criterion, stated in the *Declaration on the Rights of Man* in 1789 for example—and a similar provision is found in all comparable declarations, such as the Convention of Europe for the Protection of the Rights of Man and Fundamental Liberties.[6] An honestly erroneous conscience must be obeyed, but those who invoke the demands of conscience against the state to the point of provoking public disorder have to accept that the state has rights too. The question of how citizens with a genuine and deeply conscientious objection to the decisions of properly constituted authority may register their dissent is extremely complex, and some effort is made to summarize the position in a later section.[7] In this matter, the attitude of St. Thomas More is instructive. He sought only to have the right to think what he thought privately, without disturbing the good faith of others. It was because he was of this mind and showed that he lived by it even in the most difficult circumstances that he was able with good conscience, when he held public office, to proceed against those religious dissenters who disturbed the consciences of others and the public order with their beliefs.[8]

[4] On the philosophy of liberalism see below, pp. 91 ff. and on the conflict between liberalism and the Church in the nineteenth century, chap. 4, pp. 238 ff.

[5] The relationship between the natural and the divine law is discussed below, pp. 60 ff.

[6] Vorgrimler, ed., *Commentary on the Documents*, 4:74.

[7] See below chap. 4, pp. 215 ff.

[8] R. W. Chambers, *Thomas More* (London, 1963), pp. 262, 350.

In practice, therefore, there must be some restraint on human freedom, and the criterion suggested by the Council is that, whatever is demanded by objective justice for the preservation of the common good, for the maintenance, that is, of a sound social structure and order, must be the norm of that restraint.[9] Secular authority recognizes that incitement to violence and crime or the taking away of another's good name by slander or libel are "freedoms" which must be denied in justice and for the sake of the public good. Similarly, where freedom in the name of religion is invoked in ways which offend against these things, the state has a right to intervene. It may be very difficult in particular circumstances to decide what "the just requirements of public order" are, but unless we agree that there is a common good which it is the state's duty to protect, and unless we agree that we can and must seek justice in society in this as in all else, political life and morality part company.[10] In other words, the right of the state to determine what constitutes genuine religious freedom can only be turned against man in his search for God in a state which either in principle or in practice disregards God's law, revealed or natural.

The careful wording of the text of the document, therefore, indicates that those who drew it up were aware of the difficulties that arise, not only from restraints upon, but also from excesses of, freedom. This awareness is shared by all who are concerned with intellectual and political freedom. All place some restraints upon it. Secular liberalism accepts its restraints for its purposes and according to its values. The Council did not bless secular liberalism. It invites men to responsible freedom under the law of God, noting that secularists and Christians can come to the same conclusion on many issues.

We may note that implicit in the question of the right to religious freedom and the just requirements of public order is the related issue of the link between law and morals.[11] The obligations of the moral law are placed upon us by our Creator—those of the law of the land by those who have a right to rule and make laws. The moral law is concerned with the heart of man, with teaching him the way to salvation through the love of God and his neighbour; it judges the secrets of the heart through conscience and the word of God, interpreted by those entrusted by him with the task. The law of the land is concerned with providing for the

---

[9] *Dignitatis Humanae*, pars. 4–8 passim.

[10] The nature, origin and proper use of political authority and the foundations of political ethics are discussed in chapter 4, below.

[11] In this context we are not concerned with the moral obligation to obey the law but with the extent to which law can or should enforce morals. The question of the moral obligation to obey the law, and when we may in conscience disobey, is dealt with in considering political ethics—below, pp. 213 ff.

common good, making regulations which will enable the citizens to live together in peace and tranquillity. Its ordinances are indeed to be judged by the moral law, revealed and natural, but it must make its rules with regard to the needs of all men, not only those of believers, and it is also concerned with the external rules that all must obey for the good of all, even though the moral law is not directly involved. We may take, for example, the laws regarding the speed limit for motor vehicles. To ignore the existing law in this regard could lead to sin if, through disregarding it, serious injury is done to someone. The law itself, however, could be changed. There is nothing sacrosanct about a particular speed limit. Yet, law and sin are not in all cases disassociated. Some crimes (perjury for example) are sins also and are backed up by the residual belief anyway in divine sanctions. The form of the oath that witnesses take in a court of law indicates that here the knowledge that God is my witness is invoked in order to prevent the socially unacceptable crime of telling lies in court. It is because Western civilization was so profoundly influenced in its foundations by Christian belief that the administration of justice in this particular was affected in this way. There are other examples. Lecky noted the effect of Christian teaching on sex and marriage in Western culture and perceptively predicted what would happen if it was lessened.[12]

There are then central issues which affect human society, on which law must pronounce, and which require something more than the sanctions of positive law if they are to remain secure.[13] A Christian must see these essentials in the light of the Ten Commandments.[14] The precepts four to ten of those Commandments are of both natural and divine positive law. Any positive legislation dealing with these matters, therefore, should be for the Christian in accord with the precepts in question. But any society must get its values from a source other than positive law, or else be prepared to accept, sooner or later, arbitrariness or tyranny—because it is only an appeal to an unchanging standard which enables us to judge law as good or bad. Roman jurisprudence adapted the concept of natural law in an attempt to find its enduring basis. Christian scriptural, dogmatic and moral theology put this in the context of a divine positive (or revealed)

[12] W. H. Lecky, *History of European Morals* (London, 1911), 2:147. "Christianity taught, as a religious dogma . . . independent of all utilitarian considerations, that all forms of intercourse of the sexes, other than lifelong unions, were criminal; no other branch of ethics has been so largely determined by special dogmatic theology, and none would be so deeply affected by its decay."

[13] "Law and morality are bound by strong ties. In order to be healthy, the life of the people must . . . rest on a foundation of morality." R. Sohm, *Institutes of Roman Law* (O.U.P., 1907), p. 23.

[14] The nature of the commandments and their binding force is discussed below, pp. 55 ff.

moral law, with an authentic interpreter in the Church. Liberalism undermined this synthesis which still, however, structures so much of Western
thinking on law and morals; for example, the idea of right reason, natural
law, lingers on in modern jurisprudence. [15]

But if it is true that law must have a firm basis in morality, it would
seem to be equally true that it will only have an effective basis when
society possesses an effective consensus concerning the origin and nature
of moral law and its interpretation. Positive law is necessarily coercive.
Laws that are without sanction are of no value, yet man's conscience
cannot be forced, it can only be led by the forces and motives which
lie behind religious conviction or whatever other non-religious criteria
society recognizes as giving man the incentive to act righteously. Only
when society is agreed that some moral offences are so socially grievous
that the law must take action against them, can the law enforce morals.
Where the consensus does not exist, those who see the need for law to
enforce moral principles may certainly seek, in accordance with the right
to persuade and influence which is open to them in a constitutional state,
to ensure that the law may do this. But they will hardly succeed unless
society accepts the moral principles on which they base their case.

Given the close connection between moral consensus and key principles
of legislation, it is not surprising that the decline in Christian belief and
practice in society at large, which has been so marked a characteristic of
Western society in recent years, should have had its effect in the debate
about the reform of aspects of the law. In England it was with the
deliberations of the Wolfenden Committee on Homosexual Offences and
Prostitution, and the legislation which resulted, [16] that the debate came to
a head, [17] raising in the most acute form all those questions about the
relationship between morality and law which till then to many seemed so
academic.

That, until the reform, the treatment that homosexuals could receive as
a result of the working of the law was unjust, there can be no dispute. But

[15] "Natural law, or a like principle under another name, is an essential underlying
principle of the art of legislation." J. C. Brierly, *The Law of Nations* (O.U.P., 1963), p. 63.

[16] The Committee reported in 1957 (Cmd 257) and the Sexual Offences Act which was
partly based on it came into force in 1967.

[17] There has been a flood of literature in recent years. For example, H. L. A. Hart,
"Positivism and the Separation of Law and Morals", *Harvard Law Review* (February 1958).
P. Devlin, *The Enforcement of Morals* (London, 1959). N. St. John Stevas, *Life, Death and the
Law* (London, 1961), chap. 1, "Law and Morals". B. Mitchell, *Law, Morality and Religion in
a Secular Society* (O.U.P., 1970). R. A. Wasserstrom, *Morality and Law* (Belmont, Cali-
fornia, 1971). *The Hastings Constitutional Law Quarterly* (University of California, 1976),
vol. 3, no. 4. discusses the issues in an American context. See especially W. J. Bennett, "The
Constitution and the Moral Order".

that the effect of a change has had unforeseen effects equally seems to be beyond doubt. To say it is a matter of tolerant freedom for all is too simple: when social attitudes on a fundamental matter change and a new set of such values emerges, its very existence may in fact threaten injustice to another group or challenge the common good. For example, placing before the young the idea that society accepts homosexual and hetero-sexual love as of equal value runs the risk of undermining the very basis of society, the family. The generosity and sacrifice that is required if young couples are to undertake the task of bringing a family into the world and loving and caring for it requires every support from the community at large. Anything which separates sex from this context of family undermines the difficult ideal upon which we all ultimately depend—and the acceptance of homosexual love as equal to heterosexual effects that separation in the most comprehensive way. That in Britain before 1967 homosexuals were subject to blackmail and persecution is unfortunately true, and a change was needed, but for the reasons stated we must not swing to the other extreme and allow it to be suggested that society can accept the two forms of love as of equal value. A way has to be found of protecting homosexuals from persecution if they do not wish to try to change their orientation or abandon homosexual practices,[18] while main-taining the moral supremacy of heterosexual love in marriage. It re-quires tolerance and understanding of the homosexual's problem by society, but one which stops short of suggesting that homosexual love should be actively condoned or encouraged. Homosexuals for their part must recognize that toleration depends on those of their number who do insist on active relationships of this kind exercising discretion.

The same sort of conflict arises in other disputed areas of the relation-ship between personal and social moral values. Those who wish to make abortion[19] more easily available are forcing the consciences of those who are opposed to it in that the medical services that are used for this purpose are a community resource and in most cases are paid for at least in part by taxes to which all contribute; further, those resources are in limited

[18] John Paul II reaffirmed the Catholic teaching that "homosexual activity, as distin-guished from a homosexual orientation" is wrong, *USA: Message of Justice, Love and Peace* (Boston, 1979), p. 184, (Address to the American Bishops, Chicago, October 5); see also the *Declaration on Certain Questions Concerning Sexual Ethics* (London: CTS, 1975).

[19] T. J. O'Donnell, S.J., *Medicine and Christian Morality* (New York, 1976), pp. 137 ff. R. Shaw, *Abortion on Trial* (Dayton, Ohio, 1968). J. M. Finnis and C. W. A. Flynn, *What Do You Know About Abortion?* (Oxford, 1977). H. Peschke, *Christian Ethics*, 2:353 ff. discusses some of the recent Catholic questionings of the traditional teaching. The Joint Statement of the Catholic Archbishops of Great Britain, *Abortion and the Right to Live* (London: CTS, 1980) and the Sacred Congregation for the Doctrine of the Faith's *Declaration on Abortion*, (*L'Osservatore Romano* [English edition], 3 December 1974) restate that teaching clearly and persuasively.

supply, and any diversion for abortion purposes prevents other medical needs being satisfied. More fundamentally, when the community gives to its medical personnel the right to destroy innocent life, it does violence to the consciences of those who are opposed to such a course of action, since it is precisely in the name of the community of which they are part that the evil is being done. In the matter of homosexuality and abortion, there is no tolerant easy balance, but a conflict of fundamental values. The Christians, and those who hold similar views to theirs, would like the law to reflect their convictions; their opponents would like to see it reflect theirs. It cannot do both.

Euthanasia, or the threat of it, represents a similar dilemma.[20] We need to be careful what we mean by euthanasia. We are not obliged to use extraordinary means to keep alive when death is imminent, and the judgement as to what is extraordinary or not leaves room for interpretation according to the desire of the patient, the wishes of relatives, the implications of medical ethics and expertise and the guidance of the Church's moral theology. But euthanasia would permit denying the ordinary means (for example, food to a spina bifida baby) or giving a treatment which would actually kill—for example, a lethal injection or overdose of drugs to someone sick or senile. This again must be distinguished morally from giving pain-killing drugs to relieve suffering, even when we know the dosage necessary may well result in the death of the patient. Here the intention is to relieve pain, not to cause death. Euthanasia is precisely the direct intention to kill the sick or the senile simply because they are so.

A society which allows doctors officially to practise euthanasia in this sense would again be doing violence to the consciences of those who think it wrong; licensed by society as doctors are, in our name, to practise medicine, they would be making us unwilling participators in the evil. If supporters of euthanasia object that, if euthanasia is not allowed, their consciences are being violated because they think that existence for some is a burden of which they should be relieved, then this exactly illustrates the point made here—that on these fundamental issues the law cannot separate crime and sin. What it allows or does not allow touches precisely on one's view of what is moral and what is not, and each has the right to defend his or her fundamental values by constitutional means. Euthanasia, the direct intention of taking an innocent life which would go on were that action not taken, is against the revealed moral law as the Catholic moral

[20] Peschke, op. cit., 2:351 ff. O'Donnell, op. cit., chap. 3. J. Gould, *Your Death Warrant?: The Implications of Euthanasia* (London, 1971). D. J. Horan and D. Mall, *Death, Dying and Euthanasia* (Washington, D.C., 1977). Stevas, op. cit., pp. 262 ff. The Sacred Congregation for the Doctrine of the Faith's *Declaration on Euthanasia* (London: CTS, 1980).

tradition, with sound reason, sees it. Those who support voluntary euthanasia do so with a deceptive "humanity" which takes no account of the implications of, for example, putting the old out of their misery "for their own sake". The principle once accepted would be an invitation to abuses that could change the whole nature of such misguided "compassion".

The need for law to have a moral basis, and the need for that basis to be sufficiently acceptable to all to ensure that the law is respected, points to another fundamental issue—agreement on what the basis of moral law is. That, however imperfectly, Western civilisation until recently accepted the essentials of the traditional Christian, and indeed Catholic Christian, view meant that we had some such basis.[21] It is because we no longer accept that view in any coherent or effective form that we are now facing this crisis concerning the relationship between law and morals. Morality, in other words, cannot stand alone. It needs a sound theology or metaphysic. It was the achievement of the Catholic synthesis that it blended pagan, natural law insights with those of revealed ethics. It is not surprising that, with the rejection of the theological virtues of faith, hope and charity, the pagan or cardinal virtues of prudence, justice, fortitude and temperance are undermined also. Those virtues rely upon a belief in an objective, unchanging morality that positivism and relativism reject.

B. THE CHURCH AND FREEDOM:
SOME HISTORICAL QUESTIONS

1. The Early Church and Roman Society

The freedom under the law of Christ that the Church offered to its members was one of the things which made it so attractive, humanly speaking, to the citizens of a society increasingly fettered by bureaucracy.[22] The growth of centralization and the controls that accompanied it had been constant since the time of Augustus, but the anarchy of the third century resulted in the despotism of Diocletian (284–305) and a considerable tightening of restrictions on ordinary life.[23] The Church, by

[21] "Christianity sets the way Westerners, even those who would hate to think of themselves as Christian, think and feel about morals . . . that the individual, endowed with an immortal soul, is a free agent . . . (who) . . . once he is mature, knows by the grace of God and the teachings of the Church, right from wrong", Crane Brinton, *A History of Western Morals* (London, 1959), p. 169.

[22] C. Dawson, *The Making of Europe* (London, 1932), pp. 29, 35.

[23] *Cambridge Medieval History* (C.U.P., 1911), vol. 1, chap. 2; Dawson, loc. cit. The provinces were grouped into twelve dioceses and a huge bureaucracy directly responsible to the emperor, was created.

contrast, offered a free personal commitment in the Christian community, accepting all the self-discipline involved, and relying on the grace of God to make the attainment of the ideal possible.[24] The power of assimilation and the compactness of organisation which she possessed was the result of a freely accepted discipline—and, by the third century, nothing in the Empire, save the army itself, matched the resulting social strength and cohesion of the Christian Church.[25]

By the beginning of the fourth century, this third race, the Christian community, seems to have been in control of public opinion in the most populous parts of the Empire, and it was its all-pervasive social influence which made it such a useful ally for the disintegrating state. The Church did not need the Empire. It was the state which needed her. She entered into the alliance because of the logic of events,[26] and it was a mixed blessing from the first. Acceptance meant that there were secular advantages in Church membership and office and, inevitably, both became desirable for the wrong motives. Doctrinal and moral defects, which had never been absent from her life even in the most heroic times, flourished the more. Acceptance also meant increasing political interference in her affairs. These, then, were the drawbacks. But two things should be noted. Firstly, having insisted that she was not an enemy of the secular order as such, but capable of encouraging honest citizenship subject to God's law, it would have been unreasonable of her, even if she could have stopped the course of history, to have rejected the friendship of Rome. Secondly, not all the effects of the alliance were by any means bad. Once she was no longer persecuted she could carry on her mission openly and more effectively, and this was especially true of her works of charity.[27]

[24] "Christians were to be pure men, who do not cling to their possessions, they were also to be truthful and brave." A. Harnack, *The Mission and Expansion of Christianity in the First Three Centuries* (London, 1904), 1:208.

[25] *Cambridge Medieval History*, 1:96.

[26] 313 A.D. was the year in which Christianity was formally recognized. Constantine's motives were mixed. Certainly the alliance with the Church strengthened the state. G. H. Sabine (*History of Political Theory* [London, 1963], p. 186) sees this as Constantine's motive. On the subject see also *Cambridge Medieval History*, vol. 1, chap. 1. H. Daniel Rops, *The Church of the Apostles and Martyrs* (London, 1960), chap. 9. Mortimer Chambers et al., *The Western Experience* (New York, 1979), p. 151, concludes that "Constantine's conversion was a political as well as a psychological event . . . the Christian Church had shown itself strong enough to survive persecution. In modern terminology, Constantine was trying to bring the opposition into the government. As emperor of what was still a pagan state he continued to use pagan titles and symbols on his coinage; his personal life was hardly one of strict morality; and he delayed baptism until the year of his death, 337. He seems to have accepted the cult of Christ as one among many sources of divine help. Only gradually did he recognize its claim to be the one true faith."

[27] H. Dopsch, *The Economic and Social Foundations of European Civilisation* (London, 1937), pp. 248–49.

Christian influence on legislation was also possible now, and it became increasingly marked.[28] The alliance with the Roman State and the inheritance that she received from it better equipped her to undertake the task of evangelising the barbarian tribes as they settled in Europe. The Church took and preserved what was best in Roman life and order, and the barbarians saw belief in Christ allied to what was left of the civilisation whose achievements they wanted to share; in this way the Church's mission was helped.

The Roman inheritance aided the Church in many ways. The monastic law-making genius of Benedict, together with the patrician talents of Pope Gregory the Great, were instrumental in the formation of Western culture and civilisation. Gregory sent the Benedictines to evangelise the English, and it was an English Benedictine monk, St. Boniface (680–754), who, in turn, evangelised the Germans, working in close conjunction with the Roman See.[29] The link then forged between the international Church and the Frankish Kings through the agency of Boniface opened the way for the Franks to take the lead in the Latin West and save the infant new civilisation from the many forces which sought to destroy it from the outside.

Before entering into the alliance, however, the Church had already established, following the example of her master Christ[30] and through the testimony of her martyrs, the principle of the separation of the powers of Church and state which was to be a foundation stone of our modern ideas of individual freedom. In refusing to grant to Caesar what was not his to demand, the martyrs gave witness to the existence of an alternative organised force in society capable of resisting the totalitarian state. After the recognition of the Church by Rome, the tension between the two powers remained and it was in time rationalised into the theory of the two powers—that Church and state are each autonomous in their own spheres, and each is forbidden to trespass upon the other's rightful area of influence. The clearest early statement of the doctrine of the two powers is

---

[28] *Cambridge Medieval History*, 1:592 ff. Less despotic government, better treatment of slaves, suppression of the immorality of stage and arena, help for the poor in all its forms, and an increase in respect for woman are listed as examples of such legislation.

[29] St. Boniface was born in Devon and entered the Benedictine monastery of Nursling there. After teaching in the monastic school, he left for the mission in Friesland in 716 but had little success. Travelling to Rome in 719 he received the blessing of Pope Gregory II and returned to evangelise both Germany and Friesland, with great effect, as well as reforming the Frankish Church. Dawson, op. cit., pp. 201 ff. W. Levison, *England and the Continent in the Eighth Century* (O.U.P., 1946). J. C. Sladden, *Boniface of Devon Apostle of Germany* (Exeter, 1980).

[30] Mt 22:21. "Render to Caesar the things that are Caesar's, to God the things that are God's."

given in the Letter of Pope Gelasius (492–496) to the Byzantine Emperor Anastasius the First.

According to the elaborated theory,[31] there were two divinely instituted, separate and independent, but mutually supportive, powers in society—that of the Church for spiritual matters, that of the state for temporal. This notion of the independence of the Church, as the guardian of society's spiritual and moral values, helped to focus the political thought of the West on the idea of freedom because, in classical antiquity, the religious authority was precisely subject to the dominant social institution, the state. In Europe, the problems that arose concerning the relationship of Church and state have contributed very considerably to the development of Western political thought and practice. Indeed, without the controversies concerning that relationship, it is not easy to see how modern ideas of individual liberty could have emerged.[32] Belief in spiritual and intellectual freedom, and the idea of personal, individual freedom that follows from it, did not become embedded in Western thought in modern times. As the right of all men, not only the favoured few as in classical antiquity, it is based on the witness and example of the martyrs defying the almighty state.

The so-called Gelasian theory of the two powers remained the basic assumption of Christendom in the ninth and tenth centuries as it had done in the fifth and sixth. The theocratic character of the Frankish monarchy under Charlemagne was an interlude, the result of his highly personal conception of the role of the Church in his kingdom. His willingness and readiness to try to subject the Church to the state, for however laudable a purpose, underlined the difficulties and the conflicts that lay in the idea of one Christian society in which there were two autonomous and independent powers.[33] The clash between the emperor and the papacy which developed from the eleventh century was simply the most startling and important of these conflicts.

[31] Sabine, op. cit., pp. 194 ff. R. W. and A. J. Carlyle, *A History of Medieval Political Theory in the West*, (London, 1903), 1:188 ff. See below p. 230.

[32] It is revealing to note that G. Ruggiero in his *European Liberalism* (O.U.P., 1927), p. 403, testifies to the capacity of the Church to remain a bastion against tyranny. Commenting on Leo XIII's *Libertas Praestantissimum*—a document of which he by no means fully approved—he notes its assertion of the Catholic doctrine that legitimate power is of God and concludes that "where the right to command is absent, it becomes a duty to disobey men in order to obey God: in this way, the road being blocked to tyrannical governments the State cannot concentrate everything in itself . . . no one who reflects on the harshly authoritarian character of modern democratic civilisation can deny that the resistance of the Church to the tyranny of the state, though far from liberal in its inmost motive, may represent in point of fact a protection and defence of liberty."

[33] Carlyle and Carlyle, op. cit., 1:256 ff.

2. The Church and Medieval Society

Church and society: a general view

The medieval period was given the title "Middle Ages" during the Renaissance, when Europe was rediscovering the glories of Greece and Rome; the eighteenth-century Enlightenment continued to call them by this name, seeing in them only superstition, irrationality and deficient aesthetic sense. The view is no longer tenable. The period was one in which the distinguishing characteristics of Western culture emerged, a period in many ways comparable to the formative ages of Greece and Rome, and in the development of this culture the Church had the dominant role.[34] She exercised many of the functions of the state and did so on a supra-national scale: politics, jurisprudence, art, literature, civilised life and its refinements, agricultural, economic and urban development were all deeply influenced by her.[35] Medieval society was one into which one came by baptism,[36] and Christendom itself was an attempt, however imperfectly realised, to see the Christian ideal realised in every sphere of life.

The Middle Ages fall into three main periods: early (500–1000), central (1000–1350) and late (1350–1500). The beginnings lay in the invasions of the Empire by the Germans in 230 and 260 A.D. In 410 Rome itself was sacked.[37] The Muslim invasions of the West began in the seventh century and continued until they were checked at Poitiers by Charles Martel in 732. The invasions of the Vikings in the ninth and tenth, which were accompanied by those of the Magyars from the East and a resurgence of attacks on Italy by the Muslims (Rome itself was sacked in 846), were the

[34] S. B. Clough and R. T. Rapp, *European Economic History* (London, 1975), p. 38. M. Chambers et al., op. cit., chaps. 6, 8. In his introduction to *Medieval Europe: A Short History* (New York, 1978), p. 1, Professor C. W. Hollister remarks that one hundred years ago "the Middle Ages were seen as a thousand years of superstition and gloom that divided the Roman Empire from the new golden Age of the Renaissance—historians now realize that medieval Europe was tremendously creative . . . by about 1500 Europe's technology and political and economic organization had given her an edge over all other civilisations on earth . . . during the Middle Ages Europe grew from an under-developed rural slum into a powerful, compelling civilisation."

[35] H. W. Bussell, *Christian Theology and Social Progress* (the Bampton Lectures, London, 1907), p. 58–59. He notes that it was the sixteenth century which destroyed the unity of art, science and religion forged in the medieval period.

[36] K. S. Latourette, *A History of the Expansion of Christianity*, 2:347–48.

[37] In 476, with the imprisonment of the Western Emperor Romulus Augustulus by Frankish mercenaries under Odoacer, the Western Empire ceased to be. The Roman Empire was henceforth Byzantine, based on Constantinople, founded by Constantine in 330 A.D. The city and the flourishing civilisation lasted over 1000 years during which the barbarian West was painfully forming a new culture. M. Chambers et al., op. cit., chaps. 7, 10.

last and most terrible of all. This is the background to the period; it was out of the bloodshed of these incursions that the new order was born.

The conversion of the Frankish King Clovis in 498 opened the way for the formation of a new policy in Europe to fill the gap left by the Roman collapse. More than two centuries later, the English monk, St. Boniface, was sent by Pope Gregory to convert the Germans, and he also reformed the Frankish Church. When Pepin, the younger son of Charles Martel, sought to legitimize his seizure of power from the hands of the enfeebled Merovingians, Boniface anointed him King of the Franks at Soissons in 752. Later the Franks intervened in Italy at the Pope's request, in 754 and 756, to save the spiritual and political independence of the papacy from the Lombards; so was laid the foundation of that alliance that led to the crowning of Charlemagne Holy Roman Emperor and the emergence of Christendom.

Under Charlemagne, King of the Franks in 771 and Emperor in 800, Central Europe saw a degree of centralized and efficient government once more. The fifty-three campaigns that he waged marked the life and death struggle of Christendom and the Latin Church—German, Gaulish, Roman and Spanish—against the anti-Christian forces which sought to crush it.[38] It was in this period above all that Christendom was given its seige mentality; only by continued and military struggle did it survive. Charlemagne's kingdom itself, however, was not lasting, and after his death in 814 it disintegrated. The invasions of the ninth and tenth centuries brought chaos once more until the warlike Northmen and Magyars were, in their turn, converted and settled.[39]

From about the year 1000, a new growth is discernible. The slow process of reform in the Church, which was to come to a head in the papacy of Gregory VII (Hildebrand), owed much to the influence of the Abbey of Cluny founded in 910; by 1105, 314 monasteries followed its rule. The formalised feudalism which evolved from about 1000 meanwhile provided the framework of economic, social, political and military progress. It was a system suited to the needs of a disrupted and warlike time, when the power of the centralized state was limited or non-existent.

Accompanying the reform of the Church and the development of a system of feudal government was a vigorous economic growth. The subsistence manorial economy, which had been the characteristic of the early Middle Ages, was succeeded by the growth of towns, trade, manufacture and commerce. The reclamation of waste land, the development of agriculture and the increase in population went hand in hand throughout

[38] See H. A. L. Fisher, *A History of Europe* (London, 1976), 1:175.

[39] C. Dawson, *Religion and the Rise of Western Culture*, chap. 5. *The Making of Europe*, chap. 13. C. W. Hollister, *Medieval Europe*, chap. 7.

Europe with the process of urbanisation,[40] and the twelfth and thirteenth centuries also witnessed a revival of that learning that had briefly flowered during Charlemagne's time. About the turn of the fourteenth century there were signs of a change. The Avignon Papacy (1309–1377), followed by the Great Schism, highlighted the problems of the Church. The Black Death (1348–49), the Hundred Years' War between France and England (1338–1453) and the evidence of economic stagnation indicated the existence of a deep-seated social malaise. Intellectually, the nominalist movement undermined the synthesis so brilliantly erected by the scholastics— by St. Thomas particularly. But the fourteenth century saw also a new growth of intellectual, artistic and literary life in the Renaissance, and the fifteenth century was the age when European seamen began to open up the oceans of the world. In the sixteenth century, the corruption of the Church and the resultant theological controversies combined with the ambitions of those riding the new cultural and economic forces to bring about the Reformation.[41]

Throughout these formative years, it was the Church, her existence, her order, her influence, which, despite lapses, was the constant support of civilised values. In the early Middle Ages, she alone had been able to provide the organisation, the administration and the continuity upon which any hope of preserving civilisation and providing the precondition for its expansion rested.[42] Her services in this period cannot be overestimated. We take it for granted that, after the welter of invasions, the anarchy and the bloodshed that recurred through the six hundred years up to 1000, there would have arisen a new culture, a new civilisation. There was nothing inevitable about it. Civilisations had disappeared without trace before. Without the Church's influence, exercised in a very practical way, it is impossible to see how the Greek and Roman legacy could have survived in Europe and then, when the full glories of it were realised in the twelfth and thirteenth centuries, it was possible for it to be absorbed into the life and mind of the new order. Even more fundamentally, the moral and spiritual values which the Church gave to the barbarian invaders were the foundations of cultural unity and vitality.

[40] *Cambridge Economic History of Medieval Europe* (C.U.P., 1965), vol. 1, chap. 7; vol. 3, chap. 1. M. Chambers et al., op. cit., chap. 9.

[41] *New Cambridge Modern History*, vol. 2, "The Reformation". W. G. Hoskins, *The Age of Plunder* (London, 1976). M. Chambers et al., op. cit., chap. 14.

[42] "Only the Church retained a central organization and a universal character, able to maintain its cohesion while the Empire crumbled. It was, therefore, the main bastion of order and administration, able to take charge of cities and regions. This ability, together with its unique spiritual authority, was to make the Church the most influential power in preserving the past and in refashioning the future." G. Leff. *Medieval Thought* (London, 1970), pp. 25–26.

As noted, it was the link between the papacy and the Franks which was the key to the new European political order we call Christendom[43] and, throughout the development of that order, the Church was at hand to provide those responsible for the direction of secular affairs with the trained thinkers, educators and administrators they needed in their task. Charlemagne, who brought back to Europe once more the idea and reality of a strong civilised government, concerned to promote religion and secure justice and to redress the wrongs of subjects,[44] turned to the Church, and to Alcuin[45] in particular, for the education which he realised would be the basis of a sound political organisation. More dubiously, he drew upon the organisational strength of the Church in making dioceses and monasteries an essential link in the civil administration.[46] More dubiously still, he believed in making Christians by force. Alfred of Wessex[47] (849–899), whose defeat of the Danes marked the turning of the tide against the Vikings and the beginning of their conversion, also drew on the intellectual and moral resources of the Church to help him to restore the shattered civil order and build up a more stable civilised state. In addition to its influence upon men like these, one can say that the thread of civilised life was generally maintained, not by the civil authorities but by the Church. The monasteries were, for several hundred years, the most influential social institutions. The state lost contact with the urban tradition; theocratic government in the form of rule of the bishops replaced the municipal regimes of the classical world, and it was their significance as episcopal sees, rather than as political and commercial centres,[48] to which many cities owed their continued existence.

A fundamental work of the Church for society was in the services she provided for the slow and unspectacular rebuilding of the foundations of the moral life of Europe. St. Gregory of Tours[49] (538–594) details

[43] M. Keen, *The Pelican History of Medieval Europe*, chap. 1, analyses this concept and briefly examines the historical reality behind it.

[44] Fisher, op. cit., 1:176.

[45] Born Northumbria 735, died Tours 804. Alcuin had been educated in the monastery school at York. His achievements were as an educator, theologian and liturgical reformer.

[46] H. Daniel Rops, *The Church in the Dark Ages*, pp. 413 ff. There was never any doubt that the bishops and counts were regarded by Charles as equally officials of the state. The king's envoys were frequently ecclesiastics and the Emperor regarded himself not only as the supervisor of the Church's discipline but also of its doctrine. *Cambridge Medieval History*, 2:616, 682, 679. The great abbeys were likewise an integral part of the state organisation; see, for example, J. M. Clark, *The Abbey of St. Gall* (C.U.P., 1926), p. 5. H. Fichtenau, *The Carolingian Empire* (Blackwell, 1957), pp. 129 ff.

[47] E. S. Duckett, *Alfred the Great* (London, 1976), chap. 6.

[48] Dawson. *The Making of Europe*, pp. 268–9.

[49] O. M. Dalton, ed., *History of the Franks* (O.U.P., 1927). J. M. Wallace Hadrill, *The Long Haired Kings* (London, 1962), pp. 185 ff.

the moral collapse against which the Church was the only bastion. St. Bede (673–735) illustrates how, in preaching Christ and the life of grace, the monks gradually won over "an ungovernable people of an obstinate and barbarous temperament"[50] and taught them the Christian values. St. Boniface carried on the same task among the inhabitants of Frisia, and among the Germans and the Franks. The Viking invasions, however, once more reduced large parts of Europe to their former anarchy—to the despair of the Church leaders.[51] When these invasions ceased, and the invaders gradually settled and were in their turn converted, she once more set about her task of spiritual and moral revival.

This work for society grew directly out of her spiritual mission. The services she could offer civil rulers when they wished to advance education and good government likewise grew out of that mission. In pursuit, then, of her primary task of evangelisation and sanctification, she was also the agent of civil order and human culture at a time when political and civil authority and structures were weak and unstable.[52] The foundation of dioceses and parishes, of monasteries and nunneries, confessional work, preaching, works of piety, spiritual and moral education through the liturgy, apart from the formal education of the parish, monastic and cathedral schools, effected a slow transformation of ideals and morals and gradually renewed the fabric of society.[53] In the darkest period of the ninth and tenth centuries particularly, it was the monasteries alone which secured the tenuous links of civilised life amid the chaos.[54] In England, the Church councils were the first national assemblies, and under the Church's influence the first national code of law was formed. Here too, by the thirteenth century, parish organisation had laid the foundations of local government.[55]

[50] *A History of the English Church and People*, (London), p. 149.

[51] Dawson, *The Making of Europe*, p. 266.

[52] Daniel Rops, *The Church in the Dark Ages*, pp. 280 ff. "The organisation of the Church in the West". Latourette, op. cit. (London, 1940), 2:347 ff.

[53] M. Chambers et al., op. cit., p. 181, points out that the monks rejected both the classical system of values with its contempt for manual work and the barbarian approach with its love of violence, so laying the basis for a new set of values.

[54] "All through the darkness and distress from 850 to 950, the monasteries of Central Europe, such as St. Gall, Reichanau and Corvey, kept alive the flame of civilisation." Dawson, *The Making of Europe*, p. 233.

[55] Fisher, op. cit., 1:138. Dawson, *The Making of Europe*, p. 210. S. and B. Webb, *English Local Government: English Poor Law History*, pt. 1, "Old Poor Law" (London, 1927), p. 6. In Dawson's words: "In England the Church embodied the whole inheritance of Roman culture as compared with the weak and barbarous tribal states. It was the Church rather than the State that led the way to national unity through its common organisation, its annual synods and its tradition of administration," loc. cit.

The decline of slavery

The decline of slavery is a notable fact of the history of Western Europe—
and one of the greatest achievements of the slow work of moral reconstruction, growing out of the Church's own spiritual life and her organisation as a eucharistic community, was the undermining of the intellectual
and social foundations of that institution. She did not openly oppose it
as such. To argue that she should have and so brought about a change is
to transpose ideas and means of social and political action and organisation
that have developed only in the last two centuries into circumstances
where they could not have existed or worked—even if the prime task of
the Church, given to her by Christ, was one of social reform—which it
was not. The institution of slavery in the Roman Empire could not have
been overthrown by protest movements, even had there been a possibility
of organising such movements. And after Rome's collapse, the intellectual and social foundations of slavery had to be undermined before the
institution could be effectively challenged. That institution was the product of certain causes and unless those causes were attacked at the root, the
institution would remain.

   The intellectual foundation of slavery was the belief in the essential
inferiority of some human beings,[56] a belief which conveniently corres-
ponded with (if it was not produced by) the conviction that some types of
manual work especially were essential for the maintenance of civilised life,
but were unworthy of free men.[57] Sophists and Stoics challenged the idea
of the natural inferiority of some individuals, and Christianity, teaching
that all men were one in Christ, did the same; but Christianity's advantage
over Stoicism and other secular idealisms was that it did not stop at
preaching its ideal: its institutions and life embodied those ideals. Stoicism
had indeed taught the dignity of man, but it did not organise a living cell
comparable to the Christian eucharistic community in which that dignity
was evidenced in practice. In the life of the Church, the slave was entitled
to the same treatment as free men. Further, the influence of the Church
gave an unprecedented impetus to the age-old practice of emancipation,

---

   [56] The case is argued in Aristotle's *Politics* 1.5. "The natural slave is one qualified to be
and, therefore, is the property of another or who is only so far a human being as to
understand reason without himself possessing it."

   [57] "The ordinary Athenian had a deeply ingrained feeling that it was impossible for a free
man to work directly for another as his master . . . in the broadest sense slavery was basic to
Greek civilisation, in the sense that to abolish it and substitute free labour would have done
away with the leisure of the upper classes of Athens and Sparta." A. Andrewes, *Greek Society*
(London, 1971), p. 146. On the other hand, Greek thinkers were the first to question the
moral justification of slavery. W. de Burgh, *The Legacy of the Ancient World* (London, 1967),
p. 185.

because Christian belief gave a much more powerful spur to the en-couragement of the practice.[58] Since medieval society was the first major civilisation which had a uniformity of religion throughout its extent and embracing all ranks in society,[59] the permeative effect of Church organisa-tion on social attitudes regarding slavery, as on all else, was immense.

As to removing the stigma attached to honest labour, it was in the monasteries, centres of dedicated Christian life, that the ideal of free labour was born, and from them it first went out into the world.[60] In the monasteries, any service of the community, however humble, was re-garded as sanctifying, and no member of the community was exempt from such service simply on the grounds of birth or rank. For the Benedictine monk, agricultural labour in time became very much the exception—his manual work was of the domestic and workshop type. The Cistercian, on the other hand, stressed heavy manual labour. In both cases, the monastic ideal and the dignity of honest work went hand in hand.

As an institution, the Church helped in other ways to undermine slavery. Mark Bloch[61] notes that the overall decline in slavery in Roman and Christian Europe was due to three factors—the military, the religious and the economic. War captives had ever been the main source of slaves, and the comparative peace of the first years of the Empire reduced the supply. The Middle Ages were warlike enough but a new factor inter-vened to prevent its replenishment. It is one of the greatest triumphs of Christian ethics that the Church was able to impress on the minds of a crude and violent people that to make a slave of a fellow Catholic was not acceptable.[62] Slaves were still taken from among pagans and schismatics, but not from among their fellow Catholics, however nominal that Cathol-icism was.

Apart from the reduction in the supply of slaves and the influence of Christian values, the institution of slavery was being challenged by economic forces too. Slaves were a very inefficient form of labour, and common sense indicated that some form of non-slave, if not in our sense

---

[58] Lecky, op. cit., 2:30. These and other effects of the Church's influence gradually mitigated the lot of the slaves and helped produce the cultural atmosphere in which the institution was undermined. The Carlyles note that, while still defending the institution in theory in the ninth century, the overall effect of the Church's influence was to improve the lot of the slaves. Carlyle and Carlyle, op. cit., 1:208. See also K. S. Latourette, op. cit., 2:369.

[59] International Encyclopedia of the Social Sciences, vol. 2, s.v. "Christianity".

[60] E. Troeltsch, The Social Teaching of the Christian Churches (London, 1930), 1:163.

[61] Cambridge Economic History of Europe, 1:247. See also his Slavery and Serfdom in the Middle Ages (London, 1975).

[62] Cambridge Economic History of Europe, 1:249.

of "free" labour, was preferable. Yet it would be unwise to say that com-
monsense considerations would alone have brought about the change,
had the supply of slaves been maintained. It is significant that, when such a
supply on a large scale from non-Christian sources (that is, from among
the African tribes) became available, they were immediately seen as useful
in the exploitation of the wealth of the New World. Here the settlers were
effectively out of the control of the Church and the social conventions of
Christendom. The slave trade, and the building of an economy on it,
became profitable and possible once more, and every subterfuge was used
to justify it.

Another way in which the Church stressed the dignity of free labour in
theory and in practice, so helping to establish it as an alternative to slavery,
was by encouraging a free peasantry capable of managing its own affairs
and undertaking the responsibilities of ownership. Needing to develop
the land they owned, the monasteries in France in the early Middle Ages
pioneered the settlement of colonists or *hospites*, and these in time formed
villages of independent peasant farmers. Nor was it only economic and
development motives which led the monks to act in this way; they also
wished to help those who were fleeing from the injustice of their overlords and to identify with and help the poor and the landless by giving
them the means of independence.[63] Later there is evidence that the revolt
of the peasants against the feudal burdens they bore was one directed
particularly against the monasteries—though different authorities interpret the information available in different ways.[64] Since many monasteries did in fact fall very short of their ideal by this time, it is not
surprising that they were wanting in this particular also.[65]

One of the results of the gradual break up of the feudal system was an
increase in personal freedom through the decline of serfdom. But with
freedom came greater insecurity for many. If the serf had been tied to the
land, the land had been tied to the serf and provided him and his family

[63] Ibid., 1:45 ff, 71 ff.

[64] Compare J. W. Thompson, *An Economic and Social History of the Middle Ages* (London,
1928), p. 679, with Eileen Power in *The Cambridge Medieval History*, 7:738. Overall "feudal
lords knew how to take care of themselves, there was precious little safety for anyone else
. . . the Church showed far more comprehension of the peasant's point of view than the
nobility." *Cambridge Economic History*, 1:69–70.

[65] For example J. M. Clark in his *The Abbey of St. Gall* (C.U.P., 1926), p. 16, "by the
13th and 14th Centuries . . . the monks were men of noble birth to whom asceticism did not
appeal. The abbots were barons in monastic garb." See D. Knowles, *The Monastic Order in
England* (C.U.P., 1949), p. 686 ff. However, we must keep a sense of proportion. Though
there is plenty of evidence that the religious spirit waned in many monasteries in the later
Middle Ages, still, at the time of the dissolution of the monasteries in sixteenth-century
England, for example, historians are not persuaded that the monastic system was beyond
reform (David Edwards, *Christian England* [London, 1981], p. 297).

with the essentials of a meagre existence.[66] Freedom for the poor man was not always a blessing; change, especially rapid change, brought problems then[67] as now. What had been needed was a transition to greater freedom which avoided the creation of a proletariat. Christian Europe did not achieve this. But her achievements in terms of freedom were considerable, and in them the Church played a full part. She had undermined the intellectual foundations of slavery by giving a firmer base for the understanding of human dignity and the true equality of all, by teaching and practising the dignity of labour; above all, by permeating society effectively so that precept and practice went hand in hand, the Church prepared the way for a civilisation without slaves. By ensuring that the warlike Middle Ages would not make slaves of their Christian captives and so provide the cheap supply which is the requisite for a slave economy, she helped to prevent its re-emergence, and when the medieval economy underwent its period of great growth, 1000 to 1300, the free labour system grew too.[68] And the ordinary worker was demanding, and getting, a share in the control of affairs—the first time in history when this was done on such a scale.[69]

Given that Christian influences, combined with social and economic forces, gradually undermined and then virtually eliminated slavery by the thirteenth century, by which time serfdom was being undermined too, the question can be asked—why did not theologians and the Church condemn slavery in principle?[70]

[66] B. Tierney, *Medieval Poor Law* (Berkeley, California, 1959) p. 25.

[67] According to Eileen Power, *Cambridge Medieval History*, 7:733, there were two: firstly, the steady subdivision of holdings (and consequent inefficiency) and, secondly, the growing numbers of landless labourers "the formation of a rural proletariat".

[68] Byzantine civilisation likewise was based on free labour (M. Chambers, op. cit., p. 205).

[69] P. Boissonade, *Life and Work in Medieval Europe* (London, 1927), pp. 334–35, "For the first time the masses became associations of freemen . . . fitted by their intelligent activity to collaborate in all spheres . . . in tasks which aristocracies alone believed themselves able to fulfill."

[70] The Church's attitude to slavery over the centuries is the subject of John Maxwell's *Slavery and the Catholic Church* (London, 1975). This otherwise excellent little book suffers from its failure to see the documents with which it deals in their historical and sociological context. Its proper title should in fact be *Slavery in the Documents of the Catholic Church*—and there is far more to the Church's witness in this as in all other aspects of its life than what appears in her documents. Further, the book curiously sees its subject in the light of some of the less sensible aspects of the debate in the Church that has gone on since the Second Vatican Council. Thus, to say that, regarding abolition, "lay reformers won without much help from the teaching authority of the Church" (p. 119), is to ignore the fact that it was pressure on the Church authorities from laymen—slavers, slave owners and their friends which made it difficult to change the emphasis in her teaching earlier than she in fact did. The question is discussed further below pp. 149 ff.

The question is, in fact, less reasonable than it seems. The record of the African slave trade and all that it entailed has made the modern European conscience rightfully sensitive on the matter of slavery, since it was modern Europe which encouraged it and benefitted from it most. Medieval Europe, on the other hand, could look back on a gradual elimination of the institution from its own life by slow process of attrition. Theologians, canonists, councils of the Middle Ages, as their counterparts in every age, were taken up with urgent problems of their time; slavery was not one of them, it had almost entirely disappeared from their midst. To expect them to be as agitated about slavery as the European conscience has been in the last two centuries is then more than a little unhistorical. Further, when we ask what it was in Western thought and culture which made it possible for Europe to challenge the institution world wide, not only on economic and political grounds, but on intellectual and moral grounds too, we find that it was precisely attitudes, conventions and institutions which had been inherited from its medieval and Christian past. They are summed up in the idea of personal freedom which, in Britain and America, was particularly strong. It is no accident that it was the bringing of slaves to Britain from the West Indies which led to the first serious legal and moral challenge to slavery in the late eighteenth century. Similarly, it was when the possibility that slavery might challenge the free worker in the United States was fully realised that the war between the North and South over slavery became inevitable. Other factors were at work in challenging slavery in the nineteenth century, it is true, but it was the interaction of these with the realisation of the challenge to freedom which slavery presented, that brought about its demise.[71]

There are good grounds for saying that this idea of personal freedom that became embedded in the Western consciousness over the centuries took its origins in the example of the martyrs in the early Church. Their refusal to concede to Caesar what was not his to demand, and the later conflict between the Church and the state in the Middle Ages which was a continuation of the same struggle, "left a residuum without which modern ideas of individual liberty would scarcely be intelligible".[72] This idea of personal freedom and dignity, based on man's obligations before

[71] See below pp. 149 ff.

[72] Sabine, op. cit., p. 196. The full context of this comment is worth considering. According to the author, the idea of a universal society which was transmitted by the Fathers of the Church to the Middle Ages was that "mankind formed a single society under two governments . . . this conception differed from any that prevailed in pre-Christian antiquity because it divided men's loyalty and obedience between two ideals and two rulerships . . . thus it placed the Christian under a twofold law and twofold government. This double

God, permeated the growing social institutions of medieval Europe.[73] The dignity of free labour was first evidenced and became a socially accepted value through the example of the ideal Christian life in the monastery. In welcoming the slave into the eucharistic community as an equal with free men, the Church, which was to mould the mind of Europe, gave to it a practical example of the theory of spiritual equality. The contribution of the monasteries to the growth of a free peasantry, the sanctification of labour in the religious practices of the guilds, the elements in the Church's life which encouraged representative government, her influential place in the towns and the cities which spearheaded the move-ment to freedom, all pointed to the importance of her life and teaching in the growth of this European ideal. That there were aspects of her life and practice which were less positive in this matter, there is no denying. Each must judge whether they outweigh the contributions made on the posi-tive side.

Twentieth-century man, and the twentieth-century Christian particu-larly, still finds it hard to understand why medieval theologians did not turn their minds to questioning the moral basis for slavery. True, they had no reason to justify it as had the Greeks and the Romans; medieval society, unlike Greek and Roman, did not rest on an economy that was slave-based. But this fact could be seen as an added reason why the theoretical justification of the institution should have been challenged. One difficulty was that the Scriptures seemed to teach that slavery in some form could be justified temporarily—provided it was deprived of those cruelties and injustices which always seemed to accompany it.[74] Probably more influ-ential was the evidence that the greatest thinkers of antiquity found it possible to justify it, and that as knowledge of Roman law increased, there was found a mass of apparently sound reasons for accepting that slavery in some circumstances was just; capture in war, penal enslavement, birth of a slave mother were some of the reasons adduced.[75] Whatever the reason,

---

aspect of Christian society produced a unique problem which in the end contributed perhaps more than any other to be specific properties of European political thought. Far beyond the period in which the relation of the two authorities was a chief controversial issue, the belief in spiritual autonomy and the right of spiritual freedom, left a residuum without which modern ideas of individual privacy and liberty would scarcely be intelligible."

[73] See below p. 47. Modern ideas of freedom under the law and equal justice for all, common law rights and trial by jury were formulated in medieval times. It was a time when the rights and freedoms of the ordinary average freeman were given importance.

[74] R. de Vaux, *Ancient Israel* (London, 1973), pp. 80 ff. R. Schnackenburg, *The Moral Teaching of the New Testament* (London, 1975), pp. 244 ff. J. F. Maxwell, *Slavery and the Catholic Church*, pp. 22 ff., 27 ff. See below pp. 149 ff.

[75] Maxwell, op. cit., pp. 44 ff.

we can certainly say that if theologians on the whole did not defend the institution positively, neither did they find it necessary to repudiate the classical arguments in favour of it. In the *Summa*, for example, St. Thomas notes but does not comment on Aristotle's theory of natural slavery, simply observing that utility and positive law seemed to commend it.[76] However, since all utility and positive law were to be judged according to the requirements of the natural and revealed laws, such a qualified acceptance must be understood accordingly; it was precisely because in practice the institution of slavery more often than not offended against one or another of these laws that theoretical justifications of it were ultimately irrelevant.

Education

The Church's educational work marked her most important contribution to the development of intellectual freedom, although it was learning for the service of God and the Church which was its whole intention from the beginning. There were two elements in this work, the basic one of schooling which was the function of the parish and the cathedral school, and the more advanced theological and philosophical task which was originally the work of the monks. The education of the young for the service of the Church required that they have a sufficiency of learning and, from the sixth century, provision for such was made by Church councils. Fulfilling these obligations fell mainly upon the parochial and the cathedral schools, although the monasteries were also involved with the education of the young.[77]

It was to the Irish monks that Northern Europe mainly owed the maintenance of the thread of learning in the sixth and seventh centuries.[78] In Ireland the Roman writ had not run and the monks had to bring to their converts all the arts that went with the assimilation of Christian culture, including the knowledge of the Latin tongue, the language of the international Church, and they kept the language alive after the Roman collapse. But all their cultural efforts had an apostolic purpose. They were tireless missionaries. St. Columba founded Iona about the year 563, and from there the evangelisation of the North of England and Scotland took place. St. Columban (543–615) began his missionary work in Burgundy in 591, founding three monasteries, including that at Luxeuil, which in

[76] St. Thomas Aquinas, *Summa Theologica*, II–II, q. 57, art. 3, ad 2; q. 104, art. 5, ad 2; I–II, q. 94, art. 5, ad 3.
[77] *Cambridge Medieval History*, vol. 5, chap. 22.
[78] Dawson, *The Making of Europe*, chap. 11.

time gave rise to scores of other foundations. He was expelled for his censures on the King's concubinage, passed to Zurich and thence to Bobbio in Italy.

In time, however, the gentler rule of St. Benedict (480–547) became the norm of monastic life;[79] though in his own lifetime only three monasteries followed his rule, that rule eventually was recognized as most suitable as a general basis for religious life. St. Bede of Jarrow (673–735), Alcuin of York (735–804) and St. Anselm of Bec (1033–1109) were torchbearers of the great tradition of Benedictine learning.[80] Monastic schools were dominant in higher education until the eleventh century, when those attached to the cathedrals in Northern France began to take the leadership, and it was from the latter that many of the new universities such as that at Paris developed; between 1150 and 1500 some eighty such universities were set up throughout Europe. Paris (famous for theology and philosophy) emerged in the first part of the twelfth century and later in that same century came Oxford (Arts) and Montpellier (Medicine). Cambridge, Salamanca, Padua and Toulouse followed in the thirteenth century. The Italian universities of Salerno and Bologna predate the period of great growth, although they were revitalised by it; Bologna, through its influence in the field of canon law and civil law, played a crucial part in the development of European culture. Its graduates dominated both the Church and the state through their masters of both civil and canon law.[81]

A great impetus to the intellectual revitalisation of Europe came with the impact of the Jewish and Arab influences and the rediscovery of the corpus of Aristotle's writings through these channels.[82] The non-Christian origins of the rediscovered learning stimulated the teachers and thinkers of the Christian West. They had to show that what was good in the new influx of knowledge could be reconciled with Christian belief and how what was not so sound could be combated. There is no greater evidence of the intellectual vitality of medieval Christianity than the

[79] L. J. Daly, *Benedictine Monasticism* (New York, 1965). E. C. Butler, *Benedictine Monachism* (London, 1923).

[80] M. Chambers et al., *The Western Experience to 1715*, p. 190 ff., 293 ff. F. C. Copleston, *A History of Philosophy* (London, 1959), vol. 2, chaps. 11, 15. Leff, op. cit., chaps. 3, 5.

[81] Dawson, *Religion and the Rise of Western Culture*, chap. 10. *Cambridge Medieval History*, vol. 6, chap. 17. C. H. Haskins, *The Rise of the Universities* (London, 1978).

[82] Avicenna (980–1037) and Averroes (1126–1198) were the most prominent Muslim, Avicebron (c. 1020–c. 1057) and Maimonedes (1135–1204) the most prominent Jewish thinkers. Translations of the main Greek classics began in Syria in the eighth century and reached Spain through the Muslims there.

rapidity with which Aristotle was not merely received but absorbed into, and became part of, the Church's intellectual tradition.[83]

The intellectual synthesis that emerged in the thirteenth century was simply the last stage in a long process of the development of Catholic theology and philosophy—the foundations laid by the Fathers and Doctors of the Church were the basis, but a new growth was discernible from the time of Charlemagne. John the Scot (c. 850) produced a philosophical system, but founded no lasting school. With the work of St. Anselm (1053–1108) and Peter Abelard (1079–1142), however, a systematic and distinctive new approach began. Anselm spoke of "faith seeking understanding" and gave to the world the ontological argument for the existence of God. Abelard, in his *Sic et Non* ("Yes and No"), assembled the views of the various authorities on key theological issues, pointing out their discrepancies and leaving the resulting problems seeking for a solution. The development of the dialectical, the scholastic, method in philosophy and theology provided it.[84]

It was into this situation that the new learning of the ancient world made its entrance in the thirteenth century.[85] The recovery of that inheritance from classical times, and the intellectual vigour of the universities, provided the stimulus to intellectual growth; but it was the energy of the papacy and the availability of trained philosophers and the theologians in the new orders of friars, the Dominicans and Franciscans, which were the dominant influences in producing the required synthesis of faith and reason. When the Aristotelean teaching, filtered through Muslim and Jewish scholarship, seemed to be threatening the intellectual hegemony of the Christian world, Dominicans and Franciscans were sent by Rome to Paris, Bologna, Oxford and Toulouse and, from the middle of the thirteenth century, the leading theologians and philosophers were friars; it was through their efforts that the unity and vitality of Christian thought was maintained.[86]

The university system within which the scholastics worked had faculties of arts (initially based on the *trivium* of grammar, rhetoric and logic, and the *quadrivium* of arithmetic, astronomy, geometry and music),

[83] Sabine, op. cit., p. 247. Keen, op. cit., pp. 152 ff., comments that the Arabic philosophers were condemned by their own religious authorities; after the same attempt was made to prevent the use of Aristotle in the schools, the more active intellects, especially St. Thomas, were able to show how to reconcile the philosophy to Christian belief, and to supply for the deficiencies of the newly discovered system where Christian insights demanded new approaches. See below pp. 61 ff.

[84] M. Chambers et al., *The Western Experience to 1715*, p. 260.

[85] W. de Burgh, *The Legacy of the Ancient World*, p. 452. Leff, op. cit., chap. 7. Copleston, op. cit., vol. 2, pt. 5.

[86] Dawson, *Religion and the Rise of Western Culture*, p. 234.

theology, medicine and the law—canonical and civil. The natural sciences, as such, had no part in their formal curriculum, yet two things especially helped prepare the ground for modern scientific thinking and concern with the natural sciences. The first was the distinction between reason and faith, which we owe particularly to St. Thomas. By making such a clear distinction, he secured the freedom of the scholar to seek the truth wherever it was to be found, so throwing open the door for the advance of the physical sciences;[87] given such a distinction, they were independent of the authority of a discipline which proceeded from the postulates of faith, which was concerned with revealed truth. The second was the methodology of the schools. Higher studies in the university were dominated by the practice of submitting every question to the process of intellectual mastication in public disputation or debate.[88] Though, like all aspects of scholasticism, it deteriorated rapidly, the habit of disciplined thinking and systematic investigation, which it demanded, opened up the way for the development of the scientific method and the technological civilisation based upon it.[89] Modern science, it has been claimed, not without some justification, is the child of medieval science.[90]

It is in this context that the later errors of the churchmen in their treatment of Galileo have to be considered. The pioneers of medieval science were of necessity clerics. Robert Grosseteste (1175–1253), arguably the founder of modern experimental science, was a priest as well as an academic and became Bishop of Lincoln.[91] Galileo's heliocentrism was not a new theory: it had been anticipated by the fifteenth-century Cardinal Nicholas of Cusa and the sixteenth-century Canon Copernicus, who had

[87] De Burgh, op. cit., p. 459.

[88] Dawson, *Religion and the Rise of Western Culture*, p. 230.

[89] E. Heer, *Medieval Civilisation*, p. 231. It is worth remembering how comparatively widespread university education was in the Middle Ages. According to the *Cambridge Medieval History* (6:600–601), "It is possible that a larger proportion of the population received a university education at the close of the Middle Ages than is now the case in modern countries . . . the popular conception of the Middle Ages is far too favourable on the side of religion and morality . . . far too grudging on the intellectual side." Granted that the author was writing in 1929 when a university education was a rare privilege for the few, it remains a remarkable tribute to the late Middle Ages that a scholar of Rashdall's standing could make such a judgement.

[90] R. C. Dales, *The Scientific Achievement of the Middle Ages*, p. 176. See Copleston, op. cit., vol. 3, chap. 10.

[91] Roger Bacon (1214–1292) was his pupil. Grosseteste began lecturing at Oxford in 1200 and was Chancellor in 1215. He developed a method of investigating physical phenomena and made scientific experiments in pursuit of his interest in light metaphysics. A. C. Crombie, *Robert Grosseteste and the Origins of Experimental Science 1100–1700* (O.U.P., 1953). The objections to Dr. Crombie's thesis are considered in R. C. Dales, *The Scientific Achievements of the Middle Ages*, pp. 172 ff.

both challenged the theory that the earth was stationary and that the rest of the heavens revolved around it. Galileo's advantage was that, with the aid of a newly developed telescope, he was able to demonstrate the truth of heliocentrism. He was initially well received in Rome, but the apparent conflict between his findings and some statements of Scripture led to his being denounced to the Inquisition in 1616 and again in 1633. There is some controversy over whether he was forbidden to teach the heliocentric theory altogether or simply to stop teaching it as proven. However that may be, he signed an abduration and served out his imprisonment to his death in 1642, either at his villa in Florence or staying with friends.[92]

The Galileo case reflects no credit upon the Church authorities—though not even his most ardent admirers would deny that some of Galileo's own personal characteristics contributed to his difficulties. However that may be, it was a matter of scientific fact which was at issue, in determining which theologians, as such, had no competence. The Reformation had made the Church a little too cautious. Had she possessed theologians of the capacity of Alfred the Great and Aquinas and an intellectual vitality equal to that of the thirteenth century, the situation would not have arisen.[93] The earlier challenge of Aristotelianism had been much greater, but under the guidance of men like Aquinas it had been overcome. As it is, the Galileo incident had been left to stand in condemnation of the Church's obscurantism, despite the centuries of effort in education that were the foundation of the European intellectual tradition and bore fruit particularly in that uniquely European institution—the University.

3. The Secular Power of the Church and Its Consequences

The Investiture Controversy

The leadership the Church was able to give in educational matters during the medieval period was due to the completeness of her integration into the social, political and economic order of society, the feudal system. She had not needed the power of the state to establish herself under the Roman Empire in the first instance, neither did she depend on the feudal order for

[92] L. Geymonat, *Galileo Galilei* (London, 1965). J. Brodrick, S.J., *Galileo* (London, 1964).

[93] J. G. Bewkes et al., *The Western Heritage of Faith and Reason* (London, 1963), p. 509. In his address at the Pontifical Academy of Science's Commemoration of the Birth of Albert Einstein, Pope John Paul II pointed out that Vatican II had, in paragraph 36 of *Gaudium et Spes*, regretted such mistakes as the Galileo incident. He expressed the hope that the illusion of the conflict between faith and science, which many think still exists, would disappear as a result of collaboration. *L'Osservatore Romano* [English Weekly Edition], 26 November 1979, p. 9.

her existence—it was a case of the Roman Empire leaning upon her, rather than she upon it. Likewise, she did not choose the secular role which the Middle Ages gave her; it was thrust on her by events. To take but one example, Charlemagne made the bishops and abbots, and the structure and organisation of the Church generally, an integral part of his state organisation. It is not possible to see how the Church could have prevented him doing this—and while there is no doubt of the benefits that the cooperation brought to the state, there is equally no doubt that, whatever temporary advantages the Church gained, her over-involvement in secular affairs did great spiritual damage in the long run.

The key figures in the development of the Church's international political influence before the link with the Franks were Leo the Great and Gregory the Great. Leo was asked by the Emperor of the West, Valentinian III, to take part in an embassy seeking to negotiate with Attila the Hun in 452.[94] The negotiations were successful, and the tradition thereafter attributed that success to Leo. The political influence gained by the papacy at this time was thenceforth never lost. St. Gregory the Great[95] (590–604) reigned at a time of even greater confusion and despair, and his temporal leadership was exercised on a more massive and consistent scale. It was then the real authority and achievement of these men, responding to the needs of the time, rather than seeking to possess temporal power for its own sake, that secured for the papacy its political role.

The popes looked to the East for protection for themselves and for the effective direction of temporal affairs in Italy, but increasingly the weakened Empire passed over its temporal responsibilities there to the bishops of Rome; examination of the papal documents of the eighth century reveals the reluctance on the part of the papacy to accept the role.[96] The break finally came over the Byzantine Emperor's support of the iconoclast[97] heresy which was at its height under Constantine V (740–775). It was this, combined with the political weakness of the Empire in Italy, which threw the papacy into the arms of the Franks.

As the imperial hold on Italy weakened, the considerable, but ill-defined, political power of the papacy came under pressure from the Lombards who filled the vacuum left by the retreat of the Byzantines. Fearing that subjection to the Lombards would lead to the same attempt to interfere in Church affairs that had occurred under the Byzantines,

[94] *Cambridge Medieval History*, vol. 1, chap. 14. Daniel Rops, *The Church in the Dark Ages*, chap. 2.

[95] *Cambridge Medieval History*, vol. 2, chap. 7. F. H. Dudden, *Gregory the Great* (London, 1905), 2 vols.

[96] Carlyle and Carlyle, op. cit., 1:289.

[97] Daniel Rops, *The Church in the Dark Ages*, pp. 356 ff. D. Knowles and D. Obolensky, *The Middle Ages*, pp. 86 ff.

the popes appealed to the Franks for assistance against the new threat.[98] Pepin, who had been anointed king by Boniface with Rome's support, responded, expelled the Lombards in 756 and handed over to the pope the lands that had been taken by the latter from the Byzantines. The Papal States had come into being.[99]

The temporal power which now passed to the popes, then, was a result of the political weakness of the Empire and the confusion of political affairs in Italy. To the desire of the papacy for freedom from interference was added the self-interest of the Romans, the local nobility seeing in the papal domains a source of wealth and influence for its members. From this situation came many evils—the papacy itself was now a feudal princedom and by the ninth century was afflicted by the corruptions of the time. Though the need for a sphere of political independence by the popes so that they could exercise their spiritual responsibilities freely was real, it was to be another twelve hundred years before the problems raised by that independence could be satisfactorily solved.

It had been the confusion that followed the collapse of centralized political power in Italy that had forced the papacy to assume a role as *de facto* temporal ruler and which set in motion the events that led to the formation of the Papal States. In like manner, it was the ability of the monks especially to take a lead in the organisation and improvement of agriculture during the early and central Middle Ages which played a major part in establishing the Church as a great landowner. Reclaiming waste lands and making them fruitful, the monks filled a vital role in the development of the European economy, and it was one that society recognized. Grants were made to the Church for purposes of piety, stewardship or development. The Cistercians, in the central Middle Ages, underlined in a most spectacular manner this contribution of the Church to the development of the economy.[100]

Not only as agriculturalists did the monks serve the secular order. The social strength and continuity of a monastic community was a continuing

[98] P. Hughes, *History of the Church* (London, 1939), vol. 2, chap. 4, section iii, *Cambridge Medieval History*, vol. 2, chaps. 18, 22. Daniel Rops, op. cit., p. 390. *New Catholic Encyclopedia*, s.v. "States of the Church". The so-called donation of Constantine which was forged to establish the papacy's independence against Byzantium dates from about 750. It purported to show that Constantine bequeathed the Empire in the West to the pope.

[99] The "patrimony of St. Peter" was considerable at the time of Gregory the Great (Dudden, op. cit., 1:296 ff.), and had accrued through imperial grants, legacies, and gifts of the faithful. The patrimony comprised lands in Italy, Campania, Sicily, Africa, Dalmatia and Gaul.

[100] *Cambridge Economic History of Europe*, 1:76 ff. By 1152 there were over three hundred houses, all of them established in the wilderness and becoming centres of a thriving agriculture. Among their achievements the Cistercians were mainly responsible for developing the sheep farming that became the basis of the British woolen industry, some complaining they did this at the expense of existing villages (ibid., p. 81).

boon to an unstable and warlike society. The role of monasteries and Church institutions as savers and investors benefitted society as did the encouragement it gave to the arts and crafts through their building and artistic activities. But the secular work of the monks was not their first purpose. The social effect of the monks' efforts was a by-product of a Rule which enjoined work of various kinds, along with prayer, study and penance as the way to sanctity. Newman summed it up admirably.[101] St. Benedict

> found the world, physical and social, in ruins, and his mission was to restore it in the way not of science but of nature. Not as if setting about to do it by any set time or by any rare specific or by any series of strokes, but so quietly, patiently, gradually that it seemed often till the work was done it was not known to be doing. The new work he helped to create was a growth rather than a structure, silent men were observed about the country or in the forest, digging, clearing and building and other silent men, not seen, were sitting in the cold cloister tiring their eyes while they painfully copied and recopied manuscripts they had saved . . . by degrees the woody swamp became a hermitage, a religious house, a farm, a village, a seminary, a school of learning and a city.

The significance of the Church's position as a great landowner was that feudalism, the system of social organisation in the Middle Ages, was based on landholding or working in return for personal service—military or agricultural. Hence, as a major landholder, the Church was inextricably bound up with the secular order. Her abbots and bishops were key figures politically, economically and militarily, and the corruptions and problems that resulted from the Church's involvement in this way, because of wealth her labours had created or which she had received from others for the service of God, were many. That very involvement, it is true, gave her a chance to exercise her reforming influence; according to Thompson,[102] she never accepted conditions as she found them, was never simply content to let things drift, passively to tolerate abuses or corruption either in herself or in secular society. The Church possessed the leaders and the strength to initiate reforms and worked with great courage and industry, despite her lapses, to make a better feudal Europe, to redress the wrongs and abuses of secular society. Yet the implications of the secular involvement were a serious challenge to her spiritual role and leadership.

The confused intermingling of her secular and spiritual roles was particularly marked in the period of the Viking invasions of the ninth and tenth centuries, when all aspects of civilised life were threatened by the turmoil, and centralized control in Church and secular society practically

[101] *Historical Sketches* II (London, 1912), p. 410.
[102] *An Economic and Social History of the Middle Ages* (London, 1928), p. 676.

became impossible. The papacy itself underwent a period of corruption, while lay control of abbacies and bishoprics—for the sake of the wealth and military power they brought—increased to scandalous proportions.[103] The inevitable effect of having unworthy men in high office in the Church was that the spiritual and apostolic life waned; but the spirit of reform in the Church was never lacking, and from early in the tenth century, with the foundation of the monastery of Cluny, the pace quickened leading eventually to the papacy of Gregory VII, Hildebrand, in 1073.

Hildebrand saw in the practice whereby the secular lord "invested" the abbot or bishop with the insignia of his office the symbol of the corruption he so hated.[104] Trying diplomacy and persuasion at first to get Emperor Henry IV to end the simony and clerical concubinage that was a scandal to the whole world, he eventually decided that stronger measures were needed, and in 1076 he excommunicated the recalcitrant monarch.

This act of a purely ecclesiastical character had political consequences of momentous importance. Henry's feudal vassals were now free of their oaths of fealty; the Emperor was, in practical terms, deposed. It was to be the beginning of the long controversy wherein it would be claimed by some that the pope had both the fullness of temporal and spiritual power—a denial therefore of the two swords theory. More of this will be said later in dealing with political ethics. What is significant in our context is that the forces of reform in the Church were prepared to take on the mightiest monarch of their day for the sake of their spiritual ideals. It was to be a lesson in reforming zeal and its power which was to leave its mark on the European mind.

The Crusades

The involvement with the Crusades[105] is an aspect of medieval Church life the modern world finds hard to understand. There is between us and this period an enormous cultural gulf. We find it difficult to sympathise with a society so impregnated with Christian ideals, however imperfectly understood, and hard to appreciate the effects of the embattled mentality which had grown up in a developing culture so long threatened from the outside. For six hundred years Europe had undergone successive waves of

[103] Daniel Rops, *The Church in the Dark Ages*, pp. 529 ff. Dawson, *Religion and the Rise of Western Culture*, chap. 7.

[104] G. Tellenbach, *Church, State and Christian Society in the Time of the Investiture Controversy* (London, 1940). Sabine, op. cit., chaps. 12, 14. See below chap. 4, pp. 180 ff.

[105] The main ones took place in 1096, 1147 and 1189; the fourth (1201) was diverted to the capture of Constantinople: St. Louis of France died on the seventh Crusade in 1270. A good short account of this complex and contradictory movement is given in C. W. Hollister, *Medieval Europe: A Short History*, pp. 151 ff. See also M. Chambers et al., *The Western Experience to 1715*, pp. 304 ff. Both give guides to further reading on a vast subject.

THE ULTIMATE AND OBJECTIVE ETHICAL NORM

invasion; Charlemagne's campaigns against the encircling forces of the anti-Christian world were only one episode in the struggle. It is in this context that the Crusades must be viewed—the threat of being overwhelmed which had hung over Europe until the eleventh century. Further, the essential conflict predates Christian Europe; it had begun in the fifth century before Christ with the clash between Persia and Greece. Europe, still less the Church, did not create but inherited this historical antagonism, the result of an aggression from the East. The racial and political aspect of the movement was therefore as fundamental as the religious,[106] though it was the unity of Europe in one faith that made the Crusades possible and the papacy which set the armies of Europe in motion: the role of international leader fell to it inevitably because there was no other institution capable of rallying the divergent interests of Europe in a common cause.

The Church, therefore, canalised an historical antagonism into an idealistic defence of the Holy Places which unleashed some of the noblest and most unselfish instincts in man, as well as providing an opportunity for the indulgence of the basest. Any historical movement has a right to be judged by the standards of those who best represented its ideal—St. Louis, for example, and there were many others who were worthy of what they proclaimed. It is significant that today the word *crusade* still indicates a noble cause, however hopeless. And, paradoxical though it is to us, the Crusades seemed at the time to be one way of channelling the warlike instincts of the newly converted Norsemen to a more constructive end than the private feuds which disturbed the peace of Europe. The Church had tried to mitigate violence by the code of chivalry, the Truce of God and the Peace of God;[107] it now appeared that crusading would absorb warlike energies in a justifiable way. There had been appeals from the East for help, the vigour of the Seljuk Turk seemed to renew old dangers, and there was a need to protect pilgrims and the Holy Places. The warlike character of her children, it seemed, could be put to good use while relieving some of Europe's internal problems. Of such complex causes were the Crusades born.

The Inquisition

The use of force against heresy and heretics seems to many even less intelligible than crusading. Heresy was a comparative newcomer in the Middle Ages. Though the phenomenon had been known in the early

---

[106] The judgement is that of the *Cambridge Medieval History*, 5:265, and also of P. K. Hitti, *The Arabs* [10th edition] (1970), p. 635. Runciman's conclusion on the other hand in his *History of the Crusades* (London, 1971), 3:480, is that "the Holy War was nothing more than a long act of intolerance in the name of God."

[107] M. Bloch, *Feudal Society* (London, 1971), 2:312, 412 ff.

Church, there was little heresy evident in the West between the fifth and twelfth centuries; from the twelfth century it multiplied.[108] Its source was threefold: a simple revolt against the established religion (many of whose representatives were spiritually and morally lacking), an element of dualistic heterodoxy from the East preaching the evil of the flesh and, thirdly, a smaller element of systematic and sophisticated theological error. The two dominant traits at a popular level were Waldensianism and Albigensianism (or Catharism). The Waldensians started a campaign in 1170 for greater simplicity in Christian life and were initially orthodox, but errors crept in, and in the end the movement was condemned. The Albigensian or Catharist threat was much more serious and had to be crushed by military force; from 1209 a series of crusades over a period of twenty years finally succeeded in destroying it.

To judge the medieval reaction to heresy, we have to remind ourselves that in medieval times the concept of what social peace required was different from our own. Heresy was not only a religious offence, it was an attack on the whole of the Christian basis on which medieval society was founded. It was, in the circumstances, in effect a treason against the social order as well as an offence against God—and all societies fear treason as few other crimes. Neither did the Church have to create the atmosphere in which the persecution of heretics was possible. It existed in the fear of social breakdown remembered only too well by a culture that had known centuries of chaos, it was fed by the prejudices of the people and responded to by the secular authorities who initiated the first physical persecution.[109]

The reason why heresy took root lay in the corruption and moral weakness of the Church. But attack on Church corruption could be profitable; wealthy supporters of Albigensianism were only too ready to use theological disputes as an excuse to enrich themselves with the wealth of the Church. Nor was there any lack of awareness within the Church of the evils of corruption, but so embedded was she in the existing social order which had so largely contributed to the evils of her state, that she could hardly engage in reform without tremendous and violent social upheaval. Albigensianism in southern France had developed forms that made it subversive of civilisation and social order.[110] No society could

[108] D. Knowles and D. Obolensky, *The Middle Ages*, chaps. 32, 41. *Cambridge Medieval History*, vol. 6, chap. 20.

[109] "At the opening of the 11th Century, we find the secular arm meting out the punishment of death . . . sometimes indeed the people acted on their own authority. There are cases of this in 1106 at Cambrai . . . in one instance we are told the crowd burnt the heretics through fear of clerical leniency." *Cambridge Medieval History*, 6:715.

[110] J. Sumption, *The Albigensian Crusade* (London, 1978), pp. 48 ff., gives some account of the beliefs of the sect; pessimistic about life, apparently condoning suicide and con-

ignore the threat it presented, and yet the papacy was the only central authority with the prestige and power needed to protect secular society. Regarding the actuality of the threat that Albigensianism presented and the papacy's role in crushing it, the comments of two non-Catholic authors may be of interest. Lea, the American historian of the Inquisition, regarded the heresy as marking a return to primitive savagery. It was not merely a revolt against the Church, but the abdication of man before nature. Paul Labatier, in his *Life of St. Francis*, judged the papal initiative in crushing the Cathars to be a triumph of good sense and reason. [111]

The instincts of the Churchmen were initially against any use of violence, and it was only slowly under the growing size of the threat, and under the influence of the revival of Roman law, that it was reluctantly accepted. At the same time there was much superstition and ignorance in what passed for Christianity in medieval times, and it was capable of firing mob violence against real or supposed heretics as scapegoats, much as today other forms of prejudice and ignorance make other minorities scapegoats.

In the eleventh century ecclesiastical documents speak only of excommunication as a punishment, and it is the secular power which takes it upon itself to execute. In the twelfth and thirteenth centuries the mood changed; the bishops, fearful of antagonizing the powerful, often did not prosecute heresy through their courts. [112] It spread more quickly in consequence, and, to counter it bishops were instructed to make enquiry about heretics and take steps against them. A special official with the task of seeking out heretics was appointed in 1227, when the Council of Narbonne found the older system was not working. These new methods were still ineffective and, in 1233, Pope Gregory IX instituted Judge Delegates for heretical causes which in time took over the task from the local bishops altogether. The Holy Office had come into being.

At the heresy trial a notary minutely recorded the proceedings, and there were present also counsellors who were in theory a check on arbitrary action. [113] Yet the process in practice was open to abuses. While the average inquisitor was no monster, those abuses occurred and when, in 1215, the use of torture had been sanctioned at the examination of those

---

demning marriage, refusing to swear a binding oath, theirs was a profoundly anti-social message. The uprightness of the perfect, if arrogant, nonetheless stood in challenge to those who, though orthodox, were not as obviously ascetic.

[111] Quoted in Daniel Rops, *Cathedral and Crusade*, p. 534.

[112] M. Chambers et al., *The Western Experience to 1715*, p. 288.

[113] The inquisitors were "on the whole, picked men . . . high qualities of courage, probity and zeal were demanded. Bernard Guis' description of a model inquisitor is a fine one even by modern standards." *Cambridge Medieval History*, 6:720.

accused, they were compounded by the cruelty of the torturers. Of penances imposed on those judged guilty, most were of a spiritual nature, but the obdurate and the recidivists were turned over to the secular arm for the administration of the death penalty; of one inquisitor's sentences over seventeen years (613 in all), forty-five were for handing over to the secular arm. Such figures hardly support the idea that the Church itself was bloodthirsty. In truth she did not desire the death of the heretic—the inquisitor was above all a missionary and father confessor.[114] It was when the secular arm was interested in using the Inquisition as a means of secular policy, as in Spain, that the death penalty was used on a large scale.[115]

Conclusion

However we may make allowances for the circumstances of the time and discount the exaggerations with which the evils of the Inquisition have been embellished, it rightly appalls us that the Church was in any way allied with physical torture in the examination of heretics and in any way concerned with their condemnation to death. It is a warning to us of her identifying too closely with the moods and prejudices of the people of a particular social milieu. The Church was eased into the use of violence in this way gradually and by degrees, and we can now see that the secular involvement in which she was caught up, initially by no choice of her own, made it inevitable. The teaching of the Second Vatican Council represents then, not a concession to secular indifferentism, but the logical implication of the Church's desire for freedom from too close alliance with the state. Her involvement in the secular affairs of the Middle Ages was initially not willed. The effects of that involvement were a patchwork of good and bad, and it is only the knowledge of the whole picture that enables a balanced judgement to be made. She was in the first centuries a haven of free service and, for more than a thousand years, strove to enlighten, to educate and to civilise in her work of bringing man to God. In particular, the great reforming movement in the eleventh and twelfth centuries affected every aspect of life. Insistence on clerical celibacy helped to free the Church from the corruption of feudalism and was a necessary stage in the spiritualizing of Western society.[116] The reformed clergy supported the efforts to suppress private warfare, and through them the Church helped revive intellectual life as she established better educational facilities for her priests. The conflict with the Empire advanced the

---

[114] Ibid., p. 724.

[115] Daniel Rops, *Cathedral and Crusade*, p. 551. H. Kamen, *The Spanish Inquisition* (London, 1965).

[116] J. W. Thompson, *An Economic and Social History of the Middle Ages*, p. 661.

understanding of and development of the institutions of constitutional government. Above all, the Gregorian reform, the result of a good man pitting his strength against entrenched evils, gave an example of the power of good men to change the world for the better which the West thereafter never forgot.[117]

Between the end of the Middle Ages and the modern world there lies the Renaissance, the Reformation, and the Ages of Reason and Enlightenment. In a later chapter we will be considering the Church's interaction with the secular world and modern times and her response to modern ideas of political and other freedoms. It is, however, no longer possible to posit a total break between the medieval world and that of the Renaissance and Reformation which succeeded it. The cultural continuity is now more apparent than it once was, and there are many pointers to that continuity.

The medieval universities which still flourish are one, as is the scientific and technological civilisation made possible by the habits of mind formed in those universities. Representative government, which has been the main agent through which modern ideas of political freedom have developed, points to the same continuity,[118] as does the idea of freedom under the law and equal justice for all under the law, which became embedded in our institutions in medieval times. The common law and trial by jury are medieval in their origin, and clerics codified and formulated that law.[119] In this period the ordinary average man emerged into his own.[120]

> Men of one sort, free and lawful men, could be treated as the normal sort while other sorts enjoy privileges or are subject to disabilities which can be seen as exceptional. The lay Englishman, free but not a nobleman, who has come of age and who has forfeited none of his rights by crime or sin is the law's typical man.

[117] M. Chambers et al., *The Western Experience to 1715*, p. 256.

[118] E. Heer, *The Medieval World*, p. 231, and Carlyle and Carlyle, op. cit., 6:523 ff. summarize it so: "In the political structure of the Middle Ages there was always implicit . . . and sometimes expressed, the idea that the best form of government is that in which all members of the political community have their share . . . the development of representative government was taking place . . . subject to the final authority of justice and the divine and natural laws, it was the community which was supreme . . . the community which included the King, the nobles, the people. This was the principle out of which representative government grew."

[119] R. O'Sullivan, *The Spirit of the Common Law*, p. 94, quoting Pollock and Maitland, *History of the English Law*.

[120] O'Sullivan, op. cit., p. 96, quoting Holdsworth, *History of English Law* [3rd ed.], 3:457.

It was an age when, for the first time, those who worked with their hands, in field or workshop, were able to assert their rights by their own efforts and became associations of freemen, proud of their independence, conscious of the dignity and value of their labour and capable of showing that they could govern and rule themselves and others also for the commonweal.[121] The Church was suspicious of some aspects of the communal movement, on the other hand in the development of a free peasantry and the growth of the guilds, her overall influence was positive.[122] A university education was more widely available to all who had the interest and ability in the thirteenth century than at any time until our own day,[123] and we have seen how it was ecclesiastical interests and needs which developed the universities from the cathedral schools. The Church, which was responsible for social welfare, provided it on a scale not exceeded until the present century.[124]

These observation are not made to suggest that the Middle Ages was a golden age. They knew too much ignorance, poverty, squalor, brutality, famine, disease and war for us to delude ourselves with any such notion. Our purpose has been to show that this period, in which the Church was so dominant, was indeed an enormously creative one in human terms, and that there was much in that achievement which owed a direct debt to the Church. To remember only the Christian failures and to ignore the successes is to distort the picture. We have simply tried to restore the balance, to show that when the modern Church speaks about the connection between belief in God and the need for freedom, her own witness indicates that the connection is a real one.

II. The Divine Eternal Law
As the Ultimate Moral Norm:
The Teaching of the Scriptures

A. THE OLD TESTAMENT

The coming of Christ and the New Testament of his life and death can only be understood as a fulfillment of the Old. The introduction to the Christian life and truth is to be found in the teaching and events recorded

---

[121] Boissonade, op. cit., p. 334.

[122] Dawson, *Religion and Western Culture*, pp. 207 ff. *Cambridge Medieval History*, vol. 5, chap. 19. E. Lipson, *The Economic History of England* (London, 1920), vol. 1, chap. 8.

[123] *Cambridge Medieval History*, 6:601. With their "enormous intellectual enthusiasm . . . (they) . . . represent one of the greatest achievements of the medieval mind." C. H. Haskins, *The Rise of the Universities* (O.U.P., 1957), sees them as "the school of the modern spirit" (p. 22).

[124] Tierney, op. cit., p. 109.

there; though changed out of recognition and added to immeasurably by Christ's life and teaching, his death and resurrection, the continuity of testimony between the Old and New remains.

The Old Testament is an extremely complex compilation of documents which has as its core the Pentateuch, the law books (the most sacred and important part of the whole), namely Genesis, Exodus, Leviticus, Numbers and Deuteronomy.[125] Scholars dispute the dating and authorship of the parts, but, from a theological point of view what is important about the Scriptures, the Old as well as the New Testament, is their theological, spiritual and moral message, God speaking to man. This message is timeless and independent of its historical context, although that context influences the way in which the message is presented. It is doubtful whether any part of the Old Testament existed in written form before the time of David (about 1000 B.C.) when the history of the chosen people already extended over eight hundred years. The evidence indicates that the Old Testament is the result of the work of several groups of authors first in the period 950 to 850 B.C., a second group between 850 and 750 B.C., another dating from about 650 and the last which belongs to the postexilic period.[126] A formal canon of the Scriptures came to be from about 400 B.C.

The Old Testament itself is very much the history of a people and of God's dealing with that people.[127] In terms of contemporary cultures, the Jews were comparative latecomers in the ancient near East—around Jericho there had been a developed community life for over four thousand years before the history of the Israelites begins, and in that history it was the Exodus, some time early in the thirteenth century, which marks the emergence of a people. After the settlement in Canaan, the Jews were ruled by Judges, charismatic leaders, until Saul became King. David ruled after him (1000–961), and on the death of his successor Solomon in 922 the Kingdom was split in two: the Northern Kingdom (Israel) was destroyed by the Assyrians in 721 B.C., the Southern Kingdom (Judah) survived until 586 when the Babylonians conquered it and its capital Jerusalem, and the people went into exile. When the Persians defeated the Babylonians, the Jews were allowed to return to Jerusalem. In their turn, the Persians were defeated by the Greeks, and the Jews were subject to them; the Maccabean revolt secured a century of independence, 164 to 63 B.C. but,

---

125 H. Rowley, *The Growth of the Old Testament* (London, 1964). R. Davidson, *The Old Testament* (London, 1964). The Jewish canon consisted of *the law, the prophets* (Joshua, Judges, Samuel, Kings, Isaiah, Ezekiel and the shorter prophets) and *the writings* (Psalms, Proverbs, Job, Ruth, Song of Songs, Ecclesiastes, etc.). Davidson, op cit., pp. 12 ff.

126 The first group (950–850) known as the J authors (from Jahweh), the second (850–750) the E writers (Elohist), the third (650), the Deuteronomists, and the fourth, the P, the priestly writers.

127 John Bright, *The History of Israel* (London, 1964).

in the latter year, the chosen people became part of the Roman Empire. A
century later (A.D. 66 to 70), the Jewish war finally put an end to the state
and led to the dispersal of the people.

From the beginning, the demands of the Covenant had strong ethical
overtones and the prophets particularly stressed the importance of this
element in the service of Israel's God.[128] There were several such groups
of prophets. Elijah in the ninth century, Amos, and Micah in the eighth,
Jeremiah, Zepheniah, Nahum and Habakkuk in the seventh. Ezekiel and
the second Isaiah were the prophets of the sixth-century exile. The third
group (among whom are Malachi and Daniel) belong to the fifth and
fourth centuries.

Amos' message is typical of the harsh condemnation the prophets made
of false religion; God despised their feasts and took no delight in their
assemblies. He wanted justice to roll down like the waters and righteousness like an ever-flowing stream.[129] The same message was in Isaiah: God
could not endure festival and ceremony, new moons and pilgrimages. He
commanded his people to cease to do evil, to learn to do good, to search
for justice, help the oppressed and to be just to the orphan and plead for the
widow.[130] The prophets argued then, not from social necessity, good
manners or motives of utility; for them moral evil was something the
Lord abominated and this was the reason it was to be avoided above all
things. They stressed that only obedience to the moral law brought true
happiness, that God's law is for good and is unchanging. This idea of
morality linked with the nature of God, the one true God who, because he
is what he is, commands obedience, is fundamental to the whole Old
Testament idea of morality: "Jahweh is God indeed . . . in Heaven above
and earth below, He and no other . . . keep his law and commands so that
you and your children may prosper."[131]

The subjective aspect of morality is there too because, without the
freely willed acceptance of God's law, any loyalty to it was mere formal-
ism. But it is a personal response to an all holy God, whose holiness
demands absolute rectitude of life from those who say they believe in him
and serve him, which is required. The objective nature of morality and the
subjective needs of personal response intertwine; those who truly love
God show it by obeying his objective law; those who disobey that law
show that they have no love of the God who gave it. King Ahab and his
wife Jezebel plotted murder and theft in order to possess themselves of

[128] J. L. McKenzie, *The Two Edged Sword* (London, 1959), chap. 2. G. von Rad, *Old
Testament Theology* (London, 1979), vol. 2.
[129] Amos 5:21–24.   [130] Ibid., 1:13–17.
[131] Dt 4:39–40.

Naboth's vineyard, and it was the evil that they did in this matter which led to Elijah's condemnation, [132] and it was the specific injustices which led to Amos' condemnation—cheating in selling, oppression of the poor. [133]

The idea that there was only one God, that he created all, that he was holy and that his unchanging will was for good, marked a great step forward in man's understanding of the nature of God and his relationship with him. The idea of God in other Semitic cultures was either that of a personified force of nature, or of a personified human need or instinct. [134] Man first worshipped the powers of nature, then through the cultic myth of fertility he rendered sacred the animal satisfactions of the individual, or in the worship of the state or king he paid homage to the instincts and needs of the social group. The Hebrews, had they had their own way, would have had gods such as these. But the idea of the Deity that was given to them in revelation makes it clear that the true God is totally other. Yahweh did not embody the ideals of the people or represent a force of nature. He was a vital and almighty personal Lord who created all and impressed himself upon the consciousness of a people, marking them throughout their history with an awareness of his holiness and power, as other gods did not.

This Jewish vision of the oneness, the almightiness and the holiness of God bears important consequences for the whole of human history. Men were not without some natural insight into the relationship between belief in God and the acceptance of the sound moral order; the contents of the Ten Commandments and the link between moral life and belief in God certainly have their parallels in the world of their time. [135] The belief that law was given to men by God was common throughout the Ancient East. The Babylonian code of Hammurabi, for example, dates from the eighteenth century B.C., and the inscription we possess shows him receiving his laws from the Babylonian sun god, the god of justice. Such insights of man's reason are precious witnesses to God's plan. Since God rules the universe, it is inevitable that the truer the idea of God that men perceive by their natural reason, or the more sincere their search for a true moral code, the truer will be their grasp of the morality he requests of them, and the more ready their tendency to link moral life with God. But those same cultures also allowed belief in different gods, some of whom did tolerate, will or even command evil. The fertility rites, for example, involved sacred prostitution, and the capriciousness with which the gods

---

[132] I Kings 21:1–23.   [133] Ibid., 8:5–8.

[134] McKenzie, op. cit., chap. 3. E. Wright, *Biblical Archaeology* (London, 1962), chap. 7.

[135] Chambers, *The Western Experience*, pp. 4 ff. J. B. Pritchard, *Ancient Near Eastern Texts* (Princeton, 1969).

acted gave their followers no guide to intellectual and moral truth.[136]
Human sacrifice was certainly practised at some periods.[137]

The Jewish vision of God, therefore, differed essentially from that
possessed by their contemporaries in comparable cults. Firstly, in their
understanding it was God *who took the initiative*, intruding himself into
their lives; *he was not a matter for speculation, but an overwhelming fact*, and he
showed his power in terms which convinced. Secondly, *he was personal*—
not a myth, a theory, a cipher or a force of nature, but a living, personal
being. Thirdly, *he was the almighty creator of all things* who had no rival; he
was not one god among many, but the one true God who created a
meaningful world for man. Fourthly, *he was all holy, he did not deceive, he
was not capricious or unpredictable*, and he demanded the personal service of a
righteous life from all who believed in him. Finally *he was a universal God,
not simply the tribal god of the Jews*, he had a providential care for all men and
all time.

The nature of Israel's God is seen perhaps most clearly in the second
Isaiah. We have only to ponder the implications of the picture of Yahweh
there given to appreciate his uniqueness.[138]

> "To whom could you liken me and who could be my equal?" says the
> Holy One. . . . Who made these stars if not he who drills them like an
> army. . . ? So mighty is his power, so great his strength.

He has a providential care for his world and for those whom he created to
dwell in it.[139]

> Yes, thus says Yahweh, creator of the heavens, who is God, who formed the
> earth and made it, who set it firm, created it no chaos, but a place to be lived in.

He is a God of integrity, stressing that what comes from his mouth is
truth, his word irrevocable;[140] he is the God of all men, cares for all and
wishes his salvation to be for all, not only for the chosen people.[141] His
house will be the house of prayer for all the nations. Isaiah's prophecy,
that[142]

> the nations come to your light and kings to your dawning brightness. Lift
> up your eyes and look around: all are assembling and coming towards
> you. . . . Camels in throng will cover you, the dromedaries of Midian and

---

[136] McKenzie, op. cit., p. 58.
[137] W. F. Albright, *Archaeology and the Religion of Israel* (Baltimore, 1946), p. 92.
[138] Is 40:25.
[139] Is 45:18.
[140] Is 45:23.
[141] Is 56:8.
[142] Is 60:3–6.

Ephah; everyone in Sheba will come, bringing gold and incense and singing the praise of Yahweh.

A God who insisted on his uniqueness, his role as almighty creator, who was integrity itself and who claimed the allegiance of and gave providential care to all—such was the God of Israel.

These beliefs contrasted violently, not only with the capriciousness and the multiplicity of the gods of their own Semitic milieu, but even more markedly with those characteristics of the Greek and the Roman gods and religions.[143] Homer's *Iliad* and *Odyssey* and Hesiod's *Theogony* were comparable in their influence on the Greeks to that of the Bible on the Jews. Greek moral ideas were founded on the model given to them by the Olympian deities, and these gods were not notably more moral than men—and in some respects were less so. When the philosophical poet Xenophanes in the sixth century complained that adultery and deceit were to be ascribed to the gods, it was Homer and Hesiod he was blaming.[144] Among the Romans, the rules governing the relationship of the gods and the Roman people were the city's charter—in fact a codification of the religious practices of the various peoples who formed Roman society.[145] The regulations were not concerned with ethics, but simply with cultic practices; the gods would not desert Rome if the proper sacrifices were made at the proper time. The Romans found their ethical code in Epicureanism and Stoicism—the latter above all—but this offered no grounds of belief, no reason for enthusiasm, no motive for affection or sympathy.[146] It demanded that a man should save himself by his own resources and calm detachment and ignored the desperate cries of a world protesting that salvation was not contained within it.

The contrast with Israel's God is stark. This was a God of the universe who displayed his spiritual fatherhood in the righteous government of all nations of the earth. The world and all that is in it is God's—and man and all things in it have their place through his love and care. Men, individuals, did matter, and they had a God to whom they could look for help, protection and understanding. They were not the playthings of mindless fate. Belief in such a God injected into human culture a confidence in an abiding order governing the universe, so dispelling the terrors of existence without object or rule to which the pagan world was so prone.

[143] De Burgh, op. cit., p. 322, "the Graeco-Roman cults . . . were never predominantly ethical, and often definitely immoral . . . Christianity stood alone in grounding morality in religion, yet without reducing religion to a moral rule."

[144] A. Andrews, op. cit., p. 254.

[145] R. H. Barrow. *The Romans* (London, 1972), pp. 14 ff., 141 ff. J. Balsdon, *Roman Civilisation* (London, 1967), pp. 182 ff.

[146] Barrow, op. cit., p. 160.

Human beings could find a pattern and purpose in existence, because they were the sons and daughters of a creator who knew them and loved them and had given them a world in which they could serve him happily and holily. They were not animals living from day to day, fearful of beings above them whom they did not understand and who could betray them at their whim. This assurance of the rationality of things and the providence of God[147] has passed into Western intellectual tradition from its Judaeo-Christian roots. That tradition has taken its confidence in the order in things from revelation; before the people of Israel experienced that revelation, God, there was no confidence in such order in the universe. Everything that happened might be chance or accident, the gods could be ferocious or whimsical, and did not necessarily lay down clear principles for the conduct of human life. Zeus, according to Hesiod, "rules the world with restless sway and takes back tomorrow what he grants today."[148] Yahweh's moral law by contrast is not the arbitrary and temporary edict of a cultic or tribal deity, but an eternally valid way of regulating man's relationship with God and with his neighbour, in such a way that human life has true dignity.

The moral code given by God to the Jews in the Old Testament was, above all and firstly, a personal one, one which was to guide their standard of personal moral life and it was enshrined in the Ten Commandments.[149]

1. You shall have no others Gods before me.
2. You shall not take the name of the Lord in vain.
3. Keep the Sabbath holy.
4. Honour your father and your mother.
5. You shall not kill.
6. You shall not commit adultery.
7. You shall not steal.
8. You shall not bear false witness against your neighbour.
9. You shall not covet your neighbour's wife.
10. You shall not covet your neighbour's goods.

[147] W. Eichrodt, *The Theology of the Old Testament* (London, 1967), 2:98 ff., 167 ff.

[148] R. Kirk, *Roots of American Order* (Illinois: Open Court, 1974), p. 26. The Stoic idea of God as author of the unchanging natural law revealed a profound understanding of the connection between the divinity and morality, and both Aristotle and Plato had a more exalted understanding of the nature of God. To Plato he was a living and active soul, the self-moving source of the motion of the heavens, creator of the sensible universe. For Aristotle the universe had no beginning in time, therefore God was not creator: he was absolutely transcendent, a living being, eternal and most good, drawing the world to him as the goal of its desire. (De Burgh, *Legacy of the Ancient World*, pp. 174, 211–12.) Yet noble though this composite vision of God was, it lacked the power, personal warmth, coherence and clarity of Israel's.

[149] Ex 20:2–17. Dt 5:6–21.

The theology of Old Testament morality is complex. We may just note that unconditional acceptance of the decalogue was demanded of Israel. The promise of salvation was one which depended upon obedience to it. Refusal to accept the Commandments brought the curse of Yahweh in its train. Both Deuteronomy and the Holiness code make a blessing and cursing follow upon the proclamation of the Commandments. They did not require any substantiation to legitimate them before men. They bind men because they are the Commandments of Yahweh.[150]

As we have noted, there are parallels between the Covenant and the Decalogue and the codes possessed by contemporary civilisations. This argues the validity of the belief in the connection between God, the moral law and right reason—it does not challenge the uniqueness of the revelation to the Jews. Though the Commandments were given to man in time and at a particular time and enshrined in the language and forms of their cultural epoch, they comprise a code of personal morality that is given for all men and all time because it is precisely rooted in the nature of God. The will of God is the supreme norm behind all the particular requirements of morality, and that morality and its demands do not change.[151]

The moral precepts of the Old Testament are to be distinguished from the ceremonial and the judicial.[152] It is the former which pertain to the nature of morality, to right and wrong as they rule human life and as they are derived from the law of God and founded in his holiness and righteousness. These moral precepts are set forth in order to direct man to his end, which is God (and the first three Commandments do this). They are obligations placed on man by his revelation of how man is to attain his end. The obligation in the other seven Commandments reinforce the injunctions of natural law—love of parents, respect for life, for truth, for marriage and property.

The social morality of the Old Testament is contained in the judicial law, and it is with these judicial precepts that the modern mind has most difficulty. The example often taken as representative of the harshness of the personal moral standards of the Old Testament (an eye for an eye, and a tooth for a tooth) is precisely punitive legislation,[153] and is not indicative of the true spirit of personal morality in the Old Testament as God would

---

[150] Von Rad, op. cit., 1:196 ff. This does not mean that the Commandments were comprehensive of morality but that they formed the solid base that the fuller and more perfect morality built upon. See Eichrodt, op. cit., 2:319 ff.

[151] Eichrodt, op. cit. "Inasmuch as the will of God emerges as the supreme norm . . . the desired unity of the moral sphere shifts in essence to the personal activity of the covenant God . . . moral norms hold good in the history of mankind as a whole and this leads them to grasp the unconditional character of the ethical demand as an order of human life unrestricted by natural boundaries." (pp. 320–22).

[152] St. Thomas Aquinas, *Summa Theologica*, I–II. q. 99. art. 2, 3. q. 100. art. 1–12.

[153] Ex 21:23–25.

have it of his people. When Christ specifically abrogated this provision of the Old Law, [154] he was not suggesting that the personal moral code of the Jews was defective. He was indicating that the spirit of the beatitudes was in contrast to the harsh, if necessary, legalistic provisions of the judicial law of the Old Testament. We do ill then to draw too strong a contrast between the morality of the two Testaments. [155] Proof of a moral code is in its living, and the holiness and the serene acceptance of the will of God that is shown, for example, in the life of Christ's own Mother, of St. Joseph, of St. Elizabeth and of Simeon testifies to the true effect of that morality. [156]

The old law and the new law are very different, it is true. In the new law external regulations are only a secondary element, it is primarily a law of the spirit, it deepens insight into the natural and revealed moral law and gives a better understanding of the final goal and of the motives for the moral life. It also opens up sources of grace, of a faith in Christ, of the baptism which flows from it and the sacraments too—yet all these direct men to a more perfect observance of the moral pattern established by God in the Old Testament. The New builds on the foundations of the Old Testament moral code.

B. THE NEW TESTAMENT

The Old Testament was, as we have said, a complex compilation, and knowledge of the text and context, under the guidance of the Church, is necessary for its accurate interpretation. The same is true of the New Testament. It was not formed or written as modern scholarship would like to think that documents of such importance are written. The New Testament was not given to us as a comprehensive textbook of theology; Christ himself did not leave us any of his own writings, he formed a community of believers around himself and instructed them by word of mouth. In this community his followers, and those that they taught after his death and Resurrection, committed to writing partly for catechetical and partly for liturgical use what, under the guidance of the Holy Spirit, they saw as the essentials about his life and teaching. It was because it was so important for Christians through the ages to understand these essentials that, also under the guidance of the Holy Spirit in the Church, the process of the formation of what we have come to know as the canon on New Testament writings began. The New Testament is the Church's book; it

---

[154] Mt 5:38.

[155] On the link, and contrast, between the old and new law and its morality, *Summa Theologica*, I-II, q. 107. H. Peschke, op. cit., vol. 1, chap. 1, pp. 13 ff.

[156] The picture of the just man painted, for example, in Psalms 1 and 14 reflects the spirit of the Beatitudes.

was her zeal and care in sifting the true from the false from among the writings purporting to have special claim on Christian acceptance that secured for us the true teaching of Christ.

The controversy among scholars about the exact dating of the books that form the New Testament is a never-ending one.[157] It would seem that it was something like twenty years after the Resurrection before the first canonical text appeared, probably 1 Thessalonians, and about twenty years before the first book of the Gospels, probably Mark, followed. It seems likely that the Pauline letters were written between 51 and 67 A.D., the Gospels between 65 and 90 A.D. and the Catholic Epistles between 64 and 100 to 125. The Acts apparently date from the 70s or 80s and Hebrews and the Apocalypse, the 60s to 80s and 90s respectively.

Before the Church finally determined on the twenty-seven books which form the New Testament canon, a winnowing process went on—aided by the need to answer various heretical opinions and to counteract the flood of misleading apocryphal literature. There being no centralized organisation in these centuries, it was through the efforts of individual saints and scholars, and eventually councils, that agreement was in time reached. The work of St. Irenaeus of Lyons toward the end of the second century and whoever was responsible for the "Muratorian" canon about the same time (it seems to have been Roman in origin) mark a consistent development; by the late fourth century, with the lists of St. Augustine and St. Athanasius, the Councils of Hippo in 393 and Carthage in 397, major agreement among Christians was reached. For the Roman Catholic Church, the Council of Trent decided the canon definitively.

Our use of the New Testament must, therefore, be conditioned by a proper understanding of what it represents. It is, as we have said, not an exhaustive and comprehensive textbook of theology, but contains, in the Gospels, the essentials of Christ's life and teaching and, in the Acts, the Epistles and the Apocalypse, other factual information, moral and theological reasoning and teaching which, under the guidance of the Holy Spirit, has been preserved for us. We must approach the New Testament with care, therefore, but even as we do so we cannot help noticing that the startling thing about the Gospels especially is the clarity and the freshness of their message, the immediate meaningfulness to all. We need the guidance of the magisterium and the scholar to guide us through what is obscure, but sensible and prayerful reading enables the Gospels to be understood and responded to by the least learned. Christ's use of parables

---

[157] See *Peake's Commentary on the Bible*, s.v. "The Literature and Canon of the New Testament", by J. N. Sanders. *The Cambridge History of the Bible* (C.U.P., 1970), vol. 1, chap. 4, p. 10; s.v. "The New Testament Canon", by R. M. Grant; and *The Jerome Biblical Commentary* (London, 1969), vol 2, pp. 515 ff., s.v. "Canonicity".

and clear powerful stories to illustrate his teaching gives it universal appeal. And we see that the message of the New Testament is a fulfillment of the Old, as Christ said it was to be. In nothing is this more plain than in the unity of the moral teaching of the two.

The Old Testament teaching was that ethics was part and parcel of religion and inseparable from it, and that the right and the good were aspects of the will of God. The New Testament has the same perspective.[158] Christ called on his followers to be perfect as his Heavenly Father is perfect,[159] and in so doing, brought into stronger focus the implications of Old Testament morality concerning the motivation for the moral life and the means of attaining one's ideals. Non-religious ethics cannot provide an adequate moral dynamic for all, a means of fulfilling the ideal one seeks or maintaining the motivation one possesses. But Christ, in calling upon his followers to be perfect and offering them his help to be so, not only gave an ideal but also the means to obtain it. Christian morality or ethics is in fact the road to holiness, obedience to God's will and law by God's help. Pagan codes of morality may offer high ideals—but they are for the elite—love of God in Christ and the grace he gives is available to all, whatever their intellectual or cultural endowment.

That this morality which Christ preached was one and the same as the Old Testament morality is clear from many incidents recorded in the New Testament. The Pharisees and Scribes once asked him, for example, why his disciples ate with defiled hands instead of following the traditions of their ancestors. He answered by calling them hypocrites who did God honour with their lips when their hearts were far from him. He gave a particular example of the way in which they preferred their own traditions to the Commandments of God.[160]

> You put aside the commandment of God to cling to human traditions. . . .
> Moses said: Do your duty to your father and mother, and, Anyone who curses father or mother must be put to death. But you say, "If a man says to his father or mother: Anything that I have that I might have used to help you is . . . dedicated to God . . . then he is forbidden from that moment to do anything for his father or mother." In this way you make God's word null and void for the sake of your tradition which you have handed down.

He then points out to them that morality is essentially an interior thing, a matter of attitude. It is the evil that is in man's heart which defiles him, not

---

[158] L. H. Marshall, *The Challenge of New Testament Ethics* (London, 1966), p. 13. See also R. Schnackenburg's *The Moral Teaching of the New Testament*, pp. 73 ff.

[159] Mt 5:48.

[160] Mk 7:8–13.

the food he eats, and it is that evil which leads to acts against the moral law.[161]

"Can you not see that whatever goes into a man from outside cannot make him unclean, because it does not go into his heart but through his stomach. . . ." (Thus he pronounced all foods clean.) And he went on, "It is what comes out of a man that makes him unclean. For it is from within, from men's hearts, that evil intentions emerge: fornication, theft, murder, adultery, avarice, malice, deceit, indecency, envy, slander, pride, folly. . . ."

Here then he abrogated the ceremonial, purification aspects of the old law, but reasserted specifics of the moral law.

That the Commandments are the norm of morality and the foundation of holiness is shown in another passage from St. Matthew in which the young man asked Christ what he must do to inherit eternal life.[162]

"If you wish to enter into life, keep the commandments." He said, "Which?" "These": Jesus replied, "You must not kill. You must not commit adultery. You must not steal. You must not bring false witness. Honour your father and your mother, and you must love your neighbour as yourself."

The importance of the Commandments, the importance of obedience to God's law, is the constant theme of the rest of the New Testament as, for example, in Romans:[163]

All the commandments: You shall not commit adultery, you shall not kill, you shall not steal, you shall not covet, and so on, are summed up in this single command: You must love your neighbour as yourself. Love is the one thing that cannot hurt your neighbour; that is why it is the answer to every one of the commandments.

St. Paul here is reminding his listeners that, although the external observances of the law have been abrogated by Christ, the letter and the spirit of the moral law which is enshrined in the Commandments still remains valid. It is through love that the Commandments are obeyed. But they still need to be obeyed, and their specifics are still binding. So in the First Epistle of St. Peter.[164]

Do not behave in the way you liked to before you learnt the truth: make a habit of obedience: be holy in all you do, since it is the Holy One who has

[161] Mk 7:18–23.
[162] Mt 19:16–19.
[163] Rom 13:9–10.
[164] 1 Pet 1:14–17.

called you, and scripture says: Be holy, for I am holy.

If you are acknowledging as your Father one who has no favourites and judges everyone according to what he has done, you must be scrupulously careful. . . .

Throughout the Old Testament and the New Testament, therefore, the idea that the divine law, the law of God, a law based in the nature of God and revealed to man, is the norm of a good life, is all present. This law is objective, it is a standard by which man can judge his own conduct as either worthy of his belief in God or not. And it touches all men, because it is a law for all time in that it is precisely founded in the plan of God for human nature, for human beings who are God's creatures. When, therefore, the Council stated that the highest norm of human life is the divine law, eternal, objective and universal, it was restating the very essence of Christian belief as it is founded in the revealed truth of God in the Scriptures.

III. The Divine Eternal and the Natural Laws: The Council's Teaching and the Catholic Tradition

A. THE COUNCIL ON NATURAL LAW

The assumption behind the Council's documents, which is made explicit in several places, is that of the traditional Catholic understanding of man's participation in the divine law in a way especially suited to his nature, and that way is through the natural law. If we look back to the third paragraph of *Dignitatis Humanae*, which is given above, we find that the statement concerning the eternal objective and universal law of God which was the subject of the previous section is followed by one which asserts that

God has enabled man to participate in this law of his so that under the gentle disposition of Divine Providence, many may be able to arrive at a deeper and deeper knowledge of unchanging truth.

Elsewhere in the same document[165] principles of the moral law "that spring from nature itself" are referred to. We are also warned of seeking solutions to problems in ways which "transgress the natural law".[166] *Gaudium et Spes*[167] reminds us that "the natural law of peoples and its universal principles still retain their binding force" and in a slightly different context that[168]

---

[165] *Dignitatis Humanae*, par. 14.
[166] Ibid., par. 87.   [167] Ibid., par. 79.   [168] Ibid., par. 63.

The Church, in the course of centuries, has worked out in the light of the Gospel, principles of justice and equity, demanded by right reason, for individual and social life and also for international relations.

Of these excerpts, that from the third paragraph of *Dignitatis Humanae* is more important for our purpose, because it speaks of the participation of man in the divine, objective and universal law. This idea of the natural law as a participation in God's law, through right reason, is evocative of the way in which St. Thomas defines natural law, which he says is "nothing else than the rational creature's participation of the eternal law."[169]

Since this is the first point at which we rely heavily on the treatment of Catholic teaching by St. Thomas, it may be well to say a little about his importance in Catholic theology and thought generally. The reason why he is appealed to on this question of natural law and the relationship of the natural to the divine eternal and revealed laws is that his treatment of the question is a classic of its kind. There is another reason why we look to St. Thomas, and that is that he is the doctor communis, the "common doctor" in the sense that over the centuries the Church has seen in his works the fullest and most learned expression of the Christian truth in theological and philosophical terms.

St. Thomas was uniquely able, both in virtue of his intellectual abilities and by the circumstances in which providence placed him, to exert an exceptional influence on the development of Catholic theology and philosophy. Like St. Augustine, he lived at a major turning point in the Church's history, and like him, he had the required power as thinker, teacher and writer to give the Church's theology the purpose and direction the times needed. St. Thomas suffers somewhat from the fact that he has so unchallengeable a place in the Catholic tradition. He has often been put before students in an unimaginative way which obscures the real greatness of the man. One who taught that the important thing is not what authority lay behind a statement, but how the truth of the matter stands, and that the argument from human authority alone is of all arguments the weakest[170] has been ill served if the philosophy named after him can be presented as incapable of development. There was "nothing cramping for Aquinas about orthodoxy."[171] Confronted with questions

---

[169] *Summa Theologica*, I–II, q. 91, art. 2. As we noted above (p. 12) the footnotes in the English translation of the text omit the references to the *Summa*, I–II, q. 91, art. 1, and q. 93, art. 1 and 2 contained in the Latin original.

[170] De Burgh, op. cit., p. 457.

[171] Keen, op. cit., p. 154. He adds "St. Thomas' was a liberal and optimistic teaching, a great triumph for breadth of outlook in Christianity. It permitted much more than a reconciliation of Aristotle's thought with traditional theology, a reconciliation of Christian living with an immensely varied sense of priorities in the everyday life of the human world."

on which faith and reason seemed to be in conflict, his answer was to look more carefully at the question and rethink the issue. Thomas respected authority—but he was prepared to reject what was not well said and try to improve on it.[172] It was this readiness to look at things anew which led him into the fight to get Aristotle accepted by Christian thinkers.

In Leo XIII's encyclical *On the Restoration of Christian Philosophy, According to the Mind of St. Thomas*,[173] there occurs the observation: "His life was most holy and he loved the truth alone." His love of truth was shown in a determination to follow through every argument calmly and fully; the effect of reading him can be over-powering simply because of his preference for avoiding rhetoric and verbal brilliance, despite the mastery of language that his sacred poetry reveals was his.

There were many areas in which new departures were needed if the Catholic mind was to make the best of the rediscovery of the classics of Greek philosophy while maintaining the integrity of the revealed truths that had been committed to the Church's care. The juncture at which St. Thomas found himself has already been outlined above.[174] The Arab and the Jewish philosophers had already grappled with the work of Aristotle, and the result of their speculations were in some ways unsettling to Christian thinkers. In particular, Averroes had tried to reconcile the teaching of Aristotle with that of the Koran by the theory of the "double truth", namely that the truths of reason and those of theology or revelation can be contradictory, and yet each in themselves true. St. Thomas, however, refused to accept that this could be so. Grace builds on nature, it does not replace it, and revelation cannot take away the rights of reason, but builds on them.

The distinction made by Thomas between faith and reason was endorsed in principle by the leading thinkers of the next six centuries. Faith and reason are different means of apprehending truth. Faith is about things men can only partially understand, perhaps not understand at all, reason proceeds from what is clearly known by way of demonstration until it comes to a fuller understanding of that with which it is dealing. Hence, faith and reason cannot be in conflict. The physical and the theological sciences were in essential harmony; accordingly, any conflict between them could only arise from defects in the understanding of either theologians or scientists. A second way in which Thomas innovated was in his doctrine of creation, a doctrine which enables us to understand better the close link between God and created things—avoiding pantheism while preserving the transcendence of the Creator and instilling a reverence for the created world. He explains creation in terms of God's

---

[172] De Burgh, op. cit., p. 457.
[173] *Aeterni Patris* (1879).
[174] See above p. 61.

infinite wealth of being which enables him to display a limitless power to create and conserve that which owes everything to him, but yet is other than him. Similarly his theory of the analogy of being enables us to have confidence that we can understand something about God, so avoiding agnosticism, whilst, at the same time, avoiding anthropomorphism. In the controversy over universals he was a moderate realist; according to Thomas, each object in the universe is both autonomous and unique, but is also representative of a general species or class.[175]

In appealing to St. Thomas, then, the Church is appealing above all to his ability as a theologian to clarify and explain some of the implications of the truth that rest in God's revelation; at the same time his gifts as a philosopher underline the complementarity of faith and reason—his sanctity is as much an explanation of his greatness as a philosopher as were the great natural powers of mind he possessed. Many new insights have been developed by theologians and philosophers since his day, but the general structure of his approach retains its validity and his treatment of many questions remains unsurpassed—one such classic treatment is that of the relationship between the divine eternal, the divine positive or revealed and the natural law.

St. Thomas first of all defines the general nature of law and then brings out the nature of divine law under its three aspects:[176]

> A Law is nothing else but a dictate of practical reason emanating from a ruler who governs a perfect community. Now it is evident . . . that the whole community of the universe is governed by divine reason . . . the very idea of the government of things in God, the ruler of the universe, has the nature of law. And since the Divine reason's conception of things is not subject to time but is eternal . . . this kind of law must be called eternal.

In addition to the divine eternal law, there is needed a divine positive law. One reason is that[177]

---

[175] De Burgh, op. cit., pp. 458 ff. Chambers et al., op. cit., p. 294. For a fuller account of St. Thomas' thought in its context, F. Copleston, *A History of Philosophy*, vol. 2, chaps. 30 ff. Respect for St. Thomas as a thinker has grown in recent years as knowledge of him and his period has increased. For W. de Burgh (op. cit., p. 463), St. Thomas' *De unitate intellectus contra Averroistas* ranks with Plato's *Theatetus* as one of the finest achievements in the history of philosophy. A. Kenny, (*Aquinas: A Collection of Critical Essays* [London, 1970]), in his introduction, suggests that Aquinas' contributions to metaphysics, philosophical theology, philosophy of mind and moral philosophy, rank him with Plato, Aristotle, Descartes and Kant (ibid., pp. 1–2).

[176] *Summa Theologica*, I–II, q. 91, art. 1. I quote from the 1920 English version because it renders the phrase *"participatio legis aeternae in rationali creatura"* (article 2) as "participation in the divine law, etc.", the words used in both of the English translations of the Council documents.

[177] *Summa Theologica*, I–II, q. 91, art. 4.

because on account of the uncertainty of human judgement, especially on contingent and particular matters, different people form different judgements on human acts; whence different and contrary laws result . . . that man may know without any doubt what he ought to do and what he ought to avoid, it was necessary for man to be directed in his proper acts by a law given by God, for it is certain that such a law cannot err.

All things, therefore, are regulated and measured by the divine eternal law which is further specified by the divine positive law. In addition, all things share in the divine eternal law so far as they receive from it the tendencies to their own proper ends. The rational creature however[178]

is subject to divine providence in the most excellent way, in so far as it partakes of a share of providence, by being both provident for itself and others. Wherefore it has a share of the Eternal Reason whereby it has a natural inclination to its proper act and end; and this participation of the eternal law in the rational creature is called the natural law . . . the light of natural reason whereby we discern what is good and what is evil, which is the function of the natural law, is nothing else than an imprint on us of the Divine light . . . the natural law is nothing else than the rational creature's participation of the eternal law.

B. THE ORIGIN OF NATURAL LAW THEORY
AND ITS EMBODIMENT IN THE CATHOLIC TRADITION

So familiar is this concept of natural law in Catholic theology and philosophy, that it can be thought that it was hammered out to supply deficiencies of revealed morality, the divine law and its implications. The truth is that the idea had possessed such an authority in classical thought and Roman jurisprudence that there was no way in which it could be ignored. It had either to be incorporated into the Christian tradition and shown to be compatible with the Christian understanding of the nature of morality, or to stand in challenge to it. In the issue it was accepted by the Church, and accepted gratefully, as one of the most valuable legacies bequeathed by the unaided reason of pre-Christian man to the better understanding of our natural moral powers; it was seen that it complemented the Judaeo-Christian understanding of an objective morality founded in the divine reason and revealed through the Scriptures. Unless we appreciate the status of the concept, and its practical value, we will fail to understand how inevitable it was that it should find so secure a place in that tradition. From the first, Christian writers grasped the importance of

---

[178] Ibid., I–II, q. 91, art. 2. See J. Finnis, *Natural Law and Natural Rights*, pp. 398 ff.

the idea, although it was not until the twelfth and thirteenth centuries that it was adequately woven into classical theology. St. Paul, drawing on the Greek philosophical tradition, appealed to it,[179] and it is to the Greeks that we must look for our understanding of the precise meaning of the term as the pagan thinkers knew it.

Greek thought, like the fullness of the teaching of the Old Testament, was evolved through the history of a people and was fed from many sources until it reached its full flower in Socrates, Plato and Aristotle. We have already referred to Homer's *Iliad* and *Odyssey* which were written in the ninth century B.C. and Hesiod's *Theogony* which dates from the following century.[180] The epics related by Homer took place in the heroic age of early Greek history, about 1200 B.C., the time the Jews were settling in Canaan.[181] Historical Greece dates from about 776 B.C., and the subsequent development of Greek culture took place in, and was intimately concerned with, the form of political and social organisation known as the city state—of which states it was Athens which produced the most brilliant culture. The Athenian statesman Solon (c. 600 B.C.) laid the foundations of Greek democracy; later in 508 B.C. Cleisthenes extended it. After repulsing the Persians between 490 and 480, the Athenians liberated the whole of Greece, only to fall prey themselves in turn to imperialist ambitions which led to the disaster of the Peloponnesian War and the subsequent defeat of Athens.

The moral standards of the Olympian deities of the *Iliad* and the *Odyssey* came under attack from the poet Xenophanes (540–500 B.C.) and of the dramatists Aeschylus (525–456), Sophocles (496–406), and Euripedes (484–407), but it was the development of philosophy that presented mankind with its first really searching enquiry into the nature of morality, of ethics and moral life, which first put ethics on a scientific basis. The background to this ethical enquiry in the fifth century B.C. was the continuous development of the philosophical genius of the Greeks, their desire to explain all things, to know, to seek out answers. Yet they were not ivory-tower thinkers, they were pre-eminently practical also—and as they did in fact achieve great things, political and military success, they noticed that there was in human nature a tendency to overstep the mark, to destroy itself by pride precisely in the moment of triumph. This *hubris*

---

[179] "Ever since God created the world his everlasting power and deity . . . have been therefore the mind to see in the things he has made. That is why such people are without excuse, they knew God but refused to honour or thank him; instead they made nonsense out of logic . . . since they refused to see that it was rational to acknowledge God, God has left them to their own irrational ideas and monstrous behaviour," Rom 1:20–28.

[180] See above p. 53.

[181] H. D. F. Kitto, *The Greeks* (Pelican, 1977), chap. 2. A. Andrewes, *Greek Society*, (Pelican, 1971), chap. 2, 3.

closely resembles what we would call sin, indeed original sin in the sense of it being the root of all human self-will and pride.

The experience of Athens, after the liberation of Greece from the Persians and the brilliance of the age of Pericles[182] mirrored this tendency of human greatness to be the cause of its own destruction. The historian Thucydides (464–404) writing about the Peloponnesian War,[183] reveals to us the Greek mind at work, reflecting on its own follies, its pride, its *hubris*. The ultimatum given by the Athenians to Melos precisely de-lineates that arrogant will to self-destruction which is at the heart of man's moral dilemma. The subsequent disaster which befell the Athenians we are left in no doubt, was the result of their pride, their presumption on their prowess. It was against this background, this reflected-on experience of the evils that befall men whose moral sense is dulled by their own excessive self-confidence, that the philosophers did their work of seeking out the basis of a sounder morality. Speculations about the nature of morality can indeed be found in fragments of earlier Greek philosophy, in Heraclitus,[184] for example, who spoke of all human law being nourished by a divine law, but it was the searching of the Sophists[185] at the time of the rise and fall of Athenian ambitions, that first began to penetrate in depth into the nature of man's moral sense.

The word "Sophist", as applied to those who deal in ideas, was not at first the term of abuse it later became. The Sophists responded to a need for organised knowledge of all kinds that emerged as Athenian society became more complex and sophisticated. One result of the discussions which they provoked was the question of *physis* or *nomos* as the basis of ethics. Was there an unchanging moral nature, moral law or *physis*, or was morality simply a matter of convention or *nomos* which could change as people and times changed? Some Sophists such as Hippias (481–411) based moral duty upon an unwritten natural law, eternal and divine. Thrasymachus argued that by law of nature, might was right.[186]

In this context Socrates (469–399 B.C.), Plato (427–347 B.C.) and Aristotle (384–322 B.C.) developed their philosophies. For Socrates,

[182] Pericles (c. 490 to 429 B.C.) was effective leader of the democratic party from 469 and dominated Greek life and politics from 443. The Periclean Age is accounted the most brilliant in Greek history. Kitto, op. cit., chap. 7.

[183] Thucydides *The Peloponnesian War* 5.

[184] A citizen of Ephesus whose dates cannot be exactly determined, but he lived about 500 B.C. Only a few of his sayings remain. E. S. Kirk, *Heraclitus: The Cosmic Fragments* (C.U.P., 1954), p. 48.

[185] W. K. Guthrie, *The Sophists* (C.U.P., 1971).

[186] De Burgh, op. cit., p. 163. Hippias' views are expressed in Xenophon *Memorabilia* iv.4. Thrasymachus is one of the characters in Plato's *Republic* 1.3.

human nature was constant, and ethical values were constant also.[187] Plato's elaboration of a world of archetypal ideas or forms was part of his search to put the law of the city, the organised human life which was ever the concern of the Greek philosophers, on a sound and lasting basis. He used the expression "according to nature" to indicate the conformity of things to the idea or type which was its ideal form.[188] The notion of normality in all things, in morality too therefore, was brought out. And in his consideration of the four cardinal virtues of prudence, justice, fortitude and temperance,[189] around which St. Thomas structured his moral theology, he delineates a natural morality, an ideal to which man purely by right reason can attain. Aristotle observed that political justice is of two kinds, natural and conventional. The meaning of natural in this context is that some things have the same force everywhere and at all times and do not exist simply by man's thinking this or that.[190] Legal justice on the other hand, is that which was originally indifferent but which has been specified by practice.

The roots of natural law then were deep in the search of classical Greece for an unchanging truth, including an unchanging moral truth. But it was a later school, the Stoic philosophers, who made the concept of natural law their own in a particular way and, because of their understanding of it and the clearness of their idea of it, it is to them more than to any other influence that the concept obtained and retained its place in Western thought.

The founder of this school was Zeno, a Semite from Citium in Cyprus who went to Athens as a young man in 320 B.C. and taught there for more than half a century in the painted porch (Stoa Poikile)—hence the name "Stoic". The Stoic precepts were: follow nature, follow reason, follow virtue, and fundamental to their teaching was a belief in God; the law which governs the course of nature was not a blind mechanism, but the rational working out of the divine purpose, essentially good.[191] Zeno's successors were Cleanthes and Chrysippus. The Hymn of Cleanthes (331–332 B.C.) spoke of Zeus the all bountiful ruling all things righteously through a universal law: Cleanthes deepened the

[187] Copleston, op. cit., vol. I, p. 111, "Human nature is constant and ethical values are constant. Socrates realised the constancy of these values and sought to fix them in universal definitions which could be taken as a guide and norm in human conduct."

[188] J. Maritain, *Moral Philosophy*, p. 58.

[189] Plato *The Republic* 5.

[190] "Now of Justice. There are two forms of it, the natural and the conventional. It is natural when it has the same validity everywhere." Aristotle *Nicomachean Ethics* 5.7.

[191] De Burgh, op. cit., p. 219–21.

religious element in Stoicism, speaking of God as the soul of the universe. Chrysippus (c. 280–207 B.C.) put forward the idea of a city of the world in which there was one law valid for all men.[192] When the Roman writer Cicero[193] (106–43 B.C.) summarized the implications of natural law theory in a passage which was to have a powerful influence on European thought thereafter, he was drawing upon this Stoic tradition.

> There is in fact a true law, namely right reason, which is in accordance with nature, applies to all men and is unchangeable and eternal. By its commands this law summons men to the performance of their duties, by its prohibitions it restrains them from doing wrong. . . . It will not lay down one rule in Rome and another in Athens. . . . But there will be one law eternal and unchangeable, binding at all times upon all peoples. There will be, as it were, one common master and ruler of men, namely God, who is the author of this law, its interpreter and its sponsor. The man who will not obey it will abandon his better self.

Finally it was the coming together of the Greek idea of the natural law (*Ius Naturale*) with the Roman idea of the law of nations (*Ius Gentium*) which secured the concept of natural law its place in Western thought. Roman Law was originally the Civil Law (*Ius Civile*) confined to Roman citizens or to those non-Romans to whom a legal capacity had been granted by special treaty. In 242 B.C., when she had become a great power, a special official was appointed to dispense justice between non-citizens. His annual edicts, which embodied the adjustments of the Roman Civil Law to apply to alien peoples, formed the basis of the law of nations.[194] Thus *Ius Gentium* was a slow growth, the result of a fusion of the original Roman Law, building on those parts of that law which had accorded with those of other peoples, but modifying the Roman conception to suit varying conditions and enlarging its scope by degrees through assimilating Greek and other foreign elements. In this way a body of principles, suitable for application throughout the Roman world, was formed. Eventually, because of its inherent reasonableness, the law of nations replaced the Civil Law for Roman citizens too. Thus the practical Romans, with their profound and accurate insight into human nature, evolved a universal code valid for all based on a sense of natural equity.

In its formative stages therefore, the Roman legal structure had developed on the basis of practical experience, gathering together and reasoning from rules and practices based on ancient custom or designed to meet particular situations. The beginnings of a science of jurisprudence or philosophy of

---

[192] He also spoke of divine fire which animated the whole world and every man. Maritain, *Moral Philosophy*, p. 59.

[193] Quoted by Sabine, op. cit., p. 164, from Cicero's *Republic* 3.22.

[194] De Burgh, op. cit., pp. 261 ff., 298 ff. Sohm, op. cit., chap. 2.

law were first detectable about 100 B.C., and thereafter it developed constantly. The Emperor Augustus granted official recognition to the work of the jurists, and schools of jurisprudence flourished, moulding the law into a system, and using speculative ideas to help them in their task. Throughout these first three centuries a series of outstanding individuals, among them Celsus and Ulpian, organised systematic treatises on the law. It was out of their work that the later Justinian code was largely formed.[195]

It was the schools of jurisprudence which adapted the idea of the natural law (*Ius Naturale*) to clarify and provide a deeper understanding of the law of nations. The *Ius Naturale* or natural law was seen as the universal rule of conduct which flowed from the nature of man as a rational being, irrespective of race or time. So a slave, under the law of nature, had rights denied to him by the civil law and the *Ius Gentium*.[196] It is this corrective capacity of the concept of natural law which made it of the greatest practical as well as of the greatest speculative importance.

Enough has perhaps now been said to show how the concept of natural law, inherited from the Greek philosophic tradition, was used to help formulate practical law codes for the use of the greatest empire of antiquity; the particular Roman genius lay precisely in its ability to detect accurately the needs of a healthy legal code and system and to construct one accordingly. It was through her law compilations that the concept finally became firmly and unshakeably embedded in European thought— so making it necessary for the Church, in working out her own scientific law, philosophy and theology, to come to terms with it.

The code of the Emperor Justinian adopted from Ulpian a definition of natural law which went against the previous unanimous tradition which linked it with reason. Ulpian defined it as the law to which *all* animals are subject. The Carlyles note that, whereas there is a clarity about Ulpian's distinction between the *Ius Gentium* and the *Ius Naturale*, the same cannot be said of the definition of *Ius Naturale*.[197] They suggest that, from other passages in Ulpian's work, the more usual definition of natural law is apparent—that he did not in fact arrive at a complete and coherent conception of the natural law.

The Fathers and the Doctors of the Church used the concept of natural law. Origen, Tertullian, St. Ambrose, St. Hilary of Poitier spoke of the natural law as written in men's hearts.[198] St. Isidore, writing in the early seventh century and drawing on the clarifications and definitions of the

---

[195] Under the Emperor Justinian (527–565 A.D.) the entire existing law was consolidated into a single code. It comprised an introduction, the Digest and the Code itself.

[196] Carlyle and Carlyle, op. cit., 1:39.

[197] Ibid., p. 41. See also F. Pollock, *Essays in the Law* (London, 1922), p. 37.

[198] Carlyle and Carlyle, op. cit., 1:103–105.

Institutes of Justinian and of Ulpian, provided a more complete statement
of the place of natural law in Christian thought. He divided law into three
categories—natural, civil and the law of nations—defining natural law,
however, in a way which went back on Ulpian's definition of what is
common to all animals and linking it with the older right reason idea.[199]
His definition passed into Gratian's *Decretum* and so influenced all
medieval treatment of the subject. And as some Romans had identified
their *Ius Gentium* with the law of nature, so Gratian provided the insight
through which the law of nature was formally identified with the law of
God.[200]

What is to be noted is that medieval philosophers and theologians, like
the Greek and Roman theorists, did not necessarily agree on the interpretation of natural law, and their very disagreement stimulated fruitful
speculation. For the former, the general principle that the divine revealed
and the natural laws could not be in conflict was accepted since both had
their origin in the mind of God. Further, since the natural law was
discoverable by unaided reason, the widest field of enquiry was kept open
because individual thinkers could question whether such and such a
matter belonged to natural law or not, or was in accord with objective
truth and right reason. The important thing was the belief that human
reason could attain the moral truth, which was objective, unchanging and
binding on all. The question of where that truth lay on specific issues then
was the subject for a debate through which moral knowledge could grow.

St. Thomas' version of what the natural law consisted in, its specific
precepts, is as follows. He argues that the first precept is that good is to be
done and evil is to be avoided, all other precepts being based upon this
first.[201] The good he seeks is manifold, covering the needs of body and
soul, of reason and feeling—but the good is what he seeks in fulfilling all
these needs.

The first good a man seeks is that of his continuance in being, the
preservation of his life, the warding off of obstacles to it and the fostering of those things which help it. Hence a man seeks to mate with his
own kind and to found a family and to educate and bring up those to
whom he gives life. Man also seeks intellectual goods, to know the truth;

[199] Ibid., p. 108–110.

[200] Pollock, op. cit., p. 40. The identification is implicit in St. Paul and the Stoics
certainly used language that connected the natural law with the law of God, but according
to Pollock, the first time that the law of nature was formally identified with the golden
rule of the Gospel is in Gratian. See Carlyle and Carlyle, op. cit., 2:98 ff.

[201] *Summa Theologica*, I–II, q. 94, art. 2. There has been increasing interest, and dispute,
of late, concerning St. Thomas' view of natural law. See W.E. May, "The Natural Law and
Objective Morality", in *Principles of Catholic Moral Life*, edited by May (Chicago, 1980) for
an excellent treatment of the subject and assessment of the literature.

he also seeks the goods that come to him from social living. He therefore tries to dispel his ignorance in order to avoid offending those among whom he lives. St. Thomas would also say, as we shall see when we deal with political justice and economic justice, that it is natural to man not only to live in society but to live in political society and it is also natural for him to possess private property.

The fundamental idea of natural law then is that there is an objective moral truth which can be grasped by right reason and that it is binding on all men at all times. It is an idea which has undergone an eclipse in modern times since the attack on it by the philosopher David Hume. But one might say that, since it was both philosophy and jurisprudence which gave the concept its firm place in the Western tradition before Christian theology and philosophy took up the idea, it is not for philosophy alone to dismiss it.[202] It was indeed through the practical needs of the law rather than the speculations of philosophers, that it achieved its place in the Western tradition, and we have noted that the concept is still essential to a sound jurisprudence. Further, the modern interest in natural rights would not make sense unless there was an underlying belief that right reason demanded man be granted certain basic freedoms, whatever the positive law of tyrants might say.

There is one final point of crucial importance if we are to appreciate the implications of the embodiment of the natural law concept in Christian theology and philosophy. Though it was assumed, rather than strictly laid down, that the Church was the authentic interpreter of the natural law,[203] that assumption is a key to understanding the Church's use of the concept. The law of nature goes hand in hand with the divine authority of the Church to judge all on earth,[204] including ultimately the interpretation of the natural law.

[202] It is significant that a classic restatement of natural law theory has been made by John Finnis, Fellow and Praelector in Jurisprudence, University College, and Reader in Law at the University of Oxford, in the book I refer to several times throughout, *Natural Law and Natural Rights*.
[203] Pollock, op. cit., p. 41.
[204] Ibid.

CHAPTER TWO

THE PROXIMATE AND SUBJECTIVE
ETHICAL NORM

The proximate and subjective ethical norm is man's conscience (personal and social) guided by the sacred and certain teaching of the Church interpreting objective moral law (Dignitatis Humanae 14 and Gaudium et Spes 16, 17, 26, 63).

I. The Objective Moral Law as the Norm
Of Personal Conscience:
The Teaching of the Council and Its Basis

A. THE COUNCIL, OBJECTIVE MORAL LAW AND CONSCIENCE

Dignitatis Humanae stressed that a man must follow his conscience so that he may come to God as his last end. Conscience then is the nub of man's personal relationship with God and his privileges and duties in the light of that relationship. But this stress on personal conscience and the duty to follow it (and the denial of any human authority to intervene and force a man to go against his conscience) is stated in a context in which the Council also stresses that the law of God is the norm by which human life, and human conscience, should be regulated and judged. Conscience is by definition *subjective*. It may honestly tell me to do what is in fact against God's law. If so it must be followed. But Christians should strive to do God's will—not their own. The prompting of an ignorant conscience is no more to be proud of than is any other kind of ignorance. At best it is a sad, though excusable, defect—not a breakthrough into a new kind of freedom. What we want to do in this chapter is to examine a little more thoroughly the relationship between objective moral law and subjective conscience, in the light of the Council's observations which are as follows.[1]

Dignitatis Humanae

14. In order to satisfy the divine command: "Make disciples of all nations" (Mt 28:19), the Catholic Church must spare no effort in striving "that the word of the Lord may speed on and triumph" (2 Th 3:1).

The Church, therefore, earnestly urges her children first of all that "supplications, prayers, intercessions and thanksgivings be made for all

---

[1] The italics in the following are the author's.

men. . . . This is good, is acceptable in the sight of God our Saviour, who desires all men to be saved and to come to the knowledge of the truth" (I Tim 2:1-4).

However, in forming their consciences, the faithful must pay careful attention to the sacred and certain teaching of the Church.[35] *For the Catholic Church is by the will of Christ the teacher of truth. It is her duty to proclaim and teach with authority the truth which is Christ and, at the same time, to declare and confirm by her authority "the principles of the moral order which spring from human nature itself."* In addition, Christians should approach those who are outside wisely, "in the Holy Spirit, genuine love, truthful speech" (2 Cor 6:6-7) and should strive, even to the shedding of their blood, to spread the light of life with all confidence[36] and apostolic courage.

The disciple has a grave obligation to Christ, his Master, to grow daily in his knowledge of the truth he has received from him, to be faithful in announcing it and vigorous in defending it without having recourse to methods which are contrary to the spirit of the Gospel. At the same time the love of Christ urges him to treat with love, prudence and patience,[37] those who are in error or ignorance with regard to the faith. He must take into account his duties towards Christ, the life-giving Word whom he must proclaim, the rights of the human person and the measure of grace which God has given to each man through Christ in calling him freely to accept and profess the faith.

[35] Cf. Pius XII, Radio message, 23 Mar. 1952: AAS 44 (1952) pp. 270-278.
[36] Cf. Acts 4:29.
[37] Cf. John XXIII Encycl. *Pacem in Terris* 11 April 1963 AAS 55 (1963) pp. 299-300.

Gaudium et Spes

16. *Deep within his conscience man discovers a law which he has not laid upon himself but which he must obey. Its voice, ever calling him to love and to do what is good and to avoid evil, tells him inwardly at the right moment: do this, shun that. For man has in his heart a law inscribed by God. His dignity lies in observing this law, and by it he will be judged.*[9] His conscience is man's most secret core, and his sanctuary. There he is alone with God whose voice echoes in his depths.[10] By conscience, in a wonderful way, that law is made known which is fulfilled in the love of God and of one's neighbour.[11] Through loyalty to conscience, Christians are joined to other men in the search for truth and for the right solution to so many problems which arise both in the life of individuals and from social relationships.
Hence, *the more a correct conscience prevails, the more do persons and groups turn aside from blind choice and try to be guided by the objective standards of moral conduct. Yet it often happens that conscience goes astray through ignorance which it is unable to avoid, without thereby losing its dignity. This cannot be said of the man who takes little trouble to find out what is true and good, or when conscience is by degrees almost blinded through the habit of committing sin.*

17. It is, however, only in freedom that man can turn himself towards what is good. The people of our time prize freedom very highly and strive

eagerly for it. In this they are right. Yet they often cherish it improperly, as if it gave them leave to do anything they like, even when it is evil. But that which is truly freedom is an exceptional sign of the image of God in man. For God willed that man should "be left in the hand of his own counsel" [12] so that he might of his own accord seek his creator and freely attain his full and blessed perfection by cleaving to him. Man's dignity therefore requires him to act out of conscious and free choice, as moved and drawn in a personal way from within, and not by blind impulses in himself or by mere external constraint. *Man gains such dignity when, ridding himself of all slavery of the passions, he presses forward towards his goal by freely choosing what is good and, by his diligence and skill, effectively secures for himself the means suited to this end. Since human freedom has been weakened by sin, it is only by the help of God's grace that man can give his actions their full and proper relationship to God. Before the Judgement Seat of God an account of his own life will be rendered to each one according as he has done either good or evil.* [13]

[9] Cf. Rom 2:15–16.
[10] Cf. Pius XII, Radio message on rightly forming the Christian conscience in youth, 23 Mar. 1952: AAS 44 (1952), p. 271.
[11] Cf. Mt 22:37–40. Gal 5:14.
[12] Cf. Eccl 12:14.
[13] Cf. 2 Cor 5:10.

The question of objective criteria as the norm of moral action is raised also in *Gaudium et Spes* in the context of the right use of marriage. It is noted in paragraph 51 that

> It is not enough to take only the good intention and the evaluation of motives into account: the objective criteria must be used, criteria drawn from the value of the human person and human action . . . (and) . . . the teaching of the Church in its interpretation of the divine law.

In its observations on these matters the Council simply sums up the traditional Catholic teaching on conscience. There are several elements in that teaching and all must be understood and applied if the truth is to be seen and acted upon. The elements are as follows:

1. Moral choice must be free and aided by God's grace.
2. Conscience tells a man the difference between good and evil.
3. The norm of conscience is the objective law of God as interpreted by the Church. Ideally the individual's judgement of right and wrong in his conscience should conform with this objective norm.
4. Man should not be a captive of passion in making moral choices. It is precisely because we should be aware that our will does not always conform with God's that we should be suspicious of identifying what our subjective judgement tells us with what God wants when we find ourselves in conflict with those who have a right to instruct us on

these matters. God's grace is available to enable us to choose what is truly good. In any conflict that takes place in us between what is in fact self-will, trying to bend our subjective judgement away from God's law, we are not alone. We have the grace of God to help us.

5. If, however, through no fault of our own, it is impossible for our conscience to perceive the objective moral truth, then that conscience still retains its dignity; no moral blame attaches to the objectively wrong act. Inability to perceive the truth, invincible ignorance, is *not* the same as refusal to care about the truth. Likewise true lack of freedom or diminished responsibility is not the same as a conscience that has grown sightless as a result of habitual sin. If my diminished responsibility is a result of my own free choice of evil to the point where I no longer care about the difference between right and wrong, then I am responsible for having reduced myself to that state, and consequently for any sin committed as a result of my having been in that state.

B. THE BIBLICAL TEACHING ON CONSCIENCE AND ITS DEVELOPMENT IN MORAL THEOLOGY

The notion of conscience implies that man is aware of his responsibility for his actions, that he knows he is responsible for what he does freely and knowingly, and he realises that by his freely willed and committed acts he can judge himself good or bad and others can judge him good or bad. He may err, or disagree with others, about what is good or bad, but he cannot avoid thinking in these terms and, it may be, forming his conscience (rightly or wrongly) by his very disagreement with others.

The biblical understanding of conscience is expressed in several ways—heart, wisdom, prudence.[2] It is conscience to which Christ referred when he said that the pure in heart would see God. Conscience in the sense of self-consciousness, passing moral judgement, was known to Greek philosophy. The Greek term was *syneidesis*, "consciousness", and the term *synderesis* found its way into scholastic philosophy and theology, probably as a corruption of the original Greek. By degrees, *syneidesis* or *conscientia* came to mean the actual conscience (the judgement here and now) and *synderesis* the habitual conscience (the psychological power from which these judgements proceed).[3]

From the time of St. Paul the biblical notion of conscience had been clarified by the more acute Greek understanding of it as "self-consciousness

[2] P. Delhaye, *The Christian Conscience* (New York, 1968), chap. 2. See also H. Peschke, *Christian Ethics*, 1:147 ff.
[3] Delhaye, op. cit., pp. 27, 106.

passing moral judgement." In Romans Paul speaks of a law engraved on man's heart, a witness, a conscience, an inner mental dialogue, and he exhorts his fellow Christians to make their decisions without going against their conscience because he who does not act in good faith, according to his conscience, commits sin.[4]

As St. Thomas defined it, conscience is an act by which man makes moral judgements; it is a judgement of practical reason at work on matters of right and wrong.[5] There is an element of emotion or feeling in it, because when the reason decides what ought to be done, we feel emotionally drawn toward it, or emotionally repelled from it, according to whether we find it attractive or not. Likewise, when the moral reason passes judgement on an act committed, we either feel in good conscience or in bad conscience according to whether we know we have done right or wrong.

It is important to grasp that though we have an absolute duty to obey our consciences, this does not mean that conscience is infallibly right. Judgements may be corrupted by self-interest, by ignorance of the facts, or because we may simply make wrong estimates about the results of certain actions. A man is rarely a good judge in his own case and the more emotionally involved he is the more true this becomes. If we do then invoke the duty to follow conscience against the judgement of those to whom God has given the responsibility of deciding what the objective truth is, we are taking a great responsibility. We are saying that we know that what we are doing is against the objective truth but that we are quite sure that God knows, as we do, that we are in good conscience in doing it.

Difficulties of conscience are more likely to come from doubts about where the right lies rather than from the total conviction that a given course of action is absolutely right for me despite the objective moral law. Here there is a whole field of casuistry laid open with its advantages and disadvantages.[6] One may never act in a state of positive doubt about the right or wrong because this means that there is a danger of being indifferent to sin. The doubt must be resolved, by advice, reflection, prayer, until the actual conscience can commit itself to a decision, "This is the right thing to do." The nearer one comes to positively committing oneself against those who rightfully claim the authority to teach the objective moral truth, the more sure, and the more humble must the dissent be.[7] It

---

[4] Rom 2:15, 14:20–22.

[5] *Summa Theologica*, I, q. 79, art. 12, 13.

[6] Delhaye, op. cit., pt. 2, chaps. 1–3. Peschke, op. cit., 1:160 ff.

[7] Peschke, op. cit., 1:183 ff. He there quotes *Dignitatis Humanae* (paragraph 8) to the effect that "there are many who, under the pretext of freedom, seem inclined to reject all submission to authority and make light of the duty of obedience."

must also be noted that the duty of following an honestly erroneous conscience must not be allowed to obscure the importance of doing the objective moral right. Error must be tolerated for fear of forcing consciences; but error it remains and so an objective evil in God's sight.

All this teaching on conscience and its relation to the objective moral law grows out of the traditional moral theology which, in its turn, is based upon the revealed morality of the Scriptures. Natural law and right reason could take us some way to knowing the necessary moral truth about the concrete situation of humanity since Adam, but divine revelation is needed to discover the whole of man's moral obligations. Grace enlightens the mind and directs and strengthens the will to move us toward the fullness of the moral life God wants of us.

C. THE NATURE OF THE MORAL ACT
ACCORDING TO THE NEW TESTAMENT,
CLASSICAL MORAL THEOLOGY AND THE COUNCIL

It is the function of moral theology to draw out the implications of the teaching of the Scriptures concerning man's ultimate end in this life and his means to attaining it.[8] Christ's own teaching tells us that those who have disobeyed God's law in this life will, when it is over, be visited with eternal punishment while the virtuous will enter into eternal life.[9] He warned us that the way to eternal damnation was wide and spacious but that only few find the road to salvation.[10] It is "the man who stands firm to the end" who will be saved.[11] So throughout the rest of the New Testament. St. Peter warned us that God has no favourites and judges everyone according to what he has done, hence we must take care to live rightly in God's sight.[12]

The message of the New Testament, therefore, is that through showing our love for God in a practical way in this life, in doing what he wants us to do, we will come to our eternal home, our eternal kingdom, the kingdom of heaven. This means in practice that all the acts of my life for which I can be held morally responsible, all those which I do freely and

---

[8] The distinction between moral theology and philosophical ethics lies in the data each uses. The theologian looks to revelation, the Scriptures and the Christian tradition, the philosopher to the data of actual human experience and unaided human reason. Catholic moral theology recognizes the insights of right reason in natural law as God-given and respects the technique of the philosopher in elucidating both natural and supernatural moral truth.

[9] Mt 25:46.

[10] Mt 7:13–14.

[11] Mt 10:22.

[12] 1 Pet 1:17.

knowingly,[13] can be judged according to whether they are in accord with God's moral law, so taking us toward God and our eternal happiness, or taking us away from it. This is because morality, as we have seen, is grounded in the law of God which is unchanging, and by that the morality of the human act can be judged.

The good or evil of the human act[14] in itself (as distinct from the imputation of that morality to the doer of the act) is then determined by the relation of the act in question to the objective order established by God. Thus, the object of the act (the *finis operis*, literally "the end of the act" i.e. the end primarily achieved by the act) is the first determinant of morality. But the end as *intended by the doer* of the act (the *finis operantis*) and the other circumstances are to be taken into consideration. Three things then are to be taken into consideration regarding the moral imputability of the act: the object (*finis operis*), the end (*finis operantis*) and the circumstances.

The teaching on conscience then is in the context of this understanding of the essential nature of the moral act. An objectively evil act can be done without evil being imputed to the doer if (1) the doer cannot see the evil, or (2) even though he can, he is unable to act against it because his freedom to follow the right course is impeded. Such an evil act remains objectively evil, it is not made objectively good by the honest error of the doer. But since it is what I *know* and what I *freely* do, knowing what I am doing, which determines the moral imputability of the act, I am, in such a case, not morally imputable. The objectively evil act is only morally imputable when full knowledge and freedom exist.

Let us take the example of a private individual killing another human being. The right to kill another is sometimes one that the public authority may invoke—as in war or for the execution of a criminal—and in self-defence the individual, in some circumstances, may take life.[15] But a private individual who does not have such authority, and is acting other than in justifiable self-defence, may never deprive another of life and if we come upon a situation where a private individual has killed another, we know that an evil has been done. Another way of saying this is that a physical evil[16] has been done in that a human life, which would otherwise

[13] Ignorance, error and inattention can affect my knowledge; passion, fear, violence, disposition and habits my freedom. Peschke, op. cit., 1:188 ff.

[14] Ibid., pp. 199 ff. See St. Thomas Aquinas, *Summa Theologica*, I–II, qq. 1–12, 18–20.

[15] See Peschke, op. cit., 2:272 ff., 348 ff., 365 ff.

[16] Evil is not a positive something but the absence of a good that should be there (*Summa Theologica* I, q. 48, art. 1). We talk of the evil of suffering or disease; these are physical evils, evils *in things* and may or may not be the result of human action. *Moral* evil arises out of the human choice, the human act. A choice of what is in accord with God's law is morally good, of what is not, is evil. The things chosen may in themselves be good, i.e., the glutton abuses food which in itself is a good. A morally bad action (one not in conformity with God's Law)

have continued, has been ended by human action. But we cannot *impute* the moral evil of murder (direct and deliberate taking of life by a private individual) to the killer until we know how the killing happened. If, on examining the case, we find that the person who did the killing did so accidentally, then we do not ascribe to him the moral evil of murder. This is in practice the way in which the law works in deciding to what extent the private individual who kills another is to be punished. There is a whole range of verdicts, from willful murder down to accidental death, which are precisely concerned to find out just how far the person who did the killing was responsible. To repeat once more what was said above, therefore, the circumstances are important in determining the imputability of the moral quality of the act to the doer of that act. But the circumstances do not decide the goodness of the act itself. That goodness is determined essentially by the relationship of the *finis operis* to God's moral law.

A sound morality then must keep in mind (1) the objective facts, (2) the subjective intention, and (3) the circumstances. If either the object (*finis operis*, the effect the act achieves), the intention of the doer of the act (the *finis operantis*), or the circumstances are evil, the act is evil; circumstances can also increase or decrease the moral quality and imputability of the act but they cannot make a bad act good. To steal is always evil. To steal from the very poor is more evil but stealing from the rich is evil too. To intend the evil (*finis operantis*) even when the evil act itself (*finis operis*) does not succeed, means that the moral guilt is imputed as if the evil intended has been done. But to intend *good* while doing an *evil* act does not make the act morally good.

D. MODERN CATHOLIC OBJECTIONS TO THE CLASSICAL THEORY

This approach to moral theory and moral theology is then taken for granted by the Council. The good or evil of an act is determined objectively by its relationship to the objective law and will of God but intention and other circumstances may affect the moral *imputability* of the evil to the doer of the act. The evil that man knows and intends to do is the evil for which he can be blamed. It is his conscience, informed by the objective moral law, which is to be his guide to the moral act. In those cases in which a person honestly cannot see the objective moral good or, if he sees it, genuinely cannot act freely to attain it, then there is no moral blame for any objective moral evil done.

---

may be done by someone to whom its guilt is not imputed because of lack of knowledge or full consent.

Very different is the direction taken by some moral theologians in the light of the Second Vatican Council, and ostensibly using its teaching as a support for the new direction. It is their view that although the object (*finis operis*) of the act may be at first sight evil, in fact the subjective intent of the doer of the act (*finis operantis*) may make the choice of that evil good because of the circumstances. The inference is that what is against the objective moral order, God's law, can be made objectively good by the intention of the doer of the act.
Let us consider the following.[17]

> What value do our norms have with respect to the morality of the action as such, prior that is to the consideration of the circumstances and intention? We answer: *they cannot be moral norms unless circumstances and intention are taken into account*. They can be considered as moral norms only because we tacitly assume to judge the action in the light of possible circumstances and intention but since theoretically this is impossible, since, in practice, these elements of an action are necessarily incomplete, we cannot rule out the possibility that in the practical application an objectively based instance of conflict—the exceptional case—can show that the norm does not have objectively the range of validity previously supposed. The absoluteness of a norm depends more upon the objectivity of its relationship to reality than upon its universality.
>
> The end does not justify the means, that is the morally bad means. This tenet is, of course, correct. When and to the extent that it has been established that an action is morally bad, it may not be performed as a means towards attaining a good end. On the other hand, if there is a question only of evil in the pre-moral sense, such as death, wounding, dishonour, etc., intention and the realisation of a good can possibly justify the doing of an evil, e.g. the evil of a surgical operation in the interest of health or a transplant. Needless to say: (1) the performing of the evil is not judged independently of the intention as morally bad, (2) in the one human action (health care, transplant) the performing of the evil is not an isolated (human) action but only an element of the one action. Therefore, a *morally bad human action* is not being used as a means to a good end.

The observation that "moral norms are only such because we tacitly assume to judge the action in the light of possible circumstances and

[17] From J. Fuchs, S.J., "The Absoluteness of Moral Terms", *Gregorianum*, 52 (1971). The article is reproduced in *Readings in Moral Theology*, no. 1, edited by C. Curran (New York, 1979). Other moral theologians such as Curran, McCormick, Schuller and Janssens take views similar to those of Fuchs. Connery, Emerke, Quay, Grisez and May are among those critical of it. Some of these latter are contributors to *Readings in Moral Theology*. Articles by John Finnis and W. E. May in *Principles of Catholic Moral Life*, edited by W. E. May (Chicago, 1980), restate the teaching of St. Thomas and Vatican II and, in so doing, consider in footnotes and text, current controversies and literature.

intention" is hard to reconcile with the Second Vatican Council's view that objective criteria are to be used in determining morality. The statement as given in Fuchs is in fact logically incomplete, since it slides over the distinction between objective moral norms and subjective moral imputability. To say we judge *actions* in the light of *possible* circumstances and intentions is to speak too ambiguously and confusingly. What we do in practice is to judge *an act* in the light of principles known before the specific act is done and on the basis of this judgement we determine moral imputability. For full logical completeness the sentence should be reconstructed as follows: "moral norms do not mean that the moral quality of the act can be ascribed to the doer of the act until the circumstances and intention are known."

The use of confusing terms such as "pre-moral" also enables the author to fudge issues such as "doing evil to achieve good".[18] As we have shown above, killing is always a *physical* evil, the *moral* evil of which may not be imputed to anyone until proven. Similarly wounding, e.g. by a surgeon's knife, is, in itself, a physical evil. But we have carefully worked out norms that enable us to judge when the physical pain and discomfort of surgery, the physical evil of it, is justified. Causing a physical evil (mutilation, amputation), is in fact *morally* good; the surgeon does a positively good moral act in improving the patient's health by surgery that produces overall greater well-being. It is not that the surgeon's action has many aspects that might make a *morally evil act morally good*. It is precisely because we have *a priori* standards or norms that tell us when surgery is justified that we judge a physical infliction of pain in these circumstances morally good.

Further, Fr. Fuchs is precisely calling on the principle of totality, a product of the casuistry of the old moral theology, with its assumptions about absolute and objective morality. According to that principle of totality it is permissible for an injury to be done to one part of the body in order that the whole body may benefit. That surgery inflicts a *physical* evil is clear, but because we know that God has (subject to his law) given us dominion over our bodies we know also that we can allow someone to inflict that injury on us for a good cause, the cure of the whole body. We equally well know that it would be wrong to allow the infliction of

---

[18] In "Ontic Evil and Moral Evil" (*Readings in Moral Theology* [New York, 1979], vol. 1), Janssens asserts, "Of old we preferred the distinction between 'malum physicum' and 'malum morale'. Nowadays we prefer the term 'ontic evil' because the contemporary meaning of 'physical' corresponds more to the meaning of 'material'. Ontic evil is 'any lack of perfection at which we aim . . . frustrates our natural urges'," (p. 60). But a proper understanding of physical evil as "evil in things", including the human mind or psyche, covers all that "ontic" and "pre-moral" evil say without confusing the debate.

physical pain for masochistic or sadistic purposes because the infliction or the suffering of pain for its own sake is contrary to the dignity of man and the law of God. In other words, it is because we have an absolute and objective idea of morality, of what is in conformity with God's law or not, what *finis operis* and *finis operantis* is moral or not, that we can judge that the surgeon, although inflicting pain, is not doing a moral evil but a moral good. We know, before a particular surgeon starts a particular operation, what norms govern the right use of his knife and we judge accordingly. Fuchs is presuming the principle of totality, one which grows out of objective morality and sound casuistry to demonstrate that absolute and objective morality can be denied—a circumstance which does not give us confidence in his case.

E. THE ROLE OF CASUISTRY IN MORAL THEOLOGY

A sound and healthy casuistry is needed if objective morality is going to be applied in the spirit in which it has been given us by God. And it is because casuistry was either not understood, was misunderstood or misused that the present interest in situation ethics makes sense.[19] It is the plea of those Christians who hold to schools of thought which are either identified with situationism or closely allied to it, that it is because biblical morality, as interpreted by some Christians, was too rigid and unloving, that they have adopted the views they do adopt. There is indeed nothing in what is valid in the situationist's case which cannot be accommodated within a sound casuistry honestly applied and remaining within the context of an objective and absolute moral system based on the Scriptures and understood in the light of classical moral theology and the magisterium. But it has to be a sound casuistry, properly understood, and prepared to accept authoritative guidance. And as the example quoted from Fuchs above shows, it is all too easy to misinterpret the principles of casuistry and make them defeat their purpose.

The principle of totality used by Fuchs was developed as we saw in the context of determining the licitness (or illicitness) of certain intentional mutilations of the human body. Though what the principle itself states is not new, it was not referred to as the principle of totality until quite recently.[20] The principle asserts that since each part of the body exists for the good of the whole, then one part may be sacrificed or operated on if the health or well-being of the whole is improved by such an operation. The assumption is that there is due proportion between the mutilation

---

[19] See below pp. 112 ff.
[20] *New Catholic Encyclopedia*, s.v. "Totality, Principle of".

caused and the good achieved. For the sake of the whole body, therefore, amputations and other surgery can be justified. It is then a principle which refers to the totality of the *human body* and it establishes the moral acceptability of operating on one part of the body for the good of the whole providing the intention and the circumstances are good. But a principle developed in response to questions concerning physical mutilation is not valid if applied in order to try to justify doing or allowing moral evil in one area of my life in order that I might do good in another part of it. Each individual human act can be judged according to God's moral law and if the act is done freely and knowingly then its moral quality is imputed to me. I may not disobey God's law on one matter so that I might serve it better on another. I may not do moral evil that good may come of it. In the case of an operation—if the physical evil, the mutilation, takes place for a good reason and does genuinely help the whole then the mutilation is justified; even though a physical evil is done, the surgeon's act is morally good. But it can never be good to do *moral* evil for any reason whatsoever.

A second principle of sound casuistry which is often misused today is that of the "lesser of two evils".[21] The principle states that if I am in a situation in which, whatever I do, I will do physical evil, then I must choose to do the lesser of the evils open to me. The reason is obvious. The human act is a freely willed act, the purpose of which is known and accepted. In so far as I do what is evil freely, willingly and knowingly, then my act can be judged morally good or morally bad and imputed to me. I cannot be imputed if I did evil that I was not free to avoid doing. The principle of the lesser of two evils only frees me from moral blame when, because of forces I cannot control, I am not free to do *anything* but physical evil. The principle, therefore, can only be invoked where I am so constrained. If I can refrain from acting and so avoid evil I must do so. Similarly I may not misuse the principle to justify doing freely less evil than I could. Should I *freely choose* to kill one person rather than two I may not justify my action on the principle of the lesser of two evils, saying I did less evil than I could have done.

A sound application of the principle would be as follows. If the operator of a powerful piece of machinery found that it went suddenly out of control and he was faced with letting it run wild with a danger of killing someone, or deliberately stopping it by letting it do great damage to

[21] Delhaye, op. cit., pp. 233 ff. The author here discusses the principle in the light of actual cases (including that of God's command to Abraham to sacrifice his son) and concludes that most problems in their applications are a result of misunderstandings of the principle itself. We may note that the misuse of this principle to justify contraception is specifically rejected by *Humanae Vitae* (par. 14).

property but with no loss of life, he would have to let it destroy the property. The evil of destroying that valuable property would be unavoidable and so not morally imputable, and it would be a lesser evil than killing someone. The moral evil of that act would not be imputed because the operator could not help doing the physical evil in question. A degree of moral blame would attach, however, if the reason for the defect in the machinery was due to his or another's incompetence.

The principle of the lesser of two evils is often misused in order to justify an evil which someone expects of me. The argument is put forward that if I fail to do an evil that another wishes me to do then I may hurt that person in some way, hence I may freely choose to do the evil act, judging it the lesser of the evils with which I am faced. But it is clear that in this case I am in fact free, if I wish, to let the person concerned suffer from their own unwarranted expectations of me. I am free, that is, to refrain from doing a morally evil act. This I must do whatever another may think of me or expect of me. For example if someone I loved expected me to steal something for him or her, claiming that they would be offended if theft was not committed, the principle of the lesser of two evils would not be invoked.

Finally, the principle of double effect[22] is also subject to misuse. The principle states that if an individual act has two effects, one good and one bad, I may do such an act (1) provided the act in itself is morally good, (2) that the evil effect of the good act is not willed but only permitted or accepted, and (3) that there is due proportion between the unintended evil that follows the good act, and the good achieved by the act.

A clear example of the use of this principle is concerned with some operations during pregnancy. In the case of an ectopic pregnancy, when gestation takes place outside the womb, it may be necessary to perform an operation which leads to the destruction of the foetus as a secondary and unintentional effect. This can be justified on the principle of double effect.[23] The more difficult, very rare, but inevitably very emotive and controversial cases of choosing to save the life of the mother in a difficult birth by *directly* killing the unborn baby is not comparable to the other case quoted. The one accepts the death of the unborn baby as an unintended effect of a good act. The other directly kills the unborn baby—and therefore raises the issue of the destruction of innocent life.

The principle is clearly illustrated in other cases—for example, the policeman who attempts to capture an armed criminal and in so doing puts his own life at stake is doing a good thing (saving the community

---

[22] St. Thomas uses the principle in explaining the right to self-defence. *Summa Theologica*, II–II, q. 64, art. 7.

[23] T. J. O'Donnell, S.J., *Medicine and Christian Morality* (New York, 1975), pp. 198 ff.

from the violence of the man concerned) while risking an undesired evil, his own possible injury or even death. The man who tests planes in order to improve standards of safety can put his own life at risk in so doing: the doctor who treats patients affected with contagious diseases does the same without moral blame. They set out to do a good thing while running the risk of physical evil which, if it was directly willed, would be immoral, a moral evil.

II. The Objective Moral Law
As the Norm of Social Conscience:
The Teaching of the Council and Its Basis

A. CHRISTIAN PERSONALISM

The norms of personal morality which we have been so far examining stem from man's personal relationship with God and the need of his nature to live his life in such a way, after it, that personal relationship with God can be fulfilled in the eternity of happiness. Man, if he understands his nature properly, is entirely God-centred—created by God and for him. It is this fact of being created in the image and likeness of God which is the foundation of my personal worth and dignity as a human being. In all things in my life I must live by God's grace, worthy of the great inheritance that is mine as his son or daughter. This fundamental Christian personalism is not the same as individualism which tends to consider my rights and needs as a human being independent of those of others—if not in fact opposed to them. The first and the greatest Commandment is that I should love God above all things and it is in pursuing this love that my moral life develops. But the second half of that great Commandment is that I must love my neighbour as myself.[24] Both obligations stem from the same source—the fact that God made me and loves me and wants me to love him in return.

Christian ethics, Christian morality, is fundamentally personal in that it is a practical living out of my personal relationship with God. But this very personalism is social. I cannot claim my rights and dignities, I cannot live out my love of God in practical terms without giving to others in theory and practice those same rights and dignities which I claim through my relationship with God. I am created and loved by God but so are all those who bear his image and likeness, every man, woman and child created by God. This truth is restated by the Council in *Gaudium et Spes*. The part of the document which the following quotations come from is

[24] Mt 22:34–41.

that concerned with political and economic justice and we will be examining it more closely later on. For the moment we just want to see what was
in the Council's mind in making recommendations on these matters. The
main passages are from *Gaudium et Spes* firstly (paragraph 63).

> The Church in the course of centuries has worked out in the light of the
> Gospel principles of justice and equity demanded by right reason for indivi-
> dual and social life and also for international relations. The Council now
> intends to reiterate those principles in accordance with the situation of the
> world today and will outline certain guidelines, particularly with reference to
> the requirements of economic development.[1]

> [1] Pius XII Message, 23 March 1952: AAS 44 (1952) p. 273. John XXIII Allocution to the Italian
> Catholic Workers' Association, May 1959: AAS 51 (1959) p. 358.

In the same document it had already been noted (paragraph 26) that

> The social order and its development must constantly yield to the good of
> the person since the order of things must be subordinate to the order of
> persons not the other way round as the Lord suggests when He said the
> Sabbath was made for man and not man for the Sabbath.[6] The social order
> requires constant improvement: it must be founded in truth, built on justice,
> and enlivened by love. It should grow in freedom towards a more humane
> equilibrium.[7] If these objectives are to be attained there will first have to be a
> renewal of attitudes and far reaching social changes.

> [6] Mark 2:27.
> [7] John XXIII *Pacem in Terris* AAS 55 (1963) p. 266.

The criteria of social morality then are objective. There are principles of
equity and justice which the Church has worked out in the course of
centuries and in the light of the Gospel and these must govern man's life in
society, nationally and internationally. The specifics of the Council's
teaching on these matters will be considered later. Here we may just note
that it is to the documents of the social magisterium as it has developed
since *Rerum Novarum* (1891) through *Quadragesimo Anno* (1931), the
numerous radio messages of Pius XII, the encyclicals of John XXIII, *Mater
et Magistra* and *Pacem in Terris*, that the Council refers. In many respects
the Council simply comments on, or gives a summary of, the principles
contained in those documents.

Paragraph 26 of *Gaudium et Spes* emphasises the personalised orientation of the Christian ethic and the Christian social ethic. It speaks of the
social order and its development working for the benefit of the human
person. Society is for man and not man for society, hence the social order
needs constantly to be kept under review to see if it works to this end; the
social order which is capable of working to the benefit of the human
person is one founded on truth, built on justice and animated by love.

Truth, justice, love—these are the ideals that should be before man in society if that society is to be worthy of man in God's image.

The truth which is to be the foundation of the social order is the truth of God. Social ethics are based on those ultimate norms of human life, the divine, eternal, objective and universal law, as are personal ethics. In *Mater et Magistra* John XXIII made this conviction explicit:[25]

> There are some indeed that go so far as to deny the existence of a moral order which is transcendent, absolute, universal and equally binding upon all. Where the same law of justice is not adhered to by all, men cannot hope to come to open and full agreement on vital issues. . . . Mutual trust . . . cannot begin or increase except by recognition of and respect for the moral order but the moral order has no existence except in God. Cut off from God it must necessarily disintegrate.

The argument is that only when there is respect for the truth which comes from belief in a moral order founded by God can a sound social order develop. Respect for this truth alone produces principles of justice applicable to the needs of human society. *Gaudium et Spes*[26] notes that the Church is concerned not only with national, but international justice; it is her reflection on the Gospel and the application of right reason accordingly through two thousand years of experience that she has to offer. She has a social moral teaching as she has a personal moral teaching and both stem from the same source, the divine eternal law through the divine positive law and that natural law which is man's participation in the divine law.

B. JUSTICE AND CHARITY

Truth, justice and love are to be the foundation of the social order. The truth is guaranteed to us in revelation, the natural law and the tradition of the Church. Justice and love have to be put into practice in the human situation and the principles to be given positive effect by human endeavour. In this endeavour the social teaching of the Church, with its insistence on charity and justice, is to be the guide. The two ideas are complementary and neither may be in any way subordinated to the other. But logically, and in fact in the history of Christian mission, the Christian work of charity in society has come first and in this the Church has made a unique contribution to social ideals.[27] Charity is the cradle of justice, as it

[25] *Mater et Magistra* (London: C.T.S., 1963), pars. 205–208.

[26] *Gaudium et Spes*, par. 63.

[27] "The active habitual and detailed charity of private persons, which is so conspicuous a feature of all Christian societies, was scarcely known in antiquity. . . . Christianity for the first time made charity a rudimentary virtue . . . it united in the minds of men the idea of supreme goodness with that of active and constant benevolence." W. Lecky, *History of*

is of all the other virtues—to pretend to love one's neighbour and then to refuse him justice is a mockery.[28] The two cannot be separated, still less opposed. Modern man, however, in thinking of the problems of building a better social order tends to concentrate on matters of justice. The social teaching of the Church does not want to and does not in fact in practice argue with this fixation. It does ask that the question of charity not be neglected because, if it is, then true justice is not achieved. It is not achieved because a justice which is without love is harsh and penal. The community that thinks charity can be neglected will be inhuman in its administration of justice. It will give the poor claims on it in justice yet show contempt, lack of respect, of love, for them in administering it. It will degrade even its efforts to be just. And it will fail to encourage and foster the readiness in private individuals to seek out and see to the needs that officialdom is too impersonal to handle.

The interest in justice in society is as old as the scientific moral philosophy which took its origins among the Greeks. Plato placed justice among his cardinal virtues.[29] In his treatment of the subject St. Thomas defines it as "a habit whereby a man renders to each one his due by constant and perpetual will."[30] It is a virtue in that it is done voluntarily and knowingly and it is a habit in that it is determined to produce just acts. The virtue of justice, therefore, is not achieved or evidenced in one particular act but in a succession of such acts showing that my tendency, my will to give to others what is their due is constant. And since the object of justice is to keep men together in society, it implies the relationship of one man to another in that context and is concerned with ordering that relationship to the achievement of the common good.

The subdivisions of justice, common in the Western tradition since Aristotle,[31] are into legal, distributive and commutative. A fourth term "social justice" has recently been added though its value is disputed. The idea of legal justice is, at first sight, very misleading. In fact "universal justice" is a better rendering than "legal" justice. Experience teaches us that laws are not necessarily just but to speak of legal justice is to invite the inference that what is legal is just and that what is just is necessarily legal.

European Morals, 2:34–36. See also A. Harnack, *The Mission and Expansion of Christianity in the First Three Centuries*, vol. 1, chap. 4. A. Dopsch, *The Economic and Social Foundations of European Civilisation* (London, 1937), pp. 247 ff.

[28] E. Welty, *A Handbook of Christian Social Ethics* (London, 1960), 1:324. J. Messner, *Social Ethics* (London, 1965), pp. 334 ff.

[29] Plato *The Republic* 5. Aristotle *Nicomachean Ethics* 5. John Rawls, *A Theory of Justice* (O.U.P., 1971), restates more modern theories based on Locke, Rousseau and Kant.

[30] *Summa Theologica* II–II, q. 58, art. 1. See Welty, op. cit., 1:284 ff. Messner, op. cit., pp. 314 ff. Also John Finnis, *Natural Law and Natural Rights* (O.U.P., 1980), chap. 7.

[31] Aristotle *Nicomachean Ethics*. See J. Hoffner, *Fundamentals of Christian Sociology*, pp. 47 ff. Messner, op. cit., pp. 320 ff. Welty, op. cit., 1:292 ff. Finnis, op. cit., pp. 161 ff.

In fact it is fundamental to all Christian thinking (and indeed pagan thinking in natural law theory) that *justice* is the standard by which we must *judge law*. One may not assume that what the law says is permissible or necessary is in fact just.

Legal justice, universal justice, therefore properly understood, does not equiparate "legality" with "justice". The term and distinctions arise because justice is a general and not only a personal or particular virtue. Though justice, since it is concerned with giving others their rights, is primarily concerned with the person, with the individual, yet man lives in society and that society must be organised by legitimate authority for the common good. And since it is through the making of laws that political authority achieves its purpose of serving the common good, justice achieved in this way may truly be called universal or legal justice. Those who rule for the common good are subject to the divine eternal, the divine positive (or revealed) and the natural laws and, therefore, justice dispensed must be a true justice, one in conformity with revelation and right reason. This legal justice is in St. Thomas' words "in the sovereign principally and by way of a master craft, while it is secondarily and administratively in his subjects."[32] It is the duty of political authority, therefore, to ensure the common good is served. It is the duty of the citizen to obey just laws once made.

Particular justice is of two kinds, distributive and commutative. Distributive justice is concerned with the distribution of honour or wealth in society in such a way that the common good is preserved. It is a matter of proportion. Not every individual and not every group of individuals has the same place in society. Accordingly not all have equal claim on the good things it has to distribute. The distribution of wealth and honour must then take these matters into consideration in deciding the norms of distributive justice. But distributive justice is not being achieved if there are any in society who do not have enough to enable them to lead a full human existence, or who do not have the opportunity to prosper in wealth and honour according to their abilities and subject to the common good. Perversions of distributive justice, therefore, are all kinds of corruption, favouritism toward individuals or groups, all kinds of oppression, all unrelieved poverty. Commutative or contractual justice is concerned with the relationship between individuals. It is commutative justice which ensures against damage or injury to one's neighbours and gives the right of redress to those who have been offended in any way by others.

The term "social justice" came into use as public concern with the injustices in society in the nineteenth century grew. These were offences

[32] *Summa Theologica*, II–II, q. 58, art. 6.

against commutative justice (e.g. through the imbalance in the wage contract) and against distributive justice (because of the failure of the state to see that all had a share in the goods of the commonwealth sufficient to ensure for all a decent existence and opportunity to develop their talents). It is through economic and political change and progressive provision of social legislation that there has been some improvement. The trouble arose because the community was not organised under government sufficiently concerned with the common good. There was no true universal or legal justice. When constitutional, legal, political and economic factors came together to compel government to be more aware of its obligations in this regard then a greater social justice could, in theory, be achieved.[33]

III. Modern Objections to the Idea of Objective Moral Law And the Liberal Roots of These Objections

A. THE LIBERAL PHILOSOPHY

The Judaeo–Christian belief is in a morality or an ethic which, in its fundamentals is unchanging because it takes its origin not from the will of man or the temporary fashions of human culture but from God who is eternal, all holy and all truth. The essentials of this morality as a personal response to God's call for holiness were expressed in the Ten Commandments fulfilled by Christ in the new law in the context of the Counsels, the Beatitudes and the grace of faith in him.

The same essentials of Christian morality are binding on Christians today as they have been throughout the history of the Church. New aspects and emphases meet the needs of different circumstances, but the principles, founded as they are in God's unchanging law, remain the same. Many modern thinkers reject this approach to man and his relationship with the world and we must try to trace in outline the reasons for this and indicate some of the more significant men and ideas identified with the rejection. We will then be able to weigh the wisdom of the Church's faith and reason, whose assumptions are at one with the original insights of the Old Testament, confirmed by Christ and elaborated by the Christian tradition, against the collective view of the modern world. That is not to suggest that there is a collective view of the modern world in the sense of a coherent and unified alternative to the traditional Christian view. There is not. There is a conflicting mass of opinions united only in rejecting the

---

[33] The whole question of social justice is well discussed in J. Hoffner, *Fundamentals of Christian Sociology*, pp. 49 ff. His conclusion is that "social justice is legal justice properly understood."

idea of an absolute, objective and eternal law emanating from the mind of God. In trying to give a few pointers to the movements of thought that embody important modern developments away from the tradition, we must then recognize that they are united by this fact alone, and that in themselves they do not comprise an alternative, but a conflicting mass of systems.

The Church inherited from the Scriptures the notion of man created by God and for God and taking his significance as a person, as an individual, from that relationship. Man was seen as important, therefore, as a person and as an individual, precisely because he was created by God and subject to his law, and is the recipient of a love which he can reciprocate. This idea was impressed on Christian Europe at its foundation and became part of its cultural inheritance.

From about the time of the Renaissance in the fourteenth century, however, there emerged another idea, that of the autonomous individual, the individual, that is, sufficient unto himself. Some of those who favoured it conceded the possibility of a God or gods, even a creating God, but rejected any norm of morality other than the prompting of a man's own conscience. Initially, belief in natural law remained—an absolute, objective and unchanging norm governing that conscience. But, with the undermining of the philosophy and theology which had elaborated the idea of natural law, the concept itself was undermined and values became entirely subjective.

Ironically, such an idea of the autonomous individual could not have grown up on the soil of pagan classicism to which the Renaissance appealed for, as Niebuhr argues, pagan classicism had no passion for the individual person such as the Renaissance shows. The Renaissance in fact used an idea it had inherited from Christianity and merged it with a concept of reason it had taken from pagan rationalism. The result was a concept of individual autonomy unknown either to classicism or to Christianity. Pagan classicism identified man's rational powers, reason, mind (sharply distinguished from the body) with the divine; reason was the creative principle. Individuality was not a significant concept, resting as it did only on the particularity of the body.[34] It was man's participation in the creative principle identical with God which was important—not the fact that he was individual, personal. The Christian understanding of all men as made in God's image, on the other hand, gave all a value precisely as persons, as individuals, who were both soul and body. Man is not merely an intellect but a person, destined to rise again, body and soul, on the last day, and share an eternity of happiness in heaven.[35]

[34] R. Niebuhr, *The Nature and Destiny of Man* (London, 1941), 1:7.
[35] "Both Plato and Aristotle had found in reason the real man . . . but both had failed to reach an adequate concept of personality. . . . Augustine was the first to give the concept its

As it was Christianity which personalized creative reason, so it was Christianity which overcame the pessimism of the classical view of the world and provided modern man with a basis for his optimism about progress and his potentialities. We have already seen that the Israelite conviction of the goodness of God who had created the world he cared for, injected into human culture the idea of an ordered purpose in and a meaningfulness of life. By contrast, in the *Iliad* Zeus asserts that there is nothing more piteous than man, while Aristotle confessed that not to be born is the best thing and death is better than life. The Stoics for their part could conceive of happiness only for the wise. Seneca, the universalist, prayed, "Forgive the world, they are all fools."[36]

The knowledge of original sin leaves Christians with no illusions about man. But the Resurrection gives him hope and confidence in his future, happiness in this life if he obeys God, and eternal happiness in heaven where his true home and true fulfillment lie. The testimony of countless saints and martyrs tells us that adversity in this life, even adversity of the most extreme kind, is bearable with joy for those who believe in Christ. The pagan has no hope or joy except on earth where ambitions and hopes are easily disappointed. Christianity, while it demands the full development of man and his powers and offers to him the enjoyment of God's creation, also gives hope and encouragement in adversity—not only to bear suffering with courage, but to strive, with trust in providence, to overcome obstacles to happiness here on earth. It has been said of Stoicism that it succeeded because it was a philosophy of suffering but failed eventually because it was a philosophy of despair.[37] Christianity could match its understanding of suffering, but taught a trust in God's providence in this life and a vision of transcendent and triumphant hope beyond it.

The idea of the absolute autonomy of the individual which emerged from the Renaissance period, was and is the fundamental tenet of the liberal faith. As it has passed into common use, the word "liberalism" can refer either to a philosophy strictly so called (a view of man's relationship with the world and with other men), to a political philosophy (an account of the origin and nature of political authority, state and the government), or finally to an economic theory (an account of the creation and distribution of wealth). Here we are concerned with it strictly as a philosophy, of which the essential tenet is the absolute value of the individual, indepen-

---

full extension . . . as a believer in the word made flesh he could not but question the Platonic view of the bodily organism as irrelevant to man's true selfhood." W. de Burgh, *The Legacy of the Ancient World*, p. 374.

[36] Quoted in Niebuhr, op. cit., 1:10.

[37] C. Bigg, *The Christian Platonists of Alexandria* (O.U.P., 1923), p. 288. Quoted in de Burgh, op. cit., p. 342.

dent of any obligation to a transcendent power. Belief in God, who as the almighty and loving Creator of all things, expected of man a response in love and freedom to his commands, was a distinguishing mark of the medieval Catholic culture. That culture accepted that Christ had founded a Church which was able to speak and to teach in his name and to interpret to the individual what it was that God wanted of him. It was indeed the theology which grew out of such a concept of revelation and the Church, which gave liberalism its original confidence in its ability to know the truth, objective and absolute.

Liberalism we have said can be regarded as a philosophy, but no one key figure presents us with a clear and comprehensive statement of its beliefs. It is in truth better regarded as an intellectual mood or attitude which has possessed Europe over the past four centuries and has permeated every aspect of social, cultural and intellectual life. Salvadori,[38] a professed modern liberal, sees in Protestantism, philosophy (from Descartes), science (Galileo, Newton), politics and law (Locke and Grotius), typical representatives of liberal thought; Laski gives the economic influences on the formation of the liberal mind more weight.[39] But if its exact intellectual pedigree is hard to trace, the key conviction that distinguishes liberalism is not; it is, as said, the belief that man is absolutely autonomous and independent of any transcendent power with authority or the means to command him; man does not need authoritative guidance, but is fully able of himself to fulfill his potential.[40]

In facing the problem of finding a new set of relationships to replace the reciprocal rights and duties of the feudal system—in which state and society were effectively one—it was inevitable that personal freedom should be stressed. And there were numerous factors in the fifteenth and succeeding centuries which underlined the importance of the individual and his powers: the imagination, courage and creativity of individuals led to the geographical discoveries and scientific and technological advance; absolute monarchy, and the claim to govern by divine right which some theorists used to justify it, stressed the power and privilege of the individual in its most extreme form; the absolute monarchs ruling strong

[38] M. Salvadori, *The Liberal Heresy* (London, 1977), p. 70 ff.

[39] H. Laski, *The Rise of European Liberalism* (London, 1936), passim.

[40] According to G. Ruggiero, *The History of European Liberalism* (O.U.P., 1927), pp. 399–400, there is a permanent reason for the opposition between the liberal and the Catholic view of life; it is in "the authoritarian nature of the Church, as claiming to be invested with power from above; in its doctrine of sin, redemption and grace, implying the fallen character of human liberty and reason, and the need of external aid; and in the function it claims, of a supernatural mediator between man and God: whereas liberalism assumes that, without any intermediary and by his own unaided efforts, man is fully able to realize all the values of the spiritual life."

national states were in their turn supported by the rich and the powerful in those states, individuals who had increasing power and influence on affairs. The English experience perhaps best typifies the manner in which events combined to the advantage of the liberal mind and ambition—it was in England in 1688 that liberalism first triumphed politically.

However, if the break-up of the medieval social and political structures encouraged a new form of social relationship which allowed the individual in theory total freedom, a total liberalism, it was a liberalism which realised in practice that authority was necessary for the maintenance of an organised social order. Freedom, the insistence on the equality of individuals before the law and the refusal to accept tyrannical authority of any kind, was not to be allowed to decline into license. The only authority to which the liberal could submit, however, was the impersonal authority of the law. "Integral" liberalism, as one authority calls it,[41] assumed that each individual had access to eternal and absolute truths and values through the medium of his own conscience. Since all men of good will and right reason would come to the same conclusion in referring to their consciences, they could safely submit to the authority of a law which enforced such self-evident truths, truths embodied in a law derived from human nature. The irony is that such assumptions could only have been made by men who accepted the Christian world view as it was elaborated by the scholastic thinkers of the Middle Ages—even as that world view was being rejected, along with the authority and guidance of the Church which had nurtured it. The Catholic tradition taught the objectivity of moral truth as it taught that there were limits to the power of the state as well as the freedom of the individual—limits that were determinable by the revealed and the natural laws authoritatively interpreted. Liberalism was however by definition subjective; its assumption of the existence of an objective natural law discoverable by reason and compelling acceptance, did not square with its other assumptions. The autonomous individual free from an external guidance could reject the notion of natural law, or any of its postulates, if he so wished. There was in liberalism therefore from the beginning a contradiction which would in time destroy it.

Taking Grotius[42] for example as one of the key figures in the development of liberalism, Hallowell points out that he, Grotius, believed[43] there

---

[41] John Hallowell, *The Decline of Liberalism as an Ideology* (London, 1944), p. 7.

[42] See below chap. 4, p. 259. Hugo Grotius, a Dutch diplomat, statesman and jurist, published his *De Jure Belli et Pacis* in 1685. Appalled at the disorder and injustice in international relations as the result of the religious conflicts and nationalism, he sought a new basis for justice in a reformulation of the natural law. G. H. Sabine, *A History of Political Theory*, p. 421.

[43] Hallowell, op. cit., p. 9.

were certain objective values, eternal truths which were independent of human will and interest. These were derived rationally from the natural order of things. These objective values, embodied in natural law, constituted for Grotius and his contemporaries a limitation upon individual liberty. Here we have set out the inconsistency of original "integral" liberal thought. Society was assumed to be ruled by the individual wills and self-interest of the self-sufficient individuals who formed it but their access to eternal and absolute truths would prevent them from abusing their liberty. Liberalism, therefore, assumed at one and the same time that man was absolutely self-sufficient but that he was also subject to some eternal law and truth which would check his selfishness. The inconsistency arose because men of the sixteenth and seventeenth century[44]

> . . . were not far enough removed from the medieval Christian tradition to believe that law was unrelated to absolute and eternal values. Their conscience, moulded by Christian teaching, told them that law could not rest on expediency alone. They were unable, because of their Christian heritage and beliefs, to conceive of order as simply the product of the harmonizing of individual interests and wills. The medieval concept of a divine order unified by the will of God lingered in their consciousness. . . . The seventeenth century mentality therefore merged the two concepts, despite their logical inconsistency and respective self-sufficiency, into one theory which serves as the foundation of integral liberalism.

The implications of this inconsistency remained unrevealed as long as there was a cultural consensus concerning belief in objective truth and values. But once belief in such truth and values themselves was undermined, once it was accepted that only that which was physically tangible, empirically verifiable, or subject to the rigours of mathematical proof was true, and that all else was subjective and relative, the check upon the arbitrariness of human rulers would disappear. Anarchy or tyranny could be the only result.

Ruggiero's account of liberalism, written from a more sympathetic point of view than Hallowell's, nevertheless agrees that there was in liberalism a tendency to anarchy, a simple assertion of the right to do as one wants. For him however, freedom, true freedom, consists in spontaneously affirming one's consciousness of having a duty toward oneself and others. The other form of freedom, which he calls "negative" freedom, results in denying all liberty and law. Positive freedom however relates all authority and law to the intimacy of one's own mind. He goes on,[45]

[44] Ibid., pp. 9–10.
[45] Ruggiero, op. cit., p. 352.

To be a law unto one's self, or in other words autonomous; to obey an authority recognized by conscience, because arising from its own law, is to be truly free. The eternal glory of Kant is to have demonstrated that obedience to the moral law is freedom.

But Kant's triumphal assertion of the uprightness of the individual conscience and its ability to know moral truth was not the only fruit of liberalism—the philosophy of positivism by contrast rejected any idea of objective moral truth. Hallowell wrote his book under the shadow of the Nazi military threat in the Second World War and considered the significance of the rise of Hitler in a country with such a strong liberal tradition as Germany. Since then we have learned how fully another tyranny, that of Stalin, had dominated another people and how inevitable it was that such a tyranny could result from Marxist-Leninism—itself a creed that took its origin in nineteenth century liberalism. And it is not hard to see in the consumer-oriented permissive society, evidence of that anarchy which is the liberal alternative to tyranny.

It is not therefore surprising that the Church for her part has always seen in liberalism the source of most of the errors of the modern world, and most significantly the errors which have produced social injustice. In his encyclical *Divini Redemptoris* Pius XI noted that in building on the principles of liberalism and secularism, and in shaping their economic and social policies on them, modern states had seemed initially to have had success, but that Communism was their inevitable result.[46] *Mit Brennender Sorge*,[47] in pointing to the futility of dislodging moral teaching and conduct from the rock of faith, attributes the errors of Fascist racialism to the illusion that subjective human judgement is a sufficient guide to the needs of life—the illusion which was at the heart of liberalism.

B. SOME MODERN ETHICAL THEORIES

1. Moral Sense Theories, Kantianism and Positivism

Modern ethical thinking then has taken place in an intellectual atmosphere conditioned by liberalism.[48] Anthony Cooper, Earl of Shaftesbury (1671–1713) proposed a "moral sense" theory according to which the harmony and design of creation will reflect itself in man in a balance between the natural, the kindly and the generous affectations, and the selfish—with the

---

[46] *Divini Redemptoris* (London: C.T.S.), par. 53.

[47] *The Church and the Reconstruction of the Modern World: The Social Encyclicals of Pius XI* (New York: Image Books, 1957), p. 350.

[48] See J. McGlynn and J. Toner, *Modern Ethical Theories* (Milwaukee, 1961), H. Sidgwick, *Outline of the History of Ethics* (London, 1967), M. Warnock, *Ethics Since 1900* (O.U.P., 1975), and J. Maritain, *Moral Philosophy* (London, 1964).

latter being subordinated to the former. Joseph Butler (1692–1752) and
Francis Hutcheson (1694–1746) continued the moral sense line of thinking with greater precision and clarity. For David Hume (1711–1776)
morality was something sensed, it could not be understood or rationalised
but was entirely subjective and personal.[49]

Moral sense theories have the merit of rejecting selfish hedonism, and
being reconcilable with, in some cases demanding, objective morals. But
they are seriously lacking in that they do not give a rational account of
obligation. They cannot say why we must go along with the good and the
true and turn away from the evil, they rely on feeling, asking us to base
our choice on impulse.

Immanuel Kant (1724–1804) was moved by the theories of Hume and
Leibniz to elaborate his own philosophical system. One of philosophy's
greatest metaphysicians, there is also that about his moral philosophy
which gave him a special power and influence—and it is with that moral
philosophy we are here primarily concerned.[50]

In his *Critique of Pure Reason* he argues, countering the English empiri-
cists, that while all we know is the world of experience (phenomena), we
can still make universal and necessary judgements because we possess a
certain *a priori* knowledge which is independent of experience. In his
Critique of Practical Reason he transfers these ideas to morality. Any moral
norm must be known *a priori*, cannot be derived from experience which
gives only the contingent and the particular. And such *a priori* knowledge
tells us we have an obligation to obey the moral law, independently of our
wishes and desires. Moral law is a categorical imperative or command
which tells us that only one thing is absolutely good—a good will acting
from a sense of duty. The moral imperative orders a man to act as though
he was a member of a society where each person is seen as an *end* (not a
means), where each finds his fulfillment while not hindering that of
others.[51]

Paradoxically, despite his rejection of Christian theology, his high
ethical ideals were a secularisation of Christian moral values. His claim
was that he was founding an autonomous morality, but that morality was
in fact dependent on religious ideas and religious inspirations which were
the atmosphere of Kant's early life.[52] Yet he transforms the Christian

---

[49] H. Sidgwick (op. cit., p. 211) notes that it is difficult to make the views of Hume
consistent, but concludes that he "emphatically maintains that reason is no motive to action
except in so far as it directs the impulses received from appetite or inclination." See
F. Copleston, *A History of Philosophy*, vol. 5, chap. 16.

[50] J. Maritain, *Moral Philosophy*, pp. 95 ff. Copleston, op. cit., vol. 6, chap. 6.

[51] *Critique of Practical Reason*, I. 6, pp. 314 quoted in J. McGlynn and J. Toner, *Modern
Ethical Theories*, p. 35.

[52] Kant's religious background "is the source of what characterizes Kantian ethics from
the outset, its absolutism, the privilege it assigns to morality as the revealer of the absolute to

ethic: for him respect for law and reverence for the law takes the place of that love of God above all things which is the basis of the Judaeo-Christian system. As we have seen, Christian ethics are fundamentally personal in that they assume man's personal response to a God who has created him and loves him. Kant has taken this idea of an absolute based on love and transferred it to an absolute based on an impersonal law. For those who accepted Kant's fundamentally religious assumptions, there was much in his approach which is of lasting value and which has restated the rationality of objective and eternal, unchanging moral values. Yet the cost at which he did so was, many would say, too great.

In contrast to the Kantian belief in *a priori* knowledge, Auguste Comte (1798–1857) argued[53] that the mature scientific outlook or mentality was only concerned with observable facts—and even these are relative in the sense that we do not know all we should. Positivism, as Comte's philosophy came to be known, was developed by others; it asserted three central principles:[54] 1) that all human thought is conditioned by history so that no norm or judgement is universally valid; 2) that the domain of facts alone allows of objective certitude: values are purely subjective; and 3) that there are no objectively founded moral values—only a choice between adjustment to the environment or suicide.

With positivism, the liberalism that started out so confidently is undermined. The belief that the absolutely autonomous individual can forge ahead assuming that his upright conscience will lead him to the knowledge of objective truth that he can and will unerringly follow, is challenged, and liberalism cannot defend itself. The autonomous individual, having no check on his actions and those of others because of the subjectivity and relativism of all values, has to choose between whatever adjustment he can make to actuality and the temptation to reject life as a hopeless muddle. The result, as argued above, is the surrender to tyranny or permissiveness which is typical of the modern world.

2. Hegel, Marxism and Ethics

There is a Christian caste about the framework of the metaphysics of George Frederick Hegel (1770–1831)[55] as there is about Kant's moral

---

man, the saintliness with which it is clothed. . . . So many traits whose origin lies in the influence of revealed ethics and which have been transposed therefrom." Maritain, op. cit., pp. 96–97.

[53] Copleston, op. cit., vol. 9, chap. 5.

[54] Maritain, op. cit., pp. 264–66.

[55] "What he wanted was to make of the Catholic doctrine of the image of God in the world a statement of identity—for Hegel the world process of nature *was* the objective expression of infinite Spirit; Father, Son and Spirit of Christian theology are but so many pictorial representations." *Dictionary of Catholic Theology*, vol. 3, s.v. "Hegelianism".

theory. Hegel abandoned the traditional trinitarian theology and belief in
Jesus Christ as God made man, and formulated a theory in which the
process of nature was the objective expression of infinite spirit, eternal
ideas going out into the world manifested in nature and returning in spirit.
This infinite spirit manifests itself successively in ever more perfect forms
of political and social organisation and in the great historical figures who
are instrumental in shaping them. The essential mark of the infinite spirit
is freedom and it is most fully embodied in the German state under the
influence of Protestant Christianity.[56] This vision of the historical process
through which the infinite spirit was revealing itself can be formulated in
an historical dialectic,[57] and it is through the dialectic especially that
Hegelianism had its influence on Marx and Marxism. Marx (1818–1883)
adapted this idea to his own strictly materialistic purposes—in contrast to
the thorough-going idealism of its originator. The data of the dialectic
were not the manifestation of world spirit but the forces of production and
the consequent productive relationships that they bred.[58] But if the use of
the dialectic was changed or perverted by Marx, his moral theory is
closely modelled upon Hegel's. Given Hegel's view of the world evolving
politically and socially as the manifestation of the infinite spirit, the
successive laws, institutions and customary morality of the community
were absolute and objective moral norms in their time. Nothing, not even
the promptings of conscience, could be allowed to stand against the
community will since it is through that will that the truth is evolving.[59]
The laws and institutions, the customary morality of the community in
which man finds himself, however, are in a state of evolution, and they
therefore cannot contain any lasting value in the sense of natural law or
revealed morality. Morality itself can know no finality until the process of
evolution is complete.

Theoretically Marx/Engels/Leninism reflects this relativism. It is implicit in the *Manifesto* where it is argued that it requires no deep insight to
understand that changes in man's material conditions of life also change
his ideas.[60]

Undoubtedly it will be said . . . eternal truths such as freedom and justice
are common to all systems . . . but Communism abolishes these eternal

[56] *Lectures on the Philosophy of History* (London, 1888), Introduction and pt. 4.
[57] Ibid., pp. 66 ff.
[58] Marx's political and economic theories are briefly considered in chapters 3 and 4. As to
which is the "real" Marx see below p. 274, footnote.
[59] G. Hegel, *Phenomenology of Mind* (London, 1931), pp. 450–51. If the conscience tries
"testing the laws, moving the immovable, it is resisting Mind." The law is ". . . the pure and
absolute will of all . . . this will is not a command of what *ought to be* it *is* and *has* validity."
See Maritain, op. cit., p. 161.
[60] *Manifesto* in D. McClellan, *Karl Marx: Selected Writings* (O.U.P., 1977), p. 236.

values. . . . What does this all amount to? The history of all past society is the history of class antagonisms which took different forms in different epochs but whatever form they have taken the exploitation of one section by another is a fact common to all previous centuries. . . . The Communistic Revolution is the most radical rupture with traditional property relations: no wonder that in course of its development it breaks most radically with traditional ideas.

Ideas of religious liberty, liberty of conscience, therefore, merely express the rule of free competition within the domain of knowledge. The *Manifesto* does not deny that Communism abolishes eternal truths as commonly understood. But it says that, as commonly understood, such truths are the product of man's history and class antagonism, a history of exploitation, and that such so-called "eternal" truths are only a way of justifying and maintaining such injustices.

There are two classic texts in the literature of Communism which bring out this relativism more fully. The first is in Engels' *Antidühring*[61] in which it is stated that all moral theories are the result of the economic stage which society had reached at a particular epoch. Only a society rid of class antagonism produces a really human morality. The second is an address by Lenin to the Young Communist League[62] in which he specifically notes that Communism repudiates ethics and morality in so far as the bourgeoisie say that they are derived from God's commands, from some idealism or semi-idealism which amounts to the same thing. Communist morality is entirely subordinated to the interests of the class struggle. Morality is what serves to destroy the old exploiting society and create the new Communist one. There is no eternal morality.

The difficulty is that in using words like "exploitation" there is a clear appeal to some absolute idea of right and wrong which enables us to determine whether that exploitation has in fact taken place. This sense of moral outrage, of course, is evident in the *Manifesto*. Phrases like "pitilessly torn asunder", "naked self interest and callous cash payments", "unashamed", "brutal" are the expressions of moral outrage. Marxism, in other words, does appeal to natural justice and the conviction that others will respond to it.[63] Today particularly, where they are dealing with societies in which there is blatant exploitation or injustice, Marxists

[61] C. P. Dutt edition, pp. 109–10, quoted by R. W. Carew Hunt, *The Theory and Practice of Communism* (London, 1962), p. 113. "Such eternal truths as there are are trivialities . . . no one would dignify them with the solemn title of 'eternal truths' unless he wished to draw from their existence the conclusion . . . that there is an eternal moral law . . . but it is precisely this which is erroneous." Copleston, op. cit., vol. 7, p. 320.

[62] *Selected Works* [2 vols.] (London, 1947), 2:667, quoted in Hunt, op. cit.

[63] "Dialectical materialism does not hesitate to appeal to standards of ethical order . . . in order to stigmatize capitalist society." (Maritain, op. cit., p. 244.)

appeal to the universal moral instinct which enables the evils to be seen and condemned. They are thus able to act as defenders of absolute moral values. The ambivalence of Marxism's attitude, however, becomes plain in states where the Communists have total control over the people. There the party's will is absolute, there it is up to it and it alone to say what is in the interests of the class struggle and the proletariat and there can be no appeal against the party's decision on specifics.[64] This is the reason behind the cruelties of Stalinist Russia and the sufferings the Russian people endured, which have been recounted so graphically for us by Solzhenitsyn.[65]

The cruelty of Marxism in practice to those who do not wish to grant the party the absolute rights it claims over them, is then one aspect of Marxist morality, one which springs directly from the materialism on which the creed is based. Yet the ambivalence remains even in the Communist state in practice, even in Russia. The search for a "new man", the need to transform selfish individuals into the unselfish servants of others was from the early days one of Marx's aims and when Lenin faced the problems of building up a new society in the tremendously difficult circumstances of the early 1920s, the idea of such self-sacrifice for the new socialist state had a powerful appeal. The same conviction, the same insistence on the ability of the individual in response to the needs of what can only be called conscience to raise himself above the general apathy and lead others by his self-sacrificing example, has been present in the Soviet experiment since. So, for example, the programme of the Communist party of the Soviet Union in 1961[66] stressed the importance of patriotism, conscientious work for the community, helpful and humane attitudes, respect for others, honesty and love of truth, moral integrity, respect for the family, rejection of injustice, of parasitism, of greed, of race hatred— all in all an appeal to work in friendship and justice for peace at home and abroad.

Such standards are put before the Soviet people as binding and objective. Taken altogether they represent at least the best that the highest ideals

[64] "There can be no doubt that Marx's . . . proclamation of an ultimate good supported by history and his failure to recognize positive distinctions in ways of living have done much to facilitate the Philistinism and servility that characterize contemporary Marxism . . . enabled the Communist Party to seize centralized power and exercise unprincipled tyranny in the name of the new metaphysical sovereign—history itself." E. Kamenka, *Ethical Foundations of Marxism* (London, 1971), p. 198.

[65] A. Solzhenitsyn, *The Gulag Archipelago* (London, 1975). Also D. Caute, *The Fellow Travellers* (London, 1973). S. Bloch and B. Reddaway, *Russia's Political Hospitals* (London, 1977). A. Sakharov, *My Country and the World* (London, 1975). See below chap. 5, pp. 275 ff.

[66] Quoted in Klaus Bockmuehl, *The Challenge of Marxism* (Leicester, 1980), pp. 133 ff.

of Stoicism and natural law can attain and it is not hard to detect the influence of Judaeo-Christian personal and social moral norms. Yet behind them lies the flaw at the heart of Communist morality. It deceives because ultimately it is what the party says is the good of society, what is justice, truth and honesty, what is friendship to others and what are the demands of peace. And that the party can err very seriously in these matters, can be judged by those who have a standard by which to judge the party.

A sound moral theory and practice therefore require more than objective norms and absolute obligations. Those norms and obligations must stem from a law and a loyalty which transcend human history and purely human authority; they must be founded in God's eternal law and be a response to him in love, they must be *eternal* and *universal*. Finally they must have some means of interpretation, his Church guided by the Holy Spirit, and must offer the means to the achievement of the Christ ideal in grace and the Sacraments. Lacking this fuller, transcendent and at the same time more human and hopeful, moral vision and the means of attaining it, the high ideals of the Marxist new man will remain forever unattained and unattainable.

3. Utilitarianism, Darwinism and Ethics

Another approach to ethics that developed in the nineteenth century was that of the utilitarian school[67] of which the guiding principle is that the seeking of pleasure and the avoidance of pain determine our moral decisions. An act therefore is good or evil, according to its consequences: an act whose consequences are pleasurable is good, one whose consequences are painful is bad. J. S. Mill[68] explained and elaborated Bentham's theories more fully. The first principle of utilitarian ethics, the so-called "greatest happiness of the greatest number" principle is, he explains, not selfish—nor is it sensual or brutish. Unselfishness is necessary if the happiness of the greatest number is to be achieved.[69] Sympathy for others is to overcome selfish desire and this sympathy must be developed by social pressure and education. There is then an implicit determinism in Mills. If social pressures, education and external forces are

---

[67] Jeremy Bentham (1748–1832) first fully developed a utilitarian theory. His *Introduction to the Principles of Morals and Legislation* (1823) is philosophically his most important work. See M. Warnock, ed., *Utilitarianism* (London, 1962).

[68] (1806–73), son of James Mill (1733–1836) the friend and supporter of Bentham. J. S. Mill founded the Utilitarian Society in 1823. He was distinguished as an economist as well as a philosopher.

[69] Warnock, op. cit., p. 262.

to determine our actions, it is hard to see why there is need to argue for moral obligation. To say that we are morally obliged to do what in any case we are going to be conditioned to do would seem superfluous.

Utilitarianism as an ethical theory tends to that relativism and moral determinism which accords with the modern rejection of the Judaeo-Christian approach in which ethics is related to the law of God, obedience to which brings true and lasting happiness. To seek happiness for oneself and for others is very much part of the Christian view of life. But in the Christian scheme of things, that happiness lies above all in doing God's will which is known through the revealed and natural moral law properly interpreted; and it is a happiness which leads on to a much greater fulfillment in the joys of heaven. The utilitarian approach encourages the asking of the right questions; it requires a more profoundly metaphysical and theological approach to provide the right answers.

That utilitarianism should have had an effect on ethical attitudes is understandable given the influence and importance of Bentham and Mill and their expressed intention to affect this area of human thought. It is less clear why Darwinism, which is a natural scientific theory concerned with the evolution of organisms, should figure in any consideration, however brief, of influences on modern ethical thought. One answer is that any purely scientific enquiry which takes man as its object, introduces subjective, metaphysical, philosophical and moral elements into discussion because the consideration of man as an object of scientific enquiry cannot avoid raising issues concerning the purpose and nature of human life, of man as body and soul. But as we shall see there were other influences at work in Darwin's approach which ensured that theological and moral issues would be raised in the sharpest form.

Charles Darwin (1809–1882) published the *Origin of the Species* in 1859 and *The Descent of Man* in 1871. The idea of the evolution of existing life forms from other lower forms was not a new one;[70] but, by the nineteenth century, increasing knowledge of paleontology especially (the science which examines the life of past geological periods through fossil remains) argued conclusively that over very long periods of geologic time, living forms of greater complexity had emerged. Though not the first to draw on this new knowledge, Darwin was able, as a result of his intensive researches, to make a greater impact when his findings were published in 1859.

[70] Among the Greeks, Aristotle and others had speculated on the significance of fossil remains. Linnaeus, in the mid-eighteenth century, put forward a theory of evolution, and Lamarck (1744–1829) published his *Philosophie Zoologique* in 1809. P. S. Fothergill, *Historical Aspects of Organic Evolution* (London, 1952), chap. 1.

The argument was that new forms of life emerged by a process of natural selection. The fittest survived as they were able to adapt to new situations and meet the needs of new environments while the less fit were not. By this means, in time, new species came into being—a view which seemed to clash with the biblical account of creation and with the theological conclusions based upon it. The controversy over the *Origin of the Species* was fierce enough, but when, in *The Descent of Man*, it was argued that man himself had been the result of an evolutionary process, it reached a new peak. It could be argued that if the principle of the survival of the fittest applied to the human race as well as to the animal world, then any support for the weak would hold back the development of mankind.[71] Similarly it could be argued that since man himself had evolved from the lower animals, he was simply a more complicated such animal with none of the attributes that religion taught were his in virtue of his being created in the image and likeness of God: in particular he was not bound by the moral law as traditionally understood.

That Darwin's theories could be used in this way ensured that they would have their effect on ethical theory. However, there was evidence from the beginning that the use of Darwinism against aspects of Christian belief and practice was not accidental—the result of ignorant misunderstanding of the theory itself or of the Bible. A modern writer, N. C. Gillespie,[72] notes that he was struck, on his first reading of the *Origin of the Species*, at the way the author spent so much time attacking the idea of divine creation, and the awareness led to him further reflecting on how much theological content a scientific work contained. A possible explanation of the phenomenon is that, as a young man, Darwin was a conventional Christian, that by the time of writing the *Origin* he was simply a theist and that later he was an agnostic. That he seems to have fought so violently in his scientific work to eliminate any possibility of teleology or special creation may have something to do with his progression from belief to unbelief. But that the emphasis was there in his

---

[71] Friedrich Nietzsche (1844–1899) with his theories of "will to power", the superman and his attack on fundamentals of Christian morality as slave morality has been seen as an example of the effect of evolutionary assumptions on philosophy—in fact he had little respect for Darwinism. Copleston, op. cit., vol. 7, chaps. 21, 22.

[72] *Charles Darwin and the Problem of Creation* (Chicago, 1980). It is interesting that Marx presented Darwin with a copy of *Das Kapital* as a sincere admirer. As Marx understood it, evolutionary theory had provided a scientific answer to the idea of a personal creator transcending all. *Karl Marx–Friedrich Engels Briefsweckel* (1854–60), 2:548, quoted by Valentine Long in *The Homiletic and Pastoral Review*, April 1978. W. R. Thompson in his introduction to a new edition of the *Origin of the Species* (Everyman, 1956) notes (p. xxiii) its strongly anti-religious flavour.

works ensured that what would have been a subject of hot debate anyway became an intellectual obsession for a whole generation or more.

There is in fact no theological objection to the theory of evolution of man's *body* from a lower form of life. The question of how, or whether, the human body has developed from other organisms is a matter which has to be decided on the basis of scientific fact, not theological assertion. But just as the theologian cannot say anything, as theologian, about scientific theory (which is a matter for empirical testing and proof), neither can the physical scientist say anything about the origin and nature of the human soul or spiritual realities which are not susceptible to enquiry by methods adapted to physical, material reality. The theologian therefore is within his competence, and may not be challenged on natural scientific grounds, in stating that each individual soul is created directly by God. Whether God chose to infuse this soul into an existing living organism which then became man, or not, does not affect the essential nature of the soul or the essential nature of man—who is body and soul, both created by God.[73]

> The teaching of the Church leaves the doctrine of evolution an open question as long as it confines its speculations to the development, from other living matter, of the human body . . . in the present state of scientific and theological opinion this question may be legitimately canvassed . . . the reasons for and against either view . . . weighed and adjudged with all seriousness, fairness and restraint. . . .

There is then no need for Christians to think that anything that affects their relationship with God, with the world and each other has been changed by the evolution debate. Likewise there is no reason for those engaged in scientific research in the field of evolution to fear that any discoveries they may make will undermine or weaken Christian spiritual or moral truths or the conclusions to be drawn from them. But two things should be noted. There are some supporters of evolution who persist in thinking that if evolution is proved it will be irreconcilable with Christian belief.[74] The second is that not all scientists competent to judge are happy

---

[73] Pius XII, *Humani Generis* (1950). See A. Freemantle, *The Papal Encyclicals in their Historical Context* (New York, 1963), pp. 297–98. The theory of polygenism is however not reconcilable with Catholic teaching. The question is discussed in P. S. Fothergill's *Evolution and Christians* (London, 1962); Fothergill, a convinced Christian and an evolutionist, concludes that descent from one pair is what the biologist would expect (p. 321).

[74] For example, Sir Julian Huxley doubted whether de Chardin had reconciled the supernatural elements in Christianity with the implications of evolution. See P. S. Medawar, *The Art of the Soluble* (London, 1968), p. 81.

with the effects of Darwinian theory on the science of biology,[75] and not all are convinced that the theory is capable of proof or based on verifiable assumptions.

In summary, therefore, we may say that evolution of the human body is accepted, as a working hypothesis at least, by most of those qualified to judge in the varied and specialized fields of knowledge in which it is necessary to have competence to judge with authority in the matter. The theologian and the moralist are subject to the scientist regarding the scientific facts. Either the evolution of the body can be proved conclusively or it cannot; there is good scientific opinion which takes it as already effectively proved, there is good scientific opinion which is more cautious. There is some which is openly sceptical.[76] But none of this should affect the Christian's thinking about the nature of morality and man's obligations to obey God's law, which is eternal, objective and universal. It is not, however, hard to see how the theory of evolution, taken as proved beyond doubt, and taken to mean that man is limited by his material nature and possesses no spiritual, transcendent dimension, should lead some to conclude that, since he is simply a more complicated animal, then the categories of morality and behaviour that come from belief in man as possessed of an immortal soul and an immortal destiny, are no longer applicable. And that is why Darwinism, as understood in one way, has had important effects in helping to undermine the traditional Christian view of morality. But these effects are not the result of the scientific facts, they are the result of a particular interpretation of them which is not essential to the acceptance of the theory as proved or capable of proof.

[75] W. R. Thompson in the introduction to the 1956 edition of the *Origin of the Species* argues that Darwin's inability to prove his theory led to his falling back on speculative arguments; the result has been, he suggests, to give biologists an addiction to unverifiable speculation (pp. xi and xxi).

[76] P. S. Fothergill, *Historical Aspects of Organic Evolution*, pp. 347 ff., lists some of those who have had their doubts down the years. Among others are Professor Gray, Emeritus Professor of Zoology at Cambridge writing in *Nature*, February 1954; Professor Lucien Cuenot, holder of the Chair of Zoology at Nancy for many years, an evolutionist who was more and more convinced of the difficulties of the theory (Professor R. Collin in *Evolution* [London, 1959] p. 10). Collin himself Professor of Medicine and Director of the Institut d'Histologie at Nancy for many years, lists some of the "Scientific Difficulties of the General Theory of Evolution" in chapter 7 of the book quoted. Professor P. Medawar, biologist and Nobel prize winner, comments on the weakness of modern evolutionary theory in *The Art of the Soluble* (London, 1967), p. 78. Dr. G. A. Kerkut of the Department of Physiology and Biochemistry at Southampton University lists seven assumptions necessary for the acceptance of evolutionary theory, all of which he suggests are unverifiable (*Implications of Evolution* [London, 1960]). He notes that, in his experience, undergraduates are rarely aware that there are genuine difficulties in the theory from a purely scientific point of view.

4. Freud, Psychiatry and Ethics

Sigmund Freud (1856–1939) was the founder of the psychiatric school of psychology and the technique he developed to help patients overcome their psychological problems consisted in prompting them with questions, enabling them through free association to identify and overcome those problems. The view of the human psyche, as given by Freud,[77] is that there is an *id* (the sum of the personal characteristics each receives as the result of inherited traits and environment), while the *id* relates to the world around it by means of the *ego*; the *superego* is the system of right and wrong which is imposed on the child by the authority to which it is subject. It is in the *id* that there exist the two instinctive drives that govern life, *eros* and *thanatos*. The former is sexual and libidinous and the root of all that is constructive in man. The latter is the death instinct which shows itself in aggressive and destructive tendencies. The child feels sexual jealousy towards the parent of the opposite sex and the *oedipus* complex results.[78] As a result of these and other tensions that arise between the different elements in man's make-up, guilt feelings develop. He is caught up, a helpless victim in the conflict between sensual pleasure and the instinct to destroy.

Such an account of the workings of the human psyche suggests materialism and determinism.[79] Religion may try to give life a moral meaning and purpose but the human being simply seeks to enjoy pleasure and avoid pain.[80] The greatest pleasure man finds is in being loved and since sexual love is the most complete experience of this emotion, such love is the ideal of our search for happiness; all other forms of satisfaction and pleasure are a result of sex or of a rechannelling of the sexual drive in some way; so the appreciation of beauty for example, aestheticism, is derived from sexual feelings.[81] On such an analysis love is always basically self-centred and the idea of loving one's neighbour as oneself is an impossible ideal.[82]

It is not hard to find in Freud's writings equally dismissive attitudes to the other categories of morality as they have become familiar in the Western tradition. Right is merely a matter of convention and policy, the result of the union of the weaker to combat the stronger, and justice is simply the formalization of this right on behalf of the majority.[83] Civilisa-

---

[77] *An Outline of Psychoanalysis* (in *The Complete Psychological Works* [London, 1966], vol. 23), pp. 144 ff.

[78] Ibid., pp. 192 ff.

[79] A. Kaplan in B. Nelson, ed., *Freud and the 20th Century* (London, 1967), p. 214.

[80] *Civilisation and Its Discontents* (*Complete Works*, vol. 21), p. 76.

[81] Ibid., p. 83.   [82] Ibid., p. 109   [83] Ibid., p. 95.

tion develops to defend man against his own fierce instinctive drives and aggressions while conscience is simply a means of turning in on the ego, the self, the thwarted feelings of aggression towards others.[84]

Freud, like Darwin, was a scientist, not a theologian or a philosopher, but it was even more difficult for him than for Darwin to abstract from the philosophical, theological and moral assumptions about man. Man, and above all man's psyche, was the centre of his scientific interest. Hence though he stressed that he was not concerned to philosophize, he notes that in *The Future of an Illusion* published in 1927 and in *Civilisation and its Discontents* (1930) he investigated "the origins of religion and morality",[85] which was precisely a theological and philosophical quest. The results of his investigations were rather negative. God he saw as Father figure, created out of the growing individual's sense of insecurity,[86] an illusion therefore. He did not deny that God could also be real, nor that a morality or religion based on belief in him cannot be true or valuable. But his doubts hardly helped to reinforce such beliefs.

Overall the picture of the human psyche as presented by Freud is, according to his biographer,[87] that it is repressed, active, bestial, infantile, alogical and sexual. The entire instinctive life (and not simply that which is repressed, wicked or vicious) is in some sense bestial, animal. Maritain suggests[88] that it is not hard to see in this account of the human psyche and conscience, as it can be reconstructed from Freud, a punishment for the arrogance of a rationalism which assumed the moral rectitude and up-rightness of man and his conscience. Under this illusion man had denied all the evil that was in his nature so that he would be able to enjoy the self-satisfaction of his own individual autonomous conscience. Add to the Freudian vision of the human psyche as set above, his idea that God is an illusion, that materialism and determinism are the realities within which man's life is contained, his account of conscience, right and justice, and very little is left of the Christian vision of man as made in God's image, freely capable of responding to his love and living a life of moral integrity for his sake. But Freud's writings are often discursive, repetitive and obscure and these characteristics account for much that jars on the Christian mind. When those writings are seen against the background of his own life experience, and when the value of many of his techniques for the relief of mental suffering is appreciated, a truer picture of the positive

[84] Ibid., p. 123.
[85] *Autobiographical Study (Complete Works*, vol 20), pp. 59, 72.
[86] *The Future of an Illusion (Complete Works*, vol. 21), pp. 24 ff.
[87] Quoted by Maritain in Nelson, op. cit., p. 248.
[88] Ibid.

value of his work emerges. According to Kaplan,[89] Freud too often substituted speculation for verification of his dynamic insights with adequate
clinical observation. Still the effect of his treatment, and the ideal that
emerges from the process of self-knowledge it can set in train, was
intended to be, and could be, crucial in helping the patient to a better
self-understanding and consequently a healthier psychological state. All
in all, according to Kaplan, Freud saw human nature in itself as morally
neutral, rich in potential for good and evil alike. Ultimately then, the best
he can offer is the Stoic ideal of self-knowledge and self-sufficiency. Freud
admits that he has no consolation to give, only the power of healing to the
extent that he can transform neurotic despair into the general unhappiness
which is the usual lot of mankind.[90] Seen thus as helping in the revival of a
Stoic fortitude through self-knowledge, there is a positive side to Freud's
incursions into the field of moral theory. Such a morality suffers from the
same defects as any morality which is not founded in a belief in a personal
and loving God—it offers neither the hope nor the means of attaining
the high ideals it demands. But it is an improvement on the vulgar
Freudianism that suggests his theories lead inevitably and essentially to
the abandonment of moral standards of any kind.

Because of the importance that Freud and Freudianism have now
achieved in Western culture, there has been a great deal of work done in
recent years to try to better understand the context in which his theories
developed.[91] As a psychoanalyst, most of his work was done in one city,
Vienna, at one period and with one particular social and economic group.
And it was a very religious city—at least in the sense that the externals of
religion were very much in evidence and religious beliefs commonly
accepted. Inevitably then, most of the patients that Freud treated would be
religious and their religious beliefs and problems would be evident in their
illness in some form. To conclude, however, that religion was the cause of
mental ill health was going beyond the evidence; the psychologically
healthy in a "religious" city would be religious too. What seems to be true
is that it was a misunderstanding of religion and its implications in those
who professed it which could and did contribute to psychological problems. The vision of God that Freud rejected[92] was one which bore little or

---

[89] In Nelson, op. cit., p. 220. Abraham Kaplan held the post of Professor and Chairman
of the Department of Philosophy in the University of California (Los Angeles) at the time of
writing.

[90] Ibid., pp. 219, 225.

[91] R. Burke, "Does Psychology Have Room for God?" in *Catholic Mind* (September,
1979) quotes E. Wallwork and R. Johnson, *Critical Issues in Modern Religion* (Englewood
Cliffs, New Jersey, 1973), and D. Bakan, *Sigmund Freud and the Jewish Mystical Tradition*
(Princeton, 1958).

[92] Burke, op. cit., p. 29.

no reality to the God "Who is". But Freud's refusal to take a more positive view of religion, was rather an expression of his personal unbelief than the result of scientific analysis.[93] His own personal contacts with organised religion and its devotees were not the happiest. His Roman Catholic nanny seems to have been steeped in religious beliefs of a superstitious nature[94] which had little to do with the faith she professed. This would inevitably colour her young charge's understanding of religion in general and Roman Catholicism in particular. As a boy, and later in his profession, he personally suffered from anti-semitism in one form or another.

Freudianism, we can conclude, of itself tends to strengthen man's natural moral sense in so far as it helps him to face the truth about himself and encourages him to accept the implications of that truth. But the philosophical and theological construction that Freud put on his own work as an analyst can safely be disregarded. For the Christian in the Catholic tradition especially, the principles of morality are firmly founded, and rationally understood and expounded in revealed and natural law ethics. To these, Freudianism properly used can be a complement. For them it can never be a substitute.

Though Freud is the dominant figure in modern psychoanalysis, others were making their contribution to its development before him and during his lifetime. Alfred Adler studied under Freud initially but developed his own theories.[95] He argued that human beings were most influenced by ambition, hopes and strivings than built-in drives and past experiences, and it is to Adler we owe the concept of "inferiority complex". C. G. Jung (1875–1961) also worked with Freud at one period. He regarded the collective unconscious as the foundation of the personality structure and that around the archetypes in this unconscious are built up character and personality.[96] Both Jung and Adler allowed religion and spiritual values a much greater place in man's life. Jung believed that among his patients over 35, the main problem was that of finding a religious outlook on life;[97] Adler held that lack of love for others was the greatest single cause of neurosis. But neither Jung nor Adler committed themselves to the theological beliefs of Western religion.

Other writers and practitioners have brought psychiatry and Christian insights closer together. Mowrer saw the value to psychiatry of the

---

[93] P. Ricoeur, *Freud and Philosophy* (Yale, 1970), p. 524.

[94] Burke, op. cit.

[95] P. Bottome, *Alfred Adler: Apostle of Freedom* (London, 1957).

[96] Among his main works are *The Psychology of the Unconscious* (1916) and *Modern Man in Search of a Soul* (1932).

[97] *Modern Man in Search of a Soul* (London, 1932), p. 264. See R. Hostie, S.J., *Religion and the Psychology of Jung* (London, 1957).

concept of sin,[98] indeed it seemed to him that one of the mistakes of the psychologist was to have accepted too readily a form of Freudianism which sees emotional disturbance as a result, not of having done wrong, but of having been too good—of inhibiting instincts which should have been given expression. To Mowrer the rejection of the idea of sin, and the substitution of the idea of sickness to explain evil done, is to court the danger of totally disorienting man. The attempt to become amoral, ethically neutral and free runs the risk of severing the very roots of our being so that we lose our sense of identity and selfhood. He notes that some forms of Christianity have instilled the capacity to experience guilt without the means of relieving it, hence the strange affinity, as he calls it, between these forms of Christianity and Freudianism.

Many other experts in the field have found that the proper use of psychoanalysis, far from being hindered by traditional Christian moral values, is helped by their use—that these values and the insights of psychoanalytic technique can aid one another.[99] Insofar as psychoanalysis helps the individual to find out the truth about himself or herself, seeks to correct the flaws revealed by the knowledge and integrate the personality around a conscious, sincerely sought, ideal, so far it complements rather than challenges the Christian idea of conversion which is precisely the facing up to the sinfulness of self and turning to God. Without Christ and the grace that faith brings, conversion to the truth about oneself and readiness to accept the task of integration will remain at best a form of Stoicism. But that search for truth about oneself is, in itself, a step on the road to return to a Christian understanding of man as living bound by God's law, rather than a step away from it.

5. Situation Ethics

Inevitably the fundamental questionings that have gone on regarding aspects of morality over the last hundreds of years have not left Christian moralists untouched. Probably the most significant effect of the new thinking is summed up in "situation ethics" which attempts to counter

---

[98] O. H. Mowrer, *The Crisis in Psychiatry and Religion* (London, 1961), pp. 40 ff., 52 ff., 157 ff.

[99] R. May et al., *Existence: A New Dimension in Psychiatry and Religion* (London, 1965), pp. 54 ff. especially: J. A. Hadfield, *Psychology and Morals* (London, 1928). K. Menninger, *Whatever Became of Sin* (London, 1975). J. A. Jeeves, *Psychology and Religion* (Leicester, 1976). E. F. O'Doherty, *Religion and Psychology* (New York, 1978). J. C. Ford and G. Kelly, S.J., *Contemporary Moral Theology* (Cork, 1964), 1:314 ff. V. Frankl, *The Unconscious God* (London, 1978), is a therapist who believes that religion lies at the personal centre of the individual.

what is seen as the narrow legalism of traditional *a priori* morality with the more humane and, some would claim, more Christian approach to it through this ethic.[100]

It is certainly true that because of the breakdown in sound moral theology and a failure to understand its methods of reasoning, it has been all too easy for an oversimplified and harsh version of objective morality to be presented. But all that is valid in the situationist's point of view can be accommodated in the traditional teaching which, as we have seen, is careful to distinguish between objective moral norms (judgement about an act in the abstract in terms of its reference to God's law) and the moral imputability of the guilt of the act to the individual who does it. The guilt may not be imputed until the circumstances are fully known and it is clear that the individual concerned had full freedom and full knowledge in doing what he did. Only when there is full advertence and full freedom can the individual be blamed for the evil done. Further the possibility of an individual freely and knowingly doing that which is objectively evil but yet, through an honest but erroneous conscience incurring no moral guilt, is a commonplace of traditional moral theology. Yet the biblical view on which the Catholic tradition is based is that the good is what accords with God's eternal and objective law. I should strive to conform my will, my mind and my life, to the plan established by God. This conforming must be out of a sincere conviction, with love and by the help of God's grace, but it remains theocentric. The danger with situationism is that it encourages a man-centred morality.

Situation ethics would seem to be implicit in the atheistic existentialism of Sartre.[101] But, according to others, Fletcher for example, the school has specifically Christian origins in the publication of Brunner's *Divine Imperative* and Niebuhr's *Moral Men and Immoral Society* in the 1930s. Fletcher claims that Christian situationists are trying to rid Christian ethics of its legalism and to return to the love principles inculcated by Christ.[102] However as Basil Mitchell points out,[103] if love is to serve as a norm or measure, it must be able to rule out certain acts, tell us what, in a given situation, love indicates must be done and must not be done. Love cannot help us to decide between alternatives if contradictory acts in

[100] J. Fletcher, *Moral Responsibility* (London, 1967), p. 254. His *Situation Ethics: The New Morality* was published in 1966. For a view of situation ethics from the point of view of classical Catholic moral theology see Ford and Kelly, op. cit., vol. 1, chaps. 7, 8.

[101] McGlynn and Toner, op. cit., p. 100 ff.

[102] Fletcher, *Moral Responsibility*, p. 73.

[103] In *Norm and Context in Christian Ethics* (G. Outka and P. Ramsey, eds. [London, 1969]), p. 352.

particular circumstances can be ascribed to love. If love on the one hand tells me I must kill the incurably sick patient but love can also tell me that I must not kill him, clearly love is not a guide to action. It is a word which can justify any course of action I choose. Unless "love" is clearly understood and defined according to objective principles, it is useless—and the moment one starts defining it in terms of objective principles, one is back in the land of the moral theologian and the casuist.

The truth of the matter is that one is never out of the land of the casuist anyway. Behind the concept of love, as put forward by Fletcher and his school, there is an objective ideal—and that ideal is what is acceptable to the mid-twentieth century Anglo-American liberal intellectual. Among the presuppositions of situation ethics, according to Fletcher, is a pragmatism whose "idiom expresses the methods or lifestyle of American culture and of the technical scientific era."[104] That is the standard. Whatever is in accord with that ethos or lifestyle is love. Whatever is not, is not love. Some may be able to believe that Christian ethics are understood more fully and completely now that we have made them synonymous with the ideals of a professedly secular, materialistic and indeed atheistic culture. But it requires a very great act of faith to believe this; many would prefer the lesser act of faith involved in accepting the Church's idea of absolute moral values understood in the context of careful reasoning, sound moral theology and genuine care for the souls created by God and loved by him.

[104] Quoted by Mitchell, op. cit., p. 355, from Fletcher's *Situation Ethics*, p. 42.

CHAPTER THREE

THE ETHICS OF MARRIAGE AND THE FAMILY

Marriage is divinely instituted as a loving, personal, monogamous and indissoluble relationship, by nature ordained to the procreation and education of children (Gaudium et Spes, 48–50).

I. Introduction: Marriage, Its Personal and Social Dimension

The Christian understanding of marriage is that God instituted it to be the loving, lifelong partnership of one man and one woman in a total community of life so that of their love new life should come to be and be fostered to maturity. It is, therefore, a union between equals, based on the equal personal dignity of man and woman. It is also, of its nature, an institution in which the law of man in society has an interest because it is in the children born of a stable and loving marriage relationship that the hope of the future of that society lies.

Marriage is therefore: 1) God-ordained, 2) based on the equal love of the partners, 3) whose love is lifelong and whose marriage is therefore by nature indissoluble and 4) through that married love new life comes to be and can be fostered into full maturity, not only fulfilling the parents' lives and love but also forming the foundation of society: these essential marks are outlined in *Gaudium et Spes*.

48. The intimate partnership of life and the love which constitutes the married state has been established by the Creator and endowed by him with its own proper laws; it is rooted in the contract of its partners, that is in their irrevocable personal consent. It is an institution confirmed by the divine law and receiving its stability, even in the eyes of society, from the human act by which the partners mutually surrender themselves to each other; for the good of the partners, of the children, and of society this sacred bond no longer depends on human decision alone. For God himself is the author of marriage and has endowed it with various benefits and with various ends in view. . . .[1]

49. . . . Married love is uniquely expressed and perfected by the exercise of the acts proper to marriage. Hence the acts in marriage by which the intimate and chaste union of the spouses takes place are noble and honourable; the truly human performances of these acts fosters the self-giving they signify and enriches the spouses in joy and gratitude. Endorsed by mutual fidelity and, above all, consecrated by Christ's sacrament, this love abides faithfully in mind and body in prosperity and adversity and hence excludes both adultery and divorce. The unity of marriage, distinctly recognized by Our

115

Lord, is made clear in the equal personal dignity which must be accorded to man and wife in mutual and unreserved affection. . . .

50. Marriage and married love are by nature ordered to the procreation and education of children. . . . Without intending to underestimate the other ends of marriage, it must be said that true married love and the whole structure of family life which results from it is directed to disposing the spouses to cooperate valiantly with the love of the Creator and Saviour who, through them, will increase and enrich his family from day to day. . . . But marriage is not merely for the procreation of children: its nature as an indissoluble compact between two people and the good of the children demand that the mutual love of the partners be properly shown, that it should grow and mature. Even in cases where despite the intense desire of the spouses there are no children, marriage still retains its character of being a whole manner and communion of life and preserves its value and indissolubility.

[1] St. Augustine, *De bono conjugii*: PD 40, 375–376 and 394. St. Thomas, *Summa Theol.*, *Suppl.*, Quaest. 49, art. 3, ad 1: Decretum pro Armenis: Denz 702 (1327): Pius XI, Litt. Encycl. *Casti Connubii*: AAS 22 (1930), pp. 543–545: Denz. 2227–2238 (3703–3714).

From the point of view of social ethics it is on marriage as family, the basic unit of society, that we concentrate. But that aspect cannot be separated from marriage as personal—because it is from the personal commitment of the partners to one another that this social institution arises. We have seen that the whole stress of Christian morality is on the personal response to the personal love that God has shown for each one of us. This orientation of personalism remains throughout the Christian social ethic. Because God made us and loved us as persons, the whole orientation of life must be personalist. As John XXIII reminded us, individual human beings are the foundation, the cause and the end of every social institution.[1] Created by God as individuals, as persons and given by him that individuality and personality, all social institutions must foster, encourage and develop the human person. This then is the duty of the family—but if we are individual and personal, we are social beings too, coming to life in that basic social unit which is the family.

As God has planned it, it is the lasting love of one man for one woman which not only produces the physical act of procreation at a particular moment in time in that relationship, but also enables the child or children which may be born of the union, to be reared in the conditions which will best equip them, in their turn, to be useful members of society and fully developed human beings. When a man and woman, therefore, decide to join their lives in marriage they are giving testimony to the *personality* with which God has endowed them in undertaking the commitments of

[1] *Mater et Magistra* (London: C.T.S., 1963), par. 219.

the lifelong state which is Christian marriage. Marriage is, of its nature, based on a *personal* pledge made by the partners to each other. But this personal attestation has a social dimension because it is from their love and in their love that the most basic of human societies, the family, is founded. These two aspects of marriage, 1) marriage as a personal attestation of the love of two individuals for one another, and 2) marriage as the basic human society, are inextricably linked and can in no way be separated. This is true even if the marriage is in fact childless. The personal love of marriage has its values which remain even if, subject to God's law, no children are born of it. But the most fundamental orientation of marriage is that, through personal love and its fulfilment in the society of the family, it may begin and foster new life. The childless marriage is still a true marriage; its love a true love if the childlessness is no fault of the couple. But right reason, based on divine law, sees fruitful marriage as the norm.

II. The Christian Understanding
Of The Nature of Marriage
As a Loving, Personal Commitment
And the Implications of This Commitment

A. THE BIBLICAL TEACHING ON MARRIAGE

That these characteristics were implanted in marriage by God from the beginning is clear from the Genesis account;[2] rearranging the order of some of the verses to help our understanding, we get the following:

> God said, "Let us make man in our own image, in the likeness of ourselves". . . . God created man in the image of himself, in the image of God he created him, male and female he created them. . . .[3] Yahweh God said, "It is not good that the man should be alone. I will make him a helpmate." So Yahweh God made the man fall into a deep sleep. And while he slept, he took one of his ribs and enclosed it in flesh. Yahweh God built the rib he had taken from the man into a woman, and brought her to the man . . . the man exclaimed "This at last is bone from my bones, flesh from my flesh. This is to be called woman, for this was taken from man." This is why a man leaves his father and mother and joins himself to his wife, and they

---

[2] For fuller treatment of the biblical teaching on marriage than can here be given, see J. L. McKenzie, *The Two-Edged Sword* (London, 1959), chap. 4. P. Grelot, *Man and Wife in Scripture* (London, 1964) and E. Schillebeeckx, *Marriage: Secular Reality and Saving Mystery* [2 vols.] (London, 1965).

[3] Gen 1:26–27.

become one body. . . .[4] God blessed them, saying to them, "Be fruitful, multiply, fill the earth and conquer it. . . ."[5]

It is from their both being made in God's image and likeness that the personal equality of man and woman stems. This personal equality demands that their interdependence be expressed in an equal love—if woman was taken from Adam's rib it was because he needed someone like himself as a helpmate. Both being in God's image, the interdependence of marriage in which man has the role as head of the family cannot imply personal inferiority on the woman's part in a union based on the love of equals.

Marriage as monogamous and indissoluble springs from the very nature of the union of persons which God intended it to be. It is also the inevitable conclusion from the procreative purpose to which marriage is ordained. Without that loving permanence, the conditions for the responsible bearing and rearing of children do not exist. It takes anything from sixteen to twenty-one years to prepare a child for life and the responsibilities it brings. Assuming a reasonable spacing of births from first to last, from twenty to forty years of a woman's life then can be taken up by the responsibilities of home-making and child-rearing. The husband has a life and career outside the home. The more that the wife is entirely dedicated to home and family, the more she needs the assurance of her husband's lifelong love, not only when she is caring for the family, but afterwards when the family is capable of making its own way in the world. She, who has given the best years of her life to her family, in justice and charity requires to know that love and security will remain after her children are independent.[6]

This is a practical need; but there is in human nature at its best, a deep psychological and physiological need for an indissoluble union because it is only in such a union that the total community of life and love can be expressed, and the Genesis account points to this. God created man who had no helpmate suitable for himself so he created woman also. The imagery used is the taking of one of Adam's ribs and forming it into a woman and that imagery states nothing so much as the interdependence of man and woman. Man was so dependent upon Eve that until her creation he was incomplete. And that she was "his flesh" argues a unique and equal

[4] Gen 2:18–24.

[5] Gen 1:28.

[6] Some women are able to combine a full time career with motherhood and many others combine some kind of paid occupation outside the home with their family responsibilities. But few can combine the role of wife and mother with a fully independent career outside the home. Dedicated as they are to providing the essentials of a stable home life for the children of today and the citizens of tomorrow, they lose the chance of that independence. Society therefore owes them special protection. The question is discussed below, pp. 158 ff., 167 ff.

relationship. Without the special vocation to celibacy which God only gives to some, it is not good for man to be alone. And in a truly human living out of that interdependence which is marriage the two lives can only become more united as time passes. All of us know of marriages in which that happens, tragically it too often does not—but the Christian answer is to seek out the reasons why it does not and remove the causes that impede what was and is intended by God to be the norm, not the occasional ideal, of marriage.

Lifelong love and the giving of new life, therefore, are the permanent and essential values that God established in marriage from the beginning.[7] The question of the imagery used in the account of the Garden of Eden,[8] the tempting by the serpent and the subsequent fall do not undermine God's purpose and plan in which sexual love is so important. Yet it is impossible to read Genesis without being aware that behind the imagery is the assertion that some abuse of sexuality was the specific of the disobedience which led to man's loss of grace. McKenzie[9] suggests that this would have been particularly significant for the Hebrews. Fertility cults with their sexual excesses and sacred prostitution were the cultural context in which Judaism tried to maintain a deeper understanding of the nature of sexual purity, combined with a healthy appreciation of the gift of that sexuality used for love and procreation in marriage, as God has intended.

The account of the man/woman relationship, sexuality and procreation as it appears from the first two chapters of Genesis before the Fall, is on the other hand, without tensions or hint of evil of any kind. According to it, man and woman are personally equal and they come together in marriage so that they can complete one another's lives, and fulfill their love and God's purposes through bringing new life to be. But the realities of sex and marriage in surrounding cultures made the people of God aware that the symmetry, the beauty and the balance of all this had been shattered. They saw that, far from the dignity and equality of man and woman being preserved in the marriage relationship, exploitation of woman's sexuality, independent of personality and independent of marriage, was ever present.[10] They saw in the fertility cults a glorification of sexual promiscuity which was completely alien to the understanding of human sexuality

---

[7] Regarding the Genesis account, Pierre Grelot says in *Man and Wife in Scripture*, (pp. 36–37): "We can see clearly what is the direct source of the sacral nature of marriage, of love and fecundity. We no longer have the mythical archetypes imagined by contemporary pagan religions but the creative word of Jahweh, the expression of his enduring love . . . the same divine word has imposed on human sexuality a natural curb or rule . . . marriage has a human prototype created in the beginning by God."

[8] Gen 3:1–13.

[9] McKenzie, op. cit., pp. 96. ff.   [10] Ibid., pp. 94–95.

that they had received from the Covenant and revelation. It is in fact true to say that there is no biblical teaching on sex in isolation. Rather there is a teaching on marriage[11] and it is in the context of marriage that the proper use of sexuality is to be understood. That sex has a value in itself outside of marriage is alien to the Judaeo-Christian revelation. Sex was created by God for the purposes of marriage and it must always be subject to man's control for these God-given purposes; it must be humanity's servant and not its master.

By contrast, in the cultures of Mesopotamia and the ancient Semitic mythologies, sex was as primaeval as life itself and indeed the gods themselves mirrored human sexuality, its uses and abuses. The female principle was deified in the goddess of fertility who was considered to be the ideal woman—and as such she was primarily a sex object. The Hebrews could not accept this view for there was no sex in the God they worshipped. God, who is himself above sexuality as he is above all material and created things, gave the gift to man and woman for marriage and as an integral part of his plan for mankind. The fertility cults and the abuses to which they led reduced women to the status of sex objects or depersonalized symbols of fertility in a manner which was contrary to the Judaic ideal. Woman was not intended as an object of possession or sexual desire, nor simply as a child-bearer. She was, and is, primarily man's personal equal and partner. That the sexual act only makes sense between man and woman in marriage and that, out of marriage, any genital love is contrary to God's law, follows from the marital purpose that God has given it. And in marriage the use of sex is inextricably bound up with procreation—but not in such a way as to suggest depersonalized "fertility". Fruitful love in marriage of equals, with the partners seeing in their children the fulfillment of generous love, is very different from a depersonalized worship of fertility.

Christ's own teaching on marriage and the family was very clear[12]—in fact on no other social institution or human personal relationship did he teach with such emphasis. His whole life and teaching reflected his love and respect for the sacrament, and by example he showed an appreciation of its values. Though he never let his obligations to his parents interfere with his duty to fulfill his mission as Son of God, his love and respect for

[11] "Such authors as Edward Schillebeeckx, John L. Mackenzie and Pierre Grelot stress that the Yahwist account is not so much an account of creation in general as the story of the creation of the human race, in two different yet complementary beings of flesh and blood. For these writers the Yahwist account in Genesis 2 is an account of the creation of marriage." W. F. May and J. F. Harvey, "On Understanding Human Sexuality: a Critique of the C.T.S.A. Study", *Clergy Review*, August, 1978, p. 303.
[12] R. Schnackenburg, *The Moral Teaching of the New Testament*, pt. 1, chap. 4, p. 14. L. H. Marshall, *The Challenge of New Testament Ethics*, chaps. 5 (a); 10 (f).

them is evident, his subjection to them in the hidden years at Nazareth being one of the greatest mysteries of his life on earth. His choice of the marriage feast of Cana as the occasion of his first miracle indicates that, as a man of his time and his people, he was capable of entering into the joy and happiness of the young couple. And throughout the New Testament his love and respect for children is touchingly apparent.[13] Though aware of the dangers that family ties could bring—especially the tendency to put the love of one's own kind before the love of God—these were aberrations he warned against, not defects of the institution in itself as God designed it. His love and respect for the Creator's plan in marriage is clear. It is nowhere more clear than in his rejection of divorce which was becoming more common among the Jews of his time. When questioned by his disciples on this he replied that it was only because of the hardness of their hearts that it was allowed under the Old Law. Under the New, the law of love of Christ and true interior religion, it would no longer be allowed. However, in St. Matthew there occurs what appears to be an exception to this rule which is to be found in none of the other evangelists. Since the interpretation of Matthew has been a matter of some perplexity since, we must look at the teaching more closely. We read:[14]

> Some Pharisees approached him, and to test him they said, "Is it against the law for a man to divorce his wife on any pretext whatever?" He answered, "Have you not read that the creator from the beginning made them male and female and that he said, 'This is why a man must leave father and mother and cling to his wife and the two become one body'? They are no longer two therefore but one body. So then, what God has united man must not divide."
>
> They said to him, "Then why did Moses command that a writ of dismissal should be given in the cases of divorce?" "It was because you were so unteachable . . . that Moses allowed you to divorce your wives, but it was not like this from the beginning."

The whole purpose of the questioning by the Pharisees was to see whether Christ allowed divorce and Christ's answer was quite plain: it was God's intention in the first instance that the partners should remain united and that intention he now reasserted. As to the question of why Moses allowed divorce—it was simply because he found it impossible to get his people to obey God's command. The whole new dispensation of grace that Christ inaugurated was going to put at man's disposal a power to overcome the hardness of his heart and it was to this higher morality that Christ now appealed. The original ban on divorce was to be the norm for the follower of Christ. The difficulty is that the text goes on[15]

[13] For example Mt 18:2–6; Mk 5:30–43; 10:13–16.
[14] Mt 19:3–8.
[15] Mt 19:9.

"Now I say to you, the man who divorces his wife, I am not speaking of fornication, and marries another, is guilty of adultery."

A similar phrase occurs elsewhere in Matthew[16] and it is only in Matthew that the apparent exception is mentioned. Yet if the context is to make any sense, the phrase can hardly be made to support divorce.[17] Among the Jews there were two schools of thought on the question—the Hillel and the Shammai. The former was very lax in interpreting Moses' provisions while the latter would only allow divorce in the case of something serious as, for example, fornication. If Christ really meant that this was a reason for divorce, he would have been identifying with the Shammai School and the whole purpose of his strong words would have been meaningless. Yet in fact he was going much further than any current opinion as the reaction of his disciples shows; they concluded that if the case was so then it was better not to marry at all.[18]

The controversies that this text of Matthew have given rise to are very detailed and complex and it is not in our brief consideration to discuss them in detail. One suggestion has been that the clause was inserted by Matthew later. If this is the case then there are no grounds for suggesting that Christ allowed divorce. Another explanation has been that the remark was in parenthesis, meaning to stress the indissolubility against such allowances made by some. In other words, Christ was saying that the alleged case of fornication was irrelevant. Divorce was still not possible.

The clarification of the Church's mind on the question of divorce owes a great deal to St. Paul.[19]

. . . Christ is the head of the Church and saves the whole body, so is a husband the head of his wife, and as the Church submits to Christ in all things so should wives to their husbands. . . . Husbands should love their wives as Christ loved the Church . . . this mystery has many implications but I am saying it applies to Christ and the Church. . . .

This parallel allows no breaking of the marital relationship because it is inconceivable that Christ would break his relationship with his Church. It was reflection upon the implications of this passage which finally convinced St. Augustine, who had been prepared to allow divorce for adultery, that it could not be justified on any grounds.[20] Since the time of

[16] Mt 5:32
[17] For a fuller discussion of the problem, see, for example, R. Schnackenburg, op. cit., p. 136 ff. The Greek texts of Matthew 5 and 19 translate as "except for something shameful" which most Greek and some Latin fathers interpreted to mean the adultery of the wife. Dictionary of Catholic Theology, vol. 2, s. v. "Divorce", p. 174.
[18] Mt 19:10.
[19] Eph 5:22–32.
[20] Dictionary of Catholic Theology, vol. 2, s.v. "Divorce", p. 157.

Augustine, the Catholic teaching has been unequivocal and clear while the classic explanation of the difficult clause in Matthew has been given by St. Jerome—namely that it refers to separation of bed and board. The explanation is still not without difficulties because such a form of separation without remarriage was unknown among the Jews. But it probably is the best answer to what is an admittedly difficult textual problem. The matter of the indissolubility of marriage was one which came up once more at the time of the Council of Trent.[21] The answer was a reaffirmation of the traditional Catholic teaching and doctrine which the Second Vatican Council also reasserts.[22]

B. THE DEVELOPMENT OF CANON LAW
AND THE THEOLOGY OF MARRIAGE

1. Canon Law and Annulment

Given the teaching of Christ, the Church has, over the centuries, sought to ensure that the approach to marriage and the understanding of it is such that its indissolubility is axiomatic, and that every aspect of the sacrament is understood and safeguarded. The Church's understanding of marriage is theological, spiritual, sacramental—the theology of marriage which is based on Genesis and was confirmed by Christ. Inevitably, however, the need to make sure that the theological, sacramental ideal was maintained throughout all the vicissitudes of her history, has led to the evolution of a Church law on marriage, a canon law. And the difficulty with law is that while it tries to preserve and protect, its formulations can never be perfect—and if understood too rigidly can be misleading.

Logically the first step the Church had to take was to see that her children understood the nature of marriage and approached and lived it according to the Christian ideal; St. Paul's instructions on matrimony and its obligations are obvious signs of this concern from the earliest days. But the conditions in which Paul and the Church spoke did not give the ideal much support; increasingly under the Roman Empire stable and fruitful marriage was under pressure—and it took the Church nearly a thousand years of effort before monogamous and indissoluble marriage was accepted as the theoretical norm throughout Christendom. So in time the obligation of marriage before a priest and in the presence of two witnesses

---

[21] "The Church does not err in teaching that, according to the evangelical and apostolic discipline, adultery by one of the spouses does not dissolve the bond of marriage." Denziger-Bannwart, *Enchiridion Symbolorum*, p. 977.

[22] "Christ's Sacrament . . . excludes both adultery and divorce." *Gaudium et Spes*, par. 49.

was imposed after it was found that without this full public ceremony it was not possible to maintain respect for the serious obligations of the sacrament.

The canonical obligations governing marriage apply only to those baptized into the Catholic Church.[23] But baptized Christians who are not members of that Church enter into a valid and sacramental marriage. By the natural law, those who are not baptized but have honestly committed themselves to each other for life, according to that law, are validly married too.

The essence of a marriage, according to divine law, is a fully understood and accepted personal commitment to an exclusive and lasting relationship based on mutual love and openness to new life; it follows that a marriage which lacks one or more of these characteristics in the beginning cannot be called a true marriage. Accordingly the Church has had to lay down the precise conditions for determining a true marriage and decide the procedure for determining whether they were met. If careful examination reveals that an essential precondition for the marriage as God ordained it was missing from the beginning, then that marriage can be declared null, never to have existed.

The so-called Pauline privilege goes further than this, declaring that in the case of a marriage which was initially valid, it can be broken in one specific case, that of one who married as a pagan and became a Christian.[24] If the non-believing partner in the marriage does not become a Christian and is content to continue to live with the believer peacefully and without offence to the Creator, then the marriage must remain. However, if he or she is not so content, the two may separate and the Christian is then free to marry again. The Petrine privilege is a later development—the dissolution of a marriage contracted by a non-baptized to a baptized person in the case of the former becoming a Catholic after the original marriage has ended in civil divorce.[25] The Pauline and Petrine privileges are exceptional cases. In them the dissolution of a marriage in which one or both of the partners was non-baptized can be authorized by the Church in view of the power committed to her by Christ. But once a *valid* marriage is contracted between *baptized* Christians who intended to enter into Christian marriage, the possibility of dissolution does not exist because, on the testimony of Christ's words, such cannot be broken. Annulment can take place, however, if any of the essentials of marriage *can be proved to have been absent*

[23] For the general discussion of the Church's law on marriage see H. Peschke, *Christian Ethics*, 2:460 ff. *New Catholic Encyclopedia* (New York, 1967), 11:271 ff.

[24] Based on 1 Cor 7:12–15. See R. Brown, *Marriage Annulment in the Catholic Church*, pp. 98–99.

[25] *New Catholic Encyclopedia*, 9:289.

at the time of marriage. Further, for Catholics, neglect of canonical form and the existence of certain impediments specified by Church law, can invalidate also.

The traditional grounds for determining whether a marriage is null and void can be listed under four heads: 1) lack of true consent—undue pressure being brought to bear on one or both parties, 2) inability to enter into marriage because of serious mental or moral defect, 3) marriage in defiance of Church law concerning the presence of priest and witnesses, 4) existence of serious impediments, for example, blood relationship in a forbidden degree. Recently the importance of new knowledge in determining the psychological factors precluding mature and lasting commitment has been more fully realised. Though these, in principle, come under the second traditional heading (mental or moral defect), the way they are interpreted in the light of the findings of modern psychology marks a considerable development of the traditional understanding of what constitutes moral or mental defect. Assessing the effects of psychological states—alcoholism, homosexuality, psychological immaturity, for example—and judging their presence and impact *at the time of the marriage* leave room for considerable errors of judgement. But the cases outlined by Ralph Brown, and the decisions made in them, show how the norms can be applied responsibly.[26]

With the best will in the world, however, it is inevitable that delicate decisions on such matters which rely to a very large extent on human judgement, leave room for mistakes and abuse. Hence the *Apostolic Signatura* in 1977 condemned the view that the Second Vatican Council had changed the nature of consent required in marriage from one which was irrevocable to one which is continuous or existential, one that can be therefore abandoned because of the subjective feelings of one or both of the parties.[27] The need for the statement arose out of cases reversed by the *Signatura* because of the doctrinal errors evident in the original judgements. The responsible authorities in the Church have then a difficult balance to strike—to make proper use of new understandings and insights while avoiding their abuse. The new knowledge is important because it will help us to prevent mistakes in the future. It should enable us to get a clearer understanding of what true and full commitment is so that

[26] Brown, op. cit., especially chap. 4.

[27] *L'Osservatore Romano* ([English edition] 16 June 1977). In his address to the Roman Rota on 4 February 1980, Pope John Paul II warned that "no judge may pronounce a judgement in favour of nullity unless he has acquired moral certainty as to the existence of that nullity . . . every relaxation carries with it an impelling dynamism . . . which, if the practice be entertained, the way is laid open to the toleration of divorce under another name in the Church." *L'Osservatore Romano* ([English edition] 3 March 1980).

fewer of the sort of marriages that lead to annulment are contracted in the first instance.

2. The Development of the Church's Teaching on the Ends of Marriage

The fundamental theology of Christian marriage, based on the Scriptures themselves, stresses the personal nature of the commitment that is marriage and the importance of physical love that is uniquely the right of those whose lives are united so intimately. But equally that physical love was intended to be fruitful, to be the means by which new life could come to be and be fostered to the full dignity of mature manhood and womanhood. The pleasure that is sex and the attraction between man and woman it sets in train is, as a statement of fact, completed by a physical union which takes place in a way and involves the use of potentialities and powers which are clearly ordered to the conception and the bringing to birth of new life.

There is no way of explaining or understanding sex—physiologically, emotionally or psychologically—without recognizing that the pleasure it gives arises from functions that are concerned directly with the act of insemination of which the male and female bodies, in their roles, are capable. However sexual pleasure is achieved, in or out of marriage, heterosexually or homosexually, that pleasure results from the use of powers and emotions that are ordered to, essentially connected with, the human procreative capacity. This is not theological, philosophical or moral rationalisation but a statement of fact about our physical and emotional constitution. If we keep this fact in mind it is possible for us to decide what is right and what is wrong in the use of human sexuality. Forget it or ignore it and we will never find a way through the difficult and delicate problems it presents. Because there is a serious imbalance in this side of our natures, the aid of reason and grace is required if it is to be corrected.

The early Church realised that the overwhelming threat to the ideal of life in Christ and therefore to human dignity, was the moral depravity of the times, especially in that concerning the sins of the flesh.[28] Having had that lesson once taught her so well, she is not likely to forget it. Not surprisingly, this awareness of the degradation to which a misuse of sex could lead had its effects on thinking concerning the use of marriage, and today we are inclined to dismiss this as unreasonable and puritanical. But

---

[28] "Above all, the conflict undertaken by Christians was against the sins of the flesh, such as fornication, adultery and unnatural vice." A. Harnack, *The Mission and Expansion of Christianity in the First Three Centuries* (London, 1904), 1:207.

as the Anglican moral theologian Lindsay Dewar[29] points out, we have today much to learn from the attitude of the early Church with its experience of the excesses into which this emotion can lead society. There is a great deal more wisdom in the traditional attitude than some modern Christian writers, who reveal themselves as extraordinarily naive in these matters, allow. In the early Church, Christians were in no doubt that sex was a lion, magnificent but dangerous, and not the tame lap dog it is often depicted as today. The truth is that of itself marriage does not remove the imbalances from our sexual appetites. So much is common-sense and common knowledge, evident in the literature and the experience of mankind. The question of the proper use of sex in marriage then will always be one that exercises the human mind—on the one hand how to put this great gift at the service of human love, on the other hand how to prevent it being misused so that instead of being the servant of love it becomes its master.

That men and women sought the pleasures of sex while denying or rejecting its responsibilities was well known to the early moralists since contraception was widely practised in classical times. The Stoics condemned it, as from the first did the Christian moralists, in this following not only the Stoics, but a strand in the Jewish tradition.[30] The evidence which has been assembled by Noonan testifies to the continual presence of the question throughout the centuries since. This is why the moralist and the canonist have had to be concerned with clarifying the attitude of the Church to it.[31] It was not as if they were dealing with unreal or imaginary problems or speculating in the abstract. The issue has continued to be a real one.

Our first instinct as Christians in facing such an important question as the proper use of the gift of sex in marriage is to look to the Scriptures for the guidance they offer in the light of tradition. In the Old Testament, the account of the marriage of Tobit and Sarah is relevant. Tobit prayed to God on his wedding night.[32]

> It was you who created Adam, you who created Eve his wife to be his help and support, and from these two the human race was born. It was you

[29] *Moral Theology in the Modern World* (London, 1964), pp. 119–20. He refers to Canon V. A. Demant, *An Exposition of Christian Sex Ethics* (London, 1963), a brilliant and incisive explanation of traditional Christian teaching by the then Regius Professor of Moral and Pastoral Theology at Oxford University.

[30] J. T. Noonan, *Contraception* (Harvard, 1965), pp. 46 ff., 49 ff.

[31] However, as the *Dictionary of Catholic Theology* points out in its article on "Marriage", (3:245), Noonan errs in suggesting that St. Augustine walked a tightrope between Pelagianism and Manicheeism—the two were in fact on the same side in this matter as Augustine himself notes.

[32] Tob 8:6–9.

who said, "It is not good for man to be alone, let us make him a helpmate like himself." And so I do not take this sister of mine for any lustful motive. I do it in singleness of heart. Be kind enough to have pity on her and bring us to our old age together.

The clear inference is that marital relations can be dominated by lust, not true love. Some commentators suggest that it was Tobit's intention to counter it by an assertion of lifelong fidelity;[33] others that those who approach the marriage bed with a deep appreciation of the sacredness of the married state will avoid the misuse of marital sex.[34] The reference by Tobit to the creation of marriage in the first instance indicates his appreciation of the essential goodness of sexuality in this context—the whole passage indicates that sexual relations are not to be a sign of selfish gratification, irrespective of the purposes of love and procreation for which God had given us the gift.

The Song of Songs presents us with a more positive and complete presentation of the goodness of sexual love in marriage. The oldest interpretation of the Song is religious, the Covenant relationship compared to marriage, and the work has been the subject of interpretation by the Church's greatest mystics. But there is no doubt that the literal sense, which is a celebration of the faithful love between man and woman in marriage, is significant too.[35] The delicacy and yet the directness of its reference to the physical attractions and joys of love is unmistakeable, hence in our context it has great significance. Love, and the joys it brings, as the pledge of total self-giving goes to the very heart of the nature of marriage as God has ordained it. The Song then, in its literal interpretation, is not capable of an erotic or hedonistic interpretation which would set it against other aspects of marriage. Yet it is capable of bringing home to us, as it surely was meant to, that the physical joys of love in the sacrament of marriage are a pledge and a sign of the total self-giving the sacrament demands.[36]

In this regard, St. Paul has a significant passage:[37]

Yes, it is a good thing for a man not to touch a woman but since sex is always a danger, each man should have his own wife and each woman her

[33] Cambridge Bible Commentary, *The Shorter Books of the Apocrypha* (C.U.P., 1972), p. 44.

[34] *Jerome Biblical Commentary* (London, 1968), p. 623.

[35] Ibid., 1:506 ff., s.v. "Canticle of Canticles".

[36] "The song describes the creaturely splendour of human love . . . on the other hand there is no suggestion of frivolity. Great value is placed on the virgin state of the beloved (4:12; 8:8–10) and true love is expressed in unshakeable fidelity (8:6–7) "for love is as strong as death". Schillebeeckx, op. cit., 1:59. See P. Grelot, op. cit., pp. 76 ff.

[37] 1 Cor 7:1–6.

own husband. The husband must give his wife what she has the right to expect, so too the wife to the husband. The wife has no rights over her own body, it is the husband who has them. In the same way the husband has no rights over his own body, the wife has them. Do not refuse each other except by mutual consent and then only for an agreed time to leave yourselves free for prayer. Then come together again in case Satan should take advantage of your weakness and tempt you.

This is perhaps a rather low key but complete statement of the positive value of sexual love in marriage. Taking the whole passage together it is quite clear that the mutuality of sexual love and its importance in marriage is understood. Grudging it may seem to be, but there is no trace here of any suggestion that in marriage a full sexual life is anything but compatible with the Christian ideal. Among the Doctors of the Church, there was much evidence of a more pessimistic view of sexuality.[38] We remember once again the context in which the early Church had its being. Seeking to put before the people the ideal that Christ had left them, it often seemed that the defects of human sexuality as these were evidenced in the gross immorality of the time, outweighed its positive values. St. Augustine held that sexual concupiscence, sexual desire, was evil.[39] He defended the substantial goodness of marriage but, in so doing, he argued that only the desire for children justified the sexual act. Any other motive was at least a venial sin.

Clearly this teaching, which had its effect on theologians for hundreds of years afterwards, got its emphasis wrong—but we should notice two things. Firstly, writers of the time had good cause to know what sort of marriage practices were current. A Christian might well find that his or her partner had such a depraved view of what sexual practices were permissible in the married state, that indeed they might be in spiritual danger in entering into marriage. Secondly, theologians, even the greatest, can err. The Church is not bound by their teaching but sifts it over the centuries until its value is proved or disproved. Sin properly so called is mortal sin. Venial sins are at the most imperfection and cannot truly be called sin, of which the essential nature is that it cuts us off entirely from grace. When we consider the holiness of Christian married couples throughout the ages, men and women who have been faithful to one

[38] Especially St. Jerome. Although he attacked the Pelagian view that all intercourse was wrong and stressed the Christian value of marriage, he took a poor view of married love. *Dictionary of Catholic Theology*, 3:245, s.v. "Marriage". The same source notes that St. Augustine, in the last work of his life (his reply to Julian the Pagan) was developing a more positive view of the place of sexual love in married life.

[39] J. Ford and G. Kelly, *Contemporary Moral Theology* (Cork, 1973), 2:172. See *Dictionary of Catholic Theology*, loc. cit.

another throughout their lives, have never misused sex but enjoyed it honestly as God intended, it is impossible to believe that their physical desire for one another in the context of Christian marriage, should have had something about it that was not worthy. Perhaps it is the exaggerated importance that theologians sometimes receive or assume today which encourages us to overstate their influence at other times.

Whatever justification theologians therefore had for warning against the dangers of the abuse of sex in marriage, and they had good grounds for their warnings, there was never justification for making them into a general suspicion of marital love in itself. The reason is obvious. It is that the goodness of sexual pleasure was guaranteed by God who gave man the gift—asking only that it be used in marriage according to his law. In regard to the penitentials[40] which often reflect the negative attitude, we note[41] that they

> did not represent the universal teaching of the Catholic Church. They were the work of private doctors and their authority and orthodoxy varied immensely more than that of our modern manuals of moral theology. Later on the penitentials fell into disrepute and were even denounced by the bishops and particular councils. But they are witness to the kind of particular rules for conduct given by *many* priests to *many* married penitents over a long period of time.

Over the centuries, therefore, aspects of the Church's teaching in the area of sexual morality have been worked out with greater clarity. Moral theology developed as a much more precise and coherent science as time went on and to project modern notions of that precision and scientific coherence on to past times when there was much more confusion and lack of clarity is unjustified.

The great creative period in Catholic theology and thought in the twelfth and thirteenth centuries had its effect upon the theology of marriage. St. Augustine[42] had spoken of the three goods of marriage, namely *proles* (the bearing and rearing of children), the *fides* (the faithful love of the partners) and the *sacramentum* (the grace and sanctification of the partners and the family that came from the sacrament). Though he defended the essential goodness of marriage and the marriage act against the Manichees, he insisted it was only the procreative purpose which justified sexual intercourse. By contrast, the Manichees were opposed to

---

[40] The penitentials were practical handbooks of moral theology compiled by the mainly monastic confessors of the sixth to eleventh centuries.

[41] Ford and Kelly, op. cit., 2:177.

[42] F. X. Werz, *Ius Decretalium* (Prague, 1914), p. 70. R. Lawler et al., *The Teaching of Christ* (Huntingdon, Indiana, 1976), p. 507. St. Augustine, *De Nuptiis* 1.17.19 (ML. 44.424).

all such intercourse—but even more so to that which led to conception. St. Augustine's defence of marriage in all its aspects, therefore, lacked nothing in essentials, but its view of sexual love itself was negative—and it was this view which had so much influence in later years.

St. Thomas' general approach indicates the beginning of a more positive attitude, though he was respectful of, and built upon, the insights of Augustine. However, his evaluation of the sensitive appetite in human nature, his explanation of original sin without reference to concupiscence as the agency of transmission, together with his more positive theology of the passions and pleasures, all indicated a shift in emphasis.[43]

It is to St. Thomas that we owe the terminology of the three ends of marriage—the primary end (procreation and education of children) the secondary end (the good of the parents) and the tertiary end (the remedy for concupiscence).[44] But this is not to say that he formalised the conception of procreation as the purpose which alone justified sexual pleasure in marriage. So too his statement that only procreation and the rendering of the *debitum* free the partners from venial sin[45] in the pleasure of sex is set in a much more subtle context which shows that he was making a distinction between the eroticism which was a purely selfish seeking of satisfaction, and such satisfaction which was *mutual* and indicative of the union of the partners, soul as well as body. Where this was the case, love and love alone was a good motive for sexual relations, the assumption being that the procreative purpose was not excluded. What he did insist on, and what all Christian morality insists on as has Vatican II and *Humanae Vitae*, is the importance of chastity in marriage, both in the sense of control of the use of sex and the abstention from it when needful.

Aquinas fully understood the importance and the goodness of the passionate love of man and woman: "a man loves his wife more intensely than his parents because she is united with (him) as one flesh."[46] In treating of the primary/secondary distinction between the ends of marriage, his emphasis varies.[47] He says in effect that the procreation and raising of children is the primary end in the sense that it is the commitment to this which secures the good of fidelity and the permanence, the indissolubility which is the sign of grace. Nor does he make procreation a

[43] Ford and Kelly, op. cit., 2:178 quoting E. F. Sheridan, S.J., *The Morality of the Pleasure Motive in the Use of Marriage* (Rome, 1947).

[44] Werz, op. cit., p. 70. St. Thomas Aquinas, *Supplement*, q. 49, art. 2; q. 59, art. 2.

[45] St. Thomas Aquinas, *Supplement*, q. 49, art. 5, corp. See Ford and Kelly, op. cit., 2:178.

[46] Aquinas, *Summa Theologica* II–II, q. 96, art. 11.

[47] G. Grisez, "Marriage: Reflections Based on St. Thomas and Vatican Council II" in *Catholic Mind* (June, 1966).

purely biological function. As Grisez remarks, only a world shaped by
dualism and positivism, by Descartes and Hegel, makes it possible to see
human generation as merely biological. Common though the process of
procreation is to man and animals, that process in man is as far above that
of the animals as is the value of human life above theirs.

On marital intercourse Aquinas taught that, far from it being in any
sense wrong, it is meritorious and holy when it is an act of sacramental
marriage for virtuous motives—procreation being *not* the only virtuous
motive.[48] He argues that the act of conjugal love is holy in that it
participates in the sacramental character of marriage—which signifies the
union of Christ and his Church. The delight felt in the marriage act itself is
good in this context; there is no ground for puritan suspicion of sexual
pleasure in its proper place; the pleasure of a good act is good, the pleasure
of a bad act is bad.

It is in this context that his insistence on it being venially sinful to
engage in intercourse simply for the sake of pleasure, or in the response to
selfish erotic impulse, is to be seen. Provided the virtuous reason of
fidelity is there, then pleasure and eroticism are at the service of fidelity
which is one of the goods of marriage, along with (not a substitute for or
opposed to) procreation, but standing as in its own right nonetheless. Far
from being even venially sinful, such an act is meritorious and good in
itself.

And it is his teaching on conjugal chastity which puts the whole of his
teaching here in its perspective.[49] Attitude is important. To engage in an
integral act of intercourse with one's wife while being ready to have the
same with another's wife is mortally sinful. Similarly, because it is the
divine command that everything in man is subject to reason, we must not
make the measure of what does or does not offend our neighbour the
primary norm of sin or virtue. Hence in marriage it is not the wishes of
one's partner which makes for good or evil. It is what is in accord
with right reason according to the divine law. In this he indicates the
perspective which is the constant of Catholic teaching. St. Thomas did not
live to finish the *Summa* and marriage questions fell within the incomplete
section. The positive way in which he did treat of aspects of marriage in
passing in other parts of his work make us regret that we do not have his
mature and developed reflections on the subject. From what we do have,
however, we can see that his work presaged the later more positive
approaches to the use of the sacrament which were to develop.

And from the fifteenth and early sixteenth centuries, the more positive

[48] In 4 *Sent.* d. 31, q. 1, art. 3, quoted Grisez, p. 7.
[49] In 4 *Sent.* Exp. Text. d. 31, q. 2, art. 3 quoted Grisez, p. 17.

approach to sexual love in marriage becomes clearer. Cajetan (1468–1534) calls the pleasure a gift of God and, in 1633, it was being argued[50] that

> although anything from God as the author of nature is instituted principally for some definite end, yet it is also instituted at least secondarily for whatever legitimate ends it is capable of achieving. . . . Accordingly, even when we omit altogether the primary end of these things, we can use them for all legitimate ends of this kind. For on no heading can it be shown that any reason obliges us always to use every creature to achieve its principal end or to intend this end principally. Especially when we do not positively prevent this end from happening.

On this reasoning, therefore, the positive value of sexual intimacy in marriage as an act of love is evident, provided procreation was not denied by a contraceptive act. Though the more rigorous point of view still prevailed among the vast majority of moralists and theologians, this new emphasis was also taught. It was helped by the gradual extension of our knowledge concerning the working of the human body and the procreative process.[51] Once it was clear that the relationship between the individual acts of intercourse and conception was not as direct as had previously been thought, any understanding of procreation as the primary end of marriage which implied that the procreative intent must always be there in every act to justify it, had to be modified. If the very mechanism of the human body God has given us made it impossible to produce life through intercourse on all occasions, then the clear inference was that according to God's law the use of sex in marriage for love that could not produce new life was, in itself, good.

To the greater knowledge of the actual physiology of procreation were added the findings of psychology, stressing the importance of sex for human development. Presented thus with this greater knowledge about the nature of the human body and the human mind as given us by God according to his plan and purpose, it was inevitable that while both love and life giving would remain essential to marriage and neither could be denied, some readjustment in thinking about the use of marriage, and the terminology of primary and secondary ends, was necessary. By the time of the encyclical *Casti Connubi* of Pius XI in 1930,[52] the readjustment was

---

[50] Ford and Kelly, op. cit., 2:180–81.

[51] "Spermatoza were first discovered in 1677 and it was in 1875 that Oscar Hertwig demonstrated their function." Ford and Kelly, op. cit., p. 185.

[52] *Casti Connubii* (30 December 1930, "On Christian Marriage") was one of the most important of Pius XI's encyclicals. It dealt with the problems of sex and marriage that were then becoming acute and have become more acute: divorce, abortion, sterilization, "temporary" marriages, contraception.

apparent and Pius XII fulfilled the teaching of his predecessor in defending sexual pleasure as a genuine value and a legitimate motive in marriage.[53]

> In this matter, which is both delicate and difficult, *there are two tendencies to be avoided; first the one which, in examining the constituent elements of the act of generation, considers only the primary end of marriage, as though the secondary end did not exist, or were not the finis operis established by the Creator of nature himself; and secondly the one which gives the secondary end a place of equal principality*, detaching it from its essential subordination to the primary end—a view which would lead by logical necessity to deplorable consequences. In other words, the truth is intermediate, and two extremes must be avoided; on the one hand, particularly to deny or esteem too little the secondary end of marriage and of the act of generation; on the other hand, to dissociate or separate unduly the conjugal act from the primary end, to which according to its entire internal structure it is primarily and principally ordained.

As Ford and Kelly point out, this reasoning implies that the secondary and personalist ends are essential, the *finis operis* of marriage, while, at the same time, they are not such as can be allowed to obscure or contradict its procreative purposes.[54] Yet it is significant that Pius XII also stressed frequently that the current emphasis on sexual pleasure, even in its marital form, all too easily shades off into a non-Christian hedonism. These developments laid the way open for a reconsideration of the terminology in which the ends of marriage were expressed, while at the same time the implications, the essential import of that terminology, was not abandoned by the Council—for what that terminology was trying to say and did say expressed something about marriage and the marriage act which was and is fundamental to the Creator's purpose in giving this power to us.

Critics of the Church's teaching that the only place for sex is marriage and that within it sexual activity should always remain open to new life, frequently accuse her of hanging on to such a view because of a refusal to face the need for change.[55] Her position, they say, is irrational, unnecessary and wrong. The truth is that it is only by holding on to the essential link between sexual activity and procreation that sex remains in the service of true human values. The experience of the permissive society confirms this view. It is a fact that the spread of the contraceptive mentality has been accompanied by the increasing cheapening of sexuality. It is

---

[53] AAS 33 (1941), pp. 421 ff., quoted by Ford and Kelly, op. cit., 2:37. The occasion of Pope Pius' words was an address to the Roman Rota.

[54] See above, pp. 79 ff. The *finis operis* is the end of the act and as such the primary determinant of morality. Love is the *finis operis* of sex in marriage—but procreation must not be excluded from any individual act, that is the *finis operantis* (the intention of those making love) must remain open to new life.

[55] The reaction to the Vatican *Declaration on Certain Questions Concerning Sexual Ethics*, issued by the Sacred Congregation for the Doctrine of the Faith on 29 December 1975 (C.T.S.: London, 1976) demonstrated much evidence of this line of criticism.

irrelevant whether that mentality has caused this decline, or has merely accompanied it. The facts of the decline are incontrovertible. The only way to reverse it is to put sex back into marriage and, in marriage to ensure that contraception has no place. Once it is accepted that, in marriage, the partners have a right deliberately to separate the act of love from the responsibility of life giving, there can be no satisfactorily logical answer to those who wish to dismiss the institution as redundant. If sex is for pleasure only, then whether one sees marriage as useful or not is entirely a matter of personal preference. If sex on the other hand is for family in a context of loving, so that each act of sexual love remains open to new life, then the necessity of marriage is plain because the stability of family life is necessary for the proper bringing up of the children born of love. Unless society takes this proposition as one of its fundamental values and seeks to ensure that it is accepted by all for the good of each and the good of all, it is allowing its fundamental institution to be undermined in theory and in practice. It is not therefore surprising that a society which rejects this value is increasingly rejecting also the ideal of stable marriage, fidelity and the sanctity of life itself. Divorce and illegitimacy rates are increasing as is the proportion of abortions to the number of live births.[56] That an increase in the numbers of abortions should go hand in hand with the increasing spread of contraceptive practices is inevitable since, once the separation of the sex act from the responsibility of pregnancy and parenthood is admitted, abortion becomes the back-up for ineffective or non-existent contraception. If pregnancy is seen as some sort of disease then it has to be ended by the most effective means available and abortion is very effective in correcting the "mistake" of conception.[57] Meanwhile the promise of childless marriage that the contraceptive pill holds out can only be to tempt ill-prepared young people into it with the increasing likelihood that such marriages will be less stable and lasting.

The various errors and illusions of the permissive society therefore compound and reinforce one another. Thus a concept of sex education which, insofar as it provides one, assumes that vague exhortations to responsible "extra marital sex" constitute a sound and sufficient sexual

[56] Live births in England and Wales in 1969 numbered 797,538; abortions, 49,829. In 1977 the numbers were 569,000 and 102,677 respectively. In the same period illegitimate live births rose from 8.4% to 9.7% (S.P.U.C., *Human Concern*, [Winter, 1979]: figures based on those given by the Registrar General). Marriages (Great Britain) numbered 387,000 in 1961, 406,000 in 1978: they had risen to a peak in 1971 of 447,000. Divorces numbered 27,000 in 1961, 147,000 in 1979 (H.M.S.O., *Social Trends*, [1980]).

[57] Abortion is "the inevitable correlate of declining fertility. All family planning programmes begin with the least effective methods . . . if we want to stop fertility we either have to combine a reversible method to space out our pregnancies and use abortion when we have the pregnancy we don't want, or to choose sterilisation." Malcolm Potts at the World Population Conference, reported in *The Guardian*, 21 April 1979.

morality, is inadequate to say the least. A far stronger and clearer ethic is needed—and for it we have not far to seek. The principle that only those who are prepared to accept the responsibilities of bringing new life into the world are entitled to the pleasures of an active sexual life is reasonable, clear and simple, and respects the rights of man and woman, of children and society. It is also God's law. The exceptions of the childless couple are not a difficulty since genuine childlessness, through age or some defect, is clearly compatible with the principle stated; exceptions prove rules. Those who advocate adultery and fornication (and we should be honest enough to recognize that "premarital sex" is simply a rather misleading euphemism for this more honest old-fashioned word) are implicitly encouraging the spread of sexually-transmitted diseases with all that they entail; it is to be noted that it is the young who suffer most from such disease.[58] Also in the "sexual freedom for all" it is women, especially young women, who are the most vulnerable—particularly those who have few resources or charms beyond a healthy body.[59] All too easily they are the victims of the worst kind of male selfishness masquerading as "freedom". Finally it would be wrong to assume that promiscuity would be redeemed even it if did not have these intolerable effects. The very foundations of society are threatened when the family is—and when sex before marriage, and sexual infidelity within marriage are taken for granted and even positively approved, the institution is indeed being undermined. It is no training for the mutual trust and readiness to grow together which is at the heart of loving marriage (and the basis of that security and love children need) for the young to have put before them the doubtful ideal of disposable sexual relationships. Unless they are brought

[58] D. Barlow, *Sexual Transmitted Diseases* (O.U.P., 1979), considers in chapter 12 the factors leading to the "world-wide increase in all the sexually transmitted diseases . . . which is one which especially affects the young" (p. 111). It is noticeable that Michael Schofield, in *Promiscuity*, pp. 28 ff., wriggle as he might, cannot deny that "the more sexual partners you have, the more likely you are to catch venereal disease" (p. 31). He contents himself with putting the burden on everyone but the promiscuous, for: 1) reluctance of the latter to get treatment, 2) the reluctance of some medical authorities to make that treatment pleasant or socially acceptable. It apparently does not occur to him that those who deliberately put themselves in danger of getting the disease have any responsibility to stop the habits that lead to it. He just blames everyone else for the real or imagined failures to help sufferers. Insofar as the disease is sometimes contracted by perfectly innocent people, the social stigma attaching to it is regrettable. But the situation will not be improved by arguments for further sexual irresponsibility.

[59] "When a boy or a girl are out on a date, the girl has no reason for saying no . . . she can always use contraceptives, she can always get an abortion. She has no choice but . . . to be sexually tyrannised . . . this is being called women's liberation." *A Reader in Natural Family Planning* (Tokyo, 1978), 2nd ed., no. 1, p. 103. Mary Kenny in *Why Christianity Works* (London, 1981), pp. 61 ff., has some acute comments on the effect of permissiveness on young women.

up to respect the values that make for the establishment of marital fidelity, the ideal will be destroyed.

It cannot be but noted that the forces which have made for permissiveness are sad and misguided, intellectually naive, even where they are not openly and crudely commercial.[60] Those who worked to "liberate" mankind from the "tyranny" of the Christian sexual ethic had no idea where that "liberation" might lead. It was their hope that human sexuality would be sweetness and light after the "yoke" was cast off. It seems that they did not understand forces they were dealing with quite so well as the Church which has tried, over a period of some hundreds of years, to preserve the beauty and dignity of sex and marriage while, at the same time, avoiding the excesses that sex can produce.[61]

If the intellectual arguments for the destruction of the Christian ethic now seem to be less solid than they once were, the commercialism of the manufacturers of contraceptive devices and all those who stand to gain by the exploitation of sex grows more blatant all the time. A society which has allowed the sexual education of the young to be so much at the mercy of such commercialism is willing its own destruction. Sadly, many women are contributing to the moral pollution by the way in which they are allowing their sexuality to be exploited, or are leading the way themselves.[62] It is a strange paradox when so many women are dedicating themselves to the cause of women's rights, that others should be ensuring that women remain imprisoned by the oldest insult of all, that she is a mere sex object.

It is when we contemplate the degradation that can come upon humanity when sex is seen as a value in itself, that the reason for the insistence of the Church on the link between love and life giving is seen. There is no other way of giving sex its rightful place in life while avoiding enslaving mankind to its power, except in that link. This being the case, we would not expect that, much as the modern world has learned about the nature of sexuality, the Church would abandon a teaching which is the bulwark of human and sexual dignity. In fact, the Second Vatican Council did not at

[60] Kenny, op. cit., pp. 63 ff., on the commercialism behind sexual permissiveness.

[61] Joseph Epstein in *Divorce: The American Experience* (London, 1974), chap. 3, "The Bedroom Olympiad", after discussing Bertand Russell and Sigmund Freud's efforts at sexual liberation, notes that "Each would have warmly greeted a swing of the pendulum in sexual matters. Neither, of course, could have anticipated that when the pendulum finally swung it would swing so hard as to threaten to smash through the cabinet of the clock" (p. 57).

[62] One of the most blatant cases it seemed was Linda Lovelace (for example, her autobiography *Inside Linda Lovelace* [London, 1976]). However, she is now claiming in a later book (*Ordeal*, [London, 1981]), that she was under duress during the period in which films like *Deep Throat* were made. If this is true, then the cynicism and crudity with which women are exploited in the name of freedom is even more apparent.

all abandon, but reasserted it while summing up the positive developments in the old teaching that had been observed over several hundred
years but which has gathered momentum in the last twenty or thirty
years.

3. The Teaching of the
Second Vatican Council and *Humanae Vitae*
on the Ends of Marriage[a]

49. The Christian family springs from marriage,[9] which is an image and a
sharing in the partnership of love between Christ and the Church; it will
show forth to all men Christ's living presence in the world and the authentic
nature of the Church by the love and generous fruitfulness of the spouses, by
their unity and fidelity, and by the loving way in which all members of the
family co-operate with each other. . . .

50. *Marriage and married love are by nature ordered to the procreation and education
of children. Indeed children are the supreme gift of marriage and greatly contribute to
the good of the parents themselves.* God himself said: "It is not good that man
should be alone" (Gen. 2:18), and "from the beginning (he) made them male
and female" (Mt. 19:4): wishing to associate them in a special way with his
own creative work. God blessed man and woman with the words "Be
fruitful and multiply" (Gen. 1:28). *Without intending to underestimate the other
ends of marriage, it must be said that true married love and the whole structure of
family life which results from it is directed to disposing the spouses to co-operate
valiantly with the love of the Creator,* who through them will increase and
enrich his family from day to day.

*Married couples should regard it as their proper mission to transmit human life and
to educate their children: they should realise that they are thereby co-operating with the
love of God the Creator and are, in a certain sense, its interpreters.* This involves the
fulfilment of their role with a sense of human and Christian responsibility
and the formation of correct judgements through docile respect for God and
common reflection and effort; it also involves a consideration of their own
good and the good of their children already born or yet to come, an ability
to read the signs of the times and of their own situation on the material
and spiritual level, and, finally, an estimation of the good of the couple
themselves who must, in the last analysis arrive at these judgements before
God. Married people should realize that in their behaviour they may not
simply follow their own fancy, but must be ruled by conscience—and
conscience ought to be conformed to the law of God in the light of the
teaching authority of the Church, which is the authentic interpreter of divine
law. For the divine law throws light on the meaning of married love, protects
it and leads it to truly human fulfilment. *Whenever Christian spouses in a spirit of
sacrifice and trust in divine providence*[12] *carry out their duties of procreation with
generous human and Christian responsibility, they glorify the Creator and perfect
themselves in Christ. Among the married couples who thus fulfil their God-given*

mission, special mention should be made of those who, after prudent reflection and common decision, courageously undertake the proper upbringing of a large number of children. [13]

But marriage is not merely for the procreation of children: its nature as an indissoluble compact between two people and the good of the children demand that the mutual love of the parents be properly shown, that it should grow and mature. Even in cases where, despite the intense desire of the spouses there are no children, marriage still retains its character of being a whole manner and communion of life and preserves its value and indissolubility.

[a] The italics in the text quoted from *Gaudium et Spes* are mine. [Author]
[9] Eph. 5:32.
[12] Cf. 1 Cor. 7:5.
[13] Cf. Pius XII Allocution *Tra le verità* 20 Jan. 1958: AAS 50 (1958) p. 91.

A careful and calm reading of these passages can leave one with only one conclusion—that marriage is by nature ordered to the procreation of children and that the other ends of marriage, good though they are, may not be pursued by denying this. However, where the possibility of new life does *not exist*, the other ends and goods of marriage, above all the mutual love, are of the same value as when new life is possible. But it may not, therefore, be reasoned that any method of restricting births in a fruitful marriage can be used—conscience must be conformed to the law of God in the light of the teaching of the Church which is the authentic interpreter of that law. The document states:

> 51. . . . .when it is a question of harmonizing married love with the responsible transmission of life, it is not enough to take only the good intention and the evaluation of motives into account; the objective criteria must be used, criteria drawn from the nature of the human person and human action . . . all this is possible only if the virtue of married chastity is seriously practised. In questions of birth regulation, the sons of the Church . . . are forbidden to use methods disapproved of by the teaching authority of the Church in its interpretation of the Divine Law. [14]

[14] Cf. Pius XI, Litt. Encycl. *Casti Connubii*. AAS 22 (1930) pp. 559–561. Denz 2239–2241; Pius XII, *Allocution* to the Congress of Italian midwives, 23 June 1964, AAS (1964) pp. 581–9. By order of the Holy Father certain questions requiring further and more careful investigation have been given over to a commission for the study of population, the family and births, in order that the Holy Father may pass judgement when its task is completed. With the teaching of the magisterium standing as it is, the Council has no intention of proposing concrete solutions at this moment.

These key texts stress that the norms governing sexual activity in marriage need to be governed by objective standards. A sincere intention and motive is not enough. These objective standards are drawn from the nature of the human person and the human act. Observing them requires a sincere cultivation of married chastity. Methods of birth regulation which the Church teaches are against the Divine Law are to be rejected.

In the light of the controversies of the time however, especially on the question of population, further consideration of these matters was needed as footnote 14 noted. These had been referred to a commission and the Holy Father would decide on them when the work of the commission was finished. Some convince themselves that this reference indicated that the Pope knew a contradiction of the older teaching was needed and was thought to be possible. It can equally well be argued that the reference to the Commission was made in the hope that its deliberations would confirm the orthodox teaching; but neither argument is really relevant. The fact is that an advisory committee was in being and it was for the Pope to decide whether its recommendations were in accord with the truth of Catholic teaching. He decided they were not, giving his reasons for so doing, and saying:[63]

> Let no Catholic be heard to assert that the interpretation of the natural moral law is outside the competence of the Church's magisterium. It is in fact indisputable, as our predecessors have many times declared, that Jesus Christ when He communicated His divine power to Peter and the other apostles and sent them to teach all nations His Commandments, He constituted them as authentic guardians and interpreters of the whole moral law, not only that is the law of the Gospel but also the natural law, the reason being that the natural law declares the will of God and its faithful observance is necessary for man's eternal salvation.

The purpose of the Commission set up was simply to provide the evidence which would enable a reply to be given.[64]

> We could not regard as definite and requiring unequivocal acceptance the conclusions arrived at by the Commission. They were not such as to exempt us from the duty of examining personally this serious question and this because, if for no other reason, there was lacking complete agreement within the Commission itself as to what moral norms to put forward. This was all the more necessary because certain approaches and criteria for a solution to this question had emerged which were at variance with moral doctrines on marriage constantly taught by the magisterium of the Church. . . . We by virtue of the mandate entrusted to us by Christ intend to give our reply to this series of grave questions.

The tone of the teaching set out in the following paragraphs is entirely at one with more positive insights of *Gaudium et Spes*. The terminology of primary and secondary ends is avoided. Marriage is a personal choice of two people in love who show that love by the mutual self-giving which is their right, so that through this love new life can come to be and be

---

[63] *Humanae Vitae,* Par. 4. In this connection, see above p. 71.
[64] Ibid., par. 6.

fostered (paragraph 8). This love is human, a compound of sense and spirit, it is not then merely an expression of natural instinct or an emotional drive—but it is an act of free will. It is total, it is a sign of the generous sharing of all things by the partners, it is faithful and exclusive, and it is creative because it looks forward to new life (paragraph 9). Responsible parenthood therefore must be properly understood—it must have regard to the nature of human biology, to the power of reason and will over emotions and to the physical, economic, psychological and social conditions relevant to responsible parenthood—to the having of a large family or to restricting family size for a given or even an indeterminate period. This responsible parenthood must be guided by an objective moral law and a right conscience as a true interpreter of that law. Such responsibilities involve duties towards God, to the parents themselves, to their families and to society (paragraph 10), hence the partners are not free to do as they like in the service of transmitting life: God's laws are paramount. As God planned it, the infertile period means that fertility can be controlled but in any use of marriage whatever there must be no impairment of the natural capacity of sex to produce new life (paragraph 11).

The reason for this is that the marriage act is both unitive and potentially procreative. Just as reason can see that for one partner to force the use of marriage on the other without regard to his or her reasonable wishes is to deprive the act of its nature as a loving union, so it is equally unreasonable to use the divine gift of sexual love while depriving it of its potential for new life. Man does not have unlimited power over his sexuality; it is so closely connected with the creative action of God that it must be treated with special reverence (paragraphs 12, 13). And its loving and its procreative potential must both be respected at all times. Equally to be condemned, with abortion and sterilization, is

> [paragraph 14] . . . any action which either before, at the moment of, or after sexual intercourse, is specifically intended to prevent procreation —whether as an end or a means. . . .

The wrong use of the principle of totality or the principle of the lesser of two evils in this context is rejected. A moral evil may not be done in order that good may come of it. Contraceptive intercourse is intrinsically wrong;[65] the contraceptive effects of lawful medical treatment, however,

---

[65] The concept of "intrinsic immorality" has been challenged because it has been taken to mean that the immorality of an evil act can automatically be imputed to the agent. This is not so. If freedom or knowledge are seriously impaired *through no fault of the agent*, then imputability can be lessened, indeed be non-existent. The operative phrase is that in italics. Ignorance can be culpable. Lack of freedom can likewise result from past actions for which the agent is responsible. See above p. 79 ff.

since they are not directly intended, are not condemned. Equally, the use of the safe period to regulate birth for good reasons is morally acceptable (paragraphs 14, 15, 16). It cannot be denied that there is difficulty in this teaching. There is an element of self-denial in it and the Christian in marriage needs grace to aid reason and free will in making sure that married love conforms to right order. But self-discipline of this kind, if properly understood, far from hindering true love, can help it to develop (paragraph 21).

In the context of the current debate about contraception, birth control and family planning, the Catholic teaching is that neither birth control nor family planning are of themselves immoral or undesirable. They can in fact be very moral and very desirable, according to the circumstances, if the means to control births and plan families are in accordance with the objective moral law and do not produce a contraceptive mentality. What the Church does insist upon is that any deliberate interference with the human power to procreate *at a time that procreation is possible*, is against the law of God.

The use of the infertile times is the use of something which is God-given. The nature of the bodies God has given us makes it impossible for a woman to conceive at certain times and this provides married couples with a means of expressing their love even though they do not want conception for good reasons. *Accepting* a thing which we *cannot* change is one thing. No amount of human intervention would make the female body fertile when nature does not allow it. But *to intervene and take away the body's power to conceive* in order that sexual intercourse may be had without the responsibility of conception and birth is quite another matter. The importance then between accepting a thing we could not change, and causing it to happen by deliberate intervention, is logically as well as theologically clear. To use an example from another context—we will all one day die, we cannot prevent that happening. But the fact that each one of us will one day die does not mean that we can anticipate the inevitable and kill whom we choose. It is one thing to accept that another will die, it is quite another to cause that death.

Neither is the use of the infertile period a "Catholic" method of contraception. During the infertile period, conception could not take place, hence, no act at that time would be contraceptive—you cannot by human intervention prevent conception when conception is impossible anyway. Making full use of the powers of reason that God has given us then means that we need ways of ensuring that married couples are capable of expressing their love in a manner which accords with their emotional and psychological needs, the biological laws God has implanted in their bodies, and the natural law which is the right use of reason in all things human.

That the nature of the female reproductive cycle enables control of fertility without abuse of married love has been known since Old Testament times,[66] but it was not until 1923 that Dr. K. Ogino began an attempt to put natural family planning on a sound scientific basis with the calendar rhythm method. Twenty years later the knowledge of the significance of the rise in temperature that takes place around the time of the ovulation period helped make the planning of pregnancy more precise, while about the same time the observable variations in the cervical mucus, and in the position and consistency of the cervix itself were discovered to be of value to the same end.[67]

Currently there are two methods of natural family planning which are found particularly effective. The first is the Billings or ovulation method—based on the observation of the changes in the consistency of cervical mucus.[68] The second—the symptothermal method—combines these observations with others—intermenstrual pain and changes in the basal body temperature.[69]

There is increasing evidence, some would say overwhelming, that these natural methods of family planning are as effective as the use of artificial methods. They are certainly more in accord with the dignity of woman and the respect for her body. It is considerations such as these that make others, apart from Catholics, value the natural way.[70] If we can talk of an ecology of the human body, then artificial birth control is as destructive of it as natural family planning is protective. Natural family planning is in fact a method of family planning truly so called—since it can be used to achieve as well as to avoid pregnancy.

A very valuable aspect of N.F.P. (natural family planning) is that it involves both partners so intimately in a deeper knowledge of their bodies and their needs—it cannot work except through full and loving co-operation. As an inevitable by-product then it brings greater love, mutual

[66] Dr. H. P. Dunn, M.D., in *A Reader in Natural Family Planning* (Collegeville, Minnesota: Human Life Center, 1978), 2nd ed., no. 1, p. 25.

[67] Fr. A. Zimmerman, S.V.D. in *A Reader in Natural Family Planning*, p. 153.

[68] This is the method developed by Dr. J. J. Billings and his wife, Dr. Lyn Billings. See Dr. J. J. Billings, *The Control of Life* (Dunedin, New Zealand, 1975), *Atlas of the Ovulation Method* (Melbourne, 1979), 3rd ed. E. L. Billings and A. Westmore, *The Billings Method: Controlling Fertility without Drugs or Devices* (London, 1981). See also the papers in J. N. Santamaria and J. Billings, *Human Life and Human Love* (Melbourne, 1979).

[69] Dr. J. Roetzer, "Basics of the Symptothermal Method", *A Reader in Natural Family Planning*, no. 1, pp. 11 ff.

[70] *A Reader in Natural Family Planning*, pp. 7, 80, 116.

respect and understanding. It does involve a degree of periodic abstinence, but it is the testimony of the married couples who have used it and teach it to others that such abstinence is not harmful—quite the contrary, it is also compatible with expressions of physical love short of intercourse which, properly controlled, are effective as signs of tenderness during periods of abstinence.[71]

The effectiveness of the methods in terms of controlling pregnancy seem well attested. According to Mrs. Manion, a nurse and a teacher of N.F.P., a 100% record can be achieved with sympto-thermal methods.[72] Those who have worked in underdeveloped countries testify that natural methods can be taught to those with little education and living in difficult conditions. Sister Lucille Levasseur[73] tells of her success in instructing in it in her work in Fiji and Fr. Denis St. Marie of similar success with the ovulation method in El Salvador.[74] The World Health Organization[75] is evaluating natural methods from a purely technical standpoint.

An institution within the Catholic Church which under its original director, Fr. Paul Marx, O.S.B., did much to provide an effective focus for highly skilled medical expertise and the moral and spiritual forces of the Church to work together on this matter is the Human Life Center, St. John's University, Collegeville, Minnesota. It has organised conferences and published an *International Review of Natural Family Planning* in which medical experts and those experienced in propagating N.F.P. write on the issues involved.

In view of the evidence that N.F.P. is gaining acceptance on medical[76] as well as moral grounds, it is unfortunate that Fr. Bernard Haering

[71] Ibid., pp. 101 ff., the paper entitled "A Real Sexual Revolution" by Robert and Mary Joyce, who are writers and philosophers, is an outstanding presentation of the significance of N.F.P. The Couple to Couple League which works in many American dioceses was started by a married couple as a means of enabling married people better to understand the method and its advantages. Family Life Association exists in many countries. Ibid., p. 138 ff.

[72] Ibid., p. 72.   [73] Ibid., p. 54.

[74] Ibid., p. 56. In Santamaria and Billings, op. cit., pp. 229 ff., Mother Teresa tells how she persuaded the Indian government to let her provide N.F.P. facilities rather than sterilization for her poor people and how N.F.P. worked in controlling pregnancies.

[75] *A Reader in Natural Family Planning*, p. 146.

[76] There is in England, for example, a Natural Family Planning Centre at Birmingham Maternity Hospital's Department of Gynaecology. It is recognized by the Central Mid-wives' Board and the dean of postgraduate medical studies at Birmingham. It helps train overseas as well as British personnel and is cooperating with the World Health Organization's programme. A National Association of Ovulation Method Instructors was formed in Brixton, England in 1978 to teach and promote the Billings method. Programmes have been held in various centres and teachers take the World Health Organization/Billings agreed examination. Mr. K. Platt, 211 Brighton Road, Croydon, Surrey, England, organises the work in England.

should have given publicity to the view that N.F.P. increases the number of malformed children, when his grounds for doing so are scientifically shaky. Dr. Joseph Roetzer, M.D., an Austrian doctor active in N.F.P. work and assistant Professor of Pastoral Medicine at the Theological College of St. Poelton has shown that Haering based his objections on the findings of Rodrigo Guerrero and Oscar Rojas[77] which later research revealed were "largely false".[78] The fact is that N.F.P. finally removes any pragmatic grounds that were for objection to *Humanae Vitae*.

Natural family planning fulfills the requirements of true sexual love in marriage, uniting the couple in a deeper understanding of one another and of the mystery of their sexuality. It demands both a coming to terms with the excesses to which sexuality is prone while, at the same time, enabling married couples to enjoy to the full the loving and reasonable use of the power God has given them. It frees the woman particularly from dependence on drugs and the indignity of chemical and other mechanical means of avoiding conception. It does all this within the context of the Church's teaching and safeguards and strengthens the foundations of marriage and human dignity.

To sum up. The Holy See insists that the teaching it puts forth is a "right reason" teaching, one that conforms with man's natural moral sense. Natural law, as we saw, is a participation in the eternal law; it is therefore fundamentally a thing of the mind, of right reason. At the same time it is right reason applicable to man's life in this world; man is both soul and body; one of the obligations of his reason, therefore, is to reflect on the way the body God has given him works and the laws which are in it—laws of nature (as distinct from natural law) in the sense of basic tendencies and powers built into the structure of physical life itself. Hence natural law, right reason morality, when it is applied to those aspects of human life which concern the operation of biological laws, laws of physical nature, must conform its "right reason" judgements to the logic of the human body itself.

In appealing to us to respect biological laws, therefore, the magisterium is not confusing natural law (right reason) with the law of nature (physical law, biological law in this case). It is simply saying that the *subject matter*

[77] Their findings were published in the *New England Journal of Medicine*, September 1975, pp. 573–75. Dr. Roetzer's discussion of the whole matter is published in translation in *A Reader in Natural Family Planning*, no. 1, pp. 117 ff. The Chief of the Contraceptive Development Branch at the Center for Population Research, National Institute of Child Health and Human Development, Bethseda, Maryland, U.S.A., has confirmed that their researches into N.F.P. reveal no increased birth defects from its use (Letter to Dr. C. Norris, St. Vincent Medical Centre, Portland, Oregon; August 27, 1980; courtesy of Mr. K. Platt).

[78] Roetzer, op. cit., p. 123.

upon which *right reason* works must respect the plan and design of the Creator in so far as that plan works through physical law, including the biological. It must then reasonably account for the demands of love, of emotion and psychology, at the same time respecting the laws of physiology. It does this in saying that in the sexual act two things are involved—there is a unitive aspect, the love aspect, and the procreative aspect, and neither may ever be denied.

Those who come together in love then may do so when the body is fertile or when it is infertile and, if it is genuine, sincere love, then it is good and holy. But equally the means through which that love is expressed is a physical means, a biological means, a physical linking of two bodies. Since this is the case, those who use their bodies in this way must respect the power given to them at certain times to procreate because the joys of sex are inextricably linked with these procreative powers. If they wish to use sex at that time they may not deliberately intervene to prevent that power of procreation. But they may, for good reason (which excludes a "contraceptive" mentality—the continuing refusal to bear children for selfish motives) restrict their loving to times when conception is not possible. Once again this is not a Catholic form of contraception. It is not an act *against* conception (contra-ception). The whole point of it is to restrict intercourse to times when conception is not possible. To accept the naturally infertile times with gratitude is one thing. To intervene to destroy the power of the human body to procreate new life when it is possible is quite another.

It is not our purpose or function here to comment at great length on the reasons why some have chosen to reject the teaching of the Holy See on this matter,[79] but it is as well to note that those who reject it "because it is not infallible" cannot be sure that their argument holds.[80] A case can be made for saying that the specific teaching on the intrinsic evil of the individual contraceptive act, which is the most controversial aspect of the encyclical, is not proposed with the same fullness of authority that a formal *ex cathedra* exercise of the pope's extraordinary teaching authority implies. But the essential teaching as given by Paul VI in this document is not new but simply an application of principles which have been put beyond question by the authority of the ordinary magisterium of the Church which is, subject to certain conditions, infallible. Those conditions are given in *Lumen Gentium*:[81]

[79] The questionings of the papal teaching are reviewed in Peschke, op. cit., 2:475 ff. See also J. A. Komonochak, "Humanae Vitae and its Reception: Some Ecclesiological Reflections", *Theological Studies*, June 1978.

[80] John Ford and G. Grisez, "Contraception and the Infallibility of the Ordinary Magisterium", *Theological Studies*, June 1978.

[81] *Lumen Gentium*, par. 25.

Although the bishops, taken individually, do not enjoy the privilege of infallibility, they do, however, proclaim infallibly the doctrine of Christ on the following conditions: namely, when, even though dispersed throughout the world but preserving for all that amongst themselves and with Peter's successor the bond of communion, in their authoritative teaching concerning matters of faith and morals they are in agreement that a particular teaching is to be held definitively and absolutely.[40]

[40] Cf. Vatican Council I, Const. Dogm. *Dei Filius*, 3: Denz. 1712 (3011). Cf. the note added to schema I.*de Eccl*. (taken from St. Robert Bellarmine): Mansi 51.579C; also the revised schema of Const. II *de Ecclesia Christi*, with Kleutgen's commentary: Mansi 53, 313 AB. Pius IX Letter *Tuas Libenter* Denz. 1683 (2879).

The conditions, therefore, are four: 1) that the bishops remain in communion with one another and with the pope, 2) that they teach authoritatively on a matter of faith and morals, 3) that they agree in one judgement and 4) that they propose this judgement as one to be held definitively. The universality is fulfilled by a *moral* unity of the whole body of the bishops with the pope—not by *mathematical* unanimity. Neither does the lack of a present consensus among Catholic bishops on this matter, if it exists, nullify the judgement of the ordinary magisterium. The consensus of future bishops is not required for the Church to teach infallibly today. Neither is the present consensus of Catholic bishops required in order that infallible teachings of the past should be maintained.

On this understanding and interpretation of the ordinary magisterium then, for those who will accept no other authority to compel their assent, the document is infallible. As Noonan has shown,[82] until the recent controversy, no Catholic theologian, still less a bishop or group of bishops, has ever taught that contraception is an objectively good act. Down to the early 1960s the received Catholic teaching on contraception was universally proposed by Catholic bishops in communion with one another and with the successor of Peter. Those who reject the teaching of *Humanae Vitae* on the grounds that there is doubt whether the Pope was speaking infallibly must either accept that infallibility from the ordinary magisterium of the Church or be reduced to saying that the phrase "ordinary magisterium of the Church" is meaningless. If, unanimously, Catholic bishops, theologians and priests have been so wrong for so long on a matter of such importance then there is no aspect of Catholic teaching which can be trusted. This argument from consequences is one that the dissenters must answer. Yet it is not the reason why the teaching is to be accepted. That reason lies in the truth of the teaching, a truth which the

[82] J. T. Noonan, *Contraception: A History of Its Treatment by the Canonists and Theologians* (Harvard, 1965), p. 6. "No Catholic theologian has ever taught 'Contraception is a good act'."

Pope is determined to protect, as he made plain most notably to the 1980 Synod of Bishops.[83]

We cannot leave this question of the nature of Catholic moral teaching without paying some attention to the frequently made objection that since the Church's teaching has "changed" on central issues in the past, she could change here. Leaving aside the fact that the word "change" is used, by those who make this charge, to mean "contradict", we can look at the four cases quoted. Something is said below about the concept of development of doctrine which indeed does involve *change* but not *contradiction* in the teaching of the Church.

The four cases are: 1) usury, 2) slavery, 3) "no salvation outside the Church" and 4) the Galileo case. The latter has already been discussed in another context[84] where it was noted that since what was at issue here was a question of scientific fact on which the Church authorities as such had no competence to judge, errors of judgement made here cannot be used to invalidate her authority on matters of faith and morals where she does have that competence. Of the others, those of usury and slavery are more relevant in our context since they do concern moral issues. "No salvation outside the Church" is a dogmatic rather than a moral question, but it is useful to refer to it here.

All three of these cases are highly complex and involve many controversial historical as well as moral judgements. It does not, therefore, help to approach them with minds clouded by some of the sillier slogans of twentieth century theological polemics. Regarding usury for example, John Gilchrist[85] makes the point that if we are to understand Catholic teaching and its development, we must appreciate the process of clarification that went on in the historical context in which it occurred. In the central Middle Ages, when the terminology on this matter was developed, the Church was facing a new set of circumstances which required that she should maintain her moral objection to the taking of interest where it lead to injustice and to ensure that where it did not lead to such injustice it should be allowed. This was in accord with the scriptural tradition which condemned injustice in the making of money loans but did not deny the right of taking interest in principle.[86] Hence, when the canonists and theologians grappled with the problems of a more complex economy in the Middle Ages, the right to take interest on other than pure

---

[83] Address to the American Bishops at Chicago, 5 October 1979, in *U.S.A. Message of Justice, Love and Peace* (Boston, 1979), p. 183. Concluding address to the Synod of Bishops, 25 October 1980, (*L'Osservatore Romano* [English edition], 3 November 1980).

[84] See above pp. 37–38.

[85] See below p. 288.

[86] T. Divine, *Interest: An Analytical and Historical Study* (Milwaukee, 1959), pp. 8, 11.

money loans was upheld. Their terminology requires careful understanding, it is true. It is equally true that if their critics had been ready to give it that careful understanding, most of the accusations about what the Church did or did not teach would have been avoided.

These matters are discussed in more detail below.[87] Here we may simply note that since the scholastic theory on which the teaching of an encyclical like *Vix Pervenit* was based did not exclude at any time the legitimacy of making a profit on investment, it is an error to say that the Church changed her mind from saying that such interest or profit on money invested was wrong, to saying it was right. Interest taken on a pure money loan, on the other hand, remained as wrong in the eighteenth century as it had in the first.[88] But once it could be fairly assumed that anyone with money to lend was morally safe in taking the going rate of interest, that is to say, that the practice of taking that interest involved injustice to no one, then the cases which had agitated the minds of theologians and canonists, and the consciences of at least some businessmen of earlier days, were no longer relevant. But it is still possible to commit a sin of usury through charging excessive interest, or indeed any interest in the sort of circumstances that the Old Testament injunctions envisaged: those still exist in some parts of the world today.

The question of the Church's attitude to slavery needs to be approached with a similar appreciation of the changing historical circumstances and their implications. The world in which God revealed himself in the Old Testament was one in which slavery was a basic social institution, and it remained so throughout New Testament times. The Church, therefore, had to live with it; yet in both Testaments believers were instructed to treat their slaves as full personal equals in the moral and spiritual sense, whatever legal and personal status secular society gave them.[89]

From apostolic and through patristic times down to the twelfth century, there were two strands in the Catholic tradition regarding the attitude to slavery—both based on the scriptural teaching and practice. The one was to stress the proper ordering of the relationship between master and slave given that the institution was part of the scheme of things, the other was to lessen its hold on society through encouraging

---

[87] See below pp. 286 ff.

[88] L. Watt, *Usury* (Oxford, 1963), p. 33.

[89] J. F. Maxwell, *Slavery and the Catholic Church*, pp. 22–23, ". . . slavery among the Israelites was different from all other contemporary slavery; the Mosaic law lead in time to the humane treatment of all slaves." The New Testament texts taken together (e.g. Gal 3:26–28, Col 3:11; 3:22–4:1, Eph 6:5–9, 1 Tim 6:1–2, Tit 2:9–10, 1 Cor 7:20–24) show a tolerance of household slavery provided the relationship between masters and slaves is conformable with Christian belief and practice. The texts do not imply *any approval of slavery as an institution*; simply *the acceptance of a reality* that could not be at the time abolished.

emancipation.[90] From the twelfth century however, with the rediscovery of Aristotle's writings and of the corpus of Roman law, theologians and canonists had to grapple with some cogent arguments in favour of slavery in principle and also had laid before them a very carefully worked out account of justified slavery arising for example from capture in just wars, for crime or debt, the being born of a slave mother, the sale of oneself into slavery or the misfortune of having destitute parents.[91] For the reasons already given above,[92] the issue was largely one of speculative interest during the period of the most rapid and energetic development of theology in the twelfth and thirteenth centuries; medieval Europe had itself gradually eliminated slavery and the serfdom which replaced it was in its turn evolving into free labour. But in so far as they had cause to deal with slavery, the response of the theologians varied; the two elements in the Christian tradition regarding it remained apparent[93] as they remained apparent down to comparatively modern times. Ecclesiastical legislation allowed penal enslavement—ironically enough, one such crime so punishable was that of Christians selling their fellow Christians as slaves to the Muslims.[94] Increasingly, the popes and bishops were called on to prevent the enslavement of African Christians by their European co-religionists,[95] the latter arguing vehemently that this was a penalty they could be called upon to pay by being captured in a just war. Churchmen, with the best will in the world, were no match for the hard men of business seeking to make a profit. Other forms of *penal* enslavement were, however, still accepted—as for example that which made possible the provision of galley slaves for the Mediterranean naval squadrons, including those of the papal states.[96] Here convicted criminals could serve their time until discharge; non-Christian prisoners of war awaiting ransom were another source of supply as were those who had sold themselves into slavery. Such bondage was clearly different in kind from that which was visited upon the African—hunted, captured, taken away from family, culture and country, transported like cattle to the new world and there destined for a life-long plantation slavery. And though there was success in the new world in preventing the native Indians from being enslaved by the

[90] Ibid., pp. 30 ff.   [91] Ibid., pp. 44 ff.   [92] Ibid., p. 32.
[93] Ibid., p. 47. R. W. and A. J. Carlyle, *A History of Medieval Political Theory in the West*, 5:21 ff.
[94] Maxwell, op. cit., p. 48.
[95] Ibid., p. 55. R. Oliver and J. Fage, *A Short History of Africa*, (London, 1975), pp. 128 ff., mentions the appeals made by the African Christians to the popes in the sixteenth century: "several showed a personal concern . . . stern letters passed from Rome to Lisbon . . . the Portuguese government finally declared itself powerless to control its subjects in Angola", ibid., p. 130.
[96] Maxwell, op. cit., pp. 76 ff.

Portuguese and Spanish settlers who tried to use the older arguments in favour of the practice in circumstances where they were no longer even remotely applicable,[97] the scandal and the misery of the African slave trade remained.[98] It was to take the gradual erosion of the traditional economic and political support for the institution, and the need to open up the continent, before this problem could be tackled comprehensively and once for all.

A Catholic opinion critical of the traditional arguments justifying slavery developed from about 1570—not surprisingly one of the centres of such opinion was the Trinitarian Order, which was concerned with the work of ransoming slaves.[99] The Quaker movement against slavery which had such influence in the U.S.A. began in the 1760s[100] and the heroic efforts of the abolitionists in England and the U.S.A. had one great advantage over those who had opposed slavery on moral grounds in the past—the economic and political interest which had previously been strong in its favour were either weakened or divided. It was in England that the moves to outlaw slavery first had success and that success owed a great deal to the decline of the West Indian slave lobby at Westminster. By the end of the eighteenth century, competition and the decreasing effectiveness of slave labour were making the industry there less profitable, and the support for its interests was therefore undermined.[101] Once the slave trade had been outlawed by Parliament in 1807, Britain had a vested interest in preventing the trade continuing because it was so profitable that more legitimate forms of trade with Africa she wanted to develop could not do so until it was stopped.[102] The slave trade and slave labour had then been on the decline before the American civil war, but it was the effects of that war that finally ensured the practice which had disfigured the European record in Africa and the new world would cease. In America, it was the movement of the underlying political and economic forces against the institution which gave the abolitionists the hope and then the certainty of success. Free Americans realised that their freedom was at risk if they allowed the spread of slavery throughout the union. Free

[97] Ibid., pp. 63 ff.
[98] Ibid., pp. 78 ff., details the efforts of the Holy Office to use the traditional teaching to mitigate the evils of African slaving.
[99] Ibid., p. 90.
[100] Ibid., p. 91.
[101] The West Indies had another influence on the challenge to the institution. It was the habit of planters in bringing their slaves back to England which lead to radical Christians challenging the practice. In 1772 it was decided that there was no such thing as slavery in English law. It was then the tradition of personal freedom in English institutions which lead to the first notable victory of the abolitionist movement. Oliver and Fage, op. cit., p. 138.
[102] Ibid.

labour and slave labour could not exist side by side in a modern state.[103] With the victory of the North in the war, the last great market for African slaves went, and the trade was doomed.

In assessing the Church's attitude to the institution of slavery, then, we must keep in mind several things. In the first instance, the overwhelming reaction against it and of which we are still conscious was, as pointed out earlier,[104] the result of the European's shocked realisation that it was they, and Britain in particular,[105] which had developed the slave trade to the enormous proportions it reached. In the second place it was because Europeans had been able to call on an ideal of individual liberty and freedom (which was established in medieval Europe largely as a result of Christian influences through the Church) that when she finally roused herself against slavery in the eighteenth and nineteenth centuries, she had a sound secular ideological base for opposition to the institution as well as one theologically sound. In the third place we must note that in Latin America where the Church's influence was strong, she was far more effective in protecting the rights of slaves than were the more fragmented churches in North America.[106] Granted that she could no more have abolished slavery by formally condemning it outright than she

[103] "It took Lincoln a long time to make up his mind on slavery . . . but he became convinced that slavery, unless its spread was prevented, would become nation wide and, as Calhoun and Fitzhugh prophesied, eventually engulf the white labourer. Not until 1854 did Lincoln publicly denounce slavery on moral grounds . . . for Lincoln the slavery question was tied closely to the questions of union and democracy. In every recorded speech from 1854 to 1861 he repeated the warning that slavery might become national." R. B. Nye and J. E. Morpurgo, *The Growth of the U.S.A.* (London, 1965), 2:450.

[104] See above, p. 32.

[105] "By the 1960s, the demand for slaves in British colonies had become so great that Parliament threw open the traffic to independent merchants and traders . . . the stream of incoming slaves became so enormous (that) the annual flow of white servants was by 1710 virtually negligible. . . . What meaning had all this for the Negro. . . . The connection was intimate and direct: with the full development of the plantation there was nothing . . . to prevent unmitigated capitalism becoming unmitigated slavery . . . the condition of the bondsman's soul—a matter of much concern to church and civil authority in the Spanish colonies—was here quickly dropped from consideration. A series of laws enacted between 1667 and 1671 systematically removed any doubts whether conversion to Christianity should make any difference in status; henceforth it made none . . . there were no counterweights . . . (the personal rights of the slave) could not be sustained by the Church for the Church had little enough power and influence among its own white constituencies" (W. Elkins, *Slavery* [Chicago, 1971], 2nd ed., pp. 48–50).

[106] "In effect the Church on the one hand condemned slavery and with the other came to an understanding with the slave system . . . the Church, functioning in its capacity as guardian of morals, was responsible for whatever human rights were conserved for the slave . . . neither in Brazil nor in Spanish America did slavery carry with it such precise and irrevocable categories of perpetual servitude as in the United States . . . the presumption in these countries, should the status of a coloured person be in doubt, was that he was free

could have established the eight-hour work day by proclaiming it,[107] she put her influence where it could be most effective in serving the cause of those suffering as slaves. The way in which slavery was abolished makes it plain that until economic and political forces moved against it, moral and intellectual opposition to the institution would have had little or no effect. In the meantime the degree of success attained by the Church in mitigating the evils of the system where she had influence, remains the most remarkable positive achievement by any organisation which did not possess either the right to or the reality of effective political power.

To sum all this up—there was no more hope of abolishing slavery by the edict of some organisation whose only authority was moral in the nineteenth century than there had been in the first. Until the world had come to its senses on the matter by hard experience, the only effect of such a condemnation would have been to make it very difficult if not impossible for the Church to carry on doing the work that only she could do in mitigating the lot of slaves where she had the influence to do so. There were, as indicated above, two major strands in the Catholic tradition regarding the institution of slavery and both were Scripture-based. They enabled different responses to develop according to needs and situations. But it was not the nations in which the Church had an extensive nominal influence that kept the institution and its most terrible offshoot, the slave trade, alive. England and America bear that responsibility; only when they abandoned slavery did it die. The influence of the radical Christians, whose efforts did so much to bring this about, was a continuation of the undermining and destruction of the evil, which had begun in the early and the central Middle Ages through the Church's influence.

Finally, let us consider the question of "no salvation outside the Church". The argument here is that Boniface VIII (1294–1303), summing up and presenting an older teaching with greater force, asserted that there was no

---

rather than a slave" (ibid., pp. 71–72). Slaves could buy their freedom, or could be freed if they escaped and became Catholic in some circumstances. Similarly, a slave who had been too harshly punished could be freed by the magistrates and for performing meritorious acts he could likewise gain his freedom; fathers and mothers of large families could also be freed. Emancipation was regarded as a meritorious act in these countries also. The Church insisted on Christian marriage for slaves, and masters were compelled to have their slaves educated in the faith. From this education they learned of their equal dignity before God; in practical terms the Church could and did hold a watching brief for the proper treatment of baptized slaves. (Ibid., pp. 72 ff.) It is remarkable how Elkins' testimony to the practical influence of Christianity in improving the lot of the slaves in Latin America in the period in question tallies with the account given by W. H. Lecky in his *History of European Morals* ([London, 1911], vol. 2, p. 28, of how the Church achieved the same end in the first eight hundred years of her existence in Europe.

[107] Elkins, op. cit., p. 70.

salvation outside the Catholic Church.[108] Whereas now, after the Second Vatican Council, we are informed that there can indeed be salvation outside the Church. Therefore, the Church has erred on a major doctrinal issue.

In fact the two statements, while true, are incomplete and it is the incompleteness which can be thus used to support the contention that the teaching has contradicted itself. The assumption on which the first statement is based is that of formal heresy, that is to say willful and knowing rejection of the claims of Christ's Church. It was a statement conditioned by the experience of the Middle Ages when the enemies which surrounded Christendom were not only secular enemies but religious ones too. Whether it was the Norsemen sacking the monasteries or the Muslims with their Holy War, it seemed that anyone who attacked Europe militarily, was attacking her religiously also—they were not only enemies of the emergent Christendom as a secular power, but also enemies of the God in which Christendom believed. We now know that this was not an entirely correct way of looking at the matter. Further, we know how many millions today, and in former times, have never had the chance to know the fullness of God's self-revelation in Christ. Accordingly, we see how incomplete the statement is. Yet we must note what precisely it is that the Second Vatican Council says. It says that though there is salvation outside the Church yet those who "knowing that the Catholic Church was made necessary by God through Jesus Christ would refuse to enter her could not be saved";[109] there is, then, no contradiction between what was taught in the thirteenth century and what is taught now if the context of the teaching is understood. There is a greater subtlety of understanding of what was meant then and now. The teaching of Boniface VIII was true, that of Vatican II is nearer the whole truth.

The three cases, then, on which the claim that the Church changes (i.e. "contradicts") her teaching are on inspection seen to lack substance. They all in fact illustrate the importance of understanding correctly the concept of development of doctrine. Such developments have, as Newman pointed out,[110] four characteristics—one of which is that the original teaching is preserved however much the development based on it extends it and brings out new aspects. So with usury, the original objection to taking interest on money was a biblical one which warned against the injustices that such a practice can lead to. As the lengthier analysis of the teaching and its application given below shows, the teaching on usury had

[108] D. Knowles and D. Obolensky, *The Middle Ages*, p. 336.

[109] *Lumen Gentium*, par. 14.

[110] See J. H. Newman, *An Essay on the Development of Christian Doctrine* (London, 1909) part 2, chap. 5.

developed to accommodate the cases where it does not lead to injustice, while maintaining the moral objection to the practice where it does. Slavery, like usury, raises difficult historical and terminological questions. The starting point here is that the Christian tradition never accepted slavery as a good thing in itself, but found it one of the basic institutions of many of the societies in which it had to work down to modern times. The Christian teaching on the *nature and the dignity of man* by definition contradicted all that the classical theory of slavery and its practices implied. The teaching on the attitude to the *institution of slavery* had to take into account the realities of the world the Church lived in. The long term undermining of the institution could only be accomplished when the theory was discredited and the idea of personal freedom was as firmly embedded in the institutions of society as slavery had been. That the major influence in undermining the theory of slavery and establishing the practices which embodied personal freedom in Western society was the Church has been argued above; it has also been shown that, while slavery existed, the Church used her power and influence to mitigate the evils of the system in a very effective way. When the secular world finally came to its senses and abandoned the institution, she could say then that, far from having to change her teaching, it was the gradual working through in practice of the implications of that teaching that was a major influence leading to the abolition of that institution. Finally, an examination of the assumptions upon which it was stated in the fourteenth century that there was no salvation outside the Church and those upon which that same thing was said by the Vatican Council in the twentieth reveals that there is here no contradiction of the former teaching, only a different interpretation of the words "outside the Church". The former teaching is the truth, the latter is nearer the whole truth.

We can see, then, that to invoke these cases to advocate the inevitability of contradiction on another matter, the teaching on contraception, is not well-founded in theory or in fact. In the question of "no salvation outside the Church", a matter of dogmatic theology rather than moral, the unity of the Church's teaching is most clearly seen. Usury and slavery are social moral, social ethical, matters and hence more complex. Changing conditions made it more difficult to decide when the sin of usury was being committed. Regarding slavery—in theory and practice it contradicted the Christian dignity of man, but there was no way that the institution could have been opposed in principle until the secular world had come to its senses about the undesirability of it in practice. When it did so it did so above all because the Christian ideal of the personal freedom of every man had become embodied in the institutions of the Western world. To say that the Church over the years contradicted her teaching on usury and slavery is therefore wildly wrong: more—it is a line of argument which is so simplistic, so ready to cast complex historical and theoretical issues in the language of a particular kind of twentieth century theological polemic, that it discredits those who use it. And it is to be noted that it is also irrelevant to the contraception question. That is a matter of personal morality on which the issue has always been in theory and in practice extremely clear and precise in theological terms. There has never been any doubt in the minds of Catholic moralists and canonists about the nature of contraception; the usury issue, the one which most closely parallels that of contraception, is then doubly irrelevant in terms of the present debate on the latter.

There is one final comment that must be made before we leave this question of the Church's opposition to artificial methods of birth control, and that concerns its relevance to the population problem. The nature of that problem is discussed below;[111] here it may just be noted that to argue in favour of contraception *because* the need to control population growth is so great is to admit the principle of "the end justifies the means". The argument runs that "the population explosion must be controlled and, since contraception is a means of slowing it down, contraception is good". This line of argument ignores the fact that the same logic could justify infanticide, genocide and abortion. The truth is that evil may not be done that good may come of it. It would have to be proved in the first instance that contraception is a positive moral good, an act of a human being knowing it is in conformity with the mind of the Creator, in order that it may be advocated. The argument from consequences is not one that a Christian can invoke. Acts are good or bad in themselves according to the relationship to the law of God, not according to the degree to which they suit human convenience. The act of contraception is in fact wrong according to divine and natural law. Development on this matter must come from a presentation of the teaching in the context of more effective natural family planning. It cannot be used as a euphemism for the contradiction of sound moral principles.

III. MARRIAGE AS A SOCIAL INSTITUTION: THE FAMILY

A. THE COUNCIL ON THE FAMILY AND THE FAMILY AND SOCIETY TODAY

The personal commitment, the compact between two individuals that they will share their lives in fidelity and openness to new life through their sexual expression of love, is the basis of marriage as God ordained it, and

---

[111] See below pp. 344 ff.

as Christ instituted it as a sacrament. But this personal commitment is the basis of the family which in its turn is the foundation of society and its social structures.[112]

> The Christian family springs from marriage, which is an image and a sharing in partnership of love between Christ and the Church; it will show forth to all men Christ's living presence in the world and the authentic nature of the Church by the love and generous fruitfulness of the spouses, by their unity and fidelity, and by the loving way in which all members of the family co-operate with each other.

The family should, therefore, be a model of generous love and unity. It is the heart, not only of civil society, but even more fundamentally the heart of the Church. There is a very real sense in which the Christian sees his citizenship primarily in terms of his membership in the Church; secured in the life of grace and virtue through this, he can be a more effective and patriotic citizen of the civil state.

The exalted language of the text concerning every aspect of marriage as a social institution should not surprise us. What is being put before us is the high Christian ideal which every member of a family knows is rarely, if ever, achieved in all its aspects. But we are presumed to be looking for this ideal in our own family lives for the love of Christ, and it does us good to have that ideal put before us in all its almost unattainable beauty. In social terms, the family is to be the foundation of society because its bonds knit its members together in love as the firm base of the broader social unity. And it is the spiritual foundation of the family which is the source of its social strength because that foundation gives the motives and the means —grace—for the support of mutual love and help. Hence:[113]

> Children as living members of the family contribute in their own way to the sanctification of their parents. With sentiments of gratitude, affection and trust, they will repay their parents for the benefits given to them and will come to their assistance as devoted children in times of hardship and in the loneliness of old age. Widowhood, accepted courageously as a continuation of the calling to marriage, will be honoured by all.[8] Families will generously share their spiritual treasures with other families.
>
> [8] Cf. 1. Tim. 5.3.

St. Paul's observations on the natural rights and duties of the members of the family are relevant here.[114]

> Husbands should love their wives as Christ loved the Church and sacrificed himself for her. . . . Husbands must love their wives as their own bodies. . . . That is the way Christ heads the Church because it is his own

[112] *Gaudium et Spes*, par. 48.   [113] Ibid.
[114] Eph 5:25–33, 4:1–4.

body. . . . This mystery has many implications but I am saying it applies to Christ and his Church. . . . Each one of you must love his wife as he loves himself and let every wife respect her husband. Children be obedient to your parents that is your duty. . . . Honour your father and mother. . . . Parents, never drive your children to resentment but in bringing them up correct them and guide them as the Lord does.

It is around the parents that the life of the family revolves and it is largely in their power (provided they are given the help they need by Church and State) to determine whether the potentialities of the family in personal and social terms are achieved.[115]

> The family is, in a sense, a school for human enrichment. But if it is to achieve the full flowering of its life and mission, the married couple must practise an affectionate sharing of thought and common deliberation as well as eager co-operation as parents in the children's upbringing. The active presence of the father is very important for their training: *the mother too has a central role in the home, for the children, especially the younger children, depend on her considerably; this role must be safeguarded without, however, under-rating woman's legitimate social advancement.* The education of children should be such that when they grow up they will be able to follow their vocation, including a religious vocation, and choose their state of life with full con-sciousness of responsibility; and if they marry they should be capable of setting up a family in favourable moral, social and economic circumstances. It is the duty of parents and teachers to guide young people with prudent advice in the establishment of a family; their interest should make young people listen to them eagerly; and they should beware of exercising any undue influence, directly or indirectly, to force them into marriage or compel them in their choice of partner.

The stress here on the role of the wife as homemaker and mother must not, it is pointed out, be opposed to her legitimate social advancement. The balancing of these two ideals in an increasingly materialistic society is not easy and is by no means on the way to being solved. *Octogesima Adveniens*[116] paid some attention to this matter, noting that the equality of woman that the Church advocates does not mean

> . . . false equality which would deny the distinctions laid down by the Creator himself and which would be in contradiction with woman's proper role, which is of such capital importance, at the heart of the family as well as within society. Developments in legislation should, on the contrary, be directed to protecting her proper vocation and, at the same time, recognizing her independence as a person, and her equal rights to participate in cultural, economic, social and political life.

[115] *Gaudium et Spes*, par. 52.
[116] *Octogesima Adveniens* (London: C.T.S., 1971), par. 13.

This question of the woman's role in society and the need to see that she has the full liberty of human development, within and/or outside the family, is bound up with the difference between the sexes and the implications of that difference. It is also connected with the concept of the patriarchal family, of which more will be said in a moment.[117] Fundamentally, the question of "roles" is one of whether there is a specifically feminine quality of personality (whatever its basis), or whether the role that society has "forced" women into gives us an idea of that personality which is false and basically unjust to women.

It was argued by Lecky[118] that there are distinctively feminine characteristics and that Christianity raised them to a position of honour that they had not previously been given. The personal and social ideals of the Greeks were none of them (with the exception of conjugal fidelity) regarded as particularly feminine: like the Romans, the Greeks mainly admired and held up for admiration in women those qualities which made them more like men—qualities, for example, of physical courage; so the Amazons and the mother of the Gracchi were honoured for having overcome the weakness of their sex. Gentleness and love are among the virtues Lecky stresses as essentially feminine and to these Christianity gave full respect in their own right. He attributes to the influence that women consequently had in the Church and on it much of its success in converting Roman society: throughout history the example of wives and mothers strong in the faith was influential in determining the attitude of husbands and sons. The courage women showed in the face of persecution was no less than that of the men—but they triumphed through the strength of their gentleness and femininity fortified by belief in Christ, not in Amazonian or Stoic fortitude. They did not imitate men in their service of Christ; they knew that his appeal to them was precisely as women, and it was this that gave Christianity the power to achieve a new height of respect for their sex. Women were outstanding in their service of Christ also through works of charity and mercy, which call especially on the feminine virtues. Further, the Church's reverence for virginity and widowhood gave these aspects of womanhood and womanly virtues a special value in society, ensuring a greater appreciation of women and woman's role generally.

All this, it may be said by those who believe in the right of women to be treated and act in all things as men, was simply the result of social conditioning. If so, they are strangely apt to deny, or to hold in contempt, the attitude of the women themselves. It was because they saw in the

---

[117] See below pp. 167–68 where the Marx/Engels criticism of the patriarchal family is considered.

[118] Lecky, *A History of European Morals* (London, 1911), vol. 2, pp. 151–52.

Church and its values that which responded to their needs that they were attracted to it. One of the jibes sometimes made against the Christian religion is that is is "only for women". It is a jibe—but it has this truth in it, that many women find Christian beliefs and practices particularly helpful to them—as women.[119] Those who can only see in Christianity and its values a derogation of women are then in conflict with the countless women who see, and have seen, the situation quite differently.

That there are real differences of function and character between men and women which support the traditional Christian view that women's role as wife and mother is not to be given second place to whatever other roles she and society wish her to play, has been argued recently by an American sociologist. He claims that there has never been any society in which more than 7%, at a maximum, of the highest positions of authority have been held by women.[120] This, he suggests, is due not to male selfishness; what we know of the male/female differences in our endocrine structure makes it inevitable that men will usually play the dominant role;[121] this remains true, despite the many exceptions that show some women are the equals of men in exercising leadership in society. He uses language reminiscent of Lecky's regarding gentleness, kindness, love and life-sustaining abilities,[122] as womanly characteristics, as real and as necessary to society as are the harsher male virtues. On this analysis, women are equal but different: very many are happy to do the womanly things that mark them off from men. Insofar as they want a career, public service and the rest, it is not evident that the majority of these who make this choice see it as an alternative to marriage and homemaking.

The proper Christian understanding of the nature of woman created in God's image does not in fact justify any contradiction between her role as wife and mother and her desire for fulfillment in service of society in other ways. Yet in saying this, we know also that the physical and psychological

[119] Though Mary Kenny's *Why Christianity Works* is concerned to defend religion in general and Christianity in particular, rather than be a statement in defence of the properly understood Christian teaching on the role of women, it is apparent that for her that teaching is an essential bulwark of the dignity and rights of women. See chapters 5, 6, 8, 11 and 13 on "Women and the Sex Revolution", "Can Marriage Last?", "The Ecology of Contraception", "Feminism, Religion and the Virgin Mary" and "The Abortion Story".

[120] Steven Goldberg, *Male Dominance: The Inevitability of Patriarchy* (London, 1979), p. 61. The title is unfortunate; the thesis and research are sound.

[121] Ibid., pp. 86 ff.

[122] "In this and every other society [men] look to women for gentleness, kindness and love" (ibid., p. 221). He goes on, "In every society a basic male motivation is the feeling that women and children must be protected. But the feminist cannot have it both ways: if she wishes to sacrifice all this, all she will get is the right to meet men on male terms. She will lose."

differences between man and woman give them some potentialities which are correspondingly different. By the same token, however, we know that there are greater similarities than dissimilarities between the sexes; hence many more roles may be filled by both men and women.

The debate on the place of women in society is one that is bound to grow as society changes and job opportunities for women increase. Yet it would be foolish to deny that influences which encourage many women to take up some form of occupation outside the home[123] often have very little to do with the desire for fulfillment and a very great deal to do with sheer economic necessity. Society has a duty to see that the father of a family has the opportunity of earning a wage large enough to support himself and his family so that any neglect of the children and the home that is forced on the wife by the need to go out to work for purely economic reasons is removed. Parents, at the same time, have the duty to resist an excessive materialism which can lead the wife to go out to work to the neglect of her family responsibilities simply for the sake of procuring what are, properly considered, luxuries when compared with the more fundamental needs of home life.

Much of the present debate about women's role in society, therefore, is wrongly presented if it suggests that it arises entirely from the dissatisfaction of women with life as wives and mothers. The many who are completely happy with this role would be only too ready to give their full time to it if they were offered the opportunity of doing so. Yet there is no doubt either that there is a genuine and understandable resentment among many women that they are being denied opportunities simply because they are women. The problems differ from case to case. Some women manage to reconcile their roles as wife and mother with a full time career by choosing the time of marriage, child-bearing and rearing accordingly. But for many women the choice to be made is a difficult one. The unmarried state, even with all the "advantages" of a permissive society in which men and women can live together without the benefit of matrimony is still one chosen freely only by the minority. But marriage in which children are an expensive luxury, or even a burden (as they can be seen to be by women intent on job or career outside the home) falls somewhat short, to say the least, of the Christian ideal! Even in terms of society's needs it is unsatisfactory. A situation in which, because of social pressures

---

[123] The number of female employees increased by 1.5 million between 1961 and 1979, most of them part-timers and most of them with dependent children (H.M.S.O., *Social Trends*, no. 11 [1980], p. 72). The Census of Population in 1971 revealed 45% of women with one or two children working whole or part time; for those with two children the proportion working was 40%, with three, 35% and with four or more 30%. P. Abrams, *Work, Urbanization and Inequality* (London, 1978), p. 166.

and false social values, men and women are afraid to enter into the obligations of parenthood, or are prevented from discharging that responsibility with a sufficient degree of ease to encourage them to persevere, undermines the whole social fabric. Where the concept of motherhood is downgraded there is fear for the health and the future of any society.[124] The Council's reminder on the family as the basis of society is a timely one and becomes more timely with each succeeding year.[125]

> The family is the place where different generations come together and help one another to grow wiser and harmonize the rights of individuals with other demands of social life; as such it constitutes the basis of society.

The conclusion that must be drawn by all men of good will from this, the fundamental nature of the family's role in a healthy society, is clear:

> Everyone, therefore, who exercises an influence in the community and in social groups should devote himself effectively to the welfare of marriage and the family. Civil authority should consider it a sacred duty to acknowledge the true nature of marriage and the family and to protect and foster them, to safeguard public morality and promote domestic prosperity. The rights of parents to procreate and educate children in the family must be safeguarded. There should also be welfare legislation and provision of various kinds made for the protection and assistance of those who unfortunately have been deprived of the benefits of family life.

But, in practice, the civil authorities are encouraging the breakdown of the values that maintain stable family life. In Britain the 1971 Divorce Law Reform Act assumed that marriages had broken down when the parties had lived apart for more than two years and both wanted a divorce; it also allowed divorce at the petition of one partner against the wish of the other when they had lived apart for more than five years. The rise in divorce continues and the greatest increase in divorce was in the under-25s. Of those married in 1968, 11% had divorced within ten years, which is more than ten times the proportion of those married in 1953. Divorce is a disaster which affects children deeply; in 1975 the total affected was 202,475—145,000 under sixteen years old. Meanwhile, the breakdown in

---

[124] Dr. Penelope Leach, who is a wife and mother, insists that the ambivalence and the confusion of many women's liberation advocates on the subject of motherhood results in woman's role as mother either being held in contempt or seriously misunderstood. "Instead of making decent circumstances for creative motherhood a part of their package of demanded rights, many advocates of the women's movement have put motherhood on one side as a tiresome and irrelevant barrier to being exactly like men . . . a recent edition of a widely read women's liberation magazine described the full time care of a baby . . . as 'like spending all day every day in the exclusive company of an incontinent mental defective'," *Who Cares* (London, 1979), pp. 38–40.

[125] *Gaudium et Spes*, par. 52.

Christian values affects the attitude to marriage itself. The number of couples living without benefit of matrimony is not known but one recent report states that "everyone agrees it has risen considerably" and that in Sweden and Denmark more young people were living together outside of marriage than in it.[126]

Against this dismal background, it is chastening to remind ourselves that the Christian ideal of marriage was at one time accepted in theory at least in our culture. The love of the partners, modelled on the love of Christ for his Church, was meant to be lasting, and to be the stable foundation of society through a healthy family life. Unless there is some appeal other than to simple self-interest, society will not have that stable foundation. The effects of the 1971 Act were hardly envisaged. Whether the trend can be reversed now, however, is doubtful.

It is then clear that for the Council the family is the only secure basis for society. But it does not tie Catholic social ethics to any particular view of the sociology of the family and its structure, as both can develop according to need and circumstances. Like all other social institutions, the family is conditioned by the needs and influences which are present in society at a particular time, and sociological and historical research is indeed teaching us a very great deal about such conditioning and its effects.[127] The modern family in Western society today is predominantly a "nuclear" group of a man, his wife and children who have very little contact with aunts, uncles, cousins or grandparents, either because of increased social and geographical mobility, or because the parents of nuclear families were of small families themselves. Increased longevity plays its part too. The love and care required to look after an aged member of the family is sometimes not there; old people are not always welcome. Older generations, whether by choice, accident or necessity, were much more used to the extended family. Families were larger and mobility less marked. In speaking of the family as a place where the different generations come together, the Council clearly envisages that the benefits of the extended family should be available to all. But whether this is the norm in a particular society

[126] "The Breaking Bonds of Matrimony", New Society, 8 March 1979, commenting on H.M.S.O., Changing Patterns in Family Formation and Dissolution in England and Wales (1979). The Order of Christian Unity, Torn Lives (1979), puts the number of children affected much higher—close to one million. J. Wallerstein and J. Berlin, Surviving the Breakup (London, 1980), is a study of how children and parents cope with divorce, and though based on American experience, it has important lessons for other countries too. Its overwhelming message is the ill effect of divorce on children.

[127] See International Encyclopedia of the Social Sciences, vol. 5, s.v. "Family". E. Shorter, The Making of the Modern Family (London, 1976). Also L. Mair, Marriage (London, 1971). R. Fletcher, The Family and Marriage in Britain (London, 1971). G. R. Leslie, The Family in the Social Context (O.U.P., 1976).

or not, the Christian ideal, based as it is on the equal partnership of man and wife, remains the same. Indeed where the nuclear model prevails, the Christian ideal is of more importance than ever since the parents and children depend even more on one another.

B. THE SCRIPTURES, THE PATRIARCHAL FAMILY AND MODERN NEEDS

The Christian concept of the family, whether it is in practice on the nuclear or extended models, is patriarchal in the sense that the father is the head of the family. The Genesis account of the creation of man and woman and their complementarity in marriage indicates that this was the pattern that God intended. Marriage and the patriarchal family in the Old Testament differs in practice from the later refinements brought about by cultural developments, and, above all, by the effect of the Christian dispensation. The family in the Old Testament initially was patriarchal in the wider sense—a tribal structure of many families under one head. [128] Society was in a pre-political stage in which the leader of the tribe performed those functions that elected or inherited political leadership conferred in more developed social organisations with proper political structures. This patriarchy underwent several stages of development, but as it gave way to kingship, and as individualism grew among the people of God, the individual family unit remained patriarchal on the Genesis model. Monogamy, though not always the practice, was the norm to which the people were being led, and the outstanding examples of married life in the Old Testament were of monogamy and fidelity.

In Jewish society the patriarchal and monogamous family performed several functions essential for a healthy society. The prophets especially emphasized that before the state there was the family—which exists to secure certain social and personal needs, namely the regulation of sex, the regulation of property and the regulation of youth. [129] The prophets saw anything which undermined the family's rights in any of these matters as contrary to sound community life. Echoes of this teaching are detectable in *Gaudium et Spes*, particularly in the question of education or regulation of the young and a proper understanding of the place of sex in human life. [130] As we shall see when we come to consider economic ethics, the

[128] R. de Vaux, O.P., *Ancient Israel* (London, 1961), chaps. 1, 2.

[129] J. H. Chamberlayne, *Man in Society: The Old Testament Doctrine* (London, 1966), p. 122.

[130] "It is imperative to give suitable and timely instruction to young people above all in the heart of their own families about the dignity of married love, its role and its exercise. In this way they will be able to engage in honourable courtship and enter upon marriage of their own." *Gaudium et Spes*, par. 49.

idea that a family should own property in order to provide security is a central one in the Church's thinking, although it is recognized that other forms of providing that security are today available.

The New Testament concept of the family was patriarchal also. The picture we have of Joseph, the responsibility he took for his wife before the birth of the child, the planning and execution of the flight into Egypt and the instructions given to him about what course he should follow mark him out as head of this little group.[131] The same concept is reflected very closely in St. Paul's teaching on the sacrament, especially the key passages in Ephesians, chapter 5, which have already been quoted as of such importance in the development of the Christian theology of marriage.

In this type of family Christ himself grew up and throughout his ministry he showed the deepest interest and highest regard for it. His appreciation and respect for children is one of the most endearing characteristics of the Gospels.[132] For the duties of children towards their parents he had high standards. He repudiated with scorn the deceit by which, in the name of religion, a son was allowed to escape his obligation to his needy parents. For a son merely to declare that the funds needed for their support were to be regarded as dedicated to God in order to absolve himself from all filial responsibility was dismissed as the hypocrisy it was.[133] He portrays the idea of forgiveness in the welcome home given by a father to a wayward son.[134] Christ used family relationships to illustrate his religious and ethical teachings; he taught us to think of God as father and he expected that his disciples should deal with one another as brothers.[135]

On the other hand, in other ways he seems to have been less enthusiastic about family life. He himself never married and when directly questioned by his disciples as to whether or not it was better to marry, he replied that not everyone could accept the option of not marrying, "only those to whom it is granted."[136] He was aware of the dangers of blood ties, and seems at times to have spoken rather harshly to his mother when there appeared to be a question of his determination to do his Father's will.[137] He even went so far as to say that he had come to set a man at variance with his close relatives, and that unless a man was prepared to hate his own

[131] Mt 2:13–23.
[132] Mk 9:32–37, 10:13–16. Mt 18:1–8.
[133] Mk 7:9–13.
[134] Lk 16:11–12.
[135] Mt 18:15–35.
[136] Mt 19:11.
[137] Lk 2:49.

family and his own life, he could not be his disciple.[138] The fact is that family love and family life can take us away from God if it becomes a good to which all else is sacrificed. God, not family, comes first, and much family love can be disordered. Mothers can love their children possessively, exclusively and in a disordered way, simply seeing them as extensions of their own personality and need. Fathers too can love excessively, spoiling wives and children with too much ease and comfort and making them selfish. Children can be too attached to their parents for selfish motives, not wishing to make their own decisions as they grow older and have responsibility for their own lives.

The message of Christ, therefore, is that family life is not without its dangers. Like all God's gifts, it can be abused through human selfishness, made an enemy to the ideal God has given us by our waywardness. But if we turn to the model of how patriarchy, the family in which man is the head, is to work, we find in it none of those marks of male selfishness or female oppression which it is being charged today are inseparable from such a model. It is a headship modelled on Christ's love for his Church and of a man's love for his own body, his own self. From the beginning marriage was intended to be an equal partnership as the Genesis account showed. As the results of original sin took effect, that ideal of man and woman as partners in marriage was damaged as was everything else about life, but it can be restored by grace through Christ. And the sacrament of marriage is intended to do that for the man/woman relationship in the family. Any use of the concept or the reality of patriarchy as the model of Christian marriage which does not keep in mind the Genesis account of the equality and interdependence of the partners, and the reaffirmation of this relationship in the terms used by St. Paul, is alien to its real nature and intent.

Patriarchy in this sense has continued to be and is the ideal of marriage held forth by the Church. *Gaudium et Spes* did not stress it because it was not setting forth an exhaustive teaching on marriage, but only looking at specific questions.[139] For a fuller teaching on this matter we can look at *Casti Connubii,* Pius XI's encyclical, to which the Council referred in many places.

Casti Connubii reasserts the teaching of St. Paul on the analogy between Christ's headship of the Church and the man's role in marriage and that the obedience owed by the wife to the husband cannot accordingly be one that denies her personal equality or full responsibility in love and care for the family. Nor does it deny that conditions of time and place affect the way in which the relationship between man and wife in marriage on this

138 Mt 10:35-37.
139 *Gaudium et Spes*, par. 47.

model is expressed. It insists, however, on the primacy of the husband, properly understood: "the structure of the family and its fundamental law, established and confirmed by God, must always and everywhere be maintained intact."[140]

That the concept has been misused to justify un-Christian attitudes on the part of men and society there is no doubt. The way in which Victorian England treated its women is taken by many as an indication of such misuse. There are dangers, then, in misunderstanding what patriarchy in the Christian sense is really about—but the teaching of St. Paul in Ephesians, chapter 5, is essential to the Christian marriage, and it must therefore be understood properly.

Discontent with the patriarchal family (in the full Christian sense) is no longer simply one based on a cultural reaction against excesses and which could come to terms with an institution which has served us so well, once the necessary readjustments have been made. There is, on the contrary, a current of ideological opposition to the Judaeo-Christian concept of the family which is detectable in elements in the women's liberation movement, and that objection finds its inspiration in Communism.

The basis of the attack is work done by an American scholar in the nineteenth century,[141] work which took Marx's interest and led him to make extensive notes on his book. Engels later took these notes and used them as a guide in writing the *Origins of the Family, Private Property and the State*[142] of which the argument is that forms of family based on mother right had existed at one time, but that as civilisation developed, so too did private property; this institution came more and more under the control of the men whose new power enabled them to replace mother right with father right, to introduce patriarchy and all that it implies. The emancipation of women and their equality with men is then impossible so

---

[140] "On Christian Marriage", par. 29 of the translation in *The Church and the Reconstruction of the Modern World* (T. P. McLaughlin, ed. [New York, 1957]).

[141] Lewis Morgan, *Ancient Society: Researches into the Lines of Human Progress from Barbarism to Civilisation* (London, 1877).

[142] See R. N. Carew Hunt, *The Theory and Practice of Communism*, pp. 95 ff. The influence of Engels' work is apparent in, for example, R. Delmar's contribution to A. Oakley and J. Mitchell, *The Rights and Wrongs of Women* (London, 1976). Delmar notes the distance travelled since Engels' book made an appearance—but approves it "for asserting women's oppression as a problem of history" (ibid., p. 287). Assert it he may have done; prove it he did not. As Goldberg points out, the failure of evidence led to the abandonment of the Engels' thesis by most social scientists. "George Murdoch's *Social Structure* (New York, 1949, pp. 184–207) exposes Engels' assumptions as not only unjustified but inarguably incorrect." (S. Goldberg: *Male Dominance*, p. 32 ff.) To be fair to the man, Engels never claimed to have anything as hard as *evidence* for his theory: "As to how and when this revolution (i.e. of mother right to father right) took place, we have no knowledge. It falls entirely in pre-historical times." (*Origins of the Family* [London, 1940], p. 58).

long as women are excluded from socially productive work and so are dependent on their husbands. The conflict of the sexes is based on the possession of private property and will only disappear when that institution is abolished.

As with so much that is in Marx/Engelism, there was a core of truth and plausibility about an extreme thesis. The late nineteenth century was a time when women were becoming economically more emancipated as more opportunities for economic independence came their way; Morgan's and Engels' thesis seemed to be being confirmed by the experience of everyday.

Closer inspection of the realities shows the weakness of the theory. The attempt to explain the patriarchal family and the subjection of women in purely economic terms and to base the proof on "prehistorical" evidence is self-evidently unsound. What is pre-history cannot be invoked as historical proof. Further, the vagueness of the alternative to the family is lacking in conviction. So also is the argument for its inevitable disappearance as economic conditions change.[143] And Engels' suggestion that romantic love would be the only basis for marriage[144] has destructive consequences that would undermine society itself.

There is, in truth, no reason why the greater economic and social emancipation of women should not be reconciled with the true ideal of Christian patriarchy, based as it is on equality of partnership, the ideal of Christ's love for his Church. Those who truly believe in the message of the Scriptures, of Christ and his Church, will welcome conditions which offer women the fullest opportunities of personal development in or out of marriage. As to a replacement for the patriarchal family, it is extremely difficult, even in purely practical secular terms, to see what can replace it. The security and assurance which the child of a monogamous and patriarchal family enjoys provide the ideal conditions for developing the spirit of responsible freedom, with all the benefits it brings to the individual and society. It can be no accident that the Jewish people, whose

---

[143] "What we can now conjecture about the way in which sexual relations will be ordered after the impending overthrow of capitalist production is mainly of a negative character. . . . What will there be new? That will be answered when a new generation has grown up: a generation of men who never in their lives knew what it was to buy a woman's surrender with money or with any other social instrument of power . . . when these people are in the world, they will care precious little about what anybody thinks they ought to do, they will make their own practices and correspondingly public opinion . . . and there will be an end of it." *Origins of the Family*, p. 89.

[144] "If only marriage based on love is moral, then also only the marriage in which love continues. But the intense emotion of individual sex love varies very much in duration . . . especially among men. And if the affection comes to an end or is supplanted by a new passionate love, separation is a benefit . . . only then will people be spared having to wade through the useless mire of a divorce case." *Origins of the Family*, loc. cit.

concept of family life is precisely the biblical one, have shown such resilience and contributed in so many ways to the development of human culture. The energy and vigour of the European peoples, which have done so much to show man how to conquer his environment, physically and intellectually, have been similarly fostered.[145]

A consideration of what the true Christian patriarchal model involves in theory, the condition, that is, for its success in practice, demonstrates the nobility and value of its ideal. The husband takes on much responsibility beyond merely providing for the physical needs of the household. His is the responsibility for their spiritual, moral and physical well-being and one that can only be discharged through a genuine love and care for all entrusted to him. In his role as head of the family he needs the active support and initiative of his wife in those many areas where she is more competent than he. For her part, the wife is the centre of love; she can inculcate the civilised and moral virtues, especially as an example of Christian womanhood to her daughters and in inducing in her sons respect for womanhood. Children learn to obey and accept discipline in return for the love and care that their parents bestow upon them. Parents must see the children God has given them as persons in their own right, not as extensions of their, the parents, personalities. These are the demanding ideals of the family, the model society, the nucleus of all society. It is one that comes with the true understanding of patriarchy in the framework of Christian spiritual and moral values. It bespeaks above all the personal equality of the husband and wife and their readiness to develop in their children a sense of their own dignity and responsibilities accordingly as sons and daughters of God.

C. EDUCATION: THE ROLE OF PARENTS, CHURCH AND STATE

The education of children is primarily the responsibility of the parents and the family—especially in what regards religious and moral instruction. But more general education, and the supplementing of its religious and moral aspects, involve the Church and the state also.[146] Parents, Church and state, therefore, have overlapping rights and duties and each must

---

[145] L. Dewar, *Moral Theology in the Modern World* (London, 1964), p. 119. V. A. Demant, *Christian Sex Ethics: An Exposition* (London, 1964), pp. 90 ff.

[146] Education systems, and the problems that come in managing or improving them, vary so widely with different cultures and countries, that beyond stating the general principles from the Council's teaching, it would be futile to attempt further comment. On the British system, R. King, *Education* (London, 1971), and I. Reid, *Sociological Perspectives on School and Education* (London, 1978). M.P. Hornsby Smith, *Catholic Education* (London, 1978) looks at the Catholic system in this context.

respect those of the other two. The question is dealt with in the Council's decree *Gravissimum Educationis*.

> 3. As it is the parents who have given life to their children, on them lies the gravest obligation of educating their family.[11] They must therefore be recognized as being primarily and principally responsible for their education. The role of parents in education is of such importance that it is almost impossible to provide an adequate substitute. It is therefore the duty of parents to create a family atmosphere inspired by love and devotion to God and their fellow-men which will promote an integrated, personal and social education of their children. The family is therefore the principal school of the social virtues which are necessary to every society. It is therefore above all in the Christian family, inspired by the grace and the responsibility of the sacrament of matrimony, that children should be taught to know and worship God and to love their neighbour, in accordance with the faith which they have received in earliest infancy in the Sacrament of Baptism.

[11] Cf. Pius XI, Encycl. *Divini Illius Magistri*, pp. 50 ff., Encycl. *Mit Brennender Sorge*, 14 March 1937; also Pius XII, *Allocutio* to Ital. Cath. Teachers, 8 Sept. 1946: *Discorsi e Radiomessagi*, vol. 8, p. 218.

But the family needs the support of society in its demanding role; the same paragraph continues:

> The task of imparting education belongs primarily to the family, but it requires the help of society as a whole. As well as the rights of parents, and of those others to whom the parents entrust some share in their duty to educate, there are certain duties and rights vested in civil society inasmuch as it is its function to provide for the common good in temporal matters. It is its duty to promote the education of youth in various ways. It should recognize the duties and rights of parents, and of those others who who play a part in education, and provide them with the requisite assistance. In accordance with the principle of subsidiarity, when the efforts of the parents and of other organizations are inadequate it should itself undertake the duty of education, with due consideration, however, for the wishes of the parents. Finally, insofar as the common good requires it, it should establish its own schools and institutes.[13]

[13] Cf. Pius XI, Encycl. *Divini Illius Magistri*, p. 63 ff.; Pius XII, Radio Message, 1 June 1941: AAS 33 (1941) p. 200; *Allocutio* to Cath. Teachers, 8 Sept. 1946: *Discorsi e Radiomessagi*, vol. 8, p. 218; re: principle of subsidiarity, cf. John XXIII, Encycl. *Pacem in Terris*, 11 April 1963: AAS 44 (1963) p. 294.

The basic educational institutions, therefore, are of the greatest importance as is the role of the educator.

> 5. . . . the school[19] . . . in nurturing the intellectual faculties which is its special mission . . . develops a capacity for sound judgement and introduces

the pupils to the cultural heritage bequeathed to them by former generations. It fosters a sense of values and prepares them for professional life. By providing for friendly contacts between pupils of different characters and backgrounds, it encourages mutual understanding. Furthermore it constitutes a centre in whose activity and growth not only the families and teachers but also the various associations for the promotion of cultural, civil and religious life, civic society, and the entire community should take part.

Splendid, therefore, and of the highest importance is the vocation of those who help parents in carrying out their duties and act in the name of the community by undertaking a teaching career. This vocation requires special qualities of mind and heart, most careful preparation and a constant readiness to accept new ideas and to adapt the old.

[19] Cf. Pius XI, Encycl. *Divini Illius Magistri*, p. 76; Pius XII, *Allocutio* to Assoc. of Cath. Teachers of Bavaria, 31 Dec. 1956; *Discorsi e Radiomessagi*, vol. 18, p. 746.

From the assertion that responsibility for the education of children rests primarily on the parents, the conclusion that the latter have a right to freedom of choice in education follows.

6. Parents, who have a primary and inalienable duty and right to the education of their children, should enjoy the fullest liberty in their choice of school. The public authority, therefore, whose duty it is to protect and defend the liberty of the citizens, is bound according to the principles of distributive justice to ensure that public subsidies to schools are so allocated that parents are truly free to select schools for their children in accordance with their conscience.[20]

But it is the duty of the state to ensure that all its citizens have access to an adequate education and are prepared for the proper exercise of their civic rights and duties. The state itself, therefore, should safeguard the rights of children to an adequate education in schools. It should be vigilant about the ability of the teachers and the standard of teaching. It should watch over the health of the pupils and in general promote the work of the schools in its entirety. In this, however, the principle of subsidiarity must be borne in mind, and therefore there must be no monopoly of schools which would be prejudicial to the natural rights of the human person and would militate against the progress and extension of education, and the peaceful coexistence of citizens. It would, moreover, be inconsistent with the pluralism which exists today in many societies.[21]

[20] Cf. III Prov. Council of Cincinnati (1861); Pius XI Encycl. *Divini Illius Magistri*, p. 60, 63 ff.
[21] Cf. Pius XI, Encycl. *Divini Illius Magistri*, p. 63; also Encycl. *Non abbiamo bisogno*, 29 June 1931; AAS 23 (1931) p. 305; also Pius XII, Letter to 28th Ital. Social Week, 20 Sept. 1955: *L'Osservatore Romano*, 29 Sept. 1955; also Paul VI, *Allocutio* to Chr. Assoc. of Ital. Workers. 6 Oct. 1963; *Encicliche e Discorsi di Paolo VI*, vol. I, Rome, 1964., p. 230.

The role of the Catholic school meanwhile remains crucial.

8. . . . the Catholic school, taking into consideration as it should the conditions of an age of progress, prepares its pupils to contribute effectively to the welfare of the world of men and to work for the extension of the kingdom of God so that by living an exemplary and apostolic life they may be, as it were, a saving leaven in the community.

CHAPTER FOUR

THE ETHICS OF POLITICAL LIFE

The political community and the authority of the state are based on human nature and so belong to God's design, though the method of government and the appointment of rulers is left to the citizens' free choice. The Church is not identified with any particular system but must be free to teach her whole doctrine (including her social doctrine) and pass moral judgement on political issues as required (Gaudium et Spes, paragraphs 74 and 76).

I. The Origin and the Nature of Political Authority

A. THE TEACHING OF THE COUNCIL

The Council's main guidance on political ethics is contained in chapter 4 of *Gaudium et Spes*. Noting the general pattern of cultural, economic and social changes which were affecting the world, it goes on to say that these have had their effect on the political life of states, the more especially since they have been the concomitant of the demand for greater respect for human rights and dignity, an acceptance of pluralism and the awareness of the rights of minorities. Faced with the evidence of concern of this kind at all levels, the Council was impelled to look at the ethics of political life and organisation from the Christian point of view. It considers first the origin of political society and the state.[1]

> Individuals, families and the various groups which make up the civil community are aware of their inability to achieve a truly human life by their own unaided efforts; they see the need for a wider community where each one will make a specific contribution to an even broader implementation of the common good.[1] For this reason they set up various forms of political communities. *The political community, then, exists for the common good; this is its full justification and meaning and the source of its specific and basic right to exist. The common good embraces the sum total of all those conditions of social life which enable individuals, families and organisations to achieve complete and efficacious fulfillment.*[2]
>
> The persons who go to make up the political community are many and varied; quite rightly then they may veer towards widely differing points of view. Therefore lest the political community be ruined while everyone follows his own opinion, an authority is needed to guide the energies of all towards the common good. *It is clear that the political community and public authority are based on human nature and therefore that they need belong to an order*

[1] *Gaudium et Spes*, par. 74.

established by God; nevertheless the choice of the political regime and the appointment of rulers are left to the free choice of the citizens.[3]

It follows that the political authority, either within the political community as such or through organisation representing the state, must be exercised within the limits of the moral order and directed towards the common good . . . when citizens are under the oppression of a public authority which oversteps its competence, they should still not refuse to give or do what is objectively demanded of them by the common good; but it is legitimate for them to defend their rights . . . within the limits of the natural law and the law of the Gospel.

The concrete forms of structure and organisation of public authority adopted in any political community may vary according to the character of the various peoples and their historical development but their aim should always be the formation of a human person who is cultured, peace-loving and well disposed towards his fellow men. . . .

[1] Cf. John XXIII Litt. Encycl. *Mater et Magistra* AAS 53 (1961) p. 417.
[2] Cf. John XXIII ibid.
[3] Cf. Rom 13:1–5.

The reasoning, therefore, is that the origin of the political community is in the awareness individuals and families have that they cannot fulfill their human needs simply by their own unaided efforts: hence, they form such communities to this end. They exist, therefore, for the good of each and the good of all, the common good, and it is this which leads to the establishment of some authority within the community that will enable that good to be achieved. Political community and political authority are then founded in human nature and consequently they belong to an order established by God—though the choice of regime and rulers is left to the people themselves. The forms the public authority may take are accordingly as variable as times, peoples and conditions require, but the aim of all states should be to secure the common good and form mature and responsible citizens.

Though this is briefly and succinctly stated, it covers some of the thorniest and most complex problems in political theory and organisation. Some we want to look at a little more closely, taking first the Council's view on the origin of the political community and political authority. This in its turn cannot be separated from the related question of the nature of that authority—which exists to serve the common good: this we consider in more detail in the next section.

The concepts of community, society, political society, political authority, nation, the state and government are closely interconnected;[2] for our

[2] J. Maritain, *Man and the State* (Chicago, 1963). E. Welty, *A Handbook of Christian Social Ethics* (London, 1960), 1:68 ff., 114 ff., 2:196 ff. J. Messner, *Social Ethics* (London, 1964), pp. 474 ff., 541 ff. J. Hoffner, *The Fundamentals of Christian Sociology*, pp. 160 ff. In practical terms the distinction between state and government is perhaps most important. The state is a formally constituted and autonomous society of one or more ethnic and cultural groups with

purposes, it is the origin of the political society out of a pre-existing community which is of concern. There are many theories of how the political community and political authority came to be and the one adopted is decisive in determining one's attitude to the use of political authority. In historical fact we can see that states come to be in many ways, some by the natural evolution of a people, some by conquest or revolution, some by a mixture of all three. But it is possible to ask what it is, beneath all the varied moods of history, that has led man to form political society or to accept it and the authority, the coercive powers, the limitations of some aspect of freedom that are implicit in it. The price of being a member of a political society and getting its aid to live more peaceably and more fully is that we accept some limitation on the freedom that would be ours if we lived in a pre-political state. How we view the theoretical reasons for the transition from pre-political to political society, and how we view the nature of the authority to which we have subjected ourselves, helps to determine the limits of that authority.

The Council's view of the fundamental reason why we establish political societies is quite clear. It is a positive view. We set up political communities because we want to find a fuller life through them. The view on the proper use of political authority is clear also; it exists for the common good to enable all and each to secure a fuller life, and if it does not do that citizens have a right to defend themselves against it. The argument is not historical, but analytic, theoretical. It can be supported by historical fact,[3] though not conclusively. The question here is, what account of the origin of the state best and most clearly indicates the proper purpose of the state's powers. If individual and family precede the state and are given their essential rights and freedoms by God, then the state may never demand of them a loyalty which offends against their duty to the Creator. In this account of the origin of the state then is contained the essential core of theory which enables the right understanding of the rights and duties of state and citizen to develop.

B. THE HISTORICAL CONTEXT AND THE DEVELOPMENT OF CATHOLIC THOUGHT DOWN TO THE SIXTEENTH CENTURY

We find confirmation of the view that the political community and the authority of the state belong to God's design from his treatment of his

---

physically recognizable boundaries and the economic, military and other means of carrying out its obligations. The government is the body of individuals charged with making and administering laws and establishing various agencies in order that the state can discharge its functions.

[3] "The historical origins of the State, as far as research permits judgement on the subject, are by no means uniform. On the whole, however, history confirms the conclusion which

people in the Old Testament. As he led and guided them, he formed them into a political entity so that his spiritual purpose could be achieved. St. Thomas argues that the form of government established by God was partly monarchy, partly aristocracy and partly democracy[4] and he uses this argument to show the superiority of a mixed constitution. Israel's political system was, certainly initially, theocratic,[5] (that is, government by God), in that Moses was chosen directly by God and appointed by him as ruler over the people, acting in his name and for his direct purposes rather than in response to the needs of the people from below; this theocratic element was always present in Israel's political life even after the institution of the monarchy.

The fact that the people of God were bound to him equally in the first instance by the Covenant ensured that those who held authority in Israel could always be made aware of the obligation to use their power for the purpose for which it was intended, the good of the whole people. They did not always respond to this awareness, but the basic orientation of the political community, the coming together so that a united people could do collectively for the good of all and each what all and each could not do individually for themselves, was there. We can see the demand for a king as a working out of the logic of politics. The account of its origin as given in the Book of Samuel[6] suggests that the request for a monarchy was not looked on with favour, but it was nevertheless granted. And the role of the king achieved increasing importance in God's plan.[7]

The New Testament tells us that those who legitimately hold political authority in a non-Christian or pagan state were regarded as having received that authority from God. When challenged by his enemies to say whether it was permissible to pay taxes to Caesar or not, Jesus replied that to Caesar should be rendered what was Caesar's and to God what was God's.[8] In the context, which was one of direct challenge concerning the right of Caesar to levy taxes, the reply of Christ can only mean that such things as the levying of taxes and the issuing of coins were indeed legitimate functions of civil authority which happened to be embodied in the person of Caesar, and he accepted that authority as legitimate. Equally, when it was put to him by Pilate that he had power to release him or to

---

Aristotle reached on the basis of the facts available to him: the State has grown out of the family." Messner, op. cit., p. 543.

[4] *Summa Theologica*, I–II, q. 105, art. 1. The note to the new 1969 English translation comments that Thomas' view of the political forms of the Old Testament is now questioned.

[5] R. de Vaux, *Ancient Israel*, pp. 98–99. W. Eichrodt, *Theology of the Old Testament* (London, 1964), 1:55 ff., 90 ff.; 2:242 ff.

[6] 1 Sam 8:1–22, 10:18–25.

[7] 1 Sam 16:6–13. The Saviour was prophesied as being a descendant of David.

[8] Mt 22:21.

crucify him, his reply that Pilate would have had no power over him if it had not been given to him from above[9] seems to indicate that he accepted Pilate's power of life and death in this instance; it was a legitimate power belonging to him as representative of the political community, one that he could use or not at his discretion under the law.

St. Paul is very explicit regarding the attitude the Church should have to the state.[10]

> Since all government comes from God, the civil authorities were appointed by God and so anyone who resists authority is rebelling against God's decision and such an act is bound to be punished. Good behaviour is not being afraid of magistrates, only criminals have anything to fear. If you want to live without being afraid of authority you must live honestly and authority may even honour you. The State is there to serve God for your benefit.

Such strong words coming from a man who had suffered from Roman authority to a community already beginning to feel the threat of persecution soon to break out under Nero were remarkable indeed.

No less emphatic was St. Peter.[11]

> For the sake of the Lord, accept the authority of every social institution; the Emperor as the supreme authority, the Governors as commissioned by him to punish criminals and praise good citizenship. God wants you to be good citizens so as to silence what fools are saying in their ignorance. You are slaves of no-one except God, so behave like free men and never use your freedom as an excuse for wickedness. Have respect for everyone and love for your community: fear God and honour the Emperor.

Read out of context, the advice of both St. Paul and St. Peter can be taken as justification for any form of authority and of its right to demand blind obedience of its subjects. But a closer reading of the text and the consideration of the context give a different perspective. As has been said, the Scriptures are not a comprehensive textbook of theology, still less of social ethics, and what they say, therefore, has to be understood in the light of sound principles of interpretation and particularly of the Christian tradition. When St. Paul said that "all government comes from God", he was not preempting the important ethical question of what constitutes lawful authority in general—he was dealing with a specific situation in which it was possible to accept Roman power as legitimate. To interpret his words to imply that he was prepared to underwrite any *de facto* authority is clearly unjustified. He was simply making explicit what can

[9] Jn 19:11.
[10] Rom 13:1–4.
[11] I Pet 2:13–17.

be assumed from Christ's words and actions—that Roman authority was acceptable and that in all matters where there was no offence to God it was to be obeyed. To place any other construction on the texts is to stretch their meaning in a way which the context does not warrant. It is evident from the whole passage that the sort of obedience expected is such as a good citizen would show under any regime—namely living an honest life. The criminal may rightly fear authority precisely because he is a criminal. St. Paul is warning his people that adherence to the fundamentals of the Christian moral life means that they should have nothing to fear from secular authority. As to the warning about rebellion, this too was in accord with his Master's example. Christ resisted any temptation to be a social agitator even though he was put to death as one on false charges;[12] the Church's duty was to preach his Gospel, not to become politicized to the point of challenging the authority of the state; this would have been the surest way of destroying herself. As it was, even when she was subjected to unjust persecution, she did not react by violent means, but suffered patiently for Christ's sake as he had done.[13] It was this patience and heroism in the face of martyrdom which was so powerful a witness to Christ and helped the Church lay firm foundations; had she reacted violently, the Church would hardly have won acceptance, and her mission would have been compromised.

The wording of the passage from St. Peter clearly indicates the same concern as St. Paul. He too explicitly accepts the authority of Rome and urges his people to do so "for the sake of the Lord". In other words, any attempt by the early Christians to challenge the Roman State would have been used by the enemies of the Church as a means of discrediting her. St. Peter tells his people that they are slaves to God only and the freedom that this gives them should never result in wrong-doing. By living good lives, respecting others and honouring the Emperor, they would serve their master Christ faithfully: nothing less would do.

From the New Testament and the life of the early Church, therefore, we may correctly conclude that, true to the words and example of her Master, she had no political ambitions, no wish to challenge the Roman

[12] P. H. Furfey, *A History of Social Thought* (New York, 1949), pp. 133 ff.; the interpretation of Christ's life as a political activist, a subversive, a revolutionary, was rejected by Pope John Paul II at Puebla: it "does not tally with the Church's catechesis", *Puebla: Evangelization at Present and in the Future of Latin America* (London, 1980), p. 4.

[13] By the third century, "among the Christians there were politicians and statesmen, working men with strength and skill, slaves habituated to suffering, soldiers inured to war . . . writers who could . . . stir up rebellion" (P. Allard, *Ten Lectures on the Martyrs* [London, 1907], p. 172). The author comments that the effect of patience in the face of suffering was to win greater respect for and, finally, greater readiness to embrace Christianity.

State which she clearly accepted with all its faults—as a fact of life. Paradoxically, it was precisely her other-worldliness and her concentration on her spiritual task and her works of mercy which gave her the influence that in the end rebuilt the foundations of society; so strong had she become as a social organisation by the beginning of the fourth century that, as we have seen, the Roman Emperor turned to her and accepted her in his efforts to secure the crumbling Empire against disaster after his predecessors had unsuccessfully tried to destroy her through persecution.[14]

The writings of the Fathers and the Doctors of the Church were more concerned with the relationship between the Church and the state and the implications of this relationship than with the development of any coherent political theory in itself. To them the state was of divine institution—but it was the result of man's weakness in his fallen nature which made it necessary for the coercive power of the state to come to be. There was positive acceptance of the state and political authority, therefore, but theological justification was found in God's plan after the fall, not before it.[15]

As to how political authority came to be exercised by a particular man or group of men, given that political authority *in general* is of divine institution, this point was only slowly clarified in Christian thought. The New Testament texts quoted above could bear the interpretation that the Roman Emperor and, *a fortiori*, a Christian Roman Emperor, derived his authority directly from God in a way which left him accountable to God alone for his actions. The conclusion was not necessary and Christian writers did not always draw it. However, from the time of Irenaeus in the second century,[16] the theory that, as the representative of God, the ruler must be obeyed even when he is evil, found advocates—including St. Augustine and St. Isidore. But it was St. Gregory the Great, at the end of the sixth century, who drew out full implications of such a theory. He used the example of David's attitude to Saul in the Old Testament as evidence that good subjects will not even criticize rashly or violently the evil actions of the ruler; to do so would be to offend against God. Great administrator and forceful ruler though he was, he showed in his dealings with the Roman Emperor in the East that this attitude was not with him

[14] See above pp. 20 ff.

[15] "The Fathers maintained that Government is not natural and primitive and yet it is a divine institution . . . man is not now in the condition in which God made him . . . conditions (i.e. the coercive power of the State and Government) wholly contrary to his primitive nature are now necessary and useful." R. W. and A. J. Carlyle, *A History of Medieval Political Theory in the West*, 1:131.

[16] Ibid., 1:147 ff.

mere theory; he even seemed to tolerate the Emperor's right to interfere in Church affairs contrary to its canons, though he did not approve of such actions.[17]

The Carlyles suggest[18] that three things influenced the divine right theory in this period in the Church's history: the first was the tendency to anarchy, detectable in the exaggerated understanding of freedom by some Christians; the second was the special relationship between the emperor and the Church after the conversion of Constantine; and the third was the influence of the Old Testament idea of kingship in which the king was the Lord's anointed. These influences were reinforced by the anarchy that overtook Europe after the successive waves of invasions. Yet, by the ninth and tenth centuries, other ideas were making themselves felt, ideas stressing that, if the king gets his power from God, he does so through the people, and holds it on the condition that he fulfills the purpose of his authority—justice.[19]

The Investiture controversy, to which we have already briefly referred in the first chapter, and to which we will return later,[20] was directly relevant to the developing understanding of the particular origin of political authority. The controversy came to a head when Gregory VII excommunicated the Emperor Henry VI for his refusal to abandon the practice of investing bishops and abbots with their insignia of office; Gregory realised that unless he was able to end lay control of Church offices, typified in this practice, he would not be able to end corruption. But in excommunicating the Emperor because of his obduracy, he automatically freed his subjects from their oaths of fealty—so laying the Empire open to anarchy and revolt. There is no evidence that through his action Gregory meant to deny the two swords theory;[21] yet, later controversialists could conclude that his words and actions implied this. By the early twelfth century it was being argued that the temporal power derived its authority from the spiritual.[22] Defenders of the Emperor's position, on the other hand, appealed to the divine right theory—since his authority came directly from God, he could not be deposed by man. As noted, for the divine right theory they could claim the authority of Gregory the Great, who had taught that the derivation of the ruler's authority from God enjoined passivity in the face of injustice.[23] Throughout the following centuries the argument continued. Manegold

---

[17] Ibid., p. 154.   [18] Ibid., p. 157.   [19] Ibid., p. 228 ff.

[20] See above pp. 38 ff. and below pp. 231 ff.

[21] See above p. 21 f.

[22] By Honorius of Augsburg circa 1123. G. H. Sabine, A History of Political Theory, p. 236. Carlyle and Carlyle, op. cit., 4:286 ff. Honorius in his Summa Gloria was not so much concerned with the Investiture controversy as such, but with the general question of the origin and nature of the two great authorities—Church and state.

[23] Sabine, op. cit., p. 238. Carlyle and Carlyle, op. cit., 1:152.

of Lautenbach[24] and John of Salisbury[25] both stressed the difference between true kingship and tyranny; the essence of kingship is in the office, not the person, and the king who has betrayed his duty to give justice to all can be deposed. Manegold put forward a theory of contract between the king and his people which was invalidated if the former acted unjustly; this placed the holders of the divine right theory under the obligation of showing why the king should hold on to his office if he had seriously offended against justice. From the extreme papalist point of view, the argument was two-edged. The deposition of the emperor could be defended, but so could the independence of the royal power from the Church in so far as that power was rooted in the pact with the people.

Under the powerful popes of the thirteenth century (Innocent III [1198–1216] and Innocent IV [1243–1254] in particular), the claims of their office to temporal jurisdiction were given greater precision and power. The two swords theory had always had in it the potential for a major and destructive conflict between papacy and emperor; the course of events before the Investiture controversy showed that all these elements were there.[26] But now the claims of both sides were clarified. Lawyers and publicists saw the significance of what was happening in ecclesiological and political terms; theologians were less perceptive.

Innocent III[27] interpreted his role as moral guide to mean that he had the right to judge whether candidates for the imperial throne were fit for their task and to review any alleged irregularities in elections. Likewise, he claimed the right to adjudicate in treaties and agreements between rulers, to supervise the administration of justice, and a host of other related functions which could be claimed flowed out of the traditional understanding of the two swords theory but were so far reaching in the circumstances as to seem to contradict it. Innocent III did not seek to challenge the authority of rulers in general or to supersede it in its legitimate sphere—

[24] In *Ad Gebehardum* (written between 1080 and 1085), Sabine, op. cit., p. 241. The phrases used by Manegold concerning the conditional nature of the obedience sworn to the king, conditional upon his administering justice and maintaining the law, "expressed the normal principles of political theory in these centuries". Carlyle and Carlyle, op. cit., 3:169.

[25] John of Salisbury (1115–1180) had been chief minister to Thomas Becket at Canterbury. His *Policraticus* (1159) marks the first attempt at a systematic outline of a general political philosophy to be made in the Middle Ages; its underlying principle was that law rules the commonwealth—prince and people together; the public authority acts for the general good, or it loses its moral justification and can be opposed. The principle that the tyrant can be opposed, and if necessary deposed, remained fundamental to medieval political theory. It is to be noted that John of Salisbury was as critical of the excesses of power within the Church as in the state and as pointed in his suggestions for remedying them. Sabine, op. cit., p. 247. Carlyle and Carlyle, op. cit., 4:331.

[26] Carlyle and Carlyle, op. cit., 1:253 ff.

[27] On the conflicts of the thirteenth century: Sabine, op. cit., pp. 270 ff., Carlyle and Carlyle, op. cit., 5:152 ff. D. Knowles and D. Obolensky, *The Middle Ages*, pp. 329 ff.

but the effective claim to be the judge of what that legitimate sphere was marked in practice an advance in papal and ecclesiastical claims. Innocent IV took a step further in claiming a theoretical "plenitudo potestatis", derived from Christ, which gave the pope a power of supervision over all other forms of authority, secular as well as ecclesiastical; there can always be an appeal to the pope because there is no higher judge and secular judges are not always ready to give justice. It was this latter consideration that gave the claim particular plausibility. The competence and the dedication to justice that the Church's good offices could offer were often greater than the still half-formed political state had at its disposal. Yet the deeper involvement of the Church in temporal affairs was, in the long term, dangerous for her and her primary role.

The clash of rights and interests came to a head at the end of the thirteenth century between Pope Boniface VIII and Philip the Fair of France. The immediate cause was Philip's attempt to raise money by taxing the French clergy. In the bull *Clericos Laicos* of 1296, Boniface denounced Philip's action as illegal, but the French people supported their king against the Pope on the issue—a significant indication of the growth of the nationalist spirit which was to be one of the marks of the transition from medieval to Renaissance and Reformation Europe.

In facing the problem, Boniface, far from adjusting to meet the new mood, tried to revive old ideas in the strongest form, indeed to push them further. The bull *Unam Sanctam*[28] of 1302 not only asserted that the pope is supreme in the Church and that subjection to him is necessary for salvation, but that the temporal power of princes is to be used under the direction and at the command of the Church. Earthly authority is subject to the spiritual in this very direct way while the spiritual power is to be judged by God alone.

It was during this controversy between the French king and Rome that a new aspect of divine right theory, due apparently to the growing influence of the rediscovered Roman law, made its appearance.[29] According to the Roman jurists, the emperor's will had the force of law, although the constitutional fiction that he derived his power from the people who initially invested him with it was maintained. It was disputed in the thirteenth century whether, under the Roman theory, the people retained

---

[28] Sabine, op. cit., p. 273. The controversy is dealt with at length in Carlyle and Carlyle, op. cit., pp. 374 ff.

[29] Sabine, op. cit., p. 278. Carlyle and Carlyle, op. cit., 5:64 ff. John of Paris, *De Potestate Regia et Papali* (1302–1303), made the fullest and most explicit defence of the king's position. He put forward the idea of a general council to curb the power of the pope: he also brought out these secularist tendencies in Aristotle that St. Thomas' use of that philosopher's works had not emphasized. Sabine, op. cit., pp. 281 ff.

the power to make law; but however this may be, the idea was now abroad that the law expressed the will of the prince, whereas the typical medieval view was that the law was the custom of the people to which the prince too was subject.

The conflict between Philip of France and Boniface VIII ended in the kidnapping of the aged Pope, his death, the election of a French pope and the beginning of the Avignon Papacy.[30] A papacy so much under French influence did not please the other powers of Europe. The dispute with France had obscured the longer standing controversy with the Empire over the issue of papal temporal power; the former had been settled to France's satisfaction, but, given the suspicion now of French interference, any attempt of the Pope to activate his temporal claims in regard to the emperor and empire now had an added political overtone which exacerbated the situation. And such attempts were made; John XXII tried to interfere in an imperial election in 1323, and the resulting controversy brought a new generation of writers and polemicists into the fray. Two of them, Marsilio of Padua and William of Occam, made a lasting impact.

Marsilio[31] wrote as an Italian convinced that papal claims to temporal power were a prime cause of Italian disunity; to curb that influence he sought to make the Church subject to a secular ruler. He accepted the Church and its ministers as needful, a part of society, but argued that it and they should be subject to the temporal powers like all else in the state. The Church has no right to property while the hierarchy—the priests, bishops and pope—are within the control of secular society, and they possess no powers essentially different from those of other Christians. The only authority that is empowered to speak for the Christian community as a whole is a general council, which is the political executive of that community; the general councils are, in their turn, dependent on the secular state which alone possesses the means to enforce their authority.

William of Occam[32] was a Franciscan, and his conflicts with the papacy were bound up with the difficulties that beset the followers of St. Francis

---

[30] Knowles and Obolensky, op. cit., pp. 337, 405 ff. The residence of the popes at Avignon lasted from 1309 to 1377.

[31] Marsilio of Padua (c. 1275–1342). From Padua he went to Paris about 1311 to study medicine. He became rector of the University of Paris in 1312 and probably studied theology there from 1320, after a period in Italy and Avignon. He completed *Defensor Pacis*, in which he set out his political theories, in 1324. Sabine, op.cit., pp. 287 ff. Q. Skinner, *Foundations of Modern Political Thought* (C.U.P., 1979), 1:19 ff. F. C. Copleston, *A History of Philosophy*, 3:168 ff.

[32] Occam was born in Surrey about 1290 and died in 1349. On his life and works, Copleston, op. cit., 3:43 ff., 111 ff. Sabine, op. cit., pp. 287 ff. and Skinner, op. cit., 2:37 ff.

in determining the exact nature of the Franciscan life, given their founder's own unique charism and the spontaneous growth of the order. While Occam was lecturing at Oxford in 1323, some of his teachings were brought to the notice of the Holy See as suspect. Not all of them were found exceptionable, but while he was engaged in answering the queries they still raised, he became involved in the dispute between the General of the Franciscans and the papacy concerning the internal affairs of the Order and, in 1328, he was excommunicated, along with the General; he and other fugitives joined the Emperor Ludwig of Bavaria with whom Marsilio of Padua was leagued in his conflict with the Avignon Papacy.

Occam maintained the clear distinction between the spiritual and temporal powers and denied the papacy's right to validate imperial elections; political power comes from God through the people and therefore does not need any such validation. But the orthodoxy of some of his theological opinions had already been put in doubt and his plans for limiting what he saw as the excesses of papal power led him further astray. He wished to make the papacy subjct to a general council, a suggestion which was, in time, inevitably rejected by the Church.

To theorists like Marsilio of Padua and William of Occam, the general council was the answer to excessive Church and, in particular, papal involvement in secular affairs. But the conciliar movement which developed in the late fourteenth century was a response, not to the demands of theorists such as these, but to the practical need to end the scandal of the Great Schism (1378–1417) which had arisen from a variety of causes, prominent among them being the Avignon Papacy.[33] Once the Council of Constance (1414–1418) had ended the schism, and the question of the legitimate claimant to the papal throne was settled, the movement lost impetus. The attempt by the Council of Basle (1431–1439) to continue the dispute finally destroyed the conciliar movement, and Pope Eugenius IV gradually restored the authority of his office over the whole Church.

The controversy over the conciliar theory and its implications, therefore, led to speculation about, and consequently, a clarification of the origins of political and ecclesiastical authority. The development of the practice and the theory of representative government[34] marked a further such clarification. In the secular sphere, representative government was a natural growth that attended the rapid development of European culture and institutions from the eleventh and twelfth centuries—a development

[33] Knowles and Obolensky, *The Middle Ages*, pp. 415 ff.

[34] The essential principle of representative government is that "one or more persons stand or act on behalf of others." It is a principle as old as civilised or community life; but the Middle Ages for the first time made it apply widely in the political sphere. M. V. Clarke, *Medieval Representation and Consent* (London, 1936), p. 278.

summed up in the growth of the towns. But the idea of consent was fed by elements that had been in the feudal system from the first. The Merovingian capitularies made it clear as early as the sixth century that the consent of the people was needed for a change in the law[35]—and it is not unreasonable to see the principle of representative government as a logical extension of this same idea of registering consent on major issues affecting all. Similarly, the ideas of election and hereditary right were intermingled in feudal theory in the first instance, and even after the distinction became clearer, hereditary right still carried with it the obligation to preserve the laws.

The principles of the consent of the governed and the right to elect leaders were accordingly embedded in the institutions of government in the early Middle Ages and predisposed the new civilisation which was emerging from the eleventh century to the development and adaptation of these principles in the new order. The growth of representative government on a national scale, which then developed in parliamentary institutions, owes something to the feudal theory and practice; it also owes a great deal to the growth of the self-governing towns which were in many ways the antithesis of feudalism.

In the early Middle Ages, especially after the collapse of Charlemagne's empire and the incursions of the Vikings, Western Europe was almost entirely an agrarian society; feudalism, as the normal system of government, was based on landholding and working in return for services, military or agricultural. But, from the eleventh century onwards, the medieval world saw a rebirth of city life[36] and experienced its increasing influence on patterns of thought and culture. These cities reflected not only the vigorous economic growth of a new civilisation, but in themselves constituted a distinctive new form of organised social life unknown in the ancient world and only partly paralleled in the cities of the contemporary East. The cities of medieval Europe were neither based on slavery, as had been the cities of classical antiquity, nor on the serfdom of feudal agrarianism—and, according to Troeltsch,[37] they provided for the first time the conditions for a thorough-going attempt at the Christianization of social life. The medieval city was a unity, a tangible unity, of organised social life and faith as the presence of the walls protecting it and its Church or cathedral dominating it attested. Within it, the different economic activities of the citizens were organised in self-governing guilds which, in their turn and in their various forms, provided the basis of the

[35] Sabine, op. cit., p. 204.

[36] C. Dawson, *Religion and the Rise of Western Culture*, pp. 193 ff. *Cambridge Medieval History*, 5:624 ff. *Cambridge Economic History of Europe*, 3:3 ff., 230 ff.

[37] Quoted by C. Dawson, *Religion and the Rise of Western Culture*, pp. 193–94.

city's government. Each city possessed its constitution or charter and its tradition of self-rule, often hierarchical and authoritarian and often degenerating into an exploitation of the poor by the rich.[38] But Erasmus was to note that in Strasbourg, which retained the best traditions of guild and civic government, he saw monarchy without tyranny, aristocracy without factions, democracy without tumult and wealth without luxury. Would, he added, that Plato had lived to see such a Republic.[39]

The presence at the heart of a society which was still basically agrarian and feudal, of such self-governing entities as the cities—with the tradition of responsibility for their own affairs well-established, was one of the elements that made the establishment of representative government on a national scale possible. It was the appeal that the king was able to make to the citizens and burghers, as well as the knights, to enable him to counter-balance the influence of his tenants in chief, which made such a broad-based government possible.[40] Representative forms grew spontaneously throughout Europe in the twelfth and thirteenth centuries,[41] but the English version had been especially significant in itself and in the adaptability which enabled it to survive and adjust to the needs of changing circumstances.

The Anglo-Saxon influence on a political system that was to be so dominated by the results of the Norman conquest was nevertheless important. In Anglo-Saxon times, the rights of free men on the land were consolidated, and these rights survived the Norman conquest; the lord was lord "on" the land, not "over" it:[42] local rights and local order thus became the basis of that English common law which has played so large a

---

[38] *Cambridge Economic History*, vol. 3, pp. 34 ff. M. Mollat and R. Wolff, *The Popular Revolutions of the Late Middle Ages* (London, 1973).

[39] Quoted by C. Dawson, *Religion and the Rise of Western Culture*, pp. 206–7.

[40] In England, in 1254, two knights were ordered to be elected from each of the shires to say what financial help they could give the king. In 1265 two representatives of boroughs were also called, but it was 1295 before Edward I's "model" parliament revealed the evolution of the general council into a more general parliament; in addition to the bishops and abbots and the chief tenants of the old great council, two knights from the shires and two burgesses from each burgh attended; even so, only three of Edward's twenty later parliaments were of this kind: twelve of them had no representatives of the towns. Clarke, op. cit., pp. 313 ff. C. B. Adams, *Constitutional History of England* (London, 1971), pp. 174 ff.

[41] "By the latter half of the 13th Century, a development analogous to England's had produced ideas and institutions not fundamentally different in almost all parts of Christendom; from Scandinavia to the Adriatic they are found . . . in Hungary, Bohemia and Poland, no less than in Italy, Spain and the Low Countries. . . ." *Cambridge Medieval History*, 7:682 ff. The developments in Spain in the thirteenth century gave a much fuller claim by the people to a share in government than in England at this period.

[42] D. Jerrold, *England: Past, Present and Future* (London, 1950), p. 25.

part in the development of the idea of freedom of the individual under the law.

This common law was taken up into the Norman system of the administration of justice; the decisions of local justices, based on what custom decreed, formed a different but complementary source to Royal Statutes. Gradually, under the Normans, this common law came to be written down—but it still performed its function of establishing equity between generation and generation. The jury system's origins are obscure, although we know it was already established in practice when in 1215 the Lateran Council abolished trial by ordeal and substituted the Norman custom of inquest by sworn recognitors. Jury trial developed exclusively in England and is fully consonant with the common law tradition. In time, common law needed supplementing by other legal provisions, the Lord Chancellor's court in particular; the influence of Roman law also increased, not least because most judges were clerics trained in Canon Law (which had been influenced in its formation by its Roman origins) and educated in the law schools of Bologna and Padua. Roman jurisprudence, the natural law concept especially, supplemented and strengthened the common law tradition.

The importance of common law to the development of constitutional and representative government was in the power it possessed to command the respect and obedience of the mass of ordinary people. In order that law should be enforceable, it must be freely accepted by the people at large; when it is, then a stable and free social order can be established. A political power which decrees what is not acceptable to the majority of the people will not have a firm foundation in a free society. The growth of representative government in England took place on a basis of institutions and patterns of thought which, as a result of the common law tradition, assured such foundations. The English people were used to deliberating on the basis of law and accepting the decisions so made.

The principle and practice of representative government was present also in aspects of the Church's internal organisation. Her legislative assemblies, her councils and synods, in the first place, helped to preserve a juristic and organisational ability inherited from the Romans[43] and were capable in time of affecting the political institutions of the new civilisation. These assemblies were not elective; they consisted of bishops who attended in their role as leaders of the local churches—but they carried on the idea of a responsible group deliberating on behalf of the whole community. After a period of disruption by the Viking invasions, councils and synods revived and, in the conditions of the twelfth and

[43] Clarke, op. cit., p. 293.

thirteenth centuries, they became more numerous and important. Between 1123 and 1274, six general councils of the Church were held—almost a third of those which met between Nicea in 325 and Trent in 1548.[44] It is significant that this revival of the general councils "coincided with the rise of national legislative assemblies".[45] The Fourth Lateran Council in 1215 innovated in providing for the representation of Cathedral Chapters at the Council—a representation effected through the attendance of the proctors. The reason for the innovation was that it was on the Cathedral Chapters that the obligation of supporting schoolmasters was to be laid—and Innocent III believed in the principle which we have come to know as "no taxation without representation". His action ensured that the idea of representation should become known "throughout the whole of Western Europe".[46] Other provisions of the Council encouraged developments in representational government in the Church. It insisted, for example, on regular provincial synods at which the lower clergy should be present; it also extended the practice of triennial chapters to religious orders which did not have them already.

Constitutional government, which provided a basis for the development of representational forms, had been a natural growth in religious orders from the first.[47] The rule of St. Benedict made provision for the election of an abbot with responsibility to care for those in his charge with charity and justice. The Cluniac Reform[48] introduced the general chapter attended by the priors of individual abbeys who could make decrees binding on the whole order. Newer religious orders adapted these developments, some to more centralization, others to less.

One small order, that of Grandmont, founded in Limoges about 1076, adopted a method of choosing its prior which was truly representational; two of the brethren from each house were elected and they were given a mandate to act in the name of the community. In other words, they were not *ex officio* members of the higher deliberative body in virtue of the office they held in the individual houses; they were chosen for a specific purpose and given a specific mandate to exercise at their discretion. The order was too small for its example to have had any general effect—but the appearance of such provisions in the rule of a religious order showed that the logical development of their organisation was in this direction.

That development came to a head in the thirteenth century with the Dominicans and the Franciscans. The Dominicans made the representa-

---

[44] Ibid., pp. 295–96.   [45] Ibid., p. 296.   [46] Ibid.

[47] "In the Benedictine monasteries the monks became the first Europeans . . . Benedict's was the first constitutional Charter of Western Europe". E. Heer, *The Intellectual History of Europe* (London, 1966), p. 31.

[48] Clarke, op. cit., pp. 299 ff.

tive principle the keystone of their constitution, and the Franciscans adopted the same method. Chapters which ruled the order consisted of elected representatives of each house of the province; power was therefore derived from the convents and communities, not from above.[49]

In England, events following the Third Lateran Council opened up a new form of representational decision-making in the Church. The Council had forbidden the bishops to tax the clergy without their consent and to ensure that that consent was obtained, convocations were called at various times between 1229 and 1254 in which representatives of the lower clergy met with the bishops to decide on such matters.[50] It has been suggested that the decision of the English king to appeal to the commons over the heads of his tenants in chief was influenced by the appeal made to the lower clergy at this time.[51]

When, therefore, we look to St. Thomas once more to summarize for us the account of the origin and nature of political authority that his mature reflections suggested in the light of the Catholic tradition, we are not surprised to find that it is constitutional government, based on consent, that he favours. Much of his argumentation derives from Aristotle— but St. Thomas was also a child of his time, and above all a member of that Order of Preachers whose own constitution allowed an element of effective representation. The Greek experience summed up in Aristotle, the insights of Scripture and tradition, the developing institutions of the society of his time and the form of government of his own order, blended to give him a preference for a form of government which, while allowing for sound discipline and the active pursuit of the common good, was a government by consent, expressed through the principle of representation.

He did not write a comprehensive treatise on political theory as such, but his *De Regimine Principum* and parts of the *Summa Theologica*[52] provide us with the elements of one. He reasoned that, of all the animals, it was most natural for man to live in a group, in society. For other animals nature had prepared food, means of self-protection in the form of hide or

[49] St. Francis (1181–1226) founded his order in 1209, and its rule was given final form in 1223. St. Dominic (1170–1221) began what became the Order of Preachers in 1215; two general chapters at Bologna in 1220 and 1221 gave it more definite shape. The effect of the Dominican rule in terms of representative government is examined in F. Barker, *The Dominican Order and Convocation* (O.U.P., 1913), pp. 75 ff. See also J. B. Scott, *The Spanish Origins of International Law* (O.U.P., 1934), pp. 276 ff., and David Edwards, *Christian England* (London, 1981), pp. 174–75.

[50] Clarke, op. cit., pp. 307 ff.

[51] Ibid., p. 312.

[52] *De Regimine Principum* (On Kingship) in D. Bigongiari, *The Political Ideas of St. Thomas Aquinas* (New York, 1960), pp. 175 ff.

fur, horns or claws as a means of defence, or a speed of flight which gives them an advantage over natural enemies. Man alone is left without any natural provision against the elements or against his foes—instead he was endowed with reason, by the use of which he could supply for his needs in these matters. And his reason tells him that he can best supply them by combining with others of his own kind so that they can help each other. His social nature is evident in other ways: animals are more easily able to discern, by inborn skill, what is useful and what is injurious for them, but man needs much more instruction over a longer period. He needs to draw upon the knowledge that others have gathered and which is available in organised society. The power of speech, of rational communication with others, indicates an aptitude for the social commerce and organised community through which he can learn from and teach others.

Man, by nature inclined to form political societies, reasons also that it is necessary for someone to govern such societies,[53] because without a central authority each would look after his own interest rather than the common good of all and the purpose of coming together would be defeated. As to forms of government, the best is that in which all take some share, for this ensures peace among the people, commends itself to all and is most enduring. One in which there is an element of monarchy (since there is one head of all), an element of aristocracy (in so far as a number of people are set in authority), and an element of democracy (in so far as the rulers can be chosen from the people and the people have the right to choose their rulers) is to be preferred.[54] It is clear how much all of this is reflected in the thinking behind *Gaudium et Spes*, particularly the passage above quoted, that public authority is based on human nature, and hence, belongs to an order established by God, but that at the same time the choice of government and the method of selecting leaders is left to the will of the citizens.

In summary, therefore,[55] we can say that the principle that dominated the political thought of the Middle Ages was that political society was for the maintenance of justice for all, that where there is no justice, there is no commonwealth. And law, as distinguished from the merely arbitrary and capricious will of the ruler, was the norm of justice; it was axiomatic that the king is under no man, but he is under God and the law. Hence St. Thomas could say that while sedition is a mortal sin, revolt against a tyrant is not to be called sedition, for the tyrant's rule is not just.[56] Law then was not the expression of the will of the ruler, but of the habit of life

---

[53] *Summa Theologica*, I, q. 96, art. 4. I–II, q. 95, art. 1.
[54] Ibid., I–II, q. 105, art. 1.
[55] Carlyle and Carlyle, op. cit., 6:504 ff.
[56] *Summa Theologica*, II–II, q. 42, art. 2 ad 3. See below p. 222.

of the community. Though the Investiture controversy led some to stress the former (law as the expression of the will of the supreme power in the community), Bracton[57] stated the more representative view when he said that that has the force of law which has been determined by the counsel and consent of great men, the approval of the whole commonwealth and the authority of the king. Positive law was the expression of the will or consent of the whole community, including the king. The conception of the emperor as sole legislator was an innovation and against the mainstream of medieval thought.

Central also to the thinking of the Middle Ages was the idea of a contractual relationship between the ruler and the ruled. The coronation ceremonies of Western Europe from at least the eighth century included a promise by the prince to maintain not only abstract justice but the concrete law, and the people in their turn swore to obey the prince. The prince who ignored or defied the law forfeited all claim to authority because the whole body of the public laws of the community constituted the terms of the contract. And the political practice of the Middle Ages, through the evolution of representational forms, was working towards the development of a method of government in which an increasing number had a share. The supremacy of justice and law, and the conviction that these were ultimately determined, under God, by the whole community, the community which included the king, the nobles and the people as a whole, was the context in which the principles and practices of representative government, the logical development of the fundamental principles of the political civilisation of the period developed.[58] Slowly and painfully, the political genius of the new Europe sought in this way to reconcile the needs of liberty and authority in society.

With the break-up of Christendom, the Renaissance and the Reformation, the theoretical unity of thought and life which supported these developments came to an end. That unity was always fragile, as the Investiture controversy, and the conflicts of the thirteenth and fourteenth centuries we have briefly reviewed showed. Yet the ideal of unity had been there, and within that ideal, other ideals of the supremacy of justice, rule under the law, by consent and through representation, took their places. With the Renaissance and the Reformation, these ideals were challenged and to a considerable extent undermined. As Europe broke up into national states, the role of the monarch, and the power of the monarch, became the focus of interest in both theory and practice.

[57] Henry Bracton (d. 1268) was a cleric in the king's service and a judge in the king's central court. His treatise on the laws and customs of England was compiled between 1250 and 1260. See Sabine, op. cit., pp. 220 ff. and Carlyle and Carlyle, op. cit., 5:51 ff.

[58] Carlyle and Carlyle, op. cit., 5:472 ff.

Medieval political theory distrusted absolutism; even those like Marsilio of Padua and William of Occam, who stressed the rights of the state and the prince against what they regarded as excesses of ecclesiastical power, did not go to the other extreme and advocate state absolutism. But the thrust of events in the fifteenth and sixteenth centuries increasingly emphasized the absolute power of the monarch.

In England, after the Wars of the Roses, Henry VII (1485–1509) was able to establish a strong centralized monarchy; the potentialities of that centralization were realized by his son Henry VIII who, in the 1530s, used it to great effect in his disputes with Rome.[59] In Spain, the unity of the Kingdom of Aragon and Castile, through the marriage of Ferdinand and Isabella in 1469, laid the foundation of Spanish absolutism which was to reach its full glory in the reign of Charles V (1516–1556), while the end of the Hundred Years' War with England in 1453 saw the beginnings of absolutism in France also.

The final abandonment of the pretence of European unity in a Christendom made the emergence of national states inevitable, and the viability of those states was best assured by the power of a strong centralized political power which, in the circumstances of the time, could only be a monarchy. Political, social and economic forces[60] ensured that such monarchy would not only be strong but absolute. Representative assemblies had too readily degenerated into aristocratic anarchy or had become the instruments of privileged interests; in the troubled times of the late Middle Ages, the strong base of respect for law in stable society, upon which their healthy functioning relied, was too often absent. The new and old social and economic forces, and the ordinary people, were prepared to put their trust in a strong prince.

[59] See *The New Cambridge Modern History* (C.U.P., 1958), 2:233–34. R. W. Chambers, *Thomas More* (London, 1962), pp. 360 ff.

[60] Sabine, op. cit., p. 357. "Not for nothing did the monarchy receive the support of the growing middle class, but for this reason also the religious reformers were thrown into the arms of the Princes. Thus the Reformers joined the economic forces already in existence to make Royal Government, invested with absolute power at home and with a free hand abroad, the typical form of European State." W. G. Hoskins, *The Age of Plunder* (London, 1976), details England's "biggest changeover in landownership for nearly five hundred years, mainly arising from the systematic plunder of the Church at all levels and later the plunder of the Crown itself by the magnates of the realm" (p. xi). As Douglas Jerrold points out in *England: Past, Present, and Future* (London, 1950), p. 58, "The first half of the sixteenth century in England . . . saw the creation, mainly deliberate, of what we today would call a capitalistic totalitarian state." The Pilgrimage of Grace he sees as an honourable and widespread rebellion against the trend, a rebellion defeated by treachery. In the North, the monasteries were less affluent than in the South, and they did their works of charity more effectively, providing social services and poor relief. Their loss was particularly resented and formed one of the great grievances that led to the rebellion.

The ecclesiological and moral problems that were raised by the absolute monarchies taxed the wit of theologians and theorists of both "Catholic" and "Protestant" countries after the Reformation, since in both the prevailing systems of government were of this kind. On the Catholic side, the response was led by a group of Dominican and Jesuit writers.[61] They started with the natural law assumptions about the ability of man's reason to provide the moral foundations of political life—the natural law that is—in the triad of the eternal divine law, the revealed divine law and the natural law which is man's participation in eternal law. Human positive law exists within this framework and is to be judged by the conclusions that are drawn from it.

The origin of the state itself is in man's social nature. Accepting a pre-political stage in which men are free, equal and independent,[62] they reasoned that nonetheless he is disposed to the formation first of the non-political society and then of the political. This choice to live in political society is made because, although human nature is capable of perceiving and following right reason, it does not always do so. In consequence, injustices arise among men and they join themselves in political society in order that they may guard themselves against such injustices. God gives to men this power to form the commonwealth—in this general sense the political order is founded in God's will, but the validity of the enactments of any government depend upon their con-formity to the natural law. The theory, therefore, is that it is for men to establish government by consent, and it is that consent which establishes the validity of the state, which then must operate in accordance with the natural law. Suarez, for example, discusses fully the problems set by the state which is, in fact, established by force.[63] If any government is set up in defiance of the consent of the governed, the ruler has no legislative authority. Only insofar as the people accept, in time, any such govern-ment, can it have such authority. In other words, it is unrealistic to suppose that historically the state arises always in circumstances of calm deliberation: it is equally unrealistic to suppose that men who accept the over-riding obligation to observe God's law can ever simply accept a state based on force with no regard for justice. Where the state initially rests on force, it must be legitimized by acceptance of the people—which assumes either that the regime rules justly and can expect that support as of right, or that, by one means or another, it is made to rule justly before being accepted.

[61] Among them de Vitoria (1485–1546), Suarez (1548–1617), and St. Robert Bellarmine (1542–1621). See Skinner, op. cit., vol. 2, 1:135 ff. Copleston, op. cit., 3:380 ff. and below pp. 257 ff.

[62] Skinner, op. cit., 2:158.   [63] Ibid., p. 163.

Several important conclusions follow from such a theory of the origin of the state and the nature of its authority. The Lutheran view that the godliness of the ruler must be the condition of rulership is rejected and, with it, the threat of anarchy and reckless change that it implies. Political society is a man-made thing, depending not on grace but on nature. Hence non-Christian peoples can establish just and legitimate societies because all men participate in that natural law on which the state is founded. This argument was to prove a powerful weapon in the hands of those who wished to protect the rights of the Indians in the Americas.[64] It also provided an answer to Machiavelli: the idea that the prince's judgement should always be determined by the needs of the state, however amoral or immoral, is not compatible with natural law theory. It would seem that the Jesuit writers at the end of the sixteenth century were among the first to recognize the importance of Machiavellianism.[65]

The question of the temporal authority of the popes was also considered.[66] It was argued that temporal and ecclesiastical authority are different in kind, and that the ecclesiastical has no coercive role in relation to the secular. Suarez discusses these issues in the context of the historical conflicts and the decrees, for example, of Boniface VIII and concludes that, in spite of past claims, the pope has no direct temporal jurisdiction over the whole world.

The theory of the natural law basis of political authority and the needfulness of the consent of the governed carried with it not only the implication that political authority can only be legitimized by the people and that authority has to be used in accordance with the dictates of natural law, but that, failing these conditions, such authority can be overthrown; this was the teaching of St. Thomas as we have seen, but it achieved much greater immediacy in the conditions of the sixteenth and seventeenth centuries when absolute monarchy was the norm. Suarez, in particular, argued that when the very life of the community is being threatened by an unjust ruler, then the citizens have a right to resist;[67] he is stringent, very stringent, in laying down the conditions for such resistance; such a decision can only be taken by an appropriate representative assembly of the whole commonwealth—but that it can be taken he is in no doubt. The strictness of his pre-conditions have about them an air of artificiality. They could no more be met in the actual conditions in which the challenge to a particular authority was justified, than the calm and peaceful consent of the people could have been obtained for the setting up of most states. But the statement of the case in these extreme terms was made to rule out the

[64] Ibid., 2:170. See below p. 258.

[65] Skinner, op. cit., 2:172.   [66] Ibid., p. 175. Copleston, op. cit., 3:402 ff.

[67] Skinner, op. cit., 2:177. Copleston, op. cit., 3:397 ff.

possibility of populism, the decisions of a volatile mob leading to anarchy. The reconciliation of the demands of justice with the demands of orderly transference of power was what was being sought; in such a quest, artificiality in the recommended process of change was inevitable at the time. Modern methods of representative government and its machinery, however, closely follow Suarez's theoretical recommendations for peaceful change in a stable state.

Constitutionalism and government by consent was, therefore, defended by the Thomists—but it had its limits. The act by which the people transfers power to the ruler is not a delegation in the sense that the community still retains control. The ruler is granted full power—and is therefore, by definition, not bound by his own positive laws.[68] Such a theory accommodated the existing realities of absolute monarchy. But it was set against the whole theoretical background of Thomism—the assumption that the ruler was subject to the divine positive and the natural law. The monarch might choose not to be bound by his own positive laws while his subjects were. But he, no more than they, could disobey the law of God, revealed or natural. If he chose to do so and, in so doing, threatened the life of the community by consequent injustices, he and his authority could be rejected by the people. This was one safeguard in the Catholic theory of absolutism. The other was the final rejection of the idea that the monarch received his powers directly from God—the divine right theory. The origin of the state was in consent—in Bellarmine's words, "The King's power is derived from God, not immediately but by the consent of human wills."[69]

C. SOME NON–CATHOLIC AND SECULAR THINKERS SINCE THE RENAISSANCE

So far we have dealt with the developing Catholic tradition in political ethics concerning the origin and nature of political authority in the light of the Church's experience in history. But from the Renaissance and the Reformation, thinkers who owed no allegiance to the Catholic tradition, as it had been until this time understood, were making their contribution to the debate.

The first significant secular political theorist was Machiavelli.[70] Like his fellow countryman, Marsilio of Padua, he was concerned with the

---

[68] Skinner, op. cit., pp. 183–84. Copleston, loc. cit.

[69] J. Brodrick, S.J., *Blessed Robert Bellarmine* (London, 1927) 1:224.

[70] Niccolo Machiavelli (1546–1627). His political philosophy is contained mainly in *The Prince* and the *Discourses on the First Ten Books of Titius Livius*. See Copleston, op. cit., 3:315 ff. Skinner, op. cit., 1:113 ff. Sabine, op. cit., pp. 331 ff.

political confusion that existed in his own country and, like him, he blamed much of the confusion on the Church and the papacy. Though he preferred Republicanism and in theory respected the judgement of the people, his obsession with the needs of Italy, as he knew it, led him to stress the all-importance of the will and force of character of the prince; for practical purposes the origin of the state lay in this capacity of strong-minded and ruthless individuals to provide the order needed for healthy society. Despite his laudable motives and his respect for the conventional morality in theory, in practice he reasoned that, for the ruler in the pursuit of the purpose of maintaining the state, the end justified the means; force of character and will, ruthlessness and pursuit of the main chance were the essential virtues for heads of state. Seeing in practice that chaos could only be overcome by strong action, he envisaged force as the origin of the state and the prince having to use whatever means he thought necessary for the maintenance of order and security—justice, a natural law morality by which the ruler too was bound, a common good which prevented the ruler using bad means to secure his ends, these had no interest for Machiavelli.

Among the theologians and polemicists in the religious field who explored the morality of politics from the Protestant point of view, the main divide was between the Lutherans and the Calvinists.[71] The latter, in France and in Scotland, found themselves at odds with the government and, therefore, emphasized the right of revolt against the state. John Knox was eloquent on the theme, but the most influential contribution to the debate was the *Vindiciae Contra Tyrannos* published anonymously in France in 1579. The author argued that society is based on two contracts; in the first, the community—king and people together—undertake before God to form a chosen people, a Church, bound to true worship; in the other, the king contracts with the people to rule well and justly. The people, therefore, had the right to resist a ruler who would enforce a false religion or rule unjustly. On the other hand, where Calvinist influence dominated, they could invoke the teaching laid out in John Calvin's *Institutes of Christian Religion* (1536), namely, that all properly constituted authority must be obeyed absolutely with no suggestion of any right to resist. And in Geneva, where Calvin settled in 1541, this was the norm. By the time of the publication of the definitive Latin edition of the *Institutes*, however, in 1559, Calvin was changing his mind; the possibility of justifying active resistance to lawful magistrates was admitted.[72]

[71] Skinner, op. cit., 2:189 ff. Sabine, op. cit., pp. 354 ff., 372 ff.
[72] Skinner, op. cit., 2:191 ff. Eventually, the same author notes, the scholastic and Roman law traditions of government by consent were accepted by the Calvinists and "the main foundations of the Calvinist theory of revolution were constructed by their Catholic adversaries" (ibid., p. 321).

Luther's attitude to political authority showed, in his life and actions, some inconsistency—but, on the whole, the effect of both his teaching and example was to stress submission to the ruler. Having abandoned the idea of an authority in the Church such as the Catholic tradition knew, he had to accept that there was need for ecclesiastical discipline; since the Church (by definition) could not provide it, the state had to. The hope for the Church purified lay in secular rulers; secular government became the judge of needful reform and the means of securing it. The result was a National Church subject to the secular authorities.[73] The monarch had to be obeyed except when he commanded what was contrary to Scripture. Even then, the most that the subject could lawfully offer was passive resistance: rebellion was inexcusable even against the wicked and tyrannical ruler; punishment rested with God alone. As a result of conflicts with the emperor, Luther was in the issue prepared to allow opposition to imperial authority, while still insisting on absolute obedience to the subordinate princes. When the peasants of Germany rose in rebellion, Luther's response was that they should be shown no mercy. There could be no centre of authority in the state apart from the prince. The feudal idea of the state as a corporation of corporations was replaced by that of the state as a single corporation having direct control over all its subjects as individuals.

Absolutism, though it was not the product of the Reformation period but grew rather out of the conditions that accompanied the break-up of Christendom and the consequent growth of nationalism, was therefore encouraged by the Reformation. The "Protestant" states were now free of the pope and increasingly in conflict with the emperor—rejecting what was left of his pretensions of control over them. Their political and religious autonomy was for practical purposes complete, and the power of the local or national prince absolute. The advantages that went with absolutism appealed to the "Catholic" states too, even while remaining within the Catholic fold. For the Spaniards this was no problem, for they largely controlled Italian affairs and had great influence in the papal court and, through it, could influence the Church in Spain.[74] For the French it

[73] W. McGovern, *From Luther to Hitler* (London, 1946), p. 31, states that, "Luther started with a plea for reform in the concept of the church and ended with a reform in the concept of the state. He started with a plea for individual liberty and for freedom of conscience; yet his doctrines led directly to a belief in the divine right of kings and to the belief that monarchs have a right to dictate religious dogmas to the private individual. He started as an internationalist with a message to the peoples of all nations; he ended by formulating the doctrine of all-powerful national states in perpetual antagonism to one another. He started with the doctrine of the basic equality of all men and ended with the doctrine that all men should be subject to the iron will of their secular Lord."

[74] H. Daniel Rops, *The Catholic Reformation* (London, 1962), pp. 152 ff., and *The Church in the 17th Century* (London, 1963), pp. 175 ff.

was different. Their response, rooted in the conflicts of the thirteenth and fourteenth centuries, was "Gallicanism", which rejected papal control and attempted to make the French as independent as possible of the international Church. The papacy itself realised that any attempt to exert the old claims to international secular overlordship were no longer feasible; further, it was too weak to do much to resist the unjustifiable claims of the Catholic monarchs to a greater degree of control over the Church within their boundaries.

Absolutism and divine right theory went in hand because the absolutism of the times was one which centred on the claims of kings and princes—and their claim was so much the stronger if they could show that they received their authority and power directly from God without the intervention of any human agency. Though absolutism could be reconciled with the contract theory of the origin of the prince's political power, that power was clearly unassailable if the consent of the people was not needed. The divine right theory was not unknown in medieval Europe, as we have seen, but Bellarmine's arguments finally undermined its place in the Catholic tradition. Among some secular and Protestant theorists it retained a vogue however because of the situation in France and England. In France, the legitimate heir to the throne in 1589 was a Huguenot, and a claim to divine right would ensure that Catholic objections to the succession of a Protestant prince could be met. In the event, Henry IV became a Catholic in 1593 and so resolved the issue. The Huguenots, meanwhile, had become a dangerous challenge to the established order with their revolutionary theories. It was in a situation which called for the defence of monarchical rights that Jean Bodin argued for the divine right of kings.

Bodin,[75] unlike the classical and early medieval thinkers, did not look back to a golden age but, on the contrary, thought there was no limit to man's potentiality for progress. He argued that the origin of the state was in force, not in divine institution or in a social contract. Political organisation comes into being when a man or group of men strong enough to dominate or conquer their neighbours emerges. On the other hand, he thought it was advisable that rulership should be in accord with the divine and natural law and was against the forceful taking of power. To have allowed this could have told against the rights of the monarch he was defending.

His elaboration of the doctrine of sovereignty was Bodin's distinctive contribution to political philosophy. The state was to have ultimate

[75] Bodin (1530–1596) was Professor of Jurisprudence at Toulouse. His main work, *Les Six Livres de la République* (1576), represents the first modern attempt at an elaborated political theory. Sabine, op. cit., pp. 399 ff. Skinner, op. cit., 2:28 ff. McGovern, op. cit., p. 56 ff.

control over all persons and corporations within its territory and, within the state, one person or group of persons was to exercise that absolute power.[76] By implication, therefore, the sovereign is not subject to law. On the other hand, in theory, the absolute sovereignty of Bodin was very circumscribed. The power of the monarch was limited by the divine and natural laws, and if laws were made by him contrary to them, the magistrates were not required to enforce such laws. Neither could the monarch act contrary to the fundamental law of the state, the family life of his subjects or their property. There is in fact considerable confusion in Bodin's thought on the relationship between the absolute sovereignty he favours on the one hand and the limitations placed upon it on the other. Overall, given the circumstances of the time, it was the notion of the king as the Vicar of God on earth that he most favoured, not the idea of a king subject to the restraints on which he, in theory, insisted.[77]

Thomas Hobbes[78] (1588–1679), another defender of absolutism, developed his political theories in the context of a general philosophy of materialism. Animals and men were governed by irresistible impulses, the chief difference between men and animals being that man has the power of speech. Attraction and repulsion govern our moral lives; morality and moral judgements are the products of civilised convention and therefore changeable. He argued that the pre-political state of mankind, the state of nature, was one in which all men were free and equal. But this free and equal state is not an ideal one; man being motivated by self-interest only, he is at war with every other man. Far from being by nature a social animal, in a state of nature man is like a beast in the jungle. Bodin, drawing on the medieval tradition, saw natural law as essentially objective moral law, while to Hobbes it was essentially egoistic prudence: it had no connection with objective or God-given values because there were no such values.

[76] "In the ordinary popular sense, sovereignty means supremacy, the right to demand obedience; for the lawyer, the sovereign is the person or body to whose directions the law attributes legal force . . . whose authority is the law itself." J. Bryce, *Studies in the History of Jurisprudence* (London, 1901), p. 51.

[77] "Between the publication of the *Method* in 1566 and the *Six Books* a decade later . . . he deliberately withdraws all the specific constitutional safeguards . . . retreats with obvious alarm into an uncompromising defence of royal absolutism." Skinner, op. cit., 2:297–98.

[78] Hobbes' life spanned the period in which England was rent by civil war. He, like Bodin, was concerned to provide a theory that would ensure strong effective government. Hobbes graduated from Oxford in 1608 and became tutor to the Cavendish family, travelling widely in this capacity. Disagreements with the Long Parliament led to his departure to France in 1640 where he was for a while tutor to the future Charles II. The publication in 1651 of *Leviathan*, his main political work, brought him into disfavour with both Church and court in France, and he returned to England. See Sabine, op. cit., chap. 23. Copleston, op. cit., 5:1 ff.

Faced with the insecurity and the conflict that besets him in a state of nature, man seeks ways of setting up a government strong enough to punish and restrain those who threaten him. Hence, each takes it upon himself to give up all his rights to such a government—provided that all others do the same. So is formed the commonwealth, the state, Leviathan, the mortal God. The sovereign is not party to this covenant; his power to achieve the purpose for which the state is instituted must be absolute. Though Hobbes preferred monarchy, he allowed that the covenant could be to form a democracy or an aristocracy; but whatever the form of government, its powers must be absolute. This absolutism was, as Hobbes saw it, the only guarantee against the anarchy he so feared. Hobbes knew nothing of the theoretical restraints that Bodin put on sovereignty.

The origin of the commonwealth being so, and the power of the sovereign being so, the question arises—can the subject ever resist the sovereign? The answer lies in the purposes for which the covenant was formed. Since that purpose was the peace and security of the individuals who made it, the sovereign could not act, nor ask a man to act, against his peace and security. The subject then could not be ordered to commit suicide—to take an extreme example. Nor could he be called on to take up arms or to harm others, except when this was necessary to preserve the peace and security which he seeks. The absolute power of the sovereign, conditioned only by the demands of the citizen's self-preservation, these are the twin poles of Hobbes' political theory and morality.

John Locke (1632–1704), by contrast with Hobbes, was the philosopher of political liberalism.[79] In 1688, James II was forced to abdicate as a result of his political and religious policies, and the vacant throne was taken by his daughter Mary. With the expulsion of the last of the Stuart kings, belief in absolute monarchy and divine right went out of fashion in England, and the leaders of the new revolution were conscious of the need for a philosophy to support their cause and claims. Locke provided that philosophy when he published his two *Treatises of Civil Government* in 1690. The author had worked out his ideas before 1688 but they were powerful and apt tracts for the times; their intrinsic merits also ensured for them a place in the classics of political literature. Not only in England were they an influence; they also played their part in inspiring the leaders of both the American and French Revolutions.

[79] Locke graduated from Oxford in 1658 and tutored at Christ Church in Greek and philosophy, then for awhile practised medicine. He became confidential secretary to Lord Stanley in 1666 and spent some time in exile, 1675 and 1683–1688 because of his political views. Returning in 1688, he was rewarded with government office, and shortly afterwards he published his Treatises. McGovern, op. cit., pp 82 ff. Sabine, op. cit., pp. 517 ff. Copleston, op. cit., 5:123 ff.

Locke assumed at the outset that men are rational and that they are by nature equal. Like Hobbes, he believed in a pre-political condition or a state of nature, but thought that, because of man's rational and social nature, that state was, in contrast to Hobbes' idea, normally peaceful. To Locke, as to Bodin, natural law was moral law established by God and discoverable by reason. This natural law compels us to respect the life, liberty and property of other persons. Unfortunately, in a state of nature, not everyone obeys these commands of the natural law and, in order to prevent or right the consequent injustices, men eventually enter into a social contract and form a political state. The state, therefore, simply exists to see that natural rights are safeguarded and the natural law is observed.

Locke was a constitutional monarchist, not a Republican. He was, however, a democrat in the sense that he believed all government must rest on the consent of the governed, the social contract must be renewed in each generation, and all rulers and magistrates derived their authority from the people. As a final resort against despotic government, Locke insisted upon the right of armed revolution for the citizen. Central to his philosophy also was the idea that man retains full control over his life, liberty and property in entering into the social contract. It is not the function of the state to attempt to make its citizens better or wiser or wealthier. The state's function, indeed, was purely negative—punishing crime and looking after the natural rights of its citizens. Among those rights were the right to freedom of speech and writing and to religious belief, except for those who would deny these rights to others. He excluded from such toleration also those whose religious beliefs held them in obedience to foreign powers.

His teaching on the natural right of property was particularly influential. It was the natural right to which he paid most attention. Though there is controversy about what he actually said and meant, there was sufficient evidence in his writings to support the view that he had argued for innate indefeasible rights, to property especially. His qualifications about the amount of property a man may possess and on the manner in which he may use it were too easily overlooked by men of property. As a result of the "glorious revolution" they had the political power and used his theories for their own purposes in exercising that power.

The prestige of England, its growth in political and economic strength in the eighteenth century, impressed the continental Europeans and British thinkers, Locke especially, and was increasingly influential. Montesquieu[80] (1689–1755) developed the idea of the threefold division

[80] Charles Louis Joseph de Secondat Montesquieu, writer and philosophical historian. His *De L'Esprit des Lois* (1748) surveyed and reflected on social and political systems. McGovern, op. cit., pp. 89 ff. Sabine, op. cit., pp. 551 ff. Copleston, op. cit., 6:9 ff.

of government functions into the legislative, executive and judicial, elaborating on the idea of the checks and balances that this division should entail. Voltaire[81] was also much impressed by the way the English managed their affairs. He ascribed the English success to the philosophy of Newton and Locke and made this the basis of his own philosophical propaganda in France. It was Locke's metaphysics he primarily recommended; some of the political implications of Locke's views he could accept, such as those which supported the claims to freedom of men like Voltaire; but Locke's democratic ideas were not for him.

The Frenchman who put the case for democracy much more fundamentally was Jean-Jacques Rousseau (1712–1778).[82] There was a heartlessness and arrogance about the spirit of the enlightenment in men like Voltaire which alienated its leaders and their beliefs from the ordinary people[83]—Rousseau, on the other hand, was the living embodiment of their hopes and ambitions. Locke rationalised a dead and a very mild revolution—Rousseau's ideas and spirit helped give intellectual coherence to the emotional forces which lay behind the French Revolution to be. Rousseau followed Hobbes in his idea of absolute sovereignty, making the absolute sovereign, not the monarch but the people as a whole. Man was to be free from the tyranny of the monarch, but subject to the absolute control of the general will.

Rousseau idealised the state of nature as one in which all men were free and equal. This state of nature he compared with the inequality, the oppression and poverty of the mass of the people in a society in which the upper classes were corrupted by their contact with the luxuries of social life. By implication, therefore, he exalted, not merely the state of nature, but also the common man.

[81] François Marie Arouet (1694–1778), who changed his name to Voltaire, was dramatist, historian and philosopher. He had been exiled in England in 1726, there became acquainted with the writings of Locke and Newton, and developed a liking for the freedom of English life. Sabine, op. cit., pp. 560 ff. Copleston, op. cit., 6:18 ff.

[82] Rousseau, the son of a watchmaker, was apprenticed to the same trade. He ran away in 1725 and was befriended by Baronne de Warens under whose influence he was converted to Catholicism and spent some time in a hospice for catechumens. In 1745 he became acquainted with Voltaire, first achieved literary fame in 1750 with the *Discourse on the Arts and Sciences*, and renounced his Catholicism in 1754. The *Discourses on the Origin and Foundation of Inequality among Men*, in which he set out his ideas on the state of nature, appeared in 1758; in the same year there also appeared the *Discourse on Political Economy* in which he introduced the idea of the general will. In 1762 his *Social Contract* and *Emile* were published. They offended the Genevans whereon he renounced his citizenship, spent some time in England in 1766 as the guest of David Hume, but was soon back on the Continent showing increasing signs of persecution mania. He lived in France till his death in 1778. McGovern, op. cit., pp. 94 ff. Sabine, op. cit., pp. 575 ff. Copleston, op. cit., 6:59 ff.

[83] C. Dawson, *The Gods of Revolution*, pp. 30–31.

His view of the social contract was that man gives up all his rights to the community and sovereignty remained with that community; it could never thereafter be delegated or transferred to anyone. The state has a will of its own, the general will, to which all separate and particular wills must be subordinated. Rousseau assumed that the general will was directed to the common good or interest. Nor did he exclude a standard of natural moral law justice behind that will. But such qualifications were lost on those who took up his ideas; Robespierre was to identify the will of the Jacobins with the general will.[84]

G. F. Hegel[85] (1770–1831) sought to provide a completely new approach to philosophy in the light of what were modern needs, as he saw them. In the previous generation, sceptics had so undermined belief in reason that the concept of natural law was discredited. Kant had established his moral system as the basis of an imperative which he argued was self-evident, not requiring validation except from its own inner logic. Rousseau had loosed a torrent of emotional and uncontrollable optimism about the social potentialities of man once surrendered to the general will. Hegel saw these forces as tending to the dissolution of order, community and reason. In his philosophy, the dominant, the coherent and the energizing force in human development was the state.

The national spirit, the spirit of the race or nation working through the members of the race and nation, but independent of their will and intent, was the creator of all values and institutions. The history of civilisation is the history of national cultures as each makes its contribution to human development, and the state is the embodiment of a nation's will and destiny—such ideas as these were a significant influence on the development of German nationalism.[86] In practice, his theories place the state beyond the realm of law and moral criticism, and those within it and subject to it were at the mercy of the collective urges that manifested the world spirit. Hegelianism also has had its impact in politics through the use Marx made of the dialectic; both of the most virulent forms of modern totalitarianism, therefore, owe something to the intellectual inheritance of Hegelianism.

Marx then was indebted to Hegel for the dialectical method, but he used it to very different ends, to prove that it was the material and not the spiritual which moved all things. As for the state, far from it being the summit of human hopes, the embodiment of the best that destiny gave the

[84] Copleston, op. cit., 6:92.

[85] McGovern, op. cit., pp. 259 ff. Sabine, op. cit., pp. 620 ff. Copleston, op. cit., 7:159 ff.

[86] "It has long been recognized that Hegel is the spiritual father of Bismarck and Bismarckian notions regarding the duties and functions of the national state." McGovern, op. cit., p. 265.

nation to achieve, its executive was, according to the *Manifesto*, but a committee for managing the affairs of the bourgeoisie,[87] the result of the irreconcilable antagonisms of the class struggle, a machine for the oppression of one class by another. When the proletariat came to power, the nation state would disappear.[88]

Marx and Engels' initially strong convictions on this matter were underpinned by the findings of the anthropologist Lewis Morgan; Marx's appreciation of those findings and Engels' book based upon them have already been discussed in the context of the ethics of the family,[89] and Morgan's work was likewise used to undermine the idea of the bourgeois state. The logical implications (and they were specifically spelled out) of Marx and Engels' view was that the bourgeois state had to be brought down by the revolution in order that the socialist new order should come to be.[90] They were, however, not very clear on what would replace that bourgeois state. In the *Critique of the Gotha Programme* (1875), Marx said that after the abolition of that state and the establishment of a communist society, there would be a dictatorship of the proletariat[91]—but he was vague indeed on what would happen next.[92]

D. CONCLUSION

Against the confusion and contradiction of these theories, the greater coherence of the Catholic tradition is apparent. We have seen that elements of that tradition were consolidated against the background of classical pagan philosophy and practical political developments over many centuries. St. Thomas presents us with the essential elements—that political society grows out of human nature according to God's design, that the people have the right to choose their rulers and form of government, monarchy, aristocracy or democracy as they wish, though the best

[87] *The Communist Manifesto* (February 1848) in D. McClellan, *Karl Marx: Selected Writings*, p. 223.

[88] The argumentation of the *Manifesto* on the point is not as clear as it might be—but it says "the working men have no country" and that the national differences, already diminished by free trade under capitalism, will be further diminished by the advent to power of the proletariat. Ibid., p. 235.

[89] See above p. 167.

[90] In the *Manifesto* (McClellan, op. cit., p. 230) among other places.

[91] McClellen, op. cit., p. 565, "between capitalist and Communist society lies the period of the revolutionary transformation . . . a political transition period in which the state can be nothing but the revolutionary dictatorship of the proletariat."

[92] See R. N. Carew Hunt, *The Theory and Practice of Communism* (London, 1963), p. 105. "When, however, Marx goes on to describe the Communist State of the future, his language becomes as Utopian as that of the French Socialists from whose influence he never wholly freed himself."

seems to be a form which incorporates elements of all three. Whatever the form of government, it must be for the common good in accordance with the divine eternal, divine revealed and natural laws—which have their authoritative interpreter in the Church. Rulers who seriously neglect their duty of caring for the common good can be challenged and, in extreme circumstances, deposed.

Some of the modern theories we have reviewed, Bodin's and Locke's especially, contained elements of belief in natural law, while Locke, Hobbes and Rousseau took up the idea of social compact or contract. But Bodin's account of the restraints of natural law on the monarch lacked conviction; against the power of the monarch there was effectively no appeal because there was no independent source of moral authority to set against him. Locke stressed rights, including rights of property, at a time when events were already conspiring in England to give men of property a freedom to exploit their fellows in a way and on a scale which Europe had not before known. The implications of Hobbes' social contract in the light of his understanding of absolute monarchy and Rousseau's, given the potentialities for demagogic misinterpretation of the general will, have nothing to recommend them to an age which has seen how terrible the absolutism of modern despots can be. Nor can Hegel's vision of the almighty state be judged kindly in the light of Nazi militarism and Soviet expansionism.

Through having its own highly developed tradition to draw on, one that embodied many of the insights of the most sophisticated of the political theorists of antiquity, the Church's modern social philosophy has shown resilience and balance just as did the sixteenth and seventeenth century Thomism in the light of the challenges of its time. One element of the rethinking of the earlier period links up with a nineteenth century development in Catholic thought—it was one made in the light of Rousseau's influence. Against the advocates of the divine right of kings, Bellarmine had argued that whereas some power, such as that of the pope (in virtue of his being the successor of St. Peter), comes from God *immediately*, that of temporal rulers is derived from God *mediately*, through the choice of the people. As an example of designation, the cardinals do not *confer* the pope's authority upon him, they only *designate* the person upon whom God then confers it. The election and succession of princes, on the other hand, causes to be passed on to them a power which is originally invested in the people.[93] The question of whether political authority passes to those who exercise it by designation (which involves no transfer of power) or delegation (which does involve a

[93] Brodrick, op. cit., 1:224 ff, pp. 248 ff.

transfer of power) became of some importance in the light of Rousseau's version of the social contract. According to Rousseau, the authority of civil society comes immediately from the free consent of the citizens and in no way has its origin in God or is in any way dependent upon him. Further, power is delegated in the sense that the general will may always override the government at any time. In response to such conclusions the encyclical *Diuturnum Illud* was issued by Leo XIII.[94] In it, it was pointed out that the people certainly may choose for themselves the form of government which best suits their own character and their own particular traditions, but political power itself comes from God and is subject to law. Some have argued that Leo's encyclical in fact means that the people only *designate* their rulers—in other words, that political authority is not originally with the people and transferred (delegated) to the rulers. But *Diuturnum Illud* can be reconciled with Bellarmine's idea of delegation because the concept of delegation as used in the encyclical does not mean what it meant to Rousseau who argued that political authority *originated* in the consent of the people—that the people cannot elect representatives, only deputies, and every law that the people do not ratify in person is null and void.

Other practical and theoretical questions have arisen in the realm of political ethics, especially concerning the relationship between the Church and the state in a secularized society, and we will be dealing with the origin and the course of such conflicts and their resolution in later sections. But we shall also see that, in the resolution of such problems as the new situation has brought, the clear and precise ability to understand the origin and the nature of political authority has been and is a key factor in enabling the modern Church to face up to and to find a suitable solution to those problems. It is not always easy to determine exactly the true long-term situation to which a response is needed, and not until that situation has clarified and settled can the magisterium respond effectively. This makes many impatient with the Church on occasion—but her caution is necessary. Firstly, it is for the political and economic order and authorities to make the right reason decisions for the common good. These areas of life have a God-given autonomy under the natural law. The Church's role is to determine whether courses proposed and methods used are in accordance with that law. Truly, secular authorities would save themselves and their subjects much trouble if they referred initially to the needs of morality rather than expediency. But they do not always do so. The Church's role is to call them back to their duty; it is not for her to do the job which God has entrusted to politicians—under his law.

---

[94] The letter was published on 29 June 1881 and deals with the origin and nature of civil government. E. Gilson, ed., *The Church Speaks to the Modern World* (New York, 1954), pp. 140 ff.

II. The Purpose, Attitude Towards
And Proper Use of Political Authority

A. THE PURPOSE OF POLITICAL AUTHORITY:
THE COMMON GOOD

Having examined the question of the nature and origin of the political community and political authority, we now look more closely at the proper use of that authority. The purpose of the state, the reason for its being, is, as we have seen, the fulfillment of those needs of the citizens which they cannot, as individuals, families or voluntary societies, fulfill. By implication, therefore, the citizens, in entering political society, surrender to it some degree of control over their lives and liberties. The precise degree of that control and the manner of its exercise are, accordingly, of crucial importance to every citizen. Decisions concerning the quality of life, including its moral quality, are made for us by those who exercise political power. Education, the physical, moral and intellectual environment in which we lead our lives, job and leisure opportunities, all are affected by positive decisions made by politicians. Neither the individual Christian nor the Church can afford to neglect the political order; it is essential that we understand the right and wrong use of this power so that we may understand what our rights and responsibilities are in relation to it. The guidance from *Gaudium et Spes*, we recall, is as follows:[95]

> The political community exists for the common good: this is its full justification and meaning and the source of its specific and basic right to exist. The common good embraces the sum total of all those conditions of social life which enable individuals, families and organisations to achieve complete and efficacious fulfilment.[2]

> [2] Cf. John XXIII Encyclical *Mater et Magistra*: AAS 53 (1961) p. 417.

The next paragraph continues

The rights of all individuals, families and organizations and their practical implementations must be acknowledged and protected and fostered[6] together with the public duties binding on all citizens. Among these duties it is worth mentioning the obligation of rendering to the state whatever material and personal services are required for the common good. Governments should take care not to put obstacles in the way of family, cultural or social groups, or of organizations and intermediate institutions, nor to hinder their lawful and constructive activity: rather they should eagerly seek to promote such orderly activity. Citizens, on the other hand, either individually or in association, should take care not to vest too much power in the hands of public authority nor to make untimely and exaggerated demands for favours

[95] *Gaudium et Spes*, par. 74.

and subsidies, lessening in this way the responsible role of individuals, families and social groups. The growing complexity of modern situations makes it necessary for public authority to intervene more often in social, cultural and economic matters in order to bring out more favourable conditions to enable citizens and groups to pursue freely and effectively the achievement of man's well-being in its totality. The understanding of the relationship between socialization[7] and personal autonomy and progress will vary according to different areas and the development of peoples.

[6] Pius XII *Radio Message*, 1 June 1941: *AAS* 33 (1941) p. 200.
[7] Cf John XXIII Litt. Encycl. *Mater et Magistra*, *AAS* 53 (1961) p. 415–18.

The common good for which political authority exists, therefore, consists of the sum total of all those conditions of social life enabling individuals, families and organisations to fulfill their potential; but the state should not exceed its proper competence in this matter. One of the main concerns of the encyclical *Mater et Magistra*, referred to in a footnote, was precisely the question of what is referred to in its English translation as "socialisation". This term covers all those means of collective action which provide for the security, health and the education of citizens. The key Christian ideal in social ethics is that of personal responsibility, and the purpose of state action in this regard is to enable the individual to develop his powers and discharge his responsibilities to himself and to his family. As a result of the experience and inheritance of the nineteenth and twentieth centuries, in the situation of actual life, it was found that certain social provisions had to be made for things which ideally the individual should have been able to provide for himself.[96] Around this question, therefore, of socialisation (or social welfare, the welfare state) controversy had arisen before *Mater et Magistra*, and we will pay a little closer attention to the response of that document in a moment. For its part, *Gaudium et Spes* referred to socialisation in the context of "all those conditions of life" enabling individuals, families and organisations to achieve fulfillment, and of the need for the state to allow freedom for individuals and groups to exercise initiative and responsibility. In other words, any social provision which genuinely does aid the fulfillment of the person is welcome. Hence,

[96] The first steps towards the welfare state were taken in Bismarck's Germany in the 1880s (H. Friedlander and J. Oser, *Economic History of Modern Europe* [New York, 1953], pp. 336 ff. J. H. Clapham, *Economic Development of France and Germany, 1814–1915* [C.U.P., 1923], pp. 332 ff.) A. V. Dicey, *Law and Public Opinion in England* (London, 1905), gives the intellectual background to the British adjustment and D. Fraser, *The Evolution of the British Welfare State* (London, 1975), details the specifics. W. Laquer, *Europe since Hitler* (Penguin, 1970), pp. 243 ff., surveys the spread of the welfare state in Europe and T. H. Marshall, *Social Policy* (London, 1977), outlines what the policy for welfare involves. A good summary of the emergent doubts about the welfare state is in A. Marwick, *Britain in a Century of Total War* (London, 1968), pp. 428 ff.

such provisions for matters like security, health and education are not necessarily for the good of the person or for his ill. We ask what are the alternatives through which such goods could be provided and, if we see that there is no practical alternative but social provision and that on balance the effect of those provisions is to make it easier for a person to develop his potential as a human being, then we conclude these provisions are good. If a practical alternative exists which would enable that potential to be developed at least as well as the social provisions in question, then that alternative is to be preferred. Any move in the direction of self-help is to be welcomed, provided it does not undermine the rights of others.

This is another way of stating the principle of subsidiary function which is central to Christian social ethics. It was in particular developed in the encyclical *Quadragesimo Anno*,[97] in the context of the problems of industrial relations and industrial organisation. The encyclical discussed whether certain state interventions in industry in certain countries (they were not named, but Italy was a relevant example) were in conformity with the Church's guidance on social ethics or not.[98] We will be considering the industrial relations context and problem in a later section. Here we are simply concerned with the general principle of subsidiarity. It is set out as follows:[99]

> Just as it is wrong to withdraw from the individual and commit to a group what private enterprise and industry can accomplish, so too it is an injustice, a grave evil and a disturbance of right order for a larger and higher association to arrogate to itself functions which can be performed efficiently by smaller and lower societies. This is a fundamental principle of social philosophy, unshaken and unchangeable. Of its very nature the true aim of all social activity should be to help members of the social body, never to destroy or absorb them. The State, therefore, should leave to smaller groups the settlement of business of minor importance which otherwise would greatly distress it. It will thus carry out with greater freedom, power and success the task belonging to it alone because it alone can effectively accomplish these, directing, watching, stimulating, restraining, as circumstances suggest and necessity demands. Those in power, therefore, should be convinced that the

[97] Pius XI, *Quadragesimo Anno*, 15 May 1931 (London: C.T.S., 1960).

[98] The question was whether "a special syndical and corporative organisation" recently inaugurated is to be recommended. And since this special syndical organisation, as the encyclical noted, placed severe limits on the right of free association and was excessively bureaucratic and political, it could not be reconciled with a sound social ethic. (Ibid., pars. 90 ff.) On Fascist corporativism see McGovern, op. cit.

[99] *Quadragesimo Anno*, pars. 79–80. The recent interest in intermediate technology indicates the value of this principle in economic and social organisation. E. F. Schumacher, *Small is Beautiful* (London, 1973). N. Jequier, ed., *Appropriate Technology: Problems and Promises* (Paris: O.E.C.D., 1976).

more faithfully this principle of subsidiary function be followed and a graded hierarchical order exists between various associations, the greater will be both social authority and social efficiency and the happier and more prosperous the conditions of the commonwealth.

The question of whether the larger organisation, the state, was taking over functions that the individual, the family or the group could do for themselves is then clearly raised by the provisions of the modern state for old age, ill health, unemployment, education, family allowances and social security generally. The Christian ideal has always been that a man should possess sufficient security, from ownership or professional or manual skills, to enable him to meet these needs out of his property or his earnings or his savings. Was it morally desirable now that society should provide him with all or at least many of these things?

Mater et Magistra[100] considered these matters in some detail. The use of the word "socialisation" in the English translation has been the cause for some comment, but the context does not allow any party political interpretation to be put on the word. The translation here is perhaps cloudy, but careful reading enables the essential points to be clearly understood. What is at issue is the "increase in social relationships" and "mutual ties" of which a symptom and a cause is[101]

> the growing intervention of the state even in matters of such intimate concern to the individual as health and education, the choice of career . . . this sort of growth in social relationships . . . makes it possible for the individual to exercise many of his personal rights . . . such as the right to the indispensable means of earning a livelihood, preserving good health, receiving further education and a more thorough professional training, the right to housing, work and suitable leisure and recreation. . . . Must we conclude that increased social action necessarily reduces men to the condition of being mere automatons? By no means. This growth in the social life of man is not a product of natural forces working as it were by blind impulse. It is, as we saw, the creation of men who are free and autonomous by nature— though they must recognize and in a sense obey the laws of economic development and social progress and cannot altogether escape from the pressures of environment. The development of these social relationships, therefore, can and ought to be realised in a way best calculated to promote its inherent advantages and to preclude or at least minimise its attendant disadvantages.

The matter is further considered by the encyclical in the light of the traditional teaching on private property.[102] More will be said of it in the context of private ownership when we will deal with the latter below.

[100] John XXIII, *Mater et Magistra*, 15 May 1961 (London: C.T.S., 1963).
[101] Ibid., pars. 59 ff.   [102] Ibid., pars. 104 ff.

Since social institutions exist for the sake of the individual and not vice versa,[103] such institutions, including the state, should work so as to secure and develop personal initiative and potentialities. Hence the group (that is any organisation between the individual and the state) should not do for the individual what the individual can do for himself, nor should the state do what the group can do for itself—providing always that the individual, the family or the group of individuals, can perform the function for itself in a way which meets the just needs of the individual, the group and the state. It is on these practical matters that legitimate disagreement among political parties arises.

Since the state, properly considered, has care of the common good, it can be argued that it has to be perpetually on the watch to make sure that private individuals, families and groups within the state are sincerely serving the commonwealth. By the same token, private citizens, families and groups have a duty to watch out for the needless encroachments of the state. Where democracy is vigorous and respect for law is real, the resulting political conflicts enable the real issues to be debated fully and practical alternatives decided. The question of sectional interest prevailing over the common good remains; responsible freedom alone can provide the answer.

It is in this area, of course, in examining specific issues, that the services of experts in the social sciences are essential, and the particular pressure group, political or otherwise, must have full freedom to argue its case. Only when all the arguments are marshalled on both sides can the individual make up his mind whether the principle is being adequately implemented. There can be and there will be much disagreement among those who accept the same principle when it comes to applying it in particular cases. There are so many imponderables, questions of alternatives, the need to weigh the future possible consequences—and these factors make disagreement inevitable. What such a principle does is to challenge the belief that individualism is always right on the one hand, or the belief, on the other, that state intervention is always right. Cases and situations are to be considered on their merits. In this way the injustices of both individualism and collectivism can be countered.

Much more fundamentally, of course, the principle itself underlines the Christian belief that law and the political order must be founded on a firm moral basis. This has been a constant theme of the development of the Christian social ethic as our consideration of its historical evolution has demonstrated. One of the fullest, most modern restatements of the

---

[103] Ibid., par. 219, "Individual human beings are the foundation, the cause and the end of every social institution."

general principle occurs in the encyclical *Mit Brennender Sorge* of Pius XI.[104]
In dealing with Nazi racism it is pointed out[105] that

> It is part of the trend of the day to sever more and more, not only morality
> but also the foundations of law and its administration from true belief in God
> and from his revealed commandments. Here we have in mind particularly
> the so-called natural law that is written by the finger of the Creator himself
> on the tables of the hearts of men and which can be read on these tables by
> sound reason, not darkened by sin and passion. *Every positive law from
> whatever law giver it may come, can be examined as to its moral implications and,
> consequently, judged as to its moral authority to bind in conscience in the light of
> the Commandments of the natural law. Laws of man that are in direct contradiction
> with the natural law bear an initial defect that no violent means, no outward display
> of power can remedy. By this standard we must judge the principle "What helps
> people is right". A right meaning may be given to this sentence. . . . But even ancient
> paganism recognised that the sentence to be perfectly accurate should be inverted and
> read "never is anything useful if it is not at the same time morally good. Not because
> it is useful is it morally good but because it is morally good it is also useful. . . ."*[34]
> Man as a person possesses God-given rights which must be preserved from
> all attacks aimed at denying, suppressing or disregarding them. To pay no
> heed to this truth is to overlook the fact that the true public good is finally
> determined and recognised by the nature of man with his harmonious
> co-ordination of personal rights and social obligations as well as by the
> purpose of the community which, in its turn, is conditioned by the same
> human nature. The community is willed by the Creator as the means to the
> full human development of the individual and social attainments which the
> individual, in give and take, has to employ to his own good and that of
> others. Also these higher and more comprehensive values that cannot be
> realised by the individual but only by the community, in the final analysis
> are intended by the Creator for the sake of the individual, for his natural
> and supernatural development and perfection. A deviation from this order
> loosens the supports on which the community is placed and thereby imperils
> the tranquillity, security and even the existence of the community itself.

[34] Cicero *De Officiis* III. 30.

We are familiar with the difficulty of determining what the natural law
demands in particular circumstances and, in disputed cases, we have the
revealed moral law and the teaching of the Church interpreting it to guide
us. But the existence of these difficulties should not obscure the importance of the principle itself. The private good of the individual, of a group
within the state, or the supposed good of the state itself may not be
invoked against the moral law, the natural law existing in the mind of man

[104] 14 March 1937.
[105] Paragraph 35 of the translation published in *The Church and the Reconstruction of the
Modern World*, T. P. McLaughlin, ed. (New York, 1957), pp. 351–52.

and the revealed moral law contained in the Scriptures and the teaching of the Church. With this in mind, the Christian always has a norm by which to judge the actions of the state when they touch on man's eternal destiny or human rights. In this connection, it is worth stressing that it is from this structure of moral ideas that the Christian concept of human rights emerges. And indeed, any appeal to human rights is in fact an appeal to natural rights based on natural law.[106] Rights only exist under law: the assumption of human rights is that there is some law, known to all, accessible by unaided human reason, which enables the rationality and justice of the human right appeal to be recognized. This capacity to search out what is right and reasonable is the origin of the natural law concept as we saw above.[107]

B. THE ATTITUDE TOWARDS POLITICAL AUTHORITY AND THE RIGHT OF DISSENT

1. The Attitude towards Political Authority

Given the tradition of respect for legitimate authority that has been typical of Christian attitudes as a result of the example of Christ himself and his disciples, we would expect the Council to have a high regard for those who exercise it, and such indeed is the case.[108]

> It follows that political authority, either within the political community as such or through organisations representing the State, must be exercised within the limits of the moral order and directed towards the common good, (understood in the dynamic sense of the term) according to the juridical order legitimately established or due to be established. Citizens then are bound in conscience to obey.[4] Accordingly the responsibility and dignity and the importance of state rulers is clear.
>
> [4] Cf. Romans 13: 1–5.

Hence,[109] the next paragraph continues

> . . . Every citizen ought to be mindful of his right and his duty to promote the common good by using his vote. The Church praises and esteems those who devote themselves to the public good for the service of man and take

[106] See J. Finnis, *Natural Law and Natural Rights*, chap. 8 and passim. Welty, op. cit., 1:197 ff.

[107] See above pp. 66 ff.

[108] *Gaudium et Spes*, par. 74.

[109] Ibid., par. 75. Paul VI, *Octogesima Adveniens*, [*Social Problems*], 15 May 1971 (London: C.T.S., 1971), pars. 24 ff., comments on the needs and the problems of the Christian political commitment.

upon themselves the burdens of public office . . . those with a talent for the difficult yet noble art of politics[8] or whose talents in this matter can be developed, should prepare themselves for it and, forgetting their own convenience and material interest, they should engage in political activity. They must combat injustice and oppression, arbitrary domination and intolerance by individuals or political parties, they must do so with integrity and wisdom. They must dedicate themselves to the welfare of all in a spirit of sincerity and fairness, of love and of the courage demanded by political life.

[8] Cf. Pius XI. Allocution to the Directors of the Catholic University Federation: Discorsi di Pio XI edited Bertetto, Torino Vol. 1 (1960) p. 743.

The duty of the citizen to obey in conscience is clearly stated as is the respect for those who hold office. The question then arises of the possibility of dissent from decisions of legitimate authority in the state and how that dissent can be registered. The forms and degrees of such dissent are several: there is 1) the peaceful internal dissent that is institutionalised in the system of party politics, including the right of peaceful demonstration and of conscientious objection to specific policies, especially in wartime, 2) resistance to a party, a government or a policy on a scale that challenges one or all to the point of overturning them, but which uses only peaceful means, such as refusal to operate laws, or disrupts normal life by demonstration[110] and 3) finally, the issue of violent resistance or rebellion. On all these matters the mind of the good Christian can be and is taxed from time to time. The Council's guidance in the light of the traditional teaching was then needed.

On the issue of party politics in the first instance, the Council was quite explicit. Christians, it said[111]

should recognize the legitimacy of different points of view about the organisation of worldly affairs and show respect for their fellow citizens who even in association defend their opinions by legitimate means. Political parties for their part must support whatever in their opinion is conducive to the common good but must never put their own interest before the common good.

[110] In other words, it seems unreasonable to assume that, even where true political freedom exists, decisions can go unchallenged if the politicians of all parties get so seriously out of touch with the deep convictions of the people that they are unable to command their confidence on a serious issue. In those circumstances, provided pressure groups do not use unconstitutional means, they can agitate to the point where the legally constituted government and political parties have to change minds and policies. E. Welty gives some pointers concerning the issues where extra parliamentary but constitutional action could possibly be taken, "gross defects of legislation; completely inadequate economic and social policy; a foreign policy that endangers the state; using the danger of war irresponsibly as a means of policy" (op. cit., 2:330). An example of how public agitation changed a nation's policy in recent years would be that in America over the Vietnam war.

[111] Gaudium et Spes, par. 73.

The principle of party politics is therefore not incompatible with the duty of those who have the care of the state to seek the common good, though the bland statement in itself resolves none of the obvious practical difficulties the two concepts and realities raise. We will be looking at some of these issues at a little greater length when we deal with political pluralism and the Christian commitment in a later section. For the moment we want to consider these forms of resistance to legitimate authority which stop short of challenging it fundamentally.

One such is the right that citizens must have to peaceful anti-government demonstration and protest. It is the duty of the state to allow this under proper provision of law intended to protect life, property and the rights of others. The right of demonstration may well have to be curbed if tempers run so high that peace cannot be kept.[112] But governments should not be allowed to use this argument as an excuse for preventing any form of protest. The conditions that lead to curbing such freedoms should be clear to all and subject to proper legal definition and process. Another such right is that of conscientious objection to the policy pursued by the state, especially in the case of war. This issue is of such importance, especially in the light of the possibility of nuclear, biological and chemical warfare, that we must deal with it in a special section.

2. The Right of Dissent:
Conscientious Objection and the Just War Concept

In many of the issues which concern us as citizens, the slow organic process of representative government through political parties may be sufficient as a means of channelling our dissatisfaction with particular policies. But there are some issues which either cut across party lines or are of a nature which does not allow protest to be raised through normal political channels. A clear case is that of conscientious objection in war. A situation could conceivably arise in which objection to a particular war, or particular acts of war, or indeed objection to all use of violence, could be registered through the normal political process, but this is not the usual case. But where general dispute on the issue does not arise, individuals and groups of individuals must still have the right of conscientious objection, even where it is possible to argue that just war is being waged, and where good men may argue that breach of the rules of war has not occurred. Hence[113]

---

[112] The problem was acute in Britain in the inter-war years as a result of the marches and demonstrations by some organisations connected with the protest against unemployment and, later, and much more seriously, the activities of the British Union of Fascists in the East End of London. J. Stevenson and C. Cook, *The Slump* (London, 1977), pp. 218 ff.

[113] *Gaudium et Spes*, par. 79.

It seems that just laws should make humane provisions for the case of conscientious objectors who refuse to carry arms, provided they accept some form of community service.

The concept of the just war is fraught with difficulties, especially today when one can hardly imagine a major conflict in which an antagonist, possessed of modern nuclear and biological weapons, would not in desperation use them and so make nonsense of all attempts to reduce the barbarism of armed conflict. But the concept provides a useful basis on which to start consideration of the issues involved.

The conditions for a just war, as traditionally understood by theologians, are clear enough. The first requirement is that the war should be declared by a legitimate authority, the second that the cause should be a just one (the avenging of proportionate wrongs that cannot be righted in any other way), and finally, the belligerent should have a right intention, seeking to secure peace, to punish evildoers and help those who do right.[114] The right to wage war was in itself not denied by the Council.[115]

War, of course, has not ceased to be part of the human scene. As long as the danger of war persists and there is no international authority with the necessary competence or power, governments cannot be denied the right of lawful self-defence once all peaceful efforts have failed. State leaders and all who share the burdens of public administration have a duty to defend the interests of their people and to conduct such grave matters with a deep sense of responsibility. However, it is one thing to wage a war of self-defence, it is quite another to seek to impose domination on another nation. The possession of war potential does not justify the use of force for political or military objectives, nor does the mere fact that war has unfortunately broken out mean that all is fair between warring parties. All those who enter military service in loyalty to their country should look upon themselves as custodians of the security and freedom of their fellow countrymen and when they carry out their duty properly they are contributing to the maintenance of peace.

In other words, there will always be the possibility of war where there is no international authority capable of resolving disputes in any other way. In these circumstances, national governments may not be denied the right of self-defence. But this is not the whole of the question. It can be argued that modern methods of waging war are such that the older concept of self-defence is no longer valid; any modern war will end in total self-destruction or will involve the use of means which are intrinsically immoral. The document continues[116]

[114] St. Thomas Aquinas, *Summa Theologica*, II–II, q. 40, art. 1. See Welty, op. cit., 2:394 ff. Messner, op. cit., pp. 665 ff.
[115] *Gaudium et Spes*, par. 79.   [116] Ibid., par. 80.

The development of armaments by modern science has immeasurably magnified the horrors and wickedness of war. Warfare conducted with these weapons can inflict immense and indiscriminate havoc which goes far beyond the bounds of legitimate defence. Indeed if the kind of weapons now stocked in the arsenals of the great powers were to be employed to the fullest, the result would be the almost complete reciprocal slaughter of one side by the other, not to speak of the widespread devastation that would follow in the world and the deadly after-effects resulting from the use of such arms. All these factors force us to undertake a completely fresh re-appraisal of war.[2] Men of this generation should realise that they will have to render an account of their warlike behaviour: the destiny of generations to come depends largely on the decisions they make today. *With these considerations in mind, the Council, endorsing the condemnations of total warfare issued by recent Popes declares:*[3] *every act of war directed to the indiscriminate destruction of whole cities or vast areas with their inhabitants is a crime against God and man which merits firm and unequivocal condemnation.*

[2] John XXIII, *Pacem in Terris: AAS* 55 (1963) p. 291. "Therefore in this age of ours which prides itself on its atomic power, it is irrational to think that war is a proper way to obtain justice for violated rights."

[3] Pius XI, *Allocution:* 30 September 1954. *AAS* 46 (1954) p. 589. *Christmas Message* 1954 *AAS* 47 (1955) p. 15 f.: John XXIII *Pacem in Terris: AAS* 55 (1963) p. 286–91. Paul VI *Address to the United Nations*, 4 October 1965: *AAS* 57 (1965) p. 877–85.

The conclusion is obvious.[117]

It is our clear duty to spare no effort in order to work for the moment when all war will be completely outlawed by international agreement. This goal, of course, requires the establishment of a universally acknowledged public authority for all, regard for justice and respect for the law. But before this desirable authority can be constituted, it is necessary for existing international bodies to devote themselves resolutely to the exploration of better means for obtaining common security. But *since peace must be born of mutual trust between peoples instead of being forced on nations through dread of arms, all must work to put an end to the arms race and make a real beginning of disarmament, not unilaterally indeed but at an equal rate on all sides on the basis of agreements and backed up by genuine and effective guarantees.*[4]

[4] John XXIII *Pacem in Terris* where the reduction of arms is treated, *AAS* 55 (1963) p. 287.

The armaments of modern science referred to are not only those based on nuclear fission, but chemical and biological weapons also[118]—poison gases and the use of living organisms and toxic biological products to kill or incapacitate. Primitive forms of chemical and biological weaponry

[117] Ibid., par. 82.
[118] S. M. Hersh, *Chemical and Biological Warfare* (London, 1968). J. Cookson and J. Nottingham, *A Survey of Chemical and Biological Warfare* (London, 1969).

have been used since classical antiquity, while the First World War saw the widespread use of gas. But such horrors, great as they were, are nothing in comparison to those threatened by the possible use of more modern forms. Combined with the greater range and efficacy of missile delivery systems, they provide a totally new dimension to the evils of war.

Given these facts about the scale and nature of the destruction any future war would bring, it might have seemed inevitable that the Council would pronounce any future wars, or preparation for them, intrinsically immoral. Why it could not do so is clear. A blanket condemnation of all war would have meant that those who did not prepare for it in its modern form would be entirely at the mercy of their enemies. It had, therefore, to be left open to governments to pursue a policy which would deter its potential aggressor by the possession of these weapons and the readiness to use them in self-defence on military targets.

The question of whether, and to what extent, a policy of deterrence would result in the active use of nuclear and other weapons in case of war immediately arises.[119] To decide the rights and wrongs of it by public debate, access to a nation's defence secrets would have to be on such a scale that the whole purpose of deterrence, indeed legitimate self-defence, would be undermined.[120] To leave the matter entirely in the hands of politicians and military leaders is hardly a more encouraging prospect but, in the last analysis, we have to do that. In a free society we elect our rulers and give them power to act on our behalf, and on many issues we cannot hope to have full access to all the information they have. But if we cannot demand such full information, public debate and public agitation on the question of nuclear, biological and chemical warfare is a necessity, and those who encourage it and lead it are doing a public service. By the same token, those who, while hating the prospect of using such weapons, are prepared to do so if there is no other recourse, and accept the responsibility in discharge of their duty, have a right to urge the case for weapons and carry on in preparation for their use.

[119] See M. Walzer, *Just and Unjust War*, pp. 269 ff. E. B. F. Midgley, *The Natural Law Tradition and the Theory of International Relations* (London, 1975), pp. 371 ff. L. L. McCreavy, *Peace and War in Catholic Doctrine* (Oxford, 1963). W. Stein, *Nuclear Weapons and Christian Conscience* (London, 1961). H. P. Ford and F. X. Winters, *Ethics and Nuclear Strategy?* (New York, 1977). The article on "Preventing War" by Michael Quinlan, a deputy undersecretary of State, in *The Tablet*, 18 July 1981, presents a case for deterrence argued by a convinced Catholic. Walter Stein, in the same journal on 22 August 1981, made a case against it.

[120] Books like L. R. Beres *Apocalypse* (London 1980) give us some insight into the American thinking and policy while L. Freedman's *Britain and Nuclear Weapons* (London, 1980), traces the development of British government policy.

Public debate on these issues has become much more active in the early 1980s because of the increase in tension between the superpowers.[121] In Britain, the decision to update its strategic nuclear weapons capability has given an added edge to the proceedings. Yet the issues are unchanged essentially from those which faced the world the moment this type of weapon had first been used.

Could it ever be justifiable to use such weapons on military targets in towns and cities? In particular, does the Council's insistence on the absolute immorality of indiscriminate attacks on populated areas mean that any use of nuclear weapons on cities is wrong? The difficulty is that today it can be seriously and plausibly argued that any communications centre or industrial complex is a legitimate *military* target even though it is contained within a heavily populated area. The intention therefore (to destroy a military target) would, it is claimed, be morally defensible, the unintended effect (the deaths of civilians) regrettable but unavoidable. It is all too clear, however, in the light of the destructiveness of the weapons now available, that we must beware lest such an argument be used to justify any enormity in the name of military necessity. On balance it would seem that, since, on both matters of fact (what is a military target?) and on the implications of any course of action or lack of it (balancing the evil effects of nuclear destruction against the evils that could come of not using such weapons) views may very reasonably differ, so it would seem that each has to be left to the guidance of his own conscience in the matter.

Allied to this question is the related one of whether one can distinguish between tactical and strategic use of such weapons.[122] Is it possible to make any use of the weaponry in question without producing the conditions in which an all-out war of this nature would develop?

It can be doubted whether human life and culture would survive such an eventuality. Some would say that this is putting the matter at its most extreme and even pushing legitimate fears beyond reasonable limits, indeed to the point of hysteria. The capacity of humanity for survival on a world-wide scale, no matter how horrific the devastation, should not be underestimated. But, at the same time, we must remember that the sort of situation we may well have to face before long has no parallel in previous history. We simply have no means of knowing what the long-term effects will be of loosing the sort of forces now at our

[121] E. P. Thompson and Dan Smith, *Protest and Survive* (London, 1980). See also *The Listener*, 16 October 1980, the report of the B.B.C. Radio nuclear debate. On the Holy See's attitude to the developing situation, Pope John Paul II, at the United Nations (New York, 2 October 1980), published in *U.S.A., Message of Justice, Peace and Love* (Boston, 1980). *L'Osservatore Romano* [English weekly edition], 13 October 1980, "The Holy See's Intervention at the Geneva Conference on the Non-Proliferation of Nuclear Arms", 11 August, 5 September 1980.

command. We are in a totally new situation, and argument from previous experience is, therefore, doubtful in its relevance.

Given these difficulties, the question of conscientious objection in any war in the future raises problems of a new kind. The individual service-man whose finger was on the button, whose cooperation was necessary for the despatch of such weapons, might have good reason to think that the weapon was to be used indiscriminately or that a holocaust would be set in progress by his action, even though he had no conclusive proof of either fact. Yet there will also seem to be room in those circumstances to allow others, equally sincere in their Christian beliefs, to assume that the weapon was directed to a legitimate target, or that it would not have the domino effects described, even though this belief too could not be substantiated. The question is not really parallel to that of the soldier asked to cooperate in the deliberate sending of innocent civilians to their death, who yet pretends he does not know what was going to happen. In the case of nuclear weapons, there may in specific circumstances be the possibility that its particular use is morally justifiable. If a man serving his country in a nuclear war gave himself the benefit of the doubt till he had positive evidence that the weapons were being misused or would have evil effects that would be out of all proportion to any good achieved, it would seem he would not be doing a morally objectionable thing. By the same token, the conscientious objector who could not make this allowance would equally seem to have a right to that objection, even when in uniform and even when under orders—though he must be prepared to accept the consequences of such an action that might endanger his comrades and, indeed, his country.

We cannot underestimate the difficulty of the dilemma. There will be disagreements on what constitutes a legitimate military target and what the long term effects of using nuclear weapons will be, even when full knowledge is available. Among those who make policy at the highest level, therefore, and execute it at the highest level, there will be room for disagreement. Lower down the scale, the individual's right to refuse to cooperate when there are good reasons for conscientious objection must be safeguarded. Yet so must be the discipline and morale of military units whose commanders and the majority of whose men may be ready to accept that, on balance, the use of these weapons in these circumstances may be justified. One solution might be that provision for posting elsewhere could be made for the objectors; the larger the scale of the dissent however, the more difficult this would be. If such dissenters had to stay with their units, then it would seem that the only defensible course would be to permit to them the right not to cooperate, provided they did not try to propagate their views. Such a solution may be unworkable;

even in theory it is unsatisfactory; but it seems it is the least unsatisfactory of any available. We have to respect the consciences of the responsible political and military authorities and their subordinates, while allowing to those who have genuine difficulty the right to conscientious objection. Once again this situation is a new one. Conscientious objection of this nature and on this scale has hardly been a possibility in previous wars. Now that it has been foreseen, we cannot ignore the responsibility of considering the solutions, even when they seem to present us with highly impracticable alternatives.

3. The Right and Forms of Dissent on Other Issues: The Use of Non-Violent and Violent Means

The Council does not say anything specifically about the rights of resistance to legitimate authority beyond the observation that[123] it is legitimate for citizens who are oppressed "to defend their own rights and those of their fellow citizens against the abuses of authority within the limits of the natural law and the law of the Gospel". The traditional teaching[124] about the implications of the natural law and the law of the Gospel is that at least non-violent resistance is acceptable and indeed required if the state makes demands that are morally repugnant in themselves. If, for example, Christians subject to a particular state authority were compelled by that state to deny the faith, blaspheme Christ or reject any essential Christian belief and practice, they would have the duty to resist—though passive resistance; simple refusal to cooperate would here be enough. Passive resistance could also be used, for example, to protest against gross defects in legislation, or it could be used against inadequate economic or social policies and foreign policies that endanger the state. On these latter political issues good men may disagree as to the facts or to the seriousness of the problem facing the state. Some may decide against passive resistance. Others may equally decide for it. If there is a good and reasonable case for saying that normal means are inadequate to meet the needs of the situation, there the right to such passive resistance can be invoked if it has a hope of succeeding and it does not run the risk of causing more suffering than its success will prevent or remove. On these possibilities each must make up his own mind.

As to the question of violent resistance, revolution or rebellion, this again is not raised or dealt with by the Council, but in the encyclical *Populorum Progressio*, Paul VI noted that[125]

---

[123] *Gaudium et Spes*, par. 74.
[124] Welty, *A Handbook of Christian Social Ethics* 2:342 ff. Messner, op. cit., pp. 596 ff.
[125] *The Great Social Problem* (London: C.T.S., 1967), pars. 30–31.

There are certain situations when justice cries to Heaven. When whole populations, destitute of necessities, live in a state of dependence barring them from all initiative and responsibility, and all opportunity to advance culturally and share in social and political life, recourse to violence as a means to right these wrongs to human dignity is a great temptation. We know however that a revolutionary uprising, save where there is a manifest long-standing tyranny which would do great damage to the fundamental personal rights and dangerous harm to the common good of the country— produces new injustices, throws more elements out of balance and brings on new disasters. A real evil should not be fought against at the cost of greater misery.

This passage does not *rule out* the right to revolution where there is manifest long-standing tyranny which would do great damage to funda-mental personal rights and dangerous harm to the common good of the country. But it stresses that revolution can also produce new injustices and indeed bring more harm than good. It is, therefore, the most grudging of concessions—but it is made. It is made because of the fundamental nature of political authority. We have seen that that authority exists for the common good—that is its moral justification and, if those who exercise political authority do so not for the common good, but for the sectional or personal good of individuals, to the extent of seriously depriving the citizens of their human rights, then a prima facie case for revolution exists. St. Thomas argues[126]

A tyrannical government is not just, because it is directed not to the common good but to the private good of the ruler. Consequently there is no sedition in disturbing a government of this kind . . . it is the tyrant rather who is guilty of seditions among his subjects that he may laud it over them more securely. . . . For this is tyranny—being conducive to the private good of the ruler and to the injury of the multitude.

But St. Thomas also argues that the risk of suffering from the disturbance caused by the use of violence in overturning unjust government must not be so great that it produces more evil than it is intended to overcome. He also argues in another place that any such opposition to a tyrant must have some claim to represent public authority.[127] What such public authority might be in circumstances where the tyrant has not allowed adequate constitutional means to develop is difficult to say. It is conceivable that a conspiracy should have the majority of the nation behind it, that it would act as a spark to set the process going. It would be up to the individuals

[126] *Summa Theologica*, II-II, q. 42, art. 2 ad 3.
[127] *De Regimine Principum*. See D. Bigongiari, op. cit., p. xxxi. Hoffner, *Fundamentals of Christian Sociology*, pp. 177 ff.

concerned to judge whether it was reasonable for them to presume that, in taking the course of action they do, they represent what the majority of the population would want if given the freedom to express themselves.

These are all difficult matters of personal judgement. We can ask ourselves whether those who plotted against Hitler did so with the tacit approval of their fellow citizens, presuming that they had been free to express their opinions. This raises a further question. If, in fact, a minority acts against the clear will of the majority in such matters, it is possible that later events will show that the majority was so much in moral darkness as a result of their own or the tyrant's evil that the minority more clearly understood where lay the true common good. The difficulty, of course, is that this leaves a wide field open for those who, in a given situation, find themselves against the majority to claim that history will prove they were the real conscience of the people, when in fact it may prove the opposite. Those who wish to set up their own judgement in this way may no more claim history's verdict for themselves than their opponents can claim it will be against them. Both must make their claims on their present merits.

III. The Christian, the Church and Politics

A. THE INDIVIDUAL CHRISTIAN AND POLITICS

The question of Christian commitment in the political sphere is first of all one that concerns the individual Christian citizen as a member of the body politic. There are other questions, political and moral, that arise out of his membership in the Church (which is within the state), but these cannot be answered unless his relationship to the state as individual, as person, is first of all understood. The Council gives several pointers to the right sort of Christian attitude to the political order and the state. *Firstly*, Christians should be patriotic yet, at the same time, aware of the unity of the whole human race; *secondly*, in politics, they should be devoted to the general welfare; *thirdly*, they should respect those who differ from them on political matters and, *fourthly* and finally, they must remember that party politics, while acceptable, must never come before the common good.[128]

> Citizens should cultivate a generous and loyal spirit of patriotism but without narrowmindedness so that they will always keep in mind the welfare of the whole human family which is formed into one by the various kinds of links between races, peoples and nations. Christians must be conscious of their specific and proper role in the political community: they should be a

[128] *Gaudium et Spes*, par. 75.

shining example by their sense of responsibility and their dedication to the common good. . . . They should recognise the legitimacy of differing points of view about the organisation of worldly affairs and show respect for their fellow citizens, who even in association, defend their opinions by legitimate means. Political parties for their part must support whatever in their opinion is conducive to the common good, but must never put their own interests before the common good.

Love of one's own people is a Christian virtue in the fullest sense since Christ showed that he possessed this virtue.[129] The aim must be, however, to combine a genuine patriotism with a genuine universalism and respect for the national traditions and characteristics of others. The diversity of human culture is one of the glories of humanity, and this same document of the Council stresses the importance of developing and fulfilling the cultural characteristics which are the patrimony of the different human communities.[130] Culture in the sense used in this part of the document is much broader than simply national and racial characteristics—but it includes these also. It also stresses strongly, and we need to remember this, that the Church's mission is to all peoples and all places at all times, and she has no fixed or exclusive ties with any race or nation, any purely human code of customs old or new.[131]

The question of the motive for Christian involvement in politics is crucial. That motive is not to be primarily ecclesiological, but it must be to serve the common good—part of which is served indeed by protection of the Church's rights. Since the political order has its own divinely instituted autonomy and role, a genuine seeking of the common good by political action is good in God's sight. The ecclesiological implications of personal and organised Christian action in politics are important and are discussed below—but it is the logic of human nature and human society which demands Christian involvement in politics, and it is in this perspective that the ecclesiastical implications of the Christian in politics are set.

In seeking their own particular political commitment, Christians necessarily have to accept the traditions and conventions of their own country in so far as these are compatible with the moral law. The so-called "party" system has been worked out in some countries as the most practical way of providing a transition to alternative governments by peaceful means.[132]

[129] E.g. Lk 13:34.

[130] *Gaudium et Spes* (pars. 53–62), deals with "The Proper Development of Culture".

[131] "The Church has been sent to all ages and nations and, therefore, is not tied exclusively and indissolubly to any race or nation, to any one particular way of life or to any customary practice, ancient or modern." (par. 58).

[132] V. O. Key, *Politics, Parties and Pressure Groups* (New York, 1964). L. D. Epstein, *Political Parties in Western Democracies* (London, 1967). The political pattern in the developing world has been outlined in J. Y. Calvez, *Politics and Society in the Third World* (New York, 1973).

Does this party politics so contradict the principle that the state exists to serve the common good that it cannot be accepted? According to the Council, the two are not incompatible. By definition, however, the tension between party good and the common good will always be there. The judgement of the magisterium on this matter of party politics then is not a technical one which says it is the best way of organising political life, but simply one which says that Christians can work within it. It may be that in time a means can be found of serving the needs of political life more satisfactorily. But until, again by the inner logic of the rightful autonomy of man's political life in which Christians participate, that method is evolved and presented as an option to the Christian conscience, the Christian can live and work with the party political systems, seeking to make Christian influence effective in the natural development of political life as an individual.

The purpose of the state being the common good, therefore, all its institutions, including its party politics, must work to this good. The good is secured when each member of society is secured in his or her human rights and accepts the corresponding responsibilities.

The Council does not comment in detail on human rights, but John XXIII in *Pacem in Terris*[133] had treated of them at greater length. The following list of them is based on the text of the encyclical. Men and women have:

1. The right to life, to bodily integrity and the means for maintaining a decent standard of living. Hence provision is to be made for ill health, widowhood, old age, enforced unemployment and unavoidable redundancy.
2. The right to be respected and to have a good name.
3. The right to freedom in investigating the truth and, subject to the moral law and the common good, freedom of speech.
4. The right to practise any profession, subject also to the needs of the common good and the moral law.
5. The right to be accurately informed about public events.
6. The right to share in the benefits of culture, to a good general education and technical or professional training consistent with the degree of educational development of the country, and to more advanced studies for those capable of them.
7. The right to worship God in accordance with the dictates of conscience and profess their religion both in private and in public.

---

[133] *Pacem in Terris* [*Peace on Earth*], 11 April 1963 (London: C.T.S., 1965), pars. 11–27. On human rights in general, I. Brownlie, *Basic Documents on Human Rights* (O.U.P., 1971), especially pp. 106 ff., "Universal Declaration of Human Rights" of the United Nations (10 December 1948).

8. The right to choose a state of life, married or unmarried. The family is the basic cell of human society and it is a duty of society to see that it is strengthened. The support and education of their children is a right that belongs primarily to parents.
9. The right to work and to the exercise of personal initiative in working, to conditions consistent with his or her human needs of work and a wage sufficient for a family's support.
10. The right to the ownership of property, including property in productive goods.
11. The right of association through which to exercise initiative and responsibility.
12. The right to freedom of movement and residence within the confines of their country, and the right to emigrate to other countries and take up residence there when just reasons favour it.
13. The right to take an active part in public life and to make a contribution to the common welfare of its citizens.
14. The right to legal protection of rights and to justice.

The encyclical stresses[134] that commonplace of Catholic social ethics that rights involve duties. To claim one's rights and to ignore one's duties, or only half fulfill them, is like building a house with one hand and tearing it down with the other. For example—the right to life involves the duty of living in a manner befitting a human being, and the right to seek the truth carries with it the obligation to make an ever deeper and wider study of it. A healthy society needs the responsible acceptance and pursuit of rights and the freely given acceptance of the duties that go with them. Only on this basis can a free society, the only society worthy of man, be built up.

Pope John Paul II took up the question of human rights and dignity in his first encyclical *Redemptor Hominis* showing[135] how closely both ideas were linked with our knowledge of man redeemed by Christ, sharing his nature and being the beneficiary of the redemption that Christ gained for him.[136] It is this perspective which gives the Church, Christ's mystical body, the right and the duty to proclaim and defend that dignity.[137] Pope John Paul brings new insights to bear on the question of threats to man's rights. Man is not only oppressed and denied his rights by persecution and terror, but the fear he has of his own powers in a technological and consumer society challenges his essential humanity too.[138] Welcoming

---

[134] Ibid., par. 28 ff.
[135] John Paul II, *Redemptor Hominis* (London, C.T.S., 1979), pp. 27 ff.
[136] Ibid., p. 36.
[137] Ibid., p. 46.
[138] Ibid., p. 59.

the growing awareness of the need for the defence and furtherance of human rights by secular agencies, especially the United Nations,[139] the encyclical, however, reminds us that it is in the pursuit of spiritual values and in the acceptance of the sacramental life, the surest channel of God's grace and guidance, that the Christian enters into the service of his fellowmen.

B. THE CHURCH AND POLITICS: THE THEORY

According to their situation, Christians have to find their own way of committing themselves to the common good through political action. If we take this as our perspective, if we remember the legitimate sphere of autonomy of the political order, it becomes easier for us to answer what is a much more difficult question—the nature of the relationship between the Church as an organised community and the political order. Because political decisions are collective decisions which often involve many conflicts of rights and make assumptions about imponderables concerning the future, it is very rare that the dictates of a Christian conscience will indicate to each the same course of action.[140] Each must then judge what sincerely seems to him to be the right way to act in particular circumstances, put his principles into practice and follow through the implications of his options. The principles of justice are often clear enough, but it is very rarely that the individual may claim that his judgement of how to put those principles into practice is the only one that a good Christian may make. The Church's task, therefore, is not to try to make up the minds of its members in this way; it is hers to remind people of the spiritual values that should be safeguarded at all times, and to leave each to make his or her decision according to their own needs and the common good.

In dealing with this complex matter, the Council makes some points very emphatically. Christians are to take their political options within the limits allowable by the social teaching of the Church, but they must not expect to claim the Church's name or authority in support of their own opinions where good men may disagree. Further, only legitimate authority within the Church can decide to commit her as an institution upon any matter which touches on the political. As such, the Church is

---

[139] Ibid., p. 80.

[140] As previously pointed out above, p. 2, personal moral decisions, on the other hand, are subject to fewer of these uncertainties. In them I am conscious of my personal responsibility, for good or ill, for a particular act and usually aware of its direct consequences. In politics, however (e.g. when I vote), the effects of my one vote one way or another are usually minimal—nor can I sort out the exact implications of any party policy I vote for. Equally, political leaders are dependent on circumstances beyond their control in any policy they pursue.

not committed to any political system, but rather transcends all such systems; it and the state have an independence and autonomy which is God-given, and they must respect each other's rights, seeking to co-operate in meeting the needs of men, for it is the purpose of both Church and state to meet those needs under their different titles and aspects.[141]

> It is of supreme importance, especially in a pluralistic society, to work out a proper vision of the relationship between the political community and the Church and to distinguish clearly between the activities of Christians acting individually or collectively in their own name as citizens, guided by the dictates of Christian conscience and their activity acting along with their pastors in the name of the Church . . . *the Church, by reason of her role and competence, is not identified with any political community nor bound by ties to any political system. It is at once the sign and safeguard of the transcendental dimension of the human person. The political community and the Church are autonomous and independent of each other in their own fields. Nevertheless both are devoted to the personal vocation of man though under different titles.*

The statement that the political community and the Church in their respective fields are independent and autonomous, and that the Church is committed to no political system but transcends them all, touches upon the perennial problems of the relationship of Church and state with which we have tried to deal in outline. The theory is that the political and economic orders have been instituted by God to fulfill their own purposes for man and, provided a political or economic system is compatible in principle and practice with man's eternal destiny and human rights, then the Church has no reason to interfere. She can also live with any political or social structure; the dynamics of world history determine these according to the state of development of peoples. Though for many reasons urban civilisation[142] and constitutional government,[143] based on the consent of the governed, are particularly compatible with the Christian social ethic, such systems can only develop in certain conditions—and the Church can in fact live with any pattern, however simple, and however lacking in those sophistications which make democracy workable. The important thing is not the type of political or economic structure. The important thing is that, whatever that type is, it meets the needs of its people in their time according to God's law.

In saying all this, the Church is stating the norm for her relationship with the political order in an ideal society. It assumes she herself will be given the freedom to follow her own vocation and that the secular order

---

[141] *Gaudium et Spes*, par. 76. The italics in the text are the author's.

[142] See above p. 185.

[143] See above pp. 187 ff.

does not try to trespass on her legitimate prerogatives for its own ends. It assumes also that she possesses in her leaders and in her ordinary member-ship men and women capable of accepting this theory in principle and putting it into practice in reality. Needless to say, there has never been a time when all of these conditions, or indeed a majority of them, have existed and, therefore, the history of the Church's relationship with the state has never been smooth.

The early Church was effectively committed to the acceptance of the structure of the Roman Empire, although in practice her organisation and life was, in many ways, undermining its traditional foundations. In the Middle Ages, the Church was firmly embedded in the political and economic structures of feudalism as a result of the part she played in civilising Europe as it developed its own new distinctive culture. But she had no choice but to be embedded in those structures. History ensured that it was she who largely provided, in the course of events, the cement which held Europe together after the Roman collapse. And it was events, not choice, which gave her her influential role in rebuilding Europe after the barbarian invasion. It is not then that she chose the role history demanded of her; she was led and thrust into it. That said, many Church-men chose to play the role too enthusiastically.

In more modern times, the experience of the Church in regard to the changing political scene in the twentieth century has been very varied.[144] The experience of German, Italian and Spanish Fascism and of Latin America in the nineteenth century is still relevant, but what is happening in Poland today makes it apparent that it is not necessary to assume that because the Church accepts a dominant political structure she necessarily authenticates it. She just lives with it. If in such a situation the majority of the members of the Church in a particular state are, as individuals, politically inclined to accept the beliefs of the dominant system or party, then the Church will necessarily appear to be committed to it. If there are aspects of that system which are contrary to Christian belief and practice, then scandal is given by this commitment of the Church (as a sociological fact) to that system. If, on the other hand, the majority of members of the Church are, as individuals, politically not inclined to accept the beliefs of the dominant system, it may be an option open to them as *individuals* to decide to attempt to overturn that system on the conditions discussed above. But this would not be a declaration of the Church as a teaching, spiritual, eucharistic entity against an existing structure, it would be the

[144] H. Daniel Rops, *A Fight for God*, pp. 296 ff. A. Rhodes, *The Vatican in the Age of the Dictators* (London, 1973). M. Power, *Religion in the Reich* (London, 1939). R. Aubert, *The Church in a Secularized Society*, pp. 321 ff. J. N. Moody, *Church and Society* (New York, 1958), pp. 325 ff., 721 ff. T. Prittie, *Germans Against Hitler* (London, 1964).

collective decision of individual Christians taking a legitimate option that is open to them within the limits of that teaching—and events may prove they took the wrong option.

As it stands then, the statement that the Church is not identified with any political community, nor bound by ties to any political system, is the statement of the ideal rather than a judgement of historical fact, as we are aware. We must now try to bring together the relevant elements in the Church's experience in order to appreciate the importance of the Council's directive.

C. THE CHURCH AND POLITICS:
THE EXPERIENCE IN THE MIDDLE AGES

Before 313 A.D., when the Roman authorities accepted her, the Church concentrated on her own life and did not attempt to influence the political order by overt action. She taught her people to obey the emperor and civil authorities, even when the state persecuted and martyred her members. It was not that she was lacking in the power effectively to resist. By the third century, her strength as a social organisation was so great that nothing else in the Empire, the army alone excepted, could rival it, and the state itself saw that strength as a support for its own weaknesses. By this time then, controlling public opinion in the most populous areas of the Empire and having in her ranks the leaders, the soldiers, the ex-slaves hardened by suffering—in other words, having the means to carry on an active resistance, she chose not to do so.

Once accepted by the Roman Empire, the two swords, or the Gelasian theory,[145] assumed that the state was strong, well-organised and independent and capable of looking after secular affairs. The weakness of the Roman Empire in the West in the fifth century, when the theory was elaborated, could be seen as a temporary aberration. In fact, events were to show that it presaged total collapse. Until the emergence of the feudal state in its fully organised form from the twelfth century, there was, with the exceptions of Charlemagne's reign on the Continent and periods in Alfred's England and after, no such strong and well-organised state capable of looking after secular affairs in the West.

[145] See above pp. 22 ff. Pope Gelasius (492–496), seeking to prevent the Emperor Anastasius I from interfering in Church affairs in the Eastern Empire argued that the world is chiefly ruled by the sacred authority of the priesthood and by the authority of kings—each authority being of divine origin. While each is autonomous however, they are dependent on each other and each has some authority over the other in so far as the Church is subject to just civil laws and the Emperor to the spiritual jurisdiction of the Church. Carlyle and Carlyle, op. cit., 1:188 ff. Sabine, op. cit., (pp. 194 ff.) points out that this theory is generally representative of the teaching of the Fathers of the Church.

It was this vacuum left by the collapse of an effective secular authority, an effective state, which compelled the Church on one hand to undertake many of the tasks of civil government and, on the other hand, to be the sole bearer of the traditions of culture and learning. She was also the only agent capable of giving a lead in international affairs and the only social organisation which was coherently organised throughout the West. Inevitably, then, she was forced into a secular role, and the fact that land-holding was the only source of wealth and stable order in this period meant that her Church offices and the estates that went with them were the object of secular ambition and too often were bought and sold like any other form of property.

The result of this intermingling of the Church with the world meant that too many unworthy men found their way into ecclesiastical office, from the humblest parish priest to the highest ranks of the hierarchy. The scandal and the corruption reached its peak during the period of the Viking, Muslim and Magyar invasions in the ninth and tenth centuries, when centralized order in the Church collapsed almost entirely, and the papacy itself was, for a period, a feudal fief corrupted and squabbled over by the local aristocracy.[146] Gregory VII, after having tried to get the cooperation of the Emperor in reforming the Church, decided to go to the root of the matter, as he saw it—the practice of allowing the feudal lord the right of investing clerics with their insignia of office.[147] Such elements in the practice of investiture as at the time were justified had been grossly abused, and Gregory's attack on it was forced on him by these abuses. There was no way of telling when the Emperor Henry IV was excommunicated,[148] or what the implications would be, and only gradually did their far-reaching nature become apparent. The resulting over-involvement of

[146] C. Dawson, *Religion and the Rise of Western Culture* (London, 1950), pp. 143 ff. H. Daniel Rops, *The Church in the Dark Ages*, pp. 534 ff. C. W. Hollister, *Medieval Europe*, pp. 178 ff.

[147] Knowles and Obolensky, op. cit., pp. 165 ff. *Cambridge Medieval History*, 5:1 ff. Heer, op. cit., calls the Gregorian reform "the most momentous of all the actions and movements of modern European history" (p. 70). M. Chambers et al., *The Western Experience*, (p. 256) note the effect of the reform in improving the quality of the clergy and reducing the violence of the times by suppressing private warfare; they also suggest that the honest reforming spirit embodied in the Gregorian movement had a lasting effect on Western culture and cultural attitudes.

[148] The Emperor was released from his excommunication in the famous scene at Canossa in 1077 but was soon once more in conflict with the Pope. The Investiture controversy was, theoretically, settled by the Concordat of Worms in 1122 when the canonical freedom of ecclesiastical appointments was guaranteed while the prince was promised feudal obedience for temporalities. But the dispute over the primacy of power remained. Knowles and Obolensky, op. cit., pp. 182–83. See above pp. 39 ff.

the Church, the papacy particularly, with worldly affairs, and the confirmation of her role as a dominant force in international relations until the sixteenth century contributed to that corruption in the Church that led to the Reformation.

The course of the controversy between the Church and state in the three centuries after the death of Gregory VII was dictated by the rise and decline of papal power, the development of nationalism and the consequent disintegration of Christendom. The success of the papacy resulted in the growth of centralized administrative machinery and a complex network of representation and links throughout the Christian world: the papacy had reformed the Church, had given an impetus to the intellectual revival in the improvement of clerical education with its consequent effect on the growth of the universities; it also had helped Europe achieve a sense of identity through its leadership in the Crusades.

To direct the affairs of the great organisation that the Church had become demanded of the pope diplomatic and political skills of a high order. In Innocent III she found a man who possessed them,[149] and with his ward, Frederick II, becoming emperor in 1214,[150] it seemed at last as though papacy and empire would work in harmony. But after Innocent III's death in 1216, Frederick was in conflict with the Church until he himself died in 1250, and from the conflict it was the Church that emerged triumphant.[151] When, however, Boniface VIII (1294–1303) tried to reassert the old claims against Philip of France in the bull *Unam Sanctam*, he was kidnapped and died shortly afterwards. Thereafter the popes were exiles in Avignon; ironically it was the objection of the German electors to the claim of a French-influenced Avignon pope, John XXII (1316–1334)[152]

[149] It was Innocent III (1198–1216) who launched the Albigensian crusade. He also forced Philip of France to return to his first wife after excommunicating him and putting the country under an interdict; likewise he put King John's England under interdict and threatened to depose him. In Church affairs he was vigorous and far-sighted. He called the Fourth Lateran Council which produced legislation beneficial to the spiritual and moral health of the Church.

[150] In the previous century the popes had struggled to prevent Frederick Barbarossa from controlling Italy and hence bringing the papacy too much under the Empire's influence. The sudden death of the new emperor Henry VI in 1197 left the young Frederick as the heir—and the ward of Innocent III.

[151] Frederick was excommunicated and deposed in 1227, restored to communion with the Church in 1230, fell under the ban again in 1239, had a crusade proclaimed against him in 1240 and was solemnly deposed by the Council of Lyons in 1245. Thereafter, Innocent IV (1243–1254) deployed all his forces against the emperor. Knowles and Obolensky, op. cit., pp. 297 ff.

[152] John was already involved in conflict with Lewis the Bavarian over the support given to a faction of the Franciscans who had rejected the Pope's decision in an internal dispute in the order. See above pp. 183–84.

to a voice in the election of the emperor which led, after a long struggle, to Innocent VI (1352–1362) effectively abandoning any such claim by the papacy.[153]

The popes involved in the conflicts with the emperors and the French king were not representative of the decadence which later surrounded the office at times in the Renaissance period. They were irreproachable in their personal lives and honest in their policies and motives.[154] It is not so evident that this was always the case with those they opposed; for example, Henry IV's submission at Canossa in 1077 was less than whole-hearted. He soon disregarded his word and was disposing of abbeys and sees in the old way.[155] Philip, though pious and observant in his private religious practices, was in political and ecclesiastical policy ruthless and avaricious, aided by unscrupulous ministers. The methods he used to suppress the Templars, with the connivance of the weak Pope Clement V, revealed his brutality and rapacity at its worst. The Templars, if lacking in their early fervour and guilty of arrogance, were, as an order, guiltless of the charges laid against them.[156] But this mattered nothing to Philip—it was their wealth he had coveted, and any means he needed to use to try to get his hands on it seemed to him good.

As an institution then, and in its motives and actions, the papacy cannot be accused of worldly ambition for its own sake, though in the Avignon period the luxury of the papal court caused scandal. Further, however personally innocent popes may have been, the over-involvement of the Church in secular affairs over hundreds of years lessened its authority in spiritual matters. That over-involvement carries with it lessons valid down to today. The papacy was eager to try to bring order into a disordered world. In Professor Hollister's words, the popes[157]

> not satisfied to chide society by innocuous moralizing from the sidelines, plunged into the world to sanctify it. Tragically, perhaps inevitably, they soiled their hands.

Inevitably, too, as they did soil their hands with secular affairs, the life of the Church suffered. The Church and the papacy had in the first instance achieved their influence and power because of their spiritual and moral leadership. With the collapse of the civil authority in the early

---

[153] The "Golden Bull" of Charles IV (1356) established the rights of the electors: the pope's role was not repudiated—but neither was he mentioned. The prelates among the electors were, however, powerful and influential. Knowles and Obolensky, op. cit., p. 409.

[154] Ibid., p. 406.

[155] P. Hughes, *History of the Church* (London, 1935) 2:262.

[156] Knowles and Obolensky, op. cit., pp. 407–8.

[157] C. W. Hollister, *Medieval Europe*, p. 200.

Middle Ages and the seething troubles of a new political and economic order in the central and high middle ages, her stability, resources and skills gave her a secular role that some of her leaders failed to see would take her away from, and in the end seriously undermine her, in her primarily other-worldly task. The approach taken by the Second Vatican Council to secular affairs, tempered by several hundred years more experience, shows that her firm conviction is now to avoid direct involvement, as an institution, in political affairs. Such was the teaching of her master, Christ, which only the collapse of civilised order after the demise of the Roman Empire edged her into, if not abandoning, then at least forgetting. How much modern secular man owes to the lead forced on her, the history of Europe shows. It may be said that she has only abandoned her secular role because she no longer has the power to sustain it. The events would support that view—but then they would also support the one given here, that the Church has learned the lessons of her history.

D. THE CHURCH AND POLITICS:
RENAISSANCE AND REFORMATION TO TODAY

The post-Reformation political pattern in Europe was dominated by absolute monarchies; in "Protestant" countries the Church was completely subject to the state, and in "Catholic" countries the rulers were equally interested in exerting the maximum control over it.[158] It is, therefore, a mistake to think of the Church as somehow "choosing" absolute monarchy as her ally. Absolute monarchies were a fact of the situation with which the Church had to live. The idea that the predominantly Catholic countries put the Church and their religion first and their politics second is far from the truth. Had they chosen to unite, they could have "saved" Europe for Catholicism[159] (presuming that a Catholicism so saved would have been worthy of its mission), but they did not. They put their national politics and policies first. The Church's good was very secondary.

Within the "Catholic" states of France, Austria and Spain, the relationship between Church and state varied according to national tradition. In Spain the identification of Catholicism with the national spirit in the

---

[158] See above pp. 197–98 and see also McGovern, op. cit., p. 50. H. Daniel Rops, *The Church in the 17th Century*, pp. 178–79, "Wherever absolutism triumphed, problems arise over its relationship with the Church . . . one fact has always been evident since the time of Constantine and Byzantium: the identification of personal interests with those of the Church is the invariable and fatal consequence of absolutism no matter how Christian and Catholic it may claim to be."

[159] H. A. L. Fisher, *A History of Europe* (Fontana Edition), 2:444.

re-conquest of the land from the Moors ensured that Catholicism was not only the state religion, but also the religion without which neither state nor Spanish people could imagine themselves. The kings, nevertheless, although they too regarded themselves as good Catholics, increasingly were in conflict with the Holy See in their attempts to control the Church.[160]

In France Louis XIV[161] had sought to put the Catholic Church, as well as the Huguenots, under his control. In 1682, in the document known as the "Declaration in Four Articles", he rejected papal interference in temporal affairs, asserted the superiority of the general council to the pope and the inviolability of the rights and customs of the Gallican Church. The King was prevailed upon eventually not to enforce the claims, but Gallicanism remained a problem.

In 1763, the auxiliary Bishop of Trier, using the pseudonym Febronius, published *De Statu Ecclesiae*, which took up positions more extreme even than Gallicanism.[162] The pope, he argued, was merely the first among his peers; his power had to be diminished while that of the bishops extended. The bishops, in their turn, are the delegates of the community of the faithful to which authority in the Church belongs. These views won wide acceptance especially with the three Prince Bishops of Cologne, Trier and Mainz who, in 1786, organised an out and out rebellion against the Holy See. Only the advent of the French Revolution stopped their actions from bringing about the full chaos they seemed to portend.

It was, however, the Hapsburgs of Austria, in Joseph II (1741–1790), who produced the most complete attempt to subordinate the Catholic Church to the state. Joseph II was concerned with the problems of his empire and the growing menace of Prussia, and, as part of his programme of up-dating and strengthening the state, he wanted to treat the Church simply as part of the empire's administrative machinery. Rome's influence was to be reduced to a minimum, the pope left with residual powers in matters of dogma, but discipline and administration was the state's affair.[163] Given the experience of the Church under Gallicanism, Febronianism and Josephism, it can hardly be said that she had any reason to regret the passing of absolute monarchy—and with the French Revolution the first assault on that institution began.

---

[160] Daniel Rops, *The Church in the 18th Century*, p. 227 ff., 300 ff.

[161] Louis XIV (1638–1715) came to the throne in 1643, his mother acting as Regent. On the death of Mazarin, his chief minister, in 1661, he began his period of personal government. His great-grandson Louis XV succeeded him in 1715 and reigned until 1774. The conflict with Rome on the "Declaration in Four Articles" is detailed in Daniel Rops, *The Church in the 17th Century*, pp. 215 ff.

[162] Daniel Rops, *The Church in the 18th Century*, pp. 230 ff.   [163] Ibid.

The rejection of the old regime in France, represented by the events of 1789, was massive, and, as a sociological fact, the Church there was caught up in the general mood. It was the decision of the lower clergy to ally with the Third Estate which led to the first flouting of royal authority in June 1789 when the National Assembly rejected the limitations of its mandate and resolved not to disperse until it had given France a constitution.[164] It was only when the anti-clerical forces at work in that Assembly passed the *Civil Constitution on the Clergy*, in July 1790, that the break with the Church came. The Constitution specifically intended to subject the Church to the authority of the state: bishops and clergy were to be elected like other state officials, and the pope was to be deprived of all powers over them.[165] From that moment the possibility of further cooperation with the revolution became impossible, although it was several months before Rome, fearful of the consequences of confrontation, openly condemned the Constitution and its implication. The terror that was launched against the Church and the reaction in violence of the rising in the Vendee[166] merged into the general confusion and bloodshed that the various phases of the revolution underwent until Napoleon's emergence as First Consul.

The experience of the Church in Europe in the 1600s and 1700s, first under the Catholic absolute monarchies and then the Revolution, was, therefore, not a happy one. The papacy especially was beleaguered and under assault. The achievement of the Catholic powers, in league with the philosophic spirit, in persuading a pope to suppress the Society of Jesus in 1773 is simply one astonishing example of the hatred that Catholic monarchs had for any institution or organisation which threatened to limit them and their prerogatives. Their influence over the papacy at that time outlined excruciatingly the weakness of that institution, a weakness which was the result of attacks upon it from within the Church. The unhappy Clement XIV, who had suppressed the Society, had hoped by this act to appease the powers but, in fact, the suppression was the signal for a renewed attack on him and his office.[167]

The Church then has had little cause to trust the absolute monarchies, but it was her experience that, little cause though she had to trust them,

[164] Daniel Rops, *The Church in an Age of Revolution*, p. 3.

[165] Daniel Rops, op. cit., p. 9. Dawson, *The Gods of Revolution*, pp. 67 ff.

[166] The revolt began in February 1791. "It was a spontaneous movement which owed nothing to counter revolutionary plots or aristocratic intrigue but sprang directly from the faith and emotions of the people." Dawson, *The Gods of Revolution*, pp. 89–90. pp. 89–90.

[167] Daniel Rops, *The Church in the 18th Century*, p. 210 ff. There were many criticisms of the Society (see F. Heyer, *The Catholic Church from 1648 to 1870*, pp. 61 ff.) but it was because "an organization as firmly united behind the Pope as the Jesuit order . . . did not fit in with the absolutists' authoritarian ideas of State Churches" (Ibid., p. 62), that it was attacked and suppressed.

she had even less cause to trust the revolutionaries and their allies. Between two evils the papacy and the Church had to choose which they thought was the lesser, and they chose the one that was least likely to try to destroy her, however much they might humble and shackle her; she therefore saw the monarchies as less of a threat to her existence. In the first instance, however, it was not apparent that the French Revolution was to be anti-clerical or atheist. Only when a section within the revolutionary movement decided to work out their anti-clerical prejudices under the guise of the Revolution did the real clash with the Church come.

The experience of the Church in dealing with revolution and nationalism elsewhere in the period varied. In Poland and Ireland, and to a lesser extent, Belgium, the local church was a rallying point for nationalism. In Latin America her connection with the colonial era set the leaders of the revolution against her. But it was the experience and aftermath of the French revolution, and then the struggle for Italian unity, which was most immediate and influential. The latter especially was important because of its effects on the future of the Papal States and all that this meant to the papacy in terms of its spiritual freedom.

When Napoleon was voted in as First Consul in the last weeks of 1799, he restored the Church's freedom of worship as part of his plan to pacify and reorganise a state reduced to chaos by ten years of violence and anarchy. He also began the negotiations with the Holy See that led to the Concordat of 1801.[168] But alliance with the Emperor reduced the French Church, all too willingly, to a role of subservience as great, if not greater, than that which she had suffered under the old regime. The Concordat embroiled the papacy and the Papal States in Napoleon's wars despite everything that Pius VII could do to prevent this. In 1809 the Emperor's forces annexed the Papal States, arrested the Pope and had him transferred to a small town near Genoa. Only after the defeat in Russia was the Pope able to return to Rome, more convinced than ever that political independence, freedom from the influence of a powerful state, was essential to the exercise of the papacy's spiritual liberty.[169]

At the Congress of Vienna in 1815,[170] most of the territory of the Papal States was returned, and the problem of their administration had to be

---

[168] Daniel Rops, *The Church in an Age of Revolution*, p. 75 ff. E. E. Y. Hales, *The Catholic Church in the Modern World* (New York, 1958), pp. 59 ff. The papacy was desperate for some agreement that would allow the French Church respite and would head off outright Gallicanism.

[169] Daniel Rops, *The Church in an Age of Revolution*, p. 82, asserts that Napoleon outdid Constantine, Justinian, Charlemagne or Louis XIV, in his desire to use the Church as an instrument of government.

[170] E. Ergang, *Europe since Waterloo* (Boston, 1965). The Congress believed that "the old system of divine right government made for order and stability and sought to restore pre-revolutionary conditions as far as possible." Ibid., p. 37.

faced. The manner of that administration before 1809 had allowed for no self-determination or devolution of power. There were those who wanted this situation restored while others, including Consalvi, Secretary of State, desired changes. A purely constitutional regime was out of the question because of the impossible position the pope would be in if a representative assembly voted or acted contrary to his wishes on any matter affecting the good of the Church. The eventual compromise satisfied neither conservatives nor liberals: secret societies flourished, and there were revolts in 1816, 1817 and 1820.[171] Pius VII's successor, Leo XII (1823–1829), followed a more conservative policy. The control of the Papal States was returned to the clergy and the nobles, and the consequent resentment of the liberals led to more revolutionary fervour. In his external policies Leo likewise encouraged those seeking to restore the old regime and oppose the forces of liberalism.

In France, the restored Bourbons[172] had embarked on a policy of alliance with the Church which was intended to strengthen the position of the dynasty and keep the Church in its place, while offering it privileges— a move which once more fired the liberal zeal for change. The revolution of 1830 in France led to a bourgeois monarchy under Louis Philippe who was prepared to accept the political effects of the revolution much more positively and lay the foundations of a modern democratic state. Pius VIII also accepted the events of 1830 because he realised that an accommodation with the new order was needed. But he died in 1831, and it was his successor Gregory XVI who had to begin to grapple with the problems of coming to terms, as a temporal ruler, with the ideals of nationalism and political liberalism which were gradually gaining an irresistible momentum. These ideals were being put before him not only by the pressures for Italian national unity, but also from within the French Church by those who saw the need to accept the changing order of things, forget the alliance of "throne and altar" and ally with what was good in liberalism. But when Gregory ascended the papal throne, the Papal States were threatened by political disturbances instigated by liberals. It was also a time when the Catholic Poles were fighting for their freedom against Russian oppression. Gregory could not, as he saw it, countenance the revolution of the Poles while opposing forces in his own state which he saw as having the same aims. He was not able, in other words, to separate his role as temporal ruler from that of spiritual leader, and he counselled

[171] See *The New Catholic Encyclopedia*, vol. 13, s.v. "States of the Church" for an account of the problems of the time.
[172] Louis XVIII reigned from 1814 to 1824. Charles X who succeeded him was more reactionary. It was the unconstitutional changes he tried to introduce in 1830 (with the Gallicanized Church's support) that brought about the revolution of that year. A. R. Vidler, *The Church in an Age of Revolution*, p. 68. Fisher, op. cit., 2:977.

the Poles to obey their legitimate ruler—the Czar.[173] When he later discovered he had been tricked by the Russians, he sought to redress the damage done—but the tragedy and the dilemma of his position highlighted the difficulty of adjustment of the nineteenth century papacy.

It was de Lammenais[174] who took the lead in the French Church in seeking a rapprochement with liberalism and the Revolution. He wanted to end Gallicanism, to separate the powers of Church and state and finally destroy that influence of the state over the Church which he saw as being the cause of most problems of the Church in the previous century.[175] Much of his analysis was accurate, and many of his prescriptions have now come to be taken for granted. But his vision did not sufficiently recognize the limitations of the man and the time. Gregory XVI was a temporal ruler faced with a revolt in his own dominions, a revolt which was in the name of a liberalism which espoused many of the ideals which de Lammenais was putting forward, but which was in practice anti-clerical and anti-Christian in a way de Lammenais did not apparently appreciate. Gregory was not, therefore, a sympathetic listener to the Frenchman, and the encyclical Singulari Nos (1834)[176] condemned him and his ideas. The Pope could not accept state indifference in matters of religion, nor grant liberty of conscience while these implied positive anti-clerical and anti-Christian attitudes. Liberty of the press and separation of the Church and the state were likewise rejected absolutely because of their secularist implications. This was the essence of the papal dilemma: popes, as vicars of Christ, could hardly recommend policies which, if put into practice in their own states, would link them with men and ideas both anti-clerical and anti-religious. Only when the question of temporal power of the papacy had been solved, and when it became clear that the Italian liberals' demands for freedom and national unity were not a disguised attack upon religion itself and the rights of the Church, could the situation satisfactorily be resolved.

Pius IX, who succeeded Gregory XVI in 1848,[177] at first adopted a very liberal approach to Italian nationalism, setting up a consultative assembly

[173] Daniel Rops, The Church in an Age of Revolution, p. 214. Hales, op. cit., pp. 88–89.

[174] Félicité Robert de Lamennais (1782–1854), converted in 1804 and ordained priest in 1816, founded the paper L'Avenir in 1830 to promote the liberty of the Church from the state. After the conflict with Gregory XVI he abandoned the Church for politics and died unreconciled.

[175] A. R. Vidler, The Church in an Age of Revolution, pp. 68 ff. Daniel Rops, The Church in an Age of Revolution, pp. 162 ff., 199 ff. Hales, op. cit., pp. 90 ff.

[176] A. Freemantle, The Papal Encyclicals in their Historical Context (New York, 1956), pp. 126 ff. A previous encyclical, Mirari Vos (1832), had dealt obliquely with de Lamennais in its condemnation of liberalism as fundamentally irreligious.

[177] Vidler, op. cit., pp. 146 ff. Hales, op. cit., pp. 100 ff. Daniel Rops, The Church in an Age of Revolution, pp. 235 ff.

to help with the government of the Papal States—the constitution of 1848 providing it with power to veto the Pope's proposals. In doing this, he left himself open to the danger already mentioned—of being forced into a course of action as a temporal ruler at the insistence of an elected assembly, which as spiritual head of the Church he could not approve. It was precisely on this matter, the desire of Italian nationalism to get rid of Austrian influence, that Pius IX had his first conflict with the Liberals when they pressed him to commit the small papal armed forces against the Austrians. This he refused to do and his popularity with the Liberals disappeared overnight. The final break came when a member of the Chamber of Deputies was murdered by volunteers returned from the north and the rest of the deputies showed a callous disregard for the murder, even mocking the man's widow. For a while, the Pope was besieged in the Quirinal Palace, and he was forced to flee in 1849. Garibaldi and Mazzini were determined to declare Rome a republic, and it was only the threat of French power which prevented this being done. When the Pope eventually returned to Rome in 1850, he ruled thenceforth without the help of the assembly. King Emmanuel's prime minister, Cavour, began the positive work of the unification of Italy after the Congress of Paris in 1856 in co-operation with the French, and in 1861 the King of Piedmont was proclaimed King of Italy.[178] The withdrawal of French troops in 1870 at the outbreak of the war with Germany removed the last hope of the maintenance of papal temporal power, and the popes became the "prisoners in the Vatican".[179]

Meanwhile, the Pope had had to deal with the continuing threat, as he saw it, of liberalism as a philosophy, a philosophy which was indeed, to him, the origin of his immediate political problems. In 1864 therefore, there had been issued the *Syllabus of Errors*, which consisted of condemnations of eighty or so propositions, each one of which was taken from a previous papal document referring to a specific situation. Thus the proposition that it was an error to say that the Roman Pontiff can and should reconcile himself with and accommodate himself to progress, liberalism and modern civilisation was taken from an encyclical of March 1861 denouncing the extension of the anti-clerical laws of Piedmont to the rest of Italy—laws which said that monasteries, convents, the sacramental view

[178] Ergang, op. cit., pp. 153 ff.

[179] In November 1870 the Italian government introduced the Law of Guarantees. Pius IX rejected it, including the financial compensation which would have been of great value to him in view of the loss of revenues from the Papal States. He considered that the idea of a "free Church in a free state" was an illusion in that no bishop could be invested with his temporalities without the state's consent. The Italian State remained anti-clerical though it was respectful enough towards the papacy because of international opinion. Hales, op. cit., pp. 144–45. Aubert, *The Church in a Secularized Society*, p. 83.

of marriage and any belief in the place of religion in education were out of date.[180] Clearly, if this was progress, liberalism and modern civilisation, no pope could accept it.

That the *Syllabus* was issued at all in the form it was issued, however, did not help the Church's case. The casual reader could not be expected to know the context of the original condemnations. But if some of the propositions required a great deal of understanding of the background in order to make them acceptable, many of the others were clearly of universal application and were well within the pope's terms of reference as head of the Church. So, in condemning the errors of atheism, pantheism or those who deny the divinity of our Lord, his unequivocal condemnations were justified. But such points were overlooked in the general outrage caused by the document. Monsignor Dupanloup's commentary[181] on it, of which the Pope himself approved, enabled it to be properly understood, but many preferred to misunderstand it.

It is now so plain that the cause of Italian nationalism and the liberal state was destined to succeed that we find the attitude of Pius IX, conscious of his role as a temporal ruler, hard to understand. And as temporal rulers, the popes are to be judged as other temporal rulers—on their human wisdom and practical effectiveness as just administrators. The divine guidance that guarantees their spiritual and moral judgement in their role as the head of the Church does not extend to temporal matters. Inevitably, however, it was difficult at the time to see where the one ended and the other began.

Regarding the central issue at the time—the reluctance of the popes to countenance the surrender of their temporal power—the papacy knew with the experience of over a thousand years, that, unless it had political freedom, freedom from domination by a powerful state, it would not effectively do its work as spiritual leader. In an institution with as long a history as the papacy, and with such a capacity thrust upon it by its very nature for taking the long view, it is not fanciful to say that the experience of the eighth century and the threat of the Lombard dominance and that of the fourteenth century and the memory of Avignon was relevant in the nineteenth—that of the experience under Napoleon even more so. It simply was not clear how this over-riding need of freedom from undue influence by a particular national authority could be secured while allowing Italian nationalism and the cause of Italian unity, its head. It is of crucial importance to keep in mind also that the liberals who were leading the movement were liberals in the classic sense, men who not only held to the absolute autonomy of the individual conscience (which some believed

[180] Hales, op. cit., pp. 123 ff.
[181] Hales, op. cit., p. 126. Aubert, *The Church in a Secularized Society*, pp. 39-40.

could be reconciled with Christianity), but who were also strongly atheist and anti-clerical.[182] It was not to be expected that the papacy would think well of political reforms urged by such men.

We must note that the behaviour of the liberals themselves did not encourage cooperation by the papacy. Pius IX's experience demonstrates this. Nor was it a simple case of clerical autocracy against liberal democracy. The nationalists were not above calling on the propertied and powerful to use force against the peasants. Italian liberty, when it came, was shown also to be simply another pursuit of party privilege in the name of high ideals. The common people, whose support had enabled the movement led by Garibaldi and Cavour to succeed, were abandoned once it had done so. The ordinary people were irrelevant to nationalism. Liberalism was associated with the interests of the rich.[183]

To summarise finally—we remember first of all that the papacy in the nineteenth century was coming out of a period in which its authority had been constantly challenged on all counts by the absolute monarchies of Europe. It had, on the other hand, seen that the threats to the Church from the absolute monarchs were less to be feared than were those from the revolutionary and liberal movements of the time. The absolute monarchies allowed the Church to exist and then sought to control it. The revolutionary and liberal movements were, at best, too ready to force conditions on the Church which she would not possibly tolerate, and at worst, offer her physical violence by seizing her property and attacking the clergy and religious. Clearly, given the choice between these evils, the evil of absolutism was preferable.

We have to remember too that experience had shown how essential to the execution of the pope's office of spiritual and moral leadership his political independence was, and that it was not clear at the time how this role could be reconciled with a papal constitutional monarchy or with the claims of Italian national unity which had to include the Papal States. There was right and justice on both sides, and it was well into the twentieth century before a compromise which suited the Italian State and the Vatican could be worked out. Finally, and perhaps most importantly, we must remember the point made above, that those who led the nationalists' and liberal movement were not simply liberals in the tolerant Anglo-Saxon sense, but were expressly atheistic and anti-clerical. Only when

---

[182] "The atheism and strong anti-clericalism prevalent among French and other continental liberals have been more influential than the tolerant Christianity and humanistic agnosticism of the liberals of the English-speaking nations", M. Salvadori, *The Liberal Heresy* (London, 1977), p. 117.

[183] D. Mack Smith, *Italy: A Modern History* (Ann Arbor, 1969), pp. 41–43. John Bowle in his *A History of Europe* (London, 1979), p. 542, notes that "the sentimental view of the *Risorgimento* long accepted has now given place to a more realistic appraisal."

the Church's right to exist and work was tolerated could the good that was in liberalism be accepted.

To present the nineteenth century conflicts of the papacy with the secular movements of the time as simple obscurantism and an indication of how the Church needed to be taught the lessons of justice and freedom by the secular world, is, therefore, to present a very distorted view. What the papacy was trying to do was to pick its way carefully through an age of revolution so that its temporal power remained as an essential bulwark of its spiritual power. Many of the judgements of individual popes in these difficult circumstances can be questioned, but none affected the essential role of the papacy as the Church's leader and guide in matters of faith, morals and discipline. They were either mistakes in their political judgement as temporal rulers or misjudgements of timing in approaching the solution of the Church's doctrinal and disciplinary problems. They did not and do not invalidate the magisterium. And once the secular state made it clear that it still did wish to allow the Church its essential freedoms, then it was possible for the Church to come to terms with it. In fact, from the time that Pius IX's successor, Leo XIII, took office in 1878,[184] the rapprochement of the Church with the secular state, which was summed up by Vatican II, began to take place.

E. THE CHURCH AND POLITICS TODAY

The historical experience of the Church has taught her that it is extremely difficult for her to avoid entanglement in politics, and that such entanglements are detrimental to her mission. The more powerful and influential she is, the more secular authorities will want to control her, and the more inevitable it is for her to have direct influence on political affairs, even where she would prefer not to have it. And when she is weak then it is all the easier for the state to prevent her exercising her legitimate rights when it chooses to do so. But the theory of the relationship between Church and state, the ideal that she would like to see existing, has been reaffirmed by Vatican II. A clear distinction is drawn by the Council firstly between the activities of Christians as individuals and what they do directly in the name of the Church.[185]

> . . . The Church, by reason of her rule and competence, is not identified with any political system . . . the political community and the Church are autonomous and independent of each other in their own fields.

---

[184] Aubert, *The Church in a Secularized Society*, pp. 8 ff. E. T. Gargan, *Leo XIII and the Modern World* (New York, 1961).
[185] *Gaudium et Spes*, par. 76.

Accordingly, although there are close links between earthly concerns and those which transcend them, and although she uses temporal things in so far as her mission requires it, nevertheless the Church:[186]

> . . . never places hopes in any privileges accorded to it by civil authority: indeed it will give up the exercise of certain legitimate rights whenever it is clear that their use will compromise the sincerity of its witness and whenever new circumstances call for a revised approach. But at all times and in all places the Church should have true freedom to preach the faith, to proclaim its teaching about society, to carry out its task among men without hindrance and to pass moral judgements, even on matters relating to politics, whenever the fundamental rights of man or the salvation of souls requires it. The means, and the only means, she may use are those which are in accord with the Gospel and the welfare of all men according to times and circumstances.

Her position in the modern world, her gradual disentanglement from the relics of old political alliances such as we have been considering previously, makes it easier for her to state her position clearly and hope that she may be able to maintain it. She is indifferent to political systems as such, but she must remain free to teach the whole of her truth, including her social teaching, and pass moral judgement on political issues when the salvation of souls and the fundamental rights of man require it. Even as one states the theory, it is apparent that she will be more at home with systems that are more in conformity with her social teaching than those that are less so. Yet the statement of her independence makes it possible for her to work peacefully with the latter if she is allowed to do so. It also helps to ensure her right to speak out against any system which on specific issues is attacking fundamental human rights or spiritual/moral truth. The Council also made it clear that, for both clergy and laity, it is her social doctrine that is to be the guide to political and economic morality[187] and to action accordingly. In this it was taking up a point made forcefully by John XXIII in his encyclical *Mater et Magistra*.[188]

> *The permanent validity of the Catholic Church's social teaching admits of no doubt* . . . she has propounded a social doctrine which points out with clarity the sure way to social reconstruction. The principles she gives are of universal application, for they take human nature into account, and the varying conditions in which man's life is lived. They also take into account the principal characteristics of contemporary society, and are thus acceptable to all. But today, more than ever, it is essential that this doctrine be known,

[186] Ibid.

[187] See above p. 86. The main reference to the social teaching of the Church is in paragraph 63 of *Gaudium et Spes*; the social encyclicals are the basis of its social teaching throughout.

[188] *Mater et Magistra*, pars. 218–22.

assimilated, and put into effect in the form and manner that the different situations allow and demand. . . . *We must affirm most strongly that this Catholic social doctrine is an integral part of the Christian conception of life.*

However, in the years after the Council, some took it upon themselves to ignore, or even undermine, this teaching[189] and to seek Christian social commitment by using other guides. In this connection, we can note that the Council deplored the use of violence. In saying that she will only use means which are conformable with the Gospel, when it is necessary for her to intervene in politics for the purposes outlined,[190] she is precisely ruling out the possibility of any use of violence, any support or encouragement of it for political ends. But, as we have seen from our consideration of the nature of political authority, its origin and its proper use, the right of the individual to decide that violence is the only way to achieve justice is one that can be defended in principle according to the reservations and safeguards the principle implies.[191] It is here that the distinction between what individuals may decide to do and what the Church's official leadership may decide to do must be clearly understood and acted on.

Given the right to use violence in specified circumstances, it is entirely conceivable that in the future as in the past, political communities which are predominantly Catholic may decide to resort to revolution to achieve justice. In such circumstances, the Church, while not denying the right, must never, if she is to be true to Christ, encourage it. Her role must be that of peacemaker through truth and justice.

In the light of this inability, in loyalty to Christ, ever to give a lead in revolutionary violence and in the light of the perduring validity of her social teaching, the phenomenon of the school of liberation theology within the Church must be considered.[192] It is not easy to understand what precisely this term means. Its genesis is also mysterious. Apparently, it came into use sometime between 1965 and 1968. According to Assmann,[193] until the eve of the Medellin Conference in 1968, it was the Church's official view that development (gradual reform and social economic change) was the word that described the process Latin America had to undergo to achieve justice; but before then, unofficially, the term

[189] As has been pointed out above, p. 4, footnote, John Paul II commented on this at Puebla.

[190] *Gaudium et Spes,* par 76.

[191] See above pp. 222–23.

[192] Many names are connected with this movement; among those most widely known are G. Gutierrez, *A Theology of Liberation* (London, 1974), H. Assmann, *Practical Theology of Liberation* (London, 1975), and J. L. Segundo, *The Liberation of Theology* (Dublin, 1977).

[193] Assmann, op. cit., p. 45.

"liberation" had gained acceptance; the change of terminology indicated that what was needed was not development in the sense of gradual change from within aided by external factors, but the abolition of the state of dependence in which peoples and countries were being kept by external forces beyond their control, especially the economic power of wealthier nations.[194]

After Medellin, the word "liberation" was used increasingly in episcopal documents, and it argues, according to Assmann, for a freedom, a liberty denied in the present state of affairs. It implies refusal to accept the existing situation and the determination to change it by other than gradual development. "The very notion [i.e. of liberation] implies a judgement. It is a word of confrontation and conflict."[195] Immediately, however, the author adds that

> one cannot presuppose the existence of a detailed analytic judgement on, say, the phenomenon of under-development behind every use of the word, which implies a general condemnation of the existing state of affairs and the need for change. On its own it can be either reforming or revolutionary.

It is this lack of precision, verging on incoherence, that runs throughout the writings of the liberation theologians, that confuses. Either they believe that in specific cases (and they should name situations and countries) confrontation and conflict should be pressed, or they do not. If they do, they should tell us what they mean by "confrontation" and "conflict". Passive resistance, demonstration, violent revolution? If they think that some cases of lack of liberation are tolerable on the principle of the lesser of two evils and that in these cases it is better to wait for slow reform, again they should say so. But they are most reluctant to come to the point.

On one matter Assmann gives cold comfort. He denies that the language of liberation is a spontaneous product of the climate of reform after the Second Vatican Council. Other factors have exercised a far more direct influence.[196]

[194] The first meeting of CELAM (the General Conference of Latin American Bishops) was held in 1955, the second was at Medellin in 1968. Puebla was the third. It is not apparent from the Medellin documents themselves that the reforms and changes proposed at that conference required any abandonment of the social teaching of the Church. J. Gremillion, "The Medellin Documents", in *The Gospel of Peace and Justice* (New York, 1976), pp. 445 ff., especially pp. 448, 450, 457–58. The documents were published in full by the National Conference of Catholic Bishops (Washington D.C., 1979), under the title of *The Church in the Present Day Transformation of Latin America in the Light of the Council*.

[195] Assmann, op. cit., p. 47.

[196] Ibid., p. 48. He gives some examples of the international congresses referred to: an international symposium on the theology of liberation, March 1970; an ecumenical seminar on the theme, Buenos Aires, August 1970; a seminar at Ciudad Juarez (Mexico), October 1970, in which Harvey Cox and others took part.

> The language of the revolutionary movements of the left, the Marxist vocabulary of Latin American "New Marxism" . . . the terms used by student movements . . . the writings of Herbert Marcuse . . . and the documents from international congresses on the dialectics of liberation.

The Latin American liberation theologians are convinced that their case and situation is unique and needs unique remedies. The "progressive" theology of the developed world is irrelevant to Latin American needs.[197] The experience of the unrelenting forces of domination is the stronger influence on the movement.[198]

From these brief comments based on extracts from one of the leading exponents of liberation theology, it would seem that the movement accepts that the developmental approach, the reformist approach to social improvement and change, must be abandoned and that some affinity with Marxist theory, analysis and methodology must be accepted: It accounts for this emphasis and change of direction by the uniqueness of the Latin American situation. But is that situation unique? If Catholic communities have before today achieved greater justice without the need of ideologies such as Marxism, which are at odds with Christian belief, then perhaps the Latin Americans have something to learn.

That the use of violence may be an option that an individual may take in certain extreme circumstances to achieve justice has already been demonstrated. But the motive, the method, and the intended outcome of the use of this violence would be different not in degree but in kind from that of the Marxists. To ally with Marxism in a revolutionary situation requires particular caution as to the limits and the intention.[199] And it does

---

[197] Ibid., pp. 50–51.

[198] The forces of domination referred to are, in particular, American national and business interests allied with right wing regimes. See e.g. J. D. Cockroft et al., *Dependence and Under-Development: Latin America's Political Economy* (New York, 1972). A. Gilbert, *Latin American Development* (London, 1977), gives a more dispassionate account of the general picture and its implications.

[199] The experience of European fellow travellers in the 1920s and 1930s is still relevant. The euphoria of the near Marxists or would-be allies of Marxism clouds the judgement of the socially conscious. Anyone who doubts this should read D. Caute, *The Fellow Travellers* (London, 1973). The enthusiasm for the Chinese cultural revolution of the 1960s apparent in many quarters shows that Communist social experiments, which turn out to have been disastrous in human terms, can still appeal to the uncritical left—at a comfortable distance. On the point of theory, Paul VI, in *Octogesima Adveniens*, stressed that the Christian "cannot adhere to Marxist ideology, its atheistic materialism to its dialectic of violence and to the way it absorbs individual freedom in the collectivity at the same time denying all transcendence to man" ([London: C.T.S.], par. 26). In the same paragraph, liberal capitalism is rejected equally as strongly. And dialogue with communism does not mean acceptance of its errors. See "The Pontifical Magisterium and Marxist Atheism" (*L'Osservatore Romano* [English edition], 31 March 1977), "Forty Years after *Divini Redemptoris*: The Essential Continuity of

not appear from the writings of the theologians in question that they are aware of the relevant experience of their co-religionists in other countries and other times who succeeded without Marxism—indeed, against it. Their plea is the uniqueness of the situation. That every case of oppression has its uniqueness, no one will deny. But the liberation theologians' insistence that the uniqueness of the Latin American situation is not of *degree* but of kind is hard, indeed impossible to substantiate. It would be impossible to show that the difficulties facing the Latin American poor, part of whose problems stem from the economic domination of foreign firms, countries or economic systems, were any greater than those faced by the European working classes in the nineteenth century—difficulties which produced injustices in those countries so great that Marx used the situation as the model for his plan of revolution. The worker in the industrial areas of Britain, Germany and France was, in principle, just as much the victim of the international economic order as is the worker in modern Latin America. The collusion of governments in the oppression of the wage-earner by the maintenance of policies which deprived him of protection was real enough in the nineteenth century too.[200] Yet in facing the social problem of this period, Catholics, successfully as events proved, were able to find in their own theological and philosophical tradition, and in the spiritual resources of the Church, the means to fight the war for greater justice.[201]

The industrial revolution did not begin to have a major impact on countries with considerable Catholic populations, such as France and Germany, till the period 1830–1850,[202] and only when it did so could the members of the Church—laity, priests and bishops—begin to work together to find Christian answers to problems posed by the totally new

---

the Doctrine of the Church" (21 April 1977), "Two Documents on the Relationship between Communism and Religion" (28 April 1977). "Christianity and Marxism" (9 June 1977), "Marxism, Man and Christian Faith" (11 August 1977), "Primacy of the Spiritual and Primacy of the Temporal" (29 April 1976) and "Collaboration between Christians and Marxists" (16 September 1976).

[200] See below pp. 269 ff.

[201] For the experience of the Church in general in various countries, see J. M. Moody, *Church and Society* (New York, 1953). Daniel Rops, *A Fight for God*, pp. 128 ff, *The Church in an Age of Revolution*, pp. 343 ff. Aubert, *The Church in a Secularised Society*, pp. 144 ff. Vidler, *A Century of Social Catholicism* (London, 1964).

[202] In France, though there was a flourishing iron industry before 1850 and a strong textile sector too, it was the growth of the railways and the increase in mechanisation after that date that marked the great leap forward. Germany was rather slower to develop initially than France because of her long-term political problems, but between 1848 and 1870 huge strides were made so that, by the 1870s, she had overtaken France as an iron producer, for example. By 1900 she had also overtaken Britain both in the production of iron and of steel. Friedlander and Oser, op. cit., pp. 82 ff., 90 ff., 221 ff.

power to create wealth through machine production for mass markets, which was revolutionising society in all its aspects, and to whose problems we still seek the full answer. The French Catholic social movement had roots going back to the 1820s; the Christian socialists like Buchez and the Democrats like Ozanam had enough impact on society, together with the liberal Catholics, to ensure that the revolution of 1848 was favourable to the Church.[203] But, fearful of the ambitions of the industrial workers as represented by the sentiments of the Communist *Manifesto* (1848) the French Church, with its roots predominantly in the rural peasantry and the bourgeois in the towns, was soon supporting the factions which set up the second Empire under Louis Napoleon in 1852. The attitude of that regime, and those who supported it, to the growing industrial working class, was a paternalism that expected the wage-earner to accept his disadvantages as natural and inevitable. Not until after the national defeat in the Franco-Prussian War in 1871 did the Catholic Social Movement in France begin to revive, as the nation as a whole became more aware of the importance of the problems of industrialisation. Albert de Mun and La Tour du Pin were two of the figures identified with the Catholic revival; having been prisoners together during the war, they decided to work together after it for greater justice for their fellow countrymen. However, they took rather different directions in their later interest.

La Tour du Pin's remedy for overcoming the problems of industrialisation was a form of modified guild organisation or corporativism in industry; de Mun, along with others, was convinced that a greater degree of state intervention was needed, that the problems were too great for self-help to overcome them alone. The two schools of thought, the former named after the city of Angers in which it was centred, the latter after the city of Liège in which it was centred, came together in the Union of Fribourg in a series of meetings between 1884 and 1891. It was on their deliberations, and the documentation that grew out of them, that Leo XIII and his advisers were able to draw in writing the encyclical *Rerum Novarum*.[204]

Among those who supported the Liègois approach to the needed social reform was the München Gladbach Group, centred on the work of Franz Hitze, who organised the German Catholic Labour movement.[205] It was

[203] D. Thompson, *Europe since Napoleon*, pp. 206 ff. Moody, op. cit., pp. 126 ff.

[204] R. Ergang, *Europe since Waterloo* (New York, 1965), pp. 128 ff., 577 ff. Moody, op. cit., pp. 130 ff. Daniel Rops, *A Fight for God*, pp. 141 ff. Vidler, *Social Catholicism*, pp. 119 ff.

[205] Hitze (1851–1921) was the priest who, more than any other individual, influenced the development of trade unionism among German Catholic workers, a movement which became increasingly influential from the 1880s and did much to form the social conscience of the Catholic community thereafter. Moody, op. cit., pp. 422 ff.

indeed in Germany, not only the sound ideas of the Liégois that were more fully expanded, but also that the experience of putting, or seeing them put into practice was greater.

As the French reaction to the social problems of the nineteenth century was tempered by the experience of events of 1848 and 1870–1871, so the German Catholic social movement was largely shaped by the events leading up to the unification of Germany and the emergence of Prussia as the dominant force in that new Germany. Yet the intrinsic social strength of German Catholicism was greater than that of its French counterpart. It was among the German Catholics that an effective movement for social reform first developed in a sizeable Catholic community in the Western world.

The Catholic Church, in the Rhineland and Westphalia especially, entered the period of German nationalistic growth in the mid-nineteenth century with an inbuilt suspicion of the exaggerated respect for the state that it involved, a suspicion which Pinson notes was a direct result of its Catholic philosophy.[206] After the crushing of Austria in 1866, this feeling was intensified, while the growing economic liberalism of the time was repugnant to Catholic social philosophy. Franz Baader had been the first German writer to refer to the industrial working classes as the proletariat, and he strongly attacked capitalism and its excesses in the light of Catholic social ethics.[207] The implications of Catholic belief, therefore, taken with the pressures that existed in mid-nineteenth century Germany, gave the Church a keen and effective social conscience, one which was to be prophetic of future developments in the mitigation of the evils of capitalism.

It was in Adolf Kolping (1813–1865) and in William Ketteler (1811–1877) that German social Catholicism found the men who were to give it its first firm basis. Kolping was born of a poor family and worked as a journeyman before starting his studies for the priesthood. It was the Katholische Gesellenvreine (Catholic Journeyman's Associations) that he later founded which were to be his particular contribution to influencing the social conscience and social action of the German workers. Franz Hitze was later to develop a genuine trade union movement among German Catholic workers, but Kolping's work in its time was crucial.[208]

[206] K. Pinson, *Modern Germany*, p. 175.

[207] Ibid., pp. 181 ff. and Moody, op. cit., pp. 410 ff.

[208] Moody, op. cit., p. 417 and Vidler, *Social Catholicism*, pp. 104 ff. Pinson, op. cit., pp. 181, quotes the German Socialist leader Bebel (who was a member of such a Catholic association) on their openness to men of all faiths, their effectiveness as educational institutions and unique way in which their chaplains led them.

Bishop Ketteler was, by contrast, born of an aristocratic land-owning family and, after his university studies, joined the Prussian Civil Service from which he resigned in 1837 when the conflict with the Church began. He then found his vocation to the priesthood, and in his work as a priest he was also able to fulfill the desire he had long felt—to devote himself particularly to the problems of the people. His series of sermons in the cathedral at Mainz in 1848 so annoyed Marx that he could not thereafter speak of the preacher without anger.[209] Basing himself on traditional Catholic teaching about the social responsibility of private ownership, he rejected the economic liberalism that ignored these responsibilities. Convinced of the need of effective trade unionism, he had by 1869 also come to support the need for greater state legislation to mitigate the evils of capitalism—a programme of social legislation to provide protection and economic security for the working classes was, he said, required. It was on policies such as these that the Catholic Centre Party was founded when it was launched in 1870.[210] The profusion and vitality of Catholic social thought and action had influence beyond the Church. The social legislation of Bismarck and of the Wilhelmian epoch "bears the import of Catholic influence".[211] That legislation was the beginning of the modern welfare state which, in its turn, helped to prevent the threatened socialist take over that Marx had predicted. The German Church's social thought therefore may be said to have had a direct influence on one of the two key factors that have mitigated the evils of capitalism. And unlike Bismarck, the Church, partly through the influence of the Catholic communities in America and Britain where free trade unionism had taken root, accepted this institution positively too.[212] It well accorded with that right of association that is fundamental to Catholic social theory. Since it was the development of welfare economics, the welfare state and trade unionism which tamed the worst excesses of capitalism, it can be said that the Church, in her teaching and her members, worked with these developments to produce greater social justice.

[209] Moody, op. cit., p. 414. See also Vidler, *Social Catholicism*, pp. 101 ff. A full account of Ketteler's work, life and thought is given in G. Metlake, *Christian Social Reform* (Philadelphia, 1912).

[210] Pinson, op. cit., pp. 183 ff. Moody, op. cit., pp. 446 ff.

[211] Pinson, op. cit., p. 185.

[212] The effectiveness of British trade unionism had been noted with approval by social Catholics on the Continent. It was Cardinal Manning in England and Cardinal Gibbons in the U.S.A. who were noted in their defence of the right of association in free trade unions, and their defence had its influence as part of the background to *Rerum Novarum*. V. A. McClelland, *Cardinal Manning* (London, 1962), pp. 153 ff. A. S. Will, *The Life of Cardinal Gibbons* (New York, 1922) 1:320 ff.

Though the fundamental evils of welfare capitalism remain since it cannot shake off its materialist origins, and today runs to gross consumerism in consequence, it is clear that within it it contains the important principle of freedom which men are loath to abandon given the choice. It is the Marxist states which have to build walls to keep their people in. The question of which economic system is more compatible with the Catholic social ethic overall is discussed in another place. What we simply want here to point out is that, given the same conflict in nineteenth century Europe as the Latin American Church is now undergoing in principle, Catholics, by sticking close to their Catholic social philosophy, were able to make a marked contribution to the task of bringing greater justice and prosperity to their fellow men. They also preserved the all-important spiritual and intellectual freedoms Marxism denies to those who embrace it. It was then out of the experience of Catholics facing social injustice that the teaching of *Rerum Novarum* was born. At the very time that Marx was seeking the destruction of the current economic order, the Catholic social movement found inspiration in Christ and the Catholic tradition to save what was good in it—above all freedom—while fighting its injustices. Perhaps the Catholics of Latin America could learn from the experience of their co-religionists in a similar situation earlier—that commitment to justice does not demand an ideology alien to Christian belief. They may retort, with the Marxists, that only imperial expansion provided the means to improve the living standards of the European working class. Whether one agrees with this analysis or not, the fact of the current imbalance between the developed and underdeveloped world is indisputable, and every effort has to be made to redress it. What is not clear is that Marxist economics or Marxist revolution would improve matters. On the evidence of the experience of Eastern Europe or Castro's Cuba, such revolutions, or alliance with the Soviet bloc, produces a dependence as marked, if not more so, than the worst that liberal capitalism imposed and imposes. Only those blinded by ideology would be capable of seeing exploitation in the one and not in the other. The example of their fellow Christians who have lived through revolutions in economics and politics such as they now face and have found a way through without recourse to ideologies at variance with Christianity should give Latin American Christians hope.

All this could have been said at any time in the past ten years. But Pope John Paul II, on his visit to Mexico, forced home that it is in loyalty to the truth of the tradition of Catholic social doctrine, and in it alone, that the answer to the quest for social justice lies. He spoke often during his visit, in his speeches to the poor, the people generally, the clergy and to the specialist groups, of the need for justice and true liberation, for human fulfillment.[213] But he did not appeal to a particular political ideology—he appealed to Christ, the charity of the faithful and their thirst for justice. This is most clearly seen in his keynote address at Puebla to the Third General Conferences of the Latin American Episcopate—that meeting of CELAM which was the successor of that held in Medellin in 1968.

In his address, he took Medellin as his starting point—its conclusions, with all the positive elements they contained, but without "ignoring the incorrect interpretations . . . that call for calm discernment, opportune criticism and clear choices of position."[214]

He spoke of the "authentic liberation of man"—saying that the truth will make us free.[215] Truth indeed was the keynote of the address. Truth first concerning Jesus Christ—a sound Christology, rejecting that which sees him as "a revolutionary, the subversive from Nazareth". On the contrary, Christ rejected violence and opened the way of conversion to all—including the Publicans.[216] Sound doctrine is then the first requisite —and above all sound doctrine about Christ. Another requisite is sound ecclesiology; there can be no sound evangelisation without ready and sincere reverence for the magisterium.[217] The Kingdom of God is not to be confused with the worldly kingdom—political, economic and social liberation does not coincide with salvation in Jesus Christ.[218] Sound doctrine and sound ecclesiology demand a connection between evangelization and human advancement or liberation. But the Church does not need to have recourse to ideological systems in order to love, defend and collaborate in the liberation of man; the Christian perspective and the Church's social teaching are to be the guide.[219]

> Whatever the miseries or sufferings that afflict man, it is not through violence, the interplay of power and political systems, but through the truth concerning man, that he journeys towards a better future.

In particular, the Catholic teaching regarding the proper use of private property is appealed to—through St. Ambrose, St. Thomas, through *Populorum Progressio* and *Mater et Magistra*. And he reasserted the stress of Paul VI—that development is the new name for peace. In the light of Assmann's comments that liberation theology has gone beyond this, this is an interesting re-emphasis. Again, appealing to Paul VI, this time in

---

[213] "Address to the Poor of Los Minos", 26 January 1979; "Address to the Catholic Organizations of Mexico", 29 January; "Address to a Meeting at Guadalajara", 30 January; "Address to the Seminarium at Guadalajara", 30 January; "Meeting at Monterrey", 31 January, as in *Puebla: Pilgrimage of Faith* (New York, 1979), pp. 33 ff., 127 ff., 152 ff., 175 ff., 182 ff.

[214] Ibid., p. 95. [215] Ibid., p. 97, quoting Jn 8:33.
[216] Ibid., p. 100. [217] Ibid., p. 105.
[218] Ibid., p. 107. [219] Ibid., p. 116.

Evangelii Nuntiandi, he warns that any notion of liberation that leaves the Church open to manipulation by ideological systems is to be rejected. We should distinguish between liberation which is truly Christian and liberation which is tied to ideologies that rob us of the evangelical view of man.[220]

He sums up this part of the message by saying:[221]

> What we have already recalled constitutes a rich and complete heritage. . . .
> The Social Doctrine or Social Teaching of the Church . . . placing responsible confidence in this social doctrine—even though some people seek to sow doubt and lack of confidence in it—to give it serious study, to try to apply it, to teach it, to be faithful to it: all this is the guarantee in a member of the Church, of his commitment in the delicate and demanding social tasks, and of his efforts in favour of the liberation or advancement of his brothers or sisters.

The result of the Conference was a document of lasting interest and of value to the whole Church, though it was of its nature primarily concerned with the Latin American situation. It comes to grips with the realities of the social economic and political situation as it is all too bitterly experienced in the Latin American Church, yet it does so in a way which reflects the Church's evangelical concern. It is then at one with the great social encyclicals, the documents of Vatican II and with the words of the Holy Father in his opening address; it owes everything to the Church's own understanding of her mission and her spiritual and moral responsibilities, drawing, as she has always done, on the language and expertise of the times to help her in her understanding and guidance, but placing it in the context of the Gospel and that transcendent vision of man and his destiny of which she is the guardian.

In dealing with the fundamental question of "Evangelization and Ideology", the statement clearly takes its inspiration from the Pope's opening address. It states the Church's refusal to identify with liberal capitalism, Marxist Communism or the national security state. It warns of allowing the Church to become the tool of political pressure groups of whatever colour. The social teaching of the Church is to be our guide in the task of liberation,[222] and the teaching of *Gaudium et Spes* on the different roles of the laity and the clergy/religious in the political fields is repeated. Priests and religious should be a sign of unity, which would be jeopardized if they indulged in partisan politics—except in exceptional circumstances and with the approval of proper authority. Bishops, priests and religious who are close to God will know how to act for justice

---

[220] Ibid., p. 121.   [221] Ibid., p. 122.

[222] Third General Conference of Latin American Bishops, *Puebla: Evangelization at Present and in the Future of Latin America: Conclusions* (London, 1980), p. 103.

without sacrificing the Church's true mission. In the specifics of their own vocation lies the best way to serve God and his people.[223]

The document is wide-ranging in its concern for the good of the Church; it deals with catechetics, liturgy, education, social communications and many other matters. We have only touched on those aspects directly relevant to the social teaching of the Church and the controversies over its role in the bringing of justice to man. It is a sign of the guidance of the Spirit in the Church when the bishops of the whole of this important sub-continent, after many years of debate and open discussion, set out in some detail their plan for the Church's role in the promotion of justice and they produce a document which in its tone and content is truly evangelical, truly Catholic and truly at one with the social magisterium. It is in these characteristics that the value and the efficacy of its directives lies.

The Church in Latin America, and in other areas such as the Philippines,[224] is going to be, in the next decades, faced with the problems of redressing social injustice and faced with them in their most acute and violent forms. Under the guidance of their bishops in union with Rome, the individual countries will have to each find their own way through the many problems, and each will be faced with many crucial choices. The option for violence, failing all else, remains as the choice of the individual and informed conscience. It can never be the choice of the Church. Where a sufficient number of Christians make this choice as individuals, then as a sociological fact, it may be said that the Church takes this option: but here the distinction between what individuals do, even collectively, and what the Church does, must be maintained. As a eucharistic community, as man's guide to salvation, the Church, which is Christ, must always resist any attempt to use her influence to encourage or support the use of violence.

As to working with those whose policies are based on a different concept of man, society and the role of both, individual Christians and the Church must always remain open to work with any group with which, on specifics, it shares common aims; Communism, Fascism, liberal capitalism, the national security state, there is some good in all of them. But with none of them can the Church identify because of their defective overall philosophies. The Church has her own understanding of man

[223] Ibid., p. 111.
[224] E. Kim and L. Ziring, *An Introduction to Asian Politics* (Englewood Cliffs, New Jersey, 1977), pp. 333 ff., give the essential background. P. S. Manglapus, *The Silenced Democracy* (New York, 1976), an impassioned account of the defects of the Marcos dictatorship. W. Buhlmann, *The Coming of the Third Church* (New York, 1978), surveys the role of the Church in the third world. One does not have to agree with all the author's judgements on the past or prescriptions for the future to appreciate the breadth of his vision and to learn a great deal from what he has to say.

and his needs based on the teaching of Christ. This understanding has developed a social and moral teaching which is to be the real guide to Christian action for justice.

IV. INTERNATIONAL LAW
AND INTERNATIONAL RELATIONS

So far in this chapter on political ethics we have been mainly concerned with the nature of the national state and the attitude of the Christian to it. We must now look a little more closely at the Christian attitude to international relations, because we are members of an international Church and therefore have a perspective accordingly.

The Council gives a great deal of prominence to the question of establishing an international community. In considering the possibility and the desirability of the total outlawing of war, it speaks[225] of the need for

> the establishment of the universally acknowledged public authority, vested with the effective power to ensure security for all, regard for justice and respect for law. But before this desirable authority can be constituted, it is necessary for existing international bodies to devote themselves resolutely to the exploration of better means for obtaining common security. . . . One must not underestimate the efforts already being made . . . support should be given to the goodwill of numerous individuals who are making every effort to eliminate the havoc of war. In our time this work demands that they enlarge their thoughts and their spirit beyond the confines of their own country, that they put aside nationalistic selfishness and ambitions to dominate other nations, that they cultivate deep reverence for the whole of mankind which is painstakingly advancing towards greater maturity . . . existing international and regional organisations certainly deserve well of the human race. They represent the first attempts at laying the foundations on an international level for a community of all men to work towards the solutions of the very serious problems of our time.

In showing its concern, therefore, for the international order, the Church is reflecting the responsibility for all people that it possesses in virtue of the role given to her by Christ.

History has compelled her to accept her responsibilities in this matter, even in ways she would not have chosen. We have seen how the collapse of the Roman Empire left the Church alone as an international organisation throughout the extent of that former empire, capable of bringing home to men their obligations to mankind beyond the narrow confines of their own tribal or national boundaries. In the course of time, it was the

[225] *Gaudium et Spes*, pars. 82, 84.

link between the papacy, the missionary Benedictines and the Frankish kings which enabled Europe to emerge as a Christendom in which the various countries acknowledged the overall obligations of a larger community. As a consequence of the growth of nationalism and other factors that led to a breakdown of the medieval order, the role of the Church and the papacy as international arbiter was increasingly challenged and was finally ignored. Many aspects of her influence on international politics had negative effects on her spiritual role, but the international nature of the papacy and of the Church gives both a direct concern in these matters in which they have still a valuable part to play; the concern for justice and peace for the whole world must always be a mark of Christ's Church.

It is from the fundamental nature of the Church, therefore, that her interest in international relations springs. The Christian understanding of the origin, nature and end of man stresses the idea of the oneness of all in Christ and of all peoples as a natural community under Christ. St. Augustine developed the idea of the society of nations, and under his influence, the theologians of the Middle Ages saw the nucleus of that society in the Holy Roman Empire.[226] Dante in *De Monarchia* looked for a world state governed by an international authority,[227] but theologians thought rather in terms of a society of nations, a society that is of independent political societies; with this approach they were able, in a world opening up in the sixteenth and seventeenth centuries, to lay the foundations of international law. The Dominicans, Francis de Vitoria (1483–1564)[228] and Dominic de Soto (1494–1560),[229] together with the Jesuit, Francis Suarez (1548–1617),[230] made outstanding contributions in this field.

---

[226] Messner, op. cit., p. 493. The name Holy Roman Empire was applied to that founded by Charlemagne, of which he was formally crowned Emperor by the Pope in 800 A.D. The Empire of Charlemagne effectively died with him. In the tenth century France became separated from the Empire, and it was Otto the Great, a German king, who revived Charlemagne's conception of the Holy Roman Empire—being crowned Emperor in 962 A.D. M. Keen, *The Pelican History of Medieval Europe*, pp. 11 ff., 29 ff.

[227] Messner, loc. cit.

[228] De Vitoria was professor of theology at Salamanca from 1526 to 1546 when it was the outstanding theological centre of Catholic Europe. His lectures, *De Indis* and *De Jure Belli*, delivered in this period, give him claim to be the founder of modern international law. J. B. Scott, *The Spanish Origins of International Law: Francis de Vitoria and the Law of Nations* (Oxford, 1934).

[229] Lecturer and professor of theology at Salamanca from 1532 to 1556 and imperial theologian at the Council of Trent. His *De Iustitia et Jure* went through twenty-eight editions between 1553 and 1600.

[230] Professor of theology at Coimbra from 1597 to 1615. His *Tractatus de legibus ac Deo Legislative* (1612) and *Defensio Fidei* (1613) contain his main contributions to legal and political theory. H. Wright, ed., *Francisco Suarez: Addresses in Commemoration of his Con-*

The logic of the need for an international law and international community having been clear to the Christian mind from the beginning, the form which it has taken has varied as different phases of historical experience have brought different aspects of the truth to notice. The unity of law and political organisation in the Roman Empire, inherited and Christianised by the Church, at once expressed and reinforced the conception of humanity as one, and under the stress of attack from outside, particularly by the Muslims, it was inevitable that there should be concern with the morality of war.[231] But the theory and practice of peace-making within Christendom was also developed through the peace of God and the truce of God and the attempt by the Church to soften the brutality of the times.[232] The idea of Christendom did not survive the conditions of the central Middle Ages. The divisions within the Empire itself, the Investiture controversy and the practical inability of the Empire to maintain political unity, gradually separated the papacy from the concept of a Christian empire as the means of realising the political union of all peoples. With the break-up of the Empire, the strength of national sentiment increased and the rights of national states were to be urged. Theologians, therefore, sought, in the natural law in the light of the Christian tradition, to delineate the true rights and duties of the national monarchs and the independent states they ruled and, at the same time, work out the conditions for a true international government.

Through the concept of the *Ius Gentium*, the Catholic tradition sought to come to terms with the needs of international law in the modern world. To this law of nations Vitoria, de Soto, Bartolomé de las Casas and Suarez appealed in the dispute over the rights of Indians in the Americas. So Suarez[233] writes:

> The reason for the law of nations . . . is that the human race, though divided into no matter how many different peoples and nations, has for all that a certain unity, a unity not merely physical but also in a sense political and moral. This is shown by the natural precept of mutual love and mercy which extends to all men including foreigners of every way of thinking. Wherefore though any one state, republic or kingdom be in itself a perfect community and constant in its members, nevertheless each of the states is also a member in a certain manner of the world as far as the human race is concerned. For none of these communities are ever sufficient unto them-

tribution to International Law and Politics (Washington, 1933). John Eppstein, *The Catholic Tradition of the Law of Nations* (London, 1935), pp. 107 ff., 164 ff., 262 ff. Copleston, op. cit., vol. 3, chap. 23.

[231] Eppstein, op. cit., p. 248.
[232] Ibid., pp. 187 ff.
[233] Quoted in Eppstein, op. cit., p. 265.

selves to such a degree that they do not require some mutual help, society or communication, either to their greater advantage or from moral necessity and need as is evident from custom. For this reason, therefore, they need some law whereby they may be directed and rightly ruled in this kind of communication and society. Although this in great part comes from natural law, yet it is not sufficient or direct enough for all purposes. Therefore it has been found possible to introduce some special laws by the customs of the peoples themselves. For as in one state or province, customs introduced law, so in the whole human race international laws could be introduced by custom.

It is then to the scholastics of this period, and to Vitoria in particular, that we owe the foundations of modern international law. Vitoria in *De Indis* and *De Bello* proclaimed the existence of an international law, no longer limited to Christianity, but applying to all states without reference to geography, creed or race. The great Dutch jurist, Hugo Grotius, published his *De Jure Belli et Pacis* in 1625—nearly one hundred years after Vitoria began his work. Grotius can claim to be the first systematic expounder of modern international law, but, in drawing up his treatise, he had at hand and before his eyes the system set forth by Vitoria.[234]

The general Catholic teaching regarding international relations and international law in the modern world is summarised in the encyclical *Pacem in Terris*,[235] to which *Gaudium et Spes* referred. It pointed out first of all that order between political communities must be founded on the moral law which is revealed in nature by the Creator himself and engraved indelibly on men's hearts.[236] Hence, ties between states must be governed by truth, and that truth demands the elimination of every trace of racial discrimination and the recognition of the principle that all states are by nature equal in dignity. Each state accordingly, even the smallest, has equal right to exist, to develop and to possess the necessary means and accept the primary responsibility for that development. Just as between individuals differences may arise, so, too, they may arise between states and, when differences of this sort arise, they must be settled in a human way, not by armed force or by fraud or duplicity. There must be mutual assessment of the arguments and feelings on both sides, a mature and objective investigation of the situation and an equitable reconciliation of opposing views.[237]

[234] Scott, op. cit., pp. 10a, 3, 287–88. Long extracts from *De Indis* are given in Eppstein, op. cit., pp. 432 ff.

[235] John XXIII, *Peace on Earth*, 11 April 1963 (London: C.T.S., 1963). On the background to modern international relations and international law, F. S. Northedge and M. J. Grieve, *A Hundred Years of International Relations* (London, 1974). J. Brierly, *The Law of Nations* (O.U.P., 1963).

[236] *Pacen in Terris*, par. 85.   [237] Ibid., pars. 91–93.

The hard practical lesson of the modern situation is that no state can pursue its own interests isolated from the rest even if it wishes. So interdependent are they that they require some means of working together under an international public authority. But this general authority must be set up by the consent of all nations, and, if its work is to be effective, it must operate with fairness, absolute impartiality and with dedication to the common good of all peoples. The principle of subsidiarity must operate in that the universal authority must only be concerned to do what the individual states themselves cannot do. Its essential purpose is to create world conditions in which not only the public authorities of every nation, but also its citizens as members of intermediate groups can carry out their tasks, fulfill their duties and claim their rights with greater security. The United Nations Organization, with its Declaration of Human Rights, together with its varied economic, cultural, educational and health activities, is welcomed as the first stage of the development of this world authority, whatever its limitations and defects. The hope is that it will be able to adapt its structure and methods to the magnitude and nobility of its task.[238]

The papal approval of the United Nations does not involve an obligation on all Catholics to agree with the assessment: many may be more impressed by its weakness, ineffectiveness or misguidedness. On such practical matters of political judgement we each make up our own minds. What is incumbent on Catholics, what is a matter of moral principle, is the search for a better world order and an effective means of supra-national government which respects the rights of individual nations while supplying those services for all nations that they cannot provide for themselves. The world is too small for the simple doctrine of national sovereignty, complete unto itself, to be valid any longer. If we are exasperated with the United Nations, we should be seeking better alternatives, not contenting ourselves with criticism of that organisation's obvious defects. It is not, however, apparent that any such alternative exists at the present or is likely to exist in the near or distant future. Far better then to make the most of U.N.O. and see it as a staging post to a more effective organisation in the future.

[238] Ibid., pars 142–45. John Paul II, as Paul VI, has continued this strong encouragement for the United Nations. See, for example, his "Address to the General Assembly", October 1979, *U.S.A. Message of Justice, Peace and Love*, Boston, 1979, pp. 35 ff. On the work of U.N.O., A. Boyd, *United Nations: Piety, Myth and Truth* (London, 1964). H. G. Nicholas, *The United Nations as a Political Institution* (O.U.P., 1975).

CHAPTER FIVE

THE ETHICS OF ECONOMIC LIFE

The purpose of economics is the service of men, their material needs and those of their moral, spiritual and religious life. Economic activity is to be carried out according to its own methods and laws but within the limits of morality (Gaudium et Spes, paragraph 64).

I. INTRODUCTION:
CHRISTIAN ECONOMIC ETHICS AND IDEALS

The Gospel's warnings about the danger of wealth, of riches, must colour the Christian approach to economics and economic affairs, concerned as they are with the factors affecting the production and distribution of wealth. It should be axiomatic for the Christian that those who create, own and control wealth have particular cause to fear for their eternal salvation, simply because the possibilities of misuse of worldly riches were stressed both by the Old and the New Testaments as spiritually dangerous, not least as the result of injustice to others—the poor, the weak, the defenceless.[1] The section of *Gaudium et Spes*[2] which deals with economic morality refers in a footnote to the teaching of the New Testament where these dangers are stressed.

Today, more than ever before . . . we must encourage technical progress and the spirit of enterprise, we must foster the eagerness for creativity and improvement . . . elements that contribute to economic progress. *The ultimate and basic purpose of economic production does not consist merely in the increase in goods produced, nor in profit, nor in prestige; it is directed to the service of man, of man that is, in his totality, taking into account his material needs and the requirements of his intellectual, moral, spiritual and religious life, of all men and . . . every group of men of whatever race or from whatever part of the world. Therefore economic activity is to be carried out in accordance with techniques and methods belonging to the moral order*[2] *so that God's plan for mankind may be fulfilled. . . .*[3] Economic developments must remain under man's direction; it must not be left to a few individuals or groups possessing too much economic power, nor of the political community alone, nor of a few strong nations . . . all nations should participate in decision making . . . the voluntary initiatives of individuals and of free groups should be integrated with state enterprises . . . nor should development be left to the almost mechanical

[1] See below pp. 302 ff.
[2] Pars. 64–65.

evolution of economic activity nor to the decision of public authority. Hence we must renounce as false, doctrines which stand in the way of all reform on the pretext of a false notion of freedom as well as those which subordinate the basic rights of individuals and groups to the collective organization of production.[4] All citizens should remember that they have the right and the duty to contribute according to their ability to the genuine progress of their own community and this must be recognized by the civil authority. Above all in areas of retarded economic progress, where all resources must be urgently exploited, the common good is seriously endangered by those who hoard their resources unproductively and those who (apart from the case of every man's right of migration) deprive their community of much needed material and spiritual assistance.

[2] Pius XI Litt. Encycl. *Quadragesimo Anno AAS* 23 (1931) p. 190 f. Pius XII *Message* 23 March 1952 *AAS* 44 (1952) p. 276 ff. John XXIII Litt. Encycl. *Mater et Magistra AAS* 53 (1961) p. 45. Vatican Council II Decrees *Inter Mirifica*, ch. 1, no. 6 *AAS* 56 (1964) p. 147.

[3] Cf. Matt. 16:26; Lk. 16:1–31; Col. 3:17.

[4] Cf. Leo XIII Litt. Encycl. *Libertas Praestantissimum* 20 June 1888 *AAS* 20 (1887–1888), p. 597 ff: Pius XI Litt. Encycl. *Quadragesimo Anno AAS* 23 (1931) p. 191 ff: Pius XI *Divini Redemptoris AAS* 39 (1937) pp. 65 ff: Pius XII *Christmas Message* 1941: *AAS* 34 (1942) pp. 10 ff: John XXIII Litt. Encycl. *Mater et Magistra AAS* 53 (1961) 401–64.

It is the third footnote which makes reference to passages in the Scriptures warning against the dangers of riches. In Matthew, chapter 16, Christ tells us not to get our priorities wrong. What, he asks, does it profit a man if he gains the whole world and suffers the loss of his soul? The question, and the context, represent Christ challenging the wisdom of the worldly wise for whom possessions are an end in themselves, the real purpose of life. In Luke, the same challenge comes in a more vivid form—the account of Dives and Lazarus. Christ had used the example of the unjust steward to demonstrate to the Pharisees that they must use their worldly wealth well. If, he says, an evil man such as the unjust steward is generous in the use of the power he has in money terms over others so that they may benefit from his generosity, how much more should those who claim to be righteous, friends of God, use their possessions to help, not to their damnation, but to their salvation? In retort, the Pharisees who "were fond of riches" scorned him. and Christ therefore drew the contrast between the fates of Dives and Lazarus. Dives had refused to obey the law of Moses in his lifetime and was damned: nor could he get any mercy for his brothers who were, while still alive, acting as he had done. Given the context, the teaching is clear. Dives and his brothers were condemned for their misuse of wealth. The conclusion is, not that riches are in themselves evil or lead to damnation, or that excessive poverty is a good thing. It is that the man who selfishly, and to the neglect of the law of God, enjoys riches on earth, is in danger of damnation. It is a lesson to shock the worldly wise, not to justify the avoidable poverty of others for false spiritual reasons.

It is against this background of the scriptural warnings on the need to have a right attitude to wealth, that the general norms governing economic life are given by the Council. Those norms have been the concern of the modern social encyclicals and other papal documents which are also referred to in the footnotes. Firstly, there is recognition of the value of the economic process in itself—but it is stressed that that does not merely consist in the production of more goods, more profit, or prestige. It has to serve the needs of the whole man, material, intellectual, moral and spiritual. It must work for the good of the individual, groups within the state, the state itself and of the international community, and none of these various interests should so dominate that they harm the others. The extremes of individualism and central control are to be avoided, and resources are to be used for the good of all; this means, among other things, that none should be underused as a result of the selfishness of the few.

The points made in these two paragraphs encompass some of the most controversial and important issues of principle in economics and economic policy that have agitated the minds of men and nations in the past and continue to do so today. The truth is that economics, in its modern development, which was initially liberal capitalist, knew nothing of the conscious restraints of morality from either revealed or natural law. Only slowly, pragmatically and therefore patchily, were more humane considerations forced on it or grew, in spite of itself, out of it. Meanwhile, the evil and injustice which resulted from liberal capitalist economics were countered by Marxist socialism and that, in its turn, has proved no less contemptuous of human rights and needs, born as it was of the same contempt for God and his law.

II. LIBERAL CAPITALISM AND MARXIST SOCIALISM: THEIR ETHICS AND IDEALS IN THEORY AND IN PRACTICE

A. LIBERAL CAPITALISM

Modern economic theory developed in a period of rapid industrial and commercial growth in the eighteenth and nineteenth centuries,[3] and in an intellectual and cultural context which assumed that the good of the commonwealth could be secured if each man of property was left to seek his own self-interest. The assumption was that a beneficent natural economic order existed which, if left free to operate unhindered, would

[3] P. Mantoux, *The Industrial Revolution in the 18th Century* (London, 1961), pp. 91 ff. M. Beard, *A History of Business* (Ann Arbor, 1961), 1:325 ff.

work for the good of all. This assumption, and its effects, was to have far ranging implications for the new economic order.

The word *economics* is a Greek derivative; Aristotle, for example, had something to say on the subject,[4] though he looked at economic activity as ordered to the needs of the household; he was suspicious of the businessman, the trader and the financier. However, as society and its needs became more complex, it was necessary that the study of the economic life of man should be developed and a more positive understanding of industry, commerce and finance accompany that development. The canonists and the theologians of the Middle Ages examined commercial and business ethics in great detail[5] and with a more tolerant eye, but, like Aristotle, they could not, and did not, conceive of it as independent of conscious social moral control. Quite the contrary, they inherited the ingrained suspicion of wealth and the wealthy that comes to us from the Scriptures and the Fathers of the Church. By the time that Adam Smith (1723–1790), who may be regarded as the real founder of modern economics, emerged, other presuppositions dominated the minds of the men of property.

Smith[6] elaborated his economic theory as part of his general philosophy; his academic career and writings were concerned with social ethics, moral philosophy and political science, as well as economics. His assumption of the natural harmony in economic life was the by-product of the influence of the natural sciences—the Copernican revolution, Newtonian physics and the development of mathematics. Men were fascinated by the order in the working of the physical world and, in the way that culturally dominant ideas influence other areas of thought and life of their time, the belief that this same harmony was at work passed over into the developing science of economics[7]—even though it is not directly comparable with the physical sciences in data, purpose or degree of scientific predictability and accuracy. Smith, however, saw no contra-

---

[4] *Politics* 1.8–13. *Ethics*, 5.3–5.

[5] J. A. Schumpeter, *A History of Economic Analysis* (London, 1963), pp. 73 ff. St. Antoninus of Florence was perhaps "the first man to whom it is possible to ascribe a comprehensive vision of the economic process in all its aspects." Ibid., p. 95.

[6] He studied at Glasgow and Oxford Universities and later lectured at Edinburgh and Glasgow in logic and moral philosophy. His *On the Theory of Moral Sentiments* was published in 1759. It was during a tour of Europe in 1764 that he came in contact with the French school of economists who were disciples of Quesnay. His classic *The Wealth of Nations* was published in 1776. Though Smith is regarded as the founder of the modern science, his ideas were developed in the context of the previous history of economic thought with which he was, of course, familiar. E. Heimann, *History of Economic Doctrines*, pp. 22 ff., 48 ff. J. Schumpeter, op. cit., pp. 181 ff. R. Heilbroner, *The Worldly Philosophers*, pp. 28 ff.

[7] Heimann, op. cit., pp. 48 ff.

diction between his ethical approach to the study of economics and his belief that economic individualism was a better guarantor of the common good than any form of social supervision.

His particular target in his day was the ruling economic doctrine, namely mercantilism[8]—not so much a unified body of ideas as a series of practical assumptions that developed as nation states sought economic prosperity and security. The stress was on a strong state which would expand markets and protect commercial interests. The monarch and his advisers favoured monopolies and control of wages and prices and sought to increase the amount of bullion the nation possessed. There was much more to be said in defence of mercantilism than its critics, Smith included, allowed; but it was destined to give way to the new economic forces which were threatening not only it, but also the power of the prince. In the years after the Glorious Revolution in England in 1688, sovereignty passed to Parliament, controlled by the old and the new landed gentry and their bourgeois allies;[9] the pressure for greater freedom to exploit their position of power became irresistible, and they found in Smith a sophisticated and persuasive advocate of the policies they wished to pursue. In the observation that "man is led by an invisible hand to promote that which was no part of his intention",[10] Smith provided the intellectual justification of the policy of laissez faire; in seeking out their own expressly selfish and individualistic ends men are, at the same time, inevitably led by forces over which they have no control (but which rather control them) to secure the common good.

Smith was not a special pleader beyond the unconscious special pleading that people of a particular era indulge in because of their cultural assumptions. But, given the circumstances, the power and the comprehensiveness of his view of economic truth, he was bound to achieve a rather lopsided authority beyond his intention. He certainly did not set out to be the spokesman of the new economic interests. There runs throughout his book a strain of deep cynicism concerning the motives and attitudes of the capitalist, especially in his tendency to combination—which he sees is in the nature of the competitive system.[11] Even in his

[8] Ibid., pp. 24 ff. Schumpeter, op. cit., pp. 335 ff.

[9] Of the "Glorious Revolution" Christopher Dawson says: "Never was the influence of selfish class interests and selfish greed more nakedly revealed in political action; it was the victory of oligarchy and privilege over monarchy and prerogative," *The Gods of Revolution*, p. 17. The result of the victory is depicted in J. H. Plumb, *England in the 18th Century* (London, 1979), pp. 11 ff.

[10] *The Wealth of Nations* (New York: Cannan edition, 1937), p. 423.

[11] "We rarely hear of . . . combination of masters but frequently of those of workmen. But whoever imagines on this account that masters rarely combine is as ignorant of the world as of the subject." Ibid., p. 66.

positive advocacy of measures which appealed to the men of property, he was less dogmatic than many who later invoked his authority. Legitimate national interest, he saw, could demand restrictions on international free trade[12] just as growing industrialism demanded universal education. This was needed for the workers' adjustment to that greater specialisation that Smith saw was necessary for the improvement of industrial productivity.[13] Nor can the later belief in an iron law of wages, which became the justification of much maltreatment of labour, be assigned to Smith.[14]

It was the later development of classical economics, with its greater specialisation, which lead to the science assuming a harsher aspect. The French economist J. B. Say[15] (1767–1832) formulated the principle that supply creates its own demand, diverting attention from the problem of underused resources and its consequences, especially unemployment. Malthus[16] (1766–1834) made gloomy predictions about the outstripping of the food supply by population growth; human adaptability and ingenuity, the discovery of new techniques in agriculture, the opening up of new areas in North and South America and in Australia and New Zealand, and the application of industrial technology to farming, proved that prediction wrong. Ricardo[17] (1772–1823) applied Malthus' doctrines and argued that the press of population would force society to use the poorer soils, rents would rise and the iron law of wages would limit the return to labour so that all it could expect was minimal subsistence.

With John Stuart Mill[18] (1806–1873), something of the broader perspective within which Smith conceived the science returned. Mill was a

[12] Ibid., pp. 429–31, 434–35.   [13] Ibid., p. 734.

[14] Chapter 8 of Book One on "The Wages of Labour" concludes that higher wages are an advantage to society and that "no society can be flourishing and happy in which the greater part are poor and miserable. It is but equity that they who feed and clothe and lodge the whole body of the people should have such a share of the produce of their own labour as to be tolerably well fed, clothed and lodged" (Ibid., p. 79). In his advocacy of freedom he adds the rider "as long as (he) does not violate the laws of justice" a man is free to pursue his own interests (Ibid., p. 651). Such nuances were lost on those who were interested in growing rich, justice or no justice.

[15] Say was led to the study of economics by reading Smith. His *Treatise on Political Economy* was published in 1803, and he later visited England to study conditions here.

[16] T. R. Malthus was a clergyman and Professor of Political Economics at Haileybury. His *Essay on the Principle of Population* was published in 1798. On its use by opponents of the poor laws, see B. Inglis, *Poverty and the Industrial Revolution* (London: Panther edition, 1972), pp. 126 ff.

[17] David Ricardo was born in London and educated in Holland. A stockbroker, he retired early to give his full time to economics. The *Principles of Political Economy and Taxation* was published in 1817.

[18] John Stuart Mill was the son of James Mill, the writer on utilitarianism and political economy and the great friend of Jeremy Bentham (1748–1832). J. S. Mill's *Principles of Political Economy* (1848) was a review of the science as it was known in his day, but contained much that was Mill's own original thought.

classical liberal, yet he adapted the original teaching to meet new needs; his rejection of the wage fund theory, for example, removed one of the bases for intellectual objection to trade unionism.[19] His approach was also in tune with the growing acceptance of the need for reform through state intervention; from the 1830s the first effective factory legislation appeared, and the need for government action to improve public health in the large towns spawned by the industrial revolution was accepted too. Meanwhile, the safety demands of mining, and the need for regulation of railways, made them the subject of increasing government concern.[20]

Economic theory after Mill continued to develop in the direction of what later became known as welfare economics. Smith had seen the science as concerned with the ordered knowledge of the social phenomena through which man becomes more effective in acquiring and using material wealth.[21] His was not a non-normative approach to the science; his book was full of prescriptions. Nor, as we have seen, was he so specialized in his concern with the techniques that he forgot its human aspect. Yet his approach was capable of bearing the rather narrower interpretation that was put upon it by those later writers who concentrated on the techniques of the creation of material wealth without regard to human welfare.[22] Alfred Marshall[23] (1842–1924), the Cambridge economist of the late nineteenth century, however, saw economics as concerned with the procurement and the use of the material requisites of *well-being*, so introducing a more humane emphasis. Later Lionel Robbins defined it in terms of the allocation of scarce resources between alternative ends.[24] Robbins' approach stresses that economics should not be normative, that is to say, it should attempt to deal with what *is* and not what *should be*. The economist can tell the politician, the moralist, or anyone else, just exactly what the best use of particular resources in a particular situation is in purely economic terms. It is then for the politician, the moralist or whoever to decide whether decisions are to be made on other

[19] E. Heimann, op. cit., p. 120.

[20] J. H. Clapham, *An Economic History of Modern Britain* (C.U.P., 1939), vol. 1, chaps. 9, 10, and 11, vol. 2, chap. 10.

[21] The full title of his book *An Inquiry into the Nature and Causes of the Wealth of Nations* indicates his understanding of the subject.

[22] "The classical economists examined the economic process as bound up with the genesis of wealth . . . but there is one serious omission in their study of wealth and of its genesis: *man*. 'The living garment of divinity' becomes in their hands a sackcloth thrown over the goods. . . ." J. Messner, *Social Ethics*, p. 747.

[23] Marshall came to economics from mathematics and then ethics. He had been told that "the resources of production do not suffice for affording to the great body of the people the leisure and opportunity for study." J. M. Keynes, *Essays in Biography* (London, 1961), p. 138.

[24] *Principles of Economics*, p. 1.

than strictly economic grounds and how the resultant extra costs are to be met.

Properly considered, there should be no contradiction between such a non-normative approach and the needs of humanity and morality; a non-normative approach which is concerned to tell us what can be achieved most efficiently by alternative dispositions of resources, clears the way for overall decision making. However, it is incomplete; in itself it fails to take sufficient account of the fact that economics is a human science and its abstractions, even when justified, must never overlook this. The concept of welfare embraces, on the other hand, both the technical and scientific aspects of the science together with the human. This concept, as Schumpeter points out,[25] resurfaced in the nineteenth century, first through the approach that Marshall took and then more formally through the works of Arthur Pigou (1877–1959),[26] who provided criteria whereby economic policies could be judged according to their contributions to social welfare.

The theories of John Maynard Keynes (1883–1946)[27] departed much more fundamentally from the classical tradition—but his intention was not to destroy that tradition or the capitalism bred of it, but rather to correct certain of its wrong assumptions. The classical theory assumed that the economy was self-regulating through the working of the market, the price system, the gold standard and free trade. Keynes, concerned as he was with the fact of unemployment, said that it was not so, that the economy did not necessarily operate at the level of the full employment of labour and resources.[28] He argued that the state needed to intervene in order to encourage consumption, initiate public and encourage private investment and lower the rate of interest.[29] It is apparent to us now that in a society with free trade unions and a liberal democratic system, we also

[25] Schumpeter, op. cit., p. 97. "In the applied economics of the scholastic doctors the pivotal concept was the public good—barring technique, exactly the same thing as the welfare concept of modern economics, Professor Pigou's for example."

[26] Pigou was Marshall's pupil and his successor as Professor of Political Economy at Cambridge. His *Economics of Welfare* was published in 1920.

[27] Keynes studied philosophy and economics at Cambridge and there came under Marshall's influence. In his own work he was increasingly concerned with finding an answer to the problem of unemployment—in the inter-war years it was never less than 10% in Britain and in the early years of the 1930s reached 20% B. R. Mitchell and P. Deane, *Abstract of British Historical Statistics* (C.U.P., 1962), p. 67. Keynes, *General Theory of Employment Interest and Money* was published in 1936. R. F. Harrod, *The Life of J. M. Keynes* (London, 1972). M. Stewart, *Keynes and After* (Pelican, 1970). Schumpeter, op. cit., pp. 1170 ff.

[28] He was not the first to do so. Among the pre-Marxians, John Gray was aware of the problem. Alexander Gray, *The Socialist Tradition* (London, 1963), p. 294. See also R. Freedman, *Marx on Economics* (London, 1962), p. 146 ff.

[29] D. Dillard, *The Economics of J. M. Keynes* (London, 1966), p. 327.

THE ETHICS OF ECONOMIC LIFE 269

need to know how to prevent wages from drifting upwards when full employment is reached.[30] The sociological and institutional elements in an economic, political and industrial structure need to be modified considerably if the two desiderata of full employment and an acceptable rate of inflation are to be secured. We have yet to find a satisfactory way of doing this.[31]

The development of economic thought and policy in the Western social democracies in this century, therefore, has tended to an increasing sophistication in the methods of analysis, and through the concept of welfare economics, a more sophisticated approach to the social implications of the science has emerged.[32] However, all this took time. In the formative period of Western industrial society the older, harsher views prevailed, and the effects of those harsher views are still with us. Secondly, welfare capitalism remained and remains materialist. A society which, like Western society, sees economic well-being as an end in itself, fails to satisfy the deeper needs of its own people and all too easily does injustice to others beyond its boundaries.

The baleful effects of a lopsided interpretation to which Smith was too open, are seen in the way in which, during the agricultural and industrial revolutions in Britain in the eighteenth and nineteenth centuries, he was used as an authority who justified opposition to any attempt by the state to interfere with the workings of imagined economic laws on behalf of the common good. When Whitbread proposed a minimum wages bill in 1795, Pitt criticised him on a point of economic principle derived from the teachings of Adam Smith, under whose influence he had come while at Cambridge. The point was, according to Pitt, that the price of labour was regulated by supply and demand and that any interference with the invisible hand of providence in economic matters was unthinkable.[33] Ironically enough, the doctrines of political economy also prevented any state action to reduce the impact of the suffering caused to the agricultural labourer by the enclosure movement,[34] despite the fact that it was that

---

[30] Messner, op. cit., pp. 780, 798 (footnote). Where, in practice, Keynes was involved with wartime economic policy, he was well aware of the problems of inflation and full employment. S. Pollard, *The Development of the British Economy* (London, 1962), p. 325.

[31] A. Jones, *The New Inflation* (London, 1973), surveys the situation that has arisen in the light of welfare state policies in one country. More recently: F. T. Blackby, *The Future of Pay Policy* (London, 1980). D. J. Mitchell and and R. E. Azevedo, *Wage Price Control and Labor Market Distortions* (Berkeley: University of California, 1976) looks at the American experience of wage control.

[32] G. Dalton, *Economic Systems and Society* (Penguin, 1978), pp. 143 ff.

[33] Inglis, op. cit., pp. 81–82.

[34] Arthur Young (1741–1820), the agriculturalist who, in 1793, had been secretary of the Board of Agriculture, had initially been one of the strongest supporters of the enclosure system, but he saw how injurious the effect on the poor had been. "It was not that enclosures

legislation itself which had caused the suffering in the first instance. In other words, under the influence of sectional interests, the invisible hand and the working of natural economic forces could be interfered with to provide legislation for the enclosures of the land which helped the men of property, but legislation could not interfere with that interference.

The principle of buying labour in the cheapest market also had a brutal and dehumanizing effect upon the working classes in the early stages of the Industrial Revolution and on children especially; the cheapest labour was child labour, and it was on child labour that the wealth of the new cotton textile industry was built. Between two-thirds and three-quarters of the workers in the early factories were under the age of eighteen, lucky if they earned halfpenny an hour, and for this being made to work as children had never been made to work before, eleven hours a day being the norm.[35] In the same way, political economy was invoked against the attempts of the industrial workers to combine in their own defence and also to oppose any maintenance of the older tradition of public action in determining wages and conditions.[36]

The political economy of Smith was, therefore, made to serve as an excuse for injustice during the Industrial Revolution in Britain. And similar misuse of the new theory was made wherever the liberal state allowed the capitalist the same freedom. In America a double standard was accepted. If businessmen combined to further their own purposes, this was in accordance with natural law, but if labour did the same, it was a conspiracy. Likewise, monopoly was good business, but the closed shop for trade unionists was un-American. The government had a responsibility to aid business and protect its interests, but if it did the same for labour then that was socialism. That business should influence politics was considered common-sense—but that labour should, was un-American. Those who owned property had a natural right to get a fair return on it—but all labour might demand was simply the going market price. Hence, appeals to protect or to develop property interests were reasonable, but if the same was invoked in labour's favour, then this was unreasonable.[37] And what was true of economic and industrial

---

were at fault . . . it was the fact that compensation for them had been inadequate and of the wrong kind—money rather than land. . . ." The whole enclosure system, Young had come to realize, was rigged by the landowners for their benefit. Ibid., pp. 120–21.

[35] Ibid., p. 138. Children had been exploited before industrialisation. What was new was that they were herded into factories and the cruelties inflicted on them were, according to the conventional wisdom, justifiable in the name of economic laws.

[36] Ibid., p. 119.

[37] S. E. Morison and H. S. Commager, *The Growth of the American Republic*, (O.U.P., 1962), 2:232. Because of the particular conditions of American economic development, the

development in America and Britain was true of continental Europe too. In France, after the revolution of 1848, and still more after the Paris Commune of 1871, fears of organised working class action in the cities became obsessive and hindered the acceptance of trade unionism—which was only grudgingly legalized in 1884. The delay and the deep antagonism resulted in an increasing alienation of the French working class from the state; when it emerged, the French trade union movement was dominated by the belief in the national strike as a means of bringing that state to its knees.[38]

In Germany, the Marxist-orientated Social Democratic Party found in the evils created by German industrialisation a fruitful source through which to build up its strength.[39] When Bismarck became the first European statesman to realise that through a programme of social insurance some of the evils of that early industrialisation could be corrected and people weaned away from violent Marxist solutions, he was, in his way, accepting the indictment of capitalism that was summed up in the Marxist response. Much more positive social action was needed to secure justice for the wage earner than liberal social theory had allowed.

The attempt to develop the economy of the modern world by using a philosophy which pretended that positive intervention by the state in economic affairs, in the name of justice and morality, was not necessary, was shown then to be in error. Abandonment of the attempt to enforce moral rule of any kind, in the naive belief that absolute freedom brought equal benefits to all, meant that selfish needs were pursued by the strong to their logical conclusion and to the total disregard of the needs of the weaker members of society.

We must not, however, make the mistake of underestimating the benefits that, in material terms, the industrial revolution through liberal capitalism brought to the people at large.[40] For example, the standard of living, in material terms, increased dramatically in nineteenth century Britain; a wider range of goods was available to a larger number than ever

---

American worker was spared the mass poverty that Europe experienced, but all the other injustices that the wage earner was suffering in Europe were experienced in their measure by him too.

[38] V. R. Lorwin, *The French Labour Movement* (Harvard, 1954). H. Friedlander and J. Oser, *Economic History of Modern Europe* (New York, 1953), pp. 174, 330. J. H. Clapham, *Economic Development of France and Germany 1815–1914*, (C.U.P., 1936), pp. 265 ff., 270 ff.

[39] Friedlander and Oser, op. cit., pp. 176 ff., 332 ff. Clapham, op. cit., pp. 322 ff., 328 ff. K. S. Pinson, *Modern Germany* (London, 1961), pp. 240 ff.

[40] The controversy among economic historians concerning the effect of the Industrial Revolution in Britain is well summarized in the Foreword to Brian Inglis' *Poverty and the Industrial Revolution*. On the distribution of income and quality of life generally, E. H. Phelps Brown, *The Growth of British Industrial Relations* (London, 1960), pp. 13 ff.

before. But neither should the scale of these achievements prevent us from recognizing that what the common people had to suffer to achieve this end in the long run was morally unacceptable and the actual *quality of life* still left a great deal to be desired. Nor, in either absolute or relative terms, do the needs of distributive justice seem to have been met. Too many did not receive enough from the wealth that they created to support life decently; at the turn of the century some 25% of the adult male wage earners in Britain were receiving barely a living wage. Overall, one-quarter of the income earners took two-thirds of the national income; the manual workers, who comprised the other three-quarters, took one-third.[41]

Liberal capitalism, therefore, in the first instance treated the industrial and agricultural worker all too badly, and though it did bring real benefits in material terms and was modified in theory and practice as time went on, at the beginning of this century it still bore too harshly on the ordinary people. It was, therefore, defective in its materialistic purpose—of increasing the wealth of the nation in a way that fairly benefited all. But the more fundamental flaw in liberal capitalism, one that increases rather than decreases as it realises its materialistic aim and achieves a wider distribution of economic benefits, is that it remains, as we have said, not merely an economic philosophy, but a complete philosophy of life. It is its poverty in this respect which condemns it for the Christian. As a philosophy, liberalism denies the transcendent dimension, the metaphysical and theological perspective that it had inherited from its Christian past. By the nineteenth century, liberalism for every man meant simple materialism.[42]

> For the idea of the end of the world, nineteenth century capitalist society substituted the idea of progress. Progress means, moreover, the progressive betterment of man's material status. The aim is simply to provide man with an increasingly better furnished dwelling place, and this is regarded as an end in itself. With the growth of the capitalist system, profits are substituted for the virtues of human personality, and material values are made the measure of all things. Capitalism, as Tillich remarks, aims to provide the greatest possible number of men with the greatest possible amount of economic goods and seeks to arouse and to satisfy ever increasing demands without raising the question as to the meaning of the process which claimed the service of all spiritual and physical human abilities. Few question why men should have more and more economic goods or the meaning of the eternal striving for profits. Material comfort and the accumulation of wealth is a self-sufficient end.

[41] See Phelps-Brown, pp. 26 and 54.
[42] J. Hallowell, *The Decline of Liberalism as an Ideology* (London), pp. 71–72. See above pp. 92 ff.

It is this materialist, capitalist ethos that is our inheritance; modified in its harshness by welfare capitalism, it remains capable of its old inhumanity. Even where this is avoided, it gives us no vision that enables man to overcome his innate selfishness. Rather it encourages and panders to it—offering "more" as its only ideal.

B. MARXIST SOCIALISM

Against this welfare capitalist vision of life, the modern world sees set the Marxist socialist alternative—an alternative that is embodied today in the powerful states of Russia and Eastern Europe especially, where industrial sophistication is approaching Western standards in some major areas and equalling it in others. This system took its theoretical origins from the works of Marx and Engels who developed their ideas through the critique of the classical economic system and theory in its early stages.

The starting point of the Marxist economic analysis was the labour theory of value, a concept inherited by the classical economists from Locke and adapted by Ricardo who argued, with qualifications, that the value of a commodity depended on the relative quantity of labour necessary for its production. Marx called the part of the value created which went to the employer "surplus value" and presented it as theft from the worker. The commentators do not exactly agree on the significance of the labour theory of value as it is used by Marx, but it played a key role in his predictions of capitalist self-destruction.[43]

Profits, according to the theory, are derived from unpaid labour time, yet since capitalists are driven by competition to accumulate capital and thus become more efficient in production, capital becomes concentrated in fewer and fewer hands. As it does so, the profits of capital are reduced as labour saving machinery replaces the labour from whose unpaid time profits are derived; hence, the army of the unemployed grows, swollen by the ruined small capitalist and the workers displaced by machines. The flood of goods created by ever more productive capitalist industry meanwhile finds fewer buyers as more and more are workless, and wages are

---

[43] Relevant texts from *Capital* are given in R. Freedman, *Marx on Economics*, pp. 27 ff., 69 ff. H. W. B. Joseph, *The Labour Theory of Value in Karl Marx* (London, 1923) analyses Marx's use of the concept. Joan Robinson, *Marxian Economics* (London, 1942), p. 22, argues that "no point of substance . . . depends on the labour theory of value. . . . Marx's penetrating insight and bitter hatred of oppression supply the arsenic, the labour theory of value supplies the incantation." Schumpeter, *Ten Great Economists*, p. 27, gives the more obvious view that Marx made this theory "the cornerstone of his theoretical structure". See also Schumpeter's *History of Economic Analysis*, pp. 590 ff.

squeezed. United in their anger and misery, the masses rise up in revolt: "the knell of capitalist private property sounds, the expropriators are expropriated."[44]

The labour theory of value was in time abandoned by the classical liberal school.[45] Meanwhile, the predictions that Marx based on it have not yet been realised, though the hope that they will has not been entirely abandoned by some; every type of crisis in the capitalist world is seen by them as presaging total collapse.[46] In the meantime, far from the development of big business eliminating the middle class, it has strengthened it—the joint stock company and the stock exchange enabling the bourgeoisie to participate in the increasing wealth created by the new industrial machine without their having to exercise the old entrepreneurial skills. So far was Marx wide of his prediction that a later writer,[47] who owes his inspiration to him and indeed calls himself a Marxist, has been arguing that the capitalist system has so effectively satisfied the material needs of the workers that they have lost their revolutionary fervour and consequently need to be stimulated and led once more by such deprived groups as remain in an affluent and greedy society.

The point is not that one cannot criticize some of the effects of affluence. One can, on good Christian grounds, and indeed must. The point is that Marx predicted that the capitalist system would not produce soporific self-satisfaction through the fruits of the consumer society, but that it would produce an ever widening sea of desperate men ready to rise up to destroy the system. Marx's doom, like Malthus', was wide of the mark. While recognizing the massiveness of Marx's genius, his contributions to the development of the social and historical sciences and the masterly way in which he disposed of some of the more obvious weaknesses in the logic of the classical economists, we must recognize his limitations too.

The main import of Marx's thinking,[48] therefore, was that the capitalist system was bound to destroy itself and give way to socialism. It is,

[44] R. Freedman, op. cit., p. 170. McClellan, op. cit., p. 487. The quotation is from *Capital*, 1:31.

[45] The idea of an objective, absolute value, gave way to the subjective, marginal utility theory of neo-classicism which gained acceptance in the 1870s. Schumpeter, *History of Economic Analysis*, pp. 184 ff., 909 ff.

[46] A. Glyn and J. Harrison, *The British Economic Disaster* (London, 1980) is a good illustration of this tendency.

[47] H. Marcuse, *One Dimensional Man* (London, 1964). See A. MacIntyre, *Marcuse* (London: Fontana, 1972), pp. 62 ff.

[48] I am taking the mature Marx as the representative Marx. In Aron's words (*Main Currents in Sociological Thought* [London, 1965], 1:114), "One must be very sure of one's genius to be convinced of understanding a great writer so much better than he understood himself . . . it is better to begin by understanding the writer as he understood himself and thus assign the central place in Marxism to *Capital* and not to the *Economic and Philosophic*

accordingly, stronger in its criticisms in this direction than it is in its account of the exact nature of the socialist alternative. From scattered references to the shape of that alternative, which we find in Marx, we gather that when production is under the control of a planned society the market price of goods will equal their value in terms of the social labour time employed in their production[49] and prices will be the same as under capitalism, but the surplus of price over value will go to the state, not the capitalist.[50] Money will be abolished; producers may receive cheques so that they can obtain what they want from the social supplies of means of consumption, a share corresponding to their labour time. But such cheques will not be the equivalent of money; they will not circulate.[51]

The problem of distribution where production is for use and not for exchange/profit is to be solved by reserving part of what is produced for social use—industrial expansion, insurance and reserves, costs of administration, community services and schools, health services and unemployment. Thereafter, the remainder will be distributed, not according to production input or labour time, but on the principle of "from each according to his ability, to each according to his needs."[52]

Such, then, is the outline theory of the Marxist society. The reality is rather different. Marx was as much an optimist about the nature of socialist man as the advocates of laissez faire were about the nature of liberal capitalist, economic man. Both assumed in their objects of veneration a perfection of human nature that has not been there since the Fall, as the Christian sees it, or since man was overwhelmed by the *hubris* that the Greeks saw rooted in human nature.

Marxism grew out of the reaction to the evils of liberal capitalism at its worst, but because, in Kamenka's words, it has raised up a new metaphysical sovereign—history itself—it is therefore able to exercise, at its whim, unprincipled tyranny.[53] In fact, it also came into its kingdom in Russia through a series of events which were neither foreseen by Marx or Engels nor bore any relationship to their theory of how socialism would come to be.

It was the social, economic and political situation existing in Czarist Russia before the 1914 war, and the effects of that on the situation, which

---

Manuscripts or to *The German Ideology* the incomplete (though perhaps highly original) rough drafts of a young man speculating on Hegel and capitalism at a time when he certainly knew Hegel better than he knew capitalism."

[49] *Capital*, 3:10. R. Freedman, op. cit., p. 229.

[50] *Capital*, 3:3–9. R. Freedman, op. cit., p. 230–31.

[51] *Capital*, 2:18. R. Freedman, op. cit., p. 231.

[52] *A Critique of the Gotha Programme*, vol. I. Freedman, op cit., p. 241.

[53] See above p. 102, footnote.

provided Lenin with the opportunity to use Marx's theories, or elements
of them, as the intellectual guide to the takeover of a Russian revolution
which had already in essentials succeeded.[54] It was the Communist party
which saved Marxism from undergoing the fate of many another nineteenth century philosophy, by turning it into a faith.[55] How far it was the
theories themselves, and how far it was Lenin's shrewdness in adapting
the concept of the dictatorship of the proletariat[56] to a particular set of
circumstances and ruthlessly exploiting it which changed a philosophy
into a faith, is a matter for speculation.

When Lenin and the Bolsheviks were faced with the problem of
running a country ravaged first by the German war and then by an even
more debilitating civil war that lasted until 1921, they had little to guide
them as to their immediate course of action. The assumption had been that
the revolution would take place in highly industrialised states in which the
centralization of economic power through the accumulation of capital in
fewer and fewer hands would ease the takeover by the revolution,[57]
which would then simply have the task of transferring the means of
production to public ownership. No such situation was inherited by the
revolutionaries. Though Russia possessed a strong industrial base, it
was not an industrialised economy, and beyond the general notions of
collective or centralized ownership and distribution according to need,
there was little to guide the country's new masters as to how to proceed in
economic matters. It was left to the Russian people to pay the cost
involved in being the laboratory of Marxist Socialism.

During the civil war conditions demanded war Communism, that is to
say, an all out organisation for the war effort which in theory went
on under centralized control and direction.[58] Once the war was over
a reaction set in; there were strikes and unrest and, under the New
Economic Plan, (1921–1927),[59] though industry in general and the central
financial institutions remained under central control and certain elements
of overall national planning continued, there were concessions to the
peasants, private enterprise and the consumer. The period also allowed
the consolidation of the power of the party; it saw the emergence, too, of
Stalin as the leader of that party. With the first full five year plan that was

[54] G. F. Hudson, *Fifty Years of Communism* (Pelican, 1971), pp. 48 ff. L. Shapiro, *The Communist Party of the Soviet Union* (London, 1966), pp. 141 ff.
[55] F. C. Copleston, *A History of Philosophy*, 7:65. Schumpeter, *Great Economists*, p. 5. "In an important sense, Marxism is a religion . . . a system of ultimate ends . . . a guide to those ends which implies a plan of salvation."
[56] See above p. 204.
[57] A. Nove, *The Soviet Economic System* (London, 1978), p. 1.
[58] Nove, *An Economic History of the U.S.S.R.* (Pelican, 1976), pp. 46 ff.
[59] Ibid., pp. 83 ff.

launched under his direction, the full ruthlessness of Soviet Communism was revealed. The aim of the plan and all it involved was to speed industrialisation and, in particular, the development of large scale heavy industry. But Russia was still an agricultural country, and the problem of farming had to be tackled also—and it was.

In the late 1920s individual farming was almost the universal pattern, the state and collective farms in 1928 being responsible for less than 2% of the total grain crop.[60] The means used to bring about the collectivisation of agriculture were the selection of so-called rich peasants (or kulaks) as the scapegoats, asserting that they were an exploiting class, battening on their fellow peasants and the community. On this group, some 5 or 6% of the farmers in all,[61] was concentrated all the hatred and fear that the term traditionally struck in Russian hearts because of the money-lending practices and mortgaging injustices of the true kulaks. Such practices were in fact no longer permissible under the revolution so that justification for the attack on the evils of the kulaks disappeared too. The excuse of their imagined excesses was being used as a means of destroying traditional peasant life and independence.[62] To do this it was necessary, above all, to attack the wealthier peasants, the traditional leaders of village life and the natural rivals of the Soviet administration which the party was trying to establish in the countryside.

In 1927 came first signs of an attempt to undermine the position of the kulaks, and thereafter their subjugation and that of the peasants in general was accomplished at breakneck speed. In 1929 only 4.1% of households were in collectives; by 1934 the proportion was nearly 75%. Local Soviets were given power to confiscate the property of kulaks and banish them, and the operation was in the hands of the political police, the O.G.P.U. How many millions were involved in this brutal process is not known, but the deported alone numbered 5 million, and Stalin himself was quoted as saying that the bulk of 10 million peasants were "dealt with" in this period and were wiped out by their labourers.[63]

The collectivisation of farming illustrates one effect of a separation of economics and morals in Soviet Russia; the forced labour of the camps illustrates another. Conservatively estimated, the labour camp population was 8 million by the end of 1938 and, given an average death rate of about

[60] Ibid., p. 150.

[61] M. Dobb, *Soviet Economic Development Since 1917* (London, 1966), p. 228.

[62] Schapiro, op. cit., pp. 383–85. A Solzhenitsyn, *Gulag Archipelago*, 1:54 ff. Neither could deficiency in marketable grain surpluses be attributed to the kulaks—85% of the grain production was in the hands of the middle and poor peasants. Dobb, op. cit., p. 215.

[63] Schapiro, op. cit., p. 386. The figures were used by Stalin in conversation with Churchill and recorded in volume 4 of his *The Second World War* (London, 1951), pp., 447–48. Nove, *Economic History of U.S.S.R.*, pp. 160 ff.

10% each year in those camps, some 12 million people died in them between 1936 and 1950. If to this 12 million is added the 1.5 million who were shot in the various purges and the several millions who were killed or died from starvation during the collectivisation of agriculture,[64] it would seem that the achievement of the Socialist ideal conceded nothing, in its cost in human terms, to the achievements of capitalism at the worst.

The industrial worker in Soviet Russia, meanwhile, was denied that right of association which is the basis of independent trade unionism; a country facing the throes of industrialisation needed to have a strong free trade union movement if the rights of the industrial worker were not to be disregarded. In fact, from the beginning, trade unions in Soviet Russia have been the instruments of party policy rather than the representative of the needs and wishes of the workers. The party controlled union membership, and since an expelled worker lost his employment, a worker could do nothing against the party's wishes if he desired to keep his job.[65] Every means was used to curb independence and initiative. Solzhenitsyn tells how the skilled workers, the technical intelligentsia, as he calls them, suspected of being enemies of the revolution, were made scapegoats for the defects of planners and punished by imprisonment in the terrible conditions of the labour camps. The trust of a man in his own skill and knowledge and in his competence in using it could not be allowed to stand against the instinct of self-preservation that possessed the bureaucrats who dominated his life. These functionaries were shielded from all criticism, and ways were found of blaming the men upon whose technical knowledge and skill they relied. At this time people still had their pride and were not so easily convinced that morality was a relative class concept. They were punished without mercy for their temerity.[66]

III. ETHICS AND ECONOMIC SYSTEMS: THE MARKET ECONOMY, BASIC LOGIC, CONCEPTS AND ETHICS

The logic of the modern mature free enterprise economy, which has more and more abandoned its classical liberal assumptions, can be stated in its essence simply as follows. The economy works better for the good of all if

[64] D. Caute, *The Fellow Travellers* (London, 1973), p. 107. Dobb, *Soviet Economic Development*, p. 229 concludes, "The birth pangs were sharp: the attendant midwifery was rough, indeed brutal. But . . . may well come to be regarded as the turning point in the economic history both of Europe and Asia in the 20th Century." A strange, muted comment indeed on the actual events by a Marxist—paralleled by similar apologia for liberal capitalism made by its friends, explaining, one would suspect, that ends justify means.

[65] Schapiro, op. cit., p. 333.

[66] Solzhenitsyn, op. cit., p. 1:43 ff.

productive goods are mainly owned by private individuals or companies and operate, subject to the laws of competition, in a "free" market. The owners or managers of companies then respond to the needs of the consumer through the price system and, according to their efficiency in responding to those needs, they are profitable and, being profitable, flourish. Firms which are not profitable go out of business. Investment decisions are made in the main by private interests in response to market needs. Government has an economic role in a mixed economy, but it should be as limited as possible.

Such is the simple picture and, like all simple pictures, it leaves much unsaid. For example, the "free" market is nothing like as free as once thought.[67] However, there is clearly a difference between a system in which the major part of the nation's investment decisions are made by private individuals and companies who ultimately bear the financial responsibility, and one in which some state or central body makes all investment and other important decisions. Insofar as the private person or company has less freedom in manipulating other aspects of state machinery in order to cover up his deficiencies in business, he is clearly under a stricter discipline than the state agency; even where such an agency adopts the profit yardstick, failure is not as directly penalized as through market failure in a free enterprise economy. On the other hand, making what is, theoretically, a free market system respond to the needs of competition is a problem which exercises the responsible public authorities in capitalist countries. The system is self-correcting to some extent. Change in public tastes and the development of new products and materials are a constant challenge to the oligopolist or the monopolist.[68]

In order to explore some of the main ethical issues that arise in dealing with the market economy,[69] we must make some attempt to understand key concepts and their implications; only in this way can we isolate the ethical issues and see their import. We may start with the productive process itself. *Production* has traditionally been seen to involve three factors —labour, land and capital—and, with certain reservations, the use of these categories is still the most useful way to approach a consideration of this fundamental economic process. *Labour* is, of course, the human

---

[67] J. H. Robinson, *Economics of Imperfect Competition* (London, 1933). E. H. Chamberlin, *Theory of Monopolistic Competition* (London, 1933).

[68] Some economists argue that the progressive policies followed by monopolistic firms act as a motor for economic growth and that this advantage more than balances any disadvantages monopoly brings. R. G. Lipsey, *An Introduction to Positive Economics* (London, 1979), chap. 23. See also Schumpeter, *Capitalism, Socialism and Democracy* (London, 1976), chap. 8.

[69] Basic textbooks such as A. Cairncross, *An Introduction to Economics* [5th edition] (London, 1978), and J. Hicks, *The Social Framework* (O.U.P., 1965), deal with the general outline of the system.

factor, and under it such things as the supply of labour and its efficient use through the division of labour are considered. *Land* refers not only to the agricultural and mineral element in production but also to all the raw material requisites, while *capital* covers the supply of finance, equipment and tools.

Production is for the *market* in which the goods produced are sold; it can be a small local market or one that is national or international. In this market *demand and supply* come into play, the ratio between the one and the other establishing the price the goods bring.[70] Supply can be affected by natural factors (such as a shortage caused by weather conditions), by artificial factors (such as oligopoly or monopoly), or by the complex pattern of causes which produce the trade cycle. Demand is subject to fluctuation due to change in income, taste and the price of other goods. The prices in the market affect income in their turn, because it is from them that the factors of production are rewarded through wages, interest, rent and profits.

Under *money and banking*[71] are subsumed all aspects of finance and credit, whether provided by the commercial banks or by those controlled by the state, the central banks. *International trade and finance* is a special area of study with its own economic theory; under its heading are included questions such as the balance of payments, exchange rates between currencies, the factors affecting comparative industrial and agricultural efficiency and costs, the flow of funds from one country to another.

Although the original assumption of the market economy and market economics was and is that the system works independently of any concerted government action, this assumption has been modified in the light of the needs of actual economic life. In the period between the 1914 and 1939 wars, the experience of mass unemployment and the degradation it brought to those affected by it bred in the Western democracies and their leaders a determination to find another way—and John Maynard Keynes provided the theoretical justification for a policy of state action to manage the economy by managing demand.[72] In the last ten years, however, under the experience of inflation and faltering economic growth, the Keynesian analysis has been increasingly challenged, and the policies based on it have been under fire accordingly. It is being suggested that full employment, as we have known it, is not possible without inflation, and that there is a natural rate of employment consistent with

---

[70] Cairncross, op. cit., pp. 186 ff.   [71] Ibid., pp. 468 ff.

[72] See above p. 268. E. Heimann, op. cit., pp. 229 ff., surveys briefly the development of economic theory after the First World War and puts Keynes in this context. See also R. F. Harrod, *The Life of John Maynard Keynes* (London, 1966) and Michael Stewart, *Keynes and After* (London, 1967).

constant real wage costs. The key to economic expansion without inflation, therefore, is moderate expansion of the money supply—the so-called
monetarist theory.[73]

The debate on the exact role the government should play in the control
of the economy and the theoretical guidelines it should use in determining
that policy is, therefore, disputable. The role itself, and the importance of
it, is not. There are large non-controversial areas in which government
responsibility is taken for granted, and others in which the dispute is over
degree or direction rather than principle. Government agencies collect
statistics on various aspects of economic life, and those statistics are
essential in the determination of national policy. Government is involved
in provision of goods and services through the industries it controls
and owns, it provides incentives for particular industries and regions
according to national and local need and is increasingly concerned with a
policy for wages, indirectly or directly. Through the budget, the control
of bank rate and money supply, through its concern with the balance of
payments and exchange rates, it has further responsibilities for guiding
the economy.

These ideas and institutions and the system of economic organisation in
which they are embodied present for us some of the key issues in
economic ethics. The notion of the free market itself is one which has to be
handled very carefully if it is to serve true human values rather than to
debase them. We have noted that the word itself can refer to the physical
location in which the exchange takes place, whether it is a local weekly
market or an international commodity market where raw materials are
bought, or it can refer to the whole mass of exchange relationships which
exist throughout society.[74] The idea of totally free and unbridled competition is rejected by the Catholic social ethic. The strongest condemnation
comes perhaps in *Quadragesimo Anno*.[75]

> The proper ordering of economic life cannot be left to free competition.
> From this contaminated source have proceeded in the past all the errors of the
> economic individualist school. This school, ignorant or forgetful of the
> social and moral aspect of economic life, held that this must be considered
> and treated by the state as absolutely free and independent, because it
> possesses in free competition and the open market, a principle of self
> direction better able to control it than any human ingenuity . . . free

[73] The name particularly connected with this theory is that of M. Friedman, *The Optimum
Quantity of Money and Other Essays* (London, 1969) and *Unemployment and Inflation* (London,
1975). See also F. A. Hayek, *New Studies in the Philosophy of Politics, Economics, and the
History of Ideas* (London, 1978).

[74] See across, p. 280.

[75] *Quadragesimo Anno* (London: C.T.S.), pars. 88, 109.

competition has destroyed itself; economic domination has taken the place of the open market . . . the whole economic regime has become hard, cruel and relentless in a ghastly manner.

This was a judgement made at the time of economic upheaval in the early 1930s. Many of the defects that validated this judgement have been removed. But wherever competition exists, it has a tendency to override justice and charity, and we must always beware of this. Certainly in the relationship of the third with the developed world it is evident that the placing of profit and the virtues of competition ahead of the human values of the economic system has not disappeared. Hence, in *Populorum Progressio*, the evils of liberal capitalism are once more condemned, and while it is recognized that economic freedom in itself has contributed much to human progress, the idea of free trade is no longer equitable given the disparity of economic power between nations.[76]

According to market theory, price is settled by the working of the law of supply and demand. There are several moral issues that arise here. Artificial restraints on supply through the activity of monopolies or oligopolies, and the consequent power to influence prices, can penalize the consumer and the community. This restriction on the market concept was brought out by the writers above mentioned,[77] and the need to ensure by public action that advantage is not taken of the consumer by the use of monopoly or other restraints on trade is accepted by welfare capitalism.

The question of the use of advertising also raises problems.[78] That the advertiser in bringing to the notice of the people a new and useful product can perform a useful function there is no dispute. The problems arise when methods of advertising or the sort of goods advertised arouse impossible expectations or induce an unreal sense of deprivation; the advertising of goods which are in practical terms useless or even physically and morally harmful raises more fundamental problems still. Consumer ethics demands that the consumer should be rational enough, and articulate enough in choice and statement of preference that the dishonest or wasteful type of advertiser is made aware that his efforts and the product he markets are not worthwhile. The consumer, we know, is

[76] (London, C.T.S.), pars. 26, 58. The encyclical does not deny the value of competition, but it stresses the need for planning and central direction too. In other words, the market economy and social control and direction should move closer together and complement rather than oppose one another (pars. 32–33, 56–60).

[77] See above pp. 279, footnote; see also Messner, op. cit., pp. 859 ff.

[78] Messner, op. cit., p. 763. *Quadragesimo Anno*, in commenting on the evils of "the unquenchable thirst for riches and temporal possessions" castigates those who "indifferent as to whether their trade provides anything really useful, do not hesitate to stimulate human desires and . . . make use of them for their profit" ([London, C.T.S.], par. 132).

not always capable of acting sufficiently rationally and therefore needs informing by public and private agencies and to be protected where necessary.

Presuming, however, that a fair and free market exists, the question of the just price also has to be considered.[79] There has to be a balance between the subjective (or utility) value to the buyer and objective (or cost) value to the producer; a proper exchange value must relate the one to the other and both to the needs of society.[80] Where the methods and conditions of production are both fair to the producers and efficient in terms of unit costs, and the market is operating in a socially responsible manner, then supply and demand, determining market price, meet the demands of justice. The community has the right and the duty to see that these conditions exist.

The distribution of national income,[81] by definition, raises questions of justice; distributive justice is, we remember, concerned precisely with the fair distribution, among the members of society, of the wealth and the honours it has to offer. Though modern statistical methods and the greater availability of the information out of which it is compiled have made the calculation of national income possible, the concept itself is not without its difficulties of definition. Basically, however, it is true to say that national income can be calculated as is personal or business income— namely, by adding together all the various items that contribute to it. Yet, with a nation, the compilation has to take into account a much more complex array of factors; wages, dividends, interest, rent, undistributed profits, public income from property (less national debt interest) give us the national income before taxation and this taxation effects a redistribution of income, just or unjust according to the norms applied. Taxation must not crush initiative; there is considerable scope for disagreement about the point at which it begins to do this.

Taxation, as a manner of correcting injustices in the distribution of national income, can only be marginal to the question of the fair distribution of wealth as a whole. The more fundamental issues concern the

[79] Messner, *Social Ethics*, pp. 789 ff. The just price has been a concern of the moral theologian since this aspect of theology emerged as a specialisation. John Gilchrist, *Church and Economic Activity in the Middle Ages* (New York, 1969), pp. 58 ff., discusses the evolution of Catholic theory in great detail. He points out that the just price did not disguise a labour theory of value—on the contrary "utility and need were the fundamental determinants of price." Economic growth was not impeded by teaching on price regulation. The concept of a just price involved a concept of an unjust price too—prices kept high by monopoly and other unjustifiable trade practices.

[80] Messner, op. cit., pp. 791 ff.

[81] Hicks, op. cit., pp. 114 ff. Cairncross, op. cit., pp. 350 ff.

distribution of property and the reasons for the failure to ensure a fair income distribution which leads to the need for corrective action by the state. It was and is the assumption of the defender of liberal capitalism that the way in which wealth is distributed in the societies which have been built on its principles basically leaves nothing to be desired. That is not the judgement of the social magisterium which has frequently called attention to the historic injustices embodied in the inherited situation.[82]

Questions about justice are, therefore, implicit in any consideration of the factors affecting the distribution of national wealth and income. In terms of economic analysis, however, the three elements in the productive process (labour, land and capital)[83] have traditionally been seen as getting their due reward through the working out of the laws of economics. The triad established itself as important in economic analysis in the middle of the nineteenth century and maintained its popularity through Alfred Marshall's influence. It is still useful to aid an elementary understanding of economics such as we need in order to pinpoint some of the ethical issues involved. We can, therefore, look at the rewards of the factors of production under these three heads.

Land in this context means all the gifts of nature which yield an income—agricultural and building land, mines and minerals, fisheries and so on.[84] Payment for the use of land or natural resources in the productive process constitutes a rent of some kind, and the function of that rent in the national economy is to lead to an economically sound use of the factor which produced it. Insofar as those who own natural resources fulfill this function of encouraging its economic use, rents charged in proportion to effort are acceptable. But speculation in land (such as arises from socially created values as a result of planning decisions) is an abuse which must be subject to social control.[85]

There is then no ethical objection to rents provided that the way they operate does benefit the common good as well as the good of the owner. It is for society through positive law to ensure that all aspects of economic life serve to ensure that this happens. Moralists, mindful of the corruption of riches, must insist that all profit, including profit from rents, is

[82] For example *Quadragesimo Anno*, pars. 54 ff., *Mater et Magistra*, 115 ff., *Populorum Progressio*, pp. 22 ff.

[83] Hicks, op. cit., pp. 12 ff., 38 ff. Cairncross, op. cit., pp. 38 ff. Land, considered as a factor of production, has decreased considerably in importance from the days when, in the early stages of the industrial revolution, the majority of people still worked on the land. The discussions of rent by Smith, Ricardo and Mill have no comparable importance in any modern textbook on economics.

[84] Cairncross, op. cit., pp. 53 ff.

[85] J. R. Hoffner, *Fundamentals of Christian Sociology* (Cork, 1962), p. 147.

proportionate to effort. Windfalls that accrue simply by accident, therefore, are not to be defended.

The concept of labour as a factor of production by implication suggests
that there is an absolute distinction between those who own the means of
production and those who operate them, and that all those who do operate
them can be sensibly classified in one overall category. Neither implication reflects the realities. Some owners do manage, i.e. work or "labour",
to make the capital goods produce that profit, while among the workers
by hand and brain who are not owners of any kind there are the highest
salaried directors and technical staffs as well as the lowest paid manual or
clerical workers. Only in the very broadest sense, then, is the concept of
"labour" of use in modern economics.

A proper understanding of what labour can claim as a factor of production is of key importance as is clear from the use Marx made of the labour
theory of value. We remember he argued that since subsistence was all that
labour in fact received in return for its efforts, the difference between this
and the value of goods produced was a surplus appropriated wrongly by
the capitalists. The idea that somehow labour was cheated out of whatever
went to the other factors of production had its influence in Catholic circles
in the early part of this century, and the encyclical *Quadragesimo Anno* had
to show the falsity of the claim.[86] That is to say, it had to defend in moral
principle the right of the capital and land to a just reward (beyond mere
replacement), just as the labour element had a right to a just reward which
was beyond mere subsistence. However, this reassertion had nothing to
say about the actual rewards received by the factors in particular circumstances beyond saying, in general terms, that the wealth of nations was
very unfairly distributed. As we shall see when we consider the Christian
attitude to work, the reward due to labour is in fact a just wage;[87] the
concept of a subsistence wage is not compatible with the Christian ethic.

By capital[88] we mean society's stock of man-made material wealth and
resources which enables it to provide for its future needs. It can be
commercial or industrial capital, which is divisible into fixed capital
(factories, plant, equipment, the means of transport and communications),

[86] Pars. 55–58.
[87] See below pp. 318 ff. The inadequacy of the free market concept of labour and its
rewards is shown also where the disparity of such reward between occupations does not
reflect the social value of the occupations in question and frequently gives enormous rewards
to those who respond to ephemeral, if not useless and even socially harmful, trends. And
though the industrial relations system of welfare capitalism embodies the right of association
in free trade unions—the way the system works is far from the Christian ideal. See below
pp. 329 ff.
[88] Cairncross, op. cit., pp. 60 ff.

or working capital (raw materials, fuel, goods in process of manufacture, stocks, the cash needed to meet current needs). It can be financial capital or resources—the funds or the credit facilities available for financing new projects or maintaining those in being.

The state can and does own capital in all these senses and is, in consequence, as subject to the same moral norms in their use as is the private owner, but the Church's teaching in this matter of property has developed mainly in response to issues arising out of private ownership. We will have to deal with that teaching in more detail shortly. For the moment, we can note that the right to own property, including property in productive goods, is central to Christian social ethics, though this teaching precludes any moral justification of that liberal capitalism which considered rights of property to be absolute. On the same principles, the right to own and to live off the interest on investment is morally defensible. Investment is a particular form of private ownership and should not arouse in the Christian an automatic suspicion. It is not a pejorative word in itself, therefore, though it can be, in practice, morally objectionable because of the rejection by the investor of the moral responsibilities that attach to such ownership.[89]

The question of interest leads us on to a consideration of that related question of usury which is of such great importance in the history of economic ethics. The word "interest" is a Latin derivative (id quod interest) and referred originally to the compensation for loss suffered by a creditor because of the failure of a debtor to return a loan. Usury, also a Latin derivative (usura), signified the payment for the use of money itself.[90] That money was a "fungible" thing, used up in a single use of it (whereas other items, such as clothes, houses, etc., perdure through many times of use), was one reason for objection to making a profit on it. The reasoning was that it was wrong to make a charge for a thing that would be used up in being used, and this reasoning is clear enough when one is dealing with something like the loan of, for example, foodstuffs which clearly are used up in being used. The second reason for objection to making a profit on a money loan was that money was sterile, it could not produce anything of itself. Whatever one's view of the value of such an analysis, the reality that lay behind the objection to usury was clear enough. There could be injustice in money lending where weakness on the one hand and greed

---

[89] This was a point made with particular emphasis by *Quadragesimo Anno*: "immense power and despotic domination are concentrated in the hands of the few who, for the most part, are not owners, but only the trustees and directors of invested funds . . . grasping in their hands as it were, the very soul of production so that no one can breathe against their will" ([London: C.T.S.], pars. 105–6).

[90] T. Divine, *Interest: An Historical and Analytic Study* (Milwaukee, 1959), pp. 5–6.

on the other were present. It was against this injustice that regulations regarding usury were directed. And those who object to calling money sterile[91] can agree that money of itself can produce nothing; it requires human skill and effort to make it produce. A way of thinking that defended investment in principle while holding in suspicion those who wished to grow rich by exploiting the needs of the poor or without taking any risk or making effort themselves had much to commend it. The terminology here used is part of a more complex such terminology and analysis that developed over the centuries as the theologians, moralists and canonists tried to work out an effective morality of money and, in so doing, called upon classical writers and thinkers to help them.[92] But the basic objection to the practice of taking a profit on loans was to be found in the teaching of the Old Testament and the basis of this objection seems not to have been the nature of money itself, but the circumstances of the loan—the rich man being the creditor, the debtor, the poor man in his need. Far from there being a right to charge for money in those circumstances, the duty of the good man was even to make an outright gift.[93]

That the original moral objection to usury lay in the circumstances of the loan rather than the nature of money seems to be confirmed by the evidence we have that in the early Middle Ages, interest on commercial loans was allowed. But with the rediscovery of Aristotle, his analysis of money was adapted to enable canonists and lawyers to sort out the increasingly complex problems that the rights and wrongs of taking interest presented as commercial and industrial life developed. Out of this came the idea that while you cannot, strictly speaking, lend something which is used up in the use, and, therefore, you could not reclaim both the equivalent of what was loaned and make a charge for it, you could in a commercial situation make a charge for an inconvenience you suffered by foregoing the use of the money on alternative purposes until it was repaid. In technical language, money as a fungible thing was subject to the contract of *mutuum*; hence, you could not charge for it itself, but you could claim compensation for foregoing its use through *extrinsic* title.[94] At the same time, it was recognized that other types of contract, such as a *societas*, in which the investor retained ownership of his money, could return a profit by *intrinsic* title.

[91] Schumpeter, *History of Economic Analysis*, p. 105, suggests that St. Antoninus of Florence by implication questions this Aristotelian concept.
[92] Divine, op. cit., pp. 45 ff. St. Thomas Aquinas, *Summa Theologica*, II–II, q. 61, art. 3 and q. 78, arts. 1–4.
[93] Divine, op. cit., p. 9.
[94] Ibid., p. 47. L. Watt, *Usury* (Oxford, 1963), pp. 22–23.

All this indicates that, as the economic situation changed, the teaching developed to meet new needs. In other words, the textbook definitions were subject to interpretation to meet circumstances which they had not envisaged. To this end,[95]

> the method of canonists and theologians consisted of making exceptions to the laws of usury. This is of course fairly typical of medieval canon law and theology and it is the failure of modern historians to understand this which leads them to make such bald unqualified statements as the taking of interest was forbidden in the Middle Ages, or that the Church came later to change its doctrine. Without asking which was meant by interest or was there ever such a thing as "doctrine" of usury, which people usually take to mean a sort of infallibly defined teaching, however wrong they may be, then only confusion and misunderstanding result.

This process of adaptation, however, still raised problems which led, in 1745, to the issuing by the then Pope Benedict XIV, of an encyclical *Vix Pervenit* which dealt comprehensively with usury in the light of the teaching of the canonists and moral theologians that had been evolving since the twelfth century. He defined usury as the sin which[96]

> consists in this: solely on the grounds of *mutuum*, the nature of which is to require that only so much be returned as was received, a person demands that more be returned to him than was received: and so maintains that, solely on the grounds of *mutuum*, some profit is owed to him above the principal.

Given this definition, we would not expect that the encyclical ruled out the moral legitimacy of taking interest on money in other circumstances where the *mutuum* was not involved, or on taking it by extrinsic title where the *mutuum* was involved.[97] Given this, the way was open to further developments in the light of changing circumstances. Since the fifteenth century there had been an opinion developing among canonists and moralists that in any region where opportunities of investment were frequent it might reasonably be assumed that anyone who lent his money by *mutuum* thereby forfeited a chance to employ it profitably in commerce or industry by *societas*. *Vix Pervenit* left the option open though it recommended that it be used rather restrictively. However, it gradually came to be accepted that[98]

> given good reason to believe that economic conditions provide widespread opportunity for the investment of money in business enterprises, an owner of money who, instead of investing it lends (i.e. parts with ownership) to

[95] J. Gilchrist, *The Church and Economic Activity in the Middle Ages*, p. 65.
[96] Watt, op. cit., p. 17.
[97] Ibid., pp. 20 ff.   [98] Ibid., p. 31.

another is not guilty of usury if he demands interest by way of compensation for loss of probable profit. Permission by the civil law to charge interest was regarded as evidence that such economic conditions actually exist.

For those who are not prepared to understand how hard theologians, canonists and popes were trying to ensure that justice should be done to lender, borrower and society at large, the account of the development of the Church's teaching on this matter is of no interest. But more careful minds, aware of the continuing problem of ensuring justice in this matter, have been ready to pay tribute to the perceptiveness of the Catholic tradition.[99] On the more general question of profit, the view of St. Thomas Aquinas can stand as typical.[100]

Nothing prevents gain from being directed to some necessary and even virtuous end, and thus trading becomes lawful. Thus, for instance, a man may intend to moderate gain which he seeks to acquire by trading for the

[99] Werner Sombart, the German sociologist and economic historian (1863–1941) noted that "the very simple formula in which ecclesiastical authority expressed its attitude to the question of profit making is this; interest on a pure money loan, in any form, is forbidden: profit on capital in any form is permitted whether it flows from commercial, business or from an industrial undertaking . . . or from insurance against transport risks or shareholding in an enterprise . . . basically this is by no means astonishing when we consider more closely the men we know as scholastics. We have been prepared to do them a great injustice in regarding them as unpractical abstruse minded bookworms, treating of unreal topics with endless repetitions and intolerable prolixity. If one attentively peruses the writings of the scholastics . . . especially the work of . . . St. Thomas Aquinas . . . one gains the impression that the work of education that they had at heart was something different from our education in middle class respectability; that it was the education of their contemporaries to be upright, courageous, alert and energetic men" (See Messner, op. cit., pp. 818–19). Keynes is also quoted by Messner. He (Keynes) says (*General Theory of Employment Interest and Money* [London, 1946], pp. 351 ff.) he was brought up to believe that "the attitude of the medieval Church to the rate of interest was inherently absurd and that the subtle discussions aimed at distinguishing the returns on loans from the return for active investment were merely Jesuitical attempts to find a practical escape from a foolish theory. But I now read these discussions as an honest intellectual effort to keep separate what the classical theory has inextricably confused, namely the rate of interest and the marginal efficiency of capital. For it now seems clear that the disquisitions of the schoolmen were directed to the elucidation of a formula which would allow the schedule of the marginal efficiency of capital to be high, while using rule and the moral law to keep the rate of interest down."

[100] *Summa Theologica* II–II, q. 77, art. 4. In *Quadragesimo Anno* it is noted that "Those who are engaged in production are not forbidden to increase their fortunes in a lawful and just manner, indeed it is right that he who renders service to society should himself have a proportionate share . . . provided . . . he respects the laws of God and the rights of others and uses his property in accord with faith and right reason" (par. 136). It is "the unquenchable thirst for riches . . . which has indeed at all times impelled men to break the law of God . . . some have become so hardened against the stings of conscience as to hold all means good which enable them to increase their profits . . . easy returns, to make rapid profits with least labour" (Ibid., par. 132).

upkeep of his household, or the assistance of the needy, or again a man may trade for some public advantage, for instance lest his country lack the necessities of life and seek gain, not as an end, but as a payment for his labour.

The aspects of modern capitalism which so easily arouse the anger of those who have no sympathy with capitalism—"unearned" income and profit of any kind—reflect a suspicion of these concepts then which is deeply ingrained in traditional Catholic moral theology. There is too much evidence that high rates of profit, out of which shareholders can receive high dividends, can be and have been sought regardless of the social responsibility of profit making. But the abuse of a good thing should not blind us to the value of that thing in itself. Defending as it does the right to own property in productive goods and to put this property to use, the Church seeks to limit the abuses that undoubtedly occur, but she does not want to see abolished an institution, private property, which she sees as the bulwark of all the human freedoms. Too often the strident criticism of the real abuses of capitalism hide the desire to destroy not only those real abuses, but all private ownership of productive goods. The alternative to social responsibility of private ownership of productive goods in a mixed economy however is total social ownership—which means state ownership in which a ruling party or group exercise control over the lives of their fellow citizens. The Catholic approach is to work for both freedom and social responsibility, because both demand the best of man made in God's image. To abandon freedom in search of an earthly socialist paradise or to abandon social responsibility in search of an earthly individualistic paradise dehumanizes man who is, in truth, the end and purpose of every social organisation, not a means to that end.

IV. ETHICS AND ECONOMIC SYSTEMS:
THE CENTRALLY PLANNED ECONOMY,
BASIC LOGIC, CONCEPTS AND ETHICS

The only apparent alternative to the market economy (at least in countries which wish to develop or manage a modern industrial state) would seem to be one that is centrally planned. Since the Russian experiment in this field began in the wake of the revolution, their system has been rightly seen as the most comprehensive example of an economy run on these lines.[101] There are other planned economies, it is true, but the Soviet system has influenced them and remains the most significant still.

[101] Nove, *Soviet Economic System* and *Economic History of U.S.S.R.* Dobb, op. cit. *International Encyclopedia of the Social Sciences*, s.v. "Communism", "Economic Organ-

The basic difference between the Soviet approach and that of the mixed economy, the modified capitalism of the Western democracies, is that in the former it is the central organisation, the state, which determines the pattern of economic activity through a system of planning, whereas, as we have seen, capitalism assumes that market forces, the consumer's wishes expressed through demand, is the determinant of that activity. Neither Marxist economies nor capitalist economies work exactly according to plan or theory: each involves something of the other's approach. As we have seen already, in the mixed economy market forces are always limited to some extent, and today there is an increasing degree of government concern with the regulation of economic life in all its aspects. But the differences between the two systems are more marked than the similarities, and the key difference is in the dominance of central government decisions in the one and the dominance of private economic forces in the other.

The centralized organisation of the Soviet economy was the outcome of the first five-year plan (1929–1932). Under Stalin the plan and its implications had the urgency of a military operation and the force of law. Despite much change and adaptation, this principle of the overall power of centralized planning has been the mark of the Soviet approach to the economy since.

The planning itself is at all stages subject to the all-pervasive control of the party; in the Soviet system all political and economic power is in its hands. Under the Politburo at the summit, the government, the Council of Ministers, through state committees and economic ministries, issue orders to the descending ranks of industrial and economic bureaucracy.[102] What to produce, to whom to deliver it and how to obtain the wherewithal to produce and deliver, is all laid down. The general planning committee, Gosplan,[103] in conjunction with the various agencies in the fifteen constitutive republics of the Union, has the task of formulating and seeing the plans fulfilled. Other key agencies are the central Statistical Administration and the Ministry of Finance and State Bank.

Industry is state-owned and administered by state officials within the general overall policy determined from above and affecting operations from the highest levels down to the individual plants. Farming is a mixture of state and cooperative ownership; in 1973 *kolkhozy* (collectives) were responsible for 39.9% of the output of agriculture, the *soukhozy* (or state farms), 29.8%. There is also, in practice, a private agricultural sector

ization". G. Dalton, *Economic Systems and Society* (1978). B. N. Ward, *The Socialist Economy: A Study of Organizational Alternatives* (New York, 1967).
[102] Nove, *Soviet Economic System*, p. 23.   [103] Ibid., pp. 60 ff.

in which publicly owned land is cultivated or grazed, with the products and the livestock being genuinely private possessions. This private enterprise in fact accounts for 25% of agricultural production.[104] The cooperative and state-owned farms also allow their members to sell what they wish of the supplies distributed to their workers or members. Private ownership in the form of housing is also extensive.

Money plays almost as important a role in the life of the private Soviet citizen as in the capitalist economy.[105] Workers receive money wages, and the individual or the family has to pay for its ordinary needs, though education and health care are free. Within the enterprise, records are kept of costs, income and profit. To finance the commercial services, defence, internal security and the rest, taxes are levied, in particular sales taxes. Industry is usually expected to help finance investment out of its own resources subject to the overall plan.

So much for the general picture: as noted, the key to it, in terms of comparison with its capitalist alternative, is central planning, in contrast to the latter's great reliance on market forces. But although the theory is that central planners work out in detail what is to be done, in practice there is considerable give and take. The targets set are to some extent negotiable between principals at the various levels of administration because realistic targets need to be set. Another way of saying this is that since fulfillment of planned output is the criterion on which management bonuses and standing depend, the lower levels of the structure have a vested interest in keeping targets as low as possible.

The weaknesses of such a system are obvious enough. Planning targets are aggregates, and management fulfills its task whether or not the aggregate decided on meets the needs of efficient production and service of the consumer. The Russian literature shows that the defects are recognized. The "case of the waterpipes" is a typical example.[106] Efforts were made by those responsible for their production to see that a lighter and more efficient type was produced, so saving in materials and in installation costs. But the new pipes contradicted the plan indicators of the wholesalers, project makers and installers; they were, therefore, reluctant to use them, and so the scheme failed.

There has been no lack of effort within the Soviet and other Communist economies to make adjustments in the light of experience. In 1965, experiments were introduced in Russia primarily to correct the tendency of management to set low targets—but they failed because the incentive offered did not offset the much greater advantages that seemed to lie in playing safe.[107] Reforms, therefore, work on the assumption also that the

[104] Ibid., pp. 27, 123.   [105] Ibid., pp. 24, 172 ff., 199 ff.
[106] Ibid., p. 94, quoting an article from *Pravda*.
[107] Ibid., p. 103. Dalton, op. cit., pp. 168 ff.

system itself is not deficient, but only the way it is administered—yet there is a good case for saying that the system itself is destined to failure because it is built on the illusion that the centre can always know, and know best, what is good for everyone and in every circumstance. Manifestly it cannot, and that it cannot is most evident in planning the supply of consumer goods to be sold on the open market where prices are relied on to limit demand. The shortages, the queues and premiums above official prices also testify to the failure of the system.

As for rewards for work and choice of occupation, there has been substantial freedom of choice of jobs since 1956, and to attract necessary workers to new or less attractive occupations pay scales have been made more flexible. Overall, there is a national grading scheme applicable to all types of work which are done in more than one industry; trades specific to a particular industry are provided for in regulations governing them alone.

Though within the Russian system itself there is a constant seeking for improvement, it is the changes and adaptations made in other Communist countries that are perhaps more significant. Hungary, in the period from 1950 to 1955, had been working according to the strict Russian Soviet model. The shock of the 1956 revolution led to change—large scale decollectivisation of agriculture and a revision of industrial planning.[108] Agriculture was later recollectivised in a manner allowing for much greater consideration of the peasants' needs and interests, while the approach to planning was revised to allow prices, profitability and commercial considerations more play; obligatory production indicators were abandoned. The readjustments were not always popular because competition hurt the inefficient, and those hurt complained. The less successful companies had, therefore, to be shielded from the effects of their inefficiency. Above all, job security was seen to be at risk when change challenged old routines; at the same time, the workers liked the freedom to move to new jobs when they chose. "One-sided flexibility" was the phrase coined by one economist.[109] The experiment met with other difficulties—not the least were the international price rises, (1973–74). But the basic elements in the reform remained—the abandonment of the imposition of targets from above and greater freedom for management.

Yugoslavia[110] had also departed from the Soviet model with its greater role for market forces and its stress on worker participation. The trust in the former reached a high peak in the years 1965 to 1971, since then central control has been re-emphasized, with the general pattern however much

[108] D. Granick, *Enterprise Guidance in Eastern Europe* (Princeton, 1976). O. Gadd, ed., *Reform of the Economic Mechanism in Hungary, Development 1968/1971* (Budapest, 1972).

[109] Quoted by Nove, *Soviet Economic System*, p. 296.

[110] Granick, op. cit. Dalton, op. cit., pp. 171 ff. Nove, *Soviet Economic System*, pp. 299 ff.

more market-determined than the Hungarian system, let alone the Soviet. In East Germany,[111] cartels—industrial associations of firms making similar products—exercised more authority than one single central planning authority; problems in the early 1970s resulted in greater emphasis being placed on central control and planning, though the cartels retained a significant role. The Polish leadership, influenced by the riots of 1970, studied the East German and the Hungarian systems and introduced reforms along the same lines;[112] the scale of its failure is now evident to the world. It remains to be seen whether the fundamental social reforms forced on the Polish authorities by the strikes of the summer of 1980 are going to work. It looks to the outsider as if they challenge the whole system.

Polish agriculture had been left largely in private hands after the Communist takeover, but the authorities showed their preference for the state and collectivised sector by giving them preferential treatment in the supply of new equipment. When this discrimination was ended in the late 1960s, the small size of the holdings and the attachment to traditional methods left them unable or unwilling to modernize.

Comparison between the economic performance of the free enterprise and the Communist systems is extraordinarily difficult. Given that Russia started much later and from a much narrower base and had all the problems of compressing so much into so short a time after the revolution, the achievements of the Soviet system are in overall terms staggeringly impressive.[113] Whether overall since 1928 the cost, in human terms, was worth it is another question, as it is with the staggeringly impressive achievements of nineteenth century capitalism. With the agricultural sector there is difficulty in determining how much the historical problems of agriculture in the Soviet Union, problems which are connected with the physical conditions of this sector,[114] irrespective of the type of ownership and management involved, have been made more or less

[111] Granick, op. cit., pt. 2. Nove, Soviet Economic System, pp. 303 ff.

[112] J. Zielinski, Economic Reforms in Polish Industry (London, 1973). Nove, Soviet Economic System, pp. 304–5.

[113] "Industrial output per head is now above the British level and moving towards the U.S. level for some important producer goods. . . . The Industrial Revolution has been accompanied by major social changes: (a) in 1928, two-thirds of the population was illiterate; now, nearly everyone can read and write, (b) in 1928, some three million persons were employed in industrial labour; it is now (1965) over 25 million, (c) in 1928, some 5 percent of the state-employed labour force, i.e. excluding peasants and collective farmers, had received professional or semi-professional education; the figure is now about 15 per cent. The technological situation is different—the long-term trend (is) for labour to become a more scarce factor of production . . . the highly centralized planning structure has become less efficient and less workable." Dalton, op. cit., p. 168, quoting from R. W. Davies and M. Bornstein, Comparative Economic Systems (London, 1969).

[114] See R. Pipe's Russia Under the Old Regime, pp. 1 ff.

manageable as a result of Communism.[115] The gap between the agricultural achievements of the free enterprise countries and those of the Soviet Union must remain one of the question marks against it. If there is a conclusive economic argument against Soviet Communism, it would seem to lie in this failure. It can be reasonably argued that, so close is the connection between productivity, innovation and private ownership in this, the most fundamental of man's economic activities, Communism is simply incapable of meeting the material needs of its own people.

But whatever the objective truth about the Soviet achievement, there is no gainsaying the undeniable attraction that centralized, government-led economic development has to the countries desperately needing to increase their wealth. This enthusiasm often overlooks crucial facts—as for example, that when the first plan was launched in 1928 in Russia, though it was not an industrialized nation in the Western sense, it possessed a considerable industrial sector with the personnel and techniques required to run it, together with an extensive railway system and a food surplus. There are dangers, therefore, for underdeveloped countries in rationalising too superficially from the Soviet experience. China more nearly provides an accurate model for the underdeveloped countries to advance rapidly, but China has been in such turmoil in the last ten or twenty years, precisely because of her attempts at such rapid development, that it would be a little rash to say that she has worked out the problems in a way others could imitate.[116] The latest turn of events among her leaders should indeed seem to indicate that they are more ready to learn from the capitalist system than the Communist.

Cuba has remained truer to the Soviet model, initially attempting radical industrial diversification, but even sympathetic opinion agrees that initially her conversion was far too radical.[117] There has been a reaction in favour of increasing the efficiency of the sugar industry and the improvement of the rural areas. However, the close alliance with Russia and the almost total dependence of her economy on that ally's help as a market and as a supplier make it unwise to take Cuba as a model for third world development.

Finally, it would be unwise and risk obscuring the total truth about the use to which the basic tenets of Communism can be put in underdeveloped countries by failing to mention recent events in Southeast Asia. The callousness of Communist Vietnam's treatment of the "boat people" in 1979 was no accident: it follows directly from the ethic of Marxism

[115] Dalton, op. cit., p. 133. "Soviet policy goals, instruments and basic institutions all contributed to poor agricultural performance."

[116] Ibid., pp. 173 ff.

[117] Nove, Soviet Economic System, p. 307, quoting P. Sweezy and C. Bettelheim. Monthly Review, 1970–1971, vol. 22, no. 7; vol. 23, no. 1.

in which the good of the collectivity, as that good is understood by the party, acting as the instrument of the dictatorship of the proletariat, sees it. And the tragedy of Kampuchea proves the same point more strongly.[118]

In the early 1950s, a left-wing student in Paris, Khiev Samphan, reasoned that peoples like the Khmers in Cambodia would always be exploited as long as their economy was geared to an international market. When the Khmer Rouge captured Phnom Penh in 1975, they put this theory into practice, driving millions from the cities into make-shift collectives to enable the country to become independent. The pattern was repeated elsewhere. In June 1979, the Khmer Rouge foreign minister admitted to three million dead—exterminated because they were old, infirm or opposed to the process to which they were subject. It was, in the minister's words, "a mistake".[119]

Pol Pot, who was prime minister while this policy of extermination was being carried out, is something of a mystery, but he seems to be the same as one Saloth Sar, born of a peasant family, educated at a technical school in Phnom Penh and winning a scholarship to Paris for technical studies. When in Paris, he became attracted by Marxist Leninism as an answer to colonialism as he saw it. He returned to Cambodia early in the 1950s and worked at bringing about the revolution which enabled him to put the plan described into action.

The factors which came together to give Pol Pot and the Khmer Rouge the freedom to act with such cruelty were several, and those who created the situation into which he could inject his evil bear some of the blame. But the real blame lies with the ethics of Marxism—having created the most absolute of metaphysical sovereigns in the march of history and, in the dictatorship of the proletariat, a political machine that owes no loyalty apart from its own conception of Marxism, the way always lies open to terror on the scale of a Stalin—or a Pol Pot.

V. CONCLUSION: THE MARKET ECONOMY, SOVIET PLANNING AND CATHOLIC SOCIAL ETHICS

If we compare the two systems, therefore, the modified free market system of modern welfare capitalism and the Soviet planned economy, there is little doubt that insofar as the former can mean socially responsible

[118] F. Ponchard, *Cambodia Year* (Penguin, 1978). D. Bloodworth, "The Man who Brought Death", *Observer*, 20 January 1980. For the complicated political background to Indo-Chinese politics see C. I. Kim and L. Ziring, *An Introduction to Asian Politics* (Englewood Cliffs, New Jersey, 1977), pp. 2, 6 ff.

[119] Quoted by Bloodworth, loc. cit. In reviewing F. Ponchard's, *Cambodia: Year Zero* for the *New York Review of Books*, 31 March 1977, Jean Lacouture observes that "when men who

and widely distributed private ownership in a mixed economy, it better accords with the Catholic social ethic.[120] But, in practice such modified capitalism still bears within it the defects of the liberal tradition out of which it grew, namely, its materialism and its rejection of a law beyond itself. Further, that Catholic social ethics has this preference does not mean that the Church cannot live with Communism if she has to—the experience of Communist Poland demonstrates that beyond doubt. It is also conceivable that, overall, given some of the positive aspects of the Soviet economic system, it might be just as easy, or perhaps even easier, for the Church to live with it than with a free enterprise structure which encourages permissiveness, anarchy or gross social injustice to the point where the evils outweigh the evils of Communism. But the comparative working of economic systems is not the whole story. One does not get the Soviet type economy without a Soviet type organisation of the state, and that organisation does not allow for any working for an alternative or for effective intellectual and spiritual freedoms. All in all then, with the transcendent values paramount and freedom essential to their preservation (though the Christian puts the freedom under the law of God and does not accept the liberal heresy of absolute autonomy), the Church will prefer the political and social system that is more likely to allow the individual to seek the truth in freedom. This is not to deny that there are merits of the Soviet system. It can offer a more even-handed economic justice in some respects and a healthier moral climate in others. A centralized economy has advantages. In specific cases, it can more readily direct resources where they are needed and will serve a more useful social purpose. Resources, which under the market economy might go where profits are higher but social need less, can be directed under the Soviet system. It can, in theory, better avoid the boom and depression to which the free economy is prone, and so prevent the human and material loss that results from unemployment. Monopolistic and oligopolistic advantages cannot be used against the common good by private interests. Nor does the system depend so much on advertising which is not only too

---

talk of Marxism are able to say that only 1.5 million young Cambodians (out of 6 million) will be enough to rebuild a pure society . . . one can no longer speak of barbarism . . . what barbarians ever acted in this way?" Ponchard himself (op. cit., pp. 13 ff.) notes that some Western writers, Noam Chomsky among them, still refuse to accept what has happened, preferring to believe the bland official statements.

[120] The reasons are discussed more fully below, pp. 301 ff., 305 ff., 308 ff. But the social teaching of the Church does not assume private initiative alone is enough. On the contrary. "Individual initiative alone and the mere free play of competition could never assure proper development . . . it pertains to the public authorities to choose, even to lay down the objectives to be pursued, the ends . . . and means . . . but let them take care to associate private initiative . . . avoid the danger of complete collectivisation or arbitrary planning . . ." (*Populorum Progressio*, par. 33).

frequently wasteful in terms of what is advertised, but can morally deprave, or popularize goods which undermine health and debase tastes.

It is not hard either to see that there are advantages as well as disadvantages in the way labour is organised. Needless strikes, conflict that arises out of pointless disagreement and bitterness, strikes that affect the well-being of whole communities, even a nation, because of a disagreement affecting a few are avoided. Equity is easier to maintain in other spheres; those who have broken the law cannot employ high paid lawyers to enable them to escape the punishment they deserve, nor can experts be used to cheat the community by tax avoidance. The system of wage and salary determination has, in many ways, a better chance of reflecting the social value of a service performed than that which exists in a free economy. Finally, when we say that nonetheless Christians can live more easily with a market economy, we cannot forget that it is not only an economic system, but a philosophy of life, one which has inherited from the nineteenth century the idea that material progress is the be all and end all of life. For the Christian then it is a choice between two evils, rather than between a positive good on the one hand and a positive evil on the other. Yet, when the balance is weighed, it seems that the lesser evil lies with the system which does allow us the greater degree of spiritual and intellectual freedom, and that is the non-Communist system which, for want of a better description, we can call welfare capitalism. In practice, because of its origins and its defective philosophy, we must be suspicious of it. In this, as in so many other things, Pope John Paul II, who has lived with the reality of the Communist state and—while fighting by every means open to him to maintain the Church's spiritual freedom, avoided open conflict—is in a particularly advantageous position to warn us, immersed as we are in the consumer society, of the dangers of our situation.[121]

> A critical analysis of our modern civilisation shows that in the last hundred years it has contributed, as never before, to the development of material goods but that it has given rise, both in theory and practice, to a series of attitudes in which sensitivity to the spiritual dimension of human existence is diminished to a greater or lesser extent as a result of certain premises which reduce the meaning of human life, chiefly to the many different material and economic factors—I mean to the demands of production, the market, consumption, the accumulation of riches or of the growing bureaucracy with which an attempt is made to regulate these very processes. Is this not the result of having subordinated man to one single conception and sphere of values?

[121] Pope John Paul II, "Address to the United Nations", U.S.A.: The Message of Justice, Peace and Love, p. 50.

The reference to the "growing bureaucracy with which an attempt is made to regulate these processes" is, it would seem, a reference to the experience of a planned economy—but speaking as he was in the country which is regarded par excellence as the home of capitalism, it is the subjection to market capitalism, consumerism, which is more pointedly criticized.

If, then, we make a choice for economic freedom, it is freedom under God's law giving justice to all, and not abusing man by any of the excesses of capitalism, including consumerism. It was the English socialist, Laski, who noted that, within the confines of medieval culture, the idea of capitalism could not be contained.[122] We do not identify medievalism with Christian Catholic culture or values. But Laski made a valid point in stressing that some of the values impressed upon the culture of the Middle Ages were the direct result of Christian influence—and one was that private ownership had to be socially responsible. It was because private ownership became irresponsible that we experienced the social evils of the industrial revolution, and that we reaped the whirlwind in Marxism. If we now insist on freedom, including economic freedom as the basic human and social value, we do so conscious that the culture in which we are embedded does not understand freedom in the Catholic sense. With welfare capitalism and its liberal origins, we are only slightly more comfortable bedfellows than we would be with Marxist socialism. Both deny God his due place—the former only slightly less emphatically than the latter.

VI. THE MORAL LAWS GOVERNING PRIVATE PROPERTY: ITS OWNERSHIP AND USE[123]

In paragraphs 69 to 71 of *Gaudium et Spes* we read the following:

> God destined the earth and all it contains for all men and all peoples so that all created things would be shared fairly by all mankind under the guidance of justice tempered by charity.[8] No matter what the structures of property are in different peoples, according to various and changing circumstances and adapted to their lawful institutions, we must never lose sight of this universal destination of earthly goods. In his use of things man should regard the external goods he

---

[122] H. Laski, *The Rise of European Liberalism* (London, 1963), p. 18.

[123] In what follows "private property" is to be understood as distinguished from property which is owned by the state or the government (national or local). The right to private property certainly includes the right to individual private ownership, but is not limited to that form. The family, the tribe, the cooperative, the company, all these are "private" as opposed to "public" owners.

legitimately owns not merely as exclusive to himself but common to others also, in the sense that they can benefit others as well as himself.[9] Therefore every man has the right to possess a sufficient amount of the earth's goods for himself and his family. . . . When a person is in extreme necessity he has the right to supply himself with what he needs out of the riches of others.[11] . . . Investment in its turn should be directed to providing employment and ensuring sufficient income for the people of today and of the future. Those responsible for investment and the planning of the economy (individuals, associations, public authority) must keep these objectives in mind. . . .

[8] Cf. Pius XII, Litt. Encycl. *Sertum Laetitiae*: *AAS* 31 (1939), p. 642; John XXIII, *Consistorial Allocution*: *AAS* 52 (1969), pp. 5–11; John XXIII, Litt. Encycl. *Mater et Magistra*: *AAS* 53 (1961), p. 411.

[9] Cf. St. Thomas, *Summa Theol.*, II–II, q. 32, a. 5 ad 2; ibid., q. 66, a. 2; cf. the explanation in Leo XIII, Litt. Encycl. *Rerum Novarum*: *AAS* 23 (1890–1891) p. 651, cf. also Pius XII, *Allocution*, 1 June 1941; *AAS* 33 (1941), p. 199; Pius XII, *Christmas Message*, 1954; *AAS* 47 (1955), p. 27.

[11] In this case the old principle holds good: "in extreme necessity all goods are common, that is, they are to be shared." On the other hand for the scope, the extension, and the way, this principle is to be applied in the text, besides accepted modern authors, cf. St. Thomas, *Summa Theol.*, II–II, q. 66, a. 7. Clearly, for the correct application of the principle all the moral conditions required must be fulfilled.

The lawfulness of private ownership is not opposed to the various forms of public ownership. But the transfer of goods from private to public ownership may be undertaken only by competent authority, in accordance with the demands and within the limits of the common good, and it must be accompanied by adequate compensation. Furthermore, the state has the duty to prevent anyone from abusing his private property to the detriment of the common good.[14] By its nature, private property has a social dimension which is based on the law of common destination of earthly goods.[15] Whenever the social aspect is forgotten, ownership can often become the source of greed and serious disorder, so that its opponents easily find a pretext for calling the right itself into question. *In several economically retarded areas there exist large and sometimes very extensive rural estates which are only slightly cultivated or not cultivated at all for the sake of profit while the majority of the population have no land or possess only very small holdings. . . . Reforms are called for in these different situations . . . estates insufficiently cultivated must even be divided up and given to those who will be able to make them productive.* In this event the necessary resources and equipment must be supplied, especially educational facilities and proper cooperative organizations. However, when the common good calls for expropriation, compensation must be made and is to be calculated according to equity, with all circumstances taken into account.

[14] Cf. Pius XI, Litt. Encycl. *Quadragesimo Anno*: *AAS* 23 (1931), p. 214; John XXIII, Litt. Encycl. *Mater et Magistra*: *AAS* 53 (1961), p. 429.

[15] Cf. Pius XII, *Radio Message* of Pentecost 1941: *AAS* 44 (1931) p. 199; John XXIII, Litt. Encycl. *Mater et Magistra*: *AAS* 53 (1961), p. 430.

This being the teaching, it is clear that there is a world of difference between the Church's defence of private property and liberal capitalism's understanding of that institution and its rights. Systems based on private property must provide a good human life for all.[124] If they do not, they may not be defended as being in conformity with Catholic teaching.[125] But if the Church's teaching on private property may not be used to defend abuses of ownership, neither may those abuses be made the excuse for arguing against private property in principle. It is the Christian insight, justified by the Scriptures and by her experience of human society over two thousand years, that where the right to own private property (including private property in productive goods) does not exist, it is not possible for the other human freedoms to be maintained.

To those who say there has never been a situation in which true justice and private property have been reconciled, the Christian can answer that this is just another way of saying that men have never sufficiently obeyed their Creator. The Christian believes in the possibility of achieving justice by human effort with the aid of the grace of God but does not believe that human nature or human society is perfectible; he knows that the weakness of original sin that is in us all means that there will be some corruption and injustice in all human social, political and economic systems. The Marxist, building on the tradition of liberalism out of which his philosophy grew, believes that, on the contrary, human nature is perfectible; if only the system of private ownership of productive goods gives way to socialism, man will have a heaven on earth. But there is no evidence that the Marxist will be able to achieve his ideal—certainly on the evidence so far, he has hardly succeeded. He acts on faith in the future. In saying then that it is possible for man to use private property in accordance with justice, the Catholic position is reasonable in theory, and there is in practice much evidence that individuals can use their wealth with social

---

[124] *Rerum Novarum* by contrast saw the nineteenth century situation as one in which "the working man has been surrendered, isolated and helpless, to the hard heartedness of employers and the greed of unchecked competition . . . a small number of very rich men have been able to lay open the teeming masses, a yoke little better than that of slavery itself" (par. 2). *Quadragesimo Anno* said that "free competition has destroyed itself—the whole economic regime has become hard, cruel and relentless in a ghastly measure" (par. 109), and castigated those who "abuse religion . . . trying to cloak their own unjust impositions under its name, that they may protect themselves against the just protest of their employees" (par. 125).

[125] "There have been, and are . . . some who, while professing themselves to be Catholics, are well nigh unmindful of the . . . law of charity and justice . . . abuse religion itself, trying to cloak their own unjust impositions in its name" (*Quadragesimo Anno*, par. 125).

responsibility—either by choice[126] or persuaded by the judicious use of the law. Welfare capitalism has gone a long way to make private ownership more generally aware of its social responsibilities. It retains its defects which we can work to remove. Marxism which depends on the unattainable ideal of total human perfection is doomed to end in the frustration of its believers for this reason.

The Christian's belief in the moral acceptability of private property as an institution is based on scriptural evidence. Property, including the ownership of land and goods apart from household goods, was acceptable to the Jews under the Covenant in the old Law; two of the Commandments (the seventh and the tenth) were concerned with the injunction not to steal or covet the goods of another. Wealth came from the land, and the land had been shared out between the families, each of which guarded its property jealously. Though during the days when the Jews were desert nomads inequalities in wealth were evident, there does not seem to have been gross inequity in its distribution; but the settlement led, by the eighth century B.C., to methods of acquiring and using riches which resulted in injustice to the poor,[127] hence, the condemnation of the prophets of social evils of this kind. They denounced particularly those who bought up the land and who added "house to house and joined field to field till there is no room left."[128] But if the prophets denounced the abuses of the institution of private property, they did not condemn the institution itself. They were strong in their condemnation of those who gained it wrongly and used it wrongly, but private possession was in justice accepted.

In the New Testament Christ often condemned the abuse of riches and pointed out the dangers of riches to his followers. Yet his dealings with men like Nicodemus, one of the rulers of the Jews, Joseph of Arimathea and Zaccheus, show that the possession of riches itself was not condemned.[129] The Zaccheus incident is particularly interesting in that, on his conversion and acceptance by Jesus, he vowed to give half his property to the poor and to right the wrongs that he had caused to anyone. But he would still have remained a wealthy man in retaining half his property. In the rest of the New Testament we see the example of common ownership in the Church in Jerusalem,[130] but the Jerusalem practice was apparently not general. Paul warns the rich to do good, to be rich in good works, to

---

[126] At the height of the industrial revolution there were men like Robert Owen and Titus Salt who were able to combine their role as prosperous manufacturers, with a real attempt and no little success in proper treatment of their workers. G. D. H. Cole, *Life of Robert Owen* (London, 1965). *Dictionary of National Biography*, s.v. "Titus Salt".

[127] R. de Vaux, *Ancient Israel*, p. 72.

[128] Is 5:8.

[129] Jn 3:1–15, 19:38–42; Lk 23:50–53, 19:8–10.

[130] Acts 4:32.

be generous and willing to share and not to look down on others who are not as rich as they; but he allowed they could remain rich.[131] Hence, we cannot conclude from the one incident described in the Acts that Christian belief from the first involved the abandonment of the right to private ownership or riches.

The Church from the time of Clement of Alexandria (c. 150 A.D. to c. 215) had to grapple with the problems of the rich Christian, as she had attracted to herself more and more members, many of them wealthy. Several of the Doctors and Fathers of the Church who wrote on the matter, for example Sts. Cyprian and Ambrose, had given up great wealth in order to follow Christ, but they did not, for that, deny the right of ownership to others. They stressed, as did their master Christ, the danger of riches, developed the principle of responsible use of ownership, and they exhorted to the evangelical counsels, poverty among them. They did not condemn private ownership or wealth in itself.[132]

Clement taught the need to be detached from riches, to be generous in alms-giving, prompt in the payment of wages and avoiding ostentation in one's way of life. St. Cyprian of Carthage (born in 210 A.D.) likewise, while inveighing against the selfishness of the rich, nevertheless encourages detachment from wealth rather than its total abandonment by everyone. St. Basil (329–379) and St. Ambrose (340–397) worked strenuously for the poor and condemned their oppression by the rich, yet they too denounced the abuse of riches rather than riches themselves. St. John Chrysostom (347–407) recommended the holding of goods in common as a practical ideal for Christian communities, although he did not make this an obligation. St. Jerome (342–420) and St. Augustine (354–430) argued that, while Christians might own property, the better way is to hold goods in common.

If, however, the Fathers and Doctors of the Church were not prepared to condemn the concept of private property in principle, they did not have a very high estimation of its moral value. It represented both the fall of man from his primitive innocence and the greed and avarice which makes it impossible for men to accept the ideal of the common ownership of things. It is a method by which the acquisitiveness of human nature may be controlled and regulated rather than a good thing in itself. The natural condition is that of common ownership and individual use. This is the more perfect way, and one of the reasons why the monastic life was taken as the ideal was because it worked on this principle. It was recognized,

---

[131] 1 Tim 6:17.

[132] P. H. Furfey, *A History of Social Thought* (New York, 1949), pp. 156 ff., and R. Schlatter, *Private Property: The History of an Idea* (London, 1951). Both give detailed reference to the sources.

however, that not all could live this way; hence, for mankind in general some organisation of ownership was needed and the state and its laws which could decide the conditions and limitations of ownership.[133]

From the beginning, then, it was the Christian view that the laws governing private property can be made and changed by the state. But the suspicion and reservations of the Fathers of the Church concerning the institution itself must not be misinterpreted. Though they regarded it as "unnatural", they did not regard it as practical to abolish it. On the contrary, private property was a fact of life, a necessity of the real world after the Fall, and the question was to make sure it was properly controlled and regulated.

As in so many other things, St. Thomas was able, in the unique situation in which he found himself at the crossroads of theological and philosophical development in the thirteenth century, to present the traditional teaching in a more coherent way and to develop it in the light of the philosophical speculations and findings of the time. Thomas himself was born into one of the richest and most powerful houses of Europe and could have enjoyed a very comfortable and prosperous life had he wished. He in fact chose that of a poor friar and lived it according to its original spirit. Yet, unlike the earlier Christian writers, he defended the naturalness of private property, that is to say he underlined the positive value of the institution to human nature. At the same time, in accordance with the tradition, he argued that the common life, freely undertaken for the love of God, was more in accord with the Gospel. To Thomas, private property was only unnatural in the sense that wearing of clothes was unnatural—namely, that nature did not provide us with clothes and we had to make them for ourselves. In the same way, nature did not bestow private property on people, but men have discovered that the best way to fulfill the original gift of God to all was to develop this institution. Private property, therefore, was not so much unnatural as *in addition* to nature. It was the best way of fulfilling God's plan in giving the world to all to share in common. It was through the institution of private property that men were better able to make the earth serve the purposes for which God had created it.[134]

[133] Schlatter, op. cit., pp. 38–39, quoting A. J. Carlyle's essay "The Theory of Private Property in Medieval Theology" published in *Property: Its Rights and Duties* (New York, 1922), "For mankind in general, some organization of ownership became necessary, and this was provided by the State and its laws, which have decided the conditions and limitations of ownership. Private property is, therefore, practically the creation of the State and is defined, limited and changed by the State". Ibid., p. 40.

[134] Schlatter, op. cit. *Summa Theologica* I–II, q. 94, art. 5 ad 3, q. 105, art. 2 ad 3. II–II, q. 57, art. 3, q. 66, art. 2.

In Catholic theory the question of whether private property is "natural" to man is, therefore, one that can be argued either way. But whether we see it, as did the Fathers, as a result of sin, or with St. Thomas as compatible with human nature before the Fall, Catholic teaching, based on that of Christ and St. Paul, has accepted the right to private property, while stressing the social responsibilities of the concept. The mind of the Church, therefore, has never been that private property should not exist. The Fathers saw it as unnatural in the sense of being the result of the Fall, but, after the Fall, inevitable and acceptable. St. Thomas saw it as natural in the sense that it was a natural conclusion from God's gift of the world to all in common. Both, therefore, accepted private property as inevitable, although their evaluation of its moral worth varied, Thomas' being the more positive.

The fundamental principles of the traditional teaching were invoked by the Church in response to the economic problems of the nineteenth century, in particular in the encyclical *Rerum Novarum*. The practical arguments in defence of the principle of private ownership of productive goods given in this document[135] are almost entirely clothed in terms of the importance of land-owning as a means of personal and family security. Since the majority of people throughout the world still lived and worked on the land, technically the argument from land ownership was justified—but was less apt for the actual situation with which the Pope was concerned—industrialised society where "return to the land" was impracticable. However, if we look from the examples used to *explain* the teaching and ask ourselves what *principles* they were illustrating, we can see that those principles were applicable to the industrial worker and situation too. In summary, the arguments were as follows: private property is to be defended because 1) the possibility of increasing one's ownership is an incentive to work harder and so benefit not only yourself in the community,[136] 2) property is important as an extension of personality,[137] 3) there is evidence from the history of mankind that this institution is natural to man in the sense that all ages seem to have found it necessary,[138] and 4) the possession of private property can give a man and his family the security they need.[139]

As we will see in a moment, the fundamental moral justification of the institution, however, as it has been evolved and developed in later teachings of the magisterium, is not so much in its personal implications, although these are still important. The justification is now seen in much

[135] Leo XIII, *Rerum Novarum* (London, C.T.S.), pars. 4 ff.
[136] Ibid., pars. 9, 7.   [137] Ibid., par. 8.
[138] Ibid.   [139] Ibid., par. 10.

more general terms—without economic freedom through private property, the other freedoms go. The reason for the change of emphasis is the changing situation. As industrialisation progressed, it was no longer possible to provide for the essential security of the individual and his family from the ownership of land or from the efforts of the worker in small scale craft-based industry. And it was in time found that the way to respond to the problems of poverty caused by industrialisation was through organised social provision.[140] However, this does not mean that the principle of private ownership is now no longer valid. Given that their principle is still valid, then capitalism in the sense of socially responsible private ownership of productive goods in a mixed economy is not to be condemned. That the capitalism of the nineteenth century was not of this sort, and wherever its characteristics re-appear they are morally unacceptable, does not invalidate the moral acceptability of "reformed" capitalism, even though we reject its materialistic presumptions. It is well to remember, however, that there are obligations of charity arising out of private ownership, as well as those of justice. Assuming that the wealth of an individual (including wealth in industrial capital) is justly obtained, there is an obligation in charity (which for the Christian is *greater even* than the obligation in justice) to be generous with one's wealth once the normal requirements of one's state of life have been met. Hence, it is the duty of those who are possessed of a large share of the good things of this life to be generous in giving of their surplus to good causes.[141] It belongs to commutative or contractual justice not to encroach on the rights of another by exceeding the limits of one's own right of property once it is rightfully in one's possession.[142]

Given the original common purpose of all created things, it is for the state, in protecting the common good, to oversee the operation of this institution of private property. The limits of private possessions are, therefore, to be determined by the state, and the way in which they can be used is for it to decide, always provided that the natural right to private ownership, including that in productive goods, remains intact in theory and in practice. All this is summed up in *Gaudium et Spes*, as we have seen, and is based on the Catholic teaching developing from the Scriptures.

---

[140] *Mater et Magistra* notes that "this growth in the social life of men is not a product of blind forces working, as it were, by blind impulse. It is in the creation of men who are free and autonomous. . . ." (par. 63).

[141] *Rerum Novarum*, par. 19.

[142] In the case of the employer, the assumption is that he pays a living wage. His "great and principle duty is to give everyone what is just . . . to gather one's profit out of the need of another is condemned by all laws, human and divine" (*Rerum Novarum*, par. 17).

The moral responsibility of private ownership does not only affect the obligations regarding physical property or property in industrial capital, but also affects those who control financial resouces, those who invest. The question of this responsibility was forcefully raised in the circumstances of the 1920s leading up to the Great Crash in 1929.

In *Quadragesimo Anno* Pius XI noted[143] how

> immense power and despotic economic domination are concentrated in the hands of a few who for the most part are not the owners, but only the trustees and directors of invested funds, which they administer at their own good pleasure. This domination is most powerfully exercised by those who, because they hold and control money, also govern credit and determine its allotment supplying, so to speak, the life blood of the entire economic body. . . . This accumulation of power, the characteristic note of the modern economic order, is a natural result of limitless free competition which permits the survival of only those who are strongest and this often means those who fight most relentlessly, who pay least heed to the dictates of conscience. . . .

Those, therefore, who own wealth in money form—finance—are on the one hand morally bound to invest it so that the whole community may benefit from the use of their wealth, and those who control these funds are to be subject to moral control. In this principle is contained the whole modern demand for social responsibility by great companies—a responsibility hard to ensure because of the very scale and complexity of their operations.[144]

The reasoned argument in favour of a system based on economic freedom is summed up in *Gaudium et Spes*.[145] It is a summary and extension of the key ideas found in previous documents of the social magisterium, as the footnote indicates.

> Property and other forms of private ownership of external goods contribute to the expression of personality and provide man with the opportunity of exercising his role in society and the economy; it is very important, then, that the acquisition of some form of ownership of external goods by individuals and communities is fostered. Private property or some form of ownership of external goods assures a person a highly necessary sphere for the exercise of his personal and family autonomy and ought to be considered as an extension of human freedom. Lastly, in stimulating exercise of responsibility, it constitutes one of the conditions for civil liberty.[13] Nowadays the

[143] (London: C.T.S.), pars. 105–7.
[144] C. Tugendhat, *The Multinationals* (London, 1971). P. J. O'Mahony, *Multinationals and Human Rights* (Great Wakering, Essex, England, 1980).
[145] Par. 71.

forms of such ownership of property are varied and are becoming more diversified every day. In spite of the social security, the rights, and the services guaranteed by society, all these forms of ownership are still a source of security which must not be underestimated. And this applies not only to ownership of material goods but also to the possession of professional skills.

[13] Cf. Leo XIII Litt. Encyc. *Rerum Novarum: AAS* 23 (1890–1) pp. 643–6; Pius XI Litt. Encyc. *Quadragesimo Anno AAS* 23 (1931) p. 191: Pius XII *Radio Message* 1 June 1941: *AAS* 33 (1941) p. 199: Pius XII *Christmas Message* 1942: *AAS* 35 (1943) p. 17; Pius XII *Radio Message*, Sept. 1944: *AAS* 36 (1944) p. 253; John XXIII Litt. Encycl. *Mater et Magistra*; *AAS* 53 (1961), pp. 428 ff.

Property therefore, is 1) *an expression of personality*, affords 2) *opportunities for social and economic service*, provides 3) *incentives* to responsible work and is in a sense 4) *a condition of civil liberties*. 5) This right to *property remains an important element in security*, despite modern developments.

Since Catholic social ethics start with the person in his relationship to his Creator first of all, and then to others in society, it is inevitable that the impact upon the personality is the norm by which the Church judges all social institutions. This is so for private property. It is a fact that some men and women are particularly gifted with those skills which we call entrepreneurial and that the use of those skills gives them great satisfaction. They should then be allowed the opportunity of using their initiative in putting their skills into practice. It is also clear that some men, given the incentive of working for themselves, work with a purpose and a will which they would not otherwise exert, and in so doing prove more useful members of society. Since these talents are God-given, they are also developing their personalities by working in this way.

That this is a rational case is clear from our knowledge of human nature and from human experience. The socialist contention that human needs can be fulfilled without the use of this institution is yet to be proved, if proved it can be. Marxist socialist societies are at the most sixty years old and were built on the foundations and experience of private enterprise systems. It is by no means certain that socialist societies will show, over a comparable period, the same flexibility and the same energy in developing the world for the service of man that has been shown by the free societies. There is indeed, as we have seen, evidence that Marxist socialism is trying to develop greater flexibility by encouraging initiative and greater financial incentive and rewards, just as liberal capitalism has learned the need for social control and planning as political and social opposition to its abuse grew.

The contention that without the right to own the agricultural or industrial means of production a man cannot support himself and his family was central to the argumentation of *Rerum Novarum*, and we have noted that, in the context, the argument was perhaps overstressed. But if it is hard to see how, in the modern economy, that control over his destiny that was once exercised by the peasant or the master craftsman can be regained, it remains true that without a considerable proportion of the agricultural and industrial means of production remaining in non-government hands—in the form of individual or family holdings, partnerships or companies, limited or unlimited, private or public—then there is little hope for human freedom in other spheres. Where the means of livelihood are all under the control of the public authority, it is in practice impossible in the long run for any group within society to oppose state authority on a matter in which the state is determined to exert its will, however unjustly. At this point the person is swallowed up by the collectivity.

All this is said without denying any of the abuses of private ownership of productive goods that have occurred in the recent past and have been, and continue to be, condemned by the magisterium. But it is not clear how the transfer of ownership and control of all economic resources to the state will in the end be of more benefit to mankind either in economic or other terms. The ultimate natural law argument, therefore, in defence of private property is that unless we hold on to the principle and see it given in effective practice, it is impossible to see how other civil liberties— intellectual, cultural and spiritual freedoms—can remain. Because of the greed and ruthlessness of those private interests which control economic resources, there is still a battle for freedom and justice to be fought against them where economic freedom exists. But at least they can be fought because, demanding freedom themselves, they cannot entirely deny it to their opponents. But the injustice of state agencies, when all resources are under the power of the state, cannot be counter-balanced. All that the individual can do is suffer in silence. To say that these resources are always used for the good of all because the almighty state rules on behalf of all is, of course, a fiction which the bitter experience of this century shows is as evil as it is dangerous. As we have said above,[146] the Church can live with Marxist socialist systems if she has to and, indeed, there may be, in particular circumstances, advantages in her doing so. But, in the long term, it is freedom that matters—and that freedom cannot be guaranteed unless it includes socially responsible economic freedom.

The question arose in the 1950s and 1960s as to whether the advent of the welfare state had invalidated the argument for private property in productive goods. Security being provided by social benefits, by provision of adequate pensions and by a higher level of employment, increased skills and professional abilities—was ownership of productive

[146] See above pp. 297 ff.

goods still to be defended now that the argument that it was needed for security was no longer as relevant as it once was? *Mater et Magistra* considered this question and concluded:[147]

> The right of private ownership of goods, including productive goods, has a permanent validity. . . . History and experience testify that in those political regimes which do not recognise the rights of private ownership of goods, productive included, the exercise of freedom in almost every other direction is suppressed or stifled. This suggests surely that the exercise or freedom finds its guarantees and incentive in the right of ownership.

There is no reason, therefore, why we should see the security provisions of social welfare and private ownership of productive goods as in any way in conflict. It is not the mind of the Church to make the two opposed, but rather to see each is given a due place—and what that due place is we can disagree about in a free society.

Private ownership of productive goods is, therefore, to be maintained and safeguarded even in the conditions of the modern economy while, at the same time, that important principle is not to be made the basis for ideological opposition to the right of the state to own and work productive goods either. As the passage from *Gaudium et Spes* quoted tells us, the lawfulness of private ownership is not opposed to the various forms of public ownership.[148] This question arose in the context of the changing nature of the capitalist system. It was seen that some forms of property gave such power over the community that it could be questioned whether they should be in private hands. *Quadragesimo Anno*[149] therefore reminded us that

> it is rightly contended that certain forms of property must be reserved to the State since they carry with them the power too great to be left to private individuals without injury to the community at large. Just demands and desires of this kind contain nothing opposed to Christian truth. Much less are they peculiar to socialism.

It can always be a fair question to ask then whether a particular form of private ownership, which carries with it great power over the community, is indeed one conducive to the common good, or does not rather militate against it. Whether or not it is answered in the affirmative depends on the circumstances—and good men can read those circumstances entirely differently. But the knowledge of such a principle prevents the bitter and futile ideological debates which assume that any form of defence of

[147] Par. 109.
[148] Par. 71.
[149] Pars. 114–15.

public ownership is by definition a good thing or, on the contrary, that any form of public ownership is by definition a bad thing.

It is well then to recall the teaching of the Council more fully once more.[150]

> The right of private property is no obstacle to the right inherent in various forms of public ownership. The transference of wealth to public ownership cannot be made except by competent authority and within the limits of the common good, as well as with fair compensation. Moreover it is the business of the public authority to see that no-one abuses private ownership against the common interest. Private ownership has naturally a certain social character, founded in the law that goods are destined for all in common. If this social aspect is neglected, property often becomes the occasion of greed and serious disturbance and its opponents are given excuse to call the right itself into question. In many underdeveloped regions there are large, even vast, country estates poorly cultivated, for reasons of gain, left uncultivated while the majority of people have no land and only small plots—all this when an increase in productivity is evidently urgent . . . whenever the common good requires confiscation, compensation should be fairly estimated according to all the circumstances.

The question a Christian should be asking first of all, if a new proposal for nationalisation or public ownership comes up is, is it justified in terms of the common good? Similarly, concerning the workings of a particular nationalised industry we should be asking if it is truly working to the public advantage. To treat all public ownership, all nationalised industries, with derision is as bad as treating them all as beyond criticism. In principle, they are a socially necessary institution in a free society, and they must be assessed on their record, not dismissed out of hand or accepted uncritically.

The particular situation envisaged in the paragraph quoted—where there are large country estates that are poorly cultivated while poor people lack necessities—is one which might justify confiscation, as is pointed out. The encyclical *Populorum Progressio*[151] dealt further with this question, noting that

> property does not constitute for anyone an absolute and unconditioned right. . . . The right to property must never be exercised to the detriment of the common good. . . . If certain landed estates impede the general prosperity because they are extensive and used or poorly used, or because they bring hardship to people or are detrimental to the use of the country, the common good sometimes demands their expropriation. . . . It is unacceptable that citizens with abundant incomes and resources should transfer

[150] *Gaudium et Spes*, par. 71.
[151] Pars. 23–24.

a considerable part of this income abroad purely for their advantage, without care for the manifest wrong that they inflict on their country by doing this.

That those who do not use their property to the advantage of the common good are still entitled to receive compensation, provided they have a just title to the property in question, follows from the moral acceptability of the institution in itself. Because I have a fair title to a thing does not mean that I can use it as I wish. By the same token, if the state wishes to deprive me of what I own because I am not using it properly, it must in justice compensate me for what is rightfully mine. Precisely what the basis of compensation should be in the circumstances is a matter for positive law. The rights and needs of the community and private owner have to be considered.

The right of the state to intervene and take over private property, either because its use involves too much power or because it has been badly used, is, therefore, perfectly compatible with the moral defence of the institution. Similarly, it is justifiable for the state to intervene and lay down conditions upon which the property which remains in private hands is to be used for the common good. These rights of the community through the state are not to be seen, in principle, as infringements of the right to private ownership. They are an essential concomitant of that right.

VII. WORK, ITS SPIRITUAL AND MORAL SIGNIFICANCE, ITS RIGHTS AND ITS DUTIES

In its consideration of the place of work in human life, the Council brought to mind that[152]

> human work . . . proceeds from the human person, who as it were impresses his seal on the things of nature and reduces them to his will. . . . We believe by faith that through the homage of work offered to God, man is associated with the redemptive work of Jesus Christ whose labour with his hands greatly ennobled the dignity of work. This is the source of every man's duty to work loyally as well as his right to work.

Manual labour had always been held in greater respect among the Jews than it had in the classical world of Greece and Rome. Hence, there was nothing incongruous in Christ, the carpenter, preaching and teaching in the synagogue. In the same way, too, the apostles, most of them manual workers also, could undertake the spreading of the message of the Gospel; they could be accepted as leaders in the Jewish community, because in that

---

[152] *Gaudium et Spes*, par. 67.

community knowledge of the things of God and dedication to him had their own authority. St. Paul in fact linked the effectiveness of his ministry with his ability to earn his own living and exhorted his fellow Christians to give good example by their diligence in this.[153] From the first, the Church, though it was never class conscious and welcomed all into its ranks provided only that they wished to live by the standards Christ had taught them, was especially attractive to the poor, the slaves, the ex-slaves, the humbler artisans and shopkeepers.[154] The majority of the early martyrs were men and women of very humble origin;[155] they had found in their attachment to Christ a dignity and strength that the world could not offer them. When, therefore, the monastery and the monastic life began to develop from the third century, the respect for and value of humble honest work, physical and mental, naturally found its place in this, the perfection of Christian life as it came to be regarded. It was in the monasteries that the idea of free labour and the demand that a livelihood should be based upon labour was first clearly recognized and from there it spread into the world.[156] In the Christian Middle Ages the emancipated workers learned the formidable power that rested in the right of associa-tion, and the twelfth to the fourteenth centuries were, for them, a period of remarkable achievement.[157]

First the townsmen and then the rural classes grew wealthier and increased their social and political influence.[158] In industry especially, labour gained a new dignity—the economic historian Lipson stresses the safeguards built into the guild system for proper rewards and conditions of labour.[159] The system was a natural growth out of the economic, social

[153] "Try to find some useful manual work . . . and do some good by helping others in need . . ." (Eph 4:28). "Make a point of living quietly . . . earning your living as we told you to do" (1 Thess 4:11). John Paul II in *Laborem Exercens* (London: C.T.S., 1981) p. 21, stresses the importance of work in this respect.

[154] "At first the word had mainly affected very humble folk, the small wage earners, the fullers, cobblers and woolcarders who had often been Christ's witnesses and martyrs", H. Daniel Rops, *The Church of Apostles and Martyrs* (London, 1960), p. 200.

[155] Paul Allard, *Ten Lectures on the Martyrs* (London, 1907), p. 155.

[156] E. Troeltsch, *The Social Teaching of the Christian Churches* (London, 1930), p. 163.

[157] See above. pp. 31 and 47–48.

[158] P. Boissonade, *Life and Work in Medieval Europe* (London, 1927), pp. 332 ff.

[159] F. Lipson, *The Economic History of England* (London, 1945), 1:308 ff., 438–39. The guild system did not, in the long term, prevent class conflict. For a brief account of that conflict, M. Keen, *Pelican History of Medieval Europe*, pp. 229 ff., at more length, M. Mollat and P. Wolff, *The Popular Revolutions of the Later Middle Ages* (London, 1973): what it could at its best achieve is indicated by Erasmus' words about Strasburg under the guild system, "I saw monarchy without tyranny, aristocracy without factions, democracy without tumult and wealth without luxury," (quoted by C. Dawson, *Religion and the Rise of Western Culture*, p. 207). The achievement was all the greater because, unlike the Greek *polis*, the leisured class in the medieval city was not supported by slave labour.

and industrial needs of the time, but the link between the guilds and the Church[160] suggests that the latter influenced them considerably.

The idea that in return for being treated as a full human being a man should work loyally for those who employ him is then central to the Christian understanding of the wage contract which is discussed in more detail below. But, as modern wage work developed, it was in many ways completely devoid of the human conditions and the human rewards which would give the employer the moral right to demand of those who work for him such loyal service. Although there has been considerable improvement, the structure of modern industry and the attitudes which have grown up in the wake of the Industrial Revolution still do not allow for a full human involvement of all workers.[161] The Christian faced with this situation, therefore, must do the best he can to bring out the dignity of work and to change those aspects of modern industrial practices which militate against it. In looking, therefore, at the Christian theory of work, the theology of work, we are abstracting for the moment from the question of how far the actual conditions of work today are compatible with Christian ideals. We want to get behind the modern perversions of work where they exist to what God intended work to be.

If we consider the first chapters of Genesis, we find that God himself is depicted as "at work" creating the world. As the imagery of Genesis puts it,[162] he made the light first of all, then divided the waters and created heaven and earth, which he made fruitful and gave to man so that he could, in his turn, control the good things that God had given him. Tilling the soil was an activity in which man was engaged before the Fall, and, therefore, manual work is not to be seen simply as a result of the Fall. Quite the contrary, God gave Adam and Eve a garden of delight to cultivate and tend, and it was only after they disobeyed him and fell from grace that the tilling of the soil was attended with pain and suffering.[163]

The original injunction to man to till the earth, to work, as part of God's plan for him before the Fall, and the work which is for him a penance as a result of his Fall—both these elements then come together in the Christian theology of work, and this insight is borne out by the facts of experience. Many achieve very great fulfillment through their daily occupations,

---

[160] See e.g. R. Blackham, *The London Livery Companies* (London, 1931), "Religious feeling permeated the guilds from the outset and their meetings were associated with Church rites" (p. 5).

[161] The Marxist concept of alienation, which stressed the way in which capitalism made men experience their work and what they produced as something alien to them, a force directing them from outside, sums up the extreme view, which had of course much truth in it. McClellan, op. cit., pp. 77 ff. *Laborem Exercens*, part II, "Work and Man", examines the Christian answer to this problem of alienation.

[162] Gen 1:3–5.   [163] Ibid., 2:5,15, 3:7–19.

whether they are artistic, intellectual, professional or manual. At the same time there is for many, and indeed for all at some time, an element of real hardship and difficulty in persevering with necessary work. We should, therefore, always seek the fullness of satisfaction in the work we do and not be surprised if, at times, even the most satisfying and fulfilling of occupations is hard on our human natures. The Christian, who has a mature and balanced view of life, will remember that the difficulty of work is a reminder that, as a result of original sin, pain and toil in this life can never be escaped. The point was made in the encyclical *Rerum Novarum*, and it is an essential part of our perspective.[164]

The same mature and sound spiritual view of life will enable the Christian to see such difficulties, as he sees all such difficulties, as things to be accepted in atonement for the sins of mankind and joined, as *Gaudium et Spes* reminds us, in the redemptive work of Christ. Such an attitude is not in conflict with every human effort to lighten the toil of work and human drudgery—rather, human dignity demands that we do not passively accept those aspects of life which impede man's pursuit of happiness, but strive always to overcome them. The Christian is not doomed to the frustration that always comes to those who seek heaven on earth. That he accepts the result of the Fall does not prevent him believing in the possibility of a happy and fulfilled human existence through overcoming, as far as possible, the difficulties of human life and accepting, with trust in God's providence, those things which cannot be changed or improved.

In looking at the positive side of human work, at the joy and fulfillment that so many get in it, we can see in it a means of glorifying God. If in any use of the talents God has given us we make honest use for a good honest purpose, we do this. To work honestly, in any occupation, however humble or thankless, is in a full sense to pray. Man cannot be so alienated either by conditions or by the nature of his work from seeking and finding God through that work—so seeking and finding his own self fulfillment. The more the fulfillment is evident from the nature of the work, the more it accords with God's plan, but the Christian who has to spend his time in doing work of a less congenial nature, while seeking means of improving his situation can still find Christ in the service of others in that work. A heavy burden of responsibility meanwhile rests on those who control the work and livelihood of others to ensure that those who are subject to them in this way are ennobled and not degraded by their work.

The fact that work is necessary for life brings with it important implications in consideration of the rewards that come to a man from it.

---

[164] Par. 14. "Even had man never fallen from a state of innocence, he would not have been wholly unoccupied; but that which would have been a free choice and his delight became afterwards compulsory, and the painful expiation of his disobedience."

Rerum Novarum[165] points out firstly that man's labour is *personal* in the sense that it is his exclusive property under God's law, he is a free agent, it is his work and an extension and a fulfillment of his humanity. But labour is also *necessary* because in the normal course of events it is only through work of some kind that a man can live and can fulfill his obligations. From the fact that work is necessary, we deduce society's duty to make sure that all of those who are engaged in it should get from it the means of a decent life. Any other view of work and human labour is not, and never can be, compatible with the Christian view of work.

Society has this duty because our work has a social dimension; through it we do our part towards the commonweal and can expect that society should see we get justice in doing it. By the same token, it is the fact that human nature is involved with it, and human personality should be fulfilled through it, which demands that society respect all honest work, however menial it is. The Christian should not be possessed of that snobbery which regards only certain kinds of occupation as really worthy of man's dignity. Inevitably, some jobs or professions will stand higher in public estimation than others. This "league table" of respect for work is in itself innocent enough and, in its way, necessary, but it must not lead to lack of respect for those who have neither the talent nor the opportunity for the more highly regarded occupations and do what are necessary tasks, upon which those engaged in more respected professions rely. This very fact—that we all rely on each other—should prevent any underestimation of the human value of all honest work, wherever it stands in the scale of social estimation.

The necessity of work is linked to the right to enjoy leisure time—God is depicted in Genesis as "resting" from his labours. Thus, work and leisure should complement one another, recreations refreshing us so that we can work more effectively, and our work in turn giving us the means—financially and otherwise—to develop our talents and abilities in other directions—so re-creating ourselves. The injunction of the Old Testament to have one day of rest in seven mirrors the imagery of God resting after his labours and indicates a deep human need for suitable leisure time. The obligation to keep Sunday holy reminds us that such time provides us the opportunity for fulfilling our duty of worship and spiritual renewal. There is then this direct link between leisure time and time for God. There is also an indirect but real link—leisure properly used, like work, can give glory to God and can be a form of worship. Cultural and other differences will affect aspects of both, but this two-fold aspect of recreation, the physical/psychological and the spiritual, remain in the Christian mind intertwined.

[165] Par. 34.

The idea that work is necessary to man implies also the right to work. The classical economic theory that dominated in the nineteenth century assumed that the economy was self-regulating and that if only economic forces were given full play then in time there would be employment for all. The state's job was to make sure that the various parts of the naturally working economic system were working without hindrance. It was believed that it was not possible in normal circumstances to have a state of equilibrium below the level of the full employment of capital and labour as a result of their being insufficient demand for the goods that could be produced. Any such fall away from the level of full employment of capital and labour was temporary and due to the hindrances on the working of the natural laws of supply and demand. The experience of mass unemployment in the inter-war years and the theories of economists such as Keynes brought about a change in mind and heart and readjustments in public policy. As popularized in the form of public policy at least, Keynesianism has its problems too, as we have noted. Yet the idea of the right to work remains—independent of a particular economic theory.[166]

Another implication of work as necessary is the concept of a just wage. Initially, classical economics did not look at it this way: wages should be left to find their own level.[167] Implicit in this view was the notion that there was no decent minimum below which wages should not be allowed to fall. The idea of the subsistence level of wage ignored a man's family needs and any appreciation of labour's right to a human existence beyond simple physical maintenance in being. That does not mean that all or the majority of wages were inadequate. It did mean that it was possible to advocate policies which ignored human needs, and that there was a tradition in some trades of low wages and bad working conditions.[168] The situation in the nineteenth century was, it is true, complex and ever-changing. The rapidly rising population at the time and the sudden impact

[166] On the problem of unemployment and the difficulties of reducing it: M. Scott with R. A. Laslett, *Can We Get Back to Full Employment?* (London, 1978). R. Rothwell and W. Zegfeld, *Technical Change and Unemployment* (London, 1979). B. Showler and A. Sinfield, *The Workless State* (Oxford, 1981).

[167] The theory was influential down to the 1930s. "Had the classical laws been allowed to operate, there would have been no 'intractable' unemployment since, according to classical theory, no equilibrium was possible short of full employment. What would have happened was that the unemployed in the depressed industries would have sought work in the non-depressed industries and forced wages down there." R. Skidelsky, *Politicians and the Slump* (London, 1967), p. 207.

[168] Hence the so-called "sweated trades", of which the House of Lords Committee said in 1889–1890, "The earnings of the lowest class of workers are barely sufficient to sustain existence. The hours of labour are such as to make the lives of the worker periods of almost ceaseless toil." Brown, op. cit., p. 197. On the results of the growing discontent with the conventional wisdom, see my *The Development of Industrial Relations in Britain 1911–1939* (London, 1973), pp. 37 ff.

of industrialisation on individual countries and the world economy made it difficult to make the required adjustments. But it was not only the difficulty of grappling with a new situation which caused the problems—the ideological conviction that nothing could be done to affect the laws of supply and demand played their part too.

Rerum Novarum[169] by contrast insisted that wages should be sufficient to enable the worker to comfortably support himself, his wife and his children and, by saving, gradually to become a property owner himself. From the concept of work as necessary it was concluded that there was a minimum below which no worker, however menial or limited his talents, provided he worked loyally at a job which society wanted him to do could be given. Those who had greater talent and greater ability and opportunity, of course, could get more. Egalitarianism is not a Christian ideal. But a generous minimum must be available to all—and how cruelly too often it was not is evident from the records of the time.

Quadragesimo Anno[170] went into the whole matter much more fully. Three things, it said, are to be taken into account in calculating a just wage. The first is that wages are sufficient to support the family man. The second is that the state of the business should be taken into consideration so that excessive rises in wages do not harm it; the rider however is added—if it is the inefficiency of the management or injustices in society which prevent the business from earning enough to pay decent wages, then the workers cannot be expected to forego their just demands; rather it is the duty of employers and society to make sure that the means of paying sufficient wages are there. Finally, the requirements of the common good are to be taken into account in determining what a just wage is; a proper balance needs to be kept between one sector and another. It is for particular societies, according to time and circumstances, to decide how to adjust the often conflicting demands of these three.[171] It was and is the task of the Church as moral guide to indicate the rights of the parties. It is for the parties themselves, through the working of the normal processes of political, economic and industrial life, to decide how the reconciliation is to be affected.

Implicit also in the idea of work as an extension and expression of human personality and as necessary for its existence is the idea that if

[169] Par. 34. The theme of a family wage or of wages supplemented to this end by social grants is one developed in *Laborem Exercens*, p. 69.

[170] Pars. 63 ff.

[171] The attempts at wage policy in the affluent societies are showing just how relevant these guidelines are. The literature on Britain's efforts is already considerable. See for example Jones, op. cit. J. Mitchell, *The National Board for Prices and Incomes* (London, 1977). S. Brittan and P. Livesey, *The Delusion of Incomes Policy* (London, 1977) argues the case against such policies.

private action cannot secure decent conditions, as well as decent wages, then it is the state's duty to intervene to see that such conditions are obtained. Not only the physical conditions of work are to be adequate,[172] but the psychological conditions, the full involvement of the person in work should be sought. Man's alienation needs to be overcome, he needs to cooperate with others in his work, and he needs to be personally identified and fulfilled through any undertaking in which his labour, by hand or brain, is involved.[173] In other words, work has an inbuilt *social* as well as an inbuilt *personal* element: it is therefore not only necessary to man economically, but psychologically and spiritually too—it is an extension of his personality in much the same way that private property is. The nature of work and the structure of the organisation within which the individual works then must meet these needs. Considering what they are and how they are to be fulfilled leads us on to the question of the worker's place in the enterprise, and that can only be considered in a broader context of the nature of the enterprise and industrial organisation and the rights and duties of labour and capital, under the general super-vision of the community through provisions made by the state and its agencies.

VIII. THE ENTERPRISE AND INDUSTRIAL ORGANISATION: THE RIGHTS AND DUTIES OF CAPITAL AND LABOUR

Given the evolution of modern industry out of a revolution which in its ethic and ideology were in many ways fundamentally un-Christian, the resulting pattern of industrial organisation possessed, and still possesses from a Christian point of view, many characteristics which are unac-ceptable. The Christian ideal of industrial organisation is set forth by the Council as follows.[174]

> *In business enterprises it is persons who associate together, that is, men who are free and autonomous, created in the image of God. Therefore, while taking into account the role of every person concerned—owners, employers, management, and employees—and without weakening the necessary executive unity, the active partic-ipation of everybody in administration is to be encouraged.*[7] More often, however, decisions concerning economic and social conditions are made, not so much

---

[172] *Rerum Novarum*, par. 33.
[173] *Quadragesimo Anno*, pars. 65, 69.
[174] *Gaudium et Spes*, par. 68. The analysis made in *Laborem Exercens* provides an ex-tremely important new dimension in Catholic social theory in this matter. On the traditional teaching see J. Y. Calvez and J. Perrin, *The Church and Social Justice*, pp. 226 ff., 279 ff., 252 ff.; Messner, op. cit., pp. 821 ff., 834 ff., 840 ff., 846 ff.

within the business itself but by institutions at a higher level, and since it is on these that the future of the workers and their children depend, the latter ought to have a say in decision-making either in person or through their representatives. *Among the fundamental rights of the individual must be numbered the right of workers to form themselves into associations which truly represent them and are able to co-operate in organizing economic life properly, and the right to play their part in the activities of such associations without risk of reprisal.* Thanks to such organized participation, along with progressive economic and social education, there will be a growing awareness among all people of their role and their responsibility, and, according to the capacity and aptitudes of each one, they will feel that they have an active part to play in the whole task of economic and social development and in the achievement of the common good as a whole. *In the event of economic-social disputes, all should strive to arrive at peaceful settlements. The first step is to engage in sincere discussion between all sides; but the strike remains even in the circumstances of today a necessary (although an ultimate) means for the defence of workers' rights and the satisfaction of their lawful aspirations. As soon as possible, however, avenues should be explored to resume negotiations and effect reconciliation.*

[7] Cf. John XXIII, Litt. Encycl. *Mater et Magistra: AAS* 53 (1961) pp. 408, 424, 427; the word "curatione" used in the original text is taken from the Latin version of the Encyclical *Quadragesimo Anno: AAS* 23 (1931) p. 199. For the evolution of the question cf. also Pius XII, *Allocution*, 3 June 1950: *AAS* 42 (1950) pp. 484–88; Paul VI, *Allocution* 8 June 1964: *AAS* 56 (1964), pp. 574–79.

Industrial relations therefore must not be seen as an area of necessary and inevitable class conflict which has to be encouraged because it indicates a determination and a need to change the whole social and economic structure.[175] The possibility of strike action or lock out is implicit in a free society, as are other forms of conflict, personal or collective, random or institutionalized, that result from the life of society in which free men are free to disagree. But such freedom is under the law and within the agreement to respect the law as the guardian of the common good—not "freedom" to bring about a state of affairs wherein the whole social fabric, including the law which maintains it, is brought down.

Given that the unions and the employers retain their autonomy and the right to seek their interests according to just norms, the overall context must be one which reflects the reality—that it is *persons* who work together, persons, therefore, subject to the same moral law and, by this, capable of co-operating with one another. Because this is so, it is not

[175] The view is not shared by all. Take the following: "For the striker the only real solution to the strike problem lies in the transformation of the status of the worker and the whole structure of control in industry . . . industrial disputes are only one aspect of contemporary resistance to the goals and the structure of the political economy of modern capitalism." R. Hyman, *Strikes* (Fontana, 1972), p. 171. It is difficult to know how seriously such an observation is intended to be taken. In any case it indicates an approach and an understanding of the nature of strike action that the Christian in the Catholic tradition cannot accept.

acceptable to see the enterprise or industry as one simply in which some issue orders and others take them. So long as unity of direction is ensured, there must be some way in which all, not only the proprietors, employers and managers, but the wage-earners too, should have a share in management. Further, all should also have a voice in the deliberations of those organisations beyond the enterprise, and indeed the industry, in which the decisions that so often determine the economic future of both are taken.

Within this context, the right to free trade unions, which genuinely represent the needs of the workers, is a fundamental human one which contributes to the proper organisation of economic life. Strikes can remain a necessary last resort of the wage-earner in protecting rights and getting rightful demands accepted, though they should be a *last* resort and, even when justified, ways and means should be sought to resume negotiations and bring about reconciliation as quickly as possible.

The nature of the enterprise, as it developed in the nineteenth century under the impact of limited liability,[176] resulted in the division of those who participate in (and benefit from) its working into three groups: shareholders, managers and the workers. The distinction between shareholders and salaried managers is reasonably clear (though managers can be and often are shareholders) but it is often difficult to decide where management (those who give directions) ends and workers (those who are directed) begin. Foremen form the first line of management but they are "promoted from the ranks" and in many respects still retain a greater affinity to the rank and file than to the other levels of managerial staff. Skilled workers very often have a very considerable scope for decision-making in their own right while the activities of shop stewards and other trade union representatives mark a real participation in (some would say an infringement of) managerial prerogatives. Yet the three divisions retain their general validity, and there is, in principle, no reason why all three should not work together for the common good. Unfortunately, the nineteenth century inheritance has meant that the enterprise is too frequently marred by that selfish individualism and class antagonism, muted or open, which is contrary to the Christian vision of man in society.

The dangers of social irresponsibility by the modern company were very much the concern of the encyclical *Quadragesimo Anno*. After noting

[176] The limited company (or business corporation as it is called in America), is a body corporate with a common seal carrying on its operations managed by a board of salaried directors and owned by those who have bought shares in that company. Cairncross, op. cit., p. 138. The institution developed in the nineteenth century to meet the needs of financing and administering the increasingly large industrial unit demanded by the growing scale of production. Clapham, *An Economic History of Modern Britain* (O.U.P., 1963), 3:201 ff. H. Faulkner, *American Economic History* (New York, 1960), pp. 420 ff. Friedlander and Oser, op. cit., pp. 220 ff., 235 ff.

that a system of production in which some owned capital and others worked for the owners of such capital was not incompatible with the Christian vision and the nature of man, the document goes on to say:[177]

> It violates right order whenever capital employs the workers . . . with a view and on such terms as to direct business and economic activity entirely at its own arbitrary will and to its own advantage, without any regard to the human dignity of the workers, the social character of the economic regime, social justice and the common good . . . in our days it is patent that not wealth alone is accumulated, but immense power and despotic domination are concentrated in the hands of a few, who for the most part are not the owners, but only the trustees and directors of invested funds which they administer at their own good pleasure . . . (one result is) . . . a detestable internationalism or international imperialism in financial affairs which holds that where a man's fortune is, there is his country . . . economic power must be brought under the effective control of the public authority . . . the public institutions of society must be such as to make the whole of human society conform to the needs of the common good, that is, to the standard of social justice.

The principles here laid down justify the intervention of responsible authorities in ensuring that the managers and the shareholders accept the social responsibilities of their power and privilege.[178] If some Christians have not been as sensitive as they should to their responsibilities in this regard, they should be grateful for being made aware of where they have failed to put into practice what is the clear teaching of the Church regarding the responsibilities of ownership. They should not be too disturbed if it seems that many of those who protest the social irresponsibility of companies are less interested in seeing them made responsible than they are in undermining confidence in the mixed economy. It would not be the first time that the real deficiencies of a system have been pointed out by its enemies—to its long term benefit.

How the participation of everyone in the enterprise can be achieved is a question which has concerned the teaching Church since Rerum Novarum. In fact, one of the background controversies to that encyclical was whether the Church should identify herself with a revival of something which can best be described as a modernised guild system.[179] In the issue it

[177] Pars. 100–111.

[178] George Goyder's suggestions in The Responsible Company (London, 1971) still seem pertinent. On business ethics in general, Towards a Code of Business Ethics (London: C.A.B.E., 1972). The question of moral responsibility of companies is complicated by the size and scale of some. See P. J. O'Mahoney, Multinationals and Human Rights (Great Wakening, 1980).

[179] E. T. Gargan, Leo XIII and the Modern World (New York, 1961), pp. 76 ff. Daniel Rops, A Fight for God 1870–1939 (London, 1966), pp. 141 ff. A. Vidler, A History of Social Catholicism (London, 1964), pp. 144 ff. See above p. 248 ff.

was those who accepted the structure of modern industry, the wage contract, and the trade unions looking after the rights of their members, who prevailed. However, the deep awareness that there was something fundamentally inhuman and un-Christian about the working of the industrial system in the nineteenth century, even if it could be persuaded to give rough economic justice to its wage earners, remained. Hence *Quadragesimo Anno* asserted:[180]

> In the present state of human society we deem it advisable that the wage contract should when possible be modified somewhat by a contract of partnership, as has already been tried in various ways to the no small gain both to the wage earners and employers. In this way wage earners and other employees participate in the ownership or management or in some way share in the profits.

Mater et Magistra took up the idea again,[181] recommending profit sharing and worker shareholding so that the wage earners become full participants in the enterprise.

> We are in no two minds as to the need for giving workers an active share in the business or the company for which they work—be it a private or a public one. Every effort must be made to ensure that the community is indeed a true community of persons concerned about the needs, the activities and the standing of each of its members.

The use of the word "community" in this context raises questions for some,[182] but it is clear from the context that what is being proposed is not any new point of doctrine, still less of industrial sociology, but the familiar idea that persons are the end and purpose of every organisation in which they are involved, not vice versa. It is not sufficient simply for a man to be a wage earner. He must have a full human involvement in his work and is entitled to share in its prosperity and also to take what part he usefully can and wants in the direction of the firm, saving the unity of direction of the managers. The document is content to make suggestions, not saying whether profit sharing is meant to be a norm or ideal, or whether the share in prosperity should be taken through bonuses or shareholding. The widest possible latitude must be left to those who wish to put the principles into practice. Any more precise language would give those who had a particular scheme in mind (which may not be the best in

---

[180] Par. 65.

[181] Par. 91. See *Laborem Exercens*, pp. 49 ff. The question of worker participation is now a live issue in Europe. For a useful brief introduction, D. J. Farnham and J. Pimlott *Understanding Industrial Relations* (London, 1979) Part IV. Exhaustively, *Industrial Democracy in Europe* (O.U.P., 1981).

[182] The question is discussed in J. Y. Calvez, *The Social Teaching of John XXIII* (Chicago, 1964), pp. 41–42.

the circumstances, but may be good for certain circumstances) opportunity to narrow down the options open to the Christian in this matter.

Quadragesimo Anno was concerned not only with the provision of a
more humane relationship and attitude within the firm, but also with such
relationships in the organisation of industry in the economy as a whole.
The idea was for what, in translation, came to be known as organisational
groups, vocational groups,[183] or corporative organisation, but which, in
the British context, are better called industrial councils.

> As things now are, the wage system divides men in what is called the
> labour market in two sections resembling armies, and the disputes between
> these sections transform this labour market into an arena where the two
> armies are engaged in fierce combat. . . . But there cannot be question of any
> perfect cure unless this opposition can be done away with and well organised
> members of the social body be constituted: organisational groups claiming
> the allegiance of men not according to the position they occupy in the labour
> market but according to the diverse functions which they exercise in
> society. . . . The common interest of the whole vocational group must
> predominate and among those interests, the most important is to promote as
> much as possible the contribution of each trade or profession to the common
> good of the State. Regarding cases which may occur in which the particular
> interests of employers or employees call for special care and protection, the
> two parties will be able to deliberate separately or to come to such decisions
> as the matter may require.

The key idea, therefore, is that each industry, while having its separate
trade unions and employers' organisations, should possess some overall
organisation which would enable such common interests as do exist
between employers and employees to be built upon. There is nothing in
principle in this idea which is against the experience of industry in free
societies. In the inter-war years, at the time *Quadragesimo Anno* was
written, there were efforts in Britain through the Whitley Councils and
through various other schemes, to bring some kind of an overall organisation into being.[184] There was a form of cooperative organisation in
existence in Italy at the time the encyclical was written too. But since the
type supported by the encyclical was one based on free association and
stressed the value of such organisations in relieving the state of many of its
burdens, the Italian/Fascist type of corporatism, which was both imposed
from above and denied the right of association in free trade unions, far
from being recommended was in fact being condemned.[185]

---

[183] *Quadragesimo Anno*, pars. 84–85.

[184] See my *The Development of Industrial Relations in Britain, 1911–1939* (London, 1973), pp. 77 ff.

[185] W. McGovern, "Fascism and the Corporate State", *From Luther to Hitler* (London,
1951), pp. 584 ff. "Corporatism to the Fascist means that the control over the economic and

The observation of *Gaudium et Spes* about the right of the workers to participate in higher level institutions whose decisions affect the lives of the workers goes further than the "corporative" idea, seeking to give the workers a place in the deliberations of any organisation about the level of the industry. This recommendation that the principle of cooperation should be extended beyond the firm or industry was not moralistic projection which had no contact with reality. In various ways, different countries were already experimenting with methods of ensuring more rationalised overall cooperation in individual industries and over whole areas of the economy, even over the whole economy. [186] It was this sort of "right reason" practical approach which the encyclical recommended as being worth pursuing to achieve great cooperation.

Rerum Novarum asserted that the right of association in free trade unions was to be defended, and subsequent documents, particularly *Quadragesimo Anno*, developed this principle. But this right of association in free trade unions must be ordained to the maximum of cooperation with the employers that is compatible with the obligation of the union to defend its members' interest and the obligation of the employer to make sure that he exercises effective control. It is not for the magisterium to say precisely *how* unions, employers and the state should organise in order to achieve this end, because these are highly technical matters. It must, however, insist that this end is accepted. Once again, while the rights of capital to organise for profit are defended, and the rights of labour to organise its own best interests is defended also, capital and labour are not to be seen as naturally antagonistic in a Marxist sense, but ready to seek a reduction of needless conflicts and cooperate where interests coincide—while each side reserves the right to defend its own vital interests.

The question of the strike is becoming an increasingly important one, given the complexities of modern society. There is no doubt that since the option of striking is one that must remain open to the wage earner, we can talk about a "right" to strike. There would be no point in the right

---

social life of the nation shall lie in the hands of a number of occupational groups, each of which in turn is under governmental supervision and control" (Ibid., p. 587). "Similarly, the right of association in syndicates (trade unions) belongs only to those who accept the Fascist as the only form, and its subordination to the State." Since such principles are directly contrary to those of subsidiarity and the right of association in free trade unions, only the perverse can claim that *Quadragesimo Anno* supported Fascist corporatism.

[186] In Britain we have had, since 1964, the *National Economic Development Council* with counterpart in individual industries, as well as increasing government cooperation with the C.B.I. and the T.U.C. on major policy issues. The degree and the manner in which various governments use or do not use these organisations and conventions varies—but the overall trend since the Second World War has been to closer cooperation and consultation, the ups and downs of particular periods notwithstanding.

of association if the right to use the ultimate sanction that those who work for others have was denied to them in pursuing the aims of their association. That this has always been the implication of trade union organisation was confirmed by *Octogesima Adveniens*. The same document voiced the concern that is being evidenced in many quarters concerning the proper use of this right.[187]

> Here and there a temptation can arise of profiting from a position of strength to impose, particularly by strikes, the right to which, as a final means of defence, remains certainly recognised, conditions which are too burdensome for the overall economy and for the social body, or the desire to obtain in this way demands of directly political nature. When it is a question of public services required for the life of an entire nation, it is necessary to be able to assess the limit beyond which the harm caused to society becomes inadmissable.

That the right to strike has always possessed within it serious anti-social implications has been obvious in theory and practice since the development of modern industrial relations in the individualistic context of the nineteenth century,[188] hence, the attempts of labour law in its various ways to rationalise, to organise and to set limits upon union action in the strike situation.[189] But given the sociology of industry, given the different traditions and attitudes in various firms and industries, let alone in different countries, it is extraordinarily hard to give general guidance which will enable particular strikes to be judged justified or unjustified.

It has been customary to use the analogy of the just war theory to decide the general principles governing strike action.[190] On this, two things should be noted. The first is that nowhere in the documents of the magisterium, the encyclicals or any pronouncement of equal comparable authority, is this theory appealed to. Its value then rests entirely on the authority of the theologians and moralists who use it and on that alone. Individuals may therefore reject the analogy as inexact and any set of rules based on it as irrelevant. The second is that, insofar as the analogy is

---

[187] *Rerum Novarum*, par. 14. See also *Laborem Exercens*, p. 76.

[188] The Webbs (*Industrial Democracy* [London, 1926], p. 221) noted that "The perpetual liability to end in a strike or lock out is a grave drawback to the method of collective bargaining. So long as the parties to a bargain are free to agree or not to agree, it is inevitable then, human nature being what it is, there should now and again come a deadlock leading to a trial of strength and endurance that is beyond bargaining." They concluded that only legislation would solve the dilemma.

[189] The complexity of labour law is not to be underestimated. For a good brief introduction to the British situation: Farnham and Pimlott, op. cit., pp. 124 ff.

[190] Messner, op. cit., p. 463, discusses the right to strike in the context of natural law theory. H. Peschke, *Christian Ethics*, 2:509, applies the just war theory to the strike situation without reference however to the context.

accepted, it may not be taken to indicate that the social teaching of the Church sees industrial relations as a cockpit of the class war. That said, in the absence of any other concept or categories offered by traditional moral theory which is at first sight remotely relevant to industrial relations problems, the analogy has something to recommend it. Granted that the two sides are not to be seen as at war, the fact that on specifics they can be opposed, and that they both possess a collective power and influence when so opposed which may be likened to that at the disposal of nations, the search for a first set of principles to guide us concerning the morality of strike or lock out action may well lead us to the just war theory.

According to the theory, for a war to be just, it must be called by proper authority in a just cause (namely the redress of a grievance and not for any aggressive purposes) and with a right intention—it must, therefore, use just means in pursuing its just aim; in particular, it must not cause more evil in pursuit of a just claim by just means than the evil it intends to overcome.

So much for the general principles—which can be clearly stated. The difficulty comes in applying them. The actual situation in which a strike takes place is very rarely one in which the issues are clear enough for the immediate and successful application of any such general principles. The problems of the actual situation are clearly indicated by the British experience. In it, all the essential issues arise, though different countries face them in different ways.

Let us take first of all the question of proper authority. The relationship between unions, their officials and their members on the shop floor is one that we in this country find difficult to rationalise satisfactorily. If unions are voluntary associations, the members only obey their leaders insofar as they wish, but if they are given corporate status, the members can in theory be more effectively disciplined. Because of the problems raised by corporate status, we have chosen to regard unions as voluntary associations.[191] This has meant that leaders have very little in the way of sanctions against members—but corporate status would not solve that problem. It would be very difficult, if not impossible, for union leaders to compel their members to act against their will. Even where the state itself has tried to use the full weight of the law under wartime conditions, it has not been able to do so.[192] The question of effective authority in trade

[191] K. M. Wedderburn, *The Worker and the Law* (London, 1971), pp. 313 ff. Brian Weekes et al., *Industrial Relations and the Limits of Law* (Oxford, 1975), pp. 95 ff.

[192] *Royal Commission on Trade Unions and Employers Associations Report* [Donovan Commission] (1968), pp. 131 and Appendix 6. The case of the prosecution of the Betteshanger Colliery men for going on strike in 1941 was the one in point. It proved impossible to prosecute 4,000 men: coercion did work in some cases—where the numbers were few or the cause generally unpopular (J. Parker, *Manpower* [London, 1957], pp. 464 ff.).

unions is, therefore, more difficult than appears at first sight. It cannot be assumed that trade union leaders can get the men out on strike or that they can stop them from striking. It depends very much on the union, the situation and the mood of the moment.

So too with the just cause, i.e. the redress of a grievance and not the pursuit of any aggressive intent. The fact of the matter is that society has not yet been able to determine what the requirements of justice in specific cases of industrial conflict are.[193] The collective bargaining system, of which most free countries are in their measure justly proud, developed as a collective reaction to a situation in which workers knew from hard experience that they had to fight to maintain minimum standards when economic conditions were against them, and that wage claims, even if justified, were opposed in principle. The attempt to procure justice then was conceived by each side in terms of its own immediate needs and strength, and the idea of any norm of justice by which both should be subject to the common interest was not given any practical effect. If we are going to expect our unions to act militantly only in response to just causes, then we must be quite clear about what just causes are. The same problem occurs with considering just means. This is particularly true in the question of picketing and, in a broader context than the strike situation but invoking the same principles, the question of a closed shop.[194]

The right to peaceful persuasion that is the justification of picketing must not degenerate into brutal intimidation or extend so far beyond the actual point of dispute that all sense of proportion is lost. But it must be recognized that where tempers are high, even peaceful picketing, in a justified situation, is unpleasant for those who disagree with its purposes; objection to the excesses of picketing should not be the occasion for demonstrating a dislike, even a hatred, of pickets and picketing.

So too with the closed shop. No one can deny that, on the evidence, the institution can lead to injustice. By the same token, it can serve a useful purpose.[195] Where it has grown and flourished, society's concern should

---

[193] See the quotation from the Webbs, above p. 326.

[194] Perhaps the best discussion of both these issues is in the Donovan Commission *Report*, pars. 855 ff., 588 ff. See also Wedderburn, op. cit., pp. 321 ff., 451 ff. Bitter ideological opposition to the closed shop on the grounds of individualist libertarian political principle ignores the realities of industrial relations. Attempts to curb it by general legislation only have the effect of further entrenching it by retaliatory legislation as the 1971 Industrial Relations Act showed; further it results in bitterness that the industrial relations system could well do without. The 1980 Employment Act stopped short of what libertarian political ideology would have wanted; the closed shop remained. The decision of the European Court in the summer of 1981 in the case of the three railwaymen did not condemn the institution in principle. But one fears that the misguided attempts to abolish it altogether will continue.

[195] See the Donovan Commission *Report*, par. 602. "In our view prohibition of the closed shop must be rejected. It is better to recognise that under proper safeguards a closed shop can

be to make sure that its abuses are brought under control, but the institution itself should not be challenged where it can improve orderly and equitable collective bargaining and industrial relations, and work with justice for all.

It is unfortunately true that in Britain industrial relations issues are highly politicized—and political ideology is notoriously unhelpful in resolving industrial relations problems. If society, through its politicians and others, was as concerned in peaceful times to develop the consensus out of which alone reform of industrial relations and labour law can grow, and in virtue of which alone it would be obeyed, one would be more impressed with the anguish of society's publicists when large scale industrial conflict arises.[196]

Finally, when we look at the question of there being a proper proportion between any inconvenience a strike would cause and any possible benefits that may accrue from it, we are once again up against the problem of socially acceptable norms understood by all and applicable to the strike situation. Assuming that society accepts the right to strike, as it must, it must also be prepared to seek ways of convincing those whose strikes can do immense harm to the public good that they will lose nothing of their rightful claim to justice by surrendering their right in some or all circumstances. That certain groups of workers (one need only think of those who control our essential public services, such as hospitals) automatically put the community at risk in whole or in part, many countries have ample reason to remember in recent years. It is also being increasingly recognized that if we deny to such people the right to strike in some or in all circumstances, then we must do something to make sure that their legitimate claims are treated properly once they have foregone the right or had it denied them in law. All this is simply to state the obvious and point a way forward. However, it is an obvious way forward which, until recently, has been too little considered. Perhaps, as the full logic of the unsatisfactory nature of our industrial relation and collective bargaining system is brought home, we will be constrained to put right the defects we have too long ignored.

It is, in fact, possible to suggest how an industrial relations system in a free society should function in order that we may detect the faults of

---

serve a useful purpose and devise alternative means of overcoming the disadvantages which accompany it."

[196] "If, since the War, government and industry had given industrial relations—in the widest sense—a top priority label, the world would not be looking at Britain today as a nation of humpty dumpties . . . law cannot create qualities of leadership, and it is the right sort of leadership particularly in management, which above all determines the quality of human relations", *Fair Deal at Work* (London: Conservative Political Centre, 1968), p. 5.

existing systems and make suggestions of how they may be put right so that needless strikes are avoided and inevitable strikes properly ordered. Such an "ideal" structure can be shown to be compatible with, indeed built out of elements of, existing structures. It is in fact necessary that this should be so. The vast complex of industrial relations that exists in free societies cannot be wished away in some well intentioned but hopeless quest for a perfect order established from scratch. Yet it is not only a matter of accepting what is because there is no hope of improvement. It can be seen from analysis and examination, in the light of the freedoms that we expect men to have, that the existing structures do give us something positive to build on in the quest for a more human and rational system of industrial relations. What follows is based on my own work in the historical sociology of British industrial relations.[197] But since its findings parallel the conclusions and theories of some American writers it can fairly be taken as having a relevance beyond this country.[198]

An ideal pattern must be based first of all upon the existing collective bargaining structures. These have been built up over the years to enable unions and employers to agree to the terms and conditions of work. In principle, such a system is compatible with the Christian social ethic—but in practice, collective bargaining can be very defective; it is a system which can only be rationally defended if it does indeed enable the two sides to resolve differences which are resolvable by peaceful means with the maximum ease and expedition and provides an organised and socially acceptable way of conducting disputes (strikes or lockouts), when they cannot be avoided. We all know that the lack of confidence in our industrial relations system arises from our knowledge that too often collective bargaining does not work like this. We need then to set out the conditions a collective bargaining system must meet if it is to serve the parties to it, and the community, well.

The issues that arise in such bargaining may usefully be distinguished into the *procedural* (who is to bargain, how they are to be organised to bargain, and how the bargaining and industrial relations, including strike action, are to be conducted) and the *substantive* (on what specific issues the bargaining takes place, and what is the content of resulting agreements). Procedural questions, of course, often appear as substantive issues in the bargaining process and in agreements that result.

In the order of how things actually happen, a proper system of industrial relations depends first of all on the attitude of mind of those who enter into negotiations. The unions and the employers must be prepared to cooperate with one another in a positive way. Put in technical language

---

[197] R. Charles, *The Development of Industrial Relations in Britain, 1911–1939* (London, 1973).

[198] For example N. W. Chamberlain and J. Kuhn, *Collective Bargaining* (New York, 1965), pp. 429 ff.

we call this the *primary procedural norm*.[199] It is procedural in that it is concerned with the "how" of collective bargaining and, in all else that involves human relations and judgement, the attitude of mind of the parties will decide the quality of those relations. If unions and employers accept each other positively rather than as necessary evils, then it is likely that the procedures and agreements they operate will be helpful to both. Where one resents the other, bargaining will be ineffective and half-hearted and agreements unsatisfactory. Given this primary procedural norm,[200] secondary ones follow; there must be organisation of both sides at all levels to ensure effective procedures and the proper observance of agreements. Logic also demands that there must be an overall national organisation, based on the voluntary principle, to monitor the system, and there must be codification of agreements to form a case law and proper provision for interpreting agreements once made.

Substantive agreements[201] must firstly provide satisfactory standards of wages and conditions—above all on what the minimum wages and conditions are (the *minimum wages and conditions norm*) and, beyond that, how the wage structure is built up on this basis. Secondly, there must be agreement on the norms which cover the adjustment in existing agreements, the *adjustment norm*. Regarding the first, the *minimum wages and conditions norm*, wage structures have been, in the past, largely determined by inherited patterns, and more sophisticated standards will have to be developed in the future; some work has already been done towards evolving them.[202] The *adjustment norm* must be linked with political decisions. Governments in the welfare state have increasingly been drawn into some form of wage policy, and there is no escaping the long-term implications of this. Just as we need some kind of national organisation to monitor procedures in the ultimate, so do we need one to monitor and synchronise the system on substantive issues.

These substantive norms of *minimum wages* and *adjustment* may be called the *primary substantive norms*. There are secondary ones too. To restrict collective bargaining to wages and conditions is too limited. Fringe and welfare benefits should come into its scope as should matters like safety and productivity. In their turn these then can lead on into a consideration of worker participation in management in some form. Hence what we may call co-operative collective bargaining is not to be opposed, but is complementary to, worker participation and all that that involves.

That the elements which would enable us to build up such a system exist is evident from the close relationship of its basic ideas and structures to the system many advanced industrial countries possess; in fact, as

---

[199] R. Charles, *The Development of Industrial Relations in Britain, 1911–1939* (London, 1973), p. 28.   [200] Ibid., pp. 29 ff.   [201] Ibid., pp. 31 ff.

[202] For example, E. Jacques, *Equitable Payment* (London, 1970).

pointed out, the theory here sketched is based upon the experience of the more positive elements in the British system. Adapting what we have in Britain to this more sophisticated, but basically the same, pattern presents immense difficulties, but given the need to produce a new spirit in those relations, the pains of such adaptation would be worthwhile.

Whether or not that can be done, such a framework of ideas does give us some better chance of understanding when particular strikes are justified. If the system of industrial relations in which strikes occur is deficient in any important respect in the light of such a set of norms, then the strike itself can be assumed in principle to be justified. Whether it is justified to vindicate the principle by strike action in practice will depend upon one's judgement and point of view, and good men may well differ on this. Yet it does help to a rational consideration of justifiable or non-justifiable strikes to have such norms. A parallel may illustrate. If, for example, a plane crashes because of defective maintenance or design, we do not necessarily blame the crew, even though they are also proved to be incompetent. Whatever their incompetence in such a situation, their responsibility for an accident would be marginal if the plane was destined for trouble anyway because of reasons beyond their control. So it is in industrial relations. Given groups of workers or managers may not be prepossessing, but if they are expected to administer a system which is fundamentally organised to produce industrial unrest or is not designed to ensure effective negotiations to take place on issues which arise, then any resultant difficulties are to be blamed upon the system itself rather than upon those who administer it.

If we look more closely at the implication of the norms as above set out we will, I think, be able to judge better the right and wrong of particular strikes. To take first the primary procedural norm—that the collective bargainers enter into negotiations with a positive acceptance of the other's right to exist and in a cooperative frame of mind. Clearly where there are conflicts over issues of principle regarding the right of a man to join a union, or disputes over the closed shop or an inability to go beyond the narrowest range of subjects of collective bargaining, then this norm is not accepted. Where it is not, it is not possible to build up the right structure of organisation and agreements. Such procedures as are established will be limited and defective. They might, in fact, be a mask for the antagonism of one side to another. There will also be failure to codify agreements and to establish a true case law if attitudes are defective. If a strike takes place in a firm or an industry where attitudes and procedures are so defective, it is more than likely that strike action is the only way to register protest or get anything done, even though the real causes remain untouched by the strike.

So, too, with the substantive norms. There may be fundamental disagreement on minimum wages and conditions and consequent troubles
with the wages structure. Where there is, and where there is no peaceful
way of resolution of the problem, to expect anything but strike action
eventually is unrealistic. And on the adjustment norms we still, as a
society, do not have any way in which a standard can be agreed upon
which meets the demands of justice. For the parties to the agreement see
them and the community as a whole. If in "winters of discontent" we are
appalled at the conflict and the "greed" of particular groups of workers in
defying what we, as outsiders, see as the national interest, then we must
accept the implications of our attitude. We must be prepared, as a
community, to establish standards, norms, by which wages may be
adjusted in such a way that these conflicts are avoided or processed in a
more positive and less destructive way. We cannot have it both ways; if
we are going to be outraged at the supposed "greed" of some groups of
workers or their excessive vigour in pursuing their claim, then we must
offer them a better means of determining what their claim should be and
deciding when they are justified in pursuing it by strike action.

IX. INTERNATIONAL ECONOMICS:
THE DEVELOPED AND UNDERDEVELOPED COUNTRIES

A. DEVELOPMENT AND UNDERDEVELOPMENT:
THE FACTS AND THE ETHICAL ISSUES

Economic development in the broadest sense is the context in which the
Council's teaching on economic ethics occurs[203]—and its concern is with
ending the economic inequalities that exist throughout the world, within
countries and between countries.[204] The question of the relationship
between the developed and the underdeveloped countries is dealt with in
the general context of international relations.[205] The argument is that, if
there is to be peace between nations, then injustices must be removed, and
one of the causes of such injustice is economic inequality,[206] to overcome
which international cooperation is needed.[207]

> The present solidarity of mankind calls for greater international coopera-
> tion in economic matters . . . although nearly all peoples have achieved
> political independence, they are far from being free of excessive inequalities
> . . . from undue dependence . . . and serious internal difficulties. . . . The

[203] *Gaudium et Spes,* pars. 63 ff.   [204] Ibid., par. 66.
[205] Ibid., pars. 77 ff.   [206] Ibid., par. 82.   [207] Ibid., pars. 85, 86.

development of a nation depends upon human and financial resources . . .
citizens must be prepared by educational and professional training . . . this
involves the help of experts from abroad . . . as fellow workers. . . .
*Material aid for developing nations will not be forthcoming unless there is a
profound change in the prevailing conventions of commerce today. . . . [Affluent
nations] should look to the welfare of the weaker and poorer nations in business
dealings with them, for the revenues the latter make from the sale of home produced
goods are needed for their own support. . . . But while the ability to earn their own
living by trade is the over-riding need, there is still need also for grants, loans or
investments: they should be given in the spirit of generosity and without greed. . . .*
The establishment of an authentic economic order on a world-wide scale can
only come about by abolishing profiteering, nationalistic ambitions, greed
for political domination, schemes of military strategy, and intrigues for
spreading and imposing ideologies. . . . Developing nations . . . should not
forget that progress is based not only on foreign aid but on the full exploitation of native resources and on the development of their own talents
and traditions. . . . In many instances there exists a pressing need to
reassess economic and social structures, but caution must be exercised
regarding proposed solutions which may be untimely, especially those
which offer material advantage while militating against man's spiritual
nature and advancement. . . .

Briefly then the argument is that the solidarity of mankind requires
greater cooperation, but this cooperation must not produce a new dependence, nor can it achieve its aim unless the internal problems of the
countries concerned are taken in hand and their own resources and talents
recruited for the task. Where aid is needed in terms of training, grants,
loans and investments and in better trading opportunities, it should
go hand in hand with the establishment of an authentic international
economic order and with abandonment of nationalistic goals, desire for
domination and military and ideological ambitions.

The encyclical of Pope Paul VI, *Populorum Progressio*, published in 1967,
took up the theme of development and dealt with it in greater depth.
Stating the essence of development as seeking "to do more and know
more and have more in order to be more,"[208] the document warns against
one of the errors of developmental thinking:[209]

Development cannot be limited to mere economic growth . . . it must be
complete . . . promote the good of every man and of the whole man. In the
design of God every man is called to develop and fulfill himself, for every life
is a vocation . . . endowed with intelligence and freedom as he is for his
salvation . . . this self-fulfillment is not something optional. . . . But each
man is a member of society, he is part of the whole of mankind . . . so we

[208] Par. 6.
[209] Pars. 14–17.

have inherited from past generations and we have benefitted from the work
of contemporaries . . . and for this reason we have obligations towards all.

All economic growth is ambivalent. It is essential for man's development,
but if it becomes his master, and he its slave, then that desire for economic
growth becomes mere avarice.[210]

> . . . both for nations and for individual men, avarice is the most evident
> form of moral under-development. . . . Less human conditions are lack of
> material needs, moral deficiencies, oppressive social structures. Conditions
> that are more human are, possession of necessities, victory over social evils,
> the growth of knowledge, the acquisition of culture, esteem for others . . .
> the spirit of poverty, cooperation for the common good, the acknowledge-
> ment of the supreme values and of God as their source and finality.

The encyclical considered the problems of socially irresponsible private
ownership, the right of the state to expropriate, and the selfishness of
those who do not use their wealth and resources for the common good,[211]
while recognizing how much has been achieved by capital and labour in
development. The right of the national government to concern itself with
population control is accepted, but the means to that end must be in
accordance with God's law.[212] And the duty of human solidarity demands
that the rich should help the poor.[213]

> The struggle against destitution, though urgent and necessary, is not
> enough. It is a question rather of building a world where every man no
> matter what his race, religion or nationality can live a full human life, freed
> from servitude imposed on him by other men or by natural forces over which
> he has not sufficient control. . . . Let each one examine his conscience. . . .
> Is he prepared to support out of his own pocket, works and undertakings
> organised in favour of the most destitute? Is he ready to pay higher taxes so
> that the public authorities can intensify their efforts in favour of develop-
> ment? Is he ready to pay a higher price for imported goods, so that the
> producer may be justly rewarded, or to leave his country, if necessary, and if
> he is young, in order to assist in this development of young nations?

As individuals, so nations have this responsibility to care for others.
While seeking to give their own people a decent standard of living, they
must contribute to the development of the human race. A world fund of
the money otherwise spent on armaments suggests itself as an obvious
necessity. Agreements between nations should be free of the will to
dominate. Developing countries should not be overwhelmed by excessive

[210] Pars. 18, 19, 21.
[211] Pars. 23–24, 26–28.
[212] Par. 37. See *Mater et Magistra*, pars. 185 ff.
[213] Par. 47.

rates of interest on their debts, and those who provide capital must be assured that it will be used for the purposes agreed and with reasonable efficiency.[214]

The importance of equity in trade relations is emphasized. To be a *fair* contract, the positions of the contracting parties must be equal; international competition, therefore, is tolerable only if it allows justice to all.[215] The question of racial prejudice is relevant in this context.[216]

> It is still an obstacle to collaboration . . . and a cause of division . . . where individuals and families see the inviolable rights of the human person held in scorn as they themselves are unjustly subjected to a regime of discrimination because of their race or their colour.

By contrast, universal charity is shown in a spirit of true brotherliness, nationally and internationally. Particularly must visitors from foreign countries be welcomed, and those who give technical assistance in countries overseas should do so with due respect for those they are helping. Between civilisations, as between persons, sincere dialogue creates brotherhood. The service that many young people are giving to the developing nations is especially to be praised. There must still be a hope for, and a working towards, an adequate world authority.[217]

Populorum Progressio reminds us that important though the economic element in development is, it is not the only or indeed the main indicator of progress from underdevelopment to development. It is a means to the end of development, not the end in itself. Without an adequacy of material resources, human life remains stunted—but it is stunted too if quality of life is judged purely in material terms. In looking at the material indicators of development, the quantifiable, the statistical, we must keep this in mind. That said, the statistics do give a useful first indication of the extent to which some areas and countries are deprived of the material needs of a fully human existence. There are several such indicators; taken together, they give us an initial guide to the nature of underdevelopment. Literacy rates, life expectancy, calorie intake and annual average income per head are useful and obvious such indicators.[218]

We find that in the 1970s, developed countries as a whole had a literacy rate of 97%, the underdeveloped 50%, with life expectancy of 71 years as opposed to 48, and a calorie intake, in the case of the developed countries,

[214] Pars. 48–54.
[215] Pars. 56–61.
[216] Par. 63.
[217] Pars. 66–79.
[218] A Physical Quality of Life Index based on an infant mortality, life expectancy and basic literacy has been worked out by the U.N. and O.E.C.D. to give a more precise guide. M. D. Morris, *Measuring the Condition of the World's Poor* (Oxford, 1979).

16% above established standards, 2% below in the case of the under-developed. Per capita income ranged from $5,971 in Switzerland to $88 in Indonesia and $87 in Ethiopia.[219] By any standards, such disparities between the rich and the poor argue emphatically that we have not fulfilled the Creator's plan that the riches of this world should be generally available to all his people—the more so since the overall statistics disguise the suffering from the deprivation and malnutrition which afflict specific areas. Cretinism, pellagra, protein energy due to Vitamin A deficiencies, all these diseases are to be found endemic in parts of Asia, Africa and Latin America,[220] while the natural hazards of flood and drought occur in areas often afflicted already by poverty and other forms of deprivation. Against this perfectly accurate picture of poverty, there has to be set the considerable achievement of the third world over the last three decades. Average income has doubled, life expectancy over all has increased from 43 to 53 years and 50% of the adults are literate as opposed to 30% previously. Yet still so much remains to be done. Some 750 million are still living at subsistence level, and in low income countries life expectancy is still 24 years below that of those living in industrialised areas. There too some 600 million are illiterate and one-third of primary school age children do not get the opportunity of such schooling.[221]

The general picture of the difference between the two groups of nations, however, does not reflect the true complexity of the situation.[222] There are vast differences between regions and within regions. *South Asia* (India, Bangladesh, Pakistan, Burma, Afghanistan, Sri Lanka, Nepal and Bhutan) is perhaps most uniformly underdeveloped—though India has a considerable industrial sector and potential. *East and Southeast Asia* (South Korea, Taiwan, Hong Kong, Singapore, Indonesia, Philippines, Thailand, Malaysia, Vietnam, North Korea, Laos and Cambodia) are more varied. Here South Korea, Taiwan, Hong Kong and Singapore are highly industrialised, strong exporters and comparatively high in national income per head. Indonesia, on the other hand, is underdeveloped by any standards.

Latin America (Brazil, Mexico, Argentina, Venezuela, Colombia, Ecuador, Peru, Chile, Bolivia, Paraguay, Uraguay, Guyana, Surinam)

---

[219] G. M. Meier, *Leading Issues in Economic Development* (New York, 1976), pp. 12 ff. L. Wolf Philips, "Why Third World", *The Third World Review*, January 1979, gives basic data on 115 middle and low income developing countries.

[220] On health and nutrition in developing countries, Meier, op. cit., pp. 496 ff. *North/South: A Programme for Survival*, [The Brandt Report] (London, 1980), pp. 90 ff. *Development Report 1980* (O.U.P., 1980), pp. 59 ff.

[221] *World Development Report*, pp. 1–2.

[222] See the O.E.C.D., *Facing the Future* (Paris, 1979), pp. 197 ff., and Meier, op. cit., pp. 12–13.

and *Central America and the Caribbean Islands* (Mexico, Guatemala, Honduras, Nicaragua, El Salvador, Costa Rica, Panama, Cuba, Jamaica and the smaller islands) present the widest contrasts—Brazil, Mexico and Argentina being responsible for over 40% of the developing world's total industrial production in the mid-1970s, while Venezuela had the highest income per head ($2,570) in 1976 because of its oil riches. Yet dependence on external economic forces, and multinational companies especially, has had adverse effects on the course of development in the past and too often works against the good of the people as a whole.[223] There is every indication that this unfortunate pattern is likely to continue in the future and give credence to those seeking revolutionary change.

North Africa and the Middle East present a contrast between oil rich countries such as Saudi Arabia, Kuwait, Iraq, Iran and Libya, and those not so blessed (the Yemens, Egypt) with countries like Morocco and Lebanon in between. *Subsaharan Africa* presents, with South Asia, the greatest problems of poverty in the underdeveloped world. The 48 countries in this region, with the exception of South Africa and to a lesser extent Nigeria, Ghana, the Gold Coast and Kenya, are almost uniformly deficient in all the important indicators of development.

Such then, in overall terms, are the facts and the ethical issues concerning the contrast between the developed and underdeveloped countries. The duty of the developed countries is to do their part through technical assistance, aid in the forms of goods or investment, and justice in trade, to help the underdeveloped countries achieve the level of material well-being that the release of their free human potential requires. The duty of the less developed countries is to look to the good of the whole of their people rather than any sectional good and to put basic human requirements before grandiose schemes of national glory that can only be maintained at the expense of these basic human requirements.

B. AID, TRADE AND DEVELOPMENT

It is convenient to make a distinction between "aid" on the one hand and "trade" on the other in considering the ways in which the developed countries can help the underdeveloped—though like all such distinctions there is a tendency for the two concepts to overlap. Aid can take several forms—technical assistance, goods or supplies (aid in kind, in other words) or the transfer of financial resources through loans or grants. The help that is given under the heading of "trade" likewise takes several forms. It can consist in ensuring fairer terms for the trade they already do

[223] O.E.C.D. *Report*, p. 213. M. Niedergang, *The 20 Latin Americas* (London, 1976), 1:14. J. D. Cockroft et al., *Dependence and Under-Development* (New York, 1972).

with the developed world, or in some way helping them to overcome particular difficulties they face in the type of trade they do—or assisting them to find new ways of increasing their overseas earnings by developing new export markets while at the same time encouraging home industry. This latter may have the added advantage of reducing dependence on imports.[224] Clearly, in practice, these types of aid and trade overlap. The technical assistance enables the agricultural and industrial sectors to become more efficient in saving imports or developing exports. Investment and the development of trade in their turn assist and produce the conditions in which more skilled workers and technicians can be trained. But the examination of the sort of assistance that can be given by the developed to the underdeveloped under these separate headings helps us through a complex subject.

The idea of "aid" from one nation to another first became an important factor in the relationship between states through the Marshall Plan[225]— America's way of helping Europe to secure itself economically after the ravages of the Second World War. It included technical assistance; for example, through the Anglo-American Productivity Council, British industry was encouraged to learn what it could from the American way of doing things; but the aid given was primarily financial, through loans and grants.

The awareness of the problems of the third world[226] and the need for a response to them came in the late 1950s and early 1960s and was partly the result of the interplay between the super-powers in the context of the cold war. The basic mechanism of international economic cooperation had been established in a very limited form in the immediate post-war period. At the Bretton Woods Conference in 1944,[227] which was concerned with working out the economic implications of the Atlantic Charter, Keynes suggested the creation of an international currency by converting the existing ones into a new international form. The scheme did not go

[224] The difficulties of "import substitution" have become apparent in recent years, "only with the most meticulous economic planning and in situations in which domestic competition is present can the import substitution strategy lead to real economic development". C. P. Kindleberger and B. Herrick, *Economic Development* (London, 1977), p. 285.

[225] Friedlander and Oser, op. cit., pp. 577 ff. D. Thomson, *Europe since Waterloo*, pp. 823 ff. H. B. Price, *The Marshall Plan and its Meaning* (O.U.P., 1955). On 5 June 1947, George Marshall, the American Secretary of State, announced that European trade had to be restored by American assistance or else America as well as Europe would be threatened. Between December 1947 and the conclusion of the Plan in 1951, some $15 billion, most of it in grants, had been poured into Europe.

[226] On the meaning of the phrase see *Third World Quarterly*, January 1979, article by Leslie Wolf Philips.

[227] Harrod, op. cit., pp. 525 ff. W. Ashworth, *A Short History of the International Economy* (London, 1965), pp. 263 ff.

through, but an International Monetary Fund and an International Bank for Reconstruction and Development were established, the first to provide loans to members to help them meet their balance of payment deficiencies, the second to make loans for overseas investment at commercial rates. The International Development Association was set up in 1960 to make soft loans at lower rates and longer periods. These institutions, together with the International Finance Corporation, established in 1956 to encourage the flow of private capital in the underdeveloped countries, constitute the World Bank.[228]

In 1976, the amount invested by the developed countries in the third world was about $53 billion and this accounted for some 18% of the total investment in those countries; for the poorest, the proportion was as high as one-third. Overall, between 1960 and 1976, the proportion of the Gross National Product of the underdeveloped countries accounted for by outside investment was increased from 2% to 4.5%. Yet official aid hardly increased at all—the growth came from O.P.E.C. and bank loans; official aid had accounted for 64% of the inflow in 1960, in 1977 it was only 32%. Most of the absolute increase in investment had gone to the higher income countries; but since the loans in question were mainly nonconcessional at commercial rates, they imposed a heavy burden of repayment, even on those comparatively wealthier countries.[229]

The concessional loans have gone mainly to the poorer countries, which is as it should be, but overall the performance of the developed nations in this regard has become worse rather than better. In 1970 the United Nations suggested that 1% of the Gross National Product of the richer nations should be devoted to aid, of which 0.7% should be official development or grants. The overall figure has been reached—but official aid has declined. With the honourable exception of the Scandinavian countries and the Netherlands, the European performance has been poor. Instead of the 0.7% of G.N.P. recommended, official aid has only amounted to 0.35%. In the light of the criticism that much aid is misused and that, therefore, we are justified in being less than enthusiastic about it, it is interesting to note that the Brandt Report concluded[230]

> it would be wrong not to recognise that the overwhelming proportion of aid is usefully spent for the problems for which it was intended and aid has already done much to diminish hardships in low income countries and to help them provide a basis for progress in rural development, health and education. For the poorest, aid is essential for survival.

[228] F. S. Northedge and M. J. Grieve, *A Hundred Years of International Relations* (London, 1974), pp. 319 ff. *North/South: A Programme for Survival*, pp. 201 ff. H. G. Johnson, *Economic Policies Towards Less Developed Countries* (London, 1967), pp. 16 ff.
[229] *O.E.C.D. Report*, p. 270. *North/South: A Programme for Survival*, p. 223.
[230] P. 226.

Private investment by large corporations, especially the multinationals, plays a considerable and controversial part in the investment input of the first to the third worlds. Some 12% of the total of such investments came from this source in the 1970s. It mainly went to countries which could offer greater political stability and adequate economic incentives, places like Brazil and Mexico, Singapore and Hong Kong—70% of it going to just 15 such countries.[231] One author has made a point of delivering an indictment of the role of such companies overall, seeing it as almost entirely negative. The case is overstated though it has much truth in it; she is able, however, to quote one instance where, given the right conditions (a strong government ready to ensure that the company meets its responsibilities), the exploitation and other evils she detects can be controlled and a partnership valuable to all parties is possible.[232] Since the third world needs all the help it can get, it is better to encourage multinationals to invest, subject to effective social controls, than to dismiss them out of hand as incorrigible.

Technical aid can take several forms. Organisations like the British Council in this country, for example, help to finance students from overseas who are studying scientific and technical subjects, the Inter-university Council provides British staff for universities in third world countries, while the Technical, Educational and Training Organisation helps third world institutions develop their own staffs, facilities and curricula. The Overseas Development Association also has an extensive programme for financing those studying agriculture, medicine, science and technology in Britain. There are also organisations like Oxfam and Christian Aid which are able to work with local people in developing their own basic skills to improve housing, agriculture and develop small scale industrial projects. The whole field of intermediate technology is of immediate relevance here[233] and the developing countries themselves are beginning to see the advantage of it.

The overall aim of all forms of aid should be to help the recipient nations to help themselves by developing their own resources. In cases of emergency they may need material aid, machines, medicine, temporary housing, food, but dependence on external sources for food, for example, in normal times is an intolerable situation for the country concerned. There is no more urgent task than that of helping those countries which

---

[231] North/South: A Programme for Survival, p. 187. See also O.E.C.D. Report, pp. 260 ff.

[232] Susan George, How the Other Half Dies (London, 1977). The case of effective partnership was between that of the Kenyan Government, Booker McConnell and various development agencies, in the development of the sugar industry (op. cit., pp. 182 ff.).

[233] A. Moyes, The Poor Man's Wisdom (Oxfam, 1979). N. Jequier, Appropriate Technology: Problems and Promises (Paris: O.E.C.D., 1976). K. Darrow and R. Pam, Appropriate Technology: Sourcebook, vol. 1. (Stanford, California, 1978).

need to develop their food production potential to do so, and we will consider this matter more at length when we deal with agricultural economics. For the moment, we will concern ourselves with what needs to be done to develop these other aspects—the industry and trade of the third world—so that it can strengthen its economies.

There are two issues involved in improving the trading position of the underdeveloped countries. The first is making sure that the prices they receive for the commodities and raw materials they export are fair and stable; since most of their export earnings come from this source, getting justice here is the key to their trading future. The second is making sure that the third world gets a chance to develop its manufacturing industry.

Commodities (for example cocoa, coffee, sugar, jute, fibres, rubber, tin, copper and other minerals and metals) account for nearly 60% of third world exports. Oil accounts for another 20%—which is provided by a group of the wealthier states in the Near East, Africa and Latin America. Of the manufactures which account for the rest of third world earnings, these too come from a very small number of countries in Southeast Asia and Latin America. Of the 150 plus nations who are members of the United Nations Committee for Trade, Aid and Development (made up of the third world countries), less than twenty are in the position of being oil exporters or manufacturers with an export market on any scale.

Commodity prices are notorious for the wild way in which they fluctuate, in the 1960s and 1970s for example, sugar oscillated between £12 and £650, and copper between £300 and £1,200 a ton. These fluctuations make proper planning difficult, encourage profligacy in time of affluence and despair in time of slump. One solution that seems to have much to recommend it is the building up of buffer stocks so that the heights and hollows of production and the market can be levelled off, to the benefit of the producer and the customer.

Industrial development can be of two kinds—firstly, the building up of modern industries to turn over the products of, and use the techniques learned from the mature economies; secondly, by developing local industries on the basis of potential or traditional skills and local needs, but with the addition of those aspects of modern technology and organisation which help improve efficiency; and finally, by processing raw materials in the country of their origin so that the greater value that goes into them produces higher prices when exported.[234] The problem is that the rich nations alone have the resources to finance the buffer stocks, while any trading competition from the developing industries of the third

---

[234] O.E.C.D. Report, pp. 261 ff.; North/South: A Programme for Survival, pp. 172 ff. Meier, op. cit., pp. 395 ff., 735 ff., 753 ff. Kindleberger and Herrick, op. cit., pp. 129 ff., pp. 202 ff.

world naturally has repercussions at home which can be registered in political terms and induce caution on the part of politicians beholden to an electorate.[235]

The tremendous growth in world economic activity and trade in the period between 1948 and 1970 highlighted the injustices of the world monetary and international trading system. World output doubled between 1870 and 1939, between 1948 and 1957 it doubled again, and between 1957 and 1974 it had increased by a further 150%.[236] But with 90% of the trade in manufactured goods taking place between the industrialised nations, the third world was largely shut out from sharing in the increased wealth that the growth in production and trade brought with it, while commodity prices fluctuated or lagged.

In the early 1960s, the third world, realising that nothing would be done for it unless it did it for itself, decided to combine to try to pressure their richer nations into giving them a fairer deal. They formed the United Nations Commission on Trade, Aid and Development and, in 1964, this became an official part of the United Nations Organization. The first meeting was attended by fifty-five nations, the second, in December 1978/January 1979, by 132, and it has met at three or four yearly intervals since. The last, at Manilla in May 1979, was attended by 152 nations. There it was agreed to finance buffer stocks, though less liberally than the third world had hoped, while they agreed also to assist in the processing of commodities to increase the trading effectiveness of the producers.[237] Gradually, then, it would seem the light is dawning; whether it is enough or in time remains to be seen.

Increased food production and the development of industry and trade are then the keys to a better life for the poorer nations. But the concern of the 1960s and 1970s for the environment and the apparent danger of running out of essential raw materials seemed to cast doubt on further industrial development, while many saw the answer to food shortages, and the other problems of development, in population control. Let us take the latter first. The Council referred to this question as follows:[238]

Since there is a widespread opinion that the population expansion of the world or at least some particular countries, should be kept in check by all

[235] It is calculated that only 2% of the work force in the industries concerned has been affected by cheap textile imports into Great Britain. But as *North/South: A Programme for Survival* (p. 176) points out, proper cooperation and provision is required if such displacements are to be acceptable.

[236] *Annual Register* (1974), pp. 476–77.

[237] *North/South: A Programme for Survival*, p. 150.

[238] Par. 87. As indicated above, it was further commented on in *Populorum Progressio*. *Mater et Magistra*, pars. 185 ff., is also relevant.

possible means, by every kind of intervention and by public authority, the
Council exhorts all men to beware of all solutions, whether uttered in public
or in private, or imposed at any time which transgress the natural law . . . it
is of great importance that all should have an opportunity to cultivate a
genuinely human sense of responsibility which will take account of the
circumstances of the time and situation and will respect the divine law . . .
people should be discreetly informed of scientific advances in research into
the methods of birth regulation, whenever the value of these methods
has been thoroughly proved and their conformity with the moral order
established.

The facts about the increase in world population have been so well
rehearsed and publicized of late that there is hardly need to dwell upon
them. Briefly, between 1650 and 1850 world population doubled from
about 600 million to 12 hundred million (1.2 billion). Between 1850 and
1950 it doubled again from 1.2 to 2.4 billion; estimates of what the
population will be by the end of the century vary from 5.5 to 6.5
billion.[239]

A complex of factors affect population growth—adequate resources of
food and the other requirements of a decent existence, a stable social order
free of wars and serious internal disturbance, and an ability to prevent
or control drought, flood and natural disasters, but it is the decline in
mortality which has been the most influential factor in recent global
population growth. Improvements in medical technology and in public
health provisions have been the main causes. The case of Ceylon, where
anti-malarial spraying more than halved the death rate in the first post-war
decade, illustrates the momentous impact of such advances.

Demographers note, on the basis of the experience of Western Europe,
the various stages of population growth and decline. In the first phase,
death rates and birth rates are about equal. In phase two, with the advent
of a higher standard of living, improvement in public health and control
of disease, death rates fall while birth rates remain as before. In phase three
the two come nearer together again so that population growth slows.
Phase four results in an increasingly ageing and declining population.[240]

Nothing is more certain in population statistics than the fallibility of
predictions about the future. The only real guide we have is what has

[239] J. H. Lowry, *World Population and Food Supply* (London, 1976), p. 1. C. M. Cipolla,
The Economic History of World Population (London, 1964), pp. 99 ff.

[240] Lowry, op. cit., pp. 4 ff. R. Pressat, *Population* (London, 1973), p. 15. Stage four
produces the problem of the decline in the number of young people to support the growing
number of aged. A nation needs a birth rate of 16.8 per thousand if it is to grow rather than
stagnate or decline. The latest U.N. data show that throughout Europe, with the exception
of the South, the birthrate is lower than 16.8 per thousand. (R. Sassone, *Handbook on
Population* [4th ed.] [Santa Ana, California, 1978], p. 111).

happened in the past; the demographic transition experienced in Europe which first underwent the population explosion would indicate that as the standard of living of the population generally rises, the birth rate declines to become more nearly equal with the death rate. This seems now to be happening internationally and, what is more, it seems to be happening even in underdeveloped countries.

The Director of the United Nations Fund for population activities, Rafael Salas, reported that the birth rate had fallen by as much as 15% in countries that account for more than two-thirds of the population of the third world since the 1960s. *The Conference on Trends in the World's Population* came to the same conclusion at its meeting in London in November 1978.[241] The causes for the decline in population, once the economic conditions improve, are not clear—but several factors may be suggested. Any decline in recent years, especially in the developed countries, is clearly partly or largely due to the availability of contraceptive devices. Whether contraceptive techniques had much effect on the decline in birth rate that ocurred in Europe in the period after about 1880 (stage three of demographic transition outlined above) is more problematical. A movement to make contraceptive practices more widely known was evident early in the century, and evidence is available that the nobility of France, under the old regime, and the bourgeois of Geneva, were indulging in such methods of family limitation at an earlier stage.[242] Whether these practices were widely enough known throughout society as a whole to effect birth rate so widely and, if not, what other factors affected either fertility or marital relationships, we have no means of knowing with certainty.[243]

The reason for family limitation being practised in affluent societies is connected with the desire to give children better opportunities, the reluctance of women to be so bound to home and family as before, recognition of the difficulty of bringing children up, a preference for spending incomes on better living conditions and leisure opportunities—a mixture, therefore, of idealism and selfishness. Family planning is compatible with the ideal of Christian marriage, indeed properly understood it is essential to it. But, as we have seen, the means and the motives must be compatible with God's law.

---

[241] The fear that world population will continue to double in increasingly shorter periods is not borne out by U.N. predictions which project a world population of 9 billion by 2025, 11 billion by 2050 and a stabilizing thereafter at 12 billion. *O.E.C.D. Report*, p. 15.

[242] Pressat, op. cit., pp. 56 ff.

[243] Recent evidence from Sri Lanka suggests that breast feeding is a more effective element in family planning than all official efforts to spread knowledge of modern means of contraception. Malcolm Potts, *The Guardian*, 25 April 1979.

The paradox is that the surest way to bring about a slowing of population growth where this is desirable is to see that the standard of living for all rises.[244] Until this happens, traditional peasant societies, where poverty means that the only security in old age is one's children, will continue to resist such family planning as is morally justifiable. It is, however, unfortunately true that much of the concern with family limitation is not moved by moral motives, but by a blind and irrational fear of the future. If unchecked, this fear will inevitably lead to the decline of particular societies with all the problems that involves. If the case for an increasing population, as a general proposition always and everywhere in all circumstances is not convincing, neither is the case for population stability, still less decline. There is a case for slowing the growth or stabilising it where the immediate strain on resources in a particular country is too great, while welcoming the encouragement of population increase in countries which have the potential to provide for a larger population. A general will for "global control" of population is as arrogant in its assumptions in theory as it is impossible of achievement in practice.

As we shall shortly see, the evidence is that sufficient food and resources are available (and will continue to be available in the future if past experience, the only rational basis for prediction, is anything to go by) to meet the needs of increase in the world's population in the foreseeable future. This being so, the present concern with controlling population by practically any means can only be regarded as a panic reaction. Already the wilder predictions of doomsters have been proved wrong. Paul Ehrlich predicted in 1968 that hundreds of millions would starve to death in the 1970s.[245] Disaster on that scale did not take place—and starvation where it occurs is usually a result of human mismanagement. So far from being incapable of supporting present and future population, a responsible official of the Food and Agricultural Organisation of the United Nations has reckoned that the world's resources would enable food production to be increased by a factor of 50 over the next century if proper steps were taken.[246] This figure exceeds Colin Clark's estimation that the world's potential agricultural and forest land could supply 47 billion at American

[244] According to the *World Development Report 1980* "once a high enough level of development has been reached, fertility has fallen without exception. Where there is strong religious or cultural resistance to contraception, as in Ireland, fertility fell through delays in the age of marriage and an increase in life long celibacy, rather than through family planning" (p. 67).

[245] P. Ehrlich, *The Population Bomb* (New York, 1968), p. 39.

[246] Dr. Pawley at the Scandinavian Economists' Conference, 1971. His address was later published in *Ceres* the F.A.O. Journal, no. 22 (July/August, 1971) under the title "In the Year 2070".

and 157 billion at Asian standards.[247] It is also confirmed by recent experience. In the last twenty-five years food production has more than kept pace with population growth on a global scale.[248]

But if the fears of overall *global* starvation are not founded in fact or the sufferings that come from malnutrition do not occur on a global, but on a local and particularised scale, at this level they are very real; here population control by moral means may be required. But population control is not enough. It is necessary also to make food supplies available to the people who suffer in this way. However, this can only be a first aid. More fundamentally, the real need is to make each country self-supporting in food by the development of its own agricultural resources.

Apart from the question of food supplies, fear has been expressed in recent years about the inadequacy of other resources or the damage to the environment that will result from our trying to meet the ever-increasing demands of a growing world population seeking an ever higher standard of living which depends on complex technology. On this question, the Council has nothing specific to say—although its observations on economic progress and production indicate the proper moral context of such an answer to these questions.[249]

> The ultimate and basic purpose of economic production does not consist merely in the increase in goods produced nor in profit, nor prestige, it is directed to the service of man, in his totality, taking into account his material needs and the requirements of his intellectual, moral, spiritual and religious life. . . .

The Apostolic Letter of Paul VI, *Octogesimo Adveniens* (1971), deals specifically with the issues[250] which had become an increasing cause for comment by the end of the 1960s.

> Man is suddenly becoming aware that by an ill-considered exploitation of nature he risks destroying it and becoming in his turn the victim of this degradation. Not only is the material environment becoming a permanent menace—pollution and refuse, new illnesses and absolute destructive capacity —but the human framework is no longer under man's control, thus creating an environment for tomorrow which may well be intolerable. This is a

---

[247] *Population Growth and Land Use* (London, 1977), p. 153.

[248] *O.E.C.D. Report* gives the increase in food production as 130% over 25 years (pp. 17, 245). In the period 1950 to 1970 world population increased from 2,400 million to 3,632 million—just over 50% (Sassone, op. cit., p. 109, quoting U.N. figures). Between 1960 and 1970 and 1970 and 1980, population growth in developing countries declined from 2.5 to 2.4% (*World Development Report*, p. 99).

[249] *Gaudium et Spes*, par. 64.

[250] Par. 21.

wide-ranging social problem which concerns the entire human family. The Christian must turn to these new perceptions in order to take on responsibility, together with the rest of men, for a destiny which from now on is shared by all.

Doubts about the adequacies of the world's resources of things needful for life—apart from food—have at first sight a basic plausibility. As Professor Beckerman has noted, since they are by definition finite, they can be imagined as coming to an end. He also noted, however, that this exhausting of resources has not stopped economic development taking place since the time of Pericles.[251] The reasons are two-fold. Man has always been able to find substitute substances or sources of supply for the essentials. More fundamentally, the exhaustibility of the earth's resources is only notional. The calculation of the potential supplies of the ninety or so elements from which all our material needs are supplied is given in such gigantic figures that thousands, even millions of years, would be needed to exhaust them.

Examples of man's ability to find substitutes for materials that are no longer so readily available or are more expensive are with us everywhere today—not least in the plastics which in so many ways serve the purposes that until a short while ago only wood or metal could. That the land, sea and air still contain limitless quantities of the elements from which all things are made is to the laymen less evident until the calculations of the obvious works of reference regarding such resources are considered.[252] And we must keep in mind that nothing, apart from what is used in nuclear fission, is ever destroyed in use—it becomes available to us in another form, often potentially reclaimable.

That the facts concerning the resources theoretically available to us is very impressive is one thing—making them available is another. How much of this vast wealth in the earth's surface is reclaimable is a matter for

[251] In his inaugural lecture as Professor of Political Economy at London University (*Times*, 31 May 1974), he was particularly scathing of the statistical methods used in the Club of Rome's *Limits to Growth*.

[252] Sassone, op. cit., pp. 66 ff., takes the figures from the *U.S. Minerals Yearbook, Encyclopedia Brittanica* and the *Handbook of Chemistry and Physics* and shows that, "When we compare the amount available to the amount produced each year, we find that the lithosphere of the earth contains enough of each element to last more than 900 million years at the present rate of use." See also B. F. Skinner, *Earth Resources* [2nd ed.] (Englewood Cliffs, 1976), and *O.E.C.D. Report*, pp. 26 ff., which predicts energy resources will be sufficient for long term world consumption needs at ten to fifteen times the present level, that overall physical scarcity of raw materials is not likely and the protection of the physical environment does not look like imposing insuperable problems. In all these areas however, specific problems exist that are a cause for concern and require constant effort; but they do not justify overall gloom and doom.

investigation. What is to be noted is that the scares raised by predictions of imminent disaster exist because those who raise them base their prediction on the exhausting of the easily accessible supplies; only 20% of the earth's surface has been prospected, the most easily accessible resources have been exploited first.

Colin Clark notes that he drew up a paper for the United Nations Conference on Resources (U.N.S.C.U.R.) in 1949 in which, based on the best information available, he attempted to predict the rate of exhaustion of basic resources. Had he been correct, lead, zinc, copper, oil and chromium ore would already have run out.[253] There are real problems about finding new supplies, or adequate substitutes for some materials (for example, tin, tungsten and mercury)[254] and while both short and long term fossil fuel resources (coal, oil, gas) are abundant, the more easily accessible have been exploited first—which means increased difficulty and increased costs in extraction of the remainder. As to alternatives, there are sources of energy still untouched which will more than satisfy future demand.[255]

There are then problems concerning man's ability to wrest needful supplies from the world God has given him, but these have been there from the beginning. However, human ingenuity, proper husbanding and technological advance overcame this problem in the past. The reasonable assumption is that, spurred on by our increasing awareness of the dangers which face us if we are complacent, we will do the same in the future. We cannot be certain we will—nor can we be certain we will not—but while despair breeds fatalism, hope breeds the resolve to succeed.

Another of the problems that is raised by economic development, particularly through industrial and technological advance, is that of environmental pollution. The air can be affected by chemicals such as carbon monoxide, hydrocarbons and nitrogen oxides and by thermal pollution, while the noise and the smog of cities is unhealthy and dangerous. Water, into which substances such as mercury, D.D.T., oil and oil refinery effluents, acids, radio-activity, detergents, sewage find their way, and land similarly polluted by chemicals, salt and radio-activity pose similar problems.[256]

[253] *Population Growth* (Santa Ana, California, 1975), p. 8.

[254] Skinner, op. cit., pp. 75 ff.

[255] See *O.E.C.D. Report*, p. 29. Skinner, op. cit., asserts "there is neither an energy crisis nor an energy shortage: we have vast amounts of energy, more than we could ever use" (p. 53).

[256] The various kinds and sources of pollution are discussed in L. Hodges, *Environmental Pollution* (New York, 1977). The book is concerned with the situation in the U.S.A. but is relevant in principle to any industrialised society.

The fact of environmental pollution is indisputable, and the dangers it presents are likewise indisputable. Yet it has been shown that, given the will to reduce it, it can be done and can be done very effectively. The classic case is London's fog and London's river. Until the early 1960s the pea-soupers in London, the result of the natural climatic conditions at certain times of the year together with industrial and domestic smog, were a regular recurrence. But Londoners have not had a pea-souper since the 1960s because of the enforcement of an effective clean air policy. The cleanliness of the Thames is becoming, year by year, more apparent; the return of fish to its waters is one of the signs of a more hygienic habitat for them. There are costs involved in the control of pollution certainly, but the savings that result in terms of better health and less inconvenience more than compensate for them in the long run.[257]

X. Agricultural Economics and the Ethics of Agricultural Development

So far in this chapter on the ethics of economic life we have been mainly concerned with industry and its problems and potentialities. The perspective is given us by modern economics, which is indeed largely concerned with the industrial aspects and implications of wealth creation and distribution; agriculture tends to be seen as a junior partner. To some extent this is inevitable since it is in the capacity of man to manufacture goods on a scale which would enable him to supply mass markets which has led to the take-off in economic development since the nineteenth century. The economic revolution which has changed the world has been seen precisely as the *industrial* revolution—yet in truth it has been agricultural too; it is man's capacity to exploit the world's natural resources through agriculture and mining which has stoked the industrial growth. For that reason, therefore, agriculture and agricultural development is a key factor in modern industrial expansion. More significantly and fundamentally, it is the food production capacity of the human race which, more than anything else, will determine whether the huge population the world now contains, and will continue to contain, will be properly nourished. Nothing added a sharper edge to the arguments of those who predicted doom in the 1960s and 1970s than the apparent impossibility they saw in

[257] See Hodges, op. cit., passim, but p. 442, "Although one often hears claim that pollution control will be enormously expensive . . . if the people of the U.S.A. would be willing to forego one average year's rise in the standard of living as it is customarily measured (neglecting social costs) a vastly improved environment—with all its benefits—would be possible."

the world continuing to produce the food needed. In the short run they were proven wrong,[258] but the long term problems remain.

The Council, in considering the question of economic justice, did not neglect the rights and responsibilities of the agriculturalist.[259]

> To fulfil the requirements of justice and equity, every effort must be made to put an end, as soon as possible, to the immense economic inequalities which exist in the world and increase from day to day. . . . In view of the special difficulties in production and marketing in agriculture, country people must be helped to improve methods of production and marketing, introduce necessary developments and renewal and to achieve fair return for their products, lest they continue as often happens, in the state of inferior citizens. The farmers themselves, especially young farmers, ought to apply themselves eagerly to bettering their professional skill without which the advancement of farming is impossible. . . . In several economically retarded areas there exist large and sometimes very extensive rural estates which are only slightly cultivated or not cultivated at all . . . while the majority of the population have no land or possess very small holdings. . . . Not infrequently those who are hired as labourers or till a portion of the land as tenants receive a wage or income unworthy of a human being. . . . Reforms are called for in these different situations. . . . Estates if insufficiently cultivated must even be divided up and given to those who will be able to make them productive. In this event the necessary resources and equipment must be supplied, especially educational facilities and proper cooperative organisations. However, when the common good calls for expropriation, compensation must be made and is to be calculated according to equity with all the circumstances taken into account.

The observations of the Council, therefore, look to distinct types of problems facing agriculture. The first is in giving aid to farmers, agricultural workers and peasants who are not oppressed by unjust systems of land tenure but who, for reasons peculiar to the nature of agriculture, cannot alone organise themselves sufficiently to meet the needs of modern production in agriculture and, therefore, fulfill the role society requires of them. The second type of problem envisaged is precisely that where the system of land tenure and the general social conditions are so unjust that

---

[258] Two countries, America and Canada, produce 80% of the wheat traded on the world market. In the late 1960s and early 1970s these countries ran down their stocks so that when in 1972/1973 there was drought in Africa and poor harvests forced the Soviet Union to buy extensively on world markets, prices more than doubled in two years. Not until 1976 did something like normality return to international wheat trading. North/South: A Programme for Survival, p. 98.

[259] Gaudium et Spes, pars. 66, 71. The question of agricultural economics and ethics was extensively dealt with in Mater et Magistra, the encyclical of Pope John XXIII in 1963.

large numbers who get their living from the land are subjected to inhuman conditions of life and work.

The question of the proper treatment for the rural areas in developed economies is very much connected with that of urbanisation; here the concern is to keep the right balance between rural and urban living for many reasons—some of them economic, some of them social.[260] It is a concern that constantly exercises their legislative ingenuity. The underdeveloped nations also have this problem of urbanisation, one compounded for them by a fast growing population in both town and country and the absence of the rapid industrial development that led to the growth of cities in Europe and America.[261]

The concern of the nations of Europe with protection of agriculture began in the last quarter of the nineteenth century and it again became acute in the 1930s; legislation developed gradually over that period but, as with care for the industrial worker, it was the end of the 1939 war which ushered in a new deal for farmers and peasants—aid for the consolidation of farms into larger units, re-afforestation, land clearance, irrigation, providing early retirement pensions, market subsidies for fuels and fertilisers, and scientific services and the provision of low interest loans for farmers. The degree of subsidy for agricultural products has also grown and has become a matter of increasing political controversy.

Despite all this progress in Europe, for example, it is still reckoned that from one-third to one-half of agricultural land needs to be reallocated or consolidated if the technical effectiveness of labour and capital is to reach the level required.[262] European nations face a dilemma—the increasing need of government intervention to provide economic justice for the farmer, but the difficulties that intervention leads to in terms of butter "mountains" and wine "lakes" and subsidies which seem to benefit the farmer, but do not so clearly contribute to the common good. Meanwhile the agricultural sector itself is becoming increasingly industrialised and subject to the same stresses and strains that affect industrialised sectors of the economy—dependence upon fuel supplies and disruption by industrial disputes, for example.

The problem of justice, for the farmer, the agriculturalist, the peasant in the developed societies of the West, therefore, is a pressing one. But it pales to insignificance in the light of the needs of the agriculturalist in the

[260] F. E. Huggett, *The Land Question and European Society* (London, 1975). A. Martin, *Economics and Agriculture* (London, 1958). S. H. Franklin, *European Peasantry: The Last Phase* (London, 1969).

[261] D. Herbert, *Urban Geography* (Newton Abbott, 1977).

[262] Huggett, op. cit., p. 157.

third world. Here the question of agrarian reform is first of all crucial while the problems of making agriculture efficient are immensely more complex and fundamental than in the more sophisticated societies of the West.[263]

The parts of the world in which agricultural holdings are very small and often incapable of giving full employment to the families which occupy them are, above all, in the underdeveloped regions such as the Middle and Far East and Latin America.[264] Many such farmers do not own the land which they cultivate. In many areas there is little understanding of individual land-ownership—an individual having his share of a communal holding and also a part interest in the potentially useful but uncultivated land belonging to his group. Communal rights, however, can prevent the energetic or able individual members of the group from acquiring more land at the expense of the indolent or unproductive. They can also make it difficult to use land holdings as a security for loans in order to purchase the tools and equipment to improve it. There is also less interest by the individual in spending money to improve land which is likely to be periodically allotted. Nor does communal ownership encourage proper use of the communal land. It tends to be overgrazed and to discourage the improvement and quality of cattle.[265]

In monsoon Asia, Latin America and parts of Southern Europe the land tenure known as metayage is common. In its most basic form this is a co-partnership between the peasant who provides labour and stock in return for a fixed share of the produce and the owner who provides the land, the buildings, the equipment and seed. There are wide varieties of such systems, but the feature common to them all is that the people who actually work the land have only an indirect control over their earnings. Frequently the peasant's share in a good year is hardly enough for the needs of his own family and, in a bad one, can fall below the minimum. Whether the owner, and how much the owner, pays on repairs and maintenance is for him to decide and, if he is greedy and unintelligent, little is done for the tenant.

Such a system of tenure is a bar to economic progress, but reform is often difficult. If the land is turned over to the worker he will usually not have the resources to develop it efficiently, even if he has the will and the

[263] *The Internationalist*, February 1979, and *The Courier* September/October 1979, survey the program of land reform in the third world.

[264] Lowry, op. cit., pp. 102 ff. J. W. Mellor, *The Economics of Agricultural Development* (Cornell, 1974).

[265] P. T. Bauer and B. S. Yamey, *The Economics of Under-Developed Countries* (Cambridge), p. 52, quoted Lowry, op. cit., p. 102.

opportunity. If it is not turned over to the worker but is worked more efficiently and justly under another reformed system, unemployment and displacement result, and alternative employment is often hard to find.

In parts of Southern Europe and Latin America, enormous privately owned estates which are cultivated little, if at all, can exist side by side with small over-populated and intensively worked family farm plots. The alienation of vast areas of useful land from cultivation is most marked in Latin America where the control of land has traditionally been associated with prestige and with political and economic power, rather than with healthy development for the service of the community.

Mexico's efforts at agrarian reform have superficially been among the most successful and are often appealed to as a model for action in other places. Basically the Mexican method was the establishment of the government of an *egido*, a community or a village with its lands granted to the community.[266] In each egido there are usually 20 to 100 families and each family cultivates (but does not own) a certain area of land. The right to cultivate is inherited, but the land may not be sold, rented, mortgaged, given away, nor may the occupancy be modified in any way. This type of reform has effectively curbed the political and economic power of the wealthy private landowners and has given many Mexicans, who before did not have it, a stake in the land. On the other hand, productivity has not improved sufficiently under the system. There is inadequate capital and credit, excessive fragmentation of land, and a consequent difficulty in applying scientific agriculture and technology.

Reform in the rest of South America has had a chequered career. Venezuela, with 45% of its work force on farms, has attempted a measure of such reform, but it has been neither extensive nor effective.[267] Chile's Christian Democratic land reform did make some progress. The top 5% of landowners had their holdings reduced to 77% from 87% and 25,000 new peasant proprietors emerged.[268] In comparison with many other Latin American programmes, the Chilean achievement was impressive.

Bolivia, where well over half the people depend on the land, also experienced effective land reform in 1953; nearly 200,000 families received land; the social impact was therefore considerable, but in terms of improving economic efficiency it was less successful.[269] Brazil suffers from an antiquated land tenure system—the huge latifundias alternating with the inefficient minifundias. The Land Reform Institute has done little to distribute the land more equitably. Colonization and increases in productivity have been of more interest to the government than re-distribution.[270]

[266] See Lowry, op. cit., pp. 104 ff.
[267] A. Gilbert, *Latin American Development: A Geographical Perspective* (London, 1977), p. 161. Cockroft et al., op. cit., p. 161.
[268] Gilbert, op. cit., p. 162–63.   [269] Ibid., p. 158.   [270] Ibid., p. 162.

Colombia, where 42% of the people are engaged in agriculture, does not suffer from the inequalities of land tenure on the same scale as some other parts of the continent, but the minifundias, existing side by side with vast plantations, present a very marked contrast, and the projected reform under INCORA, the land reform agency set up in 1960, has made little progress; its main purpose has been to encourage colonization.[271]

In Peru, half of the people live in rural areas, and agrarian reform has resulted in some expropriation of estates of large landowners, which have been turned over to cooperatives, to individuals or communities.[272] In Argentina, something like 38% of the population possess 10% of the land in holdings of less than 25 hectares, while 6% own 74% of the land in holdings of over 1,000 hectares. The country is divided over land reform. Where there are many minifundias the case seems clear for radical change. The problem of the big farm is whether their break-up would generate more poverty and injustice.

In Europe it is in parts of Italy, notably in the lower Po Delta, in Sicily, Sardinia and the Southern Peninsula and the Maremma, that the social and economic problems resulting from the latifundia system have been most effectively tackled.[273] In the Maremma, the coastal lowlands between Leghorn and Rome, the landscape has been radically altered by two decades of such reforms. All but the most efficient large estates have been broken up, the former owners keeping one-third of their land on condition they improve it, the remaining two-thirds being taken over by the state and allocated to landless labourers. Once again the good social effects of such change have been counter-balanced by the economic inefficiency of large numbers of small farm units. Reforms in land tenure in other words, must be integrated into a general scheme to encourage efficiency, if it is to be really effective.

At the 1974 World Food Conference in Bucharest, Pope Paul VI urged that the emphasis on the world economic development should shift from industrialisation to agriculture and life on the land.[274] It is certain that the world food problem cannot be solved by relying everlastingly upon the bounty of the harvests of North America. It can only be solved by improving the low acre yields of millions of those who operate small farms in the developing world. There is indeed no contradiction between

[271] Ibid., p. 161.

[272] Ibid., p. 164. *The Internationalist*, p. 25, concludes that Peru's experience has been a failure.

[273] Lowry, op. cit., p. 105.

[274] "Address of His Holiness Paul VI to Participants of the World Food Conference", 9 November 1974, *L'Osservatore Romano* [English edition] 21 November 1974. Harford Thomas, *The Guardian*, 18 November 1974, summarized it by saying that "The Pope argued that nothing less than new orientations were needed . . . a reorientation of first priorities away from industries to the natural life of agriculture."

farming on a small scale and productive efficiency if the incentive and assistance is provided. Egypt, Taiwan, Japan and South Korea are countries in which the majority of farms are between 2 and 12 acres, yet they have been able to achieve yields of up to, and in excess of, the 3,000 pounds of grain an acre which the larger and more mechanized farms of the U.S.A. or Europe can achieve. Egypt's land reforms of the 1950s/60s limiting land ownership to 84, then 42 hectares, was accompanied by the setting up of cooperatives to assist with livestock, equipment and fertiliser.[275] The country remains a net importer of food because of its rapidly growing population—but its achievement in improving agricultural productivity is impressive. Japanese farms average as small as one hectare; the land reform of 1964 failed to encourage the enlargement or consolidation of holdings, but did make the Japanese farmer an owner-cultivator rather than a tenant, and yields of rice per hectare remain among the world's highest.

Taiwan intensified its agriculture in the 1950s when the Nationalists took over, and an extensive land reform was carried out, limiting the size of farms and placing the land in the hands of the peasant farmers—70% of it being now so owned.[276] South Korea has introduced a measure of land reform in redistributing land to peasant families; irrigation and agricultural techniques have been improved with the result that rice production increased by 50% between 1955 and 1975.[277] However, the area remains a net food importer because of the high population growth.

The mechanics of an agricultural development which enables the small farmer to make a full contribution to the life of the community and to provide for its needs as efficiently as the large farmer are clear enough. Such success as countries in which the majority of farmers are small holders have had in achieving agricultural improvement have been based upon a more equitable system of land tenure, together with the application of modern techniques adapted to the needs of the small farmer—Egypt and Taiwan have been particularly successful in developing and adapting farm machinery and tools to supplement, not replace, human effort.

The various African countries have their own problems of agricultural development and are working out their own solutions. Two countries are of particular interest: Tanzania and Kenya. In Tanzania, where 90% of the people depend on agriculture, land has traditionally been a community

[275] R. Mabro, *The Egyptian Economy 1952–72* (O.U.P., 1974).

[276] A. Y. Koo, *The Role of Land Reform: Economic Development, Case Study of Taiwan* (New York, 1968).

[277] D. C. Cole and P. N. Lymon, *Korean Development: The Interplay of Politics and Economics* (London, 1971).

resource and the concept been adapted to modern needs; the state owns the land and the local communities allocate the right to use it. In 1970 the government began an extensive rural settlement scheme encouraging the formation of communal villages. The aim was good—to co-ordinate development, raise living standards, improve crop production and develop agro-industries. But the disruption to traditional agriculture and the onset of serious drought has led to a serious decline in output.[278]

In Kenya, where 66% of the people are dependent on agriculture, the effort has been to encourage individual ownership on Western lines, and vast sums have been spent on registering individual ownership of land so that the peasant can get enough security to obtain loans for development purposes. Co-operatives have been established to work estates formerly owned by Britons.[279]

In summary, adequate government assistance in improving productive efficiency of the small farms (and the equitable tax system to finance it), equitable land tenure and effective cooperation between the farmers, a firm and clear law of contracts, property and liability, integrity in the administration and accounting of farmers' funds and all aspects of government assistance—these are the general conditions of success in helping the rural community to play its full part in economic development. The emphasis between communal and individual effort varies between cultures as they face up to the problems of making agriculture more effective. But without a clear and definite improvement in justice done and seen to be done to the farmer and the community, the desired improvement is not forthcoming.

[278] Meier, op. cit., pp. 114 ff.
[279] C. Leys, *Under-Development in Kenya* (London, 1975).

CHAPTER SIX

SUMMARY AND CONCLUSIONS

The Structure of the Study

In the introduction it was said that the purpose of the book was to consider the main points of the social teaching of Vatican II and examine the evolution of that teaching from the Scriptures and through the Church's experience in history. In so doing, it would compare the Catholic with other traditions, and it would examine the relevance of the social teaching of the Church to the needs of the modern world.

The first task that had to be undertaken was to look at the teaching of the Council on the principles of morality or ethics in general, since the particular social moral or social ethical teaching grows out of these principles and depends on them. This done, we looked at the central questions in social ethics—namely those of the family, of political life and of economic life.

The structure of the study, then, has centred on five main propositions which are taken from the documents of the Council. The first stated the standard, the norm, of the Christian morality to be the law of God, which is eternal, and in which man participates by using his right reason in the search for truth. This then, the divine law, is the ultimate ethical norm. The second proposition concerns the proximate and subjective ethical norm (conscience) which is to be guided by the sacred and certain teaching of the Church interpreting objective moral law. In the Catholic tradition, then, objective morality and subjective judgement are not to be opposed. The former is the rule by which we measure the soundness of the latter.

These two propositions constitute the basic principles of the Council's moral teaching. The next three propositions are concerned with their application to problems of social, political and economic justice.

We started with ethics of marriage and the family since the family is the basis of all social organisation. The family is of divine institution, given its own laws and purposes by God who intended it to be a loving, personal, monogamous and indissoluble relationship providing the proper context in which new life can come to be and be fostered to maturity. The fourth proposition is concerned with the role of politics, political life, the state and all that it involves in the same plan. These third and fourth propositions are, in fact interlinked, in that the Church understands the political society as arising out of the needs of the person in the context of the family. The state is formed precisely because man alone cannot provide for himself, and those who depend on him, all that is needed for a good and full life. The state then is part of God's plan, since it is rooted in the human nature he created. The form of government and the method of appointing rulers, however, is left to the free choice of the people—government, in other words, must rest on the consent of the governed, but this does not exclude their choosing or preferring forms other than representative democracy. Regarding the relationship of the Church to the state—like the latter, the Church is divinely instituted; hence, both Church and state have a legitimate autonomy the other cannot challenge. However, on any matter which touches on the law of God or the essential rights of the human being created in his image, the Church has a right and a duty to defend the truth against a state which challenges it. She always must have, too, the right to teach the whole of her doctrine freely including her social doctrine. In any conflict with the secular powers, she can only use methods which are in harmony with her primary spiritual role.

The fifth and last proposition concerns economic life and economic ethics. As man was given the earth and the wealth it contains so that all men could enjoy a good life from it, economics, being concerned with the factors affecting the production and distribution of wealth, has its own God-given autonomy also, but those must always chime with the needs of the moral law as given by the same God. Economics must be in the service, not simply of profit or growth, but of man as a whole—his material needs, but those of his moral, spiritual and religious life too.

Though each one of the five propositions can be stated with reasonable clarity in principle, deeper analysis reveals that they cover highly controversial and complex theoretical and practical matters. It is necessary then that each be seen in the light of historical experience and development—which does not indeed alter the truth of each proposition, but helps to a better understanding of them. We accordingly looked at some of the main such theoretical and historical questions and controversies affecting each.

Chapter One: *The ultimate and objective ethical norm is the divine law— eternal, objective and universal, and man participates in this law through the natural law.*

The context in which the Council made its observations regarding the objective ethical norm was that of religious freedom. This gave us firstly the opportunity to look at the relationship between law and morals—a relationship important in social ethical theory. The law must have a moral basis, but in order that this be possible, a moral consensus has to exist in society at large. Secondly, it also gave us the opportunity of considering objections to the Church's record as a friend of justice and peace. That the Church has at times, willingly or unwillingly, been repressive and has been manoeuvered into using violence in pursuit of her ends is historical fact. The Inquisition and the Crusades attest to it. Yet the same historical record shows that she has been a very positive force overall in the establishment of human freedom and dignity. Indeed those Western ideas of personal freedom (and it is those ideas which have become the modern ideal of human freedom) were founded in the testimony of the martyrs under the Roman Empire. For the first time in history a mass of humble people, for it is from them that the majority of the early martyrs came, were able to defy the might of totalitarian state, that of Rome. Pagan ideas of freedom were noble, but they were essentially elitist, appealing to the intellectual superiority of the few. They were not for every man. Christian dignity and freedom was.

After the collapse of the Roman Empire in the West and the waves of invasion which followed it, the Church by her very presence and work provided the spiritual, moral and intellectual leadership, as well as the main administrative skills, that enabled "a new and compelling civilisation" to emerge from an "underdeveloped rural slum" in the period 1000 to 1350. And it is that civilisation which has given us, in fact, the key ideas and institutions of modern freedom—in particular, the universities which embody our tradition of free intellectual enquiry and our representative government which sums up our tradition of personal freedom under the law. Of the universities, it can be said that in their formation and development the Church was the most important single influence. The scholastic disputation with its method of free searching and logical enquiry, the insistence, under the influence of St. Thomas especially, that faith and reason are different ways of knowing truth and may not be used against one another, did far more to secure the Western mind in its search for truth in freedom than any activities of the Inquisition can be shown to have held it back. Representative government was a spontaneous political development, but with the monasteries giving the example of constitutional government and the orders of friars from the thirteenth century developing representative forms, with the example of the councils of the Church as great deliberative assemblies of Christendom, the Church showed that she favoured this form, and her example encouraged its development. In this period, human dignity and freedom developed in other ways. The decline of slavery during it was significant. The challenge to the intellectual foundations of slavery was there from the beginning in the Christian teaching on the equality of all men in Christ and in the Church's insistence on the dignity of free labour. Her influence was also crucial in reducing the supply of slaves from war captives—always the only sure way of maintaining a slave economy in the long run. At the same time, she gave the practice of emancipation a new and more powerful motive and so extended it considerably. By the thirteenth and fourteenth centuries slavery had almost disappeared from Europe. The great civilisations of antiquity had been slave based. The life of the medieval serf, the rural and the urban labourer, the journeyman was harsh and limited. There was no golden age. Yet it was in this period that, for the first time, those who worked with their hands in field or workshop were able to assert their rights by their own efforts, conscious of the dignity of and the value of their labour and capable of showing, through guild organisation, that they could govern themselves and others. Add to this that in the thirteenth century a more effective system of social welfare (mainly Church provided, but certainly the result of the example of the Church) was available to more than in any age down to today, and that the same can be said of a university education, we can say that great progress was made. Common law and trial by jury were also medieval in origin. In England especially it was established that free men of common birth were the law's typical men. Other kinds, their social betters, enjoyed privileges or were subject to disabilities which were seen as exceptional.

The digression on the Church and freedom was necessary because the importance of freedom was the context in which the statement on the divine law as the ultimate ethical norm was made. The real purpose of this first chapter, however, was to explore the basis of the Council's teaching concerning the ultimate ethical norm. We saw that the foundation of this belief was in God's self-revelation in the Old Testament, in which he insisted that the mark of true belief in him was the personal service of a righteous life—following his law for love of him. The code of personal morality set out in the Ten Commandments is normative, not only for the Jews of the Old Testament, but for all men for all time—just as the God of Abraham, Isaac and Jacob is the God for all men for all time. The idea of the ultimate ethical norm being the divine law, eternal, objective and universal, which we find in the documents of the Second Vatican Council, is a restatement of the basic moral theology of the Old and New Testaments. It was the ceremonial and the judicial law of the Old Testament which was abrogated by Christ; he reasserted its basic moral teachings. To him ethics was part and parcel of religion and inseparable from it. Through the redemption he achieved for us, morality (as all other aspects of religious belief and practice) was transformed—but the effect of grace in Christ is to enable us to perceive more fully the truth of the Ten Commandments and follow them more sincerely for love of Christ. It does not replace them.

The other elements in the Council's conviction concerning the nature of morality is that apart from a revealed moral code there is one which is founded in human nature, a natural law which is objective, eternal and binding on all. This idea has its origin in Greek philosophy, in Socrates, Plato and Aristotle, but more particularly in the later Stoic school. In its mature form this natural law theory argued to an objective moral truth attainable by right reason, founded in and given to us by God, its author, ruling all men for all time, unchangeable and eternal. It was an idea put to good service by Roman jurisprudence. It was used by the Doctors and Fathers of the Church also as complementing the revealed moral law. The authority and value of the concept as developed by the Greek philosophers and Roman legal philosophers forced the theology of the Church, maturing in the twelfth and thirteenth centuries when the classical inheritance was being rediscovered, to find a firm place for it.

St. Thomas' statement of natural law theory, and his setting of it in the context of divine eternal and divine positive law, remains a classic. Law, he said, is a dictate of practical reason issued by the ruler of a perfect community. Since the whole of creation is governed by God, then this law must be eternal, because God's concept of things is eternal. The divine positive law (the revealed moral law) is necessary, however, because human judgement on moral matters is wayward, while we need to know what moral truth is without risk of error; since God cannot err, the revelation of his law provides man with the means to know such moral truth. However, insofar as man is moved by right reason to choose what is truly good, that is "the rational creature's participation of the eternal law". This natural law, according to St. Thomas, moves us first to see that good is to be done and evil avoided. From this general precept the others follow—the need to preserve life, to foster family life, to encourage education and the virtues that enable man to live peaceably with others. About the details of the natural law men may argue. What is essential to the idea was outlined to us by the pagan writers cited: there is a law which is eternal and unchangeable, which men of good will may understand by right reason and which has God as its author. It encapsulates the conviction that right reason will enable man to know the essentials of a God-based morality which is unchanging. The depth and strength of the intellectual pedigree of natural law theory enables us to withstand modern attacks on it. It is indispensable in practice for a sound jurisprudence and for any effective theory of human rights. Finally we noted that when Catholic thinkers absorbed the idea into their tradition, it was assumed that the Church was the authentic interpreter of natural law, because she possessed divine authority to judge all on earth in the light of its relationship to God's law.

Chapter Two: *The proximate and subjective ethical norm is man's conscience guided by the sacred and certain teaching of the Church interpreting objective moral law.*

If the ultimate and objective ethical norm is the divine law, the proximate and subjective such norm is man's conscience, the power he has of judging right from wrong and which moves him to choose the good and avoid the evil. As subjective, as the product of my own personal reflection, conscience can err as the law of God cannot. It must be followed even when it errs, but an erroneous conscience is a defective conscience. Through conscience the objective law of God should be reflected in our own souls, be known by us and be embraced by us personally and applied in our daily lives. The directives of the objective moral law, as interpreted by the sacred and certain teaching of the Church, and the promptings of my conscience should indicate to us the same course of action.

The morality of a human act, the act of a man who knows what he is doing and deliberately sets about to do it, is determined by measuring what is actually *done* against what we know, through revealed moral law and the teaching Church, God wants us to do. If what is done freely by a human being is contrary to the law of God, then that is a morally bad act, an act unworthy of man because man is made to know love, reverence and serve God by loving obedience to his law. But we do not attribute the moral evil of the act to the individual who did it until we know that it was done freely and knowingly. Ignorance, error and inattention can affect my awareness of what I am doing; my knowledge, feelings (fear, disordered emotions) and past experience can likewise inhibit my freedom. These are to be taken into account when judging moral imputability. In technical language, it is the end that is achieved by the act (the *finis operis*) which tells me whether it is in conformity with the law of God. It is the intention of the doer of the act (the *finis operantis*) plus the circumstances which determine whether the moral evil will be attributed to the doer of the act. Evil is the absence of a good that should be there. All such absence is "physical" evil, in the old terminology, whether it is the evil of famine or disease or the evil of men who cause harm or suffering to others. Only the latter, the doing of a real, a physical evil freely and knowingly is a *moral* evil because it is a free decision to go against God's law.

Judging morality, therefore, requires careful thought and judgement in examining cases, hence "casuistry" as the moral/theological method. The principles of casuistry, however, need to be properly understood and applied. For example, the principle of the lesser of two evils means that *if forced* to choose between doing physical evils, I must do the lesser. It does not mean that I *can freely* choose to do one evil while restraining myself from freely choosing to do a greater.

Man's conscience is guided by the teaching of the Church, not only in his personal ethics, but in his social ethics too. The Council reiterates the principles of justice and equity in this sphere that have been worked out by the Church, in the light of the Gospel, over the centuries. The social order must be founded on truth, justice and love. The truth is the truth of Christ in his objective moral law. Justice, the giving to others what is their due, has several aspects. Distributive justice concerns the proper distribution among its citizens of the wealth and honour the community has at its disposal; general or legal justice covers the duty of the state in preserving the true common good on the one hand and the obligation of the citizens to obey just laws on the other; commutative justice regulates the personal relation between citizens; social justice is best seen as a properly functioning general justice.

The idea of an objective moral law, founded in God, authoritatively interpreted by his Church and binding on all men for all time, which is insisted on by the Council, and which we have been examining in these first two chapters, is not one that finds much favour outside the Church today. In particular it is rejected by many of the other living traditions of Western culture, and the reason for the rejection lies in the liberal idea of the autonomous individual who recognizes no law superior to his own subjective conscience. Liberalism can refer to a general philosophy of life—man's relationship to others and the world around him. We can also speak of a liberal political theory and a liberal economic theory, and these we examine in the chapters on political and economic ethics. For the moment, we are concerned only with liberalism as a general philosophy.

The liberal ideal developed during the Renaissance and the Reformation when the assumptions of classical Catholic theology and moral philosophy were taken for granted. Hence, the first liberals assumed that the stress on the absolute rights of the subjective individual conscience would leave objective moral law intact, knowable to all. They could not conceive of conscience being wrong. Yet, as subjective, it of course can be wrong, can err. In time, when scepticism advanced to the point where some philosophers questioned the very existence of objective truth, including objective moral truth, the contradiction was revealed. If there is no objective moral truth to which the subjective conscience can attain, then it has no guide. All is subjective and relative, and anarchy and tyranny are the only alternatives. That the twentieth century, which has finally seen the proof of the contradiction in liberalism, should be faced increasingly with the choice between tyranny and anarchy, especially in the political fields, is then not surprising.

The specific stages in the undermining of the belief in a God-given objective morality, binding on all for all time and authentically interpreted by the Church, can be variously traced. Moral philosophy and theology was one of the first casualties. Moral sense theories lead to the equation of morality with feelings, emotions. Kantianism assumed the ability of the subjective conscience to lead man to absolute moral truth unerringly in practice—against the evidence of human experience. Comte, by contrast, rejected all values as subjective. Hegel assumed that the expression of the will of the national community constituted an objective moral value which conscience had not the right to stand against. His objectivity was not, however, unchanging; as the infinite spirit manifested itself ever more perfectly, morality changed accordingly. The idea of an evolutionary morality was built into Marxist theory and remains there, clashing with the belief that when socialism is achieved moral certainty will be achieved too. In practice the will of the party determines what is moral and what is not. In invoking a new metaphysical sovereign, history itself, and making the party the sole interpreter of what history says, unprincipled tyranny has a terrifying new certainty.

Utilitarianism, another nineteenth century moral theory, argued from the pleasure motive; the seeking of pleasure and the avoidance of pain determine our moral decisions. Darwinism, a scientific theory concerning the evolution of life, was made to have moral implications which undermined the traditional Christian beliefs. If man evolves, then morality cannot be certain; further if man is descended from apes, then he is only a more complicated kind of animal and his obedience to any higher power or ideal, moral or other, is denied. In fact, there is no essential contradiction between Darwinism and Christianity—if both are properly understood. If the evolution of man's body from other forms of life is proved, then nothing essential in the Christian understanding of man, his relationship to God and his moral life is changed. A scientific theory concerning man's physical evolution can tell us nothing about his spiritual or moral life. The other science which has been made to tell against the older beliefs about morality is Freudianism. Once again, this has only happened because of the way that psychiatry has been misused. The proper use of psychiatric theory and method can help man to become more Christian, not less. Only when psychiatry and the psychiatrist go beyond their legitimate fields and try to take over the role of theologians and moral theologians does the trouble arise.

Finally, situation ethics, the claim that there are no moral absolutes that cannot, in difficult cases, be put aside in the light of the "love" norm, is opposed to the traditional Christian understanding restated by the Council. In fact, situationism does have its objective norms—those of the mid-twentieth century Anglo-American liberal. What they find acceptable constitutes the norm of morality we are told.

Chapter Three: *Marriage is divinely instituted as a loving, personal and indissoluble monogamous relationship, by nature ordained to the procreation and education of children.*

The Council's statement of the ideal of marriage is based upon Scripture and the traditional teaching of the Church, but there is every reason for saying also that it responds to the best in human nature. Only when sex is seen as being for marriage and children, in the context of lifelong monogamy based on love of the partners, are true human values preserved. Such a union expresses the full personal equality of man and woman, makes sex the servant of human dignity, not its master, and provides children with the context they need in order to grow to full personal maturity.

The Genesis account of God's purpose in giving sex and marriage to mankind is to be set against a cultural context in which sex was defined in the fertility cults, which reduced woman to the role of sex object. Far from the Genesis account depicting God as sexual, it tells us sex was created for man. There could be no sexuality in God, the supreme spirit. The paternity of God is a purely spiritual and intellectual one which carries with it none of the implications of human physical paternity.

Christ referred to the Genesis account to reassert the original teaching on the indissolubility of marriage in the face of the growing Jewish resort to divorce. After some initial controversy on the indissolubility question in the early Church as a result of doubt over the meaning of the "fornication clause" in Matthew's Gospel, the conclusion was reached that divorce was not possible in any circumstances; the observations of St. Paul in chapter 5 of Ephesians, where he likened Christ's relationship with his Church to marriage between man and wife, were influential in leading the Church to this conclusion. The Pauline and Petrine privileges do not challenge the indissolubility of sacramental marriage. Annulment likewise is concerned with deciding if marriage existed in the first instance. Proof of moral or mental defect, lack of true consent, defects in observance of the Church's laws or the existence of serious impediment based on blood relationship are the grounds for such annulments.

The proper use of sex in marriage has always been the concern of the moralist, since the sexual faculty is capable of being abused even in the marriage context for which it is given to us. That sexual pleasure and procreative power are closely linked, the simple truth about our bodies and sexual emotions testify. And that some have sought sexual pleasure in marriage by denying the life-giving potential of sex is a fact of marital life that has always been a subject of concern for the moralist. Sexual pleasure in marriage is in itself good as is evident from Genesis itself and the Song of Songs, though the book of Tobit also shows that the possibility of lust in marriage was recognized too. Because in the early Church there was great danger to the Christian ideal from the poor sexual moral standards of the time, including those current in marriage, the emphasis in the Fathers and Doctors of the Church was on the threat that indulgence in sexual pleasure posed to the Christian ideal. The same attitude is evident in the penitentials, the handbooks of moral theology in use by many confessors in the Middle Ages. But they could not tell against the word of God which testifies to the goodness of marriage and honest love within it.

The idea of the ends of marriage was elaborated by St. Thomas as his theology developed—the three such ends being the bearing and rearing of children, the love of the parents and the proper ordering of sexual desire. The identification of children as the primary end of marriage in St. Thomas is in the light of the need for a stable love between the partners. The love that issues in children secures the couple in their love for each other; this is the norm the tradition seeks to establish. Increasingly, in the light of the greater knowledge of the human body and psyche, the possibility that acts of love which were not capable of beginning new life (but which were not actively closed to it) were positively good was realised. By the time of Pope Pius XII and then the Second Vatican Council, moral theology had developed accordingly. However, this development does not justify the acceptance of contraception as morally good. That natural family planning enables the couple to work together to express their love sexually only when the wife cannot conceive is morally very different from causing the infertility. The teaching of Humanae Vitae reasserts the truth to meet the new questionings. Just as it is self-evident that to use sex in marriage while deliberately denying love to one's partner is irrational, wrong and against natural justice, so it is wrong to use sex in marriage while deliberately denying the procreative potential it possesses. The use of historical and other arguments to urge that this time Catholic teaching will change (i.e. contradict itself) as it has done in other areas is misleading. Such arguments are in fact erroneous. In the first instance, to equate a change in doctrine with a contradiction of previous teaching is to fail to notice that one of the principles of sound doctrinal development is that the original teaching remains intact. In the second place, the examination of the arguments themselves shows that the appeal to historical parallels does not hold up. The Galileo case is irrelevant in that what was at issue here was a matter of scientific fact—in determining which the Church has not been given special competence by Christ; the errors of the teaching authorities in the Church here, then, should not be taken as undermining that authority where its competence is guaranteed by Christ—as it is on moral matters. Regarding the argument from the change (i.e. the supposed contradiction) in the teaching on usury—such a contradiction has not occurred. Usury remains a sin. What has changed is, not the teaching, but the circumstances which have limited the possibilities of injustice in the taking of interest on loans. But where that injustice still exists, the sin of usury can be committed. On slavery, again it is not true to say that the Church has contradicted her teaching. That slavery could be tolerated as an institution where there was no possibility of challenging it was a lesson the Church had learned from the Scriptures. Like her master Christ she tolerated it, but, in being faithful to his teaching, she undermined it. Her influence on emancipation, on the reduction in the supply of slaves from war captives and on bettering the lot of slaves, worked to this end. Meanwhile, when countries which had grown rich on the transatlantic slave trade abandoned it, they did so above all because of the threat that individual freedom and free labour faced from the institution. And it was largely through the Church's influence that these ideals of individual freedom and the dignity of labour had become embedded in the traditions of the countries concerned. The Church, then, did not need to change her teaching on slavery: she never defended it as a positive good, but only a regrettable necessity, a necessity that testified to the greed and cruelty of man to man which she had always tried to combat. When the men of power finally saw sense her hopes and attitude were vindicated.

The proper understanding of the statement concerning "no salvation outside the Church" as it was made in the early fourteenth century, and the proper understanding of what the Second Vatican Council said, shows again there is no contradiction. The assumption of the earlier statement was that those who remained outside the Church did so even though they knew the role given it by Christ. The assumption of the second was that this is not necessarily the case; but the Council goes on to say that those who did remain outside the Church, knowing what role Christ had given her, could not be saved. The first statement is true—the second is nearer the whole truth. There is no contradiction between them. Finally the appeal is sometimes made that the Church should change her teaching on the use of marriage because of the population problem. But this is to make the end justify the means. A similar argument could be used to defend genocide or abortion. The argument begs the question—contraception must be shown to be moral before it can be advocated.

Marriage and the family are then very personal things. They are based on the love of two people for one another—and the children are a witness to their love. But marriage is also a social institution, the foundation of society. Its well being is then very much the concern of the society. Several questions arise here. Firstly the role of women both in the family and outside of it is one that concerns all. The family of which the father is head, as it is outlined in Genesis, the New Testament and above all in Ephesians, chapter 5, is the Christian model, although, regrettably, abuses of this patriarchal ideal do occur. Yet equally that the ideal of the man as head of the family is compatible with that of the wife's full personal equality is evident from the lived experience of many families. There are difficulties in ensuring that a woman who wishes to combine a career or a job outside the home with the role of wife and mother can do so, but it is in society's interest to see that such a combination of roles does not lead to an undervaluing of the latter, which is indispensable for the health of society and is one which woman alone can fill.

Much of the modern questioning of the role of women in society and in the family, however, arises not from the difficulties that result from an abuse of patriarchy in practice, but from a fundamental questioning of the whole concept of patriarchy—a questioning which arises from Marxist sources. The claim is that patriarchy arose with the development of private property which the men managed to control. The argument is not based on historical fact, but it remains attractive to many for all that. Yet there is no evidence that the non-patriarchal family will serve society as well, especially a complex modern society. There are many forms the patriarchal family can take according to the nature of the society in question. Our culture seems to prefer the nuclear model—man and wife with children and with little or no contact with or dependence on any other relations by blood or marriage. But whatever the model, the norm for the Christian is the man as head of the family in which the wife is a full personal equal.

The concern of society with the family is evident in the responsibility the latter has for education. This remains with the parents primarily, but it is not one that they can possibly fulfill without the aid of the state. The state must ensure the fact that all children have access to an adequate education, supplementing the efforts of parents and Church to the end. The Church's role is to provide school for its own people, to care for its children who are in non-Catholic schools and to have a strong presence in higher education.

Chapter Four: *The political community and the authority of the state are based on human nature and so belong to God's design but the method of government and the appointment of rulers is left to the citizens' free choice. The Church is not identified with any particular system, but must be free to teach her whole doctrine (including her social doctrine) and pass moral judgement on political issues as required.*

The political community, the state, like the family, is, according to the Council, God-ordained. It is there to fulfill those needs that man on his own cannot meet. Its origins give it its essential purpose—to serve the common good on the basis of the pre-existing and God-given rights of the person in the context of the family.

Both Old and New Testaments give evidence of respect for those who govern political society, but they do not provide us with a complete

political ethic. That grew as the Church elaborated her theology and reflected on the wisdom of the Greek and Roman thinkers to help her children
who faced problems in principle the same as they had faced. Christ himself
rejected any political ambition as did the early Church but after she had
conquered by her holiness, and Constantine had accepted her, she could
not escape political involvement; later when Roman power collapsed in
the West and Europe descended into chaos, further political responsibilities and powers became hers whether she wanted them or not. Her
role as landowner in a time when land was the basis of political power
exerted one pressure to this end. The papacy meanwhile was increasingly
compelled to provide civic leadership in Italy from the fourth century.
Then, from the eighth century, the political and economic weakness of
Byzantium, together with the need to guard against the theological
ambitions of the emperors, combined with the threat of Lombards in
Northern Italy that they would reduce the popes to the role of royal
chaplains, led them to rely increasingly on the Franks. Using the English
monk Boniface initially as an intermediary, the papacy forged the links
with the latter that were to lay the foundation of Christendom and the new
European civilisation. In the central Middle Ages (1000–1350) the papacy
and the Holy Roman Emperor clashed. Initially, the popes seemed to have
triumphed, but eventually and inevitably they were challenged by the
secular powers in the person of Philip of France. It was against this
background that the Church's political ethics were hammered out.

The Fathers and the Doctors of the Church saw the state as of divine
institution to meet the needs of man after the Fall. St. Thomas was more
positive. The state was essential to man's development as man, whether
he had fallen from grace or not. Drawn to such society by nature, man
reasons that he needs someone to govern the society so formed and
concludes that the best government is partly ruled by one, partly ruled by
many, with the rulers being able to be chosen from the people by the
people. Such authority must rule for the true common good, and if it does
not, but clearly favours the ruler, or some private group good against the
commonwealth, then the tyrant, in certain circumstances and subject to
stringent conditions, may be overthrown.

St. Thomas reasoned against the background of the medieval experience—
the controversy between the emperor and the pope over investitures, the
development of urban civilisation based on personal freedom and the
growth of representative government in Church and state. Until the
Council of Basle (1431–1439) marked the end of the conciliar movement,
theories such as those of Marsilio of Padua (1273?–1342?) and William of
Occam (1290–1349) attacked the papal pretensions to temporal power and
so helped clarify the proper roles of Church and state.

The essential ethic of medieval politics, worked out by theorists who were clerics, was that political society existed to serve the common good, the good of all, and that the prince, who ruled as a result of a social compact or contract, was under the law of God and the Church; if he did not rule for the common good, but for a private or sectional good, he could in certain circumstances be deposed. The divine right theory (that the ruler received his power directly from God, and not through the people) never died out. But it was not the typical view. With the breakup of Christendom, however, from the fourteenth century and the rise of the absolutist national monarchies, the divine right theory was revived in some quarters. The neo-scholastics such as Suarez, however, argued that government should be by the consent of the governed—though that did not prevent them from choosing absolutist monarchs. Non-Catholic thinkers were to be found on both sides. Lutherans tended to be for absolutist and divine right, Calvinists for the right to revolt. Bodin (1530–1596) supported absolutism and so did Hobbes (1588–1679), while Locke (1632–1704) and Rousseau (1712–1797), in their very different ways, argued for democracy. Hegel deified the state by making it the manifestation of the infinite spirit, while Marx rejected it as the executive of the bourgeoisie.

That the state exists to do justice and seek the common good is the guiding principle of Catholic political ethics. How the state secures this common good depends on the different circumstances of the times. The Catholic inclination is to encourage personal responsibility—to prefer to have people do things for themselves rather than have them done for them—this is the essential import of the subsidiarity. However, in the circumstances in which the welfare state developed, it is wrong to assume that this undermines the principle in question. With proper safeguards the welfare state can serve personal responsibility rather than undermine it.

As the purpose of the state can be realised in different ways in different circumstances, so the organisation of the state can vary too. The party political system is preferred by many modern states which have a tradition of personal freedom under the law. Such a method is certainly compatible with the Catholic social ethic, but that does not mean that a better one may not be evolved or that it is the only one with which the Church can live.

The respect which the Christian tradition has always had for legitimately constituted political authority is reflected in the documents of the Council. But the right of political dissent is defended too. The party system is in itself an institutionalized form of such dissent. There are other forms, the peaceful and the violent. Stressing always the need for solving problems by peaceful means, the traditional teaching on the right to use violence in certain extreme cases remains valid.

A crucial issue in this context is the right to dissent by conscientious objection. The right was reasserted by the Council, but the possibility of war with nuclear weapons gives it a new dimension. A defensive war may be prepared for, leaving open the right to prepare nuclear and other modern weapons for use but many doubt if there is ever going to be any possibility of legitimate uses of modern weaponry. The debate must go on and the rights of the conscientious objector to refuse to serve in nuclear war must be stressed. But the right of self-defence by moral means which may include nuclear means remains also. The impossibility of anyone having all the information needed and of being able to weigh all the options accurately means that each must be left free to make up his own mind on this subject, unless and until it is clear that the primary intention of those using such weapons is to terrorize civilian populations.

The Council did not explore the problem of political violence, but the encyclical *Populorum Progressio* of Paul VI reasserted the traditional teaching that violence may in extreme cases be an option open to the individual.

Such, then, are the general directives that are to guide the Christian in his personal political commitment. In that commitment he must have regard for the general welfare, and he must show respect for his political opponents; likewise in party politics, the common good must never be subjected to the party good. And that common good is fulfilled when all citizens have their full human rights and accept the responsibilities attached to them. The Council document does not expatiate on human rights, but the encyclical *Pacem in Terris* had done so very fully. John Paul II also developed human rights theory in his encyclical *Redemptor Hominis*.

In his political commitment, the Christian must accept the difficulties that arise in seeking to act according to moral principle in politics. For example, it is rarely possible to have full knowledge of the implication of any course of political action; the imponderables that surround them are so much more complex than in personal decisions. Similarly, personal responsibility is more remote in collective decisions. For my own personal such decisions I am directly and fully responsible. When I join my own vote or voice to those of many others, that personal responsibility is not the same. I must nonetheless seek to do what I think is right in these circumstances according to my conscience.

The Church itself is not to be identified with any particular party or political system, but transcends them all. However, as the historical record shows, it has not always been possible for her to stick to this ideal.

Similarly today, when individual Catholics in a particular country choose overwhelmingly the same political option, the Church as a sociological fact may seem to be taking that option. But the Church leaders must ensure that as Christ's representative, as the guide for all men to their salvation, she must not be so committed to one faction.

The height of the Church's political involvement came in the Middle Ages. Thereafter her influence declined and Gallicanism in the seventeenth century, Febronianism in the 1760s and Josephism in the 1780s marked attempts by the "Catholic" absolute monarchs to limit the pope's authority over the Church even in ecclesiastical matters. The Church lived uneasily with the absolute monarchs insofar as she insisted on her right to a universal jurisdiction.

Her role in regard to the nationalist and revolutionary movements of modern Europe varied according to her situation in each country. In Ireland, Poland and Belgium she was identified with the nationalist movements because most Catholics in these countries were so identified. In France, once the revolution had shown its anti-clerical and atheist nature, the Church clashed with it. But it was in Italy that the most bitter confrontations took place. The papacy there had two problems. One was how to admit what was legitimate in the claim of the Italian nationalists without surrendering that element of true political independence, secured by her temporal possessions in central Italy, which the Church knew was necessary for her spiritual mission. The other was to reconcile itself to the legitimate claims of a movement which was not only anti-clerical but also professedly atheistic. It is now accepted that the romantic view of the risorgimento was mistaken. The liberals were self-seekers—they were for the rich and their allies, the poor, gained little from the achievement of Italian national unity.

A political role for the Church is being stressed today by the liberation theologians. One difficulty in considering their case is that it is not at all clear what it is precisely that they are saying. It would, however, seem that they reject the social teaching of the Church as having little or no relevance to the situation in which the Church is faced in Latin America especially. They seem to be advocating some kind of Marxist analysis or praxis, though again what precisely is not very clear. Their claim is that the situation in Latin America is unique and requires unique remedies. One wonders if this is so. If they looked at the achievements of the Catholic social movement in nineteenth and twentieth century Europe when the problems of social injustice in the wake of industrialization were faced, they would be less dogmatic. At Puebla Pope John Paul II, whose experience with Marxism, as with Nazi racialism, is first hand, restated the importance of the social teaching of the Church, adherence to which is a sign of generous commitment to social justice by Catholics.

Finally, the Church and international relations and international law: her concern with these matters is a direct result of the mission given to her by Christ and the role she has had in history in the light of that mission. Committed as she is to the service of all mankind, she cannot but be interested in all that would make international life and international relations more just. She insists that order between states must be founded in the moral law and that each state, however small, has an equal right to exist and be respected. Disputes between nations should be resolved where possible by peaceful means, indeed the logic of the human situation demands that we look for the establishment of an international public order based on the consent of the sovereign state and the principle of subsidiarity. The United Nations Organization, for all its defects, has always been highly regarded and encouraged by the Holy See which sees it among other things as a hope that in time something better will be achieved.

Chapter Five: *The purpose of economics is the service of men, their material needs and those of their moral, spiritual and religious life. Economic activity is to be carried out according to its own methods and laws but within the limits of morality.*

The capitalist economic theory, with the economic organisation based on it, which has done so much to form the world we live in, was the economic counterpart of a philosophical and political liberalism of which the basic assumption was belief in the absolute autonomy of the individual. It assumed that individual men of property, left free to seek their own interests, would act so as to secure justice and prosperity for all. Such an assumption knew nothing of the warnings of the Gospel about the corrupting powers of wealth. The Council however, in introducing its observations on economic life, reminds us of these injunctions. The fundamental assumptions of liberal capitalism then are not compatible with the Christian ethic. Capitalism is above all materialistic. It has made the ideal of life the pursuit of ever increasing material progress and wealth. The Christian vision, by contrast, is of enjoying God's creation here and his bounty, but doing so with the awareness that here we have no abiding city. In the light of the Gospel warnings mentioned, the knowledge that we will have to give an account of life to our Maker at the end should enable us to guard against doing injustice to others through our selfishness. The capitalist who puts worldly success measured in profit first is subject to no such restraints.

Given this antipathy between economic liberalism or capitalism and the Christian ethic, we cannot assume that since the Church defends the right to own private property, and capitalism embodies the right, the Church therefore defends, still less is responsible for capitalism. Her concept of the social responsibility of private ownership, which is compatible with her insistence that the state too has a right to own and run some sections of the economy, demands the very safeguards which were absent from capitalism in its heyday, an absence which led to the injustices it created.

The tremendous power for wealth creation implicit in the application of machines to the production of goods for mass markets (the industrial revolution) was released by men who assumed that unlimited freedom for them would serve all. It did not. The workers on the land and in industry, though they shared an increase in the material standard of living too often did not get a *just* share, while the quality of life—the condition in which they lived and worked, the opportunities open to them for cultural and moral improvement—by no means reflected the part they played in increasing the wealth of nations. That the reaction against the evils of the time should take the form of socialist extremism, summed up in the works of Marx and Engels, is not, therefore, surprising. However, Marx/Engels/Leninism has in practice been shown to be as hard, if not a harder taskmaster, than raw capitalism. Some apologists for Marxism claim that it has never been given a fair trial. But the excesses of Stalinist Russia, or of a Pol Pot's Cambodia, are directly traceable to the faulty ethics of Marx himself. A creed which makes history a sovereign more absolute than any royal absolutism of the past and concedes to those who interpret it a power more complete than any laissez-faire capitalist claimed over his workers is responsible for all the evils that those who appeal to its logic and authority commit.

Today the choice for nations which are seeking to develop modern economies would seem to be between the modified welfare capitalism of the Western democracies and the state socialism of the Soviet and Communist states. The former regards the market as the best regulator of the economy for the good of all. The factors of production—basically those who own and control wealth in its various forms, and those who work for them—are rewarded insofar as they provide the consumer with what he needs at a price that he wishes to pay. Investment is then influenced by the commercial success of firms. Tempered by effective trade unionism and political democracy, by an element of state control of the economy and by welfare schemes, capitalism has lost many of the characteristics that made it objectionable to the Christian. But the Christian ethos still rejects the materialism and the consumerism that lies behind it in practice. Its great positive advantage is that it embodies the principle of economic freedom which is the essential bulwark of all the other freedoms.

Marxist socialism, by contrast, works on the assumption that the wisdom of the central planner is the best determinant of economic activity. On the Russian model, under the Politbureau, the supreme political organisation in the state, the various descending orders of the hierarchy, determine what is to be produced, who is to produce it and how it is to be distributed. Industry is entirely state-owned but agriculture contains an element of private enterprise. As capitalism is tempered by an element of state control and ownership, so Soviet-type economies are tempered by an element of flexibility which makes allowances for personal and group initiative. In recent years economies in the Russian sphere of influence, as in Russia itself, have seen some adjustment to admit greater initiative at the lower levels and the profit motive in an effort to improve efficiency.

Soviet-type economies are less easily reconcilable with the Catholic social ethic precisely because of their limitations on freedom. On the other hand there are aspects of such systems which are more compatible with the Christian ideal—the more obvious excesses of consumerism and anti-social behaviour are curbed for example. And the Church can live with any political and economic system, however antipathetic to her, provided that the state allows her to do her work of trying to lead people in holiness.

The importance of private property, however, is central to the Church's social teaching and, all things also being equal, she recommends a system in which economic freedom exists. The right to such ownership (including that in productive goods—in modern terms e.g. factories, plant, financial resources for investment) is defended by the Scriptures and the Fathers and Doctors of the Church—though if by free choice all could accept goods in common, this is seen to be the higher ideal. However, in the real world it is accepted that private property is necessary for the proper ordering of society and as such it is defended and urged as a good thing in itself. However, such private property must operate for the good of all. It is not an absolute right in either ownership or use; it is subject to social control for the good of all.

The idea of the dignity of labour is another key principle of the Church's teaching. In Genesis God is depicted as working—and Christ himself was a village carpenter. The element of hardship that is in work as a result of the Fall does not obscure the essential goodness of the process and its importance for man to fulfill himself and support himself. The right to a just wage, earned in conditions that are worthy of him, are all implicit in this notion of the worker's dignity. The wage contract is compatible with it, but that contract must be modified by some form of participation in profits, ownership, management or control, saving the right to owners to own and managers to manage their companies. This modification of the wage contract in the individual firm and factory needs to be complemented by a system of industrial councils in individual works and areas up to industry and industry wide levels. Such councils should concern themselves with improving cooperation and looking after the good of the industry and the whole industry. The right to strike and lock out remains, but the emphasis should be on building up industrial relations systems which eliminate the cause of needless strikes and enable those which are inevitable to proceed with a minimum of loss to the worker, the employer and the community at large.

The Church's concern with international economics goes along with her concern for the whole of mankind—evidenced in the interest she takes in international law and international relations. The gap between the living standards and expectation of the poorer countries and those of the richer is clearly not one that can be reconciled with the Creator's plan in giving the world to all men in common that all might therefore enjoy a good life. Trade and aid are the means through which the richer nations must do their duty to the poorer, who also have a duty to see that they do all they can for themselves.

A connected problem is that of catering to the growth in the world's population. There is no global population problem in the sense that the actual or potential resource of the world cannot match any projected future growth. During the last twenty-five years when the doomsters have been most eloquent, global food supply has more than kept pace with population growth overall. The difficulties that arise in this matter are those of too rapid population growth in particular areas. A population control policy may be needed in these circumstances together with national and international cooperation to overcome the immediate problems of food supply. So too regarding the overall international picture concerning resources and the danger to the environment in exploiting them to provide the further industrial and technological development supporting the world's population needs. Once again there is no overall shortage, actual or potential, of resources, but there are specific shortages, and there are difficulties of exploitation; past experience, however, indicates that these are not insuperable. The environment too is safe if we behave responsibly.

Central to the solution of the problem of population and world food supplies is that of agricultural prosperity and efficiency. So much of the concern of mankind since the industrial revolution has been with industrial economics that we forget that the ability of people to feed themselves properly and exploit the wealth of the world for raw materials is as essential to human progress in material terms today as it ever was. And the key to improved agricultural performance world wide is encouraging the peasant on the small farm, the people who supply the world with most of its agricultural produce, to improve their efficiency. Agrarian reform, land reform above all, is crucial. But it has to be the right sort of reform backed up by proper social provision and action to ensure efficiency and improved performance. With such help the small farmers of the world can improve their productivity dramatically as the experience of Egypt, Taiwan, Japan and South Korea, for example, shows.

General Conclusions of the Whole Study

From all this we see two things clearly above all. The first is that the ethical guidance given to us by revelation and by the natural law, with the Church interpreting both, is clear in principle and practice in what concerns our personal and family lives, the areas in which we have control of our destinies whatever the social, political and economic conditions we live in. Secure in our knowledge of what is true and good in this sphere, what God asks of us in terms of the personal service of a righteous life, we are equipped to seek the holiness as he asks us. It is in this quest that we see the Church and our membership in it as our true home, our basic citizenship, because in the eucharistic community the graces are available to us to fulfill our basic obligation to God in these matters.

The second thing is that there is an essential difference between the implications of the guidance given us on matters of personal ethics and that which is given us on social ethics. It does not affect the binding nature of the guidance, the principles of the social teaching itself. It affects rather the way that we put them into practice. There can be no doubt how the Ten Commandments and their implications in our personal lives should be put into practice. There can be doubt, there is doubt, about how best to organise the state and the economy. It is inevitable that this should be, because conditions and needs in these matters change, and political society and economic society have their own legitimate autonomy in responding to meet them. Those who operate them, insofar as they are using their abilities in accord with right reason, are exercising an authority and power given them by God. It is possible to set out what sort of a social order best accords with the principles of Catholic social ethics—representative democracy, socially responsible private ownership in a mixed economy, a social pattern which allows freedom under the law and which is orientated, not to consumerism, but to the love and service of God and my neighbour for his sake, one in which the true common good is served as each is given the fullest possible opportunity to develop his or her potential, and there is injustice to none and a good life for all. We can keep this ideal pattern in mind; we must do so. But, in working to achieve it, we have to take part in collective decision-making which dilutes our power over our destiny and reduces our personal accountability. Even where we work for these ends, we may have to tolerate a situation in which one or other is denied. And we cannot always be sure that we will live in circumstances which will allow us to work openly and immediately for these ends. We may be citizens of a country so poor or backward, or subject to a regime which denies these aims, that we are not able, or free, to seek to build up a society of this kind. Even where these conditions existed, we would still have to love and serve God as best we could. The way would be open to us to lead a full Christian life in our personal and family lives, but we would have to be patient in seeking means to put Christian ethical principles into action in social life. We would then be guarded against despair, knowing that in doing what we could in the freedom allowed us we were pleasing God. We would know that, in certain strictly defined circumstances, violence to redress justice was an option open to the individual, though the Church can never counsel this, but must always work for justice by peaceful means. We would be guarded against apathy or fatalism in knowing that we had a duty to do what we could to improve our lot or that of our fellow citizens. We would be guarded against the illusions of an earthly utopia and embracing solutions which were not compatible with our Christian principles, because we would know what courses of action and what ideals we could accept and what we could not. The Christian ethic then provides a complete guide to the good life—but it remains anchored and rooted in the transcendent, the knowledge that we have a hope beyond this world. It does not then let us fall into the error of thinking that a true and complete justice can be attained here on earth; greater justice is a goal for which we must always strive. And it gives us the best motive for working for justice—belief in Christ and reliance on him in his Church, the mother and teacher of nations, for the guidance and the strength we need in our quest.

DOCUMENTATION

I

Extracts from the *Declaration on Religious Liberty* (*Dignitatis Humanae*) of the Second Vatican Council. 7 December 1965.

The translation is taken from *Vatican Council II: The Conciliar and the Post Conciliar Documents*, edited by Austin Flannery, O.P., Dublin, 1975.

The document as a whole is not a long one—there being fifteen paragraphs in all. The first section consists of just one paragraph and is entitled, "On the Rights of the Person and Communities to Social and Civil Liberty in Religious Matters". There are two chapters forming the main body of the document, chapter one (paragraphs 2 to 8), "The General Principle of Religious Freedom" and chapter two (paragraphs 9 to 15), "Religious Freedom in the Light of Revelation".

CHAPTER I

THE GENERAL PRINCIPLE OF RELIGIOUS FREEDOM

2. The Vatican Council declares that the human person has a right to religious freedom. Freedom of this kind means that all men should be immune from coercion on the part of individuals, social groups and every human power so that, within due limits, nobody is forced to act against his convictions in religious matters in private or in public, alone or in associations with others. The Council further declares that the right to religious freedom is based on the very dignity of the human person as known through the revealed word of God and by reason itself.[2] This right of the human person to religious freedom must be given such recognition in the constitutional order of society as will make it a civil right.

It is in accordance with their dignity that all men, because they are persons, that is, beings endowed with reason and free will and therefore bearing personal responsibility, are both impelled by their nature and bound by a moral obligation to seek the truth, especially religious truth. They are also bound to adhere to the truth once they come to know it and direct their whole lives in accordance with the

---

[2] Cf. John XXIII, Encycl. *Pacem in Terris*, 11 April 1963: *AAS* 55 (1963), pp. 260–261; Pius XII, Radio message, 24 Dec. 1942: *AAS* 35 (1943), p. 19; Pius XI, Encycl. *Mit brennender Sorge*, 14 March 1937: *AAS* 29 (1937), p. 160, Leo XIII, Encycl. *Libertas Praestantissimum*, 20 June 1888: *Acta Leonis XIII* 8 (1888), pp. 237–288.

demands of truth. But men cannot satisfy this obligation in a way that is in keeping with their own nature unless they enjoy both psychological freedom and immunity from external coercion. Therefore the right to religious freedom has its foundation not in the subjective attitude of the individual but in his very nature. For this reason the right to this immunity continues to exist even in those who do not live up to their obligation of seeking the truth and adhering to it. The exercise of this right cannot be interfered with as long as the just requirements of public order are observed.

3. This becomes even clearer if one considers that the highest norm of human life is the divine law itself—eternal, objective and universal, by which God orders, directs and governs the whole world and the ways of the human community according to a plan conceived in his wisdom and love. God has enabled man to participate in this law of his so that, under the gentle disposition of divine providence, many may be able to arrive at a deeper and deeper knowledge of unchangeable truth. For this reason everybody has the duty and consequently the right to seek the truth in religious matters so that, through the use of appropriate means, he may prudently form judgments of conscience which are sincere and true.

The search for truth, however, must be carried out in a manner that is appropriate to the dignity of the human person and his social nature, namely, by free enquiry with the help of teaching or instruction, communication and dialogue. It is by these means that men share with each other the truth they have discovered, or think they have discovered, in such a way that they help one another in the search for truth. Moreover, it is by personal assent that men must adhere to the truth they have discovered.

It is through his conscience that man sees and recognizes the demands of the divine law. He is bound to follow this conscience faithfully in all his activity so that he may come to God, who is his last end. Therefore he must not be forced to act contrary to his conscience. Nor must he be prevented from acting according to his conscience, especially in religious matters. The reason is because the practice of religion of its very nature consists primarily of those voluntary and free internal acts by which a man directs himself to God. Acts of this kind cannot be commanded or forbidden by any merely human authority.[3] But his own social nature requires that man give external expression to these internal acts of religion, that he communicate with others on religious matters, and profess his religion in community. Consequently to deny man the free exercise of religion in society, when the just requirements of public order are observed, is to do an injustice to the human person and to the very order established by God for men.

Furthermore, the private and public acts of religion by which men direct themselves to God according to their convictions transcend of their very nature the earthly and temporal order of things. Therefore the civil authority, the purpose of which is the care of the common good in the temporal order, must recognize and look with favor on the religious life of the citizens. But if it

---

[3] Cf. John XXIII, Encycl. *Pacem in Terris*, 11 April 1963: *AAS* 55 (1963), p. 270; Paul VI, Radio message, 22 Dec. 1964: *AAS* 57 (1965), pp. 181–182.

presumes to control or restrict religious activity it must be said to have exceeded the limits of its power.

4. The freedom or immunity from coercion in religious matters which is the right of individuals must also be accorded to men when they act in community. Religious communities are a requirement of the nature of man and of religion itself.

Therefore, provided the just requirements of public order are not violated, these groups have a right to immunity so that they may organize themselves according to their own principles. They must be allowed to honour the supreme Godhead with public worship, help their members to practice their religion and strengthen them with religious instruction, and promote institutions in which members may work together to organize their own lives according to their religious principles.

Religious communities also have the right not to be hindered by legislation or administrative action on the part of the civil authority in the selection, training, appointment and transfer of their own ministers, in communicating with religious authorities and communities in other parts of the world, in erecting buildings for religious purposes, and in the acquisition and use of the property they need.

Religious communities have the further right not to be prevented from publicly teaching and bearing witness to their beliefs by the spoken or written word. However, in spreading religious belief and in introducing religious practices everybody must at all times avoid any action which seems to suggest coercion or dishonest or unworthy persuasion especially when dealing with the uneducated or the poor. Such a manner of acting must be considered an abuse of one's own right and an infringement of the rights of others.

Also included in the right to religious freedom is the right of religious groups not to be prevented from freely demonstrating the special value of their teaching for the organization of society and the inspiration of all human activity. Finally, rooted in the social nature of man and in the very nature of religion is the right of men, prompted by their own religious sense, freely to hold meetings or establish educational, cultural, charitable and social organizations.

5. Every family, in that it is a society with its own basic rights, has the right freely to organize its own religious life in the home under the control of the parents. These have the right to decide in accordance with their own religious beliefs the form of religious upbringing which is to be given to their children. The civil authority must therefore recognize the right of parents to choose with genuine freedom schools or other means of education. Parents should not be subjected directly or indirectly to unjust burdens because of this freedom of choice. Furthermore, the rights of parents are violated if their children are compelled to attend classes which are not in agreement with the religious beliefs of the parents or if there is but a single compulsory system of education from which all religious instruction is excluded.

6. The common good of society consists in the sum total of those conditions of social life which enable men to achieve a fuller measure of perfection with greater ease. It consists especially in safeguarding the rights and duties of the human

person.[4] For this reason the protection of the right to religious freedom is the common responsibility of individual citizens, social groups, civil authorities, the Church and other religious communities. Each of these has its own special responsibility in the matter according to its particular duty to promote the common good.

The protection and promotion of the inviolable rights of man is an essential duty of every civil authority.[5] The civil authority therefore must undertake to safeguard the religious freedom of all the citizens in an effective manner by just legislation and other appropriate means. It must help to create conditions favorable to the fostering of religious life so that the citizens will be really in a position to exercise their religious rights and fulfil their religious duties and so that society itself may enjoy the benefits of justice and peace, which result from man's faithfulness to God and his holy will.[6]

If because of the circumstances of a particular people special civil recognition is given to one religious community in the constitutional organization of a State, the right of all citizens and religious communities to religious freedom must be recognized and respected as well.

Finally, the civil authority must see to it that the equality of the citizens before the law, which is itself an element of the common good of society, is never violated either openly or covertly for religious reasons and that there is no discrimination among citizens.

From this it follows that it is wrong for a public authority to compel its citizens by force or fear or by any other means to profess or repudiate any religion or to prevent anyone from joining or leaving a religious body. There is even more serious transgression of God's will and of the sacred rights of the individual person and the family of nations when force is applied to wipe out or repress religion either throughout the whole world or in a single region or in a particular community.

7. The right to freedom in matters of religion is exercised in human society. For this reason its use is subject to certain regulatory norms.

In availing of any freedom men must respect the moral principle of personal and social responsibility: in exercising their rights individual men and social groups are bound by the moral law to have regard for the rights of others, their own duties to others and the common good of all. All men must be treated with justice and humanity.

Furthermore, since civil society has the right to protect itself against possible abuses committed in the name of religious freedom the responsibility of providing such protection rests especially with the civil authority. However, this must not be done in an arbitrary manner or by the unfair practice of favoritism but in accordance with legal principles which are in conformity with the objective moral

[4] Cf. John XXIII. Encycl. *Mater et Magistra*, 15 May 1961: *AAS* 53 (1961), p. 417; Id., Encycl. *Pacem in Terris*, 11 April 1963: *AAS* 55 (1963), p. 273.

[5] Cf. John XXIII. Encycl. *Pacem in Terris*, 11 April 1963: *AAS* 55 (1963), pp. 273–274: Pius XII, Radio message, 1 June 1941: *AAS* 33 (1941), p. 200.

[6] Cf. Leo XIII, Encycl. *Immortale Dei*, 1 Nov. 1885: *AAS* 18 (1885), p. 165.

order. These principles are necessary for the effective protection of the rights of all citizens and for peaceful settlement of conflicts of rights. They are also necessary for an adequate protection of that just public peace which is to be found where men live together in good order and true justice. They are required too for the necessary protection of public morality. All these matters are basic to the common good and belong to what is called public order. For the rest, the principle of the integrity of freedom in society should continue to be upheld. According to this principle man's freedom should be given the fullest possible recognition and should not be curtailed except when and in so far as is necessary.

8. Modern man is subjected to a variety of pressures and runs the risk of being prevented from following his own free judgment. On the other hand, there are many who, under the pretext of freedom, seem inclined to reject all submission to authority and make light of the duty of obedience.

For this reason this Vatican Council urges everyone, especially those responsible for educating others, to try to form men with a respect for the moral order who will obey lawful authority and be lovers of true freedom—men, that is, who will form their own judgments in the light of truth, direct their activities with a sense of responsibility, and strive for what is true and just in willing cooperation with others.

Religious liberty therefore should have this further purpose and aim of enabling men to act with greater responsibility in fulfilling their own obligations in society.

II

Extracts from the *Pastoral Constitution on the Church in the Modern World (Gaudium et Spes)* of the Second Vatican Council, 7 December 1965.

The translation is taken from *Vatican Council II: The Conciliar and the Post Conciliar Documents*, edited by Austin Flannery, O.P., Dublin 1975.

There are 93 paragraphs in the document as a whole. They are divided into a *Preface* on the "Solidarity of the Church with the Whole Human Family" (paragraphs 1 to 3), and *Introduction* dealing with "The Situation of Man in the World Today" (paragraphs 4 to 10), and two parts. *Part One* is entitled "The Church and Man's Vocation" and consists of four chapters. *Chapter One* (paragraphs 12 to 22) is on "The Dignity of the Human Person", *Chapter Two* (paragraphs 23 to 32), on "The Community of Mankind", *Chapter Three* (paragraphs 33 to 39),"Man's Activity in the Universe" and *Chapter Four* the "Role of the Church in the Modern World".

Part Two looks at "Some More Urgent Problems". *Chapter One* (paragraphs 47 to 53) is on "The Dignity of Marriage and the Family", *Chapter Two* (paragraphs 53 to 62), "The Proper Development of Culture",

Chapter Three (paragraphs 63 to 72), "Economic and Social Life", *Chapter Four* (paragraphs 73 to 76), "The Political Community" and *Chapter Five* (paragraphs 77 to 93), "Fostering of Peace and the Establishment of a Community of Nations".

The extracts which follow are from the *Introduction* (paragraphs 4 to 10), *Part One, Chapter One* (paragraphs 15 to 17) and *Chapter Three* (paragraphs 33 to 36, 42 to 43 and 47 to 52) and from *Part Two, Chapter Three* (paragraphs 63 to 72), *Chapter Four* (paragraphs 73 to 76) and *Chapter Five* (paragraphs 77 to 90).

4. . . . In no other age has mankind enjoyed such an abundance of wealth, resources and economic well-being; and yet a huge proportion of the people of the world is plagued by hunger and extreme need while countless numbers are totally illiterate. At no time have men had such a keen sense of freedom, only to be faced by new forms of slavery in living and thinking. There is on the one hand a lively feeling of unity and of compelling solidarity of mutual dependence, and on the other a lamentable cleavage of bitterly opposing camps. We have not yet seen the last of bitter political, social, and economic hostility, and racial and ideological antagonism, nor are we free from the spectre of a war of total destruction. If there is a growing exchange of ideas, there is still widespread disagreement about the meaning of the words expressing our key concepts. There is lastly a painstaking search for a better material world, without a parallel spiritual advancement.

Small wonder then that many of our contemporaries are prevented by this complex situation from recognizing permanent values and duly applying them to recent discoveries. As a result they hover between hope and anxiety and wonder uneasily about the present course of events. It is a situation that challenges men to reply; they cannot escape.

Deep-seated Changes

5. The spiritual uneasiness of today and the changing structure of life are part of a broader upheaval, whose symptoms are the increasing part played on the intellectual level by the mathematical and natural sciences (not excluding the sciences dealing with man himself) and on the practical level by their repercussions on technology. The scientific mentality has wrought a change in the cultural sphere and on habits of thought, and the progress of technology is now reshaping the face of the earth and has its sights set on the conquest of space.

The human mind is, in a certain sense, broadening its mastery over time—over the past through the insights of history, over the future by foresight and planning. Advances in biology, psychology, and the social sciences not only lead man to greater self-awareness, but provide him with the technical means of molding the lives of whole peoples as well. At the same time the human race is giving more and more thought to the forecasting and control of its own population growth.

The accelerated pace of history is such that one can scarcely keep abreast of it. The destiny of the human race is viewed as a complete whole, no longer as it were, in the particular histories of various peoples: now it merges into a complete whole. And so mankind substitutes a dynamic and more evolutionary concept of nature for a static one, and the result is an immense series of new problems calling for a new endeavor of analysis and synthesis.

Changes in the Social Order

6. As a result the traditional structure of local communities—family, clan, tribe, village, various groupings and social relationships—is subjected to ever more sweeping changes. Industrialization is on the increase and has raised some nations to a position of affluence, while it radically transfigures ideas and social practices hallowed by centuries. Urbanization too is on the increase, both on account of the expanding number of city dwellers and the spread of an urban way of life into rural settings. Recent more efficient mass media are contributing to the spread of knowledge and the speedy diffusion far and wide of habits of thought and feeling, setting off chain reactions in their wake. One cannot underestimate the effect of emigration on those who, for whatever reason, are led to undertake a new way of life. On the whole, the bonds uniting man to his fellows multiply without ceasing, and "socialization" creates yet other bonds, without, however, a corresponding personal development, and truly personal relationships, "personalization". It is above all in countries with advanced standards of economic and social progress that these developments are evident, but there are stirrings for advancement afoot among peoples eager to share in the benefit of industrialization and urbanization. Peoples like these, especially where ancient traditions are still strong, are at the same time conscious of the need to exercise their freedom in a more mature and personal way.

Changes in Attitudes, Morals and Religion

7. A change in attitudes and structures frequently calls accepted values into question. This is true above all of young people who have grown impatient at times and, indeed, rebellious in their distress. Conscious of their own importance in the life of society, they aspire to play their part in it all the sooner.

As regards religion there is a completely new atmosphere that conditions its practice. On the one hand people are taking a hard look at all magical world-views and prevailing superstitions and demanding a more personal and active commitment of faith, so that not a few have achieved a lively sense of the divine. On the other hand greater numbers are falling away from the practice of religion. In the past it was the exception to repudiate God and religion to the point of abandoning them, and then only in individual cases; but nowadays it seems a matter of course to reject them as incompatible with scientific progress and a new kind of humanism. In many places it is not only in philosophical terms that such trends are expressed, but there are signs of them in literature, art, the humanities, the interpretation of history and even civil law: all of which is very disturbing to many people.

Imbalances in the World of Today

8. The headlong development of the world and a keener awareness of existing inequalities make for the creation and aggravation of differences and imbalances. On the personal level there often arises an imbalance between an outlook which is practical and modern and a way of thinking which fails to master and synthesize

the sum total of its ideas. Another imbalance occurs between concern for practicality and the demands of moral conscience, not to mention that between the claims of group living and the needs of individual reflection and contemplation. A third imbalance takes the form of conflict between specialization and an overall view of reality.

On the family level there are tensions arising out of demographic, economic and social pressures, out of conflicts between succeeding generations, and out of new social relationships between the sexes.

On the level of race and social class we find tensions between the affluent and the underdeveloped nations; we find them between international bodies set up in the interests of peace and the ambitions of ideological indoctrination along with national or bloc expansionism. In the midst of it all stands man, at once the author and the victim of mutual distrust, animosity, conflict and woe.

Broader Aspirations of Mankind

9. Meanwhile there is a growing conviction of mankind's ability and duty to strengthen its mastery over nature and of the need to establish a political, social, and economic order at the service of man to assert and develop the dignity proper to individuals and to societies.

Great numbers of people are acutely conscious of being deprived of the world's goods through injustice and unfair distribution and are vehemently demanding their share of them. Developing nations like the recently independent states are anxious to share in the political and economic benefits of modern civilization and to play their part freely in the world, but they are hampered by their economic dependence on the rapidly expanding richer nations and the ever widening gap between them. The hungry nations cry out to their affluent neighbors; women claim parity with men in fact as well as of rights, where they have not already obtained it; farmers and workers insist not just on the necessities of life but also on the opportunity to develop by their labor their personal talents and to play their due role in organizing economic, social, political and cultural life. Now for the first time in history people are not afraid to think that cultural benefits are for all and should be available to everybody.

These claims are but the sign of a deeper and more widespread aspiration. Man as an individual and as a member of society craves a life that is full, autonomous, and worthy of his nature as a human being; he longs to harness for his own welfare the immense resources of the modern world. Among nations there is a growing movement to set up a worldwide community.

In the light of the foregoing factors there appears the dichotomy of a world that is at once powerful and weak, capable of doing what is noble and what is base, disposed to freedom and slavery, progress and decline, brotherhood and hatred. Man is growing conscious that the forces he has unleashed are in his own hands and that it is up to him to control them or be enslaved by them. Here lies the modern dilemma.

Man's Deeper Questionings

10. The dichotomy affecting the modern world is, in fact, a symptom of the deeper dichotomy that is in man himself. He is the meeting point of many

conflicting forces. In his condition as a created being he is subject to a thousand shortcomings, but feels untrammeled in his inclinations and destined for a higher form of life. Torn by a welter of anxieties he is compelled to choose between them and repudiate some among them. Worse still, feeble and sinful as he is, he often does the very thing he hates and does not do what he wants.[1] And so he feels himself divided, and the result is a host of discords in social life. Many, it is true, fail to see the dramatic nature of this state of affairs in all its clarity for their vision is in fact blurred by materialism, or they are prevented from even thinking about it by the wretchedness of their plight. Others delude themselves that they have found peace in a world-view now fashionable. There are still others whose hopes are set on a genuine and total emancipation of mankind through human effort alone and look forward to some future earthly paradise where all the desires of their hearts will be fulfilled. Nor is it unusual to find people who having lost faith in life extol the kind of foolhardiness which would empty life of all significance in itself and invest it with a meaning of their own devising. Nonetheless, in the face of modern developments there is a growing body of men who are asking the most fundamental of all questions or are glimpsing them with a keener insight: What is man? What is the meaning of suffering, evil, death, which have not been eliminated by all this progress? What is the purpose of these achievements, purchased at so high a price? What can man contribute to society? What can he expect from it? What happens after this earthly life is ended?

The Church believes that Christ, who died and was raised for the sake of all,[2] can show man the way and strengthen him through the Spirit in order to be worthy of his destiny: nor is there any other name under heaven given among men by which they can be saved.[3] The Church likewise believes that the key, the center and the purpose of the whole of man's history is to be found in its Lord and Master. She also maintains that beneath all that changes there is much that is unchanging, much that has its ultimate foundation in Christ, who is the same yesterday, and today, and forever.[4] And that is why the Council, relying on the inspiration of Christ, the image of the invisible God, the firstborn of all creation,[5] proposes to speak to all men in order to unfold the mystery that is man and cooperate in tackling the main problems facing the world today.

PART ONE

CHAPTER ONE

THE DIGNITY OF THE HUMAN PERSON

Dignity of the Intellect, of Truth, and of Wisdom

15. Man, as sharing in the light of the divine mind, rightly affirms that by his intellect he surpasses the world of mere things. By diligent use of his talents through the ages he has indeed made progress in the empirical sciences, in technology, and in the liberal arts. In our time his attempts to search out the secrets

---

[1] Cf. Rom. 7:14 ff.
[2] Cf. 2 Cor. 5:15.
[3] Cf. Acts 4:12.
[4] Cf. Heb. 13:8.
[5] Cf. Col. 1:15.

of the material universe and to bring it under his control have been extremely successful. Yet he has always looked for, and found, truths of a higher order. For his intellect is not confined to the range of what can be observed by the senses. It can, with genuine certainty, reach to realities known only to the mind, even though, as a result of sin, its vision has been clouded and its powers weakened.

The intellectual nature of man finds at last its perfection, as it should, in wisdom, which gently draws the human mind to look for and to love what is true and good. Filled with wisdom man is led through visible realities to those which cannot be seen.

Our age, more than any of the past, needs such wisdom if all that man discovers is to be ennobled through human effort. Indeed the future of the world is in danger unless provision is made for men of greater wisdom. It should also be pointed out that many nations, poorer as far as material goods are concerned, yet richer as regards wisdom, can be of the greatest advantage to others.

It is by the gift of the Holy Spirit that man, through faith, comes to contemplate and savor the mystery of God's design.[8]

Dignity of Moral Conscience

16. Deep within his conscience man discovers a law which he has not laid upon himself but which he must obey. Its voice, ever calling him to love and to do what is good and to avoid evil, tells him inwardly at the right moment: do this, shun that. For man has in his heart a law inscribed by God. His dignity lies in observing this law, and by it he will be judged.[9] His conscience is man's most secret core, and his sanctuary. There he is alone with God whose voice echoes in his depths.[10] By conscience, in a wonderful way, that law is made known which is fulfilled in the love of God and of one's neighbour.[11] Through loyalty to conscience Christians are joined to other men in the search for truth and for the right solution to so many moral problems which arise both in the life of individuals and from social relationships. Hence, the more a correct conscience prevails, the more do persons and groups turn aside from blind choice and try to be guided by the objective standards of moral conduct. Yet it often happens that conscience goes astray through ignorance which it is unable to avoid, without thereby losing its dignity. This cannot be said of the man who takes little trouble to find out what is true and good, or when conscience is by degrees almost blinded through the habit of committing sin.

The Excellence of Freedom

17. It is, however, only in freedom that man can turn himself towards what is good. The people of our time prize freedom very highly and strive eagerly for it. In this they are right. Yet they often cherish it improperly, as if it gave them leave to do anything they like, even when it is evil. But that which is truly freedom is an

---

[8] Cf. Eccl. 17:7–8.

[9] Cf. Rom. 2:15–16.

[10] Cf. Pius XII, Radio message on rightly forming the Christian conscience in youth, 23 March 1952: *AAS* 44 (1952), p. 271.

[11] Cf. Mt. 22:37–40; Gal. 5:14.

exceptional sign of the image of God in man. For God willed that man should "be left in the hand of his own counsel"[12] so that he might of his own accord seek his creator and freely attain his full and blessed perfection by cleaving to him. Man's dignity therefore requires him to act out of conscious and free choice, as moved and drawn in a personal way from within, and not by blind impulses in himself or by mere external constraint. Man gains such dignity when, ridding himself of all slavery to the passions, he presses forward towards his goal by freely choosing what is good, and by his diligence and skill, effectively secures for himself the means suited to this end. Since human freedom has been weakened by sin it is only by the help of God's grace that man can give his actions their full and proper relationship to God. Before the judgment seat of God an account of his own life will be rendered to each one according as he has done either good or evil.[13]

CHAPTER THREE

MAN'S ACTIVITY IN THE UNIVERSE

The Problem

33. Man has always striven to develop his life through his mind and his work; today his efforts have achieved a measure of success, for he has extended and continues to extend his mastery over nearly all spheres of nature thanks to science and technology. Thanks above all to an increase in all kinds of interchange between nations the human family is gradually coming to recognize itself and constitute itself as one single community over the whole earth. As a result man now produces by his own enterprise many things which in former times he looked for from heavenly powers.

In the face of this immense enterprise now involving the whole human race men are troubled by many questionings. What is the meaning and value of this feverish activity? How ought all of these things be used? To what goal is all this individual and collective enterprise heading? The Church is guardian of the heritage of the divine Word and draws religious and moral principles from it, but she does not always have a ready answer to every question. Still, she is eager to associate the light of revelation with the experience of mankind in trying to clarify the course upon which mankind has just entered.

Value of Human Activity

34. Individual and collective activity, that monumental effort of man through the centuries to improve the circumstances of the world, presents no problem to believers: considered in itself, it corresponds to the plan of God. Man was created in God's image and was commanded to conquer the earth with all it contains and to rule the world in justice and holiness:[1] he was to acknowledge God as maker of all things and relate himself and the totality of creation to him, so that through the dominion of all things by man the name of God would be majestic in all the earth.[2]

---

[12] Cf. Eccl. 15:14.
[13] Cf. 2 Cor. 5:10.
[1] Cf. Gen. 1:26–27; 9:2–3; Wis. 9:2–3.
[2] Cf. Ps. 8:7 and 10.

This holds good also for our daily work. When men and women provide for themselves and their families in such a way as to be of service to the community as well, they can rightly look upon their work as a prolongation of the work of the creator, a service to their fellow men, and their personal contribution to the fulfillment in history of the divine plan.[3]

Far from considering the conquests of man's genius and courage as opposed to God's power as if he set himself up as a rival to the creator, Christians ought to be convinced that the achievements of the human race are a sign of God's greatness and the fulfilment of his mysterious design. With an increase in human power comes a broadening of responsibility on the part of individuals and communities: there is no question, then, of the Christian message inhibiting men from building up the world or making them disinterested in the good of their fellows: on the contrary it is an incentive to do these very things.[4]

Regulation of Human Activity

35. Human activity proceeds from man: it is also ordered to him. When he works, not only does he transform matter and society, but he fulfils himself. He learns, he develops his faculties, and he emerges from and transcends himself. Rightly understood, this kind of growth is more precious than any kind of wealth that can be amassed. It is what a man is, rather than what he has, that counts.[5] Technical progress is of less value than advances towards greater justice, wider brotherhood, and a more humane social environment. Technical progress may supply the material for human advance but it is powerless to actualize it.

Here then is the norm for human activity—to harmonize with the authentic interests of the human race, in accordance with God's will and design, and to enable men as individuals and as members of society to pursue and fulfil their total vocation.

Rightful Autonomy of Earthly Affairs

36. There seems to be some apprehension today that a close association between human activity and religion will endanger the autonomy of man, of organizations and of science. If by the autonomy of earthly affairs is meant the gradual discovery, exploitation, and ordering of the laws and values of matter and society, then the demand for autonomy is perfectly in order: it is at once the claim of modern man and the desire of the creator. By the very nature of creation, material being is endowed with its own stability, truth and excellence, its own order and laws. These man must respect as he recognizes the methods proper to every science and technique. Consequently, methodical research in all branches of knowledge, provided it is carried out in a truly scientific manner and does not override moral laws, can never conflict with the faith, because the things of the

---

[3] Cf. John XXIII. Litt. Encycl. *Pacem in Terris*, *AAS* 55 (1963), p. 297.

[4] Cf. *Message to all Men*, issued by the Fathers at the beginning of Vatican Council II, October 1962: *AAS* 54 (1962), p. 823.

[5] Cf. Paul VI, *Allocutio* to the Diplomatic Corps, 7 January 1965: *AAS* 57 (1965), p. 232.

world and the things of faith derive from the same God.[6] The humble and persevering investigator of the secrets of nature is being led, as it were, by the hand of God in spite of himself, for it is God, the conserver of all things, who made them what they are. We cannot but deplore certain attitudes (not unknown among Christians) deriving from a shortsighted view of the rightful autonomy of science; they have occasioned conflict and controversy and have misled many into opposing faith and science.[7]

However, if by the term "the autonomy of earthly affairs" is meant that material being does not depend on God and that man can use it as if it had no relation to its creator, then the falsity of such a claim will be obvious to anyone who believes in God. Without a creator there can be no creature. In any case, believers, no matter what their religion, have always recognized the voice and the revelation of God in the language of creatures. Besides, once God is forgotten, the creature is lost sight of as well.

What the Church Offers to Society

42. The union of the family of man is greatly consolidated and perfected by the unity which Christ established among the sons of God.[10]

Christ did not bequeath to the Church a mission in the political, economic, or social order: the purpose he assigned to it was a religious one.[11] But this religious mission can be the source of commitment, direction and vigor to establish and consolidate the community of men according to the law of God. In fact, the Church is able, indeed it is obliged, if times and circumstances require it, to initiate action for the benefit of all men, especially of those in need, like works of mercy and similar undertakings.

The Church, moreover, acknowledges the good to be found in the social dynamism of today, particularly progress towards unity, healthy socialization, and civil and economic cooperation. The encouragement of unity is in harmony with the deepest nature of the Church's mission, for it "is in the nature of a sacrament—a sign and instrument—that is of communion with God and of unity among all men."[12] It shows to the world that social and exterior union comes from a union of hearts and minds, from the faith and love by which its own indissoluble unity has been founded in the Holy Spirit. The impact which the Church can have on modern society, amounts to an effective living of faith and love, not to any external power exercised by purely human means.

By its nature and mission the Church is universal in that it is not committed to any one culture or to any political, economic or social system. Hence it can form a very close unifying effect on the various communities of men and nations, provided they have trust in the Church and guarantee it true freedom to carry out

[6] Cf. Vatican Council I, Dogmatic Constitution *De fide cath.*, ch. 3: *Denz.* 1785–1786 (3004–3005).

[7] Cf. Pius Paschini, *Vita e opere di Galileo Galilei*, 2 vol., Vatic., 1964.

[10] Cf. Dogmatic Constitution *Lumen Gentium*, ch. 2, n. 9: *AAS* 57 (1965), pp. 12–14.

[11] Cf. Pius XII, *Allocutio* to Historians and Artists, 9 March 1956: *AAS* 48 (1956), p. 212.

[12] Dogmatic Constitution *Lumen Gentium*, ch. 1, no. 1: *AAS* 57(1965), p. 5.

its mission. With this in view the Church calls upon its members and upon all men to put aside, in the family spirit of the children of God, all conflict between nations and races and to consolidate legitimate human organizations in themselves.

Whatever truth, goodness, and justice is to be found in past or present human institutions is held in high esteem by the Council. In addition, the Council declares that the Church is anxious to help and foster these institutions insofar as it depends on it and is compatible with its mission. The Church desires nothing more ardently than to develop itself untrammelled in the service of all men under any regime which recognizes the basic rights of the person and the family, and the needs of the common good.

What the Church Offers to Human Activity Through its Members

43. The Council exhorts Christians, as citizens of both cities, to perform their duties faithfully in the spirit of the Gospel. It is a mistake to think that, because we have here no lasting city, but seek the city which is to come, [13] we are entitled to shirk our earthly responsibilities; this is to forget that by our faith we are bound all the more to fulfil these responsibilities according to the vocation of each one. [14] But it is no less mistaken to think that we may immerse ourselves in earthly activities as if these latter were utterly foreign to religion, and religion were nothing more than the fulfilment of acts of worship and the observance of a few moral obligations. One of the gravest errors of our time is the dichotomy between the faith which many profess and the practice of their daily lives. As far back as the Old Testament the prophets vehemently denounced this scandal, [15] and in the New Testament Christ himself with greater force threatened it with severe punishment. [16] Let there, then, be no such pernicious opposition between professional and social activity on the one hand and religious life on the other. The Christian who shirks his temporal duties shirks his duties towards his neighbor, neglects God himself, and endangers his eternal salvation. Let Christians follow the example of Christ who worked as a craftsman; let them be proud of the opportunity to carry out their earthly activity in such a way as to integrate human, domestic, professional, scientific and technical enterprises with religious values, under whose supreme direction all things are ordered to the glory of God.

It is to the laity, though not exclusively to them, that secular duties and activity properly belong. When therefore, as citizens of the world, they are engaged in any activity either individually or collectively, they will not be satisfied with meeting the minimum legal requirements but will strive to become truly proficient in that sphere. They will gladly cooperate with others working towards the same objectives. Let them be aware of what their faith demands of them in these matters and derive strength from it; let them not hesitate to take the initiative at the opportune moment and put their findings into effect. It is their task to cultivate a properly informed conscience and to impress the divine law on the affairs of the

[13] Cf. Heb. 13:14.
[14] Cf. 2 Th. 3:6–13, Eph. 4:28.
[15] Cf. Is. 58:1–12.
[16] Cf. Mt. 23:3–33; Mk. 7:10–13.

earthly city. For guidance and spiritual strength let them turn to the clergy; but let them realize that their pastors will not always be so expert as to have a ready answer to every problem (even every grave problem) that arises; this is not the role of the clergy; it is rather up to the laymen to shoulder their responsibilities under the guidance of Christian wisdom and with eager attention to the teaching authority of the Church.[17]

Very often their Christian vision will suggest a certain solution in some given situation. Yet it happens rather frequently, and legitimately so, that some of the faithful, with no less sincerity, will see the problem quite differently. Now if one or other of the proposed solutions is too easily associated with the message of the Gospel, they ought to remember that in those cases no one is permitted to identify the authority of the Church exclusively with his own opinion. Let them, then, try to guide each other by sincere dialogue in a spirit of mutual charity and with anxious interest above all in the common good.

The laity are called to participate actively in the whole life of the Church; not only are they to animate the world with the spirit of Christianity, but they are to be witnesses to Christ in all circumstances and at the very heart of the community of mankind.

Bishops, to whom has been committed the task of directing the Church of God, along with their priests, are to preach the message of Christ in such a way that the light of the Gospel will shine on all activities of the faithful. Let all pastors of souls be mindful to build up by their daily behavior and concern[18] an image of the Church capable of impressing men with the power and truth of the Christian message. By their words and example and in union with religious and with the faithful, let them show that the Church with all its gifts is, by its presence alone, an inexhaustible font of all those resources of which the modern world stands in such dire need. Let them prepare themselves by careful study to meet and play their part in dialogue with the world and with men of all shades of opinion: let them have in their hearts above all these words of the Council: "Since the human race today is tending more and more towards civil, economic and social unity, it is all the more necessary that priests should unite their efforts and combine their resources under the leadership of the bishops and the supreme Pontiff and thus eliminate division and dissension in every shape and form, so that all mankind may be led into the unity of the family of God."[19]

By the power of the Holy Spirit the Church is the faithful spouse of the Lord and will never fail to be a sign of salvation in the world; but it is by no means unaware that down through the centuries there have been among its members,[20] both clerical and lay, some who were disloyal to the Spirit of God. Today as well, the Church is not blind to the discrepancy between the message it proclaims and the human weakness of those to whom the Gospel has been entrusted. Whatever is

[17] Cf. John XXIII, Litt. Encycl. *Mater et Magistra*, IV: *AAS* 53 (1961), pp. 456–7: cf. I: *AAS* loc. cit., pp. 407, 410–411.
[18] Dogmatic Constitution *Lumen Gentium*, ch. 3, n. 28: *AAS* 57 (1965), pp. 34–5.
[19] Ibid., n. 28: *AAS* loc. cit., pp. 35–6.
[20] Cf. St. Ambrose, *De virginitate*, ch. VIII, n. 48: *PL* 16, 278.

history's judgment on these shortcomings, we cannot ignore them and we must combat them earnestly, lest they hinder the spread of the Gospel. The Church also realizes how much it needs the maturing influence of centuries of past experience in order to work out its relationship to the world. Guided by the Holy Spirit the Church ceaselessly "exhorts her children to purification and renewal so that the sign of Christ may shine more brightly over the face of the Church."[21]

PART TWO

CHAPTER ONE

THE DIGNITY OF MARRIAGE AND THE FAMILY

Marriage and the Family in the Modern World

47. The well-being of the individual person and of both human and Christian society is closely bound up with the healthy state of conjugal and family life. Hence Christians are overjoyed, and so too are all who esteem conjugal and family life highly, to witness the various ways in which progress is being made in fostering those partnerships of love and in encouraging reverence for human life; there is progress too in services available to married people and parents for fulfilling their lofty calling: even greater benefits are to be expected and efforts are being made to bring them about.

However, this happy picture of the dignity of these partnerships is not reflected everywhere, but is overshadowed by polygamy, the plague of divorce, so-called free love, and similar blemishes; furthermore, married love is too often dishonoured by selfishness, hedonism, and unlawful contraceptive practices. Besides, the economic, social, psychological, and civil climate of today has a severely disturbing effect on family life. There are also the serious and alarming problems arising in many parts of the world as a result of population expansion. On all of these counts an anguish of conscience is being generated. And yet the strength and vigor of the institution of marriage and family shines forth time and again: for despite the hardships flowing from the profoundly changing conditions of society today, the true nature of marriage and of the family is revealed in one way or another.

It is for these reasons that the Council intends to present certain key points of the Church's teaching in a clearer light; and it hopes to guide and encourage Christians and all men who are trying to preserve and to foster the dignity and supremely sacred value of the married state.

Holiness of Marriage and the Family

48. The intimate partnership of life and the love which constitutes the married state has been established by the creator and endowed by him with its own proper laws: it is rooted in the contract of its partners, that is, in their irrevocable personal consent. It is an institution confirmed by the divine law and receiving its stability, even in the eyes of society, from the human act by which the partners mutually surrender themselves to each other; for the good of the partners, of the children,

---

[21] Dogmatic Constitution *Lumen Gentium*, ch. 2, n. 15: *AAS* 57 (1965), p. 20.

and of society this sacred bond no longer depends on human decision alone. For God himself is the author of marriage and has endowed it with various benefits and with various ends in view:[1] all of these have a very important bearing on the continuation of the human race, on the personal development and eternal destiny of every member of the family, on the dignity, stability, peace, and prosperity of the family and of the whole human race. By its very nature the institution of marriage and married love is ordered to the procreation and education of the offspring and it is in them that it finds its crowning glory. Thus the man and woman, who "are no longer two but one" (Mt. 19:6), help and serve each other by their marriage partnership; they become conscious of their unity and experience it more deeply from day to day. The intimate union of marriage, as a mutual giving of two persons, and the good of the children demand total fidelity from the spouses and require an unbreakable unity between them.[2]

Christ our Lord has abundantly blessed this love, which is rich in its various features, coming as it does from the spring of divine love and modeled on Christ's own union with the Church. Just as of old, God encountered his people with a covenant of love and fidelity,[3] so our Saviour, the spouse of the Church,[4] now encounters Christian spouses through the sacrament of marriage. He abides with them in order that by their mutual self-giving spouses will love each other with enduring fidelity, as he loved the Church and delivered himself for it.[5] Authentic married love is caught up into divine love and is directed and enriched by the redemptive power of Christ and the salvific action of the Church with the result that the spouses are effectively led to God and are helped and strengthened in their lofty role as fathers and mothers.[6] Spouses, therefore, are fortified and, as it were, consecrated for the duties and dignity of their state by a special sacrament;[7] fulfilling their conjugal and family role by virtue of this sacrament, spouses are penetrated with the spirit of Christ and their whole life is suffused by faith, hope and charity; thus they increasingly further their own perfection and their mutual sanctification, and together they render glory to God.

Inspired by the example and family prayer of their parents, children, and in fact everyone living under the family roof, will more easily set out upon the path of a truly human training, of salvation, and of holiness. As for the spouses, when they are given the dignity and role of fatherhood and motherhood, they will eagerly carry out their duties of education, especially religious education, which primarily devolves on them.

[1] St. Augustine, De bono coniugii: PL 40, 375–376 and 394; St. Thomas Summa Theol., Suppl. Quaest. 49, art. 3 ad 1; Decretum pro Armenis: Denz. 702 (1327); Pius XI, Litt. Encycl. Casti Connubii: AAS 22 (1930) pp. 543–545; Denz. 2227–2238 (3703–3714).

[2] Cf. Pius XI, Litt. Encycl. Casti Connubii: AAS 22 (1930), pp. 546–7: Denz. 2231 (3706).

[3] Cf. Hos. 2; Jer. 3:6–13; Eze. 16 and 23; Is. 54.

[4] Cf. Mt. 9:15; Mk. 2:19–20; Lk. 5:34–35; Jn. 3:29; 2 Cor. 11:2; Eph. 5:27; Apoc. 19:7–8; 21:2 and 9.

[5] Cf. Eph. 5:25.

[6] Cf. Vatican Council II, Dogmatic Constitution Lumen Gentium: AAS 57 (1965), pp. 15–16; 40–41; 47.

[7] Cf. Pius XI, Litt. Encycl. Casti Connubii: AAS (1930), p. 583.

Children as living members of the family contribute in their own way to the sanctification of their parents. With sentiments of gratitude, affection and trust, they will repay their parents for the benefits given to them and will come to their assistance as devoted children in times of hardship and in the loneliness of old age. Widowhood, accepted courageously as a continuation of the calling to marriage, will be honoured by all.[8] Families will generously share their spiritual treasures with other families. The Christian family springs from marriage,[9] which is an image and a sharing in the partnership of love between Christ and the Church; it will show forth to all men Christ's living presence in the world and the authentic nature of the Church by the love and generous fruitfulness of the spouses, by their unity and fidelity, and by the loving way in which all members of the family cooperate with each other.

Married Love

49. On several occasions the Word of God invites the betrothed to nourish and foster their betrothal with chaste love, and likewise spouses their marriage.[10] Many of our contemporaries, too, have a high regard for true love between husband and wife as manifested in the worthy customs of various times and peoples. Married love is an eminently human love because it is an affection between two persons rooted in the will and it embraces the good of the whole person; it can enrich the sentiments of the spirit and their physical expression with a unique dignity and ennoble them as the special elements and signs of the friendship proper to marriage. The Lord, wishing to bestow special gifts of grace and divine love on it, has restored, perfected, and elevated it. A love like that, bringing together the human and the divine, leads the partners to a free and mutual giving of self, experienced in tenderness and action, and permeates their whole lives;[11] besides, this love is actually developed and increased by the exercise of it. This is a far cry from mere erotic attraction, which is pursued in selfishness and soon fades away in wretchedness.

Married love is uniquely expressed and perfected by the exercise of the acts proper to marriage. Hence the acts in marriage by which the intimate and chaste union of the spouses takes place are noble and honorable; the truly human performance of these acts fosters the self-giving they signify and enriches the spouses in joy and gratitude. Endorsed by mutual fidelity and, above all, consecrated by Christ's sacrament, this love abides faithfully in mind and body in prosperity and adversity and hence excludes both adultery and divorce. The unity of marriage, distinctly recognized by our Lord, is made clear in the equal personal dignity which must be accorded to man and wife in mutual and unreserved affection. Outstanding courage is required for the constant fulfilment of the duties of this Christian calling; spouses, therefore, will need grace for leading a holy life:

[8] Cf. 1 Tim. 5:3.

[9] Cf. Eph. 5:32.

[10] Cf. Gen. 2:22–24; Prov. 5:18–20; 31:10–31; Tob. 8:4–8; Cant. 1:1–3; 2–16; 7:8–11; Eph. 5:25–33.

[11] Cf. Pius XI, Litt. Encycl. *Casti Connubii*: *AAS* 22 (1930), pp. 547 and 548; *Denz*. 2232 (3707).

they will eagerly practice a love that is firm, generous, and prompt to sacrifice and will ask for it in their prayers.

Authentic married love will be held in high esteem, and healthy public opinion will be quick to recognize it, if Christian spouses give outstanding witness to faithfulness and harmony in their love, if they are conspicuous in their concern for the education of their children, and if they play their part in a much needed cultural, psychological, and social renewal in matters of marriage and the family. It is imperative to give suitable timely instruction to young people, above all in the heart of their own families, about the dignity of married love, its role and its exercise; in this way they will be able to engage in honorable courtship and enter upon marriage of their own.

The Fruitfulness of Marriage

50. Marriage and married love are by nature ordered to the procreation and education of children. Indeed children are the supreme gift of marriage and greatly contribute to the good of the parents themselves. God himself said: "It is not good that man should be alone" (Gen. 2:18) and "from the beginning (he) made them male and female" (Mt. 19:4); wishing to associate them in a special way with his own creative work, God blessed man and woman with the words: "Be fruitful and multiply" (Gen. 1:28). Without intending to underestimate the other ends of marriage, it must be said that true married love and the whole structure of family life which results from it is directed to disposing the spouses to cooperate valiantly with the love of the Creator and Saviour, who through them will increase and enrich his family from day to day.

Married couples should regard it as their proper mission to transmit human life and to educate their children; they should realize that they are thereby cooperating with the love of God the Creator and are, in a certain sense, its interpreters. This involves the fulfilment of their role with a sense of human and Christian responsibility and the formation of correct judgments through docile respect for God and common reflection and effort; it also involves a consideration of their own good and the good of their children already born or yet to come, an ability to read the signs of the times and of their own situation on the material and spiritual level, and, finally, an estimation of the good of the family, of society, and of the Church. It is the married couple themselves who must in the last analysis arrive at these judgments before God. Married people should realize that in their behavior they may not simply follow their own fancy but must be ruled by conscience—and conscience ought to be conformed to the law of God in the light of the teaching authority of the Church, which is the authentic interpreter of divine law. For the divine law throws light on the meaning of married love, protects it and leads it to truly human fulfilment. Whenever Christian spouses in a spirit of sacrifice and trust in divine providence[12] carry out their duties of procreation with generous human and Christian responsibility, they glorify the Creator and perfect themselves in Christ. Among the married couples who thus fulfil their God-given mission, special mention should be made of those who after prudent reflection and

[12] Cf. 1 Cor. 7:5.

common decision courageously undertake the proper upbringing of a large number of children. [13]

But marriage is not merely for the procreation of children: its nature as an indissoluble compact between two people and the good of the children demand that the mutual love of the partners be properly shown, that it should grow and mature. Even in cases where despite the intense desire of the spouses there are no children, marriage still retains its character of being a whole manner and communion of life and preserves its value and indissolubility.

Married Love and Respect for Human Life

51. The Council realizes that married people are often hindered by certain situations in modern life from working out their married love harmoniously and that they can sometimes find themselves in a position where the number of children cannot be increased, at least for the time being: in cases like these it is quite difficult to preserve the practice of faithful love and the complete intimacy of their lives. But where the intimacy of married life is broken, it often happens that faithfulness is imperiled and the good of the children suffers: then the education of the children as well as the courage to accept more children are both endangered.

Some of the proposed solutions to these problems are shameful and some people have not hesitated to suggest the taking of life; the Church wishes to emphasize that there can be no conflict between the divine laws governing the transmission of life and the fostering of authentic married love.

God, the Lord of life, has entrusted to men the noble mission of safeguarding life, and men must carry it out in a manner worthy of themselves. Life must be protected with the utmost care from the moment of conception: abortion and infanticide are abominable crimes. Man's sexuality and the faculty of reproduction wondrously surpass the endowments of lower forms of life; therefore the acts proper to married life are to be ordered according to authentic human dignity and must be honored with the greatest reverence. When it is a question of harmonizing married love with the responsible transmission of life, it is not enough to take only the good intention and the evaluation of motives into account; the objective criteria must be used, criteria drawn from the nature of the human person and human action, criteria which respect the total meaning of mutual self-giving and human procreation in the context of true love; all this is possible only if the virtue of married chastity is seriously practiced. In questions of birth regulation the sons of the Church, faithful to these principles, are forbidden to use methods disapproved of by the teaching authority of the Church in its interpretation of the divine law. [14]

---

[13] Cf. Pius XII, Allocutio, Tra le verita, 20 Jan. 1958: AAS 50 (1958), p. 91.

[14] Cf. Pius XI. Litt. Encycl. Casti Connubii: AAS 22 (1930), pp. 559–561; Denz. 2239–2241 (3716–3718); Pius XII, Allocutio to the Congress of Italian Midwives, 29 Oct. 1951; AAS 43 (1951), pp. 835–54; Paul VI, Allocutio to the Cardinals, 23 June 1964: AAS 56 (1964), pp. 581–9. By order of the Holy Father, certain questions requiring further and more careful investigation have been given over to a commission for the study of population, the family, and births, in order that the Holy Father may pass judgment when its task is completed. With the teaching of the magisterium standing as it is, the Council has no intention of proposing concrete solutions at this moment.

Let all be convinced that human life and its transmission are realities whose meaning is not limited by the horizons of this life only: their true evaluation and full meaning can only be understood in reference to man's eternal destiny.

Fostering Marriage and the Family: A Duty for All

52. The family is, in a sense, a school for human enrichment. But if it is to achieve the full flowering of its life and mission, the married couple must practice an affectionate sharing of thought and common deliberation as well as eager co-operation as parents in the children's upbringing. The active presence of the father is very important for their training: the mother, too, has a central role in the home, for the children, especially the younger children, depend on her considerably; this role must be safeguarded without, however, underrating woman's legitimate social advancement. The education of children should be such that when they grow up they will be able to follow their vocation, including a religious vocation, and choose their state of life with full consciousness of responsibility; and if they marry they should be capable of setting up a family in favorable moral, social, and economic circumstances. It is the duty of parents and teachers to guide young people with prudent advice in the establishment of a family; their interest should make young people listen to them eagerly; and they should beware of exercising any undue influence, directly or indirectly, to force them into marriage or compel them in their choice of partner.

The family is the place where different generations come together and help one another to grow wiser and harmonize the rights of individuals with other demands of social life; as such it constitutes the basis of society. Everyone, therefore, who exercises an influence in the community and in social groups should devote himself effectively to the welfare of marriage and the family. Civil authority should consider it a sacred duty to acknowledge the true nature of marriage and the family, to protect and foster them, to safeguard public morality and promote domestic prosperity. The rights of parents to procreate and educate children in the family must be safeguarded. There should also be welfare legislation and provision of various kinds made for the protection and assistance of those who unfortunately have been deprived of the benefits of family life.

Christians, making full use of the times in which we live[15] and carefully distinguishing the everlasting from the changeable, should actively strive to promote the values of marriage and the family; it can be done by the witness of their own lives and by concerted action along with all men of good will; in this way they will overcome obstacles and make provision for the requirements and the advantages of family life arising at the present day. To this end the Christian instincts of the faithful, the right moral conscience of man, and the wisdom and skill of persons versed in the sacred sciences will have much to contribute.

Experts in other sciences, particularly biology, medicine, social science and psychology, can be of service to the welfare of marriage and the family and the peace of mind of people, if by pooling their findings they try to clarify thoroughly the different conditions favoring the proper regulation of births.

[15] Cf. Eph. 5:16; Col. 4:5.

It devolves on priests to be properly trained to deal with family matters and to nurture the vocation of married people in their married and family life by different pastoral means, by the preaching of the Word of God, by liturgy, and other spiritual assistance. They should strengthen them sympathetically and patiently in their difficulties and comfort them in charity with a view to the formation of truly radiant families.

Various organizations, especially family associations, should set out by their programs of instruction and activity to strengthen young people and especially young married people, and to prepare them for family, social and apostolic life.

Let married people themselves, who are created in the image of the living God, and constituted in an authentic personal dignity, be united together in equal affection, agreement of mind, and mutual holiness.[16] Thus, in the footsteps of Christ, the principle of life,[17] they will bear witness by their faithful love in the joys and sacrifices of their calling, to that mystery of love which the Lord revealed to the world by his death and resurrection.[18]

CHAPTER THREE
ECONOMIC AND SOCIAL LIFE

Some Characteristics of Economic Life Today

63. . . . . Like all other areas of social life, the economy of today is marked by man's growing dominion over nature, by closer and keener relationships between individuals, groups and peoples, and by the frequency of state intervention. At the same time increased efficiency in production and improved methods of distribution, of productivity and services, have rendered the economy an instrument capable of meeting the growing needs of the human family.

But the picture is not without its disturbing elements. Many people, especially in economically advanced areas, seem to be dominated by economics; almost all of their personal and social lives are permeated with a kind of economic mentality, and this is true of nations that favor a collective economy as well as of other nations. At the very same time when economic progress (provided it is directed and organized in a reasonable and human way) could do so much to reduce social inequalities, it serves all too often only to aggravate them; in some places it even leads to a decline in the position of the underprivileged and contempt for the poor. In the midst of huge numbers deprived of the absolute necessities of life there are some who live in riches and squander their wealth; and this happens in less developed areas as well. Luxury and misery exist side by side. While a few individuals enjoy an almost unlimited opportunity to choose for themselves, the vast majority have no chance whatever of exercising personal initiative and responsibility, and quite often have to live and work in conditions unworthy of human beings.

Similar economic and social imbalances exist between those engaged in agriculture, industry, and the service industries, and even between different areas of

---

[16] Cf. *Sacramentarium Gregorianum: PL* 78, 262.
[17] Cf. Rom. 5:15 and 18; 6:5–11; Gal. 2:20.
[18] Cf. Eph. 5:25–27.

the same country. The growing contrast between economically more advanced countries and others could well endanger world peace.

Our contemporaries are daily becoming more keenly aware of these discrepancies because they are thoroughly convinced that this unhappy state of affairs can and should be rectified by the greater technical and economic resources available in the world today. To achieve it much reform in economic and social life is required along with a change of mentality and of attitude by all men. It was for this reason that the Church in the course of centuries has worked out in the light of the Gospel principles of justice and equity demanded by right reason for individual and social life and also for international relations. The Council now intends to reiterate these principles in accordance with the situation of the world today and will outline certain guidelines, particularly with reference to the requirements of economic development.[1]

SECTION I: ECONOMIC DEVELOPMENT

Economic Development in the Service of Man

64. Today more than ever before there is an increase in the production of agricultural and industrial goods, and in the number of services available, and this is as it should be in view of the population expansion and growing human aspirations. Therefore we must encourage technical progress and the spirit of enterprise, we must foster the eagerness for creativity and improvement, and we must promote adaptation of production methods and all serious efforts of people engaged in production—in other words of all elements which contribute to economic progress. The ultimate and basic purpose of economic production does not consist merely in the increase of goods produced, nor in profit nor prestige; it is directed to the service of man, of man, that is, in his totality, taking into account his material needs and the requirements of his intellectual, moral, spiritual and religious life; of all men whomsoever and of every group of men of whatever race or from whatever part of the world. Therefore, economic activity is to be carried out in accordance with techniques and methods belonging to the moral order,[2] so that God's design for man may be fulfilled.[3]

Economic Development Under Man's Direction

65. Economic development must remain under man's direction; it is not to be left to the judgment of a few individuals or groups possessing too much economic power, nor of the political community alone, nor of a few strong nations. It is only right that, in matters of general interest, as many people as possible, and, in international relations, all nations, should participate actively in decision making. It is likewise necessary that the voluntary initiatives of individuals and of free groups should be integrated with state enterprises and organized in a suitable and

[1] Pius XII, Message, 23 March 1952: *AAS* 44 (1952), p. 273; John XXIII, *Allocutio* to the Italian Catholic Workers Association, 1 May 1959: *AAS* 51 (1959), p. 358.

[2] Pius XI, Litt. Encycl. *Quadragesimo Anno: AAS* 23 (1931), p. 190 f.; Pius XII, *Message*, 23 March 1952: *AAS* 44 (1952), p. 276 ff; John XXIII, Litt. Encycl. *Mater et Magistra: AAS* 53 (1961), p. 450; Vatican Council II, Decree *Inter Mirifica*, ch. 1, n. 6: *AAS* 56 (1964), p. 147.

[3] Cf. Mt. 16:26; Lk. 16:1–31; Col. 3:17.

harmonious way. Nor should development be left to the almost mechanical evolution of economic activity nor to the decision of public authority. Hence we must denounce as false doctrines which stand in the way of all reform on the pretext of a false notion of freedom, as well as those which subordinate the basic rights of individuals and of groups to the collective organization of production.[4]

All citizens should remember that they have the right and the duty to contribute according to their ability to the genuine progress of their own community and this must be recognized by the civil authority. Above all in areas of retarded economic progress, where all resources must be urgently exploited, the common good is seriously endangered by those who hoard their resources unproductively and by those who (apart from the case of every man's personal right of migration) deprive their community of much needed material and spiritual assistance.

An End to Excessive Economic and Social Differences

66. To fulfil the requirements of justice and equity, every effort must be made to put an end as soon as possible to the immense economic inequalities which exist in the world and increase from day to day, linked with individual and social discrimination, provided, of course, that the rights of individuals and the character of each people are not disturbed. Likewise in many areas, in view of the special difficulties of production and marketing in agriculture, country people must be helped to improve methods of production and marketing, to introduce necessary developments and renewal, and to achieve a fair return for their products, lest they continue, as often happens, in the state of inferior citizens. Farmers themselves, especially young farmers, ought to apply themselves eagerly to bettering their professional skill, without which the advancement of farming is impossible.[5]

Justice and equity also demand that the livelihood of individuals and their families should not become insecure and precarious through a kind of mobility which is a necessary feature of developing economies. All kinds of discrimination in wages and working conditions should be avoided in regard to workers who come from other countries or areas and contribute their work to the economic development of a people or a region. Furthermore, no one, especially public authorities, should treat them simply as mere tools of production, but as persons; they should facilitate them in having their families with them and in obtaining decent housing conditions, and they should endeavor to integrate them into the social life of the country or area to which they have come. However, employment should be found for them so far as possible in their own countries.

Nowadays when the economy is undergoing transition, as in new forms of industrialization, where, for example automation is being introduced, care must be taken to ensure that there is sufficient and suitable employment available; opportunities of appropriate technical and professional training should be pro-

[4] Cf. Leo XIII, Litt. Encycl. *Libertas Praestantissimum*, 20 June 1888: *AAS* 20 (1887–1888), p. 597 ff.; Pius XI, Litt. Encycl. *Quadragesimo Anno*: *AAS* 23 (1931), p. 191 ff.; Pius XI, *Divini Redemptoris*: *AAS* 39 (1937), p. 65 ff.; Pius XII, *Christmas Message*, 1941: *AAS* 34 (1942), p. 10 ff.; John XXIII, Litt. Encycl. *Mater et Magistra*: *AAS* 53 (1961), pp. 401–464.

[5] For the problem of agriculture cf. especially John XXIII, Litt. Encycl. *Mater et Magistra*: *AAS* 53 (1961), p. 341 ff.

vided, and safeguards should be placed so that the livelihood and human dignity should be protected of those who through age or ill health labor under serious disadvantages.

SECTION 2: SOME PRINCIPLES GOVERNING
ECONOMIC AND SOCIAL LIFE AS A WHOLE

Work, Working Conditions, Leisure

67. Human work which is exercised in the production and exchange of goods or in the provision of economic services, surpasses all other elements of economic life, for the latter are only means to an end.

Human work, whether exercised independently or in subordination to another, proceeds from the human person, who as it were impresses his seal on the things of nature and reduces them to his will. By his work a man ordinarily provides for himself and his family, associates with others as his brothers, and renders them service; he can exercise genuine charity and be a partner in the work of bringing divine creation to perfection. Moreover, we believe in faith that through the homage of work offered to God man is associated with the redemptive work of Jesus Christ, whose labor with his hands at Nazareth greatly ennobled the dignity of work. This is the source of every man's duty to work loyally as well as his right to work; moreover, it is the duty of society to see to it that, according to the prevailing circumstances, all citizens have the opportunity of finding employment. Finally, remuneration for work should guarantee man the opportunity to provide a dignified livelihood for himself and his family on the material, social, cultural and spiritual level to correspond to the role and the productivity of each, the relevant economic factors in his employment, and the common good.[6]

Since economic activity is, for the most part, the fruit of the collaboration of many men, it is unjust and inhuman to organize and direct it in such a way that some of the workers are exploited. But it frequently happens, even today, that workers are almost enslaved by the work they do. So-called laws of economics are no excuse for this kind of thing. The entire process of productive work, then, must be accommodated to the needs of the human person and the nature of his life, with special attention to domestic life and of mothers of families in particular, taking sex and age always into account. Workers should have the opportunity to develop their talents and their personalities in the very exercise of their work. While devoting their time and energy to the performance of their work with a due sense of responsibility, they should nevertheless be allowed sufficient rest and leisure to cultivate their family, cultural, social and religious life. And they should be given the opportunity to develop these energies and talents, which perhaps are not catered for in their professional work.

---

[6] Cf. Leo XIII, Litt. Encycl. *Rerum Novarum: AAS* 23 (1890–1891), pp. 649–662; Pius XI, Litt. Encycl. *Quadragesimo Anno: AAS* 23 (1931), p. 200; Pius XI, Litt. Encycl. *Divini Redemptoris: AAS* 29 (1937), p. 92; Pius XII, *Christmas Message*, 1942: *AAS* 35 (1943); Pius XII, Radio message to Spanish workers, 11 March 1951: *AAS* 43 (1951), p. 215; John XXIII, Litt. Encycl. *Mater et Magistra: AAS* 53 (1961), p. 419.

Co-Responsibility in Enterprise And in the Economic System as a Whole; Labor Disputes

68. In business enterprises it is persons who associate together, that is, men who are free and autonomous, created in the image of God. Therefore, while taking into account the role of every person concerned—owners, employers, management, and employees—and without weakening the necessary executive unity, the active participation of everybody in administration is to be encouraged.[7] More often, however, decisions concerning economic and social conditions are made not so much within the business itself but by institutions at a higher level, and since it is on these that the future of the workers and their children depends, the latter ought to have a say in decision-making either in person or through their representatives.

Among the fundamental rights of the individual must be numbered the right of workers to form themselves into associations which truly represent them and are able to cooperate in organizing economic life properly, and the right to play their part in the activities of such associations without risk of reprisal. Thanks to such organized participation, along with progressive economic and social education, there will be a growing awareness among all people of their role and their responsibility, and according to the capacity and aptitudes of each one, they will feel that they have an active part to play in the whole task of economic and social development and in the achievement of the common good as a whole.

In the event of economic-social disputes, all should strive to arrive at peaceful settlements. The first step is to engage in sincere discussion between all sides; but the strike remains even in the circumstances of today a necessary (although an ultimate) means for the defence of workers' rights and the satisfaction of their lawful aspirations. As soon as possible, however, avenues should be explored to resume negotiations and effect reconciliation.

Earthly Goods Destined for All Men

69. God destined the earth and all it contains for all men and all peoples so that all created things would be shared fairly by all mankind under the guidance of justice tempered by charity.[8] No matter what the structures of property are in different peoples, according to various and changing circumstances and adapted to their lawful institutions, we must never lose sight of this universal destination of earthly goods. In his use of things man should regard the external goods he legitimately owns not merely as exclusive to himself but common to others also, in the sense that they can benefit others as well as himself.[9] Therefore every man has the right

[7] Cf. John XXIII, Litt. Encycl. *Mater et Magistra*: AAS 53 (1961), pp. 408, 424, 427; the word "curatione" used in the original text is taken from the Latin version of the Encyclical *Quadragesimo Anno*: AAS 23 (1931), p. 199. For the evolution of the question cf. also: Pius XII, *Allocutio*, 3 June 1950: AAS 42 (1950), pp. 484–8: Paul VI, *Allocutio*, 8 June 1964. AAS 56 (1964): pp. 547–9.

[8] Cf. Pius XII, Litt. Encycl. *Sertum Laetitiae*: AAS 31 (1939), p. 642; John XXIII, Litt. Encycl. *Consistorial Allocution*: AAS 52 (1969), pp. 5–11; John XXIII, Litt. Encycl. *Mater et Magistra*: AAS 53 (1961), p. 411.

[9] Cf. St. Thomas, *Summa Theol.*, II–II, q. 32 a. 5 ad 2; ibid., q. 66, a. 2: cf. the explanation in Leo XIII, Litt. Encycl. *Rerum Novarum*: AAS 23 (1890–1891), p. 651; cf. also Pius XII, *Allocution*, 1 June 1941: AAS 33 (1941), p. 199; Pius XII, *Christmas Message*, 1954: AAS 47 (1955), p. 27.

to possess a sufficient amount of the earth's goods for himself and his family. This has been the opinion of the Fathers and Doctors of the Church, who taught that men are bound to come to the aid of the poor and to do so not merely out of their superfluous goods.[10] "When a person is in extreme necessity he has the right to supply himself with what he needs out of the riches of others."[11] Faced with a world today where so many people are suffering from want, the Council asks individuals and governments to remember the saying of the Fathers: "Feed the man dying of hunger, because if you do not feed him you are killing him,"[12] and it urges them according to their ability to share and dispose of their goods to help others, above all by giving them aid which will enable them to help and develop themselves.

In economically less developed societies it often happens that the common destination of goods is partly achieved by a system of community customs and traditions which guarantee a minimum of necessities to each one. Certain customs must not be considered sacrosanct if they no longer correspond to modern needs; on the other hand one should not rashly do away with respectable customs which if they are brought up to date can still be very useful. In the same way, in economically advanced countries the common destination of goods is achieved through a system of social institutions dealing with insurance and security. Family and social services, especially those providing for culture and education, should be further developed. In setting up these different organizations care must be taken to prevent the citizens from slipping into a kind of passivity vis-a-vis society, or of irresponsibility in their duty, or of a refusal to do their fair share.

Investment and Money

70. Investment in its turn should be directed to providing employment and ensuring sufficient income for the people of today and of the future. Those responsible for investment and the planning of the economy (individuals, associ-

[10] Cf. St. Basil, *Hom. in illud Lucae "Destruam horrea mea,"* n. 2: *PG* 31, 263; Lactantius, *Divinarum Institutionum*, bk. V on justice: *PL* 6, 565 B; St. Augustine, *In Ioann. Ev.*, tr. 50, n. 6: *PL* 35, 1760; St. Augustine, *Enerratio in Ps. CXLVII*, 12: *PL* 37, 1922; St. Gregory the Great, *Homiliae in Ev.*, hom. 20: *PL* 76, 1165; St. Gregory the Great, *Regulae Pastoralis liber*, part III, c. 21: *PL* 77, 87; St. Bonaventure, *In III Sent.*, d. 33, dub. 1 (ed. Quaracchi III, 728); St. Bonaventure, *In IV Sent.* d. 15, p. 11, a. 2, q. 1 (ed. cit. IV. 371 b); q. *de superfluo* (ms. *Assisi, Bibl., commun.* 186, ff. 112a–113a); St. Albert the Great, *In III Sent.*, d. 33, a. 3, sol. 1 (ed. Borgnet XXVIII, 611); St. Albert the Great, *In IV Sent*, d. 15, a. 16 (ed. cit. XXIX, 494–497). As regards the determination of what is superfluous today cf. John XXIII, Radio–Television Message, 11 Sept. 1962: *AAS* 54 (1962), p. 682: "It is the duty of every man, the compelling duty of Christians, to calculate what is superfluous by the measure of the needs of others and to see to it that the administration and distribution of created goods be utilized for the advantage of all."

[11] In this case the old principle holds good: "In extreme necessity all goods are common, that is, they are to be shared." On the other hand for the scope, the extension, and the way this principle is to be applied in the text, besides accepted modern authors, cf. St. Thomas, *Summa Theol.*, II-II, q. 66, a. 7. Clearly, for the correct application of the principle all the moral conditions required must be fulfilled.

[12] Cf. Gratian, *Decretum*, c. 21, dist. LXXXVI: ed. Friedberg I, 302. This axiom is found already in *PL* 54, 591a and *PL* 56, 1132b; cf. *Antonianum*, 27 (1952), 349–366.

ations, public authority) must keep these objectives in mind; they must show themselves aware of their serious obligation, on the one hand, to see to it that the necessities for living a decent life are available to individuals and to the community as a whole, and, on the other hand, to provide for the future and strike a rightful balance between the needs of present-day consumption, individual and collective, and the requirements of investment for future generations. Always before their eyes they must keep the pressing needs of underdeveloped countries and areas. In fiscal matters they must be careful not to do harm to their own country or to any other. Care must also be taken that economically weak countries do not unjustly suffer loss from a change in the value of money.

Ownership, Private Property, Large Estates

71. Property and other forms of private ownership of external goods contribute to the expression of personality and provide man with the opportunity of exercising his role in society and in the economy; it is very important, then, that the acquisition of some form of ownership of external goods by individuals and communities be fostered.

Private property or some form of ownership of external goods assures a person a highly necessary sphere for the exercise of his personal and family autonomy and ought to be considered as an extension of human freedom. Lastly, in stimulating exercise of responsibility, it constitutes one of the conditions for civil liberty.[13] Nowadays the forms of such ownership or property are varied and are becoming more diversified every day. In spite of the social security, the rights, and the services guaranteed by society, all these forms of ownership are still a source of security which must not be underestimated. And this applies not only to owner-ship of material goods but also to the possession of professional skills.

The lawfulness of private ownership is not opposed to the various forms of public ownership. But the transfer of goods from private to public ownership may be undertaken only by competent authority, in accordance with the demands and within the limits of the common good, and it must be accompanied by adequate compensation. Furthermore, the state has the duty to prevent anyone from abusing his private property to the detriment of the common good.[14] By its nature private property has a social dimension which is based on the law of common destination of earthly goods.[15] Whenever the social aspect is forgotten, ownership can often become the source of greed and serious disorder, so that its opponents easily find a pretext for calling the right itself into question.

In several economically retarded areas there exist large, and sometimes very extensive rural estates which are only slightly cultivated or not cultivated at all for

[13] Cf. Leo XII, Litt. Encycl. *Rerum Novarum*: *AAS* 23 (1890–1891), pp. 643–6; Pius XI, Litt. Encycl. *Quadragesimo Anno*: *AAS* 23 (1931), p. 191; Pius XII, Radio message, 1 June 1941: *AAS* 33 (1941), p. 199; Pius XII, *Christmas Message*, 1942: *AAS* 35 (1943), p. 17; Pius XII, Radio message, 1 Sept. 1944: *AAS* 36 (1944), p. 253; John XXIII, Litt. Encycl. *Mater et Magistra*: *AAS* 53 (1961), pp. 428 ff.

[14] Cf. Pius XI, Litt. Encycl. *Quadragesimo Anno*: *AAS* 23 (1931), p. 214; John XXIII, Litt. Encycl. *Mater et Magistra*: *AAS* 53 (1961), p. 429.

[15] Cf. Pius XII, Radio message of Pentecost 1941: *AAS* 44 (1941), p. 199; John XXIII, Litt. Encycl. *Mater et Magistra*: *AAS* 53 (1961), p. 430.

the sake of profit, while the majority of the population have no land or possess only very small holdings and the need to increase agricultural production is pressing and evident to all. Not infrequently those who are hired as labourers or who till a portion of the land as tenants receive a wage or income unworthy of the human being; they are deprived of decent living conditions and are exploited by middlemen. They lack all sense of security and live in such a state of personal dependence that almost all chance of exercising initiative and responsibility is closed to them and they are denied any cultural advancement or participation in social and political life. Reforms are called for in these different situations: incomes must be raised, working conditions improved, security in employment assured, and personal incentives to work encouraged; estates insufficiently cultivated must even be divided up and given to those who will be able to make them productive. In this event the necessary resources and equipment must be supplied, especially educational facilities and proper cooperative organizations. However, when the common good calls for expropriation, compensation must be made and is to be calculated according to equity, with all circumstances taken into account.

Economic and Social Activity and the Kingdom of Christ

72. Christians engaged actively in modern economic and social progress and in the struggle for justice and charity must be convinced that they have much to contribute to the prosperity of mankind and to world peace. Let them, as individuals and as group members, give a shining example to others. Endowed with the skill and experience so absolutely necessary for them, let them preserve a proper sense of values in their earthly activity in loyalty to Christ and his Gospel, in order that their lives, individual as well as social, may be inspired by the spirit of the Beatitudes, and in particular by the spirit of poverty.

Anyone who in obedience to Christ seeks first the kingdom of God will derive from it a stronger and purer love for helping all his brethren and for accomplishing the task of justice under the inspiration of charity.[16]

CHAPTER FOUR
THE POLITICAL COMMUNITY

Modern Public Life

73. In our times profound transformations are to be noticed in the structure and institutions of peoples; they are the accompaniment of cultural, economic, and social development. These transformations exercise a deep influence on political life, particularly as regards the rights and duties of the individual in the exercise of civil liberty and in the achievement of the common good; and they affect the organization of the relations of citizens with each other and of their position vis-a-vis the state.

A keener awareness of human dignity has given rise in various parts of the world to an eagerness to establish a politico-juridical order in which the rights of the human person in public life will be better protected—for example, the right of free

---

[16] For the right use of goods according to the teaching of the New Testament, cf. Lk. 3:11; 10:30 ff.; 11:41; Mk. 8:36; 12:29–31; 1 Pet. 5:3; Jas. 5:1–6; 1 Tim. 6:8; Eph. 4:28; 2 Cor. 8:13 f.; 1 Jn. 3:17–18.

assembly and association, the right to express one's opinions and to profess one's religion privately and publicly. The guarantee of the rights of the person is, indeed, a necessary condition for citizens, individually and collectively, to play an active part in public life and administration.

Linked with cultural, economic, and social progress there is a growing desire among many to assume greater responsibilities in the organization of political life. Many people are becoming more eager to ensure that the rights of minority groups in their country be safeguarded, without overlooking the duties of these minorities towards the political community; there is also an increase in tolerance for others who differ in opinion and religion; at the same time wider cooperation is taking place to enable all citizens, and not only a few privileged individuals, to exercise their rights effectively as persons.

Men are repudiating political systems, still prevailing in some parts of the world, which hinder civil and religious liberty or victimize their citizens through avarice and political crimes, or distort the use of authority from being at the service of the common good to benefiting the convenience of political parties or of the governing classes.

There is no better way to establish political life on a truly human basis than by encouraging an inward sense of justice, of good will, and of service to the common good, and by consolidating the basic convictions of men as to the true nature of the political community and the aim, proper exercise, and the limits of public authority.

Nature and Purpose of the Political Community

74. Individuals, families, and the various groups which make up the civil community, are aware of their inability to achieve a truly human life by their own unaided efforts; they see the need for a wider community where each one will make a specific contribution to an even broader implementation of the common good.[1] For this reason they set up various forms of political communities. The political community, then, exists for the common good; this is its full justification and meaning and the source of its specific and basic right to exist. The common good embraces the sum total of all those conditions of social life which enable individuals, families, and organizations to achieve complete and efficacious fulfilment.[2]

The persons who go to make up the political community are many and varied; quite rightly, then, they may veer towards widely differing points of view. Therefore, lest the political community be ruined while everyone follows his own opinion, an authority is needed to guide the energies of all towards the common good—not mechanically or despotically, but by acting above all as a moral force based on freedom and a sense of responsibility. It is clear that the political community and public authority are based on human nature, and therefore, that they need belong to an order established by God; nevertheless, the choice of the

[1] Cf. John XXIII, Litt. Encycl. *Mater et Magistra: AAS* 53 (1961), p. 417.
[2] Cf. John XXIII, ibid.

political regime and the appointment of rulers are left to the free decision of the citizens.[3]

It follows that political authority, either within the political community as such or through organizations representing the state, must be exercised within the limits of the moral order and directed towards the common good (understood in the dynamic sense of the term) according to the juridical order legitimately established or due to be established. Citizens, then, are bound in conscience to obey.[4] Accordingly, the responsibility, the dignity, and the importance of state rulers is clear.

When citizens are under the oppression of a public authority which oversteps its competence, they should still not refuse to give or to do whatever is objectively demanded of them by the common good; but it is legitimate for them to defend their own rights and those of their fellow citizens against abuses of this authority within the limits of the natural law and the law of the Gospel.

The concrete forms of structure and organization of public authority adopted in any political community may vary according to the character of various peoples and their historical development; but their aim should always be the formation of a human person who is cultured, peace-loving and well disposed towards his fellow men with a view to the benefit of the whole human race.

Participation by All in Public Life

75. It is fully consonant with human nature that there should be politico-juridical structures providing all citizens without any distinction with ever improving and effective opportunities to play an active part in the establishment of the juridical foundations of the political community, in the administration of public affairs, in determining the aims and the terms of reference of public bodies, and in the election of political leaders.[5] Every citizen ought to be mindful of his right and his duty to promote the common good by using his vote. The Church praises and esteems those who devote themselves to the public good for the service of men and take upon themselves the burdens of public office.

If the citizens' cooperation and their sense of responsibility are to produce the favourable results expected of them in the normal course of public life, a system of positive law is required providing for a suitable division of the functions and organs of public authority and an effective and independent protection of citizens' rights. The rights of all individuals, families and organizations and their practical implementation must be acknowledged, protected, and fostered,[6] together with the public duties binding on all citizens. Among these duties it is worth mentioning the obligation of rendering to the state whatever material and personal services

[3] Cf. Rom. 13:1-5.

[4] Cf. Rom. 13:5.

[5] Cf. Pius XII, *Christmas Message* 1942: *AAS* 35 (1043), pp. 9-24; *Christmas Message* 1944: *AAS* 37 (1945), pp. 11-17; John XXIII, Litt. Encycl. *Pacem in Terris: AAS* 55 (1963), pp. 263, 271, 277, 278.

[6] Cf. Pius XII, Radio message, 1 June 1941: *AAS* 33 (1941), p. 200; John XXIII, Litt. Encycl. *Pacem in Terris: AAS* 55 (1963), pp. 273, 274.

are required for the common good. Governments should take care not to put obstacles in the way of family, cultural or social groups, or of organizations and intermediate institutions, nor to hinder their lawful and constructive activity; rather, they should eagerly seek to promote such orderly activity. Citizens, on the other hand, either individually or in association, should take care not to vest too much power in the hands of public authority nor to make untimely and exaggerated demands for favors and subsidies, lessening in this way the responsible role of individuals, families and social groups.

The growing complexity of modern situations makes it necessary for public authority to intervene more often in social, cultural and economic matters in order to bring about more favourable conditions to enable citizens and groups to pursue freely and effectively the achievement of man's well-being in its totality. The understanding of the relationship between socialization[7] and personal autonomy and progress will vary according to different areas and the development of peoples. However, if restrictions are imposed temporarily for the common good on the exercise of human rights, these restrictions are to be lifted as soon as possible after the situation has changed. In any case it is inhuman for public authority to fall back on totalitarian methods or dictatorship which violate the rights of persons or social groups.

Citizens should cultivate a generous and loyal spirit of patriotism, but without narrow-mindedness, so that they will always keep in mind the welfare of the whole human family which is formed into one by various kinds of links between races, peoples, and nations.

Christians must be conscious of their specific and proper role in the political community; they should be a shining example by their sense of responsibility and their dedication to the common good; they should show in practice how authority can be reconciled with freedom, personal initiative and with the solidarity and the needs of the whole social framework, and the advantages of unity with profitable diversity. They should recognize the legitimacy of differing points of view about the organization of worldly affairs and show respect for their fellow citizens, who even in association defend their opinions by legitimate means. Political parties, for their part, must support whatever in their opinion is conducive to the common good, but must never put their own interests before the common good.

So that all citizens will be able to play their part in political affairs, civil and political education is vitally necessary for the population as a whole and for young people in particular, and must be diligently attended to. Those with a talent for the difficult yet noble art of politics,[8] or whose talents in this matter can be developed, should prepare themselves for it, and forgetting their own convenience and material interests, they should engage in political activity. They must combat injustice and oppression, arbitrary domination and intolerance by individuals or political parties, and they must do so with integrity and wisdom. They must

---

[7] Cf. John XXIII, Litt. Encycl. *Mater et Magistra: AAS* 53 (1961), p. 415–418.

[8] Cf. Pius XI, *Allocutio* to the Directors of the Catholic University Federation: *Discorsi di Pio XI*, ed. Bertetto, Torino, vol. 1 (1960), p. 743.

dedicate themselves to the welfare of all in a spirit of sincerity and fairness, of love and of the courage demanded by political life.

The Political Community and the Church

76. It is of supreme importance, especially in a pluralistic society, to work out a proper vision of the relationship between the political community and the Church, and to distinguish clearly between the activities of Christians, acting individually or collectively in their own name as citizens guided by the dictates of a Christian conscience, and their activity acting along with their pastors in the name of the Church.

The Church, by reason of her role and competence, is not identified with any political community nor bound by ties to any political system. It is at once the sign and the safeguard of the transcendental dimension of the human person.

The political community and the Church are autonomous and independent of each other in their own fields. Nevertheless, both are devoted to the personal vocation of man, though under different titles. This service will redound the more effectively to the welfare of all insofar as both institutions practice better cooperation according to the local and prevailing situation. For man's horizons are not bounded only by the temporal order; living on the level of human history he preserves the integrity of his eternal destiny. The Church, for its part, being founded in the love of the Redeemer, contributes towards the spread of justice and charity among nations and within the borders of the nations themselves. By preaching the truths of the Gospels and clarifying all sectors of human activity through its teaching and the witness of its members, the Church respects and encourages the political freedom and responsibility of the citizen.

Since the apostles, their successors and all who help them have been given the task of announcing Christ, Saviour of the world, to man, they rely in their apostolate on the power of God, who often shows forth the force of the Gospel in the weakness of its witnesses. If anyone wishes to devote himself to the ministry of God's Word, let him use the ways and means proper to the Gospel, which differ in many respects from those obtaining in the earthly city.

Nevertheless, there are close links between the things of earth and those things in man's condition which transcend the world, and the Church utilizes temporal realities as often as its mission requires it. But it never places its hopes in any privileges accorded to it by civil authority; indeed, it will give up the exercise of certain legitimate rights whenever it becomes clear that their use will compromise the sincerity of its witness, or whenever new circumstances call for a revised approach. But at all times and in all places the Church should have true freedom to preach the faith, to proclaim its teaching about society, to carry out its task among men without hindrance, and to pass moral judgments even in matters relating to politics, whenever the fundamental rights of man or the salvation of souls requires it. The means, the only means, it may use are those which are in accord with the Gospel and the welfare of all men according to the diversity of times and circumstances.

With loyalty to the Gospel in the fulfilment of its mission in the world, the Church, whose duty it is to foster and elevate all that is true, all that is good, and all that is beautiful in the human community,[9] consolidates peace among men for the glory of God.[10]

CHAPTER FIVE

FOSTERING OF PEACE AND ESTABLISHMENT OF A COMMUNITY OF NATIONS

INTRODUCTION

77. In our generation, which has been marked by the persistent and acute hardships and anxiety resulting from the ravages of war and the threat of war, the whole human race faces a moment of supreme crisis in its advance towards maturity. Mankind has gradually come closer together and is everywhere more conscious of its own unity; but it will not succeed in accomplishing the task awaiting it, that is, the establishment of a truly human world for all men over the entire earth, unless everyone devotes himself to the cause of true peace with renewed vigor. Thus the message of the Gospel, which epitomizes the highest ideals and aspirations of mankind, shines anew in our times when it proclaims that the advocates of peace are blessed "for they shall be called sons of God" (Mt. 5:9).

Accordingly, the Council proposes to outline the true and noble nature of peace, to condemn the savagery of war, and earnestly to exhort Christians to cooperate with all in securing a peace based on justice and charity and in promoting the means necessary to attain it, under the help of Christ, author of peace.

Nature of Peace

78. Peace is more than the absence of war: it cannot be reduced to the maintenance of a balance of power between opposing forces nor does it arise out of despotic dominion, but it is appropriately called "the effect of righteousness" (Is. 32:17). It is the fruit of that right ordering of things with which the divine founder has invested human society and which must be actualized by man thirsting after an ever more perfect reign of justice. But while the common good of mankind ultimately derives from the eternal law, it depends in the concrete upon circumstances which change as time goes on; consequently, peace will never be achieved once and for all, but must be built up continually. Since, moreover, human nature is weak and wounded by sin, the achievement of peace requires a constant effort to control the passions and unceasing vigilance by lawful authority.

But this is not enough. Peace cannot be obtained on earth unless the welfare of man is safeguarded and people freely and trustingly share with one another the riches of their minds and their talents. A firm determination to respect the dignity of other men and other peoples along with the deliberate practice of fraternal love are absolutely necessary for the achievement of peace. Accordingly, peace is also the fruit of love, for love goes beyond what justice can ensure.

[9] Cf. Vatican Council II, Dogmatic Constitution *Lumen Gentium*, n. 13: *AAS* 57 (1965), p. 17.

[10] Cf. Lk. 2:14.

Peace on earth, which flows from love of one's neighbor, symbolizes and derives from the peace of Christ who proceeds from God the Father. Christ, the Word made flesh, the prince of peace, reconciled all men to God by the cross, and, restoring the unity of all in one people and one body, he abolished hatred in his own flesh,[1] having been lifted up through his resurrection he poured forth the Spirit of love into the hearts of men. Therefore, all Christians are earnestly to speak the truth in love (cf. Eph. 4:15) and join with all peace-loving men in pleading for peace and trying to bring it about. In the same spirit we cannot but express our admiration for all who forgo the use of violence to vindicate their rights and resort to those other means of defense which are available to weaker parties, provided it can be done without harm to the rights and duties of others and of the community.

Insofar as men are sinners, the threat of war hangs over them and will so continue until the coming of Christ; but insofar as they can vanquish sin by coming together in charity, violence itself will be vanquished and they will make these words come true: "They shall beat their swords into ploughshares, and their spears into pruning hooks; nation shall not lift up sword against nation, neither shall they learn war any more" (Is. 2:4).

SECTION I: AVOIDANCE OF WAR

Curbing the Savagery of War

79. Even though recent wars have wrought immense material and moral havoc on the world, the devastation of battle still rages in some parts of the world. Indeed, now that every kind of weapon produced by modern science is used in war, the savagery of war threatens to lead the combatants to barbarities far surpassing those of former ages. Moreover, the complexity of the modern world and the intricacy of international relations cause incipient wars to develop into full-scale conflict by new methods of infiltration and subversion. In many cases terrorist methods are regarded as new strategies of war.

Faced by this deplorable state of humanity the Council wishes to remind men that the natural law of peoples and its universal principles still retain their binding force. The conscience of mankind firmly and ever more emphatically proclaims these principles. Any action which deliberately violates these principles and any order which commands such actions is criminal and blind obedience cannot excuse those who carry them out. The most infamous among these actions are those designed for the reasoned and methodical extermination of an entire race, nation, or ethnic minority. These must be condemned as frightful crimes; and we cannot commend too highly the courage of the men who openly and fearlessly resist those who issue orders of this kind.

On the question of warfare, there are various international conventions, signed by many countries, aimed at rendering military action and its consequences less inhuman; they deal with the treatment of wounded and interned prisoners of war and with various kindred questions. These agreements must be honored; indeed public authorities and specialists in these matters must do all in their power to

---

[1] Cf. Eph. 2:16; Col. 1:20–22.

improve these conventions and thus bring about a better and more effective curbing of the savagery of war. Moreover, it seems just that laws should make humane provision for the case of conscientious objectors who refuse to carry arms, provided they accept some other form of community service.

War, of course, has not ceased to be part of the human scene. As long as the danger of war persists and there is no international authority with the necessary competence and power, governments cannot be denied the right of lawful self-defense, once all peace efforts have failed. State leaders and all who share the burdens of public administration have the duty to defend the interests of their people and to conduct such grave matters with a deep sense of responsibility. However, it is one thing to wage a war of self-defense; it is quite another to seek to impose domination on another nation. The possession of war potential does not justify the use of force for political or military objectives. Nor does the mere fact that war has unfortunately broken out mean that all is fair between the warring parties.

All those who enter the military service in loyalty to their country should look upon themselves as the custodians of the security and freedom of their fellow-countrymen; and when they carry out their duty properly, they are contributing to the maintenance of peace.

Total Warfare

80. The development of armaments by modern science has immeasurably magnified the horrors and wickedness of war. Warfare conducted with these weapons can inflict immense and indiscriminate havoc which goes far beyond the bounds of legitimate defense. Indeed if the kind of weapons now stocked in the arsenals of the great powers were to be employed to the fullest, the result would be the almost complete reciprocal slaughter of one side by the other, not to speak of the widespread devastation that would follow in the world and the deadly after-effects resulting from the use of such arms.

All these factors force us to undertake a completely fresh reappraisal of war.[2] Men of this generation should realize that they will have to render an account of their warlike behavior; the destiny of generations to come depends largely on the decisions they make today.

With these considerations in mind the Council, endorsing the condemnations of total warfare issued by recent popes,[3] declares: Every act of war directed to the indiscriminate destruction of whole cities or vast areas with their inhabitants is a crime against God and man, which merits firm and unequivocal condemnation.

The hazards peculiar to modern warfare consist in the fact that they expose those possessing recently developed weapons to the risk of perpetrating crimes like these

[2] Cf. John XXIII, Litt. Encycl. *Pacem in Terris*: AAS 55 (1963), p. 291: "Therefore in this age of ours, which prides itself on its atomic power, it is irrational to think that war is a proper way to obtain justice for violated rights."
[3] Cf Pius XII, *Allocutio*, 30 Sept. 1954: AAS 46 (1954), p. 589; *Christmas Message* 1954: AAS 47 (1955), pp. 15 ff.; John XXIII, Litt. Encycl. *Pacem in Terris*: AAS 55 (1963), pp. 286–291; Paul VI, *Address to the United Nations*, 4 Oct. 1965: AAS 57 (1965), pp. 877–885.

and, by an inexorable chain of events, of urging men to even worse acts of atrocity. To obviate the possibility of this happening at any time in the future, the bishops of the world gathered together to implore all men, especially government leaders and military advisers, to give unceasing consideration to their immense responsibilities before God and before the whole human race.

The Arms Race

81. Undoubtedly, armaments are not amassed merely for use in wartime. Since the defensive strength of any nation is thought to depend on its capacity for immediate retaliation, the stockpiling of arms which grows from year to year serves, in a way hitherto unthought of, as a deterrent to potential attackers. Many people look upon this as the most effective way known at the present time for maintaining some sort of peace among nations.

Whatever one may think of this form of deterrent, people are convinced that the arms race, which quite a few countries have entered, is no infallible way of maintaining real peace and that the resulting so-called balance of power is no sure and genuine path to achieving it. Rather than eliminate the causes of war, the arms race serves only to aggravate the position. As long as extravagant sums of money are poured into the development of new weapons, it is impossible to devote adequate aid in tackling the misery which prevails at the present day in the world. Instead of eradicating international conflict once and for all, the contagion is spreading to other parts of the world. New approaches, based on reformed attitudes, will have to be chosen in order to remove this stumbling block, to free the earth from its pressing anxieties, and give back to the world a genuine peace.

Therefore, we declare once again: the arms race is one of the greatest curses on the human race and the harm it inflicts on the poor is more than can be endured. And there is every reason to fear that if it continues it will bring forth those lethal disasters which are already in preparation. Warned by the possibility of the catastrophes that man has created, let us profit by the respite we now enjoy, thanks to the divine favor, to take stock of our responsibilities and find ways of resolving controversies in a manner worthy of human beings. Providence urgently demands of us that we free ourselves from the age-old slavery of war. If we refuse to make this effort, there is no knowing where we will be led on the fatal path we have taken.

Total Outlawing of War: International Action to Prevent War

82. It is our clear duty to spare no effort in order to work for the moment when all war will be completely outlawed by international agreement. This goal, of course, requires the establishment of a universally acknowledged public authority vested with the effective power to ensure security for all, regard for justice, and respect for law. But before this desirable authority can be constituted, it is necessary for existing international bodies to devote themselves resolutely to the exploration of better means for obtaining common security. But since peace must be born of mutual trust between peoples instead of being forced on nations through dread of arms, all must work to put an end to the arms race and make a real beginning of

disarmament, not unilaterally indeed but at an equal rate on all sides, on the basis of agreements and backed up by genuine and effective guarantees.[4]

In the meantime one must not underestimate the efforts already made or now under way to eliminate the danger of war. On the contrary, support should be given to the good will of numerous individuals who are making every effort to eliminate the havoc of war; these men, although burdened by the weighty responsibilities of their high office, are motivated by a consciousness of their very grave obligations, even if they cannot ignore the complexity of the situation as it stands. We must beseech the Lord to give them the strength to tackle with perseverance and carry out with courage this task of supreme love for man which is the building up of a lasting peace in a true spirit of manhood. In our times this work demands that they enlarge their thoughts and their spirit beyond the confines of their own country, that they put aside nationalistic selfishness and ambitions to dominate other nations, and that they cultivate deep reverence for the whole of mankind which is painstakingly advancing towards greater maturity.

The problems of peace and disarmament have been treated at length with courage and untiring consultation at negotiations and international meetings; these are to be considered as the first steps towards the solutions of such important questions and must be further pursued with even greater insistence, with a view to obtaining concrete results in the future. But people should beware of leaving these problems to the efforts of a few men without putting their own attitudes in order. For state leaders, who are at once the guardians of their own people and the promoters of the welfare of the whole world, rely to a large extent on public opinion and public attitudes. Their peace-making efforts will be in vain, as long as men are divided and warring among themselves through hostility, contempt, and distrust, as well as through racial hatred and uncompromising hostilities. Hence there is a very urgent need of re-education and a new orientation of public opinion. Those engaged in the work of education, especially youth education, and the people who mold public opinion, should regard it as their most important task to educate the minds of men to renewed sentiments of peace. Every one of us needs a change of heart; we must set our gaze on the whole world and look to those tasks we can all perform together in order to bring about the betterment of our race.

But let us not be buoyed up with false hope. For unless animosity and hatred are put aside, and firm, honest agreements about world peace are concluded, humanity may, in spite of the wonders of modern science, go from the grave crisis of the present day to that dismal hour, when the only peace it will experience will be the dread peace of death. The Church, however, living in the midst of these anxieties, even as it makes these statements, has not lost hope. The Church intends to propose to our age over and over again, in season and out of season, the apostle's message: "Behold, now is the acceptable time" for a change of heart; "behold, now is the day of salvation".[5]

[4] Cf. John XXIII, Litt. Encycl. *Pacem in Terris*, where the reduction of arms is treated: *AAS* 55 (1963), p. 287.

[5] Cf. 2 Cor. 6:2.

Causes of Discord: Remedies

83. If peace is to be established, the first condition is to root out the causes of discord among men which lead to wars—in the first place, injustice. Not a few of these causes arise out of excessive economic inequalities and out of hesitation to undertake necessary correctives. Some are due to the desire for power and to contempt for people, and at a deeper level, to envy, distrust, pride, and other selfish passions. Man cannot put up with such an amount of disorder; the result is that, even when war is absent, the world is constantly beset by strife and violence between men. Since the same evils are also to be found in the relations between nations, it is of the utmost importance, if these evils are to be overcome or forestalled and if headlong violence is to be curbed, for international bodies to work more effectively and more resolutely together and to coordinate their efforts. And finally, man should work unsparingly towards the creation of bodies designed to promote the cause of peace.

The Community of Nations and International Organizations

84. At the present time when close ties of dependence between individuals and peoples all over the world are developing, the universal common good has to be pursued in an appropriate way and more effectively achieved; it is now a necessity for the community of nations to organize itself in a manner suited to its present responsibilities, with special reference to its obligations towards the many areas of the world where intolerable want still prevails. To reach this goal, organizations of the international community, for their part, should set themselves to provide for the different needs of men; this will involve the sphere of social life to which belong questions of food, hygiene, education, employment, and certain particular situations arising here and there, as for example a general need to promote the welfare of developing countries, to alleviate the miseries of refugees dispersed throughout the world, and to assist migrants and their families.

Already existing international and regional organizations certainly deserve well of the human race. They represent the first attempts at laying the foundations on an international level for a community of all men to work towards the solutions of the very serious problems of our times, and specifically towards the encouragement of progress everywhere and the prevention of wars of all kinds. The Church is glad to view the spirit of true brotherhood existing in all spheres between Christians and non-Christians as it seeks to intensify its untiring efforts to alleviate the enormity of human misery.

International Cooperation in Economic Matters

85. The present solidarity of mankind calls for greater international cooperation in economic matters. Indeed, although nearly all peoples have achieved political independence, they are far from being free from excessive inequalities and from every form of undue independence and far from being immune to serious internal difficulties.

The development of a nation depends on human and financial resources. The citizens of every nation must be prepared by education and professional training to undertake the various tasks of economic and social life. This involves the help of experts from abroad, who, while they are the bearers of assistance, should not behave as overlords but as helpers and fellow-workers. Material aid for developing nations will not be forthcoming unless there is a profound change in the prevailing conventions of commerce today. Other forms of aid from affluent nations should take the form of grants, loans, or investments: they should be given in a spirit of generosity and without greed on one side, and accepted with complete honesty on the other.

The establishment of an authentic economic order on a worldwide scale can come about only by abolishing profiteering, nationalistic ambitions, greed for political domination, schemes of military strategy, and intrigues for spreading and imposing ideologies. Different economic and social systems have been suggested; it is to be hoped that experts will find in them a common basis for a just world commerce; it will come about if all men forgo their own prejudices and show themselves ready to enter into sincere dialogue.

Some Useful Norms

86. The following norms seem useful for such cooperation:

(a) Developing nations should be firmly convinced that their express and unequivocal aim is the total human development of their citizens. They should not forget that progress has its roots and its strength before all else in the work and talent of their citizens. They should not forget that progress is based, not only on foreign aid, but on the full exploitation of native resources and on the development of their own talents and traditions. In this matter those who exert the greater influence on others should be the more outstanding by their example.

(b) The most important task of the affluent nations is to help developing nations to fulfil these commitments. Accordingly, they should undertake within their own confines the spiritual and material adjustments which are needed for the establishment of world-wide cooperation. They should look to the welfare of the weaker and poorer nations in business dealings with them, for the revenues the latter make from the sale of home-produced goods are needed for their own support.

(c) It is up to the international community to coordinate and stimulate development, but in such a way as to distribute with the maximum fairness and efficacy the resources set aside for this purpose. It is also its task to organize economic affairs on a worldwide scale, without transgressing the principle of subsidiarity, so that business will be conducted according to the norms of justice. Organizations should be set up to promote and regulate international commerce, especially with less developed nations, in order to compensate for losses resulting from excessive inequality of power between nations. This kind of organization accompanied by technical, cultural, and financial aid, should provide nations on the path of progress with all that is necessary for them to achieve adequate economic success.

(d) In many instances there exists a pressing need to reassess economic and social structure, but caution must be exercised with regard to proposed solutions which may be untimely, especially those which offer material advantage while militating against man's spiritual nature and advancement. For "Man does not live on bread alone but on every word that comes from the mouth of God" (Mt. 4:4). Every branch of the human race possesses in itself and in its nobler traditions some part of the spiritual treasure which God has entrusted to men, even though many do not know the source of it.

87. International cooperation is vitally necessary in the case of those peoples who very often in the midst of many difficulties are faced with the special problems arising out of rapid increases in population. There is a pressing need to harness the full and eager cooperation of all, particularly of the richer countries, in order to explore how the human necessities of food and suitable education can be furnished and shared with the entire human community. Some peoples could improve their standard of living considerably if they were properly trained to substitute new techniques of agricultural production for antiquated methods and adapt them prudently to their own situation. The social order would also be improved and a fairer distribution of land ownership would be assured.

The government has, assuredly, in the matter of the population of its country, its own rights and duties, within the limits of its proper competence, for instance as regards social and family legislation, the migration of country-dwellers to the city, and information concerning the state and needs of the nation. Some men nowadays are gravely disturbed by this problem; it is to be hoped that there will be Catholic experts in these matters, particularly in universities, who will diligently study the problems and pursue their researches further.

Since there is widespread opinion that the population expansion of the world, or at least some particular countries, should be kept in check by all possible means and by every kind of intervention by public authority, the Council exhorts all men to beware of all solutions, whether uttered in public or in private or imposed at any time, which transgress the natural law. Because in virtue of man's inalienable right to marriage and the procreation of children, the decision regarding the number of children depends on the judgment of the parents and is in no way to be left to the decrees of public authority. Now, since the parents' judgment presupposes a properly formed conscience, it is of great importance that all should have an opportunity to cultivate a genuinely human sense of responsibility which will take account of the circumstances of time and situation and will respect the divine law; to attain this goal a change for the better must take place in educational and social conditions and, above all, religious formations, or at least full moral training, must be available. People should be discreetly informed of scientific advances in research into methods of birth regulation, whenever the value of these methods has been thoroughly proved and their conformity with the moral order established.

Role of Christians in International Aid

88. Christians should willingly and wholeheartedly support the establishment of an international order that includes a genuine respect for legitimate freedom and friendly sentiments of brotherhood towards all men. It is all the more urgent now that the greater part of the world is in a state of such poverty that it is as if Christ himself were crying out in the mouths of these poor people to the charity of his

disciples. Let us not be guilty of the scandal of having some nations, most of whose citizens bear the name of Christians, enjoying an abundance of riches, while others lack the necessities of life and are tortured by hunger, disease, and all kinds of misery. For the spirit of poverty and charity is the glory and witness of the Church of Christ.

We must praise and assist those Christians, especially those young Christians, who volunteer their services to help other men and other peoples. Indeed it is a duty for the whole people of God, under the teaching and example of the bishops, to alleviate the hardships of our times within the limits of its means, giving generously, as was the ancient custom of the Church, not merely out of what is superfluous, but also out of what is necessary.

Without being rigid and altogether uniform in the matter, methods of collection and distribution of aid should be systematically conducted in dioceses, nations, and throughout the world and in collaboration with suitable institutes.

Effective Presence of the Church in the International Community

89. The Church, in preaching the Gospel to all men and dispensing the treasures of grace in accordance with its divine mission, makes a contribution to the strengthening of peace over the whole world and helps to consolidate the foundations of brotherly communion among men and peoples. This it does by imparting the knowledge of the divine and the natural law. Accordingly, the Church ought to be present in the community of peoples, to foster and stimulate cooperation among men; motivated by the sole desire of serving all men, it contributes both by means of its official channels and through the full and sincere collaboration of all Christians. This goal will be more effectively brought about if all the faithful are conscious of their responsibility as men and as Christians and work in their own environments to arouse generous cooperation with the international community. In their religious and civil education special attention should be given to the training of youth in this matter.

Role of Christians in International Organizations

90. For Christians one undoubtedly excellent form of international activity is the part they play, either individually or collectively, in organizations set up or on the way to being set up to foster cooperation between nations. Different Catholic international bodies can assist the community of nations on the way to peace and brotherhood; these bodies should be strengthened by enlarging the number of their well-trained members, by increasing the subsidies they need so badly, and by suitable coordination of their forces. Nowadays efficiency of action and the need for dialogue call for concerted effort. Organizations of this kind, moreover, contribute more than a little to the instilling of a feeling of universality, which is certainly appropriate for Catholics, and to the formation of truly worldwide solidarity and responsibility.

Finally, it is to be hoped that, in order to fulfil their role in the international community properly, Catholics will seek to cooperate actively and positively with our separated brethren, who profess the charity of the Gospel along with us, and also with all men thirsting for true peace.

Taking into account the immensity of the hardships which still afflict a large section of humanity, and with a view to fostering everywhere the justice and love of Christ for the poor, the Council suggests that it would be most opportune to create some organization of the universal Church whose task it would be to arouse the Catholic community to promote the progress of areas which are in want and foster social justice between nations.

III

Extracts from the *Declaration on Christian Education* (*Gravissimum Educationis*) of the Second Vatican Council, 28 October 1965.

The translation is taken from *Vatican Council II: The Conciliar and Post Conciliar Documents* edited by Austin Flannery, O.P., Dublin, 1975.

There are twelve paragraphs in all in the document. There are no chapters or subdivisions.

3. As it is the parents who have given life to their children, on them lies the gravest obligation of educating their family. [11] They must therefore be recognized as being primarily and principally responsible for their education. The role of parents in education is of such importance that it is almost impossible to provide an adequate substitute. It is therefore the duty of parents to create a family atmosphere inspired by love and devotion to God and their fellow-men which will promote an integrated, personal and social education of their children. The family is therefore the principal school of the social virtues which are necessary to every society. It is therefore above all in the Christian family, inspired by the grace and responsibility of the sacrament of matrimony, that children should be taught to know and worship God and to love their neighbor, in accordance with the faith which they have received in earliest infancy in the sacrament of Baptism. In it, also they will have their first experience of a well-balanced human society and of the Church. Finally it is through the family that they are gradually initiated into association with their fellow-men in civil life and as members of the people of God. Parents should, therefore, appreciate how important a role the truly Christian family plays in the life and progress of the whole people of God. [12]

The task of imparting education belongs primarily to the family, but it requires the help of society as a whole. As well as the rights of parents, and of those others to whom the parents entrust some share in their duty to educate, there are certain

[11] Cf. Pius XI, Encycl. *Divini Illius Magistri*, 31 Dec. 1929: *AAS* 22 (1930), p. 50 ff.; encycl. *Mit brennender Sorge*, 14 March 1937: *AAS* 29 (1937), p. 164 ff.; also Pius XII, *Allocutio* to Ital. Cath. Teachers, 7 Sept. 1946; *Discorsi e Radiomessaggi*, vol. 8, p. 218.

[12] Cf. Vatican Council II, Dogmatic Constitution on the Church, n. 11, 35: *AAS* 57 (1965) pp. 16, 40 ff.

duties and rights vested in civil society inasmuch as it is its function to provide for the common good in temporal matters. It is its duty to promote the education of youth in various ways. It should recognize the duties and rights of parents, and of those others who play a part in education, and provide them with the requisite assistance. In accordance with the principle of subsidiarity, when the efforts of the parents and of other organizations are inadequate it should itself undertake the duty of education, with due consideration, however, for the wishes of the parents. Finally, insofar as the common good requires it, it should establish its own schools and institutes.[13]

Education is, in a very special way, the concern of the Church, not only because the Church must be recognized as a human society capable of imparting education, but especially has the duty of proclaiming the way of salvation to all men, of revealing the life of Christ to those who believe, and of assisting them with unremitting care so that they may be able to attain to the fulness of that life.[14]

The Church as a mother is under an obligation, therefore, to provide for its children an education by virtue of which their whole lives may be inspired by the spirit of Christ. At the same time it will offer its assistance to all peoples for the promotion of a well-balanced perfection of the human personality, for the good of society in this world and for the development of a world more worthy of man.[15]

4. In the exercise of its functions in education the Church is appreciative of every means that may be of service, but it relies especially on those which are essentially its own. Chief among these is catechetical instruction,[16] which illumines and strengthens the faith, develops a life in harmony with the spirit of Christ, stimulates a conscious and fervent participation in the liturgical mystery[17] and encourages men to take an active part in the apostolate. The Church values highly those other educational media which belong to the common patrimony of men and which make a valuable contribution to the development of character and to the formation of men. These it seeks to ennoble by imbuing them with its own spirit. Such are the media of social communication,[18] different groups devoted to the training of mind and body, youth associations, and especially schools.

5. Among the various organs of education the school is of outstanding im-

[13] Cf. Pius XI, Encycl. *Divini Illius Magistri, loc. cit.,* p. 63 ff.; Pius XII, Radio Message 1 June 1941: *AAS* 33 (1941) p. 200; *Allocutio* to Cath. Teachers, 8 Sept. 1946: *Discorsi e Radiomessaggi,* vol. 8, p. 218; re principle of subsidiarity, cf. John XXIII, Encycl. *Pacem in Terris,* 11 April 1963: *AAS* (1963) p. 294.

[14] Cf. Pius XI, Encycl. *Divini Illius Magistri, loc. cit.,* p. 53 ff. and 56 ff., also Encycl. *Non abbiamo bisogno,* 29 June 1931: *AAS* 23 (1931) p. 311 ff.; Pius XII, Letter to Italian Social Week, 20 Sept. 1955: *L'Osservatore Romano,* 29 Sept. 1955.

[15] The Church praises civil authorities—civil, national and international—who, through an awareness of the urgent needs of the present age, work indefatigably so that all people may enjoy a fuller education and human culture. Cf. Paul VI, Allocutio to U.N. Assembly, 4 Oct. 1965: *AAS* 57 (1965) pp. 877–885.

[16] Cf. Pius XI, Motu Proprio *Orbem Catholicum,* 29 June 1923: *AAS* 15 (1923) pp. 327–329; Decree *Provido sane,* 12 Jan. 1935: *AAS* (1935) pp. 145–152; Vatican Council II, Decree on the Pastoral Function of Bishops in the Church, nn. 13–14.

[117] Cf. Vatican Council II, Constitution on the Sacred Liturgy, n. 14: *AAS* 56 (1964) p. 104.

[18] Cf. Vatican Council II, Decree on the Means of Social Communication, nn. 13–14: *AAS* 56 (1964) pp. 149 ff.

portance.[19] In nurturing the intellectual faculties which is its special mission, it develops a capacity for sound judgment and introduces the pupils to the cultural heritage bequeathed to them by former generations. It fosters a sense of values and prepares them for professional life. By providing for friendly contacts between pupils of different characters and backgrounds it encourages mutual understanding. Furthermore it constitutes a center in whose activity and growth not only the families and teachers but also the various associations for the promotion of cultural, civil and religious life, civic society, and the entire community should take part.

Splendid, therefore, and of the highest importance is the vocation of those who help parents in carrying out their duties and act in the name of the community by undertaking a teaching career. This vocation requires special qualities of mind and heart, most careful preparation and a constant readiness to accept new ideas and to adapt the old.

6. Parents, who have a primary and inalienable duty and right in regard to the education of their children, should enjoy the fullest liberty in their choice of school. The public authority, therefore, whose duty it is to protect and defend the liberty of the citizens, is bound according to the principles of distributive justice to ensure that public subsidies to schools are so allocated that parents are truly free to select schools for their children in accordance with their conscience.[20]

But it is the duty of the state to ensure that all its citizens have access to an adequate education and are prepared for the proper exercise of their civic rights and duties. The state itself, therefore, should safeguard the rights of children to an adequate education in schools. It should be vigilant about the ability of the teachers and the standard of teaching. It should watch over the health of the pupils and in general promote the work of the schools in its entirety. In this, however, the principle of subsidiarity must be borne in mind, and therefore there must be no monopoly of schools which would be prejudicial to the natural rights of the human person and would militate against the progress and extension of education, and the peaceful coexistence of citizens. It would, moreover, be inconsistent with the pluralism which exists today in many societies.[21]

Accordingly the sacred Synod urges the faithful to cooperate readily in the development of suitable methods of education and systems of study and in the training of teachers competent to give a good education to their pupils. They are urged also to further by their efforts, and especially by associations of parents, the entire activity of the schools and in particular the moral education given in them.[22]

7. Acknowledging its grave obligation to see to the moral and religious education

---

[19] Cf. Pius XI, Encycl. *Divini Illius Magistri, loc. cit.* p. 76; Pius XII, *Allocutio* to Assoc. of Cath. Teachers of Bavaria, 31 Dec. 1956: *Discorsi e Radiomessaggi*, vol. 18, p. 746.

[20] Cf. III Prov. Council of Cincinnati (1861); Pius XI, Encycl. *Divini Illius Magistri, loc. cit.*, p. 60, 63 ff.

[21] Cf. Pius XI, Encycl. *Divini Illius Magistri, loc. cit.* p. 63; also Encycl. *Non abbiamo bisogno*, 29 June 1931: *AAS* 23 (1931) p. 305; also Pius XII, Letter to 28th Ital. Social Week, 20 Sept. 1955; *L'Osservatore Romano*, 29 Sept. 1955; Also Paul VI *Allocutio* to Chr. Assoc. of Ital. Workers, 6 Oct. 1963: *Encicliche Discorsi di Paolo VI*, vol. 1, Rome, 1964, p. 230.

[22] Cf. John XXIII, Message for 30th Anniv. of *Div. Illius Magistri*, 30 Dec. 1959: *AAS* 52 (1960) p. 57.

of all its children, the Church should give special attention and help to the great number of them who are being taught in non-Catholic schools. This will be done by the living example of those who teach and have charge of these children and by the apostolic action of their fellow-students,[23] but especially by the efforts of those priests and laymen who teach them Christian doctrine in a manner suited to their age and background and who provide them with spiritual help by means of various activities adapted to the requirements of time and circumstance.

Parents are reminded of their grave obligation to make all necessary arrangements and even to insist that their children may be able to take advantage of these services and thus enjoy a balanced progress in their Christian formation and their preparation for life in the world. For this reason the Church is deeply grateful to those public authorities and associations which, taking into consideration the pluralism of contemporary society, and showing due respect for religious liberty, assist families to ensure that the education of their children in all schools is given in accordance with the moral and religious principles of the family.[24]

8. The Church's role is especially evident in Catholic schools. These are no less zealous than other schools in the promotion of culture and in the human formation of young people. It is, however, the special function of the Catholic school to develop in the school community an atmosphere animated by a spirit of liberty and charity based on the Gospel. It enables young people, while developing their own personality, to grow at the same time in that new life which has been given them in baptism. Finally it so orients the whole of human culture to the message of salvation that the knowledge which the pupils acquire of the world, of life and of men is illumined by faith.[25] Thus, the Catholic school, taking into consideration as it should the conditions of an age of progress, prepares its pupils to contribute effectively to the welfare of the world of men and to work for the extension of the kingdom of God, so that by living an exemplary and apostolic life they may be, as it were, a saving leaven in the community.

Accordingly, since the Catholic school can be of such service in developing the mission of the People of God and in promoting dialogue between the Church and the community at large to the advantage of both, it is still of vital importance even in our times. The sacred Synod therefore affirms once more the right of the Church freely to establish and conduct schools of all kinds and grades, a right which has already been asserted time and again in many documents of the Magisterium.[26] It emphasizes that the exercise of this right is of the utmost

[23] The Church places a high value upon the apostolic action which Catholic teachers and those associated with them are able to perform even in these schools.

[24] Cf. Pius XII *Allocutio* to Assoc. of Cath. Teachers of Bavaria, 31 Dec. 1956: *Discorsi e Radiomessaggi*, vol. 18, pp. 745 ff.

[25] Cf. First Prov. Council of Westminster (1852), *Collectio* Lacensis, vol. 3, col. 1334, a/b; also Pius XI, Encycl. *Div. Illius Magistri, loc. cit.,* pp. 77 ff.; also Pius XII, *Allocutio* to Assoc. of Cath. Teachers of Bavaria, *loc. cit.* p. 746; also Paul VI, *Allocutio* to Federated Institutes, 30 Dec. 1963: *Encicliche e Discorsi di Paolo VI*, vol. 1, Rome, 1964, pp. 602 ff.

[26] Cf. most importantly the documents recommended in (1); in addition, this right of the Church is proclaimed by many provincial councils and in the most recent declarations of many episcopal conferences.

importance for the preservation of liberty of conscience, for the protection of the rights of parents, and for the advancement of culture itself.

Teachers must remember that it depends chiefly on them whether the Catholic school achieves its purpose.[27] They should therefore be prepared for their work with special care, having the appropriate qualifications and adequate learning both religious and secular. They should also be skilled in the art of education in accordance with the discoveries of modern times. Possessed by charity both towards each other and towards their pupils, and inspired by an apostolic spirit, they should bear testimony by their lives and their teaching to the one Teacher, who is Christ. Above all they should work in close cooperation with the parents. In the entire educational program they should, together with the parents make full allowance for the differences of sex and for the particular role which providence has appointed to each sex in the family and in society. They should strive to awaken in their pupils a spirit of personal initiative and, even after they have left school, they should continue to help them with their advice and friendship and by the organization of special groups imbued with the true spirit of the Church. The sacred Synod declares that the services of such teachers constitute an active apostolate, one which is admirably suited to our times and indeed is very necessary. At the same time they render a valuable service to society. Catholic parents are reminded of their duty to send their children to Catholic schools wherever this is possible, to give Catholic schools all the support in their power, and to cooperate with them in their work for the good of their children.[28]

9. Although Catholic schools may assume various forms according to local circumstances, all schools which are in any way dependent on the Church should conform as far as possible to this prototype.[29] Furthermore the Church attaches particular importance to those schools, especially in the territories of newly founded Churches, which include non-Catholics among their pupils.

Moreover, in establishing and conducting Catholic schools one must keep modern developments in mind. Accordingly, while one may not neglect primary and intermediate schools, which provide the basis of education, one should attach considerable importance to those establishments which are particularly necessary nowadays, such as: professional[30] and technical colleges, institutes for adult education and for the promotion of social work, institutions for those who require special care on account of some natural handicap, and training colleges for teachers, of religion and of other branches of education.

The sacred Synod earnestly exhorts the pastors of the Church and all the faithful to spare no sacrifice in helping Catholic schools to become increasingly effective,

[27] Cf. Pius XI, Encycl. *Div. Illius Magistri, loc. cit.*, pp. 80 ff.; also Pius XII, *Allocutio* to Ital. Secondary Teachers, 5 Jan. 1954: *Discorsi e Radiomessaggi*, vol. 15, pp. 551–556; also John XXIII, *Allocutio* to Ital. Assoc. of Cath. Teachers, 5 Sept. 1959: *Discorsi, Messaggi, Colloqui*, vol. 1, Rome, 1960, pp. 427–431.

[28] Cf. Pius XII, *Allocutio* to Ital. Secondary Teachers, 5 Jan. 1954, *loc. cit.* p. 555.

[29] Cf. Paul VI, *Allocutio* to Internat. Office of Cath. Education, 25 Feb. 1964: *Encicliche e Discorsi di Paolo VI*, vol. 2, Rome, 1964, p. 232.

[30] Cf. Paul VI, *Allocutio* to Ital. Workers, 6 Oct. 1963: *loc. cit.* vol. 1 Rome, 1964, p. 229.

especially in caring for the poor, for those who are without the help and affection of family, and those who do not have the Faith.

10. The Church likewise devotes considerable care to higher-level education, especially in universities and faculties. Indeed, in the institutions under its control the Church endeavors systematically to ensure that the treatment of the individual disciplines is consonant with their own principles, their own methods, and with a true liberty of scientific enquiry. Its object is that a progressively deeper under-standing of them may be achieved, and by a careful attention to the current problems of these changing times and to the research being undertaken, the convergence of faith and reason in the one truth may be seen more clearly. This method follows the tradition of the doctors of the Church and especially St. Thomas Aquinas.[31] Thus the Christian outlook should acquire, as it were, a public stable and universal influence in the whole process of the promotion of higher culture. The graduates of these institutes should be outstanding in learning, ready to undertake the more responsible duties of society, and to be witnesses in the world to the true faith.[32]

In Catholic universities in which there is no faculty of Sacred Theology there should be an institute or course of theology in which lectures may be given suited also to the needs of lay students. Since the advance of knowledge is secured especially by research into matters of major scientific importance, every effort should be made in Catholic universities and faculties to develop departments for the advancement of scientific research.

The sacred Synod earnestly recommends the establishment of Catholic univer-sities and faculties strategically distributed throughout the world, but they should be noteworthy not so much for their numbers as for their high standards.

IV

Extracts from the *Decree on the Apostolate of Lay People* (*Apostolicam Actuositatem*) of the Second Vatican Council, 18 November 1965.

The translation is taken from *Vatican Council II: The Conciliar and the Post Conciliar Documents* edited by Austin Flannery, O.P., Dublin, 1975.

There are 33 paragraphs and they are divided into an *Introduction* (paragraph 1), *Chapter One* (paragraphs 2 to 4), "The Vocation of Lay

---

[31] Cf. Paul VI, *Allocutio* to 6th Internat. Thomistic Congr., 10 Sept. 1965: *AAS* 57 (1965) pp. 788–792.

[32] Cf. Pius XII, *Allocutio* to Higher Institutes of France, 21 Sept. 1950: *Discorsi e Radiomessaggi*, vol. 12, pp. 219–221; Letter to 22nd Congr. of *Pax Romana*, 12 Aug. 1952: *loc. cit.*, vol. 14, pp. 567–569; John XXIII, *Allocutio* to Fed. of Cath. Universities, 1 April 1959: *Discorsi, Messaggi, Colloqui*, vol. 1., Roma, 1960, pp. 226–229; Paul VI, *Allocutio* to Acad. Senate of University of Milan, 5 April 1964: *Encicliche e Discorsi di Paolo VI*, vol. 2, Rome, 1964, pp. 438–443.

People to the Apostolate", *Chapter Two* (paragraphs 5 to 8), "Objectives", *Chapter Three*, (paragraphs 9 to 14), "The Various Fields of the Apostolate", *Chapter Four*, (paragraphs 15 to 22), "The Different Forms of the Apostolate", *Chapter Five*, (paragraphs 23 to 27), "The Order to be Observed" and *Chapter Six* (paragraphs 28 to 33), "Training for the Apostolate".

Our extracts are from Chapter Two (paragraphs 6 to 7), Chapter Five (paragraphs 23 to 27) and Chapter Six (paragraphs 28 to 32).

The Apostolate of Evangelization and Sanctification

6. The Church's mission is concerned with the salvation of men; and men win salvation through the grace of Christ and faith in him. The apostolate of the Church therefore, and of each of its members, aims primarily at announcing to the world by word and action the message of Christ and communicating to it the grace of Christ. The principal means of bringing this about is the ministry of the word and of the sacraments. Committed in a special way to the clergy, it leaves room however for a highly important part for the laity, the part namely of "helping the cause of truth" (3 Jn. 8). It is in this sphere most of all that the lay apostolate and the pastoral ministry complete each other. . . .

The Renewal of the Temporal Order

7. That men, working in harmony, should renew the temporal order and make it increasingly more perfect: such is God's design for the world.

All that goes to make up the temporal order: personal and family values, culture, economic interests, the trades and professions, institutions of the political community, international relations, and so on, as well as their gradual development—all these are not merely helps to man's last end; they possess a value of their own, placed in them by God, whether considered individually or as parts of the integral temporal structure: "And God saw all that he had made and found it very good" (Gen. 1:31). This natural goodness of theirs receives an added dignity from their relation with the human person, for whose use they have been created. . . .

It is the work of the entire Church to fashion men able to establish the proper scale of values on the temporal order and direct it towards God through Christ. Pastors have the duty to set forth clearly the principles concerning the purpose of creation and the use to be made of the world, and to provide moral and spiritual helps for the renewal of the temporal order in Christ.

Laymen ought to take on themselves as their distinctive task this renewal of the temporal order. Guided by the light of the Gospel and the mind of the Church, prompted by Christian love, they should act in this domain in a direct way and in their own specific manner. As citizens among citizens they must bring to their cooperation with others their own special competence, and act on their own responsibility; everywhere and always they have to seek the justice of the kingdom of God. The temporal order is to be renewed in such a way that, while its own principles are fully respected, it is harmonized with the principles of the Christian life and adapted to the various conditions of times, places and peoples. Among the tasks of this apostolate Christian social action is preeminent. The Council desires to see it extended today to every sector of life, not forgetting the cultural sphere.[2]

CHAPTER V

THE ORDER TO BE OBSERVED

23. The lay apostolate, individual or collective, must be set in its true place within the apostolate of the whole Church. Union with those whom the Holy Spirit has appointed to rule the Church of God (cf. Acts 20:28) is an essential element of the Christian apostolate. Not less necessary is collaboration among the different undertakings of the apostolate; it is the hierarchy's place to put proper system into this collaboration.

Mutual esteem for all forms of the Church's apostolate, and good coordination, preserving nevertheless the character special to each, are in fact absolutely necessary for promoting that spirit of unity which will cause fraternal charity to shine out in the Church's whole apostolate, common aims to be reached and ruinous rivalries avoided.[1]

This is appropriate most of all when some particular action in the Church calls for the agreement and apostolic cooperation of both classes of the clergy, of religious and of the laity.

Relations with the Hierarchy

24. The hierarchy's duty is to favor the lay apostolate, furnish it with principles and spiritual assistance, direct the exercise of the apostolate to the common good of the Church, and see to it that doctrine and order are safeguarded.

Yet the lay apostolate allows of different kinds of relations with the hierarchy, depending on the various forms and objects of this apostolate.

In the Church are to be found, in fact, very many apostolic enterprises owing their origin to the free choice of the laity and run at their own discretion. Such enterprises enable the Church, in certain circumstances, to fulfil her mission more effectively; not seldom, therefore, are they praised and commended by the hierarchy.[2] But no enterprise must lay claim to the name "Catholic" if it has not the approval of legitimate ecclesiastical authority.

Certain types of the lay apostolate are explicitly recognized by the hierarchy though in different ways.

Ecclesiastical authority, looking to the needs of the common good of the Church, may also, from among apostolic associations and undertakings aiming immediately at a spiritual goal, pick out some which it will foster in a particular way; in these it assumes a special responsibility. And so, organizing the apostolate differently according to circumstances, the hierarchy brings into closer con-

[2] Cf. Leo XIII, Encyclical Letter *Rerum Novarum*: *AAS* 23 (1890–1891) p. 647; Pius XI, Encyclical Letter *Quadragesimo Anno*: *AAS* 23 (1931) p. 190; Pius XII, *Nuntius Radiophonicus*, 1 June 1941: *AAS* 33 (1941) p. 207.
[1] Cf. Pius XI, Encyclical Letter *Quamvis Nostra*, 30 April 1936: *AAS* 28 (1936) pp. 160–161.
[2] Cf. Sacred Congregation of the Council, Resolution *Corrienten.*, 13 Nov. 1920: *AAS* 13 (1921) pp. 137–140.

junction with its own apostolic functions such-and-such a form of apostolate, without, however, changing the specific nature of either or the distinction between the two, and consequently without depriving the laity of their rightful freedom to act on their own initiative. This act of the hierarchy has received the name of "mandate" in various ecclesiastical documents.

Finally, the hierarchy entrusts the laity with certain charges more closely connected with the duties of pastors: in teaching of Christian doctrine, for example, in certain liturgical actions, in the care of souls. In virtue of this mission the laity are fully subject to superior ecclesiastical control in regard to the exercise of these charges.

As for works and institutions of the temporal order, the duty of the ecclesiastical hierarchy is the teaching and authentic interpretation of the moral principles to be followed in this domain. It is also in its province to judge, after mature reflection and with the help of qualified persons, of the conformity of such works or institutions with moral principles, and to pronounce in their regard concerning what is required for the safeguard and promotion of the values of the supernatural order.

Relations with the Clergy and with Religious

25. Bishops, parish priests and other priests of the secular and regular clergy will remember that the right and duty of exercising the apostolate are common to all the faithful, whether clerics or lay; and that in the building up of the Church the laity too have parts of their own to play.[3] For this reason they will work as brothers with the laity in the Church and for the Church, and will have a special concern for the laity in the apostolic activities of the latter.[4]

A careful choice will be made of priests with the ability and appropriate training for helping special forms of the lay apostolate.[5] Those who take part in this ministry in virtue of a mission received from the hierarchy represent the hierarchy in this pastoral action of theirs. Ever faithfully attached to the spirit and teaching of the Church they will devote their energies to fostering the spiritual life and the apostolic sense of the Catholic associations confided to them; their wise advice will be there to help these along in their apostolic labors; their encouragement will be given to their enterprises. In constant dialogue with the laity they will make painstaking search for methods capable of making apostolic action more fruitful; they will develop the spirit of unity within the association, and between it and others.

Lastly, religious Brothers and Sisters will hold lay apostolic works in high regard; and will gladly help in promoting them in accordance with the spirit and rules of their institute;[6] they will strive to support, assist and complete the ministrations of the priest.

[3] Cf. Pius XII, *Ad II Conventum ex Omnibus Gentibus Laicorum Apostolatui provehendo*, 5 Oct. 1957: *AAS* 49 (1957) p. 927.
[4] Cf. Dogmatic Constitution *De Ecclesia*, chap. IV, no. 37: *AAS* 57 (1965) pp. 42–43.
[5] Cf. Pius XII, Apostolic Exhortation *Menti Nostrae*, 23 Sept. 1950: *AAS* 42 (1950) p. 660.
[6] Cf. Decree *De Accomodata renovatione vitae religiosae*, no. 8.

Special Councils

26. In dioceses, as far as possible, councils should be set up to assist the Church's apostolic work, whether in the field of evangelization and sanctification or in the fields of charity, social relations and the rest; the clergy and religious working with the laity in whatever way proves satisfactory. These councils can take care of the mutual coordinating of the various lay associations and undertakings, the autonomy and particular nature of each remaining untouched.[7]

Such councils should be found too, if possible, at parochial, inter-parochial, inter-diocesan level, and also on the national and international plane.[8]

In addition, a special secretariat should be established at the Holy See for the service and promotion of the lay apostolate. This secretariat will act as a center which, with the proper equipment, will supply information about the different apostolic initiatives of the laity. It will undertake research on the problems arising today in this domain; and with its advice will assist the hierarchy and laity in the field of apostolic activities. The various apostolic movements and institutes of the lay apostolate all the world over should be represented in this secretariat. Clerics and religious should also be there to collaborate with the laity.

Cooperation with Other Christians and Non-Christians

27. The common patrimony of the Gospel and the common duty resulting from it of bearing a Christian witness make it desirable, and often imperative, that Catholics cooperate with other Christians, either in activities or in societies; this collaboration is carried on by individuals and by ecclesial communities, and at national or international level.[9]

Not seldom also do human values common to all mankind require of Christians working for apostolic ends that they collaborate with those who do not profess Christianity but acknowledge these values.

Through this dynamic, yet prudent, cooperation,[10] which is of great importance in temporal activities, the laity bears witness to Christ the Saviour of the world, and to the unity of the human family.

CHAPTER VI

TRAINING FOR THE APOSTOLATE

28. A training, at once many-sided and complete, is indispensable if the apostolate is to attain full efficacy. This is required, not only by the continuous spiritual and doctrinal progress of the layman himself, but also by the variety of circumstances, persons and duties to which he should adapt his activity. This education to the

[7] Cf. Benedict XIV, *De Synodo Dioecesana*, book III, chap. IX, no. VII.
[8] Cf. Pius XI, Encyclical Letter *Quamvis Nostra*, 30 April 1936, *AAS* 28 (1936) pp. 160–161.
[9] Cf. John XXIII, Encyclical Letter *Mater et Magistra*, 15 May 1961: *AAS* 53 (1961) pp. 456–457; cf. Decree *De Oecumenismo*, chap. II, no. 12: *AAS* 57 (1965) pp. 99–100.
[10] Cf. Decree *De Oecumenismo*, chap. II, no. 12: *AAS* 57 (1965) p. 100; cf. also Dogmatic Constitution *De Ecclesia*, chap. II, no. 15: *AAS* 57 (1965) pp. 19–20.

apostolate must rest on those foundations which the Council has in other places set down and expounded.[1] Not a few types of apostolate require, besides the education common to all Christians, a specific and individual training, by reason of the diversity of persons and circumstances.

Principles of Training

29. Since the laity participate in the Church's mission in a way that is their own, their apostolic training acquires a special character precisely from the secularity proper to the lay state and from its particular type of spirituality.

Education for the apostolate presupposes an integral human education suited to each one's abilities and conditions. For the layman ought to be, through an intimate knowledge of the contemporary world, a member well integrated into his own society and its culture.

But in the first place he should learn to accomplish the mission of Christ and the Church, living by faith in the divine mystery of creation and redemption, moved by the Holy Spirit who gives life to the People of God and urges all men to love God the Father, and in him to love the world of men. This education must be considered the foundation and condition of any fruitful apostolate.

Besides spiritual formation, solid grounding in doctrine is required: in theology, ethics and philosophy, at least, proportioned to the age, condition and abilities of each one. The importance too of a general culture linked with a practical and technical training is something which should by no means be overlooked.

If good human relations are to be cultivated, then it is necessary for genuine human values to stand at a premium, especially the art of living and working on friendly terms with others and entering into dialogue with them.

Training for the apostolate cannot consist in theoretical teaching alone; on that account there is need, right from the start of training, to learn gradually and prudently to see all things in the light of faith, to judge and act always in its light, to improve and perfect oneself by working with others, and in this manner to enter actively into the service of the Church.[2] Inasmuch as the human person is continuously developing and new problems are forever arising, this education should be steadily perfected; it requires an ever more thorough knowledge and a continual adaptation of action. While meeting all its demands, concern for the unity and integrity of the human person must be kept always in the foreground, in order to preserve and intensify its harmony and equilibrium.

In this way the layman actively inserts himself deep into the very reality of the temporal order and takes his part competently in the work of the world. At the same time, as a living member and witness of the Church, he brings its presence and its action into the heart of the temporal sphere.[3]

[1] Cf. Dogmatic Constitution *De Ecclesia*, chaps. II, IV, V: *AAS* 57 (1965) pp. 12–21, 37–49; cf. also Decree *De Oecumenismo*, nos. 4, 6, 7, 12: *AAS* 57 (1965) pp. 94, 96, 97, 99, 100; cf. also above, no. 4.

[2] Cf. Pius XII, *Ad I Conferentiam internationalem 'boy-scouts,'* 6 June 1952: *AAS* 44 (1952) pp. 579–580; John XXIII, Encyclical Letter *Mater et Magistra*, 15 May 1961: *AAS* 53 (1961) p. 456.

[3] Cf. Dogmatic Constitution *De Ecclesia*, chap. IV, no. 33: *AAS* 57 (1965) p. 39.

Those Who Train Others for the Apostolate

30. Training for the apostolate should begin from the very start of a child's education. But it is more particularly adolescents and youth who should be initiated into the apostolate and imbued with its spirit. This training should be continued all through life, to fit them to meet the demands of fresh duties. It is clear, then, that those with responsibility for Christian education have also the duty of attending to this apostolic education.

It rests with parents to prepare their children from an early age, within the family circle, to discern God's love for all men; they will teach them little by little—and above all by their example—to have concern for their neighbors' needs, material and spiritual. The whole family, accordingly, and its community life should become a kind of apprenticeship to the apostolate.

Children must be trained, besides, to go beyond the confines of the family and take an interest in both ecclesial and temporal communities. Their integration into the local parish community should succeed in bringing them the awareness of being living, active members of the People of God. Priests, for their part, should not lose sight of this question of training for the apostolate when catechizing, preaching and directing souls, and in other functions of the pastoral ministry.

Schools and colleges and other Catholic educational institutions should foster in the young a Catholic outlook and apostolic action. If the young do not get this type of education, either because they do not attend these schools, or for some other reason, all the greater is the responsibility for it that devolves upon parents, pastoral and apostolic bodies. As for teachers and educators, who by their calling and position practice an outstanding form of lay apostolate, adequate learning and a thorough grasp of pedagogy is a prerequisite to any success in this branch of education.

The various lay groups and associations dedicated to the apostolate or to any other supernatural end should look after this education to the apostolate with care and constancy, in ways consistent with their objectives and limits.[4] Frequently they are the ordinary channel of adequate apostolic training; doctrinal, spiritual and practical. The members, gathered in small groups with their companions or friends, evaluate the methods and results of their apostolic action, and measure their everyday behavior by the Gospel.

The training should be pursued in such a way as to take account of the entire range of the lay apostolate, an apostolate that is to be exercised in all circumstances and in every sector of life—in the professional and social sectors especially—and not confined within the precincts of the associations. In point of fact, every single lay person should himself actively undertake his own preparation for the apostolate. Especially for adults does this hold true; for as the years pass, self-awareness expands and so allows each one to get a clearer view of the talents with which God has enriched his life and to bring in better results from the exercise of the charisms given him by the Holy Spirit for the good of his brothers.

---

[4] Cf. John XXIII, Encyclical Letter *Mater et Magistra*, 15 May 1961: *AAS* 53 (1961) p. 455.

Fields Calling for Specialized Training

31. Different types of apostolate require their own appropriate method of training:

(a) The apostolate of evangelization and sanctification: the laity are to be especially trained for engaging in dialogue with others, believers or non-believers, their aim being to set the message of Christ before the eyes of all.[5] But as materialism under various guises is today spreading far and wide, even among Catholics, the laity should not only make a careful study of Catholic doctrine, especially points that are called into question, but should confront materialism of every type with the witness of evangelical life.

(b) The Christian renewal of the temporal order: the laity are to be instructed in the true meaning and value of temporal goods, both in themselves and in their relation to all the aims of the human person. The laity should gain experience in the right use of goods and in the organization of institutions, paying heed always to the common good in the light of the principles of the Church's moral and social teaching. They should acquire such a knowledge of social teaching especially, its principles and conclusions, as will fit them for contributing to the best of their ability to the progress of that teaching, and for making correct application of these same principles and conclusions in individual cases.[6]

(c) Works of charity and mercy bear a most striking testimony to Christian life; therefore, an apostolic training which has as its object the performance of these works should enable the faithful to learn from very childhood how to sympathize with their brothers, and help them generously when in need.[7]

Aids to Training

32. Many aids are now at the disposal of the laity who devote themselves to the apostolate: namely, sessions, congresses, recollections, retreats, frequent meetings, conferences, books and periodicals; all these enable them to deepen their knowledge of Holy Scripture and Catholic doctrine, nourish the spiritual life, and become acquainted also with world conditions and discover and adopt suitable methods.[8]

These educational aids take into account the various types of apostolate exercised in this or that particular area.

With this end in view higher centers or institutes have been created; these have already given excellent results.

The Council rejoices at initiatives of this kind now flourishing in certain regions; it desires to see them take root in other places too, wherever the need for them makes itself felt.

[5] Cf. Pius XII, Encyclical Letter *Sertum laetitiae*, 1 Nov. 1939: *AAS* 31 (1939) pp. 635–644; cf. idem., *Ad 'Laureati' Act. Cath. It.*, 24 May 1953.

[6] Cf. Pius XII, *Ad congressum Universalem Foederationis Juventutis Femininae Catholicae*, 18 April 1952: *AAS* 44 (1952) pp. 414–419; cf. idem, *Ad Associationem Christianam Operariorum Italiae* (A.C.L.I.), 1 May 1955: *AAS* 47 (1955) pp. 403–404.

[7] Cf. Pius XII, *Ad Delegatos Conventus Sodalitatum Caritas*, 27 April 1952: *AAS* pp. 470–471.

[8] Cf. John XXIII, Encyclical Letter *Mater et Magistra*, 15 May 1961: *AAS* 53 (1961) p. 454.

Moreover, centers of documentation and research should be established, not only in theology but also in anthropology, psychology, sociology, methodology, for the benefit of all fields of the apostolate. The purpose of such centers is to create a more favorable atmosphere for developing the aptitudes of the laity, men and women, young and old.

V

Extracts from the encyclical letter *On Fostering the Development of Peoples* (*Populorum Progressio*) of Pope Paul VI, 26 March 1967.

The translation is from the C.T.S. Edition, London.

The encyclical has 87 paragraphs divided into an *Introduction* (paragraphs 1 to 5), and two parts, *Part One* "Towards Man's Complete Development" (paragraphs 6 to 42), and *Part Two* "The Development of the Human Race in a Spirit of Solidarity" (paragraphs 43 to 80). There is a short "Final Appeal" (paragraphs 81 to 87).

Christian Vision of Development

14. Development cannot be limited to mere economic growth. In order to be authentic, it must be complete, integral; that is, it has to promote the good of every man and of the whole man. As an eminent specialist has very rightly and emphatically declared: 'We do not believe in separating the economic from the human, nor development from the civilizations in which it exists. What we hold important is man, each man and each group of men, and we even include the whole of humanity'.[15]

15. In the design of God, every man is called upon to develop and fulfil himself, for every life is a vocation. At birth, everyone is granted, in germ, a set of aptitudes and qualities for him to bring to fruition. Their coming to maturity, which will be the result of education received from the environment and personal efforts, will allow each man to direct himself toward the destiny intended for him by his Creator. Endowed with intelligence and freedom, he is responsible for his fulfilment as he is for his salvation. He is aided, or sometimes impeded, by those who educate him and those with whom he lives, but each one remains, whatever be these influences affecting him, the principal agent of his own success or failure. By the unaided effort of his own intelligence and his will, each man can grow in humanity, can enhance his personal worth, can become more a person.

---

[15] Cf. L. J. Lebret, O.P., *Dynamique concrète du développement* (Paris: Economie et Humanisme, Les Editions Ouvrières, 1961), p. 28.

Personal and Communal Responsibility

16. However, this self-fulfilment is not something optional. Just as the whole of creation is ordained to its Creator, so spiritual beings should of their own accord orientate their lives to God, the first truth and the supreme good. Thus it is that human fulfilment constitutes, as it were, a summary of our duties. But there is much more: this harmonious enrichment of nature by personal and responsible effort is ordered to a further perfection. By reason of his union with Christ, the source of life, man attains to new fulfilment of himself, to a transcendent humanism which gives him his greatest possible perfection: this is the highest goal of personal development.

17. But each man is a member of society. He is part of the whole of mankind. It is not just certain individuals, but all men who are called to this fullness of development. Civilizations are born, develop and die. But humanity is advancing along the path of history like the waves of a rising tide encroaching gradually on the shore. We have inherited from past generations, and we have benefited from the work of our contemporaries: for this reason we have obligations towards all, and we cannot refuse to interest ourselves in those who will come after us to enlarge the human family. The reality of human solidarity, which is a benefit for us, also imposes a duty.

18. This personal and communal development would be threatened if the true scale of values were undermined. The desire for necessities is legitimate, and work undertaken to obtain them is a duty: 'If any one will not work, let him not eat'.[16] But the acquiring of temporal goods can lead to greed, to the insatiable desire for more, and can make increased power a tempting objective. Individuals, families and nations can be overcome by avarice, be they poor or rich, and all can fall victim to a stifling materialism.

19. Increased possessions is not the ultimate goal of nations nor of individuals. All growth is ambivalent. It is essential if man is to develop as a man, but in a way it imprisons man if he considers it the supreme good, and it restricts his vision. Then we see hearts harden and minds close, and men no longer gather together in friendship but out of self-interest, which soon leads to oppositions and disunity. The exclusive pursuit of possessions thus becomes an obstacle to individual fulfilment and to man's true greatness. Both for nations and for individual men, avarice is the most evident form of moral underdevelopment.

Towards a More Human Condition

20. If further development calls for the work of more and more technicians, even more necessary is the deep thought and reflection of wise men in search of a new humanism which will enable modern man to find himself anew by embracing the higher values of love and friendship, of prayer and contemplation.[17] This is what

[16] 2 Thess 3:10.

[17] Cf., for example, J. Maritain, *Les conditions spirituelles du progrès et de la paix*, in *Rencontre des cultures a l'UNESCO sous le signe du Concile oecumenique Vatican II* (Paris: Mame, 1966), p. 66.

will permit the fullness of authentic development, a development which is for each and all the transition from less human conditions to those which are more human.

21. Less human conditions are the lack of material necessities for those who are without the minimum essential for life; the moral deficiencies of those who are mutilated by selfishness; oppressive social structures, whether due to the abuses of ownership or to the abuses of power, to the exploitation of workers or to unjust transactions. Conditions that are more human are the passage from misery towards the possession of necessities, victory over social scourges, the growth of knowledge, the acquisition of culture. Additional conditions that are more human are increased esteem for the dignity of others, the turning towards the spirit of poverty,[18] co-operation for the common good, and will and desire for peace. Conditions that are still more human are the acknowledgement by man of supreme values, and of God their source and their finality. Conditions that, finally and above all, are more human are faith, a gift of God accepted by the good will of man, and unity in the charity of Christ, who calls us all to share as sons in the life of the living God, the Father of all men.

3. ACTION TO BE UNDERTAKEN

The Universal Purpose of Created Things

22. 'Fill the earth and subdue it':[19] the Bible, from the first page on, teaches us that the whole of creation is for man, that it is his responsibility to develop it by intelligent effort and by means of his labour to perfect it, so to speak, for his use. If the world is made to furnish each individual with the means of livelihood and the instruments for his growth and progress, each man has therefore the right to find in the world what is necessary for himself. The recent Council reminded us of this: 'God intended the earth and all it contains for the use of all men and peoples, so created goods should flow fairly to all, regulated by justice and accompanied by charity'.[20] All other rights whatsoever, including those of property and of free commerce, are to be subordinated to this principle. They should not hinder but on the contrary favour its application. It is a grave and urgent social duty to redirect them to their primary finality.

Property and Revenue

23. 'But if any one has the world's goods and sees his brother in need, yet closes his heart against him, how does God's love abide in him?'[21] It is well known how strong were the words used by the Fathers of the Church to describe the proper attitude of persons who possess anything towards persons in need. To quote Saint Ambrose: 'You are not making a gift of your possessions to the poor person. You are handing over to him what is his. For what has been given in common for the use of all, you have arrogated to yourself. The world is given to all, and not only to

---

[18] Cf. Mt 5:3.

[19] Gen 1:28.

[20] Vatican Council II, Pastoral Constitution on the Church in the World of Today, *Gaudium et Spes*, n. 69, *AAS* 58 (1966), p. 1090.

[21] 1 Jn 3:17.

the rich'.[22] That is, private property does not constitute for anyone an absolute and unconditioned right. No one is justified in keeping for his exclusive use what he does not need, when others lack necessities. In a word, 'according to the traditional doctrine as found in the Fathers of the Church and the great theologians, the right to property must never be exercised to the detriment of the common good'. If there should arise a conflict 'between acquired private rights and primary community exigencies', it is the responsibility of public authorities 'to look for a solution, with the active participation of individuals and social groups'.[23]

24. If certain landed estates impede the general prosperity because they are extensive, unused or poorly used, or because they bring hardship to peoples or are detrimental to the interests of the country, the common good sometimes demands their expropriation. While giving a clear statement on this,[24] the Council recalled no less clearly that the available revenue is not to be used in accordance with mere whim, and that no place must be given to selfish speculation. Consequently it is unacceptable that citizens with abundant incomes from the resources and activity of their country should transfer a considerable part of this income abroad purely for their own advantage, without care for the manifest wrong they inflict on their country by doing this.[25]

Industrialization

25. The introduction of industry is a necessity for economic growth and human progress; it is also a sign of development and contributes to it. By persistent work and use of his intelligence man gradually wrests nature's secrets from her and finds a better application for her riches. As his self-mastery increases, he develops a taste for research and discovery, an ability to take a calculated risk, boldness in enterprises, generosity in what he does and a sense of responsibility.

Liberal Capitalism

26. But is is unfortunate that on these new conditions of society a system has been constructed which considers profit as the key motive for economic progress, competition as the supreme law of economics, and private ownership of the means of production as an absolute right that has no limits and carries no corresponding social obligation. This unchecked liberalism leads to dictatorship rightly denounced by Pius XI as producing 'the international imperialism of money'.[26] One cannot condemn such abuses too strongly by solemnly recalling once again that the economy is at the service of man.[27] But if it is true that a type of capitalism has

[22] *De Nabuthe*, c. 12, n. 53 (P.L. 14, 747). Cf. J.-R. Palanque, *Saint Ambroise et l'empire romain* (Paris: de Boccard, 1933), pp. 366 ff.

[23] Letter to the 52nd Session of the French Social Weeks (Brest, 1965), in *L'homme et la révolution urbaine* (Lyons: *Chronique Sociale*, 1965), pp. 8 and 9. Cf. *L'Osservatore Romano*, 10 July 1965; *Documentation Catholique*, v. 62, Paris, 1965, col. 1365.

[24] Vatican Council II, Pastoral Constitution on the Church in the World of Today, *Gaudium et Spes*, n. 71, *AAS* 58 (1966), p. 1093.

[25] Cf. *ibid.*, n. 65, *AAS* 58 (1966), p. 1086.

[26] Pius XI, Encyclical *Quadragesimo Anno*, *AAS* 23 (1931), p. 212.

[27] Cf., for example, Colin Clark, *The Conditions of Economic Progress*, 3rd ed. (London: Macmillan; New York: St. Martin's Press, 1960), pp.3–6.

been the source of excessive suffering, injustices and fratricidal conflicts whose effects still persist, it would also be wrong to attribute to industrialization itself evils that belong to the woeful system which accompanied it. On the contrary one must recognize in all justice the irreplaceable contribution made by the organization of labour and of industry to what development has accomplished.

Work

27. Similarly with work: while it can sometimes be given exaggerated significance, it is for all something willed and blessed by God. Man created to his image 'must co-operate with his Creator in the perfecting of creation and communicate to the earth the spiritual imprint he himself has received'.[28] God, who has endowed man with intelligence, imagination and sensitivity, has also given him the means of completing His work in a certain way: whether he be artist or craftsman, engaged in management, industry or agriculture, everyone who works is a creator. Bent over a material that resists his efforts, a man by his work gives his imprint to it, acquiring, as he does so, perseverance, skill and a spirit of invention. Further, when work is done in common, when hope, hardship, ambition and joy are shared, it brings together and firmly unites the wills, minds and hearts of men: in its accomplishment, men find themselves to be brothers.[29]

28. Work of course can have contrary effects, for it promises money, pleasure and power, invites some to selfishness, others to revolt; it also develops professional awareness, sense of duty and charity to one's neighbour. When it is more scientific and better organized, there is a risk of its dehumanizing those who perform it, by making them its servants, for work is human only if it remains intelligent and free. John XXIII gave a reminder of the urgency of giving everyone who works his proper dignity by making him a true sharer in the work he does with others: 'every effort must be made to ensure that the company is indeed a true community of persons, concerned about the needs, the activities and the standing of each of its members'.[30] Man's labour means much more still for the Christian: the mission of sharing in the creation of the supernatural world[31] which remains incomplete until we all come to build up together that perfect man of whom Saint Paul speaks 'who realizes the fullness of Christ'.[32]

29. We must make haste as too many are suffering, and the distance is growing that separates the progress of some and the stagnation, not to say the regression, of others. Yet the work required should advance smoothly if there is not to be the

---

[28] Letter to the 51st Session of the French Social Weeks (Lyons, 1964), in *Le travail et les travailleurs dans la société contemporaine*, Lyons, Chronique Sociale, 1965, p. 6. Cf. *L'Osservatore Romano*, 10 July 1964; *Documentation Catholique*, v. 61, Paris, 1964, col. 931.

[29] Cf., for example, M. D. Chenu O.P., *Pour une théologie du travail*, Paris, Edition de Seuil, 1955. [Eng. tr.: *The Theology of Work: An Exploration* (Dublin: Gill and Son, 1963).]

[30] John XXIII, Encyclical *Mater et Magistra, AAS* 53 (1961), p. 423.

[31] Cf., for example, O. Von Nell-Breunings S.J., *Wirtschaft und Gesellschaft*, v. 1: *Grundfragen*, Freiburg, Herder, 1956, pp. 183–184.

[32] Eph 4:13.

risk of losing indispensable equilibrium. A hasty agrarian reform can fail. Industrialization if introduced suddenly can displace structures still necessary, and produce hardships in society which would be a setback in terms of human values.

Temptation to Violence

30. There are certainly situations whose injustice cries to heaven. When whole populations destitute of necessities live in a state of dependence barring them from all initiative and responsibility, and all opportunity to advance culturally and share in social and political life, recourse to violence, as a means to right these wrongs to human dignity, is a grave temptation.

31. We know, however, that a revolutionary uprising—save where there is manifest, long-standing tyranny which would do great damage to fundamental personal rights and dangerous harm to the common good of the country—produces new injustices, throws more elements out of balance and brings on new disasters. A real evil should not be fought against at the cost of greater misery.

Reform

32. We want to be clearly understood: the present situation must be faced with courage and the injustices linked with it must be fought against and overcome. Development demands bold transformations, innovations that go deep. Urgent reforms should be undertaken without delay. It is for each one to take his share in them with generosity, particularly those whose education, position and opportunities afford them wide scope for action. May they show an example, and give of their own possessions as several of Our brothers in the episcopacy have done.[33] In so doing they will live up to men's expectations and be faithful to the Spirit of God, since 'the ferment of the Gospel rouses in man's heart a demand for dignity that cannot be stifled'.[34]

Programmes and Planning

33. Individual initiative alone and the mere free play of competition could never assure successful development. One must avoid the risk of increasing still more the wealth of the rich and the dominion of the strong, whilst leaving the poor in their misery and adding to the servitude of the oppressed. Hence programmes are necessary in order 'to encourage, stimulate, co-ordinate, supplement and integrate'[35] the activity of individuals and of intermediary bodies. It pertains to the public authorities to choose, even to lay down the objectives to be pursued, the ends to be achieved, and the means for attaining these, and it is for them to stimulate all the forces engaged in this common activity. But let them take care to associate private initiative and intermediate bodies with this work. They will thus

[33] Cf., for example, Manuel Larrain Errazuriz, Bishop of Talca, Chile, President of CELAM, *Pastoral Letter on civil development and peace* (Paris: Pax Christi, 1965).

[34] Cf. Vatican Council II, Pastoral Constitution on the Church in the World of Today, *Gaudium et Spes*, n. 26, AAS 58 (1966), p. 1046.

[35] John XXIII, Encyclical *Mater et Magistra*, AAS 53 (1961), p. 414.

avoid the danger of complete collectivization or of arbitrary planning which, by denying liberty, would prevent the exercise of the fundamental rights of the human person.

34. This is true since every programme, made to increase production, has, in the last analysis, no other *raison d'être* than the service of man. Such programmes should reduce inequalities, fight discriminations, free man from various types of servitude and enable him to be the instrument of his own material betterment, of his moral progress and of his spiritual growth. To speak of development is in effect to show as much concern for social progress as for economic growth. It is not sufficient to increase overall wealth for it to be distributed equitably. It is not sufficient to promote technology to render the world a more human place in which to live. The mistakes of their predecessors should warn those on the road to development of the dangers to be avoided in this field. Tomorrow's technocracy can beget evils no less formidable than those due to the liberalism of yesterday. Economics and technology have no meaning except from man whom they should serve. And man is only truly man in as far as, master of his own acts and judge of their worth, he is author of his own advancement, in keeping with the nature which was given to him by his Creator and whose possibilities and exigencies he himself freely assumes.

Efforts to Achieve Literacy

35. It can even be affirmed that economic growth depends in the very first place upon social progress: thus basic education is the primary object of any plan of development. Indeed hunger for education is no less debasing than hunger for food; an illiterate is a person with an undernourished mind. To be able to read and write, to acquire a professional formation, means to recover confidence in oneself and to discover that one can progress along with the others. As We said in Our message to the UNESCO Congress held in 1965 at Teheran, for man literacy is 'a fundamental factor of social integration, as well as of personal enrichment, and for society it is a privileged instrument of economic progress and of development'.[36] We also rejoice at the good work accomplished in this field by private initiative, by the public authorities and by international organizations: these are the primary agents of development, because they render man capable of acting for himself.

The Family

36. But man finds his true identity only in his social milieu, where the family plays a fundamental role. The family's influence may have been excessive, at some periods of history and in some places, when it was exercised to the detriment of the fundamental rights of the individual. The long-standing social frameworks, often too rigid and badly organized, existing in developing countries, are, nevertheless, still necessary for a time, yet progressively relaxing their excessive hold on the population. But the natural family, monogamous and stable such as the divine

[36] *L'Osservatore Romano*, 11 Sept. 1965; *Documentation Catholique*, v. 62, Paris, 1965, col. 1674–1675.

plan conceived it[37] and as Christianity sanctified it, must remain the place where 'different generations live together, helping each other to acquire greater wisdom and to harmonize personal rights with other social needs'.[38]

Population

37. It is true that too frequently an accelerated increase in population adds its own difficulties to the problems of development; the size of the population increases more rapidly than available resources, and things are found to have reached apparently an impasse. From that moment the temptation is great to check the demographic increase by means of radical measures. It is certain that public authorities can intervene, within the limit of their competence, by favouring the availability of appropriate information and by adopting suitable measures, provided that these be in conformity with the moral law and that they respect the rightful freedom of married couples. Where the inalienable right to marriage and procreation is lacking, human dignity has ceased to exist. Finally, it is for the parents to decide, with full knowledge of the matter, on the number of their children, taking into account their responsibilities towards God, themselves, the children they have already brought into the world, and the community to which they belong. In all this they must follow the demands of their own conscience enlightened by God's law authentically interpreted, and sustained by confidence in Him.[39]

Professional Organizations

38. In the task of development, man, who finds his life's primary environment in the family, is often aided by professional organizations. If it is their objective to promote the interests of their members, their responsibility is also great with regard to the educative task which at the same time they can and ought to accomplish. By means of the information they provide and the formation they propose, they can do much to give to all a sense of the common good and of the consequent obligations that fall upon each person.

39. All social action involves a doctrine. The Christian cannot admit that which is based upon a materialistic and atheistic philosophy, which respects neither the religious orientation of life to its final end, nor human freedom and dignity. But, provided that these values are safeguarded, a pluralism of professional organizations and trade unions is admissible, and from certain points of view useful, if thereby liberty is protected and emulation stimulated. And We most willingly pay homage to all those who labour in them to give unselfish service to their brothers.

[37] Cf. Mt 19:6.

[38] Vatican Council II, Pastoral Constitution on the Church in the World of Today, *Gaudium et Spes*, n. 52, *AAS* 58 (1966), p. 1073.

[39] Cf. Vatican Council II, Pastoral Constitution on the Church in the World of Today, *Gaudium et Spes*, nn. 50–51 and footnote: *AAS* 58 (1966), pp. 1070–1073; cf. also n. 87, *AAS* 58 (1966), p. 1110.

Promotion of Culture

40. In addition to professional organizations, there are other institutions which are at work. Their role is no less important for the success of development. 'The future of the world is in danger', the Council gravely affirms, 'unless wiser men are to be found'. And it adds: 'many of the materially poorer nations who are richer in wisdom may be of greater profit to the rest'.[40] Rich or poor, each country possesses a civilization handed down by their ancestors: institutions called for by life in this world, and higher manifestations of the life of the spirit, manifestations of an artistic, intellectual and religious character. When the latter possess true human values, it would be a grave error to sacrifice them to the former. A people that would act in this way would thereby lose the best of its patrimony; in order to live, it would be sacrificing its reasons for living. Christ's teaching also applies to people: 'What will it profit a man, if he gains the whole world and forfeits his life?'[41]

VI

Extracts from the encyclical letter *On the Regulation of Birth* (*Humanae Vitae*) of Pope Paul VI, 25 July 1968.

The translation is that of the C.T.S. London, revised edition, 1970.

There are thirty-one paragraphs in the letter, which is divided into three parts: *Part One*, "New Aspects of the Problem and the Competency of the Magisterium" (paragraphs 1 to 6), *Part Two*, "Doctrinal Questions" (paragraphs 7 to 18) and *Part Three*, "Pastoral Directives" (paragraphs 19 to 31). Our extracts are from Parts One and Two.

New Formulation of the Problem

2. The changes that have taken place are in fact of considerable importance and concern different problems. In the first place there is the question of the rapid increase in population which has made many fear that the world population is going to grow faster than available resources, with the consequence that many families and developing countries are being faced with greater hardships. This fact can easily induce public authorities to be tempted to take radical measures to avert this danger. There is also the fact that not only working and housing conditions, but the greater demands made both in the economic and educational field require that kind of life in which it is frequently extremely difficult these days to provide for a large family.

[40] Cf. *ibid.*, n. 15, *AAS* 58 (1966), p. 1036.
[41] Mt 16:26.

It is also apparent that, with the new understanding of the dignity of woman, and her place in society, there has been an appreciation of the value of love in marriage and of the meaning of intimate married life in the light of that love.

But the most remarkable development of all is to be seen in man's stupendous progress in the domination and rational organization of the forces of nature to the point that he is endeavouring to extend this control over every aspect of his own life—over his body, over his mind and emotions, over his social life, and even over the laws that regulate the transmission of life.

New Questions

3. This new state of things gives rise to new questions. Granted the conditions of life today and taking into account the relevance of married love to the harmony and mutual fidelity of husband and wife, would it not be right to review the moral norms in force till now, especially when it is felt that these can be observed, only with the gravest difficulty, sometimes only by heroic effort?

Moreover, if one were to apply here the so-called principle of totality, could it not be accepted that the intention to have a less prolific but more rationally planned family might not transform an action which renders natural processes infertile into a licit and provident control of birth? Could it not be admitted, in other words, that procreative finality applies to the totality of married life rather than to each single act? It is being asked whether, because people are more conscious today of their responsibilities, the time has not come when the transmission of life should be regulated by their intelligence and will rather than through the specific rhythms of their own bodies.

Competency of the Magisterium

4. This kind of question required from the teaching authority of the Church a new and deeper reflection on the principles of the moral teaching on marriage—a teaching which is based on the natural law as illuminated and enriched by divine Revelation.

Let no Catholic be heard to assert that the interpretation of the natural moral law is outside the competence of the Church's Magisterium. It is in fact indisputable, as Our Predecessors have many times declared,[1] that Jesus Christ, when he communicated his divine power to Peter and the other apostles and sent them to teach all nations his commandments,[2] constituted them as the authentic guardians and interpreters of the whole moral law, not only, that is, of the law of the Gospel but also of the natural law, the reason being that the natural law declares the will of God, and its faithful observance is necessary for men's eternal salvation.[3]

---

[1] Cf. Pius XI, Encyclical *Qui pluribus: Pii IX P.M. Acta*, 1, pp. 9–10; St. Pius X, Encycl. *Singulari quadam*, *AAS* 4 (1912), p. 658; Pius XI, Encycl. *Casti Connubii*, *AAS* 22 (1930), pp. 579–581 (C.T.S. translation, nn. 107–109); Pius XII, Address *Magnificate Dominum* to the Episcopate of the Catholic World, *AAS* 46 (1954), pp. 671–672; John XXIII, Encycl. *Mater et Magistra*, *AAS* 53 (1961), p. 457 (C.T.S. translation, n. 239).

[2] Cf. Mt 28:18–19.

[3] Cf. Mt 7:21.

The Church, in carrying out this mandate, has always provided consistent teaching on the nature of marriage, on the correct use of conjugal rights, and on all the duties of husband and wife. This is especially true in recent times.[4]

Special Studies

5. The consciousness of that same responsibility induced Us to confirm and expand the Commission set up by Our Predecessor, Pope John XXIII, of happy memory, in March 1963. This Commission included married couples as well as many men, expert in the various fields pertinent to these questions. Its competence, however, was to examine views and opinions concerning married life, and especially on the correct regulation of births. But it was also intended to provide the teaching authority of the Church with such evidence as would enable it to give an apt reply in this matter, which not only the faithful but also the rest of the world were waiting for.[5]

When the evidence of the experts had been received, as well as the opinions and advice of a considerable number of Our Brethren in the Episcopate, some of whom sent their views spontaneously, while others were requested by Us to do so, We were in a position to weigh up with more precision all the aspects of this complex subject. Hence we are deeply grateful to all those concerned.

Reply of the Magisterium

6. Nevertheless, we could not regard as definitive and requiring unequivocal acceptance the conclusions arrived at by the Commission. They were not such as to exempt Us from the duty of examining personally this serious question, and this because, if for no other reason, there was lacking complete agreement within the Commission itself as to what moral norms to put forward. This was all the more necessary because certain approaches and criteria for a solution to this question had emerged which were at variance with the moral doctrines on marriage constantly taught by the Magisterium of the Church.

[4] Cf. Council of Trent Roman Catechism, Part II, ch. 8; Leo XIII, Encycl. *Arcanum*: *Acta Leonis XIII*, 2 (1880), pp. 26–29; Pius XI, Encycl. *Divini Illius Magistri*, *AAS* 22 (1930), pp. 58–61 (C.T.S. translation, nn. 32–41); Pius XI, Encycl. *Casti Connubii*, *AAS* 22 (1930), pp. 545–546 (C.T.S. translation, nn. 16–18); Pius XII, Address to the Italian Medico-Biological Union of St. Luke, *Discorsi e Radiomessaggi* VI, pp. 191–192, to the Italian Association of Catholic Midwives, *AAS* 43 (1951), pp. 835–854 (C.T.S. translation, nn. 1–71); to the Association known as the 'Family Campaign' and other Family Associations, *AAS* 43 (1951), pp. 857–859 (C.T.S. translation, nn. 6–15); to the seventh Congress of the International Society of Haematology, *AAS* 50 (1958), pp. 734–735; John XXIII, Encycl. *Mater et Magistra*, *AAS* 53 (1961), pp. 446–447 (C.T.S. translation, nn. 188–192); Vatican Council II, Pastoral Constitution on the Church in the World of Today *Gaudium et Spes*, nn. 47–52, *AAS* 58 (1966), pp. 1067–1074; Code of Canon Law, Canons 1067, 1068 1, Canon 1076 1–2.

[5] Cf. Paul VI, Address to the Sacred College of Cardinals, *AAS* 56 (1964), p. 588; to the Commission for the Study of Problems of Population, Family and Birth, *AAS* 57 (1965), p. 388; to the National Congress of the Italian Society of Obstetrics and Gynaecology, *AAS* 58 (1966), p. 1168.

Consequently now that we have sifted carefully the evidence sent to us and intently studied the whole matter, as well as prayed constantly to God, We, by virtue of the mandate entrusted to Us by Christ, intend to give our reply to this series of grave questions.

PART TWO
DOCTRINAL QUESTIONS

A Total Vision of Man

7. The question of the birth of children, like every other question which touches human life, is too large to be resolved by limited criteria, such as are provided by biology, psychology, demography or sociology. It is the whole man and the whole complex of his responsibilities that must be considered, not only what is natural and limited to this earth, but also what is supernatural and eternal. And since in the attempt to justify artificial methods of birth control many appeal to the demands of married love or of 'responsible parenthood', these two important realities of married life must be accurately defined and analyzed. This is what We mean to do, with special reference to what the Second Vatican Council taught with the highest authority in its Pastoral Constitution *Gaudium et Spes*.

Marriage is a Sacrament

8. Married love particularly reveals its true nature and nobility when we realize that it derives from God and finds its supreme origin in him who 'is Love',[6] the Father 'from whom every family in heaven and earth is named'.[7]

Marriage, then, is far from being the effect of chance or the result of the blind evolution of natural forces. It is in reality the wise and provident institution of God the Creator, whose purpose was to establish in man his loving design. As a consequence, husband and wife, through that mutual gift of themselves, which is specific and exclusive to them alone, seek to develop that kind of personal union in which they complement one another in order to co-operate with God in the generation and education of new lives.

Furthermore, the marriage of those who have been baptized is invested with the dignity of a sacramental sign of grace, for it represents the union of Christ and his Church.

Married Love

9. In the light of these facts the characteristic features and exigencies of married love are clearly indicated, and it is of the highest importance to evaluate them exactly.

This love is above all fully *human*, a compound of sense and spirit. It is not, then, merely a question of natural instinct or emotional drive. It is also, and above all, an act of the free will, whose dynamism ensures that not only does it endure through the joys and sorrows of daily life, but also that it grows, so that husband and wife

[6] Cf. 1 Jn 4:8.
[7] Eph 3:15.

become in a way one heart and one soul, and together attain their human fulfilment.

Then it is a love which is *total*—that very special form of personal friendship in which husband and wife generously share everything, allowing no unreasonable exceptions or thinking just of their own interests. Whoever really loves his partner loves not only for what he receives, but loves that partner for her own sake, content to be able to enrich the other with the gift of himself.

Again, married love is *faithful* and *exclusive* of all others, and this until death. This is how husband and wife understood it on the day on which, fully aware of what they were doing, they freely vowed themselves to one another in marriage. Though this fidelity of husband and wife sometimes presents difficulties, no one can assert that it is impossible, for it is always honourable and worthy of the highest esteem. The example of so many married persons down through the centuries shows not only that fidelity is conatural to marriage but also that it is the source of profound and enduring happiness.

And finally this love is *creative of life*, for it is not exhausted by the loving interchange of husband and wife, but also contrives to go beyond this to bring new life into being. 'Marriage and married love are by their character ordained to the procreation and bringing up of children. Children are the outstanding gift of marriage, and contribute in the highest degree to the parents' welfare.'[8]

Responsible Parenthood

10. Married love, therefore, requires of husband and wife the full awareness of their obligations in the matter of responsible parenthood, which today, rightly enough, is much insisted upon, but which, at the same time, should be rightly understood. Hence, this must be studied in the light of the various inter-related arguments which are its justification.

If first we consider it in relation to the biological processes involved, responsible parenthood is to be understood as the knowledge and observance of their specific functions. Human intelligence discovers in the faculty of procreating life, the biological laws which involve human personality.[9]

If, on the other hand, we examine the innate drives and emotions of man, responsible parenthood expresses the domination which reason and will must exert over them.

But if we then attend to relevant physical, economic, psychological and social conditions, those are considered to exercise responsible parenthood who prudently and generously decide to have a large family, or who, for serious reasons and with due respect to the moral law, choose to have no more children for the time being or even for an indeterminate period.

Responsible parenthood, moreover, in the terms in which we use the phrase, retains a further and deeper significance of paramount importance which refers to the objective moral order instituted by God,—the order of which a right conscience is the true interpreter. As a consequence the commitment to responsible

[8] Vatican Council II, Pastoral Constitution on the Church in the World of Today *Gaudium et Spes*, n. 50, *AAS* 58 (1966), pp. 1070–1072.

[9] Cf. St. Thomas, *Summa Theologica*, I–II, q. 94, art. 2.

parenthood requires that husband and wife, keeping a right order of priorities, recognize their own duties towards God, themselves, their families and human society.

From this it follows that they are not free to do as they like in the service of transmitting life, on the supposition that it is lawful for them to decide independently of other considerations what is the right course to follow. On the contrary, they are bound to ensure that what they do corresponds to the will of God the Creator. The very nature of marriage and its use makes this clear, while the constant teaching of the Church affirms it.[10]

Respect for the Nature and Purpose of the Marriage Act

11. The sexual activity, in which husband and wife are intimately and chastely united with one another, through which human life is transmitted, is, as the recent Council recalled, 'honourable and good'.[11] It does not, moreover, cease to be legitimate even when, for reasons independent of their will, it is foreseen to be infertile. For its natural adaptation to the expression and strengthening of the union of husband and wife is not thereby suppressed. The facts are, as experience shows, that new life is not the result of each and every act of sexual intercourse. God has wisely ordered the laws of nature and the incidence of fertility in such a way that successive births are already naturally spaced through the inherent operation of these laws. The Church, nevertheless, in urging men to the observance of the precepts of the natural law, which it interprets by its constant doctrine, teaches as absolutely required that *in any use whatever of marriage* there must be no impairment of its natural capacity to procreate human life.[12]

Teaching in Harmony with Human Reason

12. This particular doctrine, often expounded by the Magisterium of the Church, is based on the inseparable connection, established by God, which man on his own initiative may not break, between the unitive significance and the procreative significance which are both inherent to the marriage act.

The reason is that the marriage act, because of its fundamental structure, while it unites husband and wife in the closest intimacy, also brings into operation laws written into the actual nature of man and of woman for the generation of new life. And if each of these essential qualities, the unitive and the procreative, is preserved, the use of marriage fully retains its sense of true mutual love and its ordination to the supreme responsibility of parenthood to which man is called. We believe that our contemporaries are particularly capable of seeing that this teaching is in harmony with human reason.

Faithfulness to God's Design

13. For men rightly observe that to force the use of marriage on one's partner without regard to his or her condition or personal and reasonable wishes in the

[10] Cf. Vatican Council II, Pastoral Constitution on the Church in the World of Today *Gaudium et Spes*, nn. 50–51, *AAS* 58 (1968), pp. 1070–1073.

[11] Cf. *ibid.*, n. 49, *AAS* 58 (1966), p. 1070.

[12] Cf. Pius XI, Encycl. *Casti Connubii*, *AAS* 22 (1930), p. 560 (C.T.S. translation, n. 56); Pius XII, Address to Midwives, *AAS* 43 (1951), p. 843 (C.T.S. Translation, n. 24).

matter, is no true act of love, and therefore offends the moral order in its particular application to the intimate relationship of husband and wife. In the same way, if they reflect, they must also recognize than an act of mutual love which impairs the capacity to transmit life which God the Creator, through specific laws, has built into it, frustrates his design which constitutes the norms of marriage, and contradicts the will of the Author of life. Hence, to use this divine gift while depriving it, even if only partially, of its meaning and purpose, is equally repugnant to the nature of man and of woman, strikes at the heart of their relationship and is consequently in opposition to the plan of God and his holy will. But to experience the gift of married love while respecting the laws of conception is to acknowledge that one is not the master of the sources of life but rather the minister of the design established by the Creator. Just as man does not have unlimited dominion over his body in general, so also, and with more particular reason, he has no such dominion over his specifically sexual faculties, for these are concerned by their very nature with the generation of life, of which God is the source. For human life is sacred—all men must recognize that fact, Our Predecessor, Pope John XXIII, recalled, 'since from its first beginnings it calls for the creative action of God'.[13]

Unlawful Ways of Regulating Birth

14. Therefore we base our words on the first principles of a human and Christian doctrine of marriage when we are obliged once more to declare that the direct interruption of the generative process already begun and, above all, direct abortion, even for therapeutic reasons, are to be absolutely excluded as lawful means of controlling the birth of children.[14]

Equally to be condemned, as the Magisterium of the Church has affirmed on various occasions, is direct sterilization, whether of the man or of the woman, whether permanent or temporary.[15]

Similarly excluded is any action, which either before, at the moment of, or after sexual intercourse, is specifically intended to prevent procreation—whether as an end or as a means.[16]

[13] Cf. John XXIII, Encycl. *Mater et Magistra*, AAS 53 (1961), p. 447 (C.T.S. translation, n. 194).

[14] Cf. Council of Trent Roman Catechism, Part II, ch. 8; Pius XI, Encycl. *Casti Connubii*, AAS 22 (1930), pp. 562–564 (C.T.S. translation, nn. 62–66); Pius XII, Address to the Medico-Biological Union of St. Luke, *Discorsi e Radiomessaggi*, VI, pp. 191–192; Address to Midwives, AAS 43 (1951), pp. 842–843 (C.T.S. translation, nn. 20–26); Address to the 'Family Campaign' and other Family Associations, AAS 43 (1951), pp. 857–859 (C.T.S. translation, nn. 6–15); John XXIII, Encycl. *Pacem in Terris*, AAS 55 (1963), pp. 259–260 (C.T.S. translation, nn. 8–13); Vatican Council II, Pastoral Constitution on the Church in the World of Today *Gaudium et Spes*, n. 51, AAS 58 (1966), p. 1072.

[15] Cf. Pius XI, Encycl. *Casti Connubii*, AAS 22 (1930), p. 565 (C.T.S. translation, nn. 67–70); Decree of the Holy Office, 22 Feb. 1940, AAS 32 (1940), p. 73; Pius XII, Address to Midwives, AAS 43 (1951), pp. 843–844 (C.T.S. translation, nn. 24–28); to the Society of Haematology, AAS 50 (1958), pp. 734–735.

[16] Cf. Council of Trent Roman Catechism, Part II, ch. 8; Pius XI, Encycl. *Casti Connubii*, AAS 22 (1930), pp. 559–561 (C.T.S. translation, nn. 53–57); Pius XII, Address to Midwives, AAS 43 (1951), p. 843 (C.T.S. translation, n. 24); to the Society of Haematology,

Neither is it valid to argue, as a justification for sexual intercourse which is deliberately contraceptive, that a lesser evil is to be preferred to a greater one, or that such intercourse would merge with the normal relations of past and future to form a single entity, and so be qualified by exactly the same moral goodness as these. Though it is true that sometimes it is lawful to tolerate a lesser moral evil in order to avoid a greater or in order to promote a greater good,[17] it is never lawful, even for the gravest reasons, to do evil that good may come of it[18]—in other words, to intend positively something which intrinsically contradicts the moral order, and which must therefore be judged unworthy of man, even though the intention is to protect or promote the welfare of an individual, of a family or of society in general. Consequently it is a serious error to think that a whole married life of otherwise normal relations can justify sexual intercourse which is deliberately contraceptive and so intrinsically wrong.

Lawfulness of Therapeutic Means

15. But the Church in no way regards as unlawful therapeutic means considered necessary to cure organic diseases, even though they also have a contraceptive effect, and this is foreseen—provided that this contraceptive effect is not directly intended for any motive whatsoever.[19]

Lawfulness of Recourse to Infertile Periods

16. However, as We noted earlier (n. 3), some people today raise the objection against this particular doctrine of the Church concerning the moral laws governing marriage, that human intelligence has both the right and the responsibility to control those forces of irrational nature which come within its ambit and to direct them towards ends beneficial to man. Others ask on the same point whether it is not reasonable in so many cases to use artificial birth control if by so doing the harmony and peace of a family are better served and more suitable conditions are provided for the education of children already born. To this question we must give a clear reply. The Church is the first to praise and commend the application of human intelligence to an activity in which a rational creature such as man is so closely associated with his Creator. But she affirms that this must be done within the limits of the order of reality established by God.

If therefore there are reasonable grounds for spacing births, arising from the physical or psychological condition of husband or wife or from external circumstances, the Church teaches that then married people may take advantage of the natural cycles immanent in the reproductive system and use their marriage at

---

AAS 50 (1958), pp. 734–735; John XXIII, Encycl. *Mater et Magistra, AAS* 53 (1961), p. 447 (C.T.S. translation, n. 193).

[17] Cf. Pius XII, Address to the National Congress of the Italian Society of the Union of Catholic Jurists, *AAS* 45 (1953), pp. 798–799.

[18] Cf. Rom 3:8.

[19] Cf. Pius XII, Address to the twenty-sixth Congress of the Italian Association of Urology, *AAS* 45 (1953), pp. 674–675; to the Society of Haematology, *AAS* 50 (1958), pp. 734–735.

precisely those times that are infertile, and in this way control birth, a way which does not in the least offend the moral principles which we have just explained.[20]

Neither the Church nor her doctrine is inconsistent when she considers it lawful for married people to take advantage of the infertile period but condemns as always unlawful the use of means which directly exclude conception, even when the reasons given for the latter practice are neither trivial nor immoral. In reality, these two cases are completely different. In the former married couples rightly use a facility provided them by nature. In the latter they obstruct the natural development of the generative process. It cannot be denied that in each case married couples, for acceptable reasons, are both perfectly clear in their intention to avoid children and mean to make sure that none will be born. But it is equally true that it is exclusively in the former case that husband and wife are ready to abstain from intercourse during the fertile period as often as for reasonable motives the birth of another child is not desirable. And when the infertile period recurs, they use their married intimacy to express their mutual love and safeguard their fidelity towards one another. In doing this they certainly give proof of a true and authentic love.

Grave Consequences of Artificial Birth Control

17. Responsible men can become more deeply convinced of the truth of the doctrine laid down by the Church on this issue if they reflect on the consequences of methods and plans for the artificial restriction of increases in the birth-rate. Let them first consider how easily this course of action can lead to the way being wide open to marital infidelity and a general lowering of moral standards. Not much experience is needed to be fully aware of human weakness and to understand that men—and especially the young, who are so exposed to temptation—need incentives to keep the moral law, and it is an evil thing to make it easy for them to break that law. Another effect that gives cause for alarm is that a man who grows accustomed to the use of contraceptive methods may forget the reverence due to a woman, and, disregarding her physical and emotional equilibrium, reduce her to being a mere instrument for the satisfaction of his own desires, no longer considering her as his partner whom he should surround with care and affection.

Finally, grave consideration should be given to the danger of this power passing into the hands of those public authorities who care little for the precepts of the moral law. Who will blame a Government which in its attempt to resolve the problems affecting an entire country resorts to the same measures as are regarded as lawful by married people in the solution of a particular family difficulty? Who will prevent public authorities from favouring those contraceptive methods which they consider more effective? Should they regard this as necessary, they may even impose their use on everyone. It could well happen, therefore, that when people, either individually or in family or social life, experience the inherent difficulties of the divine law and are determined to avoid them, they may be giving into the hands of public authorities the power to intervene in the most personal and intimate responsibility of husband and wife.

Consequently, unless we are willing that the responsibility of procreating life should be left to the arbitrary decision of men, we must accept that there are

[20] Cf. Pius XII, Address to Midwives, *AAS* 43 (1951), p. 846 (C.T.S. translation, n. 36).

certain limits, beyond which it is wrong to go, to the power of man over his own body and its natural functions—limits, let it be said, which no one, whether as a private individual or as a public authority, can lawfully exceed. These limits are expressly imposed because of the reverence due to the whole human organism and its natural functions, in the light of the principles, which we stated earlier, and according to a correct understanding of the so-called 'principle of totality', enunciated by Our Predecessor, Pope Pius XII.[21]

VII

Extracts from the apostolic letter *On the Eightieth Anniversary of* Rerum Novarum (*Octogesima Adveniens*) of Paul VI, 15 May 1971.

The translation is from the London C.T.S. edition 1971.

There are fifty-two paragraphs in the letter. There is a Foreword (paragraphs 1 to 7) and four parts: *Part One*, "New Social Problems" (paragraphs 8 to 21), *Part Two*, "Fundamental Aspirations and Currents of Ideas" (paragraphs 22 to 41), *Part Three*, "Christians Face to Face with These New Problems" (paragraphs 42 to 47) and *Part Four*, "Call to Action" (paragraphs 48 to 52). Our extracts are from *Part One*, "New Social Problems".

Urbanization

8. A major phenomenon draws our attention, as much in the industrialized countries as in those which are developing: urbanization.

After long centuries, agrarian civilization is weakening. Is sufficient attention being devoted to the arrangement and improvement of the life of the country people, whose inferior and at times miserable economic situation provokes the flight to the unhappy crowded conditions of the city outskirts, where neither employment nor housing awaits them?

This unceasing flight from the land, industrial growth, continual demographic expansion and the attraction of urban centres bring about concentration of population, the extent of which is difficult to imagine, for people are already speaking in terms of a 'megalopolis' grouping together tens of millions of persons. Of course there exist medium-sized towns, the dimension of which ensures a better balance in the population. While being able to offer employment to those that progress in agriculture makes available, they permit an adjustment of the human environment which better avoids the proletarianism and crowding of the great built-up areas.

[21] Cf. Pius XII, Address to the Association of Urology, *AAS* 45 (1953), pp. 674–675; to Leaders and Members of the Italian Association of 'corneae' donors and the Italian Association of the Blind, *AAS* 48 (1956), pp. 461–462.

9. The inordinate growth of these centres accompanies industrial expansion, without being identified with it. Based on technological research and the transformation of nature, industrialization constantly goes forward, giving proof of incessant creativity. While certain enterprises develop and are concentrated, others die or change their location. Thus new social problems are created: professional or regional unemployment, redeployment and mobility of persons, permanent adaptation of workers and disparity of conditions in the different branches of industry. Unlimited competition utilizing the modern means of publicity incessantly launches new products and tries to attract the consumer, while earlier industrial installations which are still capable of functioning become useless. While very large areas of the population are unable to satisfy their primary needs, superfluous needs are ingeniously created. It can thus rightly be asked if, in spite of all his conquests, man is not turning back against himself the results of his activity. Having rationally endeavoured to control nature,[7] is he not now becoming the slave of the objects which he makes?

Christians in the City

10. Is not the rise of an urban civilization which accompanies the advance of industrial civilization a true challenge to the wisdom of man, to his capacity for organization and to his far-seeing imagination? Within industrial society urbanization upsets both the ways of life and the habitual structures of existence: the family, the neighbourhood, and the very framework of the Christian community. Man is experiencing a new loneliness; it is not in the face of a hostile nature which it has taken him centuries to subdue, but in an anonymous crowd which surrounds him and in which he feels himself a stranger. Urbanization, undoubtedly an irreversible stage in the development of human societies, confronts man with difficult problems. How is he to master its growth, regulate its organization, and successfully accomplish its animation for the good of all?

In this disordered growth, new proletariats are born. They install themselves in the heart of the cities sometimes abandoned by the rich; they dwell on the outskirts—which become a belt of misery besieging in a still silent protest the luxury which blatantly cries out from the centres of consumption and waste. Instead of favouring fraternal encounter and mutual aid, the city fosters discrimination and also indifference. It lends itself to new forms of exploitation and of domination whereby some people in speculating on the needs of others derive inadmissible profits. Behind the facades, much misery is hidden, unsuspected even by the closest neighbours; other forms of misery spread where human dignity founders: delinquency, criminality, abuse of drugs and eroticism.

11. It is in fact the weakest who are the victims of dehumanizing living conditions, degrading for conscience and endangering the existence of the family as an institution. Shared dwellings make any private family life impossible; young couples waiting in vain for a decent dwelling at a price they can afford are demoralized and even their union can thereby be endangered; the young escape from a home which is too confined and seek in the streets compensations and

[7] Cf. Encyclical Letter *Populorum Progressio*, 25: *AAS* 59 (1967), pp. 269–270.

companionships which cannot be supervised. It is the grave duty of those responsible to strive to control this process and to give it direction.

There is an urgent need to remake at the level of the street, of the neighbourhood or of the great agglomerative dwellings the social fabric whereby man may be able to develop the needs of his personality. Centres of special interest and of culture must be created or developed at the community and parish levels with different forms of associations, recreational centres, and spiritual and community gatherings where the individual can escape from isolation and form anew fraternal relationships.

12. To build up the city, the place where men and their expanded communities exist, to create new modes of neighbourliness and co-operation, to think out original applications of social justice and to undertake responsibility for this collective future, which all foresee will be difficult, is a task in which Christians must share. To those who have to live in confined urban surroundings which become intolerable it is necessary to bring a message of hope. This requires an active brotherhood and justice seen to be done. Let Christians, conscious of this new responsibility, not lose heart in view of the vast and faceless society; let them recall Jonah who traversed Nineveh, the great city, to proclaim therein the good news of God's mercy and was upheld in his weakness by the sole strength of the word of almighty God. In the Bible, the city is in fact often the place of sin and pride—the pride of man who feels secure enough to be able to build his life without God and even to affirm that he is powerful against God. But there is also the example of Jerusalem, the Holy City, the place where God is encountered, the promise of the city which comes from on high.[8]

Youth

13. Urban life and industrial change bring strongly to light questions which until now were poorly grasped. What place, for example, in this newly emerging world, should be given to youth?

Everywhere dialogue is proving to be difficult between youth, with its aspirations, its search for renewal and also its insecurity for the future, and the adult generations. It is obvious to all that here we have a source of serious conflicts, division and opting out, even within the family, and a questioning of the basis of authority, of education for freedom and of certain good and established traditions, which strikes at the deep roots of society.

The Role of Women

Similarly, in many countries a charter for women which would put an end to an actual discrimination and would establish relationships of equality in rights and of respect for their dignity is the object of study and at times of lively demands. We do not have in mind that false equality which would deny the distinctions laid down by the Creator himself and which would be in contradiction with woman's proper role, which is of such capital importance, at the heart of the family as well as within society. Developments in legislation should on the contrary be directed

---

[8] Cf. Rev 3:12; 21:2.

to protecting her proper vocation and at the same time recognizing her independence as a person, and her equal rights to participate in cultural, economic, social and political life.

Workers

14. As the Church solemnly reaffirmed in the recent Council, 'the beginning, the subject and the goal of all social institutions is and must be the human person'.[9] Every man has the right to work, to a chance to develop his qualities and his personality in the exercise of his profession, to equitable remuneration which will enable him and his family to 'lead a worthy life on the material, social, cultural and spiritual level',[10] and to assistance in case of need arising from sickness or age.

Although for the defence of these rights democratic societies accept today the principle of labour union rights, they are not always open to their exercise. The important role of union organizations must be admitted: their object is the representation of the various categories of workers, their lawful collaboration in the economic advance of society, and the development of their sense of responsibility for the realization of the common good. Their activity, however, is not without its difficulties. Here and there the temptation can arise of profiting from a position of strength to impose, particularly by strikes—the right to which as a final means of defence remains certainly recognized—conditions which are too burdensome for the overall economy and for the social body, or to desire to obtain in this way demands of a directly political nature. When it is a question of public services, required for the life of an entire nation, it is necessary to be able to assess the limit beyond which the harm caused to society becomes inadmissible.

Victims of Changes

15. In short, progress has already been made in introducing, in the area of human relationships, greater justice and greater sharing of responsibilities. But in this immense field much remains to be done. Further reflection, research and experimentation must be actively pursued, unless one is to be late in meeting the legitimate aspirations of the workers—aspirations which are being increasingly asserted according as their education, their consciousness of their dignity and the strength of their organizations increase.

Egoism and domination are permanent temptations for men. Likewise an ever finer discernment is needed, in order to strike at the roots of newly arising situations of injustice and to establish progressively a justice which will be less and less imperfect. Especially in industrial change, which demands speedy and constant adaptation, we can see that those who will find themselves injured will be ever more numerous and at a greater disadvantage from the point of view of making their voices heard. The Church directs her attention to these new 'poor' —the handicapped and the maladjusted, the old, different groups of those on the fringe of society, and so on—in order to recognize them, help them, defend their place and dignity in a society hardened by competition and the attraction of success.

[9] Vatican Council II, Pastoral Constitution *Gaudium et Spes*, 25: *AAS* 58 (1966), p. 1045.
[10] Ibid., 67, p. 1089.

Discrimination

16. Among the victims of situations of injustice—unfortunately no new phenomenon—must be placed those who are discriminated against, in law or in fact, on account of their race, origin, colour, culture, sex or religion.

Racial discrimination possesses at the moment a character of very great relevance by reason of the tension which it stirs up both within certain countries and on the international level. Men rightly consider unjustifiable and reject as inadmissible the tendency to maintain or introduce legislation or behaviour systematically inspired by racialist prejudice. The members of mankind share the same basic rights and duties, as well as the same supernatural destiny. Within a country which belongs to each one, all should be equal before the law, find equal admittance to economic, cultural, civic and social life and benefit from a fair sharing of the nation's riches.

Right To Emigrate

17. We are thinking also of the precarious situation of a great number of emigrant workers whose condition as foreigners makes it all the more difficult for them to assert their lawful social rights, in spite of their real participation in the economic effort of the country that receives them. It is urgently necessary for people to go beyond a narrowly nationalist attitude in their regard and to give them a charter which will assure them a right to emigrate, favour their integration, facilitate their professional advancement and give them access to decent housing where, when the opportunity allows, their families can join them.[11]

Linked to this category are the people who, to find work, or to escape a disaster or a hostile climate, leave their homeland and find themselves without roots among other people.

It is everyone's duty, but especially that of Christians,[12] to work with energy for the establishment of universal brotherhood, the indispensable basis for authentic justice and the conditions for enduring peace: 'We cannot in truthfulness call upon that God who is the Father of all if to some men, created in God's image, we refuse to act in a brotherly way. A man's relationship with God the Father and his relationship with his brother men are so linked together that Scripture says: "He who does not love does not know God" (1 Jn 4:8)'.[13]

Creating Employment

18. With demographic growth, which is particularly pronounced in the young nations, the number of those failing to find work and are driven to a life of misery or become hangers-on will grow in the coming years unless the conscience of man rouses itself and gives rise to a general movement of solidarity through the effective policy of investment and of organization of production and trade, as well as of education. We know the attention given to these problems within international organizations, and it is our lively wish that their members will not delay bringing their actions into line with their declarations.

[11] Cf. Encyclical Letter *Populorum Progressio*, 69: *AAS* 59 (1967), pp. 290–291.
[12] Cf. Mt 25:35.
[13] Vatican Council II, Declaration *Nostra aetate*, 5: *AAS* 58 (1966), p. 743 (C.T.S. Do 360).

It is disquieting in this regard to note a kind of fatalism which is gaining a hold even on people in positions of responsibility. This feeling sometimes leads to Malthusian solutions inculcated by active propaganda for contraception and abortion. In this critical situation, it must on the contrary be affirmed that the family, without which no society can stand, has a right to the assistance which will assure it of the conditions for a healthy development. 'It is certain', we said in our encyclical *Populorum Progressio*, 'that public authorities can intervene, within the limit of their competence, by favouring the availability of appropriate information and by adopting suitable measures, provided that these be in conformity with the moral law and that they respect the rightful freedom of married couples. Where the inalienable right to marriage and procreation is lacking, human dignity has ceased to exist.'[14]

19. In no other age have men been so explicitly called to social innovation. To this should be devoted resources of invention and capital as important as those invested for armaments or technological achievements. If man lets himself rush ahead without foreseeing in good time the emergence of new social problems, they will become too grave for a peaceful solution to be hoped for.

Media of Social Communication

20. Among the major changes of our times, we must not forget to emphasize the growing role being assumed by the media of social communication and their influence on the transformation of mentalities, of knowledge, of organizations and of society itself. Certainly they have many positive aspects. Thanks to them news from the entire world reaches us practically in an instant, establishing contacts which supersede distances and creating elements of unity among all men. A greater spread of education and culture is becoming possible. Nevertheless, by their very action the media of social communication are reaching the point of representing as it were a new power. One cannot but ask about those who really hold this power, the aims that they pursue and the means they use, and finally, about the effect of their activity on the exercise of individual liberty, both in the political and ideological spheres and in social, economic and cultural life. The men who hold this power have a grave moral responsibility with respect to the truth of the information that they spread, the needs and the reactions that they generate and the values which they put forward. In the case of television, moreover, what is coming into being is an original mode of knowledge and a new civilization: that of the image.

Naturally, the public authorities cannot ignore the growing power and influence of the media of social communication and the advantages and risks which their use involves for the development and real perfecting of the civic community.

Consequently they are called upon to perform their own positive function for the common good by encouraging every constructive expression, by supporting individual citizens and groups in defending the fundamental values of the person and of human society, and also by taking suitable steps to prevent the spread of

[14] *AAS* 59 (1967), p. 276.

what would harm the common heritage of values on which orderly progress is based.[15]

The Environment

21. While the horizon of man is thus being modified according to the images that are chosen for him, another transformation is making itself felt, one which is the dramatic and unexpected consequence of human activity. Man is suddenly becoming aware that by an ill-considered exploitation of nature he risks destroying it and becoming in his turn the victim of this degradation. Not only is the material environment becoming a permanent menace—pollution and refuse, new illnesses and absolute destructive capacity—but the human framework is no longer under man's control, thus creating an environment for tomorrow which may well be intolerable. This is a wide-ranging social problem which concerns the entire human family.

The Christian must turn to these new perceptions in order to take on responsibility, together with the rest of men, for a destiny which from now on is shared by all.

VIII

Extracts from the *Declaration on Certain Questions Concerning Sexual Ethics* issued by the Sacred Congregation for the Doctrine of the Faith, 29 December 1975.

The translation is that of the Vatican Polyglot Press distributed by the C.T.S. London.

The document runs to twenty pages; there are no subheadings.

DECLARATION ON CERTAIN QUESTIONS CONCERNING SEXUAL ETHICS

1. According to contemporary scientific research, the human person is so profoundly affected by sexuality that it must be considered as one of the factors which give to each individual's life the principal traits that distinguish it. In fact it is from sex that the human person receives the characteristics which, on the biological, psychological and spiritual levels, make that person a man or a woman, and thereby largely condition his or her progress towards maturity and insertion into society. Hence sexual matters, as is obvious to everyone, today constitute a theme frequently and openly dealt with in books, reviews, magazines and other means of social communication.

[115] Cf. Vatican Council II, Decree *Inter mirifica*, 12: *AAS* 56 (1964), p. 149 (C.T.S. Do 389).

In the present period, the corruption of morals has increased, and one of the most serious indications of this corruption is the unbridled exaltation of sex. Moreover, through the means of social communication and through public entertainment this corruption has reached the point of invading the field of education and of infecting the general mentality.

In this context certain educators, teachers and moralists have been able to contribute to a better understanding and integration into life of the values proper to each of the sexes; on the other hand there are those who have put forward concepts and modes of behaviour which are contrary to the true moral exigencies of the human person. Some members of the latter group have even gone so far as to favour a licentious hedonism.

As a result, in the course of a few years, teachings, moral criteria and modes of living hitherto faithfully preserved have been very much unsettled, even among Christians. There are many people today who, being confronted with so many widespread opinions opposed to the teaching which they received from the Church, have come to wonder what they must still hold as true.

2. The Church cannot remain indifferent to this confusion of minds and relaxation of morals. It is a question, in fact, of a matter which is of the utmost importance both for the personal lives of Christians and for the social life of our time.[1]

The Bishops are daily led to note the growing difficulties experienced by the faithful in obtaining knowledge of wholesome moral teaching, especially in sexual matters, and of the growing difficulties experienced by pastors in expounding this teaching effectively. The Bishops know that by their pastoral charge they are called upon to meet the needs of their faithful in this very serious matter, and important documents dealing with it have already been published by some of them or by Episcopal Conferences. Nevertheless, since the erroneous opinions and resulting deviations are continuing to spread everywhere, the Sacred Congregation for the Doctrine of the Faith, by virtue of its function in the universal Church[2] and by a mandate of the Supreme Pontiff, has judged it necessary to publish the present Declaration.

3. The people of our time are more and more convinced that the human person's dignity and vocation demand that they should discover, by the light of their own intelligence, the values innate in their nature, that they should ceaselessly develop these values and realize them in their lives, in order to achieve an ever greater development.

In moral matters man cannot make value judgments according to his personal whim: "In the depths of his conscience, man detects a law which he does not impose on himself, but which holds him to obedience. . . . For man has in his heart a law written by God. To obey it is the very dignity of man; according to it he will be judged".[3]

---

[1] Cf. Second Vatican Ecumenical Council, Constitution on the Church in the Modern World *Gaudium et Spes*, 47: *AAS* 58 (1966), p. 1067.

[2] Cf. Apostolic Constitution *Regimi Ecclesiae Universae*, 29 (15 August 1967) *AAS* 59 (1967), p. 897.

[3] *Gaudium et Spes*, 16: *AAS* 58 (1966), p. 1037.

Moreover, through his revelation God has made known to us Christians his plan of salvation, and he has held up to us Christ, the Saviour and Sanctifier, in his teaching and example, as the supreme and immutable Law of life: "I am the light of the world; anyone who follows me will not be walking in the dark, he will have the light of life".[4]

Therefore there can be no true promotion of man's dignity unless the essential order of his nature is respected. Of course, in the history of civilization many of the concrete conditions and needs of human life have changed and will continue to change. But all evolution of morals and every type of life must be kept within the limits imposed by the immutable principles based upon every human person's constitutive elements and essential relations—elements and relations which transcend historical contingency.

These fundamental principles, which can be grasped by reason, are contained in "the divine law—eternal, objective and universal—whereby God orders, directs and governs the entire universe and all the ways of the human community, by a plan conceived in wisdom and love. Man has been made by God to participate in this law, with the result that, under the gentle disposition of divine Providence, he can come to perceive ever increasingly the unchanging truth".[5] This divine law is accessible to our minds.

4. Hence, those many people are in error who today assert that one can find neither in human nature nor in the revealed law any absolute and immutable norm to serve for particular actions other than the one which expresses itself in the general law of charity and respect for human dignity. As a proof of their assertion they put forward the view that so-called norms of the natural law or precepts of Sacred Scripture are to be regarded only as given expressions of a form of particular culture at a certain moment of history.

But in fact, divine Revelation and, in its own proper order, philosophical wisdom, emphasize the authentic exigencies of human nature. They thereby necessarily manifest the existence of immutable laws inscribed in the constitutive elements of human nature and which are revealed to be identical in all beings endowed with reason.

Furthermore, Christ instituted his Church as "the pillar and bulwark of truth".[6] With the Holy Spirit's assistance, she ceaselessly preserves and transmits without error the truths of the moral order, and she authentically interprets not only the revealed positive law but "also those principles of the moral order which have their origin in human nature itself"[7] and which concern man's full development and sanctification. Now in fact the Church throughout her history has always

---

[4] Jn 8:12.

[5] Second Vatican Ecumenical Council, Declaration *Dignitatis Humanae*, 3: *AAS* 58 (1966), p. 931.

[6] 1 Tim 3:15.

[7] *Dignitatis Humanae*, 14: *AAS* 58 (1966), p. 940; cf. Pius XI, Encyclical Letter *Casti Connubii*, 31 December 1930: *AAS* 22 (1930), pp. 579–580; Pius XII, Allocution of 2 November 1954: *AAS* 46 (1954), pp. 671–672; John XXIII, Encyclical Letter *Mater et Magistra*, 15 May 1961: *AAS* 53 (1961), p. 457; Paul VI, Encyclical Letter *Humanae Vitae*, 4, 25 July 1968: *AAS* 60 (1968), p. 483.

considered a certain number of precepts of the natural law as having an absolute and immutable value, and in their transgression she has seen a contradiction of the teaching and spirit of the Gospel.

5. Since sexual ethics concern certain fundamental values of human and Christian life, this general teaching equally applies to sexual ethics. In this domain there exist principles and norms which the Church has always unhesitatingly transmitted as part of her teaching, however much the opinions and morals of the world may have been opposed to them. These principles and norms in no way owe their origin to a certain type of culture, but rather to knowledge of the divine law and of human nature. They therefore cannot be considered as having become out of date or doubtful under the pretext that a new cultural situation has arisen.

It is these principles which inspired the exhortations and directives given by the Second Vatican Council for an education and an organization of social life taking account of the equal dignity of man and woman while respecting their difference. [8]

Speaking of "the sexual nature of man and the human faculty of procreation", the Council noted that they "wonderfully exceed the dispositions of lower forms of life". [9] It then took particular care to expound the principles and criteria which concern human sexuality in marriage, and which are based upon the finality of the specific function of sexuality.

In this regard the Council declares that the moral goodness of the acts proper to conjugal life, acts which are ordered according to true human dignity, "does not depend solely on sincere intentions or on an evaluation of motives. It must be determined by objective standards. These, based on the nature of the human person and his acts, preserve the full sense of mutual self-giving and human procreation in the context of true love". [10]

These final words briefly sum up the Council's teaching—more fully expounded in an earlier part of the same Constitution[11]—on the finality of the sexual act and on the principal criterion of its morality: it is respect for its finality that ensures the moral goodness of this act.

This same principle, which the Church holds from divine Revelation and from her authentic interpretation of the natural law, is also the basis of her traditional doctrine, which states that the use of the sexual function has its true meaning and moral rectitude only in true marriage. [12]

6. It is not the purpose of the present declaration to deal with all the abuses of the sexual faculty, nor with all the elements involved in the practice of chastity. Its object is rather to repeat the Church's doctrine on certain particular points, in view of the urgent need to oppose serious errors and widespread aberrant modes of behaviour.

[8] Cf. Second Vatican Ecumenical Council, Declaration *Gravissimum Educationis*, 1, 8: *AAS* 58 (1966), pp. 729–730; 734–736. *Gaudium et Spes*, 29, 60, 67: *AAS* 58 (1966), pp. 1048–1049, 1080–1081, 1088–1089.

[9] *Gaudium et Spes*, 51: *AAS* 58 (1966), pp. 1072.

[10] *Ibid.*; cf. also 49: *loc. cit.*, pp. 1069–1070.

[11] *Ibid.*, 49, 50: *loc. cit.*, pp. 1069–1072.

[12] The present Declaration does not go into further detail regarding the norms of sexual life within marriage; these norms have been clearly taught in the Encyclical Letters *Casti Connubii* and *Humanae Vitae*.

7. Today there are many who vindicate the right to sexual union before marriage, at least in those cases where a firm intention to marry and an affection which is already in some way conjugal in the psychology of the subjects require this completion, which they judge to be con-natural. This is especially the case when the celebration of the marriage is impeded by circumstances or when this intimate relationship seems necessary in order for love to be preserved.

This opinion is contrary to Christian doctrine, which states that every genital act must be within the framework of marriage. However firm the intention of those who practise such premature sexual relationships may be, the fact remains that these relations cannot ensure, in sincerity and fidelity, the interpersonal relationship between a man and a woman, nor especially can they protect this relationship from whims and caprices. Now it is a stable union that Jesus willed, and he restored its original requirement, beginning with the sexual difference. "Have you not read that the creator from the beginning made them male and female and that he said: This is why a man must leave father and mother, and cling to his wife, and the two become one body? They are no longer two, therefore, but one body. So then, what God has united, man must not divide".[13] Saint Paul will be even more explicit when he shows that if unmarried people or widows cannot live chastely they have no other alternative than the stable union of marriage: ". . . it is better to marry than to be aflame with passion".[14] Through marriage, in fact, the love of married people is taken up into that love which Christ irrevocably has for the Church,[15] while dissolute sexual union[16] defiles the temple of the Holy Spirit which the Christian has become. Sexual union therefore is only legitimate if a definitive community of life has been established between the man and the woman.

This is what the Church has always understood and taught,[17] and she finds a profound agreement with her doctrine in men's reflection and in the lessons of history. . . .

IX

Address of Pope John Paul II at the Opening of the Third General Conference of Latin American Bishops (CELAM) delivered at Puebla de los Angeles, Mexico, on 28 January 1979.

The translation is from *Puebla: Evangelization at Present and in the Future of Latin America* (The Third General Conference of Latin American Bishops). Official English edition published by the CIIR and St. Paul Publications, London, 1980. The whole of the address is given.

[13] Cf. Mt 19:4–6.

[14] 1 Cor 7:9.

[15] Cf. Eph 5:25–32.

[16] Sexual intercourse outside marriage is formally condemned: 1 Cor 5:1; 6:9; 7:2; 10:8; Eph. 5:5; 1 Tim 1:10; Heb 13:4; and with explicit reasons: 1 Cor 6:12–20.

[17] Cf. Innocent IV, Letter *Sub catholica professione*, 6 March 1254, DS 835; Pius II, *Propos. damn. in Ep. Cum sicut accepimus*, 14 November 1459, DS 1367; Decrees of the Holy Office, 24 September 1665, DS 2045; 2 March 1679, DS 2148. Pius XI, Encyclical Letter *Casti Connubii*, 31 December 1930: *AAS* 22 (1930), pp. 558–559.

Beloved brothers in the episcopate:

This hour that I have the happiness to experience with you is certainly a historic one for the Church in Latin America. World opinion is aware of this; so are the faithful members of your local Churches; and you yourselves, in particular, are aware of it because you will be the protagonists and responsible leaders of this hour.

It is also an hour of grace marked by the passing by of the Lord, by a very special presence and activity of God's spirit. For this reason we have confidently invoked this Spirit as we begin our labors. For this reason also I now want to make the following plea, speaking to you as a brother to his very beloved brothers: all the days of this conference and in every one of its proceedings, let yourselves be led by the Spirit; open up to the Spirit's inspiration and impulse; let it be that Spirit and none other that guides and strengthens you.

Under the guidance of this Spirit, for the third time in the last twenty-five years you are coming together as bishops. You have come here from every country of Latin America, as representatives of the whole Latin American episcopate, to study more deeply as a group the meaning of your mission in the face of the new exigencies of your peoples.

The conference now opening was convoked by our revered Paul VI, confirmed by my unforgettable predecessor, John Paul I, and reconfirmed by me as one of the first acts of my pontificate. It is linked with the already distant conference held in Rio de Janeiro, whose most noteworthy result was the foundation of CELAM. And it is even more closely linked with your second conference in Medellin, marking its tenth anniversary.

How far humanity has travelled in those ten years! How far the Church has travelled in those ten years in the company and service of humanity! This third conference cannot disregard that fact. So it will have to take Medellin's conclusions as its point of departure, with all the positive elements contained therein, but without disregarding the incorrect interpretations that have sometimes resulted and that call for calm discernment, opportune criticism, and clear-cut stances.

In your debates you will find guidance in the working draft, which was drawn up with great care so that it might serve as a constant point of reference.

But you will also have in your hands Paul VI's Apostolic Exhortation entitled *Evangelii Nuntiandi*. How pleased and delighted that great pontiff was to give his approval to the theme of your conference: "Evangelization in Latin America's Present and Future."

Those close to him during the months when this meeting was being prepared can tell you this. They can also tell you how grateful he was when he learned that the scenario for this whole conference would be that text, into which he poured his whole pastoral soul as his life drew to a close. And now that he "has closed his eyes on this world's scene" (Testament of Paul VI), his document becomes a spiritual testament. Your conference will have to scrutinize it lovingly and diligently, making it one of your obligatory touchstones and trying to discover how you can put it into practice. The whole Church owes you a debt of gratitude for what you are doing and for the example you are giving. Perhaps other local Churches will take up that example.

The pope chooses to be with you at the start of your labors, grateful for the gift of being allowed to be with you at yesterday's solemn Mass under the maternal gaze of the Virgin of Guadalupe, and also at this morning's Mass; because "every worthwhile gift, every genuine benefit comes from above, descending from the Father of the heavenly luminaries" (James 1:17). I would very much like to stay with you in prayer, reflection, and work. Be assured that I shall stay with you in spirit while "my anxiety for all the churches" (2 Cor. 11:28) calls me elsewhere. But before I continue my pastoral visit through Mexico and then return to Rome, I want at least to leave you with a few words as a pledge of my spiritual presence. They are uttered with all the concern of a pastor and all the affection of a father. They echo my main preoccupations concerning the theme you are dealing with and the life of the Church in these beloved countries.

I. TEACHERS OF THE FAITH

It is a great consolation for the universal Pastor to see that you come together here, not as a symposium of experts or a parliament of politicians or a congress of scientists or technologists (however important such meetings may be), but rather as a fraternal gathering of church pastors. As pastors, you keenly realize that your chief duty is to be teachers of the truth: not of a human, rational truth but of the truth that comes from God. That truth includes the principle of authentic human liberation: "You will know the truth, and the truth will set you free" (John 8:32). It is the one and only truth that offers a solid basis for an adequate "praxis".

I,1. Carefully watching over purity of doctrine, basic in building up the Christian community, is therefore the primary and irreplaceable duty of the pastor, of the teacher of faith—in conjunction with the proclamation of the Gospel. How often this was emphasized by St. Paul, who was convinced of the seriousness of carrying out this obligation (1 Tim. 1:3–7; 1:18–20; 1:11–16; 2 Tim. 1:4–14)! Besides oneness in charity, oneness in truth ever remains an urgent demand upon us. In his Apostolic Exhortation *Evangelii Nuntiandi*, our very beloved Paul VI put it this way: "The Gospel that has been entrusted to us is the word of truth. This truth sets us free, and it alone provides peace of heart. It is what people are looking for when we announce the Good News. The truth about God, the truth about human beings and their mysterious destiny, the truth about the world. . . . The preacher of the Gospel will be someone who, even at the cost of renunciation and sacrifice, is always seeking the truth to be transmitted to others. Such a person never betrays or misrepresents the truth out of a desire to please people, to astonish or shock people, to display originality, or to strike a pose. . . . We are pastors of the People of God; our pastoral service bids us to preserve, defend, and communicate the truth, whatever sacrifices may be entailed" (EN:78).

The Truth about Jesus Christ

I,2. From you, pastors, the faithful of your countries expect and demand first and foremost a careful and zealous transmission of the truth about Jesus Christ. This truth is at the core of evangelization and constitutes its essential content: "There is no authentic evangelization so long as one does not announce the name, the teaching, the life, the promises, the Kingdom, the mystery of Jesus of Nazareth, the Son of God" (EN:22).

The vigor of the faith of millions of people will depend on a lively knowledge of this truth. On such knowledge will also depend the strength of their adhesion to the Church and their active presence as Christians in the world. From it will flow options, values, attitudes, and behavior patterns that can give direction and definition to our Christian living, that can create new human beings and then a new humanity through the conversion of the individual and social conscience (EN:18).

It is from a solid Christology that light must be shed on so many of the doctrinal and pastoral themes and questions that you propose to examine in the coming days.

I,3. So we must profess Christ before history and the world, displaying the same deeply felt and deeply lived conviction that Peter did in his profession: "You are the Messiah, . . . the Son of the living God" (Matt. 16:16).

This is the Good News, unique in a real sense. The Church lives by it and for it, even as the Church draws from it all that it has to offer to all human beings, regardless of nation, culture, race, epoch, age, or condition. Hence "on the basis of that profession [Peter's], the history of sacred salvation and of the People of God should take on a new dimension" (John Paul II, Inaugural homily of his pontificate, 22 October 1978).

This is the one and only Gospel. And as the apostle wrote so pointedly, "Even if we, or an angel from heaven, should preach to you a gospel not in accord with the one we delivered to you, let a curse be upon him" (Gal. 1:8).

I,4. Now today we find in many places a phenomenon that is not new. We find "re-readings" of the Gospel that are the product of theoretical speculations rather than of authentic meditation on the word of God and a genuine evangelical commitment. They cause confusion insofar as they depart from the central criteria of the Church's faith, and people have the temerity to pass them on as catechesis to Christian communities.

In some cases people are silent about Christ's divinity, or else they indulge in types of interpretation that are at variance with the Church's faith. Christ is alleged to be only a "prophet," a proclaimer of God's Kingdom and love, but not the true Son of God. Hence he allegedly is not the center and object of the gospel message itself.

In other cases people purport to depict Jesus as a political activist, as a fighter against Roman domination and the authorities, and even as someone involved in the class struggle. This conception of Christ as a political figure, a revolutionary, as the subversive from Nazareth, does not tally with the Church's catechesis. Confusing the insidious pretext of Jesus' accusers with the attitude of Jesus himself—which was very different—people claim that the cause of his death was the result of a political conflict; they say nothing about the Lord's willing self-surrender or even his awareness of his redemptive mission. The Gospels show clearly that for Jesus anything that would alter his mission as the Servant of Yahweh was a temptation (Matt. 4:8; Luke 4:5). He does not accept the position of those who mixed the things of God with merely political attitudes (Matt. 22:21; Mark 12:17; John 18:36). He unequivocally rejects recourse to violence. He opens his message of conversion to all, and he does not exclude even the publicans. The perspective of his mission goes much deeper. It has to do with complete and integral salvation through a love that brings transformation, peace, pardon, and reconciliation. And there can be no doubt that all this imposes exacting demands on the attitude of any Christians who truly wish to serve the least of their brothers and sisters, the poor, the needy, the marginalized: i.e., all those whose lives reflect the suffering countenance of the Lord (LG:8).

I,5. Against such "re-readings," therefore, and against the perhaps brilliant but fragile and inconsistent hypotheses flowing from them, "evangelization in Latin America's present and future" cannot cease to affirm the Church's faith: Jesus Christ, the Word and Son of God, becomes human to draw close to human beings and to offer them, through the power of his mystery, the great gift of God that is salvation (EN: 19, 27).

This is the faith that has informed your history, that has shaped what is best in the values of your peoples, and that must continue to animate the dynamics of their future in the most energetic terms. This is the faith that reveals the vocation to concord and unity that must banish the danger of warfare from this continent of hope, a continent in which the Church has been such a potent force for integration. This, in short, is the faith that has found such lively and varied expression among the faithful of Latin America in their religiosity or popular piety.

Rooted in this faith in Christ and in the bosom of the Church, we are capable of serving human beings and our peoples, of penetrating their culture with the Gospel, of transforming hearts, and of humanizing systems and structures.

Any form of silence, disregard, mutilation, or inadequate emphasis on the whole of the mystery of Jesus Christ that diverges from the Church's faith cannot be the valid content of evangelization. "Today, under the pretext of a piety that is false, under the deceptive appearance of a preaching of the gospel message, some people are trying to deny the Lord Jesus," wrote a great bishop in the midst of the hard crises of the fourth century. And he added: "I speak the truth, so that the cause of the confusion that we are suffering may be known to all. I cannot keep silent" (St. Hilary of Poitiers, *Ad Auxentium*, 1–4). Nor can you, the bishops of today, keep silent when this confusion occurs.

This is what Pope Paul VI recommended in his opening address at the Medellin Conference: "Speak, speak, preach, write, take a position, as is said, united in plan and intention, for the defence and elucidation of the truths of the faith, on the relevance of the Gospel, on the questions that interest the life of the faithful and the defense of Christian conduct. . . ."

To fulfill my duty to evangelize all of humanity, I myself will never tire of repeating: "Do not be afraid. Open wide the doors for Christ. To his saving power open the boundaries of State, economic and political systems, the vast fields of culture, civilization, and development" (John Paul II, Inaugural homily of his pontificate, 22 October, 1978).

The Truth about the Church's Mission

I,6. As teachers of the truth, you are expected to proclaim unceasingly, but with special vigor at this moment, the truth about the mission of the Church, an object of the Creed we profess and a basic, indispensable area of our fidelity. The Lord instituted the Church "as a fellowship of life, charity, and truth" (LG:9); as the body, *pleroma*, and sacrament of Christ, in whom dwells the fullness of divinity (LG:7).

The Church is born of our response in faith to Christ. In fact it is by sincere acceptance of the Good News that we believers gather together "in Jesus' name to seek the Kingdom together, build it up, and live it" (EN:13). The Church is the gathering together of "all those who in faith look upon Jesus as the author of salvation and the source of unity and peace" (LG:9).

But on the other hand we are born of the Church. It communicates to us the riches of life and grace entrusted to it. The Church begets us by baptism, nourishes us with the sacraments and the Word of God, prepares us for our mission, and leads us to God's plan—the reason for our existence as Christians. We are the Church's children. With just pride we call the Church our Mother, repeating a title that has come down to us through the centuries from the earliest days (Henri de Lubac, *Méditation sur l'Église*, p. 211 ff.).

So we must invoke the Church, respect it, and serve it because "one cannot have God for one's Father if one does not have the Church for one's Mother" (St. Cyprian, *De catholicae ecclesiae unitate*, 6, 8). After all, "how can one possibly love Christ without loving the Church, since the most beautiful testimony to Christ is the following statement of St. Paul: 'He loved the Church and gave himself up for it' " (EN:16). Or, as St. Augustine puts it: "One possesses the Holy Spirit to the extent that one loves the Church of Christ" (*In Joannis evangelicum*, Tractatus, 32, 8).

Love for the Church must be composed of fidelity and trust. In the first address of my pontificate, I stressed my desire to be faithful to Vatican II, and my resolve to focus my greatest concern on the area of ecclesiology. I invited all to take up once again the Dogmatic Constitution *Lumen Gentium* and "to ponder with renewed earnestness the nature and mission of the Church, its way of existing and operating . . . not only to achieve that communion of life in Christ among all those who believe and hope in him, but also to help broaden and tighten the oneness of the whole family" (John Paul II, Message to the Church and the World, 17 October 1978).

Now, at this critical moment in the evangelization of Latin America, I repeat my invitation: "Adherence to this conciliar document, which reflects the light of tradition and contains the dogmatic formulas enunciated a century ago by Vatican I, will provide all of us, both pastors and faithful, a sure pathway and a constant incentive—to say it once again—to tread the byways of life and history" (ibid.).

I,7. Without a well-grounded ecclesiology, we have no guarantee of serious and vigorous evangelizing activity.

This is so, first of all, because evangelizing is the essential mission, the specific vocation, the innermost identity of the Church, which has been evangelized in turn (EN: 14–15; LG:5). Sent out by the Lord, the Church in turn sends out evangelizers to preach" not themselves or their personal ideas, but a Gospel that neither they nor the Church own as their own absolute property, to dispose of as they may see fit . . ." (EN:15). This is so, in the second place, because "for no one is evangelizing an isolated, individual act; rather, it is a profoundly ecclesial action, . . . an action of the Church" (EN:60). Far from being subject to the discretionary authority of individualistic criteria and perspectives, it stands "in communion with the Church and its pastors" (EN:60). Hence a correct vision of the Church is indispensable for a correct view of evangelization.

How could there be any authentic evangelization in the absence of prompt, sincere respect for the sacred magisterium, a respect based on the clear realization that in submitting to it, the People of God are not accepting the word of human beings but the authentic word of God? (1 Thess. 2:13; LG:12). "The 'objective' importance of this magisterium must be kept in mind and defended against the insidious attacks that now appear here and there against some of the solid truths of our Catholic faith" (John Paul II, Message to the Church and the World, 17 October 1978).

I am well aware of your attachment and availability to the See of Peter and of the love you have always shown it. In the Lord's name I express my heartfelt thanks for the deeply ecclesial outlook implied in that, and I wish you yourselves the consolation of counting on the loyal adherence of your faithful.

I,8. In the abundant documentation that went into the preparation of this conference, and particularly in the contributions of many Churches, one sometimes notices a certain uneasiness in interpreting the nature and mission of the Church. Allusion is made, for example, to the separation that some set up between the Church and the Kingdom of God. Emptied of its full content, the Kingdom of God is understood in a rather secularist sense: i.e., we do not arrive at the Kingdom through faith and membership in the Church but rather merely by structural change and sociopolitical involvement. Where there is a certain kind of commitment and praxis for justice, there the Kingdom is already present. This view forgets that "the Church . . . receives the mission to proclaim and to establish among all peoples the kingdom of Christ and of God. She becomes on earth the initial budding forth of that kingdom" (LG:5).

In one of his beautiful catechetical intructions, Pope John Paul I alludes to the virtue of hope. Then he says: "By contrast, it is a mistake to state that political, economic, and social liberation coincide with salvation in Jesus Christ; that the *regnum Dei* is identified with the *regnum hominis*" (John Paul I, Catechetical Lesson on the Theological Virtue of Hope, 20 September 1978).

In some instances an attitude of mistrust is fostered toward the "institutional" or "official" Church, which is described as alienating. Over against it is set another, people's Church, one which "is born of the people" and is fleshed out in the poor. These positions could contain varying and not always easily measurable degrees of familiar ideological forms of conditioning. The Council has called our attention to the exact nature and mission of the Church. It has reminded us of the contribution made to its deeper oneness and its ongoing construction by those whose task is to minister to the community and who must count on the collaboration of all the people of God. But let us face the fact: "If the Gospel proclaimed by us seems to be rent by doctrinal disputes, ideological polarizations, or mutual condemnations among Christians, if it is at the mercy of their differing views about Christ and the

Church, and even on their differing conceptions of human society and its institutions, . . . how can those to whom we address our preaching fail to be disturbed, disoriented, and even scandalized?" (EN:77).

The Truth about Human Beings

I,9. The truth we owe to human beings is, first and foremost, a truth about themselves. As witnesses to Jesus Christ, we are heralds, spokesmen, and servants of this truth. We cannot reduce it to the principles of some philosophical system, or to mere political activity. We cannot forget it or betray it.

Perhaps one of the most glaring weaknesses of present-day civilization lies in an inadequate view of the human being. Undoubtedly our age is the age that has written and spoken the most about the human being; it is the age of various humanisms, the age of anthropocentrism. But paradoxically it is also the age of people's deepest anxieties about their identity and destiny; it is the age when human beings have been debased to previously unsuspected levels, when human values have been trodden underfoot as never before.

How do we explain this paradox? We can say that it is the inexorable paradox of atheistic humanism. It is the drama of people severed from an essential dimension of their being—the Absolute—and thus confronted with the worst possible diminution of their being. *Gaudium et Spes* goes to the heart of the problem when it says: "Only in the mystery of the incarnate Word does the mystery of man take on light" (GS:22).

Thanks to the Gospel, the Church possesses the truth about the human being. It is found in an anthropology that the Church never ceases to explore more deeply and to share. The primordial assertion of this anthropology is that the human being is the image of God and cannot be reduced to a mere fragment of nature or to an anonymous element in the human city (GS: 12, 14). This is the sense intended by St. Irenaeus when he wrote: "The glory of the human being is God; but the receptacle of all God's activity, wisdom and power is the human being" (St. Irenaeus, *Adversus haereses*, III, 20, 2–3).

I made especially pointed reference to this irreplaceable foundation of the Christian conception of the human being in my Christmas Message: "Christmas is the feast of the human being. . . . Viewed in quantitative terms, the human being is an object of calculation. . . . But at the same time the human being is single, unique, and unrepeatable, someone thought of and chosen from eternity, someone called and identified by name" (John Paul II, Christmas Message, 25 December 1978).

Faced with many other forms of humanism, which frequently are locked into a strictly economic, biological, or psychological view of the human being, the Church has the right and the duty to proclaim the truth about the human being that it receives from its teacher, Jesus Christ. God grant that no external coercion will prevent the Church from doing so. But above all, God grant that the Church itself will not fail to do so out of fear or doubt, or because it has let itself be contaminated by other brands of humanism, or for lack of confidence in its original message.

So when a pastor of the Church clearly and unambiguously announces the truth about the human being, which was revealed by him who knew "what was in man's heart" (John 2:25), he should be encouraged by the certainty that he is rendering the best service to human beings.

This complete truth about human beings is the basis of the Church's social teaching, even as it is the basis of authentic liberation. In the light of this truth we see that human beings are not the pawns of economic or political processes, that instead these processes are geared toward human beings and subject to them.

I have no doubt that this truth about human beings, as taught by the Church, will emerge strengthened from this pastoral meeting.

II. SIGNS AND BUILDERS OF UNITY
YOUR PASTORAL SERVICE TO THE TRUTH
IS COMPLEMENTED BY A LIKE SERVICE TO UNITY

Unity Among the Bishops

II,1. First of all, it will be a unity among you yourselves, the bishops. As one bishop, St. Cyprian, put it in an era when communion among the bishops of his country was greatly threatened: "We must guard and maintain this unity . . . we bishops, in particular, who preside over the Church, so that we may bear witness to the fact that the episcopate is one and indivisible. Let no one mislead the faithful or alter the truth. The episcopate is one . . ." St. Cyprian, *De catholica ecclesiae unitate*, 6, 8).

This episcopal unity does not come from human calculation or maneuvering but from on high: from service to one single Lord, from the inspiration of one single Spirit, from love for one and the same unique Church. It is the unity resulting from the mission that Christ has entrusted to us. Here on the Latin American continent that mission has been going on for almost half a millenium. Today you are boldly carrying it on in an age of profound transformations, as we approach the close of the second millenium of redemption and ecclesial activity. It is unity centered around the Gospel of the body and blood of the Lamb, of Peter living in his successors; all of these are different but important signs of Jesus' presence in our midst.

What an obligation you have, dear brothers, to live this pastoral unity at the conference! The conference itself is a sign and fruit of the unity that already exists; but it is also a foretaste and anticipation of what should be an even more intimate and solid unity! So begin your labors in an atmosphere of fraternal unity. Even now let this unity be a component of evangelization.

Unity with Priests, Religious, and the Faithful

II,2. Unity among the bishops finds its extension in unity with priests, religious, and the faithful laity. Priests are the immediate collaborators of the bishops in their pastoral mission. This mission would be compromised if close unity did not exist between priests and their bishops.

Men and women religious are also particularly important subjects of that unity. I know well how important their contribution to evangelization has been, and continues to be, in Latin America. They arrived here in the dawning light of discovery, and they were here when almost all your countries were taking their first steps. They have labored here continually by the side of the diocesan clergy. In some countries more than half of your priests are religious; in others the vast majority are. This alone indicates how important it is here, even more than in other parts of the world, for religious to not only accept but loyally strive for an indissoluble unity of outlook and action with their bishops. To the bishops the Lord entrusted the mission of feeding the flock. To religious belongs the task of blazing the trail for evangelization. Bishops cannot and should not fail to have the collaboration of religious, whose charism makes them all the more available as agents in the service of the Gospel. And their collaboration must be not only active and responsible, but also docile and trusting. In this connection a heavy obligation weighs on everyone in the ecclesial community to avoid parallel magisteria, which are ecclesially unacceptable and pastorally sterile.

Lay people are also subjects of this unity, whether involved as individuals or joined in organs of the apostolate for the spread of God's Kingdom. It is they who must consecrate the world to Christ in the midst of their day-to-day tasks and in their varied family and professional functions, maintaining close union with, and obedience to, their legitimate pastors.

This precious gift of ecclesial unity must be safeguarded among all those who are part of the wayfaring People of God, in line with what *Lumen Gentium* said.

III. DEFENDERS AND PROMOTERS OF HUMAN DIGNITY

III,1. Those familiar with the history of the Church know that in every age there have been admirable bishops deeply involved in the valiant defense of the human dignity of those entrusted to them by the Lord. Their activity was always mandated by their episcopal mission, because they regarded human dignity as a gospel value that cannot be despised without greatly offending the Creator.

On the level of the individual, this dignity is crushed underfoot when due regard is not maintained for such values as freedom, the right to profess one's religion, physical and psychic integrity, the right to life's necessities, and the right to life itself. On the social and political level it is crushed when human beings cannot exercise their right to participate, when they are subjected to unjust and illegitimate forms of coercion, when they are subjected to physical and psychic torture, and so forth.

I am not unaware of the many problems in this area that are being faced in Latin America today. As bishops, you cannot fail to concern yourselves with them. I know that you propose to reflect seriously on the relationships and implications existing between evangelization and human promotion or liberation, focusing on the specific nature of the Church's presence in this broad and important area.

Here is where we come to the concrete, practical application of the themes we have touched upon in talking about the truth about Christ, about the Church, and about the human being.

III,2. If the Church gets involved in defending or promoting human dignity, it does so in accordance with its mission. For even though that mission is religious in character, and not social or political, it cannot help but consider human persons in terms of their whole being. In the parable of the Good Samaritan, the Lord outlined the model way of attending to all human needs (Luke 10:30 ff.); and he said that in the last analysis he will identify himself with the disinherited—the imprisoned, the hungry, and the abandoned—to whom we have offered a helping hand (Matt. 25:31 ff.). In these and other passages of the Gospel (Mark 6:35–44), the Church has learned that an indispensable part of its evangelizing mission is made up of works on behalf of justice and human promotion (see the Final Document of the Synod of Bishops, October 1971). It has learned that evangelization and human promotion are linked together by very strong ties of an anthropological, theological, and charitable nature (EN:31). Thus "evangelization would not be complete if it did not take into account the mutual interaction that takes hold in the course of time between the Gospel and the concrete personal and social life of the human being" (EN:29).

Let us also keep in mind that the Church's activity in such areas as human promotion, development, justice, and human rights is always intended to be in the service of the human being, the human being as seen by the Church in the Christian framework of the anthropology it adopts. The Church therefore does not need to have recourse to ideological systems in order to love, defend, and collaborate in the liberation of the human being. At the center of the message of which the Church is the trustee and herald, it finds inspiration for acting in favor of brotherhood, justice, and peace; and against all forms of domination, slavery, discrimination, violence, attacks on religious liberty, and aggression against human beings and whatever attacks life (GS: 26, 27, 29).

III,3. It is therefore not out of opportunism or a thirst for novelty that the Church, the "expert in humanity" (Paul VI, Address to the United Nations, 5 October 1965) defends human rights. It is prompted by an authentically evangelical commitment which, like that of Christ, is primarily a commitment to those most in need.

In fidelity to this commitment, the Church wishes to maintain its freedom with regard to the opposing systems, in order to opt solely for the human being. Whatever the miseries or sufferings that afflict human beings, it is not through violence, power-plays, or political systems but through the truth about human beings that they will find their way to a better future.

III,4. From this arises the Church's constant preoccupation with the delicate question of property ownership. One proof of this is to be found in the writings of the Church Fathers during the first thousand years of Christianity's existence (St. Ambrose, de Nabuthae, c. 12, n. 53). It is demonstrated by the vigorous and oft reiterated teaching of St. Thomas Aquinas. In our day the Church has appealed to the same principles in such far-reaching documents as the social encyclicals of the recent popes. Pope Paul VI spoke out on this matter with particular force and profundity in his encyclical Populorum Progressio (PP:23–24; MM: 104–15).

This voice of the Church, echoing the voice of the human conscience, did not cease to make itself heard down through the centuries, amid the most varied sociocultural systems and circumstances. It deserves and needs to be heard in our age as well, when the growing affluence of a few people parallels the growing poverty of the masses.

It is then that the Church's teaching, which says that there is a social mortgage on all private property, takes on an urgent character. Insofar as this teaching is concerned, the Church has a mission to fulfill. It must preach, educate persons and groups, shape public opinion, and give direction to national officials. In so doing, it will be working for the good of society. Eventually this Christian, evangelical principle will lead to a more just and equitable distribution of goods, not only within each nation but also in the wide world as a whole. And this will prevent the stronger countries from using their power to the detriment of the weaker ones.

Those in charge of the public life of States and nations will have to realize that internal and international peace will be assured only when a social and economic system based on justice takes effect.

Christ did not remain indifferent in the face of this vast and demanding imperative of social morality. Neither could the Church. In the spirit of the Church, which is the spirit of Christ, and supported by its ample, solid teaching, let us get back to work in this field.

Here I must once again emphasize that the Church's concern is for the whole human being.

Thus an indispensable condition for a just economic system is that it foster the growth and spread of public education and culture. The juster an economy is, the deeper will be its cultural awareness. This is very much in line with the view of Vatican II; i.e., that to achieve a life worthy of a human being, one cannot limit oneself to *having more*; one must strive to *be more* (GS:35).

So drink at these authentic fonts, Brothers. Speak in the idiom of Vatican II, John XXIII, and Paul VI. For that is the idiom that embodies the experience, the suffering, and the hope of contemporary humanity.

When Paul VI declared that development is the new name for peace (PP:76–79), he was thinking of all the ties of interdependence existing, not only within nations, but also between them on a worldwide scale. He took into consideration the mechanisms that are imbued with materialism rather than authentic humanism, and that therefore lead on the international level to the ever increasing wealth of the rich at the expense of the ever increasing poverty of the poor.

There is no economic norm that can change those mechanisms in and by itself. In international life, too, one must appeal to the principles of ethics, the exigencies of justice, and the primary commandment of love. Primacy must be given to that which is moral, to that which is spiitual, to that which flows from the full truth about the human being.

I wanted to voice these reflections to you, since I regard them as very important: but they should not distract you from the central theme of this conference. We will reach human beings, we will reach justice through evangelization.

III, 5. In the light of what has been said above, the Church is profoundly grieved to see "the sometimes massive increase in violations of human rights in many parts of the world. . . . Who can deny that today there are individual persons and civil authorities who are violating fundamental rights of the human person with impunity? I refer to such rights as the right to be born; the right to life; the right to responsible procreation; the right to work; the right to peace, freedom, and social justice; and the right to participate in making decisions that affect peoples and nations. And what are we to say when we run up against individuals and groups and the physical and psychological torturing of prisoners and political dissidents? The list grows when we add examples of abduction and of kidnapping for the sake of material gain, which represent such a traumatic attack on family life and the social fabric" (John Paul II, Message to the United Nations, 2 December 1978). We cry out once more: Respect the human being, who is the image of God! Evangelize so that this may become a reality, so that the Lord may transform hearts and humanize political and economic systems, with the responsible commitment of human beings as the starting point!

III,6. Pastoral commitments in this field must be nurtured with a correct Christian conception of liberation. "The Church . . . has the duty of proclaiming the liberation of millions of human beings,. . . the duty of helping to bring about this liberation" (EN:30). But it also has the corresponding duty of proclaiming liberation in its deeper, fuller sense, the sense proclaimed and realized by Jesus (EN:31 ff.). That fuller liberation is "liberation from everything that oppresses human beings, but especially liberation from sin and the evil one, in the joy of knowing God and being known by him" (EN:9). It is liberation made up of reconciliation and forgiveness. It is liberation rooted in the fact of being the children of God, whom we are now able to call Abba, Father! (Rom. 8:15). It is liberation that enables us to recognize all human beings as our brothers or sisters, as people whose hearts can be transformed by God's mercifulness. It is liberation that pushes us, with all the force of love, toward communion; and we find the fullness and culmination of that communion in the Lord. It is liberation as the successful conquest of the forms of bondage and idols fashioned by human beings, as the growth and flowering of the new human being.

It is a liberation that, in the framework of the Church's specific mission, "cannot be reduced simply to the restricted domain of economics, politics, society, or culture . . . can never be sacrificed to the requirements of some particular strategy, some short-term praxis or gain" (EN:33).

If we are to safeguard the originality of Christian liberation and the energies that it is capable of releasing, we must at all costs avoid reductionism and ambiguity. As Paul VI pointed out: "The Church would lose its innermost meaning. Its message of liberation would have nothing original, and it would lend itself to ready manipulation and expropriation by ideological systems and political parties" (EN:32). There are many signs that help us to distinguish when the liberation in question is Christian and when, on the other hand, it is based on ideologies that make it inconsistent with an evangelical view of humanity, of things, and of events (EN:35). These signs derive from the content that the evangelizers proclaim or from the concrete attitudes that they adopt. At the level of content one must consider how faithful they are to the Word of God, to the Church's living tradition, and to its magisterium. As for attitudes, one must consider what sense of communion they feel, with the bishops first of all, and then with the other sectors of God's People. Here one must also consider what contribution they make to the real building up of community; how they channel their love into caring for the poor, the sick, the dispossessed, the neglected, the oppressed; and how, discovering in these people the image of the poor and suffering Jesus, they strive to alleviate their needs and to serve Christ in them (LG:8). Let us make no mistake about it: as if by some evangelical instinct, the humble and simple faithful spontaneously sense when the Gospel is being served in the Church and when it is being eviscerated and asphyxiated by other interests.

As you see, the whole set of observations on the theme of liberation that were made by *Evangelii Nuntiandi* retain their full validity.

III,7. All that we have recalled above constitutes a rich and complex heritage, which *Evangelii Nuntiandi* calls the social doctrine, or social teaching, of the Church (EN:38). This teaching comes into being, in the light of God's Word and the authentic magisterium, from the presence of Christians in the midst of the world's changing situations and their contact with the resultant challenges. So this social doctrine entails not only principles for reflection but also norms for judgment and guidelines for action (OA:4).

To place responsible confidence in this social doctrine, even though some people try to sow doubts and lack of confidence in it; to study it seriously; to try to apply it; to teach it and to be loyal to it: in children of the Church, all this guarantees the authenticity of their involvement in delicate and demanding social tasks, and of their efforts on behalf of the liberation or advancement of their fellow human beings.   Permit me, then, to commend to your special pastoral attention the urgency of making your faithful aware of the Church's social doctrine.

Particular care must be devoted to forming a social conscience at all levels and in all sectors. When injustices increase and the gap between rich and poor widens distressingly, then the social doctrine of the Church—in a form that is creative and open to the broad areas of the Church's presence—should be a valuable tool for formation and action. This holds true for the laity in particular: "Secular duties and activities belong properly, although not exclusively, to laymen" (GS:43). It is necessary to avoid supplanting the laity, and to study seriously just when certain ways of substituting for them retain their *raison d'être*. Is it not the laity who are called, by virtue of their vocation in the Church, to make their contribution in the political and economic areas, and to be effectively present in the safeguarding and advancing of human rights?

IV. SOME PRIORITY TASKS

You are going to consider many pastoral topics of great importance. Time prevents me from mentioning them. I have referred to some, or will do so, in my meetings with priests, religious, seminarians, and lay people.

For various reasons, the topics I mention here are of great importance. You will not fail to consider them, among the many others your pastoral perspicacity will indicate to you.

(a) The family: Make every effort to ensure that there is pastoral care for the family. Attend to this area of such priority importance, certain that evangelization in the future depends largely on the "domestic Church." The family is the school of love, of knowledge of God, of respect for life and human dignity. This pastoral field is all the more important because the family is the object of so many threats.

Think of the campaigns advocating divorce, the use of contraceptives, and abortion, which destroy society.

(b) Priestly and religious vocations: Despite an encouraging revival of vocations, the lack of vocations is a grave and chronic problem in most of your countries. There is an immense disproportion between the growing number of inhabitants and the number of workers engaged in evangelization. This is of immeasurable importance to the Christian community. Every community must acquire its vocations, just as a proof of its vitality and maturity. An intensive pastoral effort must be reactivated. Starting off from the Christian vocation in general and an enthusiastic pastoral effort among young people, such an effort will give the Church the servants it needs. Lay vocations, indispensable as they are, cannot be a satisfactory compensation. What is more, one of the proofs of the laity's commitment is the abundance of vocations to the consecrated life.

(c) Young people: How much hope the Church places in them! How much energy needed by the Church circulates through young people in Latin America! How close we pastors must be to young people, so that Christ and the Church and brotherly love may penetrate deeply into their hearts!

V. CONCLUSION

Closing this message, I cannot fail to call down once again the protection of the Mother of God upon your persons and your work during these days. The fact that this meeting of ours is taking place in the spiritual presence of Our Lady of Guadalupe—who is venerated in Mexico and in all other countries as the mother of the Church in Latin America—is a cause of joy and a source of hope for me. May she, the "star of evangelization", be your guide in the reflections you make and the decisions you arrive at. From her divine Son may she obtain for you:

—the boldness of prophets and the evangelical prudence of pastors;
—the clearsightedness of teachers and the confident certainty of guides and directors;
—courage as witnesses, and the calmness, patience, and gentleness of fathers.

May the Lord bless your labors. You are accompanied by select representatives: priests, deacons, men and women religious, lay people, experts, and observers. Their collaboration will be very useful to you. The eyes of the whole Church are on you, in confidence and hope. You intend to measure up to their expectations, in full fidelity to Christ, the Church, and humanity. The future is in God's hands. But somehow God is also placing the future of a new evangelization impetus in your hands. "Go, therefore, and make disciples of all nations" (Matt. 28:19).

X

Extracts from the *Conclusions* of the Third General Conference of Latin American Bishops (CELAM), Puebla, January–February 1979, published in *Puebla: Evangelization at Present and in the Future of Latin America*, London, 1980.

4.2. The Social Teaching of the Church

The contribution of the Church to liberation and human promotion has gradually been taking shape in a series of doctrinal guidelines and criteria for action that we now are accustomed to call "the social teaching of the Church." These teachings have their source in Sacred Scripture, in the teaching of the Fathers and major theologians of the Church, and in the magisterium (particularly that of the most recent popes). As is evident from their origin, they contain permanently valid elements that are grounded in an anthropology that derives from the message of Christ and in the perennial values of Christian ethics. But they also contain changing elements that correspond to the particular conditions of each country and each epoch.[a]

Following Paul VI (OA:4), we can formulate the matter this way: attentive to the signs of the time, which are interpreted in the light of the Gospel and the Church's magisterium, the whole Christian community is called upon to assume responsibility for concrete options and their effective implementation in order to respond to the summons presented by changing circumstances. Thus these social teachings possess a dynamic character. In their elaboration and application lay people are not to be passive executors but rather active collaborators with their pastors, contributing their experience as Christians, and their professional, scientific competence (GS:42).

Clearly, then, it is the whole Christian community, in communion with its legitimate pastors and guided by them, that is the responsible subject of evangelization, liberation, and human promotion.

The primary object of this social teaching is the personal dignity of the human being, who is the image of God, and the protection of all inalienable human rights (PP:14–21). As the need has arisen, the Church has proceeded to spell out its teaching with regard to other areas of life: social life, economics, politics, and cultural life. But the aim of this doctrine of the Church, which offers its own specific vision of the human being and humanity (PP:13), is always the promotion and integral liberation of human beings in terms of both their earthly and their transcendent dimensions. It is a contribution to the construction of the ultimate and definitive Kingdom, although it does not equate earthly progress with Christ's Kingdom (GS:39).

If our social teachings are to be credible and to be accepted by all, they must effectively respond to the serious challenges and problems arising out of the reality of Latin America. Human beings who are diminished by all sorts of deficiencies and wants are calling for urgent efforts of promotion on our part, and this makes our works of social assistance necessary. Nor can we propose our teaching without being challenged by it in turn insofar as our personal and institutional behaviour is concerned. It requires us to display consistency, creativity, boldness, and total commitment. Our social conduct is an integral part of our following of Christ. Our reflection on the Church's projection into the world as a sacrament of communion and salvation is a part of our theological reflection. For "evange-

---

[a] See the explanatory note at the start of *Gaudium et Spes*, which explains why that conciliar Constitution is called "pastoral".

lization would not be complete if it did not take into account the reciprocal appeal that arises in the course of time between the Gospel on the one hand and the concrete personal and social life of human beings on the other" (EN:29).

Human promotion entails activities that help to arouse human awareness in every dimension and to make human beings themselves the active protagonists of their own human and Christian development. It educates people in living together, it gives impetus to organization, it fosters Christian sharing of goods, and it is an effective aid to communion and participation.

If the Christian community is to bear consistent witness in its efforts for liberation and human betterment, each country and local Church will organize its social pastoral effort around ongoing and adequate organisms. These organisms will sustain and stimulate commitment to the community, ensuring the needed coordination of activities through a continuing dialogue with all the members of the Church. Caritas and other organisms, which have been doing effective work for many years, can offer valuable help to this end.

If they are to be faithful and complete, theology, preaching, and catechesis must keep in mind the whole human being and all human beings. In timely and adequate terms they must offer people today "an especially vigorous message concerning liberation" (EN:29), framing it in terms of the "overall plan of salvation" (EN:38). So it seems that we must offer some clarifying remarks about the concept of liberation itself at this present moment in the life of our continent.

4.3 Discerning the Nature of Liberation in Christ

At the Medellín Conference we saw the elucidation of a dynamic process of integral liberation. Its positive echoes were taken up by *Evangelii Nuntiandi* and by John Paul II in his message to this conference. This proclamation imposes an urgent task on the Church, and it belongs to the very core of an evangelization that seeks the authentic realization of the human being.

But there are different conceptions and applications of liberation. Though they share common traits, they contain points of view that can hardly be brought together satisfactorily. The best thing to do, therefore, is to offer criteria that derive from the magisterium and that provide us with the necessary discernment regarding the original conception of Christian liberation.

There are two complementary and inseparable elements. The first is liberation from all the forms of bondage, from personal and social sin, and from everything that tears apart the human individual and society; all this finds its source to be in egotism, in the mystery of iniquity. The second element is liberation for progressive growth in being through communion with God and other human beings; this reaches its culmination in the perfect communion of heaven, where God is all in all and weeping forever ceases.

This liberation is gradually being realized in history, in our personal history and that of our peoples. It takes in all the different dimensions of life: the social, the political, the economic, the cultural, and all their interrelationships. Through all these dimensions must flow the transforming treasure of the Gospel. It has its own specific and distinctive contribution to make, which must be safeguarded. Otherwise we would be faced with the situation described by Paul VI in *Evangelii*

Nuntiandi: "The Church would lose its innermost significance. Its message of liberation would have no originality of its own. It would be prone to takeover or manipulation by ideological systems and political parties" (EN:32).

It should be made clear that this liberation is erected on the three great pillars that John Paul II offered us as defining guidelines: i.e., the truth about Jesus Christ, the truth about the Church, and the truth about human beings.

Thus we mutilate liberation in an unpardonable way if we do not achieve liberation from sin and all its seductions and idolatry, and if we do not help to make concrete the liberation that Christ won on the cross. We do the very same thing if we forget the crux of liberative evangelization, which is to transform human beings into active subjects of their own individual and communitarian development. And we also do the very same thing if we overlook dependence and the forms of bondage that violate basic rights that come from God, the Creator and Father, rather than being bestowed by governments or institutions, however powerful they may be.

The sort of liberation we are talking about knows how to use evangelical means, which have their own distinctive efficacy. It does not resort to violence of any sort, or to the dialectics of class struggle. Instead it relies on the vigorous energy and activity of Christians, who are moved by the Spirit to respond to the cries of countless millions of their brothers and sisters.

We pastors in Latin America have the most serious reasons for pressing for liberative evangelization. It is not just that we feel obliged to remind people of individual and social sinfulness. The further reason lies in the fact that since the Medellin Conference the situation has grown worse and more acute for the vast majority of our population.

We are pleased to note many examples of efforts to live out liberative evangelization in all its fullness. One of the chief tasks involved in continuing to encourage Christian liberation is the creative search for approaches free of ambiguity and reductionism (EN:32) and fully faithful to the Word of God. Given to us in the Church, that Word stirs us to offer joyful proclamation to the poor as one of the messianic signs of Christ's Kingdom.

John Paul II has made this point well: "There are many signs that help us to distinguish when the liberation in question is Christian and when, on the other hand, it is based on ideologies that make it inconsistent with an evangelical view of humanity, of things, and of events (EN:35). These signs derive from the content that the evangelizers proclaim or from the concrete attitudes that they adopt. At the level of content one must consider how faithful they are to the Word of God, to the Church's living tradition, and to its magisterium. As for attitudes, one must consider what sense of communion they feel, with the bishops first of all, and then with the other sectors of God's People. Here one must also consider what contribution they make to the real building up of the community; how they channel their love into caring for the poor, the sick, the dispossessed, the neglected, and the oppressed; and how, discovering in these people the image of the poor and suffering Jesus, they strive to alleviate their needs and to serve Christ in them (LG:8). Let us make no mistake about it: as if by some evangelical instinct, the humble and simple faithful spontaneously sense when the Gospel is being served in the Church and when it is being eviscerated and asphyxiated by other interests" (OAP:III,6).

Those who hold to the vision of humanity offered by Christianity also take on the commitment not to measure the sacrifice it costs to ensure that all will enjoy the status of authentic children of God and brothers and sisters in Jesus Christ. Thus liberative evangelization finds its full realization in the communion of all in Christ, as the Father of all people wills.

4.4 Liberative Evangelization for a Human Societal Life Worthy of the Children of God

Other than God, nothing is divine or worthy of worship. Human beings fall into slavery when they divinize or absolutize wealth, power, the State, sex, pleasure, or anything created by God—including their own being or human reason. God himself is the source of radical liberation from all forms of idolatry, because the adoration of what is not adorable and the absolutization of the relative leads to violation of the innermost reality of human persons: i.e., their relationship with God and their personal fulfillment. Here is the liberative word par excellence: "You shall do homage to the Lord your God; him alone shall you adore" (Matt. 4:10; cf. Deut. 5:6 ff.). The collapse of idols restores to human beings their essential realm of freedom. God, who is supremely free, wants to enter into dialogue with free beings who are capable of making their own choices and exercising their responsibilities on both the individual and communitarian levels. So we have a human history that, even though it possesses its own consistency and autonomy, is called upon to be consecrated to God by humanity. Authentic liberation frees us from oppression so that we may be able to say yes to a higher good.

Humanity and earthly goods. By virtue of their origin and nature, by the will of the Creator, worldly goods and riches are meant to serve the utility and progress of each and every human being and people. Thus each and every one enjoys a primary, fundamental, and absolutely inviolable right to share in the use of these goods, insofar as that is necessary for the worthy fulfillment of the human person. All other rights, including the right of property and free trade, are subordinate to that right. As John Paul II teaches: "There is a social mortgage on all private property" (OAP:III,4). To be compatible with primordial human rights, the right of ownership must be primarily a right of use and administration; and though this does not rule out ownership and control, it does not make these absolute or unlimited. Ownership should be a source of freedom for all, but never a source of domination or special privilege. We have a grave and pressing duty to restore this right to its original and primary aim (PP:23).

Liberation from the idol of wealth. Earthly goods become an idol and a serious obstacle to the Kingdom of God (Matt. 19:23–26) when human beings devote all their attention to possessing them or even coveting them. Then earthly goods turn into an absolute, and "you cannot give yourself to God and money" (Luke 16:13).

Turned into an absolute, wealth is an obstacle to authentic freedom. The cruel contrast between luxurious wealth and extreme poverty, which is so visible throughout our continent and which is further aggravated by the corruption that often invades public and professional life, shows the great extent to which our nations are dominated by the idol of wealth.

These forms of idolatry are concretized in two opposed forms that have a common root. One is liberal capitalism. The other, a reaction against liberal capitalism, is Marxist collectivism. Both are forms of what can be called "institutionalized injustice."

Finally, as already noted, we must take cognizance of the devastating effects of an uncontrolled process of industrialization and a process of urbanization that is taking on alarming proportions. The depletion of our natural resources and the pollution of the environment will become a critical problem. Once again we affirm that the consumptionist tendencies of the more developed nations must undergo a thorough revision. They must take into account the elementary needs of the poor peoples who constitute the majority of the world's population.

The new humanism proclaimed by the Church, which rejects all forms of idolatry, "will enable our contemporaries to enjoy the higher values of love and friendship, of prayer and contemplation, and thus find themselves. This is what will guarantee humanity's authentic develoment—its transition from less than human conditions to truly human ones" (PP:20). In this way economic planning will be put in the service of human beings rather than human beings being put in the service of economics (PP:34). The latter is what happens in the two forms of idolatry mentioned above (liberal capitalism and Marxist collectivism). The former is the only way to make sure that what human beings "have" does not suffocate what they "are" (GS:35).

Human beings and power. The various forms of power in society are a basic part of the order of creation. Hence in themselves they are essentially good, insofar as they render service to the human community.

Authority, which is necessary in every society, comes from God (Rom. 13:1; John 19:11). It is the faculty of giving commands in accordance with right reason. Hence its obligatory force derives from the moral order (PT:47), and it should develop out of that ground in order to oblige people in conscience: "Authority is before all else a moral force" (PT:48; GS:74).

Sin corrupts humanity's use of power, leading people to abuse the rights of others, sometimes in more or less absolute ways. The most notorious example of this is the exercise of political power. For this is an area that involves decisions governing the overall organization of the community's temporal welfare, and it readily lends itself to abuses. Indeed it may lead not only to abuses by those in power but also to the absolutizing of power itself (GS:73) with the backing of public force. Political power is divinized when in practice it is regarded as absolute. Hence the totalitarian use of power is a form of idolatry; and as such, the Church completely rejects it (GS:75). We grieve to note the presence of many authoritarian and even oppressive regimes on our continent. They constitute one of the most serious obstacles to the full development of the rights of persons, groups, and even nations.

Unfortunately, in many instances this reaches the point where the political and economic authorities of our nations are themselves made subject to even more powerful centers that are operative on an international scale. This goes far beyond the normal range of mutual relationships. And the situation is further aggravated by the fact that these centers of power are ubiquitous, covertly organized, and easily capable of evading the control of governments and even international organisms.

There is an urgent need to liberate our peoples from the idol of absolutized power so that they may live together in a society based on justice and freedom. As a youthful people with a wealth of culture and tradition, Latin Americans must carry out the mission assigned to them by history. But if they are to do this, they need a political order that will respect human dignity and ensure harmony and peace to the community, both in its internal relations and in its relations with other communities. Among all the aspirations of our peoples, we would like to stress the following:

—Equality for all citizens. All have the right and the duty to participate in the destiny of their society and to enjoy equality of opportunity, bearing their fair share of the burdens and obeying legitimately established laws.

—The exercise of their freedoms. These should be protected by basic institutions that will stand surety for the common good and respect the fundamental rights of persons and associations.

—Legitimate self-determination for our peoples. This will permit them to organize their lives in accordance with their own genius and history (GS:74) and to cooperate in a new international order.

—The urgent necessity of re-establishing justice. We are not talking only about theoretical justice recognized merely in the abstract. We are talking also about a justice that is effectively implemented in practice by institutions that are truly operative and adequate to the task.[b]

5. Evangelization, Ideologies, and Politics

5.1 Introduction

Recent years have seen a growing deterioration in the sociopolitical life of our countries.

They are experiencing the heavy burden of economic and institutional crises, and clear symptoms of corruption and violence.

The violence is generated and fostered by two factors: (1) what can be called institutionalized injustice in various social, political, and economic systems; and (2) ideologies that use violence as a means to win power.

The latter in turn causes the proliferation of governments based on force, which often derive their inspiration from the ideology of National Security.

As a mother and teacher whose expertise is humanity, the Church must examine the conditions, systems, ideologies, and political life of our continent—shedding light on them from the standpoint of the Gospel and its own social teaching. And this must be done even though it knows that people will try to use its message as their own tool.

[b] Hedonism, too, has been set up as an absolute on our continent. Liberation from the idol of pleasure-seeking and consumptionism is an imperative demand of Christian social teaching. We shall consider this issue more fully in part three, chap. 1, when we deal with educating people for love and family life (see nos. 582–89 below).

So the Church projects the light of its message on politics and ideologies, as one more form of service to its peoples and as a sure line of orientation for all those who must assume social responsibilities in one form or another.

5.2 Evangelization and Politics

The political dimension is a constitutive dimension of human beings and a relevant area of human societal life. It has an all-embracing aspect because its aim is the common welfare of society. But that does not mean that it exhausts the gamut of social relationships.

Far from despising political activity, the Christian faith values it and holds it in high esteem.

Speaking in general, and without distinguishing between the roles that may be proper to its various members, the Church feels it has a duty and a right to be present in this area of reality. For Christianity is supposed to evangelize the whole of human life, including the political dimension. So the Church criticizes those who would restrict the scope of faith to personal or family life; who would exclude the professional, economic, social and political orders as if sin, love, prayer, and pardon had no relevance in them.

The fact is that the need for the Church's presence in the political arena flows from the very core of the Christian faith. That is to say, it flows from the lordship of Christ over the whole of life. Christ sets the seal on the definitive brotherhood of humanity, wherein every human being is of equal worth: "All are one in Christ Jesus" (Gal. 3:28).

From the integral message of Christ there flows an original anthropology and theology that takes in "the concrete personal and social life of the human being" (EN:29). It is a liberating message because it saves us from the bondage of sin, which is the root and source of all oppression, injustice, and discrimination.

These are some of the reasons why the Church is present in the political arena to enlighten consciences and to proclaim a message that is capable of transforming society.

The Church recognizes the proper autonomy of the temporal order (GS:36). This holds true for governments, parties, labor unions, and other groups in the social and political arena. The purpose that the Lord assigned to his Church is a religious one; so when it does intervene in the sociopolitical arena, it is not prompted by any aim of a political, economic, or social nature. "But out of this religious mission itself come a function, a light, and an energy which can serve to structure and consolidate the human community according to the divine law" (GS:42).

Insofar as the political arena is concerned, the Church is particularly interested in distinguishing between the specific functions of the laity, religious, and those who minister to the unity of the Church—i.e., the bishop and his priests.

5.3 Notions of Politics and Political Involvement

We must distinguish between two notions of politics and political involvement. First, in the broad sense politics seeks the common good on both the national and international plane. Its task is to spell out the fundamental values of every community—internal concord and external security—reconciling equality with freedom, public authority with the legitimate autonomy and participation of individual persons and groups, and national sovereignty with international co-existence and solidarity. It also defines the ethics and means of social relationships. In this broad sense politics is of interest to the Church, and hence to its pastors, who are ministers of unity. It is a way of paying worship to the one and only God by simultaneously desacralizing and consecrating the world to him (LG:34).

So the Church helps to foster the values that should inspire politics. In every nation it interprets the aspirations of the people, especially the yearnings of those that society tends to marginalize. And it does this with its testimony, its teaching, and its varied forms of pastoral activity.

Second, the concrete performance of this fundamental political task is normally carried out by groups of citizens. They resolve to pursue and exercise political power in order to solve economic, political, and social problems in accordance with their own criteria or ideology. Here, then, we can talk about "party politics." Now even though the ideologies elaborated by such groups may be inspired by Christian doctrine, they can come to differing conclusions. No matter how deeply inspired in church teaching, no political party can claim the right to represent all the faithful because its concrete program can never have absolute value for all (cf. Pius XI, *Catholic Action and Politics*, 1937).

Party politics is properly the realm of lay people (GS:43). Their lay status entitles them to establish and organize political parties, using an ideology and strategy that is suited to achieving their legitimate aims.

In the social teaching of the Church lay people find the proper criteria deriving from the Christian view of the human being. For its part the hierarchy will demonstrate its solidarity by contributing to their adequate formation and their spiritual life, and also by nurturing their creativity so that they can explore options that are increasingly in line with the common good and the needs of the weakest.

Pastors, on the other hand, must be concerned with unity. So they will divest themselves of every partisan political ideology that might condition their criteria and attitudes. They then will be able to evangelize the political sphere as Christ did, relying on the Gospel without any infusion of partisanship or ideologization. Christ's Gospel would not have had such an impact on history if he had not proclaimed it as a religious message: "The Gospels show clearly that for Jesus anything that would alter his mission as the Servant of Yahweh was a temptation (Matt. 4:8, Luke 4:5). He does not accept the position of those who mixed the things of God with merely political attitudes (Matt. 22:21; Mark 12:17; John 18:36)" (OAP: 1,4).

Priests, also ministers of unity, and deacons must submit to the same sort of personal renunciation. If they are active in party politics, they will run the risk of absolutizing and radicalizing such activity; for their vocation is to be "men dedicated to the Absolute." As the Medellin Conference pointed out: "In the economic and social order . . . and especially in the political order, where a variety of concrete choices is offered, the priest, as priest, should not directly concern himself with decisions or leadership nor with the structuring of solutions" (Med-PR:19). And the 1971 Synod of Bishops stated: "Leadership or active militancy on behalf of any political party is to be excluded by every priest unless, in concrete and exceptional circumstances, this is truly required by the good of the community and receives the consent of the bishop after consultation with the priests' council and, if circumstances call for it, with the episcopal conference" ("The Ministerial Priesthood," Part Two, no. 2). Certainly the present thrust of the Church is not in that direction.

By virtue of the way in which they follow Christ, and in line with the distinctive function that is theirs within the Church's mission because of their specific charism, religious also cooperate in the evangelization of the political order. Living in a society that is far from fraternal, that is taken up with consumptionism, and that has as its ultimate goal the development of its material forces of production, religious will have to give testimony of real austerity in their lifestyle, of interhuman communion, and of an intense relationship with God. They, too, will have to resist the temptation to get involved in party politics, so that they do not create confusion between the values of the Gospel and some specific ideology.

Close reflection upon the recent words of the Holy Father addressed to bishops, priests, and religious will provide valuable guidance for their service in this area: "Souls that are living in habitual contact with God and that are operating in the warm light of his love know how to defend themselves easily against the temptations of partisanship and antithesis that threaten to create painful divisions. They know how to interpret their options for the poorest and for all the victims of human egotism in the proper light of the Gospel, without succumbing to forms of sociopolitical radicalism. In the long run such radicalism is untimely, counter-productive, and generative of new abuses. Such souls know how to draw near to the people and immerse themselves in their midst without calling into question their own religious identity or obscuring the 'specific originality' of their own vocation, which flows from following the poor, chaste, and obedient Christ. A measure of real adoration has more value and spiritual fruitfulness than the most intense activity, even apostolic activity. This is the most urgent kind of 'protest' that religious should exercise against a society where efficiency has been turned into an idol on whose altar even human dignity itself is sometimes sacrificed" (RMS).

Lay leaders of pastoral action should not use their authority in support of parties or ideologies.

5.4. Reflections on Political Violence

Faced with the deplorable reality of violence in Latin America, we wish to express our view clearly. Condemnation is always the proper judgment on physical and psychological torture, kidnapping, the persecution of political dissidents or suspect persons, and the exclusion of people from public life because of their ideas. If these crimes are committed by the authorities entrusted with the task of safeguarding the common good, then they defile those who practice them, notwithstanding any reasons offered.

The Church is just as decisive in rejecting terrorist and guerilla violence, which becomes cruel and uncontrollable when it is unleashed. Criminal acts can in no way be justified as the way to liberation. Violence inexorably engenders new forms of oppression and bondage, which usually prove to be more serious than the ones people are allegedly being liberated from. But most importantly violence is an attack on life, which depends on the Creator alone. And we must also stress that when an ideology appeals to violence, it thereby admits its own weakness and inadequacy.

Our responsibility as Christians is to use all possible means to promote the implementation of nonviolent tactics in the effort to re-establish justice in economic and sociopolitical relations. This is in accordance with the teaching of Vatican II, which applies to both national and international life: "We cannot fail to praise those who renounce the use of violence in the vindication of their rights and who resort to methods of defense which are otherwise available to weaker parties too, provided that this can be done without injury to the rights and duties of others or of the community" (GS:78).

"We are obliged to state and reaffirm that violence is neither Christian nor evangelical, and that brusque, violent structural changes will be false, ineffective in themselves, and certainly inconsistent with the dignity of the people" (Paul VI, Address in Bogotá, 23 August 1968). The fact is that "the Church realizes that even the best structures and the most idealized systems quickly become inhuman if human inclinations are not improved, if there is no conversion of heart and mind on the part of those who are living in those structures or controlling them" (EN:36).

5.5 Evangelization and Ideologies

Here we shall consider the exercise of discernment with regard to the ideologies existing in Latin America and the systems inspired by them.

Of the many different definitions of ideology that might be offered, we apply the term here to any conception that offers a view of the various aspects of life from the standpoint of a specific group in society. The ideology manifests the aspirations of this group, summons its members to a certain kind of solidarity and combative struggle, and grounds the legitimacy of these aspirations on specific values. Every ideology is partial because no one group can claim to identify its aspirations with those of society as a whole. Thus an ideology will be legitimate if the interests it upholds are legitimate and if it respects the basic rights of other groups in the nation. Viewed in this positive sense, ideologies seem to be necessary for social activity, insofar as they are mediating factors leading to action.

But in themselves ideologies have a tendency to absolutize the interests they uphold, the vision they propose, and the strategy they promote. In such a case they really become "lay religions." People take refuge in ideology as an ultimate explanation of everything: "In this way they fashion a new idol, as it were, whose absolute and coercive character is maintained, sometimes unwittingly" (OA:28). In that sense it is not surprising that ideologies try to use persons and institutions as their tools in order to achieve their aims more effectively. Herein lies the ambiguous and negative side of ideologies.

But ideologies should not be analyzed solely in terms of their conceptual content. In addition, they are dynamic, living phenomena of a sweeping and contagious nature. They are currents of yearning tending toward absolutization, and they are powerful in winning people over and whipping up redemptive fervor. This confers a special "mystique" on them, and it also enables them to make their way into different milieus in a way that is often irresistible. Their slogans, typical expressions, and criteria can easily make their way into the minds of people who are far from adhering voluntarily to their doctrinal principles. Thus many people live and struggle in practice within the atmosphere of specific ideologies, without ever having taken cognizance of that fact. This aspect calls for constant vigilance and re-examination. And it applies both to ideologies that legitimate the existing situation and to those that seek to change it.

To exercise the necessary discernment and critical judgment with regard to ideologies, Christians must rely on "a rich and complex heritage, which *Evangelii Nuntiandi* calls the social doctrine, or social teaching, of the Church" (OAP:III,7).

This social doctrine or teaching of the Church is an expression of its "distinctive contribution: a global perspective on the human being and on humanity" (PP:13). The Church accepts the challenge and contribution of ideologies in their positive aspects, and in turn challenges, criticizes, and relativizes them.

Neither the Gospel nor the Church's social teaching deriving from it are ideologies. On the contrary, they represent a powerful source for challenging the limitations and ambiguities of all ideologies. The ever fresh originality of the gospel message must be continually clarified and defended against all efforts to turn it into an ideology.

The unrestricted exaltation of the State and its many abuses must not, however, cause us to forget the necessity of the functions performed by the modern State. We are talking about a State that respects basic rights and freedoms; a State that is grounded on a broad base of popular participation involving many intermediary groups; a State that promotes autonomous development of an equitable and rapid sort, so that the life of the nation can withstand undue pressure and interference on both the domestic and international fronts; a State that is capable of adopting a position of active cooperation with the forces for integration into both the continental and the international community; and finally, a State that avoids the abuse of monolithic power concentrated in the hands of a few.

In Latin America we are obliged to analyze a variety of ideologies:

(a). First, there is a capitalist liberalism, the idolatrous worship of wealth in individualistic terms. We acknowledge that it has given much encouragement to the creative capabilities of human freedom, and that it has been a stimulus to progress. But on the other side of the coin it views "profit as the chief spur to economic progress, free competition as the supreme law of economics, and private ownership of the means of production as an absolute right, having no limits nor concomitant social obligations" (PP:26). The illegitimate privileges stemming from the absolute right of ownership give rise to scandalous contrasts, and to a situation of dependence and oppression on both the national and international levels. Now it is true that in some countries its original historical form of expression has been attenuated by necessary forms of social legislation and specific instances of government intervention. But in other countries capitalist liberalism persists in its original form, or has even retrogressed to more primitive forms with even less social sensitivity.

(b). Second, there is Marxist collectivism. With its materialist presuppositions, it too leads to the idolatrous worship of wealth—but in collectivist terms. It arose as a positive criticism of commodity fetishism and of the disregard for the human value of labor. But it did not manage to get to the root of that form of idolatry, which lies in the rejection of the only God worthy of adoration: the God of love and justice.

The driving force behind its dialectics is class struggle. Its objective is a classless society, which is to be achieved through a dictatorship of the proletariat; but in the last analysis this really sets up a dictatorship of the party. All the concrete historical experiments of Marxism have been carried out within the framework of totalitarian regimes that are closed to any possibility of criticism and correction. Some believe it is possible to separate various aspects of Marxism—its doctrine and its method of analysis in particular. But we would remind people of the teaching of the papal magisterium on this point: "It would be foolish and dangerous on that account to forget that they are closely linked to each other; to embrace certain elements of Marxist analysis without taking due account of their relation with its ideology; and to become involved in the class struggle and the Marxist interpretation of it without paying attention to the kind of violent and totalitarian society to which this activity leads" (OA:34).

We must also note the risk of ideologization run by theological reflection when it is based on a praxis that has recourse to Marxist analysis. The consequences are the total politicization of Christian existence, the disintegration of the language of faith into that of the social sciences, and the draining away of the transcendental dimension of Christian salvation.

Both of the aforementioned ideologies—capitalist liberalism and Marxism— find their inspiration in brands of humanism that are closed to any transcendent perspective. One does because of its practical atheism; the other does because of its systematic profession of a militant atheism.

(c). In recent years the so-called Doctrine of National Security has taken a firm hold on our continent. In reality it is more an ideology than a doctrine. It is bound up with a specific politico-economic model with elitist and verticalist features, which suppresses the broad-based participation of the people in political decisions. In some countries of Latin America this doctrine justifies itself as the defender of the Christian civilization of the West. It elaborates a repressive system, which is in line with its concept of "permanent war." And in some cases it expresses a clear intention to exercise active geopolitical leadership.

We fully realize that fraternal coexistence requires a security system to inculcate respect for a social order that will permit all to carry out their mission with regard to the common good. This means that security measures must be under the control of an independent authority that can pass judgment on violations of the law and guarantee corrective measures.

The Doctrine of National Security, understood as an absolute ideology, would not be compatible with the Christian vision of the human being as responsible for carrying out a temporal project, and to its vision of the State as the administrator of the common good. It puts the people under the tutelage of military and political elites, who exercise authority and power; and it leads to increased inequality in sharing the benefits of development.

We again insist on the view of the Medellin Conference: "The system of liberal capitalism and the temptation of the Marxist system would appear to exhaust the possibilities of transforming the economic structures of our continent. Both systems militate against the dignity of the human person. One takes for granted the primacy of capital, its power, and its discriminatory utilization in the function of profit-making. The other, although it ideologically supports a kind of human-ism, is more concerned with collective humanity, and in practice becomes a totalitarian concentration of state power. We must denounce the fact that Latin America finds itself caught between these two options and remains dependent on one or the other of the centers of power that control its economy" (Med-JU:10).

In the face of this situation, the Church chooses "to maintain its freedom with regard to the opposing systems, in order to opt solely for the human being. Whatever the miseries or sufferings that afflict human beings, it is not through violence, power-plays, or political systems but through the truth about human beings that they will find their way to a better future" (OAP:III,3). Grounded on this humanism, Christians will find encouragement to get beyond the hard and fast either-or and to help build a new civilization that is just, fraternal, and open to the transcendent. It will also bear witness that eschatalogical hopes give vitality and meaning to human hopes.

For this bold and creative activity Christians will fortify their identity in the original values of Christian anthropology. The Church "does not need to have recourse to ideological systems in order to love, defend, and collaborate in the liberation of the human being. At the center of the message of which the Church is the trustee and herald, it finds inspiration for acting in favor of brotherhood, justice, and peace; and against all forms of domination, slavery, discrimination, violence, attacks on religious liberty, and aggression against human beings and whatever attacks life" (OAP:III.2).

Finding inspiration in these tenets of an authentic Christian anthropology, Christians must commit themselves to the elaboration of historical projects that meet the needs of a given moment and a given culture.

Christians must devote special attention and discernment to their involvement in historical movements that have arisen from various ideologies but are distinct from them. The teaching of *Pacem in Terris* (PT:55 and 152), which is reiterated in *Octogesima Adveniens*, tells us that false philosophical theories cannot be equated with the historical movements that originated in them, insofar as these historical movements can be subject to further influences as they evolve. The involvement of Christians in these movements imposes certain obligations to persevere in fidelity, and these obligations will facilitate their evangelizing role. They include:

(a). Ecclesial discernment, in communion with their pastors, as described in *Octogesima Adveniens* (OA:4).

(b). The shoring up of their identity by nourishing it with the truths of faith, their elaboration in the social teaching or doctrine of the Church, and an enriching life of prayer and participation in the sacraments.

(c) Critical awareness of the difficulties, limitations, possibilities, and values of these convergences.

5.6. The Danger of the Church and its Ministers' Activity Being Used as a Tool

In propounding an absolutized view of the human being to which everything, including human thought, is subordinated, ideologies and parties try to use the Church or deprive it of its legitimate independence. This manipulation of the Church, always a risk in political life, may derive from Christians themselves, and even from priests and religious, when they proclaim a Gospel devoid of economic, social, cultural, and political implications. In practice this mutilation comes down to a kind of complicity with the established order, however unwitting.

Other groups are tempted in the opposite direction. They are tempted to consider a given political policy to be of primary urgency, a precondition for the Church's fulfillment of its mission. They are tempted to equate the Christian message with some ideology and subordinate the former to the latter, calling for a "re-reading" of the Gospel on the basis of a political option (OAP:1,4). But the fact is that we must try to read the political scene from the standpoint of the Gospel, not vice-versa.

Traditional integrism looks for the Kingdom to come principally through a stepping back in history and reconstructing a Christian culture of a medieval cast. This would be a new Christendom, in which there was an intimate alliance between civil authority and ecclesiastical authority.

The radical thrust of groups at the other extreme falls into the same trap. It looks for the Kingdom to come from a strategic alliance between the Church and Marxism, and it rules out all other alternatives. For these people it is not simply a matter of being Marxists, but of being Marxists in the name of the faith (see nos. 543–46 above).

5.7. Conclusion

The mission of the Church is immense and more necessary than ever before, when we consider the situation at hand: conflicts that threaten the human race and the Latin American continent; violations of justice and freedom; institutionalized injustice embodied in governments adhering to opposing ideologies; and terrorist violence. Fulfillment of its mission will require activity from the Church as a whole: pastors, consecrated ministers, religious, and lay people. All must carry out their own specific tasks. Joined with Christ in prayer and abnegation, they will commit themselves to work for a better society without employing hatred and violence; and they will see that decision through to the end, whatever the consequences. For the attainment of a society that is more just, more free, and more at peace is an ardent longing of the peoples of Latin America and an indispensable fruit of any liberative evangelization.

XI

Extracts from the *Address of Pope John Paul II to the XXXIV General Assembly of the United Nations Organization*, Tuesday, 2 October 1979.

The text is that given in *John Paul II, U.S.A.: The Message of Justice, Peace and Love*, Boston, 1979.

13. In a movement that one hopes will be progressive and continuous, the Universal Declaration of Human Rights and the other international and national juridical instruments are endeavoring to create general awareness of the dignity of the human being, and to define at least some of the inalienable rights of man. Permit me to enumerate some of the most important human rights that are universally recognized: the right to life, liberty and security of person; the right to food, clothing, housing, sufficient health care, rest and leisure; the right to freedom of expression, education and culture; the right to freedom of thought, conscience and religion, and the right to manifest one's religion either individually or in community, in public or in private; the right to choose a state of life, to found a family and to enjoy all conditions necessary for family life; the right to property and work, to adequate working conditions and a just wage; the right of assembly and association; the right to freedom of movement, to internal and external migration; the right to nationality and residence; the right to political participation and the right to participate in the free choice of the political system of the people to which one belongs. All these human rights taken together are in keeping with the substance of the dignity of the human being, understood in his entirety, not as reduced to one dimension only. These rights concern the satisfaction of man's essential needs, the exercise of his freedoms, and his relationships with others; but always and everywhere they concern man, they concern man's full human dimension.

14. Man lives at the same time both in the world of material values and in that of spiritual values. For the individual living and hoping man, his needs, freedoms and relationships with others never concern one sphere of values alone, but belong to both. Material and spiritual realities may be viewed separately in order to understand better that in the concrete human being they are inseparable, and to see that any threat to human rights, whether in the field of material realities or in that of spiritual realities, is equally dangerous for peace, since in every instance it concerns man in his entirety. Permit me, distinguished ladies and gentlemen, to recall a constant rule of the history of humanity, a rule that is implicitly contained in all that I have already stated with regard to integral development and human rights. The rule is based on the relationship between spiritual values and material or economic values. In this relationship, it is the spiritual values that are preeminent, both on account of the nature of these values and also for the reasons concerning the good of man. The preeminence of the values of the spirit defines the proper

sense of earthly material goods and the way to use them. This preeminence is therefore at the basis of a just peace. It is also a contributing factor to ensuring that material development, technical development and the development of civilization are at the service of what constitutes man. This means enabling man to have full access to truth, to moral development, and to the complete possibility of enjoying the goods of culture which he has inherited, and of increasing them by his own creativity. It is easy to see that material goods do not have unlimited capacity for satisfying the needs of man: they are not in themselves easily distributed and, in the relationship between those who possess and enjoy them and those who are without them, they give rise to tension, dissension and division that will often even turn into open conflict. Spiritual goods, on the other hand, are open to unlimited enjoyment by many at the same time, without diminution of the goods themselves. Indeed, the more people share in such goods, the more they are enjoyed and drawn upon, the more then do those goods show their indestructible and immortal worth. This truth is confirmed, for example, by the works of creativity—I mean by the works of thought, poetry, music, and the figurative arts, fruits of man's spirit.

15. A critical analysis of our modern civilization shows that in the last hundred years it has contributed as never before to the development of material goods, but that it has also given rise, both in theory and still more in practice, to a series of attitudes in which sensitivity to the spiritual dimension of human existence is diminished to a greater or less extent, as a result of certain premises which reduce the meaning of human life chiefly to the many different material and economic factors—I mean to the demands of production, the market, consumption, the accumulation of riches or of the growing bureaucracy with which an attempt is made to regulate these very processes. Is this not the result of having subordinated man to one single conception and sphere of values?

16. What is the link between these reflections and the cause of peace and war? Since, as I have already stated, material goods by their very nature provoke conditionings and divisions, the struggle to obtain these goods becomes inevitable in the history of humanity. If we cultivate this one-sided subordination of man to material goods alone, we shall be incapable of overcoming this state of need. We shall be able to attenuate it and avoid it in particular cases, but we shall not succeed in eliminating it systematically and radically, unless we emphasize more and pay greater honor, before everyone's eyes, in the sight of every society, to the second dimension of the goods of man: the dimension that does not divide people but puts them into communication with each other, associates them and unites them.

I consider that the famous opening words of the Charter of the United Nations, in which "the peoples of the United Nations, determined to save succeeding generations from the scourge of war" solemnly reaffirmed "faith in fundamental human rights, in the dignity and worth of the human person, in the equal rights of men and women and of nations large and small," are meant to stress this dimension.

Indeed, the fight against incipient wars cannot be carried out on a merely superficial level, by treating the symptoms. It must be done in a radical way, by attacking the causes. The reason I have called attention to the dimension constituted by spiritual realities is my concern for the cause of peace, peace which is built up by men and women uniting around what is most fully and profoundly human, around what raises them above the world about them and determines their indestructible grandeur—indestructible in spite of the death to which everyone on earth is subject. I would like to add that the Catholic Church and, I think I can say, the whole of Christianity sees in this very domain its own particular task. The Second Vatican Council helped to establish what the Christian faith has in common with the various non-Christian religions in this aspiration. The Church is therefore grateful to all who show respect and good will with regard to this mission of hers and do not impede it or make it difficult. An analysis of the history of mankind, especially at its present stage, shows how important is the duty of revealing more fully the range of the goods that are linked with the spiritual dimension of human existence. It shows how important this task is for building peace and how serious is any threat to human rights. Any violation of them, even in a "peace situation," is a form of warfare against humanity.

It seems that in the modern world there are two main threats. Both concern human rights in the field of international relations and human rights within the individual States or societies.

17. The first of these systematic threats against human rights is linked in an overall sense with the distribution of material goods. This distribution is frequently unjust both within individual societies and on the planet as a whole. Everyone knows that these goods are given to man not only as nature's bounty: they are enjoyed by him chiefly as the fruit of his many activities, ranging from the simplest manual and physical labor to the most complicated forms of industrial production, and to the highly qualified and specialized research and study. Various forms of *inequality in the possession of material goods*, and in the enjoyment of them, can often be explained by different historical and cultural causes and circumstances. But, while these circumstances can diminish the moral responsibility of people today, they do not prevent the situations of inequality from being marked by injustice and social injury.

People must become aware that economic tensions within countries and in the relationship between States and even between entire continents contain within themselves substantial elements that restrict or violate human rights. Such elements are the exploitation of labor and many other abuses that affect the dignity of the human person. It follows that the fundamental criterion for comparing social, economic and political systems is not, *and cannot be*, the criterion of hegemony and imperialism: it can be, and indeed it must be, *the humanistic criterion*, namely, the measure in which each system is really capable of reducing, restraining and eliminating as far as possible the various forms of exploitation of man and of ensuring for him, through work, not only the just distribution of the indispensable material goods, but also a participation, in keeping with his dignity, in the whole process of production and in the social life that grows up around that process. Let us not forget that, although man depends on the resources of the material world for his life, he cannot be their slave, but he must be their master.

The words of the book of Genesis, "Fill the earth and subdue it" (Gn. 1:28), are in a sense a primary and essential directive in the field of economy and of labor policy.

18. Humanity as a whole, and the individual nations, have certainly made remarkable progress in this field during the last hundred years. But it is a field in which there is never any lack of systematic threats and violations of human rights. Disturbing factors are frequently present in the form of the frightful disparities between excessively rich individuals and groups on the one hand, and on the other hand the majority made up of the poor or indeed of the destitute, who lack food and opportunities for work and education and are in great numbers condemned to hunger and disease. And concern is also caused at times by the radical separation of work from property, by man's indifference to the production enterprise to which he is linked only by a work obligation, without feeling that he is working for a good that will be his or for himself.

It is no secret that the abyss separating the minority of the excessively rich from the multitude of the destitute is a very grave symptom in the life of any society. This must also be said with even greater insistence with regard to the abyss separating countries and regions of the earth. Surely the only way to overcome this serious disparity between areas of satiety and areas of hunger and depression is through coordinated cooperation by all countries. This requires above all else a unity inspired by an authentic perspective of peace. Everything will depend on whether these differences and contrasts in the sphere of the "possession" of goods will be systematically reduced through truly effective means, on whether the belts of hunger, malnutrition, destitution, underdevelopment, disease and illiteracy will disappear from the economic map of the earth, and on whether peaceful cooperation will avoid imposing conditions of exploitation and economic or political dependence, which would only be a form of neocolonialism.

19. I would now like to draw attention to *a second systematic threat* to man in his inalienable rights in the modern world, a threat which constitutes no less a danger than the first to the cause of peace. I refer to the various forms of injustice in the field of the spirit.

Man can indeed be wounded in his inner relationship with truth, in his conscience, in his most personal belief, in his view of the world, in his religious faith, and in the sphere of what are known as civil liberties. Decisive for these last is equality of rights without discrimination on grounds of origin, race, sex, nationality, religion, political convictions and the like. Equality of rights means the exclusion of the various forms of privilege for some and discrimination against others, whether they are people born in the same country or people from different backgrounds of history, nationality, race and ideology. For centuries the thrust of civilization has been in one direction: that of giving the life of individual political societies a form in which there can be *fully safeguarded the objective rights of the spirit, of human conscience and of human creativity, including man's relationship with God*. Yet in spite of this we still see in this field recurring threats and violations, often with no possibility of appealing to a higher authority or of obtaining an effective remedy.

Besides the acceptance of legal formulas safeguarding the principle of the freedom of the human spirit, such as freedom of thought and expression, religious freedom, and freedom of conscience, structures of social life often exist in which the practical exercise of these freedoms condemns man, in fact if not formally, to become a second-class or third-class citizen, to see compromised his chances of social advancement, his professional career or his access to certain posts of responsibility, and to lose even the possibility of educating his children freely. It is a question of the highest importance that in internal social life, as well as in international life, *all human beings* in every nation and country *should be able to enjoy effectively their full rights under any political regime or system*.

Only the safeguarding of this real completeness of rights for every human being without discrimination can ensure peace at its very roots.

20. With regard to religious freedom, which I, as Pope, am bound to have particularly at heart, precisely with a view to safeguarding peace, I would like to repeat here, as a contribution to respect for man's spiritual dimension, some principles contained in the Second Vatican Council's Declaration *Dignitatis Humanae*: "In accordance with their dignity, all human beings, because they are persons, that is, beings endowed with reason and free will and therefore bearing personal responsibility, are both impelled by their nature and bound by a moral obligation to seek the truth, especially religious truth. They are also bound to adhere to the truth once they come to know it and to direct their whole lives in accordance with its demands" (*Dignitatis Humanae*, 2).

"The practice of religion of its very nature consists primarily of those voluntary and free internal acts by which a human being directly sets his course towards God. No merely human power can either command or prohibit acts of this kind. But man's social nature itself requires that he give external expression to his internal acts of religion, that he communicate with others in religious matters and that he profess his religion in community" (*Dignitatis Humanae*, 3).

These words touch the very substance of the question. They also show how even the confrontation between *the religious view of the world and the agnostic or even atheistic view*, which is one of the "signs of the times" of the present age, could preserve honest and respectful human dimensions without violating the essential rights of conscience of any man or woman living on earth.

Respect for the dignity of the human person would seem to demand that, when the exact tenor of the exercise of religious freedom is being discussed or determined with a view to national laws or international conventions, the institutions that are by their nature at the service of religion should also be brought in. If this participation is omitted, there is a danger of imposing, in so intimate a field of man's life, rules or restrictions that are opposed to his true religious needs.

21. The United Nations Organization has proclaimed *1979 the Year of the Child*. In the presence of the representatives of so many nations of the world gathered here, I wish to express the joy that we all find in children, the springtime of life, the anticipation of the future history of each of our present earthly homelands. No country on earth, no political system can think of its own future otherwise than through the image of these new generations that will receive from their parents the

manifold heritage of values, duties and aspirations of the nation to which they belong and of the whole human family. Concern for the child, even before birth, from the first moment of conception and then throughout the years of infancy and youth, is the primary and fundamental test of the relationship of one human being to another.

And so, what better wish can I express for every nation and the whole of mankind, and for all the children of the world than *a better future* in which respect for human rights will become a complete reality throughout the third millenium, which is drawing near.

22. But in this perspective we must ask ourselves whether there will continue to accumulate over the heads of this new generation of children the threat of common extermination for which the means are in the hands of the modern States, especially the major world powers. *Are the children to receive the arms race from us* as a necessary inheritance? How are we to explain this unbridled race?

The ancients said: *Si vis pacem, para bellum*. But can our age still really believe that the breathtaking spiral of armaments is at the service of world peace? In alleging the threat of a potential enemy, is it really not rather the intention to keep for oneself a means of threat, in order to get the upper hand with the aid of one's own arsenal of destruction? Here too it is the human dimension of peace that tends to vanish *in favor of ever new possible forms of imperialism*.

It must be our solemn wish here for our children, for the children of all the nations on earth, that this point will never be reached. And for that reason I do not cease to pray to God each day so that in His mercy He may save us from so terrible a day.

23. At the close of this address, I wish to express once more before all the high representatives of the States who are present a word of esteem and deep love for all the peoples, all the nations of the earth, for all human communities. Each one has its own history and culture. I hope that they will live and grow in the freedom and truth of their own history. For that is the measure of the common good of each one of them. I hope that each person will *live and grow strong with the moral force of the community* that forms its members as citizens. I hope that the State authorities, while respecting the just rights of each citizen, will enjoy the confidence of all for the common good. I hope that all the nations, even the smallest, even those that do not yet enjoy full sovereignty, and those that have been forcibly robbed of it, will meet in full equality with the others in the United Nations Organization. I hope that the United Nations will ever remain the supreme forum of peace and justice, the authentic seat of freedom of peoples and individuals in their longing for a better future.

XII

Extract from the concluding address of Pope John Paul II to the Synod of Bishops, 25th October 1980.

From *L' Osservatore Romano* [Eng. weekly edition] 3 November 1980.

7. . . . The Synod, commenting on the pastoral ministry of those who have entered a new union after divorce, deservedly praised those spouses, who, although faced with great difficulties, nevertheless witness in their own life to the indissolubility of marriage; in their life there is carried the beautiful message of faithfulness to the love which has in Christ its strength and foundation. Besides, the Fathers of the Synod, affirming once again the indissolubility of marriage and the practice of the Church of not admitting to Eucharistic Communion those who have divorced and have—against the rule—attempted another marriage, exhort Pastors and the whole Christian community to help these brothers and sisters, who are not to be considered separate from the Church, but by virtue of their Baptism can and ought to participate in the life of the Church by praying, by hearing the word, by assisting at the Eucharistic celebration of the community, and by fostering charity and justice. Although it must not be denied that such persons can be received to the Sacrament of Penance, eventually and finally to the Eucharistic Communion, when they open themselves with a sincere heart to live in a manner which is not opposed to the indissolubility of marriage: namely, when a man and woman in this situation, who cannot fulfill the obligation to separate, take on themselves the duty to live in complete continence, that is, by abstinence from acts in which only married couples can engage, and when they avoid giving scandal; nevertheless, the deprivation of sacramental reconciliation with God should not prevent them from persevering in prayer, penance, and works of charity that they might find the grace of conversion and salvation. It is fitting that the Church present herself as a merciful mother by pouring forth prayers for these persons and by strengthening them in faith and in hope.

8. The Fathers of the Synod are not removed in mind and heart from the grave difficulties which many spouses feel in their consciences about moral laws which pertain to transmitting and fostering human life. Knowing that the divine precept carries with it both a promise and a grace, they have openly confirmed the validity and clear truth of the prophetic message, profound in meaning and pertaining to today's conditions—contained in the Encyclical Letter *Humanae Vitae*. The same Synod urged theologians to join their talents with the work of the hierarchical magisterium so that the biblical foundation and so-called "personalistic" reasons for this doctrine might be continually illustrated, explaining it so that the whole doctrine of the Church might be clearer to all persons of good will, and so that understanding might grow deeper by the day.

Directing their attention to those things which concern pastoral ministry for the good of spouses and of families, the Fathers of the Synod rejected any type of division or "dichotomy" between a pedagogy, which takes into account a certain progression in accepting the plan of God, and doctrine, proposed by the Church, with all its consequences, in which the precept of living according to the same doctrine is contained; in which case there is not a question of a desire of keeping the law as merely an ideal to be achieved in the future, but rather of the mandate of Christ the Lord that difficulties constantly be overcome. Really, the "process of gradualness", as it is called, can't be applied unless someone accepts divine law with a sincere heart and seeks those goods which are protected and promoted by the same law. Thus, the so-called *lex gradualitatis* (law of gradation) or gradual progress can't be the same as *gradualitas legis* (the gradation of the law), as if there were in divine law various levels or forms of precept for various persons and conditions.

All spouses are called to sanctity in marriage according to God's plan; but this vocation takes an effect insofar as the human person responds to the precept of God, and with a serene mind has confidence in divine grace and one's own will. Therefore, for spouses, if both are not bound by the same religious insights, it will not be enough to accommodate oneself in a passive and easy manner to existing conditions, but they must try, so that, with patience and goodwill, they might find a common willingness to be faithful to the duties of Christian marriage.

9. The Fathers of the Synod have sought a deeper awareness and consciousness either of the riches, which are found in various forms in people's cultures, or of the benefits which every culture brings with it—through which the unfathomable mystery of Christ is more fully understood. Besides, they have acknowledged, even within the purposes of marriage and family, a vast field of theological and pastoral research, so that the accommodation of the message of the Gospel to the character of each people might be fostered, and so that it might be perceived in what ways, customs, outstanding characteristics, the sense of life and the genius peculiar to each human culture are compatible with those things from which divine revelation is known (cf. *Ad Gentes Divinitus*, 22).

This inquiry, if it is instituted according to the principle of communion with the universal Church and under the impetus of local Bishops, who are joined among themselves and with St. Peter's Chair, "which presides over the universal assembly of charity" (*Lumen Gentium*, 13), will bear fruit for families.

10. In words both opportune and persuasive, the Synod has spoken of woman with reverence and a grateful spirit, especially of her dignity and vocation as a daughter of God, as a wife, and as a mother. Therefore, it commendably asked that human society be so constituted that women not be forced to engage in external work proper to a certain role or, as they say, profession, but rather, so that the family might be able to live rightly, that the mother might devote herself fully to the family.

11. If we have remembered these outstanding questions and the responses which the Synod gave to them, we would not wish to think less of other matters which the Synod treated; for it has been shown how, in many interventions through these weeks, useful and fruitful, worthy questions were treated, which are explained either in the teaching or in the pastoral ministry of the Church, with great reverence and love, full of mercy toward men and women, our brothers and sisters, who come to the Church to receive words of faith and hope. Therefore, taking the example of the Synod, Pastors should address these problems as

they exist in married and family life with the same care and firm will so that we all might "bear the truth in charity".

We now wish to add something as the fruit of labours which we have undertaken for more than four weeks: namely that no one can exercise charity other than in truth. This principle can be applied to the life and work of Pastors who really intend to serve families.

Therefore, the fruit of this Synod Session has been found in precisely this: that the roles of the Christian family, of which charity itself is the heart, are not fulfilled except in full charity. Moreover, all on whom it has been proposed to confer responsibility for a role of this type in the Church—whether lay people or clerics or religious of either sex—can do it in no other way than in truth. For truth is that which frees; truth is that which provides order; truth shows the way to holiness and justice.

It has been shown to us how great is the love of Christ and how great is the charity conferred on all those who establish any family in the Church and in the world: not only to the men and women joined in marriage, but also to children and young people, to widows and orphans, and to each and every person who participates in family life in any way.

To all these, the Church wants to be and to remain a witness and, as it were, a portal to the fullness of that life of which St. Paul speaks at the beginning of the words just read: that we have become rich in all things in Christ Jesus, in every word and in all knowledge (cf. 1 Cor 1:5).

XIII

Extracts from the Encyclical *Laborem Exercens* of John Paul II issued on September 14th 1981 to commemorate the 90th anniversary of *Rerum Novarum*. The extracts are taken from the CTS London edition 1981.

There are five parts to the encyclical: *Part One* (paragraphs 1 to 3), "Introduction", *Part Two* (paragraphs 4 to 10), "Work and Man", *Part Three* (paragraphs 11 to 15), "Conflict Between Capital and Labour in the Present Phase of History", *Part Four* (paragraphs 16 to 23), "Rights of Workers", *Part Five* (paragraphs 24 to 27), "Elements for a Spirituality of Work".

The extracts are from *Part Two* (paragraphs 6, 7 and 8), *Part Three* (paragraphs 11, 12, 13, 14 and 15), and *Part Four* (paragraphs 17, 18, 19 and 20).

II
WORK AND MAN

6. WORK IN THE SUBJECTIVE SENSE: MAN AS THE SUBJECT OF WORK

. . . Man has to subdue the earth and dominate it, because as the "image of God" he is a person, that is to say, a subjective being capable of acting in a planned and rational way, capable of deciding about himself, and with a tendency to self-realization. . . .

. . . Understood as a process whereby man and the human race subdue the earth, work corresponds to this basic biblical concept only when throughout the process man manifests himself and confirms himself *as the one who "dominates"*. This dominion, in a certain sense, refers to the subjective dimension even more than to the objective one: this dimension conditions *the very ethical nature* of work. In fact there is no doubt that human work has an ethical value of its own, which clearly and directly remains linked to the fact that the one who carries it out is a person, a conscious and free subject, that is to say a subject that decides about himself. . . .

The ancient world introduced its own typical differentiation of people into classes according to the type of work done. Work which demanded from the worker the exercise of physical strength, the work of muscles and hands, was considered unworthy of free men, and was therefore given to slaves. By broadening certain aspects that already belonged to the Old Testament, Christianity brought about a fundamental change of ideas in this field, taking the whole content of the Gospel message as its point of departure, especially the fact that the one who, while *being God*, became like us in all things[11] devoted most of the years of his life on earth to *manual work* at the carpenter's bench. This circumstance constitutes in itself the most eloquent "Gospel of work", showing that the basis for determining the value of human work is not primarily the kind of work being done but the fact that the one who is doing it is a person. The sources of the dignity of work are to be sought primarily in the subjective dimension, not in the objective one. . . .

7. A THREAT TO THE RIGHT ORDER OF VALUES

. . . In the modern period, from the beginning of the industrial age, the Christian truth about work had to oppose the various trends of *materialistic and economistic* thought.

For certain supporters of such ideas, work was understood and treated as a sort of "merchandise" that the worker—especially the industrial worker—sells to the employer, who at the same time is the possessor of the capital, that is to say, of all the working tools and means that make production possible. This way of looking at work was widespread especially in the first half of the nineteenth century. . . . The interaction between the worker and the tools and means of production has given rise to the development of various forms of capitalism—parallel with various forms of collectivism—into which other socioeconomic elements have entered as a consequence of new concrete circumstances, of the activity of workers' associations and public authorities, and of the emergence of large transnational enterprises. Nevertheless, the *danger* of treating work as a special kind of "merchandise", or as an impersonal "force" needed for production (the expression "work-force" is in fact in common use) *always exists*, especially when the whole way of looking at the question of economics is marked by the premises of materialistic economism.

A systematic opportunity for thinking and evaluating in this way, and in a certain sense a stimulus for doing so, is provided by the quickening process of development of a onesidedly materialistic civilization, which gives prime importance to the objective dimension of work, while the subjective dimension—everything in direct or indirect relationship with the subject of work—remains on a secondary level. In all cases of this sort, in every social situation of this type, there is a confusion or even a reversal of the order laid down from the beginning by the words of the Book of Genesis: *man is treated as an instrument of production*,[12] whereas he—he alone, independently of the work he does—ought to be treated as the effective subject of work and its true maker and creator. . . .

. . . the analysis of human work in the light of the words concerning man's "dominion" over the earth goes to the very heart of the ethical and social question. This concept should also find *a central place* in the whole *sphere of social and economic policy*, both within individual countries and in the wider field of international and intercontinental relationships, particularly with reference to the tensions making themselves felt in the world not only between East and West but also between North and South. Both John XXIII in the Encyclical *Mater et Magistra* and Paul VI in the Encyclical *Populorum Progressio* gave special attention to these dimensions of the modern ethical and social question.

8. WORKER SOLIDARITY

. . . Following the lines laid down by the Encyclical *Rerum Novarum* and many later documents of the Church's Magisterium, it must be frankly recognized that the reaction against the system of injustice and harm that cried to heaven for vengeance[13] and that weighed heavily upon workers in that period of rapid industrialization was justified *from the point of view of social morality*. This state of affairs was favoured by the liberal socio-political system, which, in accordance with its "economistic" premises, strengthened and safeguarded economic initiative by the possessors of capital alone, but did not pay sufficient attention to the rights of the workers, on the grounds that human work is solely an instrument of production, and that capital is the basis, efficient factor and purpose of production.

From that time, worker solidarity, together with a clearer and more committed realization by others of workers' rights, has in many cases brought about profound changes. . . . But at the same time various ideological or power systems, and new relationships which have arisen at various levels of society, *have allowed flagrant injustices to persist or have created new ones*. On the world level, the development of civilization and of communications has made possible a more complete diagnosis of the living and working conditions of man globally, but it has also revealed other forms of injustice, much more extensive than those which in the last century stimulated unity between workers for particular solidarity in the working world. This is true in countries which have completed a certain process of industrial revolution. It is also true in countries where the main working milieu continues to be *agriculture* or other similar occupations. . . .

III

CONFLICT BETWEEN LABOUR AND CAPITAL IN THE PRESENT PHASE OF HISTORY

11. DIMENSIONS OF THE CONFLICT

Throughout this period, which is by no means yet over, the issue of work has of course been posed on the basis of the great *conflict* that in the age of, and together with, industrial development emerged *between "capital" and "labour"*, that is to say between the small but highly influential group of entrepreneurs, owners or holders of the means of production, and the broader multitude of people who lacked these means and who shared in the process of production solely by their labour. . . .

This conflict, interpreted by some as a socio-economic *class conflict*, found expression in the *ideological conflict* between liberalism, understood as the ideology of capitalism, and Marxism, understood as the ideology of scientific socialism and communism, which professes to act as the spokesman for the working class and the world-wide proletariat. Thus the real conflict between labour and capital was transformed into *a systematic class struggle*, conducted not only by ideological means but also and chiefly by political means. We are familiar with the history of this conflict and with the demands of both sides. The Marxist programme, based on the philosophy of Marx and Engels, sees in class struggle the only way to eliminate class injustices in society and to eliminate the classes themselves. Putting this programme into practice presupposes *the collectivization of the means of production* so that, through the transfer of these means from private hands to the collectivity, human labour will be preserved from exploitation.

This is the goal of the struggle carried on by political as well as ideological means. In accordance with the principle of "the dictatorship of the proletariat", the groups that as political parties follow the guidance of Marxist ideology aim by the use of various kinds of influence, including revolutionary pressure, to win *a monopoly of power in each society*, in order to introduce the collectivist system into it by eliminating private ownership of the means of production. According to the principal ideologists and leaders of this broad international movement, the purpose of this programme of action is to achieve the social revolution and to introduce socialism and, finally, the communist system throughout the world.

As we touch on this extremely important field of issues, which constitute not only a theory but a whole fabric of socioeconomic, political, and international life in our age, we cannot *go into the details*, nor is this necessary, for they are known both from the vast literature on the subject and by experience. Instead, we must leave the context of these issues and go back to the fundamental issue of human work, which is the main subject of the considerations in this document. It is clear, indeed, that this issue, which is of such importance for man—it constitutes one of the fundamental dimensions of his earthly existence and of his vocation—can also be explained only by taking into account the full context of the contemporary situation.

12. THE PRIORITY OF LABOUR

. . . Further consideration of this question should confirm our conviction of *the priority of human labour over* what in the course of time we have grown accustomed to calling *capital*. Since the concept of capital includes not only the natural resources placed at man's disposal but also the whole collection of means by which man appropriates natural resources and transforms them in accordance with his needs (and thus in a sense humanizes them), it must immediately be noted that *all these means are the result of the historical heritage of human labor*. All the means of production, from the most primitive to the ultra-modern ones—it is man that has gradually developed them: man's experience and intellect. In this way there have appeared not only the simplest instruments for cultivating the earth but also, through adequate progress in science and technology, the more modern and complex ones: machines, factories, laboratories, and computers. Thus *everything that is at the service of work*, everything that in the present state of technology constitutes its ever more highly perfected "instrument", *is the result of work*. . . .

13. ECONOMISM AND MATERIALISM

. . . Opposition between labour and capital does not spring from the structure of the production process or from the structure of the economic process. . . . Working at any workbench, whether a relatively primitive or an ultra-modern one, a man can easily see that *through his work he enters into two inheritances*: the inheritance of what is given to the whole of humanity in the resources of nature, and the inheritance of what others have already developed on the basis of those resources, primarily by developing technology, that is to say, by producing a whole collection of increasingly perfect instruments for work. In working, man also "enters into the labour of others".[21] Guided both by our intelligence and by the faith that draws light from the word of God, we have no difficulty in accepting this image of the sphere and process of man's labour. It is *a consistent image, one that is humanistic as well as theological*. . . .

This *consistent image*, in which the principle of the primacy of person over things is strictly preserved, *was broken up in human thought*, sometimes after a long period of incubation in practical living. The break occurred in such a way that labour was separated from capital and set in opposition to it, and capital was set in opposition to labour, as though they were two impersonal forces, two production factors juxtaposed in the same "economistic" perspective. This way of stating the issue contained a fundamental error, what we can call *the error of economism*, that of considering human labour solely according to its economic purpose. This fundamental error of thought can and must be called *an error of materialism*, in that economism directly or indirectly includes a conviction of the primacy and superiority of the material, and directly or indirectly places the spiritual and the personal (man's activity, moral values and such matters) in a position of subordination to material reality. . . .

14. WORK AND OWNERSHIP

The historical process briefly presented here has certainly gone beyond its initial phase, but it is still taking place and indeed is spreading in the relationships between nations and continents. It needs to be specified further from another point of view. It is obvious that, when we speak of opposition between labour and capital, we are not dealing only with abstract concepts or "impersonal forces" operating in economic production. Behind both concepts are people, living, actual people: on the one side are those who do the work without being the owners of the means of production, and on the other side those who act as entrepreneurs and who own these means or represent the owners. Thus *the issue of ownership or property* enters from the beginning into the whole of this difficult historical process. The Encyclical *Rerum Novarum*, which has the social question as its theme, stresses this issue also, recalling and confirming the Church's teaching on ownership, on the right to private property even when it is a question of the means of production. The Encyclical *Mater et Magistra* did the same.

The above principle, as it was then stated and as it is still taught by the Church, *diverges* radically from the programme of *collectivism* as proclaimed by Marxism and put into practice in various countries in the decades following the time of Leo XIII's Encyclical. At the same time it differs from the programme of *capitalism* practised by liberalism and by the political systems inspired by it. In the latter case, the difference consists in the way the right to ownership or property is understood. Christian tradition has never upheld this right as absolute and untouchable. On the contrary, it has always understood this right within the broader context of the right common to all to use the goods of the whole of creation: *the right to private property is subordinated to the right to common use*, to the fact that goods are meant for everyone. . . .

In light of the above, the many proposals put forward by experts in Catholic social teaching and by the highest Magisterium of the Church take on special significance:[23] *proposals* for *joint ownership of the means of work*, sharing by the workers in the management and/or profits of businesses, so-called shareholding by labour, etc. Whether these various proposals can or cannot be applied concretely, it is clear that recognition of the proper position of labour and the worker in the production process demands various adaptations in the sphere of the right to ownership of the means of production. . . .

Therefore, while the position of "rigid" capitalism must undergo continual revision, in order to be reformed from the point of view of human rights, both human rights in the widest sense and those linked with man's work, it must be stated that, from the same point of view, these many deeply desired reforms cannot be achieved by an *a priori elimination of private ownership of the means of production*. For it must be noted that merely taking these means of production (capital) out of the hands of their private owners is not enough to ensure their satisfactory socialization. They cease to be the property of a certain social group, namely the private owners, and become the property of organized society, coming under the administration and direct control of another group of people, namely those who, though not owning them, from the fact of exercising power in society *manage* them on the level of the whole national or the local economy.

This group in authority may carry out its task satisfactorily from the point of view of the priority of labour; but it may also carry it out badly by claiming for itself *a monopoly of the administration and disposal* of the means of production and not refraining even from offending basic human rights. Thus, merely converting the means of production into State property in the collectivist system is by no means equivalent to "socializing" that property. We can speak of socializing only when the subject character of society is ensured, that is to say, when on the basis of his work each person is fully entitled to consider himself a part-owner of the great workbench at which he is working with every one else. A way towards that goal could be found by associating labour with the ownership of capital, as far as possible, and by producing a wide range of intermediate bodies with economic, social and cultural purposes; they would be bodies enjoying real autonomy with regard to the public powers, pursuing their specific aims in honest collaboration with each other and in subordination to the demands of the common good, and they would be living communities both in form and in substance, in the sense that the members of each body would be looked upon and treated as persons and encouraged to take an active part in the life of the body.[24]

15. THE "PERSONALIST" ARGUMENT

Thus, *the principle of the priority of labour* over capital is a postulate of the order of social morality. It has key importance both in the system built on the principle of private ownership of the means of production and also in the system in which private ownership of these means has been limited even in a radical way. Labour is in a sense inseparable from capital; in no way does it accept the antinomy, that is to say, the separation and opposition with regard to the means of production that has weighed upon human life in recent centuries as a result of merely economic premises. When man works, using all the means of production, he also wishes the fruit of this work to be used by himself and others, and he wishes to be able to take part in the very work process as a sharer in responsibility and creativity at the workbench to which he applies himself.

From this spring certain specific rights of workers, corresponding to the obligation of work. They will be discussed later. But here it must be emphasized, in general terms, that the person who works desires *not only* due *remuneration* for his work; he also wishes that, within the production process, provision be made for him to be able to *know* that in his work, even on something that is owned in common, he is working *"for himself"*. This awareness is extinguished within him in a system of excessive bureaucratic centralization, which makes the worker feel that he is just a cog in a huge machine moved from above, that he is for more reasons than one a mere production instrument rather than a true subject of work with an initiative of his own. The Church's teaching has always expressed the strong and deep conviction that man's work concerns not only the economy but also, and especially, personal values. The economic system itself and the production process benefit precisely when these personal values are fully respected. In the mind of Saint Thomas Aquinas,[25] this is the principal reason in favour of private ownership of the means of production. While we accept that for certain well founded reasons exceptions can be made to the principle of private ownership—in our own time we even see that the system of "socialized ownership" has been introduced—nevertheless the personalist *argument still holds good* both on the level of principles and *on the practical level*. If it is to be rational and fruitful, any socialization of the means of production must take this argument into consideration. Every effort must be made to ensure that in this kind of system also the human person can preserve his awareness of working "for himself". If this is not done, incalculable damage is inevitably done throughout the economic process, not only economic damage but first and foremost damage to man.

IV

RIGHTS OF WORKERS

17. DIRECT AND INDIRECT EMPLOYER

The concept of indirect employer includes both persons and institutions of various kinds, and also collective labour contracts and the *principles* of conduct which are laid down by these persons and institutions and which determine the whole socioeconomic *system* or are its result. The concept of "indirect employer" thus refers to many different elements. . . .

The concept of indirect employer is applicable to every society, and in the first place to the State. For it is the State that must conduct a just labour policy. However, it is common knowledge that in the present system of economic relations in the world there are numerous *links between* individual *States*, links that find expression, for instance, in the import and export process, that is to say, in the mutual exchange of economic goods, whether raw materials, semi-manufactured goods, or finished industrial products. These links also create mutual *dependence*, and as a result it would be difficult to speak, in the case of any State, even the economically most powerful, of complete self-sufficiency or autarky. . . .

It is easy to see that this framework of forms of dependence linked with the concept of the indirect employer is enormously extensive and complicated. It is determined, in a sense, by *all* the elements that are decisive for economic life *within a given society and state*, but also by much wider links and forms of dependence. The attainment of the worker's rights cannot however be doomed to be merely a result of economic systems which on a larger or smaller scale are guided chiefly by the criterion of maximum profit. On the contrary, it is respect for the objective rights of the worker—every kind of worker: manual or intellectual, industrial or agricultural, etc.—that must constitute the *adequate and fundamental criterion* for shaping the whole economy, both on the level of the individual society and State and within the whole of the world economic policy and of the systems of international relationships that derive from it. . . .

18. THE EMPLOYMENT ISSUE

. . . In order to meet the danger of unemployment and to ensure employment for all, the agents defined here as "indirect employer" must make provison for *overall planning* with regard to the different kinds of work by which not only the economic life but also the cultural life of a given society is shaped; they must also give attention to organizing that work in a correct and rational way. In the final analysis this overall concern weighs on the shoulders of the State, but it cannot mean onesided centralization by the public authorities. Instead, what is in question is a just and rational *coordination*, within the framework of which the *initiative* of individuals, free groups and local work centres and complexes must be *safeguarded*. . . .

19. WAGES AND OTHER SOCIAL BENEFITS

. . . It should also be noted that the justice of a socioeconomic system, and in each case, its just functioning, deserve in the final analysis to be evaluated by the way in which man's work is properly remunerated in the system. Here we return once more to the first principle of the whole ethical and social order, namely, *the principle of the common use of goods*. In every system, regardless of the fundamental relationships within it between capital and labour, wages, that is to say *remuneration for work*, are still a *practical means* whereby the vast majority of people can have access to those goods which are intended for common use: both the goods of nature and manufactured goods. Both kinds of goods become accessible to the worker through the wage which he receives as remuneration for his work. Hence, in every case, a just wage is the concrete means of *verifying the justice* of the whole socioeconomic system and, in any case, of checking that it is functioning justly. It is not the only means of checking, but it is a particularly important one and, in a sense, the key means.

This means of checking concerns above all the family. Just remuneration for the work of an adult who is responsible for a family means remuneration which will suffice for establishing and properly maintaining a family and for providing security for its future. Such remuneration can be given either through what is called a *family wage*—that is, a single salary given to the head of the family for his work, sufficient for the needs of the family without the other spouse having to take up gainful employment outside the home—or through *other social measures* such as family allowances or grants to mothers devoting themselves exclusively to their families. . . .

20. IMPORTANCE OF UNIONS

All these rights, together with the need for the workers themselves to secure them, give rise to yet another right: *the right of association*, that is to form associations for the purpose of defending the vital interests of those employed in the various professions. These association are called *labour* or *trade unions*. The vital interests of the workers are to a certain extent common for all of them; at the same time however each type of work, each profession, has its own specific character which should find a particular reflection in these organizations.

. . . The experience of history teaches that organizations of this type are an indispensable *element of social life*, especially in modern industrialized societies. Obviously, this does not mean that only industrial workers can set up associations of this type. . . .

Catholic social teaching does not hold that unions are no more than a reflection of the "class" structure of society and that they are a mouthpiece for a class struggle which inevitably governs social life. They are indeed *a mouthpiece for the struggle for social justice*, for the just rights of working people in accordance with their individual professions. However, this struggle should be seen as a normal endeavor "for" the just good: in the present case, for the good which corresponds to the needs and merits of working people associated by profession; but it *is not a struggle "against" others*. Even if in controversial questions the struggle takes on a character of opposition toward others, this is because it aims at the good of social justice, not for the sake of "struggle" or in order to eliminate the opponent. It is characteristic of work that it first and foremost unites people. In this consists its social power: the power to build a community. In the final analysis, both those who work and those who manage the means of production or who own them must in some way be united in this community. *In the light of this fundamental structure* of all work—in the light of the fact that, in the final analysis, labour and capital are indispensable components of the process of production in any social system—it is clear that, even if it is because of their work needs that people unite to secure their rights, their union remains a constructive factor of *social order* and *solidarity*, and it is impossible to ignore it.

Just efforts to secure the rights of workers who are united by the same profession should always take into account the limitations imposed by the general economic situation of the country. Union demands cannot be turned into a kind of *group or class "egoism"*, although they can and should also aim at correcting —with a view to the common good of the whole of society—everything defective in the system of ownership of the means of production or in the way these are managed. Social and socioeconomic life is certainly like a system of "connected vessels", and every social activity directed towards safeguarding the rights of particular groups should adapt itself to this system.

In this sense, union activity undoubtedly enters the field of *politics*, understood as *prudent concern for the common good*. However, the role of unions is not to "play politics" in the sense that the expression is commonly understood today. Unions do not have the character of political parties struggling for power; they should not be subjected to the decision of political parties or have too close links with them. In fact, in such a situation they easily lose contact with their specific role, which is to secure the just rights of workers within the framework of the common good of the whole of society; instead they become an *instrument used for other purposes*. . . .

One method used by unions in pursuing the just rights of their members, is *the strike* or work stoppage, as a kind of ultimatum to the competent bodies, especially the employers. This method is recognized by Catholic social teaching as legitimate in the proper conditions and within just limits. In this connection workers should be assured the *right to strike*, without being subjected to personal penal sanctions for taking part in a strike. While admitting that it is a legitimate means, we must at the same time emphasize that a strike remains, in a sense, an extreme means. *It must not be abused;* it must not be abused especially for "political" purposes. Furthermore it must never be forgotten that, when essential community services are in question, they must in every case be ensured, if necessary by means of appropriate legislation. Abuse of the strike weapon can lead to the paralysis of the whole of socioeconomic life, and this is contrary to the requirements of the common good of society, which also corresponds to the properly understood nature of work itself.

[11] Cf. Heb 2:17; Phil 2:5–8.
[12] Cf. Pope Pius XI, Encycl. *Quadragesimo Anno: AAS* 23 (1931), p.221.
[13] Dt 24:15; James 5:4; and also Gen 4:10.
[21] Cf. Jn 4:38.
[23] Cf. Pope Pius XI, Encycl. *Quadragesimo Anno: AAS* 23 (1931), p.199; Second Vatican Ecumenical Council, Pastoral Constitution on the Church in the Modern World *Gaudium et Spes, AAS* 58 (1966), pp. 1089–90.
[24] Cf. Pope John XXIII, Encycl. *Mater et Magistra: AAS* 53 (1961), p. 419.
[25] Cf. *Summa Theologica*, II–II, q. 65, art. 2.

READING SUGGESTIONS

Note: The purpose of these suggestions is to try to indicate the general works considered to be of most value in providing deeper knowledge of the subject matter of each chapter. Most of the volumes listed here are mentioned also in the footnotes to the text; on more specific points the footnotes indicate further reading.

CHAPTER ONE

THE ULTIMATE AND OBJECTIVE ETHICAL NORM: THE DIVINE LAW

I. THE TEACHING OF THE COUNCIL: THE DOCUMENTS

1. A. Flannery, O.P., ed. *Vatican II, The Conciliar and Post-Conciliar Documents*. Tenbury Wells, Worcester, 1975.
   The fullest compilation available in English.

2. H. Vorgrimler. *Commentary on the Documents of Vatican II*. London, 1968.
   The standard commentary on each of the documents, giving the genesis of each and the main points of discussion during the Council proceedings.

3. *Constitutiones Decreta Declarationes, Sacrosanctum Oecumenicum Concilium Vaticanum II*. Rome, 1966.
   The full Latin text of the Decrees of the Council together with related documents.

II. LAW AND MORALS: GENERAL

1. P. Devlin. *The Enforcement of Morals*. O.U.P., 1965.
   The title was that of the Maccabaean Lecture given in 1959; the book contains this lecture and other lectures stemming from it.

2. H. A. L. Hart. *Law, Liberty and Morality*. O.U.P., 1963.
   Professor Hart's criticism of the approach taken by Lord Devlin in the 1959 lecture.

3. Basil Mitchell, ed. *Law, Morality and Religion in a Secular Society*. O.U.P., 1967.

A contribution to the debate sparked off by Lord Devlin's lecture, with more emphasis on the religious aspect.

4. National Deviancy Council. *Permissiveness and Control: The Fate of the 1960s Legislation*. London, 1980.

A collection of essays based on a conference run by the Council. That entitled "Reformism and the Legislation of Consent" illustrates the close connection between law and morals in practice.

5. Norman St. John-Stevas. *Life, Death and the Law*. London, 1961.

An earlier contribution to the "Law and Morals" debate: the first chapter is particularly useful.

III. Law and Morals: Particular Issues

A. EUTHANASIA

1. J. Gould, ed. *Your Death Warrant? The Implications of Euthanasia*. London, 1971.

The findings of a study group of concerned Catholic doctors and lawyers.

2. J. M. Boyle and G. Grisez. *Life and Death with Liberty and Justice*. London, 1979.

Comprehensive of Catholic teaching in all its implications.

3. D. J. Horan and D. Mall. *Death, Dying and Euthanasia*. Washington, D.C., 1977.

An extensive collection of readings from experts of many persuasions. It includes Pius XII's address to anaesthesiologists on the prolongation of life.

4. T. J. O'Donnell, S.J. *Medicine and Christian Morality*. New York, 1975.

An updating of *Morals in Medicine*, which was many times reprinted. The author is concerned to state the Church's teaching with clarity and in full appreciation of the complexities of medical science. Chapter 3 has a section on euthanasia and suicide.

5. Sacred Congregation for the Doctrine of the Faith. *Declaration on Euthanasia*. London: C.T.S., 1980.

A brief restatement of the Catholic position on the matter and in the light of the current debate. Clear, concise, and compassionate.

B. ABORTION

1. Catholic Archbishops of Great Britain. *Abortion and the Right to Live*. London: C.T.S., 1980.

   A full and clear statement of the reasons for the traditional total prohibition of abortion and a reassertion of the reasonableness of those principles in the light of the modern situation.

2. G. Grisez. *Abortion, the Myths, the Realities and the Arguments*. New York, 1970.

   A study in depth by an outstanding Catholic moral theologian.

3. J. T. Noonan, ed. *The Morality of Abortion: Legal and Historical Perspectives*. Cambridge, Mass., 1970.

   A collection of essays by, among others, Paul Ramsey, Bernard Häring and John Finnis.

4. T. J. O'Donnell, S.J. *Medicine and Christian Morality*. New York, 1975.

   Chapter 5 is on "Moral Aspects of Pregnancy and Delivery", and gives the general principles and the medical issues involved.

5. R. Shaw. *Abortion on Trial*. Dayton, Ohio, 1968.

   A most useful short treatment of the issues in the light of the Catholic tradition.

C. HOMOSEXUALITY

1. D. Sherwin Bailey. *Homosexuality in the Western Christian Tradition*. London, 1959.

   Surveys the attitudes of ecclesiastical and civil authorities to the question, and the related shifts in public opinion.

2. M. J. Buckley. *Morality and the Homosexual*. London, 1959.

   Clear treatment of Catholic teaching, written in the light of the Wolfenden Report.

3. H. Peschke. *Christian Ethics*, volume 2. Dublin, 1978.

   A survey of the modern debate on this matter is given in chapter 4, "Sexuality and Marriage".

4. Sacred Congregation for the Doctrine of the Faith. *Declaration on Certain Questions Concerning Sexual Ethics*. London: C.T.S., 1975.

   Summarizes the Catholic teaching on sexuality including homosexuality.

5. Norman St. John-Stevas. *Life, Death and the Law*. London, 1961.

Chapter 5, "Homosexuality", examines the state of the question before the legislation based on Wolfenden was introduced.

IV. The Church and Freedom

A. IN ROMAN SOCIETY

1. *Cambridge Medieval History*, volume 1. C.U.P., 1911.
   Chapter 4, "The Triumph of Christianity", a stimulating essay on the causes for that triumph.

2. H. Chadwick. *The Early Church*. London, 1967.
   Chapter 3 on "Expansion and Growth" presents a summary of the factors which contributed to the success of the Christian mission.

3. M. Chambers et al. *The Western Experience to 1715*. New York, 1979.
   A modern study by a group of scholars of different faiths. Chapter 5, "The Empire and Christianity", provides a good introduction to the subject.

4. Christopher Dawson. *The Making of Europe*. London, 1932.
   A classic study; part I, "The Foundations", is particularly valuable in this context.

5. K. S. Latourette. *A History of the Expansion of Christianity*, volume 1. London, 1938.
   Thorough in its coverage of every aspect of the Christian mission; the interaction of Church and society is considered in chapter 6.

B. MEDIEVAL EUROPE: BACKGROUND

1. M. Mortimer Chambers et al. *The Western Experience to 1715*. New York, 1979.
   Chapter 6, "The Making of Europe", chapter 8, "Two Centuries of Creativity" and chapter 9, "The Summer of the Middles Ages" are specially recommended.

2. Christopher Dawson. *Religion and the Rise of Western Culture*. London, 1950.
   Useful throughout. Chapter 10, "Medieval City: School and University" is relevant on the subject of intellectual and social freedom.

3. Christopher Dawson. *The Making of Europe*. London, 1932.
   Part 3: "The Formation of Western Christendom" illustrates how the Church's influence affected many aspects of medieval European development.

4. C. W. Hollister. *Medieval Europe: A Short History*. Chichester, 1978.
A brief and brilliant introduction by an American scholar. Highly recommended.

C. EDUCATION

1. *Cambridge Medieval History*, volumes 5, 6, 8. C.U.P., 1927–1936.
Volume 5, chapter 22, and volume 8, chapter 23, give an account of schooling from the early to the late Middle Ages. Volume 6, chapter 17, is on the universities. The latter chapter was written by H. Rashdall whose *The Universities of Europe in the Middle Ages*, (3 volumes), O.U.P., 1936 is the standard work.

2. M. Chambers et al. *The Western Experience to 1715*. New York, 1979.
Chapter 8 contains a section on "The Cultural Revival" which outlines the development of higher learning in the Middle Ages.

3. Christopher Dawson. *Religion and the Rise of Western Culture*. London, 1950.
Chapter 10 describes the role of the school and the university in the context of city life.

4. C. H. Haskins. *The Rise of the Universities*. O.U.P., 1957.
A brief and perceptive account by a modern scholar.

5. N. Orme. *English Schools in the Middle Ages*. London, 1973.
A recent specialized study illustrating the evolution of education in England.

D. THE DECLINE OF SLAVERY

1. M. Bloch. *Slavery and Serfdom in the Middle Ages*. London, 1975.
A collection of essays on this subject by one of the outstanding medieval historians of our time.

2. *Cambridge Economic History of Europe*, volume 1. C.U.P., 1966.
This volume on "The Agrarian Life of the Middle Ages" gives in chapter 6 an account of the decline of slavery by the same author.

3. R. Cave and H. Coulson. *A Source Book of Medieval Economic History*. New York, 1965.
Texts and references in part IV on Christian attitudes to slavery and serfdom.

4. K. S. Latourette. *A History of the Expansion of Christianity*, volume 2. London, 1939.

Chapter 8 contains a brief but useful summary of the Christian attitude to slavery.

5. W. E. H. Lecky. *A History of European Morals*, volume 2. London, 1911.

His observations in chapter 4 concerning the effect of Christian belief and practice on slavery are of particular interest.

E. CHURCH AND STATE

1. A. J. and R. W. Carlyle. *A History of Medieval Political Theory in the West*, volume 4. London, 1922.

This volume is concerned with the relationship of the empire and the papacy from the tenth to the twelfth centuries.

2. C. W. Hollister. *Medieval Europe: A Short History*. Chichester, 1978.

Chapters 11 and 15 provide excellent surveys of the central issues.

3. M. Keen. *The Pelican History of Medieval Europe*. London, 1978.

Another highly recommended introductory study of the medieval period by a modern scholar. Chapters 5, 10, 12 and 15 are a little more full than Hollister's on this subject.

4. G. H. Sabine. *A History of Political Theory*. London, 1964.

A standard textbook on political theory. Chapters 11 to 16 cover the Investiture controversy and the conciliar movement.

5. R. W. Southern. *Western Society and the Church in the Middle Ages*. London, 1970.

The best and most comprehensive introductory study.

6. G. Tellenbach. *Church, State and Christian Society at the Time of the Investiture Controversy*. London, 1940.

A translation of a classic work by a German scholar.

F. THE CRUSADES

1. A. S. Atiya. *Crusades, Commerce and Culture*. London, 1962.

A look at some of the secular implications of the Crusades.

2. *Cambridge Medieval History*, volume 5.

Chapters 7 to 9 cover the first three crusades and provide an invaluable introduction.

3. M. Chambers, et al. *The Western Experience to 1715*. New York, 1979.

Chapter 10 gives a brief and scholarly survey with suggestions for further reading.

4. M. Keen. *The Pelican History of Medieval Europe*. London, 1978.
Chapters 9, 13 and 20 chart the Crusade movement and its aftermath.

5. K. M. Setton, gen. ed. *A History of the Crusades* (3 volumes). London, 1969–1975.
The most exhaustive and authoritative work in English.

G. THE INQUISITION

1. *Cambridge Medieval History*, volume 6. C.U.P, 1929.
Chapter 20 on "Heresies and the Inquisition in the Middle Ages"—a well-balanced survey.

2. H. Kamen. *The Spanish Inquisition*. London, 1965.
Kamen's study is concerned with the more politically and racially motivated activities of the Inquisition in Spain, where it was an instrument of secular policy.

3. D. Knowles and D. Obolensky. *The Christian Centuries*, volume 2, "The Middle Ages". London, 1969.
Chapters 32 and 41 place the questions of the Inquisition and heresy in the general context of Church history at the time.

4. M. D. Lambert. *Medieval Heresy*. London, 1977.
Covers the subject from about 1000 to the early fifteenth century.

5. G. Leff. *Heresy in the Later Middle Ages* (2 volumes). London, 1967.
A deeper analysis which concentrates more on the later period.

V. THE TEACHING OF THE OLD TESTAMENT ON THE ULTIMATE AND OBJECTIVE ETHICAL NORM

1. John Bright. *The History of Israel*. London, 1972.
The standard and very full treatment of the history of the people of the Old Testament.

2. R. Davidson. *The Old Testament*. London, 1964.
A brief, scholarly introduction, probably the best such.

3. W. Eichrodt. *The Theology of the Old Testament*, 2 volumes. London, 1967.
A translation of a great work by a German scholar. Chapters 17 and 22 of volume 2 on "The Maintenance of the World" and "The Effect of Piety on Conduct" are especially valuable in our context.

4. J. L. McKenzie. *The Two-edged Sword*. London, 1956.

Popularly presented, but acute and illuminating. Chapters 3, 6 and 9 stress the connection between belief in God and everyday life in the Old Testament.

5. G. von Rad. *Old Testament Theology*, 2 volumes. London, 1975.

A profound, exhaustive and scholarly study. Chapter 4 of volume 1 puts Old Testament morality in its theological context.

VI. Greece and Rome: Moral Philosophy

1. A. Andrewes. *Greek Society*. London, 1971.

A popular introduction by a modern scholar. Chapters 10 and 12 deal with the nature of social values and moral beliefs.

2. R. H. Barrow. *The Romans*. London, 1968.

Chapter 7 looks at the Roman attitude to religion and philosophy, including moral theory.

3. W. de Burgh. *The Legacy of the Ancient World*. London, 1947.

This book, first published in the 1920s, remains from many points of view the best introduction to the Western cultural tradition. Its survey of the early Eastern, Israelite, Hellenic, Roman and Christian elements puts the moral ideas of each in their context.

4. F. C. Copleston. *A History of Philosophy*, volume 1, *Greece and Rome*. London, 1947.

The author's unhurried treatment of the various individual schools of thought in Greece and Rome contains an examination of the development of the moral philosophy of each.

5. P. Huby. *Greek Ethics*. London, 1967.

A short account, stressing the contribution of Socrates, Plato and Aristotle but dealing also with the Sophists and Stoics.

6. J. Maritain. *Moral Philosophy*. London, 1964.

A thematic study which brings together the elements of Greek and Roman thought as part of its general analysis of the subject.

VII. The Teaching of the New Testament On the Ultimate and Objective Ethical Norm And the Development of Moral Theology

1. L. H. Marshall. *The Challenge of New Testament Ethics*. London, 1964.

A reprint of an older study by a Protestant writer, first published in the 1940s.

2. F. X. Murphy. *Moral Teaching in the Primitive Church*. Tenbury Wells, 1968.

A collection of documents tracing the development of early Christian moral teaching.

3. H. Peschke. *Christian Ethics*, volume 1. Dublin, 1977.

In part I, chapters 2 and 3, the moral teaching of the New Testament and evolution of moral theology is briefly surveyed.

4. R. Schnackenburg. *The Moral Teaching of the New Testament*. London, 1967.

A very thorough treatment by a Catholic scholar.

5. R. Sidgwick. *A History of Ethics*. London, 1967.

Reprinted in various forms since 1888, Professor Sidgwick's summary of the various ethical schools remains a standard. Chapter 2, "Christianity and Medieval Ethics", traces the development of Christian moral-theological reflection in its early stages.

CHAPTER TWO

THE PROXIMATE AND SUBJECTIVE ETHICAL NORM: CONSCIENCE

I. THE NATURE OF CONSCIENCE

1. St. Thomas Aquinas. *Summa Theologica*

Part I, question 79, articles 12 and 13 on "The Nature of Conscience" and part I–II, question 19, articles 5 and 6 on "Erroneous Conscience".

2. P. Delahaye. *The Christian Conscience*. New York, 1968.

A comprehensive study by a Catholic scholar. It examines the biblical foundations, the teaching of the Fathers, and the elaborated modern theory.

3. W. E. May, ed. *Principles of Catholic Moral Life*. Chicago, 1980.

Papers read at a Catholic University of America symposium, June 1979. Chapters 19 and 15 deal with the meaning of conscience and the formation of conscience.

4. *New Catholic Encyclopedia*.

Article on "Conscience": analyses the concept, its biblical foundations, and its theology.

5. H. Peschke. *Christian Ethics*, volume 1. Dublin, 1977.

Part II, chapter 3, on conscience.

II. The Nature of Morality: The Moral Act

1. St. Thomas Aquinas. *Summa Theologica*.

   I-II. The treatise on man's last end, questions 1 to 21, especially 18 to 20 on the good and evil of human acts.

2. W. Eichrodt. *Theology of the Old Testament*, volume 2. London, 1979.

   Chapter 22 deals with Old Testament morality.

3. H. Jone. *Moral Theology*. Cork, 1951.

   This older compendium shows the strengths and weaknesses of the highly formalized presentation of traditional teaching that was once the norm for moral theology textbooks and handbooks.

4. L. H. Marshall. *The Challenge of New Testament Ethics*. London, 1964.

   Chapters 1 to 4 deal with Christ's teaching on morality.

5. W. E. May, ed. *The Principles of Catholic Life*. Chicago, 1980.

   Chapters 12 and 13 are on moral methodology; highly recommended.

6. F. X. Murphy. *Moral Teaching in the Primitive Church*. Tenbury Wells, 1968.

   Valuable in illustrating the early approach to moral teaching.

7. H. Peschke. *Christian Ethics*, volume 1. Dublin, 1977.

   Good on the biblical foundations, the evolution of moral theology and its general principles.

8. G. von Rad. *Old Testament Theology*, volume 1. London, 1979.

   A section in chapter 4 of part 2 on the significance of the Commandments puts them in their theological context.

9. R. Schnackenburg. *The Moral Teaching of the New Testament*. London, 1967.

   Part one, chapters 1, 2, 3, and 5 on Christ's moral teaching.

10. H. Sidgwick. *Outline of the History of Ethics*. London, 1967.

    Stresses in chapter 2, "Christianity and Medieval Ethics", the importance the Christian community attached from the beginning to the idea of morality as a code given by God.

III. Modern Catholic Objections to the Classical Theory On the Nature of Morality and the Moral Act

1. C. Curran, ed. *Readings in Moral Theology*. New York, 1979.

   A selection of readings with contributions by those who hold to the traditional Catholic teaching as well as some of the more outstanding opponents of that teaching, in particular the article by J. Fuchs from *Gregorianum* 52, 1971, on "The Absoluteness of Moral Norms" is given, as is L. Jenssen's on "Ontic Evil and Moral Evil" from *Louvain Studies* 40, 1972.

2. C. Curran. *Christian Morality*. London, 1969.

Chapter 5 is devoted to a consideration of Bernard Häring's moral theology which, we are told, is an attempt to develop a situation ethics which does not deny the traditional absolutes of Catholic moral theology.

3. W. E. May, ed. *The Principles of Catholic Moral Life*. Chicago, 1980.

Chapters 6, 7, and 12 are particularly valuable in that they subject the writings of the better known dissenting moral theologians within the Church to the sort of exacting criticism they rarely receive.

4. T. O'Connell. *Principles for a Catholic Morality*. New York, 1978.

Argues that experience, rather than the traditional understanding of objective natural law and revelation, is to be the basis of moral reasoning.

5. H. Peschke. *Christian Ethics*, volume 1. Dublin, 1977.

There is a brief survey of the recent controversies in chapter 4 of part II.

IV. OBJECTIVE MORAL LAW, JUSTICE AND CHARITY

1. St. Thomas Aquinas. *Summa Theologica*, II–II.

Questions 57, 58 and 61 deal with right, with justice and with the divisions of justice.

2. Aristotle. *Nicomachean Ethics*.

Book 5 on justice.

3. J. Messner. *Social Ethics*. London, 1965.

Section 50 on justice and section 53 on social charity.

4. Plato. *The Republic*.

Part 5 on justice in the state and the individual.

5. J. Rawls. *A Theory of Justice*. O.U.P., 1972.

An influential study by a modern scholar, in which he elaborates on the social contract theory as advanced by Locke, Rousseau and Kant.

6. E. Welty. *A Handbook of Christian Social Ethics*. New York, 1960.

The introductory questions at the beginning of the book set out the connection between ethics and social ethics in the Catholic tradition. Part 3 deals with justice and charity and their inter-relationship.

V. Modern Secular Objections To the Idea of Objective Moral Law
And the Liberal Roots of those Objections

1. W. de Burgh. *The Legacy of the Ancient World*. London, 1964.
   The last two chapters deal with the relationship between the Christian
   legacy of the Middle Ages, Renaissance, the Reformation, and the
   modern world.

2. M. Chambers et al. *The Western Experience to 1715*. New York, 1979.
   Chapters 12 to 17 more fully detail the influences that formed the
   modern mind and world.

3. J. Hallowell. *The Decline of Liberalism as an Ideology*. London, 1949.
   Crucial for an understanding of the essential conflicts in the liberal
   ideology.

4. H. Laski. *The Rise of European Liberalism*. London, 1936.
   Stresses the economic aspects of liberalism but considers these in their
   general cultural context.

5. J. Maritain. *Moral Philosophy*. London, 1969.
   Considers the subject in the light of Thomist tradition.

6. R. Niebuhr. *The Nature and Destiny of Man*. London, 1941.
   A survey of the intellectual development of modern man.

7. G. Ruggiero. *The History of European Liberalism*. O.U.P., 1927.
   A pioneering and authoritative study of the subject.

8. M. Salvadori. *The Liberal Heresy*. London, 1977.
   A sympathetic modern interpretation of liberalism.

VI. Some Modern Ethical Theories

1. F. C. Copleston. *A History of Philosophy*. London, 1948.
   Since it is difficult to separate a philosopher's moral theories from the
   rest of his philosophy, such theories are best understood in their
   context. Fr. Copleston's books are well organised to enable the
   patient reader to do this. Volumes 4 and following cover modern
   philosophy starting with Descartes and the main philosophical influences on modern moral thinking from Hobbes through Kant,
   Hegel, Marx to Bentham, Sartre are reviewed.

2. E. F. O. Dougherty. *Religion and Psychiatry*. New York, 1978.
   A recent contribution to the debate on this subject.

3. J. Fletcher. *Situation Ethics: The New Morality*. Philadelphia, 1966.
   Moral Responsibility. London, 1968.

Two statements of the theory and its implications by one who has done much to popularise this approach to ethics.

4. J. C. Ford and G. Kelly. *Contemporary Moral Theology*, volume 1. Cork, 1958.
Has useful chapters on psychiatry and Catholicism, and the Holy See and situation ethics.

5. Sigmund Freud. *The Future of an Illusion* and *Civilisation and its Discontents*. (Complete Works, volume 1.) London, 1966.
The fullest general statement of Freud's ethical theories are contained in these two works.

6. J. Hadfield. *Psychiatry and Morals*. London, 1928.
One of the earliest studies by a psychiatrist on the relationship of his science to traditional moral values.

7. T. E. Hill. *Contemporary Ethical Theory*. New York, 1950.
A comprehensive survey of the contributions made by twentieth century ethical theorists.

8. E. Kamenka. *The Ethical Foundations of Marxism*. London, 1971.
Good analysis of its subject.

9. J. Maritain. *Moral Philosophy*. London, 1964.
The major modern thinkers reviewed in the context of the Thomist tradition.

10. A. McIntyre. *History of Ethics*. London, 1967.
A more modern treatment in outline, whose author is very conscious of the achievement of Sidgwick.

11. J. McGlynn and J. Toner. *Modern Ethical Theories*. Milwaukee, 1962.
A brief, clear treatment by two Catholic authors.

12. O M. Mowrer. *The Crisis in Psychiatry and Religion*. Princeton, 1961.
Underlines the extent to which some religious thinkers have been misled by exaggerated respect for vulgar Freudianism.

13. B. Nelson, ed. *Freud and the 20th Century*. London, 1958.
A collection of essays by individual writers on the theme. Those by Maritain and Kaplan are of especial value.

14. G. Outka and P. Ramsay, eds. *Norm and Context in Christian Ethics*. London, 1969.
A symposium to which Catholic and non-Catholic authors contributed. Basil Mitchell's "Critique of Situation Ethics" is particularly perceptive.

15. H. Sidgwick. *Outline of the History of Ethics*. London, 1967.
The last two chapters summarise the development of modern ethical theory.

CHAPTER THREE

THE ETHICS OF MARRIAGE AND THE FAMILY

I. THE CHRISTIAN UNDERSTANDING OF THE NATURE OF MARRIAGE

1. P. Grelot. *Man and Wife in Scripture*. London, 1964.
A study of the relevant texts and their significance.

2. J. L. McKenzie. *The Two-Edged Sword*. London, 1964.
Chapter 6, "Human Origins", puts the Genesis teaching in its biblical context.

3. E. Schillebeeckx. *Marriage: Secular Reality and Saving Mystery*, 2 volumes. London, 1965.
Volume 1 examines the teaching of the Scriptures.

4. R. Schnackenburg. *The Moral Teaching of the New Testament*. London, 1967.
Examines Jesus' attitude to marriage and the family, and the question of divorce, in part 1, chapter 4.

5. R. de Vaux. *Ancient Israel*. New York, 1961.
Part 1, chapter 2, deals with marriage in the Old Testament.

II. THE DEVELOPMENT OF THE THEOLOGY AND CANON LAW OF MARRIAGE

1. R. Brown. *Marriage Annulment in the Catholic Church*. London, 1977.
A sound and sympathetic account of developments in Catholic teaching and practice based on the British experience.

2. *Dictionary of Catholic Theology*.
Article on "Divorce"; the clarification of the Church's doctrine down to St. Augustine, is particularly useful.

3. Pope John Paul II. *Concluding Address to the Synod of Bishops, 1980* (*L'Osservatore Romano*, English edition, 3 November 1980).
Contains observations made by the Holy Father on the indissolubility of marriage.

4. Pope John Paul II. *Familiaris Consortio*. C.T.S., London, 1982.
Published since this book was finished and went to press, we have

unfortunately not been able to use its insights in the chapter on marriage. It is a magnificent and magisterial restatement of the Christian truth about the sacrament in the light of modern needs.

5. G. H. Joyce. *Christian Marriage: An Historical and Doctrinal Study*. London, 1948.
First published in 1933 and still standard on the approach its title indicates.

6. *New Catholic Encyclopedia*.
The article on marriage is very full on the canon law aspects.

7. H. Peschke. *Christian Ethics*. Dublin, 1978.
Volume 2 puts the teaching on marriage in the context of general moral theology down to the 1970s.

8. E. Schillebeeckx. *Marriage: Secular Reality and Saving Mystery*, volume 2. London, 1965.

III. The Teaching on the Ends of Marriage Down to Vatican II

1. D. Sherwin Bailey. *The Man/Woman Relationship in Christian Thought*. London, 1959.
Particularly valuable in bringing together the main patristic sources on sex, marriage and virginity.

2. V. A. Demant. *An Exposition of Christian Ethics*. London, 1963.
Lectures by the then Regius Professor of Moral and Pastoral Theology at the University of Oxford. Chapter 2 is particularly relevant.

3. *Dictionary of Catholic Theology*.
Article on "Marriage" is useful in giving the context of the early teaching.

4. J. Ford and G. Kelly. *Contemporary Moral Theology*, volume 2. Cork, 1958.
In part 2, chapter 9, the development of the Church's teaching on the use of marriage is outlined.

5. John F. McNeill and H. N. Gamer. *Medieval Handbooks of Penance*. New York, 1938.
This translation of the principle such handbooks enables the reader to put their sexual teaching in its proper context.

6. E. Sheridan. *The Morality of the Pleasure Motive in the Use of Marriage*. Rome, 1947.
A moralist looks at the developing understanding of this subject.

IV. The Ends of Marriage, The Teaching of Vatican II: Humanae Vitae and John Paul II

1. E. Billings and A. Westmore. *The Billings Method: Controlling Fertility without Drugs or Devices*. London, 1981.

   Dr. Billings, who with her husband, also a medical doctor, has been concerned with research in natural family planning, explains their findings.

2. J. Ford and G. Grisez. "Contraception and the Infallibility of the Ordinary Magisterium". *Theological Studies*, June 1978.

   A demonstration of the binding nature of the teaching.

3. G. Grisez. "Marriage, Reflections Based on St. Thomas and Vatican II", *Catholic Mind*. June, 1966.

   Essential to an understanding of St. Thomas on the ends of marriage in the light of the modern teaching summed up in Vatican II.

4. A. Zimmerman (co-ordinator). *Natural Family Planning*. Milwaukee, 1980 (distributed by Human Life Center, Collegeville, Minnesota).

   Part 1 on the experience of N.F.P., part 2 on the scientific data, part 3 on the theology. *Documentation* in the Appendix is useful.

5. Pope John Paul II. (a) Address to the American Bishops, Chicago, 1979. In *U.S.A. Message of Justice, Love and Peace*. Boston, 1979. (b) Concluding address to the Synod of Bishops, 1980. *L'Osservatore Romano*, English weekly edition, 3 November 1980.

6. J. Komonochak. "Humanae Vitae and its Reception: Some Ecclesio logical Reflections". *Theological Studies*, June, 1978.

   A summary of the controversy by one not favourable to the encyclical.

7. R. Lawler, ed. *The Teaching of Christ*. Huntingdon, Indiana, 1976.

   Chapter 30, "Christian Marriage", unites the traditional teaching with that of the Second Vatican Council and *Humanae Vitae*.

8. W. E. May and J. F. Harvey. "On Understanding Human Sexuality". *Clergy Review*. August, 1978.

   A consideration of the defects of some new approaches to Christian sexual ethics.

9. J. Santamaria and J. Billings. *Human Life and Human Love*. Melbourne, 1979.

   Among the many contributors to this symposium was Mother Teresa who asserts her support for natural family planning and its effectiveness among the people for whom she works.

BIBLIOGRAPHY 527

10. E. Zimmerman, ed. *A Reader in Natural Family Planning*, 2nd edition. Collegeville, Minnesota, 1980.

Testimonies to the value and effectiveness of natural family planning by a wide variety of experts, most of them married men and women.

V. MARRIAGE AS A SOCIAL INSTITUTION

1. E. Butterworth and D. Weir, ed. *The Sociology of Modern Britain*. London, 1977.

A section on the family provides selected readings on the family in Britain today.

2. J. Epstein. *Divorce: The American Experience*. London, 1971.

The cultural and other factors he describes as affecting divorce are basically common to all Western cultures.

3. R. Fletcher. *The Family and Marriage in Modern Britain*. London, 1966.

A social history of the family in one country in modern times.

4. Mary Kenny. *Why Christianity Works*. London, 1980.

Chapter 6, "Can Marriage Last?", a survey of the strains on the modern family by a Catholic writer and mother.

5. P. Leach. *Who Cares?* London, 1979.

Dr. Leach, psychologist and mother, defends the role of motherhood, which, as she points out tends to be downgraded by some defenders of women's rights.

6. G. R. Leslie. *The Family in Social Context*. O.U.P., 1976.

Looks at the varying cultural contexts, the theory and the history of the family.

7. Lucy Mair. *Marriage*. London, 1971.

Dr. Mair examines the institution in various cultures throughout the world.

8. J. Messner. *Social Ethics*. London, 1965.

Sections 69 to 80 on the family are full and detailed.

9. E. Shorter. *The Making of the Modern Family*. London, 1971.

An historian's attempt (and he is very well aware of the difficulties) to trace the evolution of the family of Everyman in the last centuries.

10. J. Wallerstein and Joan Kelly. *Surviving the Break-Up*. London, 1980.

An American study which considers the effects of divorce upon the children.

11. E. Welty. *A Handbook of Christian Social Ethics*, volume 2. New York, 1960.

Part one on "Marriage and the Family". The author's approach through the Church's documents anchors the subject well.

VI. THE SCRIPTURES AND THE PATRIARCHAL FAMILY

1. R. Chamberlayne. *Man in Society: The Old Testament Doctrine*. London, 1966.

Brings together the findings of the best of modern scholarship on all aspects of its theme, including that of marriage.

2. V. A. Demant. *An Exposition of Christian Sex Ethics*. London, 1963.

Chapter 6 on "Sex and Civilisation" argues that the patriarchal family, properly understood in the context of the Christian teaching, is the best for the individual and society.

3. F. Engels. *The Origins of the Family: Private Property and the State*. London, 1940.

The famous but often challenged thesis that patriarchy is the result of economic domination of women by men in the early stages of human development.

4. S. Goldberg. *Male Dominance: The Inevitability of Patriarchy*. London, 1979.

Rather unfortunately titled: the book is in fact a balanced statement of the case for patriarchy, based on the ascertainable facts about human society in history as well as on the physical and psychological constitutions of men and women.

5. A. Kardiner. *Sex and Morality*. London, 1965.

Kardiner, a professor of clinical psychology argues that patriarchy and monogamy provide the best opportunities for human development, especially that of the children.

6. L. Marshall. *The Challenge of New Testament Ethics*.

The question of St. Paul's attitude to women and its implications discussed in chapter 10(e).

7. A. Oakley and J. Mitchell. *The Rights and Wrongs of Women*. London, 1976.

A contribution "On looking again at Engels' *Origin of the Family, Private Property, and the State*" underlines the influence that Engels' thesis still has on some exponents of women's liberation.

8. E. Schillebeeckx. *Marriage: Secular Reality and Saving Mystery*. London, 1965.

Volume 1, chapter 5 (11), on the New Testament ethos.

9. R. Schnackenburg. *The Moral Teaching of the New Testament*. London, 1967.

The implications of the New Testament about the status of the sexes and the position of the wife in marriage are considered in part 2.

10. J. D. Unwin. *Sex and Culture*. O.U.P., 1934.

This massively learned work, surveying cultures ancient and modern, primitive and civilised, concludes that the restriction of sex to marriage, and a patriarchal model of the family, provide the best conditions for social progress.

11. R. de Vaux. *Ancient Israel*. New York, 1961.

Part 1, chapters 1 and 4 examine the role of the family among the Jews of the Old Testament.

VII. EDUCATION: THE ROLE OF PARENTS, CHURCH AND STATE

1. T. Burgess. *A Guide to English Schools*. London, 1964.

A straight-forward factual account, avoiding controversy, on the structure of the system.

2. E. Butterworth and D. Weir. *The Sociology of Modern Britain*. London, 1977.

Contributions by King, Halsey, Katz and Cotgrove highlight some of the strengths and weaknesses of, and some of the controversies surrounding, private education.

3. Institute of Economic Affairs. *Education: The Framework for Choice*. London, 1970.

Contributions by, among others, A. C. F. Beales and Mark Blaug. It argues for the private sector and its rights.

4. J. Messner. *Social Ethics*. London, 1965.

Sections 73 and 143 examine education and the cultural functions of the state.

5. Pius XI. *Divini Illius Magistri* (On the Christian Education of Youth).

This encyclical of Pius XI, published in December, 1929, remains a valuable source of guidance.

6. E. Welty. *A Handbook of Christian Social Ethics*. New York, 1960.

Volume 2, part 1, lesson 3 discusses the rights of parents in education.

7. E. G. West. *Education and the State*. London, 1970.

One of the contributors to the I.E.A. publication mentioned above argues the case at greater length.

THE ETHICS OF POLITICAL LIFE

I. The Origin and Nature of Political Authority

A. POLITICAL THEORY

1. T. Gilby. *Between Community and Society*. London, 1957.

   Subtitled "A Philosophy and Theology of the State", it examines the evolution of St. Thomas' social theories in their intellectual and cultural context.

2. J. Maritain. *Man and the State*. Chicago, 1963.

   The relationship between community and society, nation and state, is examined in chapter 1.

3. J. Messner. *Social Ethics*. London, 1965.

   Book 2, sections 114, 127 and passim deal with the origin and nature of political authority.

4. E. Welty. *A Handbook of Christian Social Ethics*, 2 volumes. London, 1964.

   Volume 1, part 1, lesson 2 examines the origin and nature of political society, and lesson 3 the relationship of individual and community. Volume 2, part 3, lesson 1, on the political community and the state.

B. THE HISTORICAL CONTEXT AND THE DEVELOPMENT OF CATHOLIC THOUGHT ON THE NATURE OF THE STATE DOWN TO THE SIXTEENTH CENTURY

(i) The Scriptures and the Early Church

> *Note*: John Paul II's *Opening Address* at the Puebla Conference and the *Conclusions* of the Conference, Section 109 and following, provide a modern commentary on the example of Christ and the role of the Church concerning political involvement. *Puebla: Evangelisation at Present and in the Future of Latin America*, London, 1980, contains the documents of the Conference.

1. P. Allard. *Ten Lectures on the Martyrs*. London, 1907.

   That on "The Social Status of the Martyrs" underlines how the early Church refused to resort to violence, and brings out the apostolic importance of this attitude.

2. St. Thomas Aquinas. *Summa Theologica*. II–II, question 52, article 1.

   St. Thomas' reflections on the nature of the political order in the Old Testament.

3. R. W. and A. J. Carlyle. *A History of Medieval Political Theory in the West*, volume 1. London, 1903.

Part 3 on "The Political Theory of the New Testament and the Fathers".

4. R. Davidson. *The Old Testament*. London, 1964.

Chapter 4 looks at the relationship between God and the community under the title of "The Responsible Society".

5. W. Eichrodt. *The Theology of the Old Testament* (2 volumes). London, 1967.

Volume 1 has chapters on the links between secular law and belief in God, and the leadership of the people of Israel from Moses to the development of monarchy. Volume 2 has one on the individual and the community in the Old Testament.

6. F. M. Furfey. *A History of Social Thought*. New York, 1949.

His consideration of "Our Lord as Social Agitator" in chapter 7 is interesting in the light of the later development of liberation theology.

7. L. H. Marshall. *The Challenge of New Testament Ethics*. London, 1964.

Chapter 5(c), on the state, brings together Christian teachings on the state.

8. J. L. McKenzie. *The Two-Edged Sword*. London, 1959.

His treatment of the national origins, the role of king and prophet and the national welfare is valuable and relevant.

9. R. Schnackenburg. *The Moral Teaching of the New Testament*. London, 1967.

Has sections on Jesus' attitude to the political order and the attitude of the early Church to the same.

10. E. Troeltsch. *The Social Teaching of the Christian Churches*, vol. 1. London, 1931.

Chapter 1, "The Foundations in the Early Church", traces the development of Catholic teaching.

11. R. de Vaux. *Ancient Israel*. London, 1973.

Part 2, chapter 4, "The Israelite Conception of the State", summarizes the Old Testament attitude.

(ii) The Medieval Church

1. D. Bigongiari. *The Political Ideas of St. Thomas Aquinas*. New York, 1960.

A useful compilation of the main relevant texts from St. Thomas.

2. *Cambridge Medieval History*, volume 7. C.U.P., 1932.

The chapters on the medieval estates and the communal movement are most useful.

3. *Cambridge Economic History of Europe*, volume 3. C.U.P., 1963.

Exhaustive in its examination of all aspects of urban life and economic organisation, the social and economic background against which medieval political theory developed.

4. R. W. and A. J. Carlyle. *A History of Medieval Political Theory in the West*, 6 volumes. London, 1903–1927.

A study still unsurpassed for its completeness and balance.

5. M. C. Clarke. *Medieval Representation and Consent*. London, 1936.

The interaction of the secular and ecclesiastical developments detailed.

6. Christopher Dawson. *The Making of Europe*. London, 1932.

Part 1: "The Foundations" and part 2: "The Formation of Western Christendom", outlines the Church's role.

7. Christopher Dawson. *Religion and the Rise of Western Culture*. London, 1950.

Chapter 9, "The Medieval City: Commune and Gild" is particularly useful.

8. D. Edwards. *Christian England*. London, 1980.

Chapter 5, "The Age of Faith", has a brief section on the development of democracy in the English context.

9. T. Gilby. *Principality and Polity: Aquinas and the Rise of State Theory in the West*. London, 1958.

Gives the theological, juridical, philosophical and social background within which St. Thomas worked, and examines his thought in that light.

10. G. L. Haskins. *The Growth of English Representative Government*. Oxford, 1948.

Chapters 2 and 3 note the influence of general councils in shaping ideas of representation and that it was only in Christian Europe that feudalism was replaced by representative government.

11. C. W. Hollister. *Medieval Europe: A Short History*. Chichester, 1978.

Short chapters on empire and papacy, the Church and state in the fourteenth and fifteenth centuries; excellent introduction.

12. M. Keen. *The Pelican History of Medieval Europe*. London, 1978.

Chapters 5, 10, 12, 14, 15 and 19 chart the course of the Church/state conflict through the general history of the period.

13. G. H. Sabine. *History of Political Theory*. London, 1964.

The chapters in part 2, "The Theory of the Universal Community", take us through from Stoicism and Cicero to the Fathers, Gregory VII, St. Thomas and Occam.

C. THE ORIGIN AND NATURE OF THE STATE: SOME NON–CATHOLIC THINKERS SINCE THE RENAISSANCE

(i) Historical Background

1. W. Ault. *Europe in Modern Times*. London, 1946.

Starts with the eclipse of the idea of Christendom at the end of the Middle Ages and surveys developments down to the present century.

2. J. Bowle. *A History of Europe*. London, 1979.

"The Rise of the Dynastic States", "The Age of the Oceans", and "Industrial Civilisation, Democracy and Nationalism", are the themes of books 4 to 6.

3. E. Ergang. *Europe since Waterloo*. Boston, 1965.

An excellent survey by an American scholar.

4. H. A. L. Fisher. *A History of Europe*. London, 1936.

This many times reprinted study remains a most useful general introduction.

5. D. Thompson. *Europe since Napoleon*. London, 1967.

A useful companion volume to that of Ergang which deals with the same period.

(ii) Political Theory

Note: The books by Ruggiero, Laski and Hallowell on modern liberalism listed in the reading suggestions for chapter 2, section 5, are also relevant here.

1. W. McGovern. *From Luther to Hitler*. London, 1946.

An account of modern political theory written when the full evil of Nazism was fresh in peoples' minds.

2. T. P. McNeill. *The Rise and Decline of Liberalism*. Milwaukee, 1953.

Valuable, among other things, for the discussion of the meaning of the term in the first chapter.

3. G. H. Sabine. *A History of Political Theory*. London, 1964.

Part 3, "The Theory of the National State", deals with developments from Machiavelli to modern Fascism.

4. M. Salvadori. *The Liberal Heresy*. London, 1977.

A modern liberal explains the evolution and the significance of the creed.

5. Q. Skinner. *The Foundations of Modern Political Thought*, 2 volumes. Cambridge, 1978.

A specialist study of the Italian Renaissance, neo-Thomism and the Calvinist and Lutheran traditions.

II. THE PURPOSE, ATTITUDE TO, AND PROPER USE OF POLITICAL AUTHORITY

A. THE PURPOSE OF POLITICAL AUTHORITY, THE COMMON GOOD

1. J. Finnis. *Natural Law and Natural Rights*. O.U.P., 1980.

Chapter 6 on "Community, Communities and the Common Good" —a recent and refreshing contribution.

2. T. Gilby. *Principal and Polity: Aquinas and the Rise of State Theory in the West*. London, 1958.

Chapter 7 examines the relationship between the personal and the common good in Aquinas.

3. J. Hoffner. *Fundamentals of Christian Sociology*. Cork, 1964.

Chapter 2 of part 1 on "The Principles of the Common Good" presents a brief historical and theoretical account.

4. J. Messner. *Social Ethics*. London, 1965.

The concept is analyzed in sections 22 to 31.

5. *New Catholic Encyclopedia*.

The article on "The Common Good" surveys the historical development of the idea and its use in the documents of the modern social magisterium.

6. E. Welty. *A Handbook of Christian Social Ethics*. London, 1964.

The idea of the common good is discussed in lessons 2 and 3 of volume 1, part 2 on the origin and nature of human society and the relationship of individual and community.

B. THE ATTITUDE TO POLITICAL AUTHORITY AND THE RIGHT OF DISSENT

1. D. Bigongiari. *The Political Ideas of Thomas Aquinas*. New York, 1960.

Contains questions 42 and 104 from the *Summa* II-II on sedition and obedience.

2. J. Messner. *Social Ethics*. London, 1965.
   Sections 131 and 132 on political obedience and the right to resist.

3. Q. Skinner. *The Foundations of Modern Political Thought*. Cambridge, 1978.
   Volume 2, chapter 6, on "The Limits of Constitutionalism", discusses the neo-Thomist theories of legitimate resistance.

4. E. Welty. *A Handbook of Christian Social Ethics*. London, 1964.
   Volume 1, part 3, lesson 6: on resistance to the authority of the state.

C. CONSCIENTIOUS OBJECTION AND THE "JUST WAR" CONCEPT TODAY

1. J. Eppstein. *The Catholic Tradition of the Law of Nations*. London, 1935.
   Part 1 examines the development of Christian doctrine on peace and war to the 1930s.

2. H. Ford and F. X. Winters, eds. *Ethics and Nuclear Strategy*. New York, 1977.
   A series of essays by scholars at Georgetown University.

3. J. Messner. *Social Ethics*. London, 1965.
   Sections 105 on international law and war with nuclear weapons and 146 on defensive war and the refusal of military service.

4. B. Midgley. *The Natural Law Tradition and the Theory of International Relations*. London, 1975.
   Chapter 12, "Concerning Nuclear Preparation" looks at deterrence and conscientious objection to unlawful policies and orders.

5. W. Stein. *Nuclear Weapons and the Christian Conscience*. London, 1961.
   A contribution to the debate by a group of Catholics.

6. E. Thomson and D. Smith. *Protest and Survive*. London, 1980.
   A comprehensive attack upon the concept and practicality of nuclear war.

7. M. Walzer. *Just and Unjust Wars*. London, 1979.
   The author, professor of government at Harvard, seeks to recapture the just war, the tradition of Aquinas, Vitoria and Grotius, for moral theory.

III. THE CHRISTIAN, THE CHURCH, AND POLITICS

A. THE INDIVIDUAL CHRISTIAN, THE CHURCH AND POLITICS

1. J. E. Calvez. *Politics and Society in the Third World*. New York, 1977.
   A comprehensive survey.

2. L. D. Eppstein. *Politics and Parties in Western Democracies*. London, 1967.

A standard study of the subject.

3. J. Finnis. *Natural Law and Natural Rights*. O.U.P., 1980.

The author points out that human rights is the contemporary idiom for natural rights. Chapter 7 on "Justice" and chapter 8 on "Rights".

4. V. O. Key. *Politics, Parties and Pressure Groups*. New York, 1964.

A textbook on the American system.

5. J. Messner. *Social Ethics*. London, 1965.

Section 51 on freedom looks at natural rights in the context of justice.

6. E. Welty. *A Handbook of Christian Social Ethics*, volume 1. London, 1964.

Part 3, lesson 1 on right in general, and lesson 2 on natural right and human right.

B. THE CHURCH AND POLITICS DOWN TO THE SIXTEENTH CENTURY

Note: See the books listed above under I (B).

C. THE CHURCH AND POLITICS: THE SEVENTEENTH TO NINETEENTH CENTURIES

Note: The books by Fisher, Bowle, Ault, Ergang and Thomson mentioned for this chapter under I(c)(i), provide the historical background here. Ault's section on the Old Regime at its height and liberalism and nationalism are a particularly valuable introduction.

1. Robert Aubert et al. *The Church in a Secularized Society*. London, 1978.

Part 1 is on the period 1848 to 1914.

2. G. R. Cragg. *The Church in the Age of Reason, 1648–1789*. London, 1966.

Useful on the background to the French Revolution and its impact on the Church.

3. H. Daniel-Rops. *The Church in the 17th Century*. London, 1963.

Deals very thoroughly with the policy of the Holy See, the development of absolutism in Europe, and particularly with Louis XIV, "the most Christian King".

4. H. Daniel-Rops. *The Church in the 18th Century*. London, 1964.

Full on the suppression of the Society of Jesus, and also on Febronianism and Josephism; also looks at the Church in countries where she was not under attack.

5. C. Dawson. *The Gods of Revolution*. London, 1973.
Particularly valuable in giving the background to the French Revolution.

6. E. E. Y. Hales. *Revolution and Papacy 1789–1846*. New York, 1960.
An in-depth study of the period from the French Revolution to the death of Gregory XVI.

7. E. E. Y. Hales. *The Catholic Church in the Modern World*. London, 1959.
Good throughout, and especially useful on the conflict between the papacy and Italian nationalism in the nineteenth century.

8. A. R. Vidler. *The Church in an Age of Revolution*. London, 1974.
Has chapters on liberal Catholicism and ultra-Montanism in France, and on the pontificate of Pius IX.

9. E. N. Williams. *The Ancien Régime in Europe*. London, 1979.
The major regimes reviewed. The author's introduction compares and contrasts the corporate with the absolute state.

D. THE CHURCH AND POLITICS IN THE TWENTIETH CENTURY

1. H. Assman. *A Practical Theology of Liberation*. London, 1975.
A useful introduction to the subject.

2. Robert Aubert. *The Church in a Secularised Society*. London, 1978.
Surveys the international Church but is stronger on the European and Anglo-Saxon world.

3. Third General Congregation of Latin American Bishops (CELAM). *Puebla: Evangelisation at Present and in the Future of Latin America*, Conclusions. London, 1980.
The address by Pope John Paul II is crucial. The conclusions themselves present a coherent and sophisticated theology and plan of action relevant not only to the Latin American situation but throughout the world, particularly the third world.

4. H. Daniel-Rops. *A Fight for God*. London, 1959.
The chapters on Pius X look at the question of Catholics in politics in France, and that on Pius XI surveys the Church's relationship to Fascism and communism up to the Second World War.

5. G. Guttierez. *A Theology of Liberation*. London, 1974.
Densely written though hardly illuminating.

6. J. N. Moody. *Church and Society*. New York, 1953.

A pioneering work in its day, looking at the Church in Europe and the Americas.

7. A. Rhodes. *The Vatican in the Age of the Dictators*. London, 1973.

A survey by a non-Catholic, probably the most balanced account available.

E. THE CHURCH, INTERNATIONAL LAW AND INTERNATIONAL RELATIONS

1. A. Boyd. *The United Nations: Piety, Myth and Truth*. London, 1969.
A frank look at the U.N. experiment.

2. J. Eppstein. *The Catholic Tradition of the Law of Nations*. London, 1935.

Still probably the best and most coherent presentation of the Catholic tradition; it is amply documented.

3. J. Messner. *Social Ethics*. London, 1965.

In dealing in sections 99 and following with the community of nations, the concept and reality of international law and the possibility of an organised community of nations are examined in some detail.

4. F. S. Northcote and M. J. Grieve. *A Hundred Years of International Relations*. London, 1974.

The chapters on the League of Nations and the United Nations provide a good introduction to these institutions in their context.

5. A. de Soras. *International Morality*. London, 1963.
Brief but comprehensive.

CHAPTER FIVE

THE ETHICS OF ECONOMIC LIFE

I. LIBERAL CAPITALISM

1. M. Beard. *A History of Business*, 2 volumes. Ann Arbor, 1961.
Really a history of the businessman in his historical context over the ages.

2. H. Faulkner. *American Economic History*. London, 1964.
Chapter 22 examines the American labour movement till 1914 and subsequent chapters, e.g. 28, 30, and 32, trace its development.

3. H. Friedlander and J. Oser. *An Economic History of Modern Europe*. New York, 1953.
Invaluable for giving both the economic context and an account of the development of labour movements and social legislation.

4. R. Heilbroner. *The Worldly Philosophers*. New York, 1961.
A popular approach, very readable and informative.

5. E. Heiman. *History of Economic Doctrines*. O.U.P., 1964.
Probably the most useful introduction to the development of economic theory generally, and classical liberalism in particular.

6. Brian Inglis. *Poverty and the Industrial Revolution*. Panther, 1972.
A comprehensive account of the effect of the British industrial revolution upon the ordinary man.

7. P. Mantoux. *The Industrial Revolution in the Eighteenth Century*. London, 1961.
A study of the roots of the Industrial Revolution in England.

8. J. A. Schumpeter. *A History of Economic Analysis*. London, 1963.
The classic and exhaustive study of the subject.

9. W. Woodruff. *The Impact of Western Man*. London, 1966.
Europe's role in the world economy 1750–1960—surveying empire, emigration, banking, technology, transport, trade etc.

II. MARXIST SOCIALISM

1. R. N. Carew Hunt. *The Theory and Practice of Communism*, 5th edition. (Preface by Leonard Schapiro.) London, 1963.
A classical interpretation of Marx/Engelism and of the development of Communism.

2. D. Caute. *The Fellow Travellers*. London, 1971.
An exhaustive account of the illusions of the fellow travellers in the inter-war years.

3. F. C. Copleston. *A History of Philosophy*, volume 7. London, 1948.
Chapter 16 on "The Transformation of Idealism" puts Marx and Engels in their philosophical context.

4. R. Freedman. *Marx on Economics*. London, 1960.
A useful selection by an American scholar.

5. Alexander Gray. *The Socialist Tradition*. London, 1964.
A very perceptive study which places Marx in his socialist context.

6. G. F. Hudson. *Fifty Years of Communism*. London, 1971.
Brief account of the Soviet experiment.

7. D. McLellan. *Karl Marx*. London, 1973.
A standard work by a modern scholar.

8. D. McLellan. *Karl Marx, Selected Writings*. O.U.P., 1979.
The main lines of Marxist thought in all its various aspects.

9. J. Robinson. *Marxian Economics*. London, 1942.
A famous essay by a writer sympathetic to Marxism.

10. L. Schapiro. *The Communist Party of the Soviet Union*. London, 1966.
Another classic study by a modern scholar.

III. ETHICS AND ECONOMIC SYSTEMS: THE MARKET ECONOMY

Note: The books by Heilbroner, Heiman and Schumpeter listed for this chapter under I. "Liberal Capitalism", are useful here also.

1. A. Cairncross. *An Introduction to Economics*.
This basic textbook, many times reprinted since 1944, provides a good introduction to the subject.

2. J. E. Calvez and J. Perrin. *The Church and Social Justice*. London, 1961.
Has useful chapters on capital, exchange, price and the market, and free enterprise.

3. D. Dillard. *The Economics of J. M. Keynes*. London, 1948.
A systematic account of the theories of this most influential modern economist.

4. T. Divine. *Interest: An Historical and Analytic Study*. Milwaukee, 1959.
A full and scholarly treatment of interest and usury in both its economic and ethical contexts.

5. M. Friedman. *The Optimum Quantity of Money and Other Essays*. London, 1969.
These essays illustrate the thinking of one of the most controversial of contemporary economists.

6. J. Gilchrist. *The Church and Economic Activity in the Middle Ages*. London, 1969.
Indispensable for those who wish to understand the Church's role in this period.

7. F. A. Hayek. *New Studies in Philosophy, Politics, Economics and the History of Ideas*. London, 1969.

A restatement of the author's absolute belief in the market economy and distrust of concepts like social justice.

8. J. Hoffner. *Fundamentals of Christian Sociology*. Cork, 1964.

   Brief and to the point in part 2 on central issues in economic ethics.

9. J. Messner. *Social Ethics*. London 1965.

   Book 4: "The Ethics of Social Economy"—Dr. Messner's majestic treatment of the subject from the standpoint of the natural law tradition.

10. Michael Stewart. *Keynes and After*. London, 1967.

    An introduction to Keynes' life and ideas.

11. L. Watt. *Usury*. Oxford, 1963.

    A short and lucidly written account.

IV. Ethics and Economic Systems: The Centrally Planned Economy

1. M. Dobb. *Soviet Economic Development Since 1917*. London, 1966.

   An examination by one sympathetic to the Soviet experiment.

2. D. Granick. *Enterprise Guidance in Eastern Europe*. Princeton, 1976.

   A scholarly study of Communist economies.

3. A. Nove. *The Soviet Economic System*. London, 1978.

   Probably the best account in English.

4. A. Nove. *Economic History of the U.S.S.R.* London, 1976.

   Brings the same expertise to bear on the development of the Soviet system.

5. F. Ponchard. *Cambodia Year Zero*. London, 1978.

   Reminds us that Marx's economic theories, allied to his general philosophy, can still inspire monsters as great, if not greater than, Stalin.

6. B. M. Ward. *The Socialist Economy. A Study of Organizational Alternatives*. New York, 1967.

   Examines the organisation and economic performance of the various socialist states.

V. The Moral Laws Governing Private Property, Its Ownership and its Use

1. St. Thomas Aquinas. *Summa Theologica*.

   II–II, question 66, articles 1 and 2 on whether it is natural for man to possess property.

2. P. H. Furfey. *A History of Social Thought*. New York, 1949.

The chapters on the New Testament and "From the Fathers to the Medieval Synthesis" examine the Catholic teaching on property in its context.

3. J. Messner. *Social Ethics*. London, 1965.

Section 171 is on the natural law theory of private property.

4. H. Peschke. *Christian Ethics*, volume 2. Dublin, 1978.

Chapter 5 provides a good summary of Catholic teaching on property.

5. R. Schlatter. *Private Property: The History of an Idea*. London, 1951.

A useful study by an American scholar—though not quite accurate in its interpretation of some aspects of the Catholic tradition.

6. R. Schnackenburg. *The Moral Teaching of the New Testament*. London, 1967.

Chapter 4, section 14, deals with Jesus' attitude toward property.

7. R. de Vaux. *Ancient Israel*. New York, 1961.

Part 2, chapter 11 on economic life analyzes attitudes to property and its distribution.

VI. WORK: ITS SPIRITUAL AND MORAL SIGNIFICANCE: ITS RIGHTS AND ITS DUTIES

1. P. Allard. *Ten Lectures on the Martyrs*. London, 1907.

The lecture on "The Social Position of the Martyrs" indicates the appeal Christianity had for the ordinary people of the time.

2. J. E. Calvez and J. Perrin. *The Church and Social Justice*.

Chapter 10 on labour summarizes the implication of the Church's social teaching on this matter from Leo XIII.

3. J. Hoffner. *Fundamentals of Christian Sociology*. Cork, 1964.

Part 2 of chapter 1. The Christian meaning of work.

4. E. Lipson. *The Economic History of England*. London, 1944.

Volume 1 deals extensively with the guilds and the importance of their role.

5. H. Peschke. *Christian Ethics*, volume 2. Dublin, 1978.

A useful summary of traditional and modern teaching is given in chapter 5.

6. R. Schnackenburg. *The Moral Teaching of the New Testament*. London, 1967.

Chapter 4, section 14, deals also with Jesus' attitude toward work.

7. E. Troeltsch. *The Social Teaching of the Christian Churches*, volume 1. London, 1931.

Chapter 1, "The Foundations of the Early Church", looks, among other things, at attitudes to work and trade.

8. R. de Vaux. *Ancient Israel*. New York, 1961.

The attitude to wage-earners and craftsmen in Old Testament times is examined in part 2, chapters 1 and 2.

9. Pope John Paul II. *Laborem Exercens*. London, C.T.S., 1981

The most comprehensive and authoritative Catholic treatment of the theology and philosophy of work.

VII. THE ENTERPRISE AND INDUSTRIAL ORGANISATION: THE RIGHTS AND DUTIES OF CAPITAL AND LABOUR

1. J. E. Calvez and J. Perrin. *The Church and Social Justice*.

Chapters 10, 13, 18 and 19 deal with various aspects of industrial organisation and relations.

2. M. W. Chamberlain and J. Kuhn. *Collective Bargaining*. New York, 1965.

A standard American text; the concept of cooperative bargaining which the authors set out is of particular interest.

3. R. Charles. *The Development of Industrial Relations in Britain 1911–1939*. London, 1973.

A study of consultation and cooperation between employers and unions in this period. Confirms, the author thinks, the validity of the Church's guidance on these matters.

4. H. Clegg. *Trade Unionism Under Collective Bargaining: A Theory Based on the Comparison of Six Countries*. Oxford, 1976.

An examinationof variations in union behaviour in Europe and the U.S.A.

5. H. Daniel-Rops. *A Fight for God*. London, 1966.

Chapter 4 on social Catholicism surveys the background to *Rerum Novarum* and the conflicting ideas on industrial organisation and industrial relations that existed at the time.

6. D. Farnham and J. Pimlott. *Understanding Industrial Relations*. London, 1979.

Part 4 on "Industrial Democracy and Current Trends in Industrial Relations" summarises the recent interest in worker participation.

7. B. Martin and E. Kassalow. *Labour Relations in Advanced Industrial Societies: Issues and Problems*. New York, 1980.

These papers read at a symposium on international labour problems in December 1977 give some idea of the current points of interest.

8. J. Messner. *Social Ethics*. London 1965.

Book 4, part 2, "The Organization of the Social Economy" considers private ownership and industrial organization, including labour organization.

Note: The question of strikes and the rights and wrongs of strikes is the only one which focuses the public mind generally upon industrial relations. Practical guidance on the matter is difficult for the reasons mentioned in the text. Attempts at theoretical guidance are given in J. Messner's *Social Ethics*, pp. 463 ff., and H. Peschke's *Christian Ethics*, volume 2, chapter 5. *The Right to Strike* (London: C.T.S., 1979), looks at the subject in the British context.

VIII. POPULATION AND RESOURCES

1. C. M. Cipolla. *The Economic History of World Population*. London, 1964.

2. C. Clark. *Population Growth and Land Use*. 1977.

A standard work since its first publication in 1967.

3. L. Hodges. *Environmental Pollution*. New York, 1977.

An American study but relevant to other countries too.

4. J. H. Lowry. *World Population and Food Supply*. London, 1976.

A brief survey useful on the technical aspects; some of its moral judgements are more dubious.

5. R. Pressat. *Population*. London, 1973.

A valuable introductory study.

6. R. Sassone. *Handbook on Population*, 4th edition. Santa Ana, California, 1978.

The author uses the question and answer method and so makes his mass of statistical and factual information very digestible.

7. B. F. Skinner. *Earth Resources*. Englewood Cliffs, 1976.

An American expert surveys the ability of the earth to supply human needs.

IX. INTERNATIONAL ECONOMICS: AND DEVELOPMENT

1. Charles P. Kindleberger and Bruce Herrick. *Economic Development*. London, 1977.
A first-rate textbook which covers all aspects, theoretical and factual.

2. Independent Commission on International Development Issues (under the chairmanship of Willy Brandt). *North/South—A Programme for Survival*. London, 1980.
The much discussed and controversial Brandt Report.

3. G. M. Meier. *International Economics*. O.U.P., 1980.
Another excellent textbook—useful for the general reader also.

4. G. M. Meier. *Leading Issues in Economic Development*. New York, 1976.
Some of the main problems identified and discussed.

5. O.E.C.D. *Facing the Future*. Paris, 1979.
The report of a research group looking into the relationship between the advanced and the developing countries.

6. World Bank. *World Development Report*. Oxford, 1980.
Extremely valuable on all aspects of development programmes and prospects.

X. AGRICULTURAL ECONOMICS AND AGRICULTURAL DEVELOPMENT

1. *The Courier*, (published bi-monthly by the E.E.C., Brussels) September/October 1979: *Dossier on Agrarian Reform and Rural Development*.

2. *The Internationalist*, (published by OXFAM/Christian Aid, Oxford). No. 81 (November, 1979), devoted to land and agrarian reform in the third world.

3. Charles Kindleberger and Bruce Herrick. *Economic Development*. London, 1977.
Chapter 13 briefly puts agricultural development and agrarian reform in its economic context.

4. J. H. Lowry. *World Population and Food Supply*. London, 1976.
Has a brief chapter on land-holding and management.

5. John W. Mellor. *The Economics of Agricultural Development*. London, 1974.
Chapter 14 considers land tenure and agrarian reform in the context of economic incentives to produce.

INDEX OF AUTHORS,
NAMES AND TITLES

Abelard, 36
Abraham, 84
Abrams, P., 161
Adam, 78, 118, 127, 314
Adams, C. B., 186
Adler, A., 111
Aeterni Patris, 62
Aeschylus, 65
Ahab, 50
Albright, W. F., 52
Alcuin, 26, 35
Alfred, King, 26, 230
Allard, P., 178, 313
Amazons, 159
Ambrose, Saint, 69, 253, 303
Amos, 50
Anastasius I, 22, 230
Andrewes, A., 28, 53
Angers, 249
Anselm, Saint, 35, 36
Antoninus, Saint, 264, 287
Aquinas, Saint Thomas, 9, 61, 62, 63,
  67, 70, 71, 81, 85, 89, 90, 131, 132,
  176, 182, 189, 190, 194, 204, 216,
  222, 253, 287, 289, 300, 304, 305,
  361, 368, 371
Aristotle, 9, 34, 35, 36, 54, 62, 63, 65,
  66, 67, 89, 92, 104, 150, 182, 189,
  264, 287, 362
Ashworth, W., 339
Assmann, 245, 246, 253
Assyrians, 49
Athanasius, Saint, 57
Athens, 28, 67, 68
Atlantic Charter, 339
Aubert, R., 229, 240, 241, 243, 248
Augustine, Saint, 9, 57, 61, 92, 122,
  123, 127, 130, 131, 179, 303
Augustus, 19, 69
Averroes, 35, 62
Avicebron, 35
Avicenna, 35
Avignon, 25, 183, 184, 232, 233, 241

Baader, 250
Babylonians, 49
Bacon, R., 37
Balsdon, J., 53
Barker, F., 189
Barlow, D., 136
Barrow, R. H. 53
Bauer, P. T. and B. S. Yamey, 353
Beard, M., 263
Bebel, 250
Beckerman, W., 348
Becket, Saint Thomas, 181
Bede, Saint, 27, 35
Bellarmine, Saint Robert, 193, 195,
  198
Benedict, Saint, 21, 35, 41, 188
Benedict XIV, 288
Benedictines, 257
Bennett, W. J., 16
Bentham, 103, 104, 266
Beres, L. R., 218, 219
Bewkes, J. G. et al., 38
Bigg, C., 93
Bigongiari, D., 189, 222
Billings, Dr. Lyn, 143
Bismarck, 203, 251, 271
Blackaby, F. T., 269
Blackham, R., 314
Bloch, M., 29, 43
Bloch, S. and B. Reddaway, 102
Bloodworth, D., 296
Bobbio, 35
Bockmuchl, K., 102
Bodin, J., 198, 199, 205, 372
Boissonade, P., 31, 48, 313
Bologna, 35, 36, 187
Bolsheviks, 276
Boniface VIII, 153, 154, 182, 183,
  194, 232
Booker McConnell, 341
Bottome, P., 111
Bourbons, 238
Bowle, J., 242

Boyd, A., 260
Bracton, 191
Brandt Report, 337
Bretton Woods Conference, 339
Brierly, J., 16, 259
Bright, J., 49
British Council, 341
Brittan, S. and P. Livesey, 318
Brodrick, J., S.J., 38, 195, 205
Brownlie, I., 225, 226
Brown, E. H. Phelps, 271, 272, 317
Brown, R., 124, 125
Brunner, 113
Bryce, J., 199
Buchez, 249
Buhlmann, W., 255
Burgh, W. de, 28, 36, 37, 53, 54, 61, 62, 63, 66, 67, 93
Burke, R., 110, 111
Bussell, H. W., 23
Butler, E.C., 35
Byzantines, 39
Byzantium, 371

Caesar, 176
Cairncross, A., 279, 280, 283, 284, 285, 321
Cajetan, 133
Calvez, J. Y., 224, 319, 323
Calvez, J. Y. and J. Perrin, 6, 319
Calvin, J., 196
Calvinists, 196, 372
Cambodia, 296, 376
Cambridge, 35
Cambridge Bible Commentary, 128
Cambridge Economic History of Europe, 25, 29, 30, 40, 185, 186
Cambridge History of the Bible, The, 57
Cambridge Medieval History, 19, 20, 21, 26, 30, 31, 34, 35, 37, 39, 40, 43, 44, 45, 48, 185, 186, 231
Canaan, 49, 65
Canossa, 231, 233
Carlyle, A. J., 304
Carlyle, R. W. and A. J., 22, 29, 39, 47, 69, 70, 150, 179, 180, 181, 182, 190, 191, 230
Casas, de las, 258
Casti Connubii, 113, 116, 139, 166, 167

Castro, 252
Catholic Centre Party, 251
Catholic Institute of Social Ethics, 4
Catholic Journeyman's Associations, 250
Catholic Mind, 110, 131
Catholic Social Movement, 249
Caute, D., 102, 247, 278
Cavour, 242
CELAM, 246, 253
Celsus, 69
Census of Population 1971, 161
Ceres, 346
Ceylon, 344
Chamberlain, N. W. and J. Kuhn, 330
Chamberlayne, J. H., 164
Chamberlin, E. H., 279
Chambers, M. et al., 20, 23, 25, 27, 31, 35, 36, 42, 45, 47, 51, 63, 164, 231
Chambers, R. W., 13, 191
Chardin, T. de, 106
Charlemagne, 22, 24, 26, 36, 43, 185, 230, 237, 257
Charles II, 199
Charles IV, 233
Charles V, 192
Charles X, 238
Charles, R., S.J., 4, 317, 324, 330, 331
Chile, 354
Chomsky, 297
Christ, 19, 21, 27, 48, 49, 56, 57, 58, 74, 91, 100, 103, 112, 113, 115, 120, 121, 122, 123, 124, 126, 132, 140, 147, 154, 157, 158, 159, 163, 165, 166, 168, 176, 178, 182 213, 221, 224, 226, 239, 245, 252, 253, 255, 256, 257, 262, 302, 303, 305, 312, 313, 315, 361, 362, 367, 368, 369, 371, 375, 377, 380
Christian Aid, 341
Chrysippus, 67, 68
Churchill, W., 277
Cicero, 68
Cipolla, C. M., 344
Cistercians, 40
Civil Constitution on the Clergy, 236
Clapham, J. H., 208, 267, 271, 321

Clark, C., 346, 349
Clark, J. M., 26, 30
Clarke, M. V., 184, 186, 187, 188, 189
Cleanthes, 67
Cleisthenes, 65
Clement of Alexandria, 303
Clement V, 233
Clement XIV, 236
Clericos Laicos, 182
Clergy Review, 120
Clough, S. B. and R. T. Rapp, 23
Clovis, 24
Cluny, 24, 42
Cockroft, J. D. et al., 247, 338, 354
Coimbra, 257
Cole, D. C. and P. N. Lymon, 356
Cole, G. D. H., 302
Columba, Saint, 34
Commune (Paris), 271
Comte, A., 99, 365
Concordat, 237
Concordat of Worms, 231
Conference on Trends in the World's Population, 345
Congress of Vienna, 237
Consalvi, 238
Constantine, 20, 180, 237, 371
Constantine V, 39
Convention of Europe, 13
Copleston, F. C., 35, 36, 37, 63, 67, 98, 99, 101, 105, 183, 194, 195, 199, 202, 203, 258, 276
Council of Basle, 184, 371
Council of Carthage, 57
Council of Constance, 184
Council of Hippo, 57
Council of Lyons, 232
Council of Narbonne, 45
Council of Trent, 57, 123
Couple to Couple League, 144
Covenant, The, 50, 55, 120, 128, 176, 302
Cox, H., 246
Crombie, A. C., 37
Cuba, 252, 295
Cuenot, L., 107
Curran, C., 81
Cyprian, Saint, 303

Dales, R. C., 37
Dalton, G., 269, 291, 292, 294, 295
Dalton, O. M., 26
Daly, L. J., 35
Daniel, 50
Daniel Rops, H., 20, 26, 27, 39, 40, 42, 45, 46, 197, 229, 231, 234, 235, 236, 237, 239, 248, 249, 313
Dante, 257
Darrow, K. and R. Pam, 341
David (King), 49, 176
Davidson, R., 49
Davies, R. W. and M. Bornstein, 294
Dawson, C., 19, 21, 24, 26, 27, 34, 35, 36, 37, 42, 48, 185, 186, 202, 231, 236, 265, 313
Declaration on Abortion, 17
Declaration on Certain Questions Concerning Sexual Ethics, 17, 134
Declaration on Euthanasia, 18
Declaration of Human Rights, 260
Declaration on the Rights of Man, 13
Decretum pro Armenis, 116
Delhaye, P., 76, 77, 84
Delmar, R., 167
Demant, V. A., 127, 169
Denmark, 163
Denziger-Bannwart, 123
Descartes, R., 63, 94, 132
Deuteronomy, 49, 55
Devlin, P., 16
Dewar, L., 127, 169
Dicey, A. V., 208
Dictionary of Catholic Theology, 99, 122, 127, 129
Dictionary of National Biography, 302
Dignitatis Humanae, 6, 9, 10, 14, 60, 61, 63, 73, 77
Dillard, D., 268
Diocletian, 19
Diuturnum Illud, 206
Dives, 262
Divine, T., 148, 286
Divini Illius Magistri, 170, 171
Divini Redemptoris, 97, 262
Divorce Law Reform Act 1971, 162, 163
Dobb, M., 277, 278, 290

Doctors of the Church, 179, 303, 363, 367, 371, 377
Dominic, Saint, 189
Dominican Fathers, 63
Dominicans 188, 193, 257
Donovan Commission Report, 327, 328–9
Dopsch, H., 20, 89
Duckett, E. S., 26
Dudden, F. H., 39
Dunn, Dr. H. P., 143
Dunning, J., 307
Dupanloup, 241
Dutt, C. P., 101

Edwards, D., 30, 189
Ehrlich, P., 346
Eichrodt, W., 54, 55, 176
Einstein, A., 38
Elizabeth, Saint, 56
Elijah, 50, 51
Elkins, W., 152, 153
Emmanuel (King), 240
Enchiridion Symbolorum, 123
Encyclopedia Britannica, 348
Engels, F., 100, 101, 167, 204, 273, 376
Ephesians 165, 167, 369
Epstein, J., 137
Epstein, L. D., 224
Eppstein, J., 258, 259
Erasmus, D., 186, 313
Ergang, E. 237, 240, 249
Eugenius IV, 184
Euripides, 65
Evangelii Nuntiandi, 254
Eve, 118, 127
Exodus, 49
Ezekiel, 50

Fair Deal at Work, 329
Family Life Association, 144
Farnham, D. J. and J. Pimlott, 323, 326
Faulkner, H., 321
Ferdinand and Isabella, 192
Fichtenau, H., 26

Finnis, J., 64, 71, 81, 89, 213
and C. W. A. Flynn, 17
Fisher, H. A. L., 24, 26, 27, 234, 238
Fletcher, J., 113, 114
Fletcher, R., 163
Ford, H. P. and F. X. Winters, 218
Ford, J. C.
and G. Grisez, 146
and G. Kelly, S.J., 112, 113, 129, 130, 131, 133, 134
Fothergill, P. S., 104, 106, 107
Francis of Assisi, Saint, 189
Franciscans, 188, 189, 232
Franco-Prussian War, 249
Frankl, V., 112
Franklin, S. H., 352
Fraser, D., 208
Frederick Barbarossa, 232
Frederick II, 232
Freedman, L., 218, 219
Freemantle, A., 106, 239
Freud, S., 108, 109, 110, 111, 137
Fribourg, 249
Friedlander, H. and J. Oser, 208, 248, 271, 321, 339
Friedman, M., 281
Freedman, R., 268, 273, 274, 275
Fuchs, Fr., 81, 82, 83
Furfey, P. H., 178, 303

Gadd, O., 293
Galileo, 37, 38, 94, 148, 368
Gargan, E. T., 243
Garibaldi, G., 240, 242
Gaudium et Spes, 5, 6, 9, 38, 60, 73, 74, 75, 87, 88, 115, 123, 139, 140, 157, 158, 162, 164, 166, 173, 190, 207, 208, 213, 215, 216, 221, 223, 224, 228, 243, 244, 245, 254, 256, 259, 261, 299, 306, 307, 311, 312, 315, 319, 325, 333, 347, 351
Gelasius, 22, 230
Genesis, 49, 117, 118, 119, 123, 138, 166, 314, 316, 367, 369, 377
Geneva, 196, 345
George, S., 341
Geymonat, L., 38
Gilbert, A., 247, 354, 355

Gilchrist, J., 148, 283, 288
Gillespie, N. C., 105
Gilson, E., 206
Glorious Revolution, 265
Glynn, A. and J. Harrison, 274
Goldberg, S., 160, 167
Gould, J., 18
Goyder, G., 322
Grandmont, 188
Granick, D., 293, 294
Grant, R. M., 57
Gratian, 70
Gravissimum Educationis, 170
Gray, A., 268
Gray, J., 268
Gray, Professor, 107
Great Schism, 184
Gregorianum, 81
Gregory II, 21
Gregory VII, 24, 42, 180, 231
Gregory IX, 45
Gregory XVI, 238, 239
Gregory the Great, Saint, 21, 39, 40, 179, 180
Gregory of Tours, Saint, 26
Grelot, P., 117, 119, 120, 128
Gremillion, J., 246
Grisez, G., 131, 132
Grosseteste, R., 37
Grotius 94, 95, 96, 259
Guardian, 135, 345, 355
Guerrero, R. and O. Rojas, 145
Guthrie, W. K., 66
Gutierrez, G., 245

Habakkuk, 50
Haering, Fr. B., 144, 145
Hales, E. E. Y., 237, 239, 240, 241
Hallowell, J., 95, 96, 97, 272
Hammurabi, 51
Hapsburgs, 235
Harnack, A., 20, 89, 126
Harrod, R. F., 268, 280, 339
Hart, H. L. A., 16
Harvard Law Review, 16
Haskins, C. H., 35, 48
Hastings Constitutional Law Quarterly, 16
Hebrews, 51, 119, 120

Heer, E., 37, 47, 188, 231
Hegel, G. F., 99, 100, 132, 203, 205, 275, 366, 372
Heilbroner, R., 264
Heimann, E., 264, 267, 280
Henry IV, 42, 198, 231, 233
Henry VI, 180, 232
Henry VII, 192
Henry VIII, 192
Heraclitus, 66
Herbert, D., 352
Hersh, S. M., 217
Hertwig, O., 133
Hesiod, 53, 54
Heyer, F., 236
Heythrop College, 4
Hicks, J., 279, 283, 284
Hilary, Saint, 69
Hillel and Shammai, 122
Hippias, 66
Hitler, A., 97
Hitti, P. K., 43
Hitze, 249, 250
H.M.S.O., 161, 163
Hobbes, T., 199, 205
Hodges, L., 349, 350
Hoffner, J., 89, 91, 174, 222, 284
Holdsworth, W. S., 47
Hollister, C. W., 23, 24, 42, 231, 233
Holy Roman Emperor, 371
Holy Roman Empire, 257
Holy See, 145, 146, 184, 219, 375
Holy Spirit, The, 56, 103
Homer, 53, 65
Homiletic and Pastoral Review, 105
Honorius of Augsburg, 180
Horan, D. J. and D. Mall, 18
Hornsby Smith, M. P., 169
Hoskins, W. G., 25, 192
Hospites, 30
Hostie, R., S.J., 111
Hudson, G. F., 276
Huggett, F. E., 352
Hughes, P., 40, 233
Huguenots, 198, 235
Human Concern, 135
Human Life Center, 144
Humanae Vitae, 84, 131, 140, 145, 146, 147, 368
Humani Generis, 106

Hume, D., 71, 98, 202
Hunt, R. W. Carew, 101, 167, 204
Hutcheson, F., 98
Huxley, Sir J., 106
Hyman, R., 320

Iliad, The, 53, 65
Inglis, B., 266, 269, 271
Innocent III, 181, 188, 232
Innocent IV, 181, 182, 232
Innocent VI, 233
Inter Mirifica, 262
International Bank for Reconstruction and Development, 340
International Encyclopedia of the Social Sciences, 29, 163, 290
International Monetary Fund, 340
International Review of Natural Family Planning, 144
Internationalist, 353, 355
Irenaeus, Saint, 57, 179
Isaiah, 50, 52
Isidore, Saint, 69, 179
Israel, 49, 50, 52, 53
Ius Decretalium, 130, 131
Ius Gentium, 68, 69, 70, 258

Jacques, E., 331
Jahweh, 50, 51, 52, 53, 54, 55, 117, 119
Janssens, 82
Jeeves, J. A., 112
Jequier, N., 209, 341
Jeremiah, 50
Jerome Biblical Commentary, The, 57, 128
Jerome, Saint, 123, 129, 303
Jerrold, D., 186, 192
Jerusalem, 49
Jezebel, 50
John Chrysostom, Saint, 303
John of Paris, 182
John of Salisbury, 181
John the Scot, 36
John XXII, 183, 232
John XXIII, 1, 6, 74, 87, 88, 116, 170, 174, 207, 208, 210, 211, 217, 225, 244, 259, 262, 300, 308, 320, 351

John Paul II, 1, 17, 38, 125, 148, 178, 226, 227, 252, 260, 298, 313, 373, 374
Johnson, H. G., 340
Joint Statement of the Catholic Archbishops of Great Britain on Abortion, 17
Jones, A., 269, 318
Joseph II, 235
Joseph of Arimathea, Saint, 302
Joseph, Saint, 56
Joyce, R. and M., 144
Judges, 49
Julian the Pagan, 129
Jung, C. G., 111
Justinian, 69, 237

Kamen, H., 46
Kamenka, E., 102, 275
Kampuchea, 296
Kant, I., 63, 89, 97, 98, 99, 203
Kaplan, A., 108, 109, 110
Keen, M., 26, 36, 61, 257
Kenny, A., 63
Kenny, M., 136, 137, 160
Kenya, 356, 357
Kerkut, Dr. G. A., 107
Ketteler, 250, 251
Key, V. O., 224
Keynes, J. M., 267, 268, 269, 280, 289, 317, 339
Khmer Rouge, 296
Kim, E. and Ziring, L., 255, 296
Kindleberger, C. P. and B. Herrick, 339, 342
King, R., 169
Kirk, E. S., 66
Kirk, R., 54
Kitto, H. D. F., 65, 66
Knowles, D., 30
Knowles, D. and D. Obolensky, 39, 44, 154, 181, 183, 184, 231, 232, 233
Knox, J., 196
Kolping, A., 250
Koo, A. Y., 356
Koran, The, 62

La Tour du Pin, 249
Labatier, P., 45
Laborem Exercens, 313, 314, 318, 319, 323, 326
Lacouture, J., 296
Lamarck, 104
Lammenais, F. R. de, 239
Laquer, W., 208
Laski, H., 94, 299
Laslett, R. A., 317
Lateran Council(s), 187, 188, 189, 232
Latourette, K. S., 23, 27, 29
Lawler, R. et al., 130
Lazarus, 262
Lea, 45
Leach, Dr. P., 162
Lecky, W. H., 15, 29, 88–9, 153, 160
Leff, G., 25, 35, 36
Leibniz, G. W., 98
Lenin, V. I., 101, 276
Leo XII, 238
Leo XIII, 4, 22, 62, 206, 243, 249, 262, 300, 305, 308
Leo the Great, 39
Leviticus, 49
Leys, C., 357
Liberals, 240
Libertas Praestantissimum, 22, 262
Liège, 249
Limoges, 188
Linnaeus, 104
Lipsey, R. G., 279
Lipson, E., 48, 313
Listener, 219
Locke, J., 89, 94, 202, 205, 372
Lombard(s), 39, 241, 371
Long, V., 105
Long Parliament, 199
Lorwin, V. R., 271
L'Osservatore Romano, 125, 148, 171, 247, 355
Louis XIV, 235, 237
Louis XV, 235
Louis XVIII, 238
Louis, Saint, 42, 43
Louis Philippe, 238
Lovelace, L., 137
Lowry, J. H., 344, 353, 354, 355
Ludwig of Bavaria, 184, 232
Lumen Gentium, 146, 154

Luther, M., 197
Lutherans, 196, 372

McClellan, D., 100, 204, 273, 274, 314
McClelland, V. A., 251
McCreavy, L. L., 218
McGlynn, J. and J. Toner, 97, 98, 113
McGovern, W., 197, 198, 202, 203, 209, 234, 324
MacIntyre, A., 274
McKenzie, J. L., 50, 51, 52, 117, 119
McLaughlin, T. P., 167, 212
McMahan, J., 219
Mabro, R., 356
Machiavelli, N., 194, 195
Mack Smith, D., 242
Magyars, 23
Mainz, 251
Malachi, 50
Malthus, T. R., 266, 274
Manegold of Lautenbach, 180–1
Manglapus, P. S., 255
Manichees, 130
Manifesto (Communist), 100, 101, 204, 249
Manion, 144
Manning, H. E. Cardinal, 251
Mantoux, P., 263
Marcuse, H., 247, 274
Marie, Fr. Denis, 144
Maritain, J., 68, 97, 98, 99, 100, 101, 109, 174
Marshall, A., 267, 268, 284
Marshall, G., 339
Marshall, L. H., 58, 120
Marshall, T. H., 208
Marsilio of Padua, 183, 184, 192, 195, 371
Martel, C., 23, 24
Martin, A., 352
Marwick, A., 208
Marx, K., 100, 102, 105, 167, 203, 204, 251, 273, 274, 275, 276, 285, 372, 376
Mater et Magistra, 1, 6, 87, 88, 116, 174, 207, 208, 210, 211, 244, 253, 262, 284, 300, 306, 308, 320, 323, 335, 343, 351

Matthew, Saint, 59, 121, 122, 123
Maxwell, J., 31, 33, 149, 150, 151
May, R. et al., 112
May, W. E., 70, 81
  and J. F. Harvey, 120
Mazzini, G. 240
Medawar, P. S., 106, 107
Medellin, 245, 246, 253
Meier, G. M., 337, 342, 357
Mellor, J. W., 353
Menninger, K., 112
Mesopotamia, 120
Messner, J., 89, 174, 176, 216, 221,
  257, 267, 269, 282, 283, 289, 326
Metlake, G., 251
Mexico, 252, 354
Micah, 50
Midgley, E. B. F., 218
Mill, J. S., 103, 104, 266, 267, 284
Mirari Vos, 239
Mit Brennender Sorge, 97, 170, 212
Mitchell, B., 16, 113, 114
Mitchell, B. R. and P. Deane, 268
Mitchell, D. J. and R. E. Azevedo,
  269
Mitchell, J., 318
Mollat, M. and R. Wolff, 186, 313
Monthly Review 1970–1971, 295
Montpellier, 35
Moody, J. N., 229, 248, 249, 250,
  251
More, Saint Thomas, 13
Morgan, L., 167, 168, 204
Morison, S. E. and H. S. Commager,
  270
Morris, M. D., 336
Moses, 121, 122, 176, 262
Mowrer, O. H., 111, 112
Moyes, A., 341
Mun, A. de, 249
Munchen Gladbach Group, 249
Muslims, 23, 150, 154, 258

Nahum, 50
Napoleon, 236, 237
National Assembly, 236
National Association of Ovulation
  Method Instructors, 144

National Economic Development
  Council, 325
Nazareth, 121
Neibuhr, R. 92, 93, 113
Nelson, B., 108, 109, 110
Nero, 177
New Cambridge Modern History, The,
  25, 191
New Catholic Encyclopedia, 40, 83,
  124, 238
New Society, 163
Newman, J. H. Cardinal, 41, 154
Newton, I., 94, 202
Nicea, 188
Nicholas of Cusa, 37
Nicholas, H. G., 260
Niedergang, M., 338
Non abbiamo bisogno, 171
Noonan, J. T., 127, 147
Northedge, F. S. and M. J. Grieve,
  259, 340
Nove, A., 276, 277, 290, 291, 292,
  293, 294, 295
Numbers, 49
Nye, R. B. and J. E. Morpurgo, 152

O'Doherty, E. F., 112
O'Donnell, T. J., 17, 18, 85
O'Mahoney, P. J., 322
O'Sullivan, R., 47
Oakley, A. and J. Mitchell, 167
Octogesima Adveniens, 1, 6, 158, 213,
  247, 326, 347
Odoacer, 23
Odyssey, The, 53, 65
O.E.C.D., 337, 338, 341
Ogino, Dr. K., 143
Old Law, The, 121
Oliver, R. and J. Fage, 150, 151
On the Restoration of Christian
  Philosophy, According to the Mind of
  St. Thomas (Aeterni Patris), 62
Order of Christian Unity, 163
Order of Preachers, 189
Origen, 69
Otto the Great, 257
Overseas Development Association,
  341
Owen, R., 302

Oxfam, 341
Oxford, 35, 36, 184, 199
Ozanam, 249

Pacem in Terris, 6, 74, 87, 170, 217, 225, 226, 259, 373
Padua, 183, 187
Papal States, 40, 237, 238, 240, 242
Paris, 35, 36, 183
Parker, J., 327
Paul, Saint, 59, 65, 70, 76, 77, 122, 123, 128, 157, 165, 166, 167, 177, 178, 305, 313, 367
Paul VI, 146, 171, 213, 217, 221, 247, 253, 260, 334, 347, 355, 373
Pawley, Dr., 346
Peake's Commentary, 57
Pentateuch, The, 49
Pepin, 24
Pericles, 66, 348
Perrin, J., 319
Persians, 49
Peschke, H., 17, 18, 56, 76, 77, 79, 124, 246, 326
Peter, Saint, 59, 78, 140, 147, 177, 178, 205
Pharisees, 58, 121, 262
Philip the Fair (Philip IV of France), 182, 183, 232, 233
Philips, L. Wolf, 337, 339
Piedmont, 240
Pigou, 268
Pilate, 176, 177
Pilgrimage of Grace, 192
Pinson, K., 250, 251, 271
Pipe, R., 294
Pitt, W., 269
Pius VII, 237, 238
Pius VIII, 238
Pius IX, 239, 240, 241, 242, 243
Pius XI, 97, 116, 133, 139, 166, 167, 170, 171, 209, 212, 214, 217, 262, 300
Pius XII, 74, 75, 87, 106, 134, 139, 171, 208, 262, 300, 368
Plato, 9, 54, 63, 65, 66, 67, 89, 92, 186, 362
Platt, K., 144
Plumb, J. H., 265

Pol Pot, 376
Politbureau, 377
Pollard, S., 269
Pollock, F., 69, 70, 71
Pollock and Maitland, 47
Ponchard, F., 296, 297
Populorum Progressio, 6, 221, 253, 282, 284, 297, 311, 334, 335, 336, 343, 373
Potts, M., 135, 345
Power, E., 30, 31
Power, M., 229
Pravda, 292
Pressat, R., 344, 345
Price, H. B., 339
Pritchard, J. B., 51
Prittie, T., 229
Puebla, 6, 253, 374

Quadragesimo Anno, 6, 87, 209, 262, 281, 282, 284, 285, 286, 289, 300, 307, 308, 310, 318, 319, 320, 321, 323, 324, 325
Quaker Movement Against Slavery, 151
Quirinal Palace, 240

Rad, G. von, 50, 55
Rawls, John, 89
Redemptor Hominis, 226, 227, 373
Reid, I., 169
Rerum Novarum, 4, 6, 87, 249, 251, 252, 300, 305, 306, 308, 315, 316, 318, 319, 322, 325, 326
Rhodes, A., 229
Ricardo, D., 266, 284
Ricoeur, P., 111
Robbins, L., 267
Robespierre, M., 203
Robinson, J. H., 273, 279
Roetzer, Dr. J., 143, 145
Roman Empire, 123, 229, 230, 234, 256, 258, 361
Roman Rota, 125, 134
Romans, 33, 53, 159
Rome, 20, 21, 23, 36, 68
Rothwell, R. and W. Zegfeld, 317

Rousseau, J. J., 89, 202, 203, 205, 206, 372
Rowley, H., 49
Ruggiero, G., 22, 94, 96
Runciman, S., 43
Russell, B., 137

Sabine, G. H., 20, 22, 32, 36, 68, 95, 180, 181, 182, 183, 185, 191, 192, 195, 196, 198, 199, 202, 203, 230
Sacraments, 103
Sacred Congregation for the Doctrine of the Faith, 17, 18, 134
St. John-Stevas, N., 16, 18
Sakharov, A., 102
Salamanca, 35, 257
Salas, Rafael, 345
Salerno, 35
Salt, T., 302
Salvadori, M., 94, 242
Samuel, 176
Sanders, J. N., 57
Santamaria, J. N. and J. Billings, 143, 144
Sartre, J.-P., 113
Sassone, R., 344, 348
Saul, 179
Say, J.B., 266
Schapiro, L., 276, 277, 278
Schillebeeckx, E., 117, 120, 128
Schlatter, R., 303, 304
Schnackenburg, R., 33, 58, 120, 122
Schofield, M., 136
Schumacher, E. F., 209
Schumpeter, J. A., 264, 265, 268, 273, 274, 276, 279, 287
Scott, J. B., 189, 257, 259
Scott, M., 317
Second Vatican Council, 1, 9, 31, 38, 46, 60, 73, 75, 78, 80, 81, 82, 86, 87, 123, 125, 131, 134, 137, 138, 147, 154, 156, 162, 163, 166, 170, 173, 174, 175, 213, 214, 216, 218, 219, 221, 223, 224, 225, 227, 230, 234, 243, 244, 245, 246, 254, 256, 262, 263, 311 319, 333, 343, 347, 350, 359, 360, 362, 364, 365, 366, 368, 369, 370, 372, 373, 375

Segundo, J. L., 245
Sertum Laetitiae, 300
Shaftesbury, Earl of, 97
Shaw, R., 17
Sheridan, E. F., 131
Shorter, E., 163
Showler, B. and A. Sinfield, 317
Sidgwick, H., 97, 98
Simeon, 56
Singulari Nos, 239
Skidelsky, R., 317
Skinner, B. F., 348, 349
Skinner, Q., 183, 193, 194, 195, 196, 198, 199
Sladden, J. C., 21
Smith, A., 264, 265, 266, 267, 270, 284
Socrates, 9, 65, 66, 362
Sohm, R., 15
Solon, 65
Solzhenitsyn, A., 102, 277, 278
Sombart, W., 289
Song of Songs, 128, 367
Sophocles, 65
Soto, D. de, 257, 258
South Asia, 337
Soviet Russia, 277, 278
Soviet Union, 102
Sparta, 28
S.P.U.C., 135
Stalin, J., 97, 277, 291, 296
Stein, W., 218
Stevenson, J. and C. Cook, 215
Stewart, M., 268, 280
Strasbourg, 186, 313
Suarez, 193, 194, 195, 257, 258, 372
Summa Theologica, 34, 37, 38, 55, 56, 61, 63, 64, 70, 77, 79, 85, 89, 90, 116, 131, 132, 176, 189, 190, 216, 222, 287, 289, 300, 304
Sumption, J., 44
Sweden, 163
Sweezy, P. and C. Bettelheim, 295
Syllabus of Errors, 240, 241
Synod of Bishops 1980, 148

Tablet, 218
Taiwan, 356, 379

Tanzania, 356
Tellenbach, G., 42
Templars, 233
Teresa of Calcutta, Mother, 144
Tertullian, 69
Theological Studies, 146
Third World Quarterly, 339
Third World Review, 337
Thomas Aquinas, Saint. *See*
  Aquinas, Saint Thomas
Thomas, H., 355
Thomists, 195
Thomson, D., 249, 339
Thompson, E. P. and D. Smith, 219
Thompson, J. W., 30, 41, 46
Thompson, W. R., 107
Thrasymachus, 66
Thucydides, 66
Tierney, B., 31, 48
Tillich, 272
Tobit, 127, 128, 367
Toulouse, 35, 36, 198
Trier, 235
Trinitarian Order, 151
Troeltsch, E., 29, 185, 313
Tugendhat, C., 307

Ulpian, 69, 70
Unam Sanctam, 182, 232
United Nations, 227, 340, 346
United Nations Committee for Trade,
  Aid and Development, 342, 343
United Nations Conference on
  Resources, 349
United Nations Organization, 260,
  343, 375

Valentinian III, 39
Vatican Council II. *See* Second Vatican
  Council
Vaux, R. de, 33, 164, 176, 302
Vidler, A. R., 238, 239, 248, 249,
  250, 251
Vietnam, 295
Vikings, 23, 185
Vindiciae Contra Tyrannos, 196
Vitoria, de, 193, 257, 258, 259
Vix Pervenit, 149, 288

Voltaire, 202
Vorgrimler, H., 12, 13

Wallace-Hadrill, J. M., 26
Wallerstein, J. and J. Berlin, 163
Wallwork, E. and R. Johnson, 110
Walzer, M., 218
Ward, B. N., 291
Warnock, M., 97, 103
Wasserstrom, R. A., 16
Watt, L., 149, 287, 288
Webb, S. and B., 27, 326, 328
Wedderburn, K. M., 327, 328
Weekes, Brian, 327
Welty, E., 6, 89, 174, 213, 214, 216,
  221
Werz, F. X., 130, 131
Whitbread, 269
Whitley Councils, 324
Will, A. S., 251
William of Occam, 183, 184, 192, 371
Wolfenden Committee, 16
World Development Report, 337, 346,
  347
World Food Conference, 355
World Health Organization, 144
World Population Conference, 135
Wright, H., 257

Xenophanes, 65
Xenophon, 66

Yahweh. *See* Jahweh
Young, A., 269, 270

Zachaeus, 302
Zeno, 67
Zepheniah, 50
Zeus, 54, 67
Zielinski, J., 294
Zimmerman, Fr. A., 143
Zurich, 35

INDEX OF SUBJECTS

Abortion, 17, 18, 135
Absolute monarchy, growth of, 192
Absolutism, 197
Adlerian psychology, 111
Agricultural reform, 353
Agriculture, 24
  in the developed world, 352
  in the underdeveloped world,
    353 ff.
Agricultural economics, 350 ff.
Agricultural development
  medieval, 24
  modern, 350 ff.
Aid to undeveloped countries, 333 ff.
Albigensianism, 44
Alienation, concept of, 314
Annulment of marriage, 123 ff.
Apostolic Signatura, 125
Aquinas, Saint Thomas
  Catholic theology, philosophy
    and, 61
  conscience, teaching on, 77
  divine law, teaching on, 63
  natural law, teaching on, 64
  political ethics and, 204
  political theory and, 189
  profit, teaching on, 289–90
  sedition, teaching on, 190
  sex and marriage, teaching on,
    131 ff.
Arab philosophers, 35
Augustine, Saint
  divorce, teaching on, 122
  sex and marriage, teaching on,
    130
Autonomy, individual, 92 ff.
  Freudianism and, 109
Avignon papacy, 25

Barbarian invasions of Europe, 23
Benedictine monasticism
  agricultural development and,
    40–41
  education and, 34
  evangelisation and, 21, 24, 27

Billings method of family planning,
  143
Biological warfare, 218
Black Death, 25
Byzantine Empire
  papacy and, 39
  Roman Empire and, 23

Caesar, tribute to, 176
Capital, 285
Capitalism, liberal
  Adam Smith and, 265
  Catholic social ethics and, 272,
    296 ff.
  classical economics and, 266, 269 ff.
  development of, 263
  industrial revolution and, 269 ff.
  Keynesianism and, 268
  welfare economics and, 267
  workers and, 270 ff.
Capitalism and medieval culture, 299
Canon law
  annulment and, 133 ff.
  civil law and, 187
Casuistry, 77 ff., 83 ff.
Catholic Church
  absolutism and, 197 ff.
  Constantine and, 20
  corruption in, 25, 41, 46
  Crusades and, 42–43
  economic ethics and, 262, 282 ff.,
    290 ff., 296 ff., 300 ff.
  education and, 26 ff., 34 ff., 169 ff.
  feudalism and, 41
  Franks and, 21, 23, 26
  French revolution and, 236
  Galileo case and, 37–38
  Greek legacy and, 25
  international law and, 256
  international relations and, 256 ff.
  Inquisition and, 43 ff.
  medieval Europe/Middle Ages
    and, 23 ff.
  nationalism and, 237, 239 ff.
  political ethics and, 173 ff., 207 ff.,
    227 ff., 230 ff., 235 ff., 243 ff.

politics and, 23 ff., 38 ff., 47 ff.,
    230 ff., 234 ff., 243 ff., 257 ff.
private property and, 300 ff.
representative government and,
    187 ff.
reform and, 24, 46
Reformation and, 25
revolution and, 190, 194, 221 ff.,
    247 ff.
sex and marriage, teaching on,
    123 ff.
social movement, nineteenth
    century and, 248 ff.
social teaching of, 1 ff., 87, 88,
    244, 254
slavery and, 28 ff., 149 ff.
state and, 20 ff., 230 ff., 235 ff.
universities and, 35–36
urban life and, 26, 185
usury and, 148, 286 ff.
Centrally planned economy, 290 ff.
Charity, 88 ff.
Christ
    danger of riches, teaching on, 302
    moral teaching of, 58
    political violence and, 178, 253
Closed shop, 328
Collective bargaining, 329–30
Collectivisation of agriculture, 277
Commandments, the Ten, 54–55. See
    also Decalogue
Commercialism and sexual morals,
    137
Common good, 15, 207 ff., 211
Community, 174
Commutative justice, 89
Competition, economic, ethics of,
    261, 281, 296 ff.
Conciliar movement, 184
Conscience, 73 ff., 86 ff., 92
    and social conscience, 86 ff.
Conscientious objection, 215 ff.
Constitutional government, 188, 195
Consumerism, 299
Corporative organisation of industry,
    320 ff.
Crusades, 42–43

Darwinism, 104 ff.
Decalogue, 15, 54 ff.

Development of doctrine, 148 ff.,
    154
Delegation of political authority, 205
Demand and supply, economic, 280
Democracy, 201–2
Demographic transition, concept of,
    344
Designation of political authority,
    205
Dialectical method, 36, 203
Dissent, political, 213 ff.
Dignity of labour, 29, 48, 312 ff.
Distributive justice, 89, 90
Divine eternal law, 9 ff., 49 ff., 60 ff.
Divine right, 179 ff.
Divorce, 121 ff., 162 ff.
Doctors of the Church
    private property, teaching on, 303
    political authority, teaching
        on, 179
    sex and marriage, teaching on,
        129
Double effect, principle of, 85

Economic development, 333 ff.
    indicators of, 336
    social teaching of the Church and,
        334
Economic planning (Marxist), 290 ff.
Economics
    defined, 267
    ethics of, 261 ff., 296 ff.
    origins of, 263
    systems, 278 ff., 290 ff.
    theory, 267
Education, 34 ff., 169 ff.
Ends of marriage, 138 ff.
Environmental pollution, 349
Epicureanism, 53
Equity in trade relations, 336
Ethics
    Christian, 1 ff., 78, 86 ff.
    classical Greece and Rome, 66 ff.
    defined, 1, 78
    economic, 261 ff., 278 ff.
    modern theories, 97 ff.
    philosophical, 78
    political, 173 ff.
    social, 1 ff., 86 ff.
    theological, 1, 78

Europe
    cultural continuity of, 47–48
    formation of, 23 ff.
European unity, Renaissance and
    Reformation, 47, 191
Euthanasia, 18 ff.
Evolution, 104 ff.
Expropriation of private property,
    311

Factors of production, economic, 284
Family
    biblical teaching on, 117 ff.
    Church's teaching on, 123 ff.
    planning, 142 ff.
    sociological models of, 163 ff.
    Vatican II and, 156 ff.
Fathers of the Church, 69
    natural law, teaching on, 69
    political ethics, teaching on, 179
    property, teaching on, 303
    sex and marriage, teaching on,
    122, 129
Febronianism, 235
Feminine characteristics, 159
Feudalism, 41, 185
Finis operantis, 79 ff.
Finis operis, 79 ff.
Franks, 21, 24, 40
Free market, economic, 279
Freedom, 10, 13 ff., 19 ff., 79, 198
Free labour, 29 ff., 48
French Revolution, 236

Galileo, 37
Gallicanism, 234
Gelasian theory, 22, 230
God
    man and, 53, 92
    morality and belief in, 50 ff.
    sexuality and, 120
God, idea of
    classical culture and, 53–54
    contemporary Old Testament
    cultures and, 53–54
    Old Testament and, 50, 52
Government, 174
Great Schism, 25
Greece, 23

Greek
    dramatists, 53, 65
    historians, 66
    philosophers, 65
Greeks, 33, 49, 65, 104, 159
    idea of justice, 89
Guilds, 185, 313, 322

Heliocentrism, 38
Hillel school, 122
Homosexuality, 16, 17
Hope, 93
Human rights, 225
Hubris, 66
Human act, 79 ff.
Hundred Years War, 25

Iconoclasm, 39
Imputability, moral, 79 ff.
Individual autonomy, 92 ff.
Industrial
    councils, 324
    development and third world, 342
    enterprise, organisation and ethics
    of, 319 ff.
    organisation and industrial
    relations, 322, 329 ff.
    relations, ethics of, 320 ff.
Industrial Revolution
    Church and, 248
    working classes and, 271–72
Infertile times and natural family
    planning, 142
integral liberalism, 95
Interest, 286
International
    economics, 333 ff.
    justice, 256
    law, 256
    trade, 280, 338 ff.
Investiture controversy, 38 ff.,
    180 ff., 231 ff.

Jewish philosophers, 35
Josephism, 235
Jungian psychology, 111
Jury, trial by, 47, 187
Just price, 283

Just wage, 317
Just war, 216 ff.
Justice, 89 ff. *See also* Ethics
Justinian code, 69

Keynesianism, 280
Killing, morality of, 79

Labour theory of value, 273, 285
Land
    reform, 353 ff.
    tenure, 353 ff.
Latin America, 354 ff.
    liberation theology and, 245
Law
    justice and, 90
    morals and, 14 ff.
Legal justice, 89–90
Lenin, 101, 276
Lesser of two evils, principle of, 84
Liberal capitalism, 263 ff., 272 ff. *See
    also* Capitalism, liberal
    Catholic social ethics and, 297 ff.,
        301, 307
Liberalism
    Church and, 13, 93 ff., 249 ff.
    classical, 263 ff.
    economic, 94, 263 ff., 272 ff.
    philosophical, 94, 97
    political, 200
Liberation theology, 245 ff.
Lombards and papacy, 39–40

Magyars, 23
Market economy, 278 ff.
Marriage
    annulment, 123 ff.
    canon law of, 123 ff.
    divorce and, 121 ff.
    ends of, 126 ff., 131 ff.
    family and, 115 ff., 156
    "goods" of, 130
    nature of, 124
    role of state regarding, 167
    social institution, as, 156

Vatican II on, 115 ff., 131, 138 ff.,
    157 ff.
Marxism
    Church and, 247
    classical economics and, 273
    dialectic and, 100
    economic theory of, 273 ff., 290
    history and, 275
    Lenin and, 276
    liberation theology and, 247
    modern socialism and, 274
    morality and, 100 ff.
    revolution and, 203–4, 273–74
    theory of state and, 203
    USSR, in, 274 ff.
Medieval/Middle Ages
    Church and, 23 ff., 34 ff.,
        42 ff., 46 ff.
    cultural continuity with, 47
    main periods of, 23
    political theory of, 190
    universities in, 35
Mercantilism, 265
Metaphysics, 9
Modern ethical theories, 97 ff.
Monetarism, 280
Money and banking, 280
Monasticism. *See also* Benedictine
    monasticism
    constitutional government and,
        188
    economic role of, 40, 41
    free labour and, 29
    ideals, effect on social values, 27
    Irish, 34
Moral absolutes and modern thinkers,
    80 ff., 91 ff., 97 ff.
Moral
    act, 78, 79, 80 ff.
    consensus and law, 16
    evil, nature of, 79
    law and, 14
    philosophy, 1, 78
    theology, 15, 78
Morality
    belief in God and, 51 ff., 56 ff.
    imputation of, 79 ff.
Morals and ethics, 1, 78
Mutilation, morality of, 82 ff.
Muslim invasions, 23

Nation, Hegel's concept of, 283
Nationalisation. *See* Public ownership
Natural family planning, 142 ff.
Natural law
  biological law and, 145
  Fathers of the Church and, 69
  Greek thinkers and, 65 ff.
  Hobbes' idea of, 199
  Isidore, Saint, and, 69, 70
  law of nature and, 145
  liberalism, integral and, 92, 96
  Locke and, 201, 205
  magisterium and, 71, 140
  New Testament and, 65
  origins of idea of, 64 ff.
  Paul, Saint, and, 65
  political morality and, 212
  precepts of, 70
  right to revolt and, 194
  Roman jurisprudence and, 68, 69
  Rousseau and, 202, 205
  Second Vatican Council on, 60 ff.
  Thomas Aquinas' teaching on,
    63–64
  Ulpian's definition of, 69
New Testament
  canon of, 57
  economic ethics and, 262–63
  moral teaching of, 58 ff.
  political ethics and, 176–77
  property, teaching on, 302
Nomos, 66
Nuclear warfare, morality of, 217 ff.

Objective, concept defined, 9
Objective moral law
  personal conscience and, 73 ff.
  liberalism and, 95, 96
  natural law and, 71, 75
  scriptures and, 50 ff., 58 ff.
  social conscience and, 86 ff.
  situation ethics and, 114
  subjective imputability and, 79,
    81 ff.
  Vatican II and, 9 ff.
Old Law/Old Testament
  ceremonial, judicial, moral
    distinction, 55
  social morality and, 55

  new law and, 56
  political ethics and, 176
  private property and, 302
Ontic evil, 82
Optimism, Christian, 93
Original sin, 93

Papacy
  absolute monarchs and, 234 ff.
  Avignon, 25, 233
  corruption and, 40, 42
  Holy Roman Empire and, 42,
    180 ff., 231 ff.
  Italian unity and, 239 ff.
  liberalism and, 238 ff.
  temporal power of, 26, 40, 237,
    241
  United Nations and, 260
Papal States, 40, 237
Parents, rights and duties of, 158 ff.
Party politics
  individual Christian and, 223 ff.
  social teaching of the Church and,
    214
Patriarchy
  abuse of, 167
  Casti Connubii and, 167
  Engels on, 167
  New Testament concept of, 165
  Old Testament concept of, 164
  understanding of the concept, 169
  women and, 166
Patriotism, 224
Paul, Saint
  conscience, teaching on, 77
  marriage and the family, teaching
    on, 122, 157
  moral teaching of, 59
  natural law and, 65
  political authority and, 177
  work, teaching on, 313
Pauline privilege, 124
Peace of God, 43
People of God, 49
Permissive society, 135 ff.
Personal freedom, 94
Personal morality/ethics, 2, 3, 78 ff.,
  86

social morality/ethics and, 2, 17, 86 ff.
Peter, Saint
  moral teaching of, 59
  political authority and, 177
Petrine privilege, 124
Philosophy
  classical Greece and, 9, 66, 67
  moral teaching of Vatican II and, 9
Physical evil, 79, 82
Physis, 66
Plenitudo potestatis, 182
Political
  authority, Christian attitude to, 213
  community, origins of, 173 ff.
  community, purpose of, 207
  order, and moral order, 211
Popes. *See* Papacy
Population
  factors affecting, 344
  food and, 343, 346
  global growth of, 344
  Malthus on, 266
  problems concerning, 156
Pregnancy, ectopic, 85
Pre-moral, concept of, 82
Price theory, 282
Private property
  early Church and, 303
  expropriation of, 310 ff.
  Fathers of the Church and, 303
  importance of, 308
  morality of, 299 ff.
  public ownership and, 310
  social teaching of the Church on, 305 ff., 335
  scriptures and, 302
  Thomas Aquinas and, 304
  welfare state and, 310
Principle of totality, 82 ff.
Procedural norms of collective bargaining, 330 ff.
Production, economic, 279
Profit, 289
Profit sharing, 323
Prophets, Old Testament, 50
Providence, 52
Psychiatry and ethics, 108 ff.

Public Order
  conscience and, 13
  religious freedom and, 13, 14
Public ownership, 310 ff.
Puebla Conference (CELAM III), 259

Racialism, 336
Reformation, 23, 47, 191, 193, 197, 234
Religious freedom, 10 ff., 43 ff.
Renaissance, 25, 47, 93, 191, 195, 233
Rent, 282
Representative government, 184 ff.
Revolution
  Locke on, 201
  Marxism and, 203, 274
  Reformers and, 196, 197
  social teaching of the Church on, 221 ff., 247
  Thomas Aquinas and, 190
Right of dissent, political, 213 ff.

Salvation outside the Church, 154
Scholasticism, 36
Science and the Middle Ages, 37
Serfdom, 31
Second Vatican Council
  conscience, teaching on, 73 ff.
  economic ethics, teaching on, 261 ff.
  marriage and the family, teaching on, 115 ff.
  political ethics, teaching on, 174 ff.
  proximate and subjective ethical norm, teaching on, 73 ff.
  natural law, teaching on, 60 ff.
  social encyclicals/social teaching and, 4, 5, 86
  ultimate and objective ethical norm, teaching on, 9 ff.
Sexuality, human. *See* Marriage
Shamai school, 122
Situation ethics, 83 ff., 113 ff.
Slavery
  abolition of, 151 ff.
  Church and, 28 ff., 149 ff.

economic inefficiency of, 29, 151
intellectual foundations of, 28
medieval Europe and, 32, 150
natural law and, 69
scriptures and, 33, 149
theology and, 31 ff., 149 ff., 155
Social
aspects of personal ethics, 2
conscience, 86, 227
contract, 185, 191, 203, 291
encyclicals, 4, 6, 86
ethics, 1 ff., 86
justice, 88 ff.
morals and personal morals, 2, 86
responsibility of the firm, 321
teaching of the Church, 1 ff., 87,
88, 244, 254
Socialist economies, 290 ff.
Socialisation, 210
Society, 174
Society of Jesus, suppression of, 236
Sovereignty, 198
Soviet Russia, 102, 276, 290
State, the
Marxism and, 204
origins of, 173 ff., 189, 191, 199 ff.
political theory and, 195 ff.
private ownership and, 306
public ownership and, 309
Thomas Aquinas on, 189, 204
Vatican II on, 174 ff.
Stoics, 53, 67 ff.
Subjective
aspects of morality, 50
defined, 9
Syneidesis, 76
Synderesis, 76
Symptothermal method of natural
family planning, 143
Starvation, 347
Strikes, 321, 325 ff.
Subsidiary function, 209
Substantive norms of collective
bargaining, 331

Taxation, 283
Technical aid to underdeveloped
countries, 341

Theocracy, 176
Theology
Cardinal Newman and, 154
development of until thirteenth
century, 36
scholasticism and, 61
Trade unions
Catholic social teaching and, 321,
324, 325, 327 ff.
collective bargaining and, 330 ff.
Europe/America,
nineteenth-century, 270–71

Universities, 36, 48
Urban civilisation and the medieval
Church, 185
USSR. See Soviet Russia
Usury, 148–49, 286 ff.

Vatican II. See Second Vatican Council
Vocational groups, 324

Waldensianism, 44
War. See Just war
War communism, 276
Welfare
capitalism, 267, 298 ff.
economics, 267
Western intellectual tradition, 54
Woman's role
Octogesima Adveniens and, 158
sociological view of, 160
Vatican II and, 158
women's rights and, 161 ff.
Work
dignity of, 28–29, 48, 314 ff.
ethics of, 312 ff.
Genesis and, 314
right to, 317
just wage and, 317
social teaching of the Church on,
317 ff.
Worker participation, 322
World
economic growth, 343
population growth. See Population
resources, 347

INDEX OF DOCUMENTATION

Abortion, 400
Absolute norms, morality and, 382, 461
Agriculture, 503
Aid, economic, 420
Aquinas, Saint Thomas, 428, 507
Arms race, 417
Atheism, 496
Automation, 404
Autonomy of earthly affairs, 392

Bishops, role of, 471

Capitalism, liberal, 439, 482, 488, 502–3, 505
Catholic Church
  failings of members of, 395–6
  faithful spouse of Christ, 395
  international community and, 417
  Latin America and, 463 ff.
  liberation and, 475, 479 ff.
  manipulation of by secular factions, 491
  mission of, true character, 467
  political violence and, 441, 466, 486 ff.
  politics and, 413 ff., 484
  sectional (party) politics and, 395, 412 ff.
  society and, 392 ff.
Catholic education, 423 ff.
CELAM II (Medellin), 485, 490
CELAM III (Puebla), 463 ff.
Charity, truth and, 500
Children, family and, 398
Christ
  dignity of work and, 501
  family and, 397
  politics and, 466
  truth about, 465
  violence and, 466
Christians, politics and, 412, 483 ff.
Class conflict, industry and, 503
Commission on Population (of John XXIII), 446

Common good, 383, 410
Community of nations, 414 ff.
Conscience, 382, 390, 443
Contraception, 444 ff.
Created things, universal purpose of, 438

Declaration on Religious Liberty (Dignitatis Humanae), 381 ff.
Declaration on Sexual Ethics, 459 ff.
Dichotomy in man, 388
Dictatorship of the proletariat, 503
Dignity
  of man, 389–90
  of work, 501
Direct employer, 507

Ecclesiology, evangelisation and, 468
Economic
  development, 403 ff.
  growth, ambivalence of, 437
  imbalance in the world today, 402
  injustice, 404
  life, general, 402 ff.
Economism, materialistic, 504
Education
  Church and, 383, 423 ff.
  parents and, 383, 423 ff.
  state and, 423 ff.
Emigration, right to, 457
Employment, creation of, 457, 508
Environment, care for, 459
Evangelisation and ideology, 483, 487
Evangelii Nuntiandi, 464, 488

Family planning
  means of, unlawful, 450
  means of, lawful, 451–52
  objective criteria and, 400

Gradualitas legis, 499
Genesis, human work and, 502

Human
  beings, truth about, 470
  dignity, 472
  labour, priority of in industry,
    504–6
  life, purpose of, 391
  rights, 410–11, 494–95
  work, 405, 500 ff.
Humanae Vitae, 444 ff., 498

Imbalance, economic, in the world
  today, 387, 402
Indirect employer, 507
Industrial enterprise, cooperation and,
  406, 505
Industrialisation, economic growth
  and, 439
Inequality in material possessions,
  494
Infertile times, family planning and,
  451
Integrism, errors of, 491
International
  aid and Christians, 421
  community, establishment of, 419
  cooperation, economic, 419
  organisation, 419
  poverty, 404 ff., 494
  public authority, 417
Investment, 407

John Paul II
  at 1980 Synod of Bishops, 498 ff.
  at Puebla, 483 ff.
  at UNO, 492 ff.
Joint ownership in industry, 406, 505
Just war, 416

Laborem Exercens, 500 ff.
Latin America
  Church and, 478 ff., 491
  ideology and, 488–89
  justice and freedom in, 477 ff.

Lay apostolate, 395, 430 ff.
Laymen, responsibility of in the world,
  395, 429
Lex gradualitatis, 499
Liberal capitalism. See Capitalism,
  liberal
Literacy, 442

Magisterium, obedience to, 469
Man and work, 405–6, 500 ff.
Marriage, 396 ff.
  indissolubility of, 498
  responsibility for life and, 400
  sanctity of partners and, 499
Married love
  chastity and, 400
  holiness and, 402
Marxism, 489 ff., 502
Mater et Magistra, 502
Materialism, 493
Materialistic economism, 504
Medellin (CELAM II)
  Marxism and, 490
  liberal capitalism and, 490
Media, 458
Modern world, characteristics of,
  386 ff.
Moral conscience, 390
Morals, changes in attitudes towards,
  387, 460
Morality and religion today, 387

National Security State, 489
Natural moral law, 382, 400, 411,
  415, 445 ff., 461

Objective moral order, 384–85, 400
  rights of workers and, 507 ff.
Octogesima Adveniens, 453 ff., 490
Ownership, private. See Private
  ownership

Pacem in Terris, 490
Pastoral Constitution on the Church in
  the Modern World, 385 ff.
Patriotism, 412
Paul VI, 444 ff., 453 ff.
Peace, nature of, 414, 418, 493, 497
Personalism, priority of labour and,
  506
Political
  authority and moral law, 411
  community, Church and, 413 ff.
  community, nature and purpose
    of, 410
  dissent, norms governing, 411
  life, role of laity and, 429, 485
  life, priests and, 485–86
  violence in Latin America, Church
    and, 486–87

Politics, Church and, 413
Population
    family planning and, 443
    growth of, 421, 444 ff.
Populorum Progressio, 436 ff.
Poverty, international, 404 ff., 494
Premarital sex, 463
Priesthood, 477
    politics and, 485–86, 491
Private ownership of the means of
    production, 439, 473
    Thomas Aquinas on, 507
    work and, 505
Private property, 406 ff., 439, 473,
    481, 505
    expropriation of, 409
    social responsibility and, 406–7,
        481, 505
Public
    order, just requirements of, 383
    ownership, 408, 505 ff.
Puebla (CELAM III)
    final report of, 477 ff.
    John Paul II's address at, 483 ff.

Racial discrimination, 457
Racial hatred, 418
Religion and the modern world, 387
Religious freedom, 381 ff.
Reform, social, 441, 481 ff.
Revolution, 411, 441, 466, 486–87,
    503
Right
    of association, 508
    to strike, 456, 509
Rights of workers, 507 ff.

Science and the modern world, 386
Scriptures
    dignity of work and, 501
    family and, 399
Secular world
    role of laity and, 394
    role of priest and, 395
Sex and marriage, 398 ff., 447 ff., 462
Sexual morals, modern attack on, 460
Social order, changes in, 387 ff.
Social teaching/doctrine of the Church,
    476, 488
    social action and, 443

Socialisation, 387, 412, 505–6
Spiritual goods, primacy of, 493
State/Church, autonomy of, 413
Strikes, 406, 456, 509
Subsidiarity, principle of, 412
Subjective sense of work, 501
Synod of Bishops 1980, 498 ff.

Teachers, role of, 427
Technology, 442
Theological education, 428
Total war, 416
Truth, man and, 382

Underdevelopment, signs of, 438
Unions
    importance of, 508 ff.
    rights and responsibilities of, 406,
        456
Universities, Catholic, importance
    of, 428
Urbanisation, 387, 453

Violence, political
    Christ and, 466–67
    Latin America, in, 486–87

Wages, 405
    the family and, 508
War
    avoidance of, 415 ff.
    modern, and the Christian, 414 ff.
Wealth, distribution of internationally,
    386–87, 404, 419 ff.
Women, role of in society, 455–56,
    499
Work
    class war and, 503
    ethics and, 501
    Genesis and, 502
    materialistic economism and, 502
    objective sense of, 507
    ownership and, 505
    right to, 405, 508
    subjective sense of, 501
Workers
    co-responsibility and, 406
    joint ownership and, 505
    rights of, 507 ff.
    solidarity and, 502 ff.